Henry Boynton Smith, William Stevens Karr

System of Christian Theology

Henry Boynton Smith, William Stevens Karr

System of Christian Theology

ISBN/EAN: 9783743305946

Manufactured in Europe, USA, Canada, Australia, Japa

Cover: Foto ©Lupo / pixelio.de

Manufactured and distributed by brebook publishing software (www.brebook.com)

Henry Boynton Smith, William Stevens Karr

System of Christian Theology

SYSTEM

OF

CHRISTIAN THEOLOGY

BY

HENRY B. SMITH, D.D., LL.D.

EDITED BY

WILLIAM S. KARR, D.D.,
Professor of Theology in Hartford Theological Seminary

SECOND EDITION.

NEW YORK:
A. C. ARMSTRONG AND SON,
714 BROADWAY.
1884.

Copyright, 1884,
BY ELIZABETH L. SMITH.

St. Johnland
Stereotype Foundry,
Suffolk Co., N Y.

Press of
J. J. Little & Co.,
10 Astor Place, N. Y.

PREFACE.

IN preparing this work use has been made of a phonographic report of the larger part of Professor Smith's lectures as they were given in the year 1857, of several full sets of notes taken by students in other years, of the whole of Professor Smith's sketches and outlines of his lectures as left in manuscript, and of a number of his unpublished sermons.[1] The result is that the following exhibition of his views in theology is much fuller than that which he was able to impart to any one class during the years of lecturing to successive classes.

The order of topics given in Chap. VI. of The Introduction to Christian Theology is observed in this volume with some few deviations. The author did not always keep with strictness to the order which he had prescribed to himself. But all the main features of the system presented in The Introduction are preserved here.

Following the two books already published,[2] this volume completes the author's statements on all the chief questions in theology, and as care has been taken to give not only his thought but his precise language in

---

[1] Selections from the sermons are inserted, for the most part, in the Second Division and at the beginning of the Third.

[2] The Apologetics and The Introduction to Christian Theology.

all cases where this was practicable, it is hoped that the work will not be found wanting in any of the characteristics which distinguish his productions. The footnotes are made up from materials found in Professor Smith's papers. In a few instances the editor has given his own impressions as to the author's views, and has added references to his published works.

The two sons of Professor Smith have rendered valuable assistance in carrying the book through the press, and the Index has been prepared by Mrs. Smith, who has thus added to her most attractive memoir of her husband a summary of his chief work.

W. S. K.

HARTFORD THEOLOGICAL SEMINARY,
March, 1884.

CONTENTS.

DIVISION FIRST.

ANTECEDENTS OF REDEMPTION.

PART I.

THE CHRISTIAN DOCTRINE RESPECTING GOD.

BOOK I.—THE DIVINE NATURE AND ATTRIBUTES.

CHAP. I.—THE DIVINE NATURE.
    § 1. Can God be known? 3
    § 2. Can God be defined? 7
    § 3. The Mode in which we gain our explicit Conception of the Deity. 7
    § 4. Anthropomorphism and Anthropopathism 9
    § 5. Scriptural Designations of the Divine Nature 10
    § 6. Theological Definitions of the Divine Nature 11
CHAP. II.—THE DIVINE ATTRIBUTES.
    § 1. The Idea of the Divine Attributes 12
    § 2. Classification of the Attributes 15
CHAP. III.—THE ATTRIBUTES OF GOD AS PURE ESSENCE OR BEING.
    § 1. Self-existence 16
    § 2. Unlimited by Space or Time 17
    § 3. Eternity of God 17
    § 4. The Divine Immensity and Omnipresence 20
    § 5. The Divine Spirituality. The Divine Simplicity . . . 21
    § 6. The Divine Unity 21
CHAP. IV.—ATTRIBUTES OF GOD AS THE SUPREME REASON AND UNDERSTANDING.
    § 1. Proof that God is the most perfect Intelligence 23
    § 2. Definition of Omniscience 23
    § 3. The Objects of the Divine Knowledge 24
    § 4. Of Scientia Media 25
    § 5. The Divine Prescience or Foreknowledge 26
    § 6. The Divine Reason 28
CHAP. V.—ATTRIBUTES OF THE DIVINE WILL.
    § 1. Idea of the Divine Will 29
    § 2. The Distinction of the Divine Will as to its Objects . . 30
    § 3. Other Distinctions as to the Mode of Manifestation of the Divine Will 31
CHAP. VI.—THE OMNIPOTENCE OF GOD 32
CHAP. VII.—THE DIVINE HOLINESS 34

CONTENTS.

Chap. VIII.—The Divine Love.
§ 1. Definitions of Divine Love 37
§ 2. Proofs of the Divine Love 37
§ 3. Divisions of the Divine Love as to its Objects 38
§ 4. Other Modifications of the Divine Love 38
§ 5. The Divine Benevolence 38
§ 6. Sources of Proof of the Divine Benevolence 40
§ 7. Objections to the Divine Benevolence from the Existence of Evil 40

Chap. IX.—The Divine Veracity 43

Chap. X.—The Divine Justice.
§ 1. General Idea of the Justice of God 44
§ 2. Proofs of the Divine Justice 45
§ 3. Distinctions in respect to the Divine Justice . . . 45
§ 4. Why does God as a Moral Governor exercise Punitive Justice? . 46

BOOK II.—THE TRINITY, OR GOD AS KNOWN IN THE WORK OF REDEMPTION.

Preliminary Remarks 48

Chap. I.—The Manifested Trinity.
§ 1. That God is One 50
§ 2. That the Father is Divine and a Distinct Person . . . 51
§ 3. That the Son is Divine and a Distinct Person from the Father . 53
§ 4. Objections to the Proof of the Divinity of Christ on the Ground of the Arian Hypothesis 63
§ 5. That the Holy Spirit is Divine and a Distinct Person from the Father and the Son 65
§ 6. The Father, Son, and Spirit, are classed together, separately from all other Beings, as Divine 71
§ 7. Result of the Biblical Evidence in respect to the Divinity of the Father, the Son, and the Holy Spirit 72

Chap. II.—The Essential Trinity.
§ 1. That the Distinctions of the Godhead are represented in the Scriptures as internal 73
§ 2. Remarks on Sabellianism 77
§ 3. That these Distinctions in the Godhead are appropriately designated as Personal Distinctions 79
§ 4. The Ecclesiastical Statements as to the distinctive Characteristics of the Persons 80
§ 5. Is the Term Son used in the Scriptures in reference to Christ's immanent Relation to the Father? 83
§ 6. How are we to conceive this Relation as an internal one in the Godhead? 87

PART II.

CHRISTIAN COSMOLOGY.

Chap. I.—Creator and Creation.
§ 1. The Scripture represents God as the Creator of the World . . 92
§ 2. The Scripture represents the Son of God as the Medium by Whom the World was brought into being 92

§ 3. God Created freely and not by necessity 92
§ 4. Creation is not from any previously extant substance . . . 92
§ 5. The Relation of God as Creator to what He has created . . 95
§ 6. The Scripture represents Creation as a plan and not as a Development 95
CHAP. II.—OF THE CREATED UNIVERSE AS SET FORTH IN SCRIPTURE . . 96
CHAP. III.—OF THE DIFFERENT ORDERS OF CREATED BEINGS . . . 98
CHAP. IV.—THE PRESERVATION OF CREATION.
§ 1. Sources of Proof of the Doctrine 102
§ 2. The Purport of the Doctrine 102
§ 3. Theory of continued Creation 103
§ 4. A Modification of the Theory of continued Creation . . . 104
§ 5. The Mechanical Theory of Preservation 105
CHAP. V.—DIVINE PROVIDENCE.
§ 1. General Statements in respect to this Doctrine 106
§ 2. Proof of the Doctrine of Providence 108
§ 3. Distinction as to general and particular Providence . . . 110
§ 4. Modes of the Divine Providence 111
CHAP. VI.—THE DECREES OF GOD 114
§ 1. Preliminary Statements 115
§ 2. Of the Terms used to denote the Doctrine 117
§ 3. Characteristics of the Divine Decree or Decrees 117
§ 4. Proof of the Doctrine of Decrees 120
§ 5. Objections to the Doctrine of the Divine Decrees . . . 122
CHAP. VII.—THE END OF GOD IN CREATION 126
§ 1. Meaning and Statement of the Question 127
§ 2. Conditions of the Solution of the Problem—if possible . . 129
§ 3. Statement of the Theories 130
§ 4. The Scriptural Argument 131
§ 5. The Supreme End of Creation is the Declarative Glory of God . 132
§ 6. Arguments in Favor of this Position 136
§ 7. Consideration of Objections 138
§ 8. The Happiness Theory 140
§ 9. The Connection between the View of the End of God in Creation and the Theory of the Nature of Virtue 142
§ 10. Some historical Statements as to Theories of God's End in Creation 143
CHAP. VIII.—THE THEODICY. THE QUESTION OF THE BEST SYSTEM . . 146
§ 1. Is Sin the necessary Means of the greatest Good? . . . 147
§ 2. Does the Nature of Free Agency account for Sin? . . . 149
§ 3. We cannot State all the Reasons for the Permission of Sin . . 153

PART III.

CHRISTIAN ANTHROPOLOGY. THE DOCTRINE RESPECTING MAN.

CHAP. I.—WHAT IS MAN AS A MORAL BEING? 161
§ 1. Of Man in his most General Relations 161
§ 2. What constitutes the Individuality of each Man? . . . 163
§ 3. Of the Union of Body and Soul in Man 163

§ 4. Of the Origin of Souls (after the Creation of the first Soul) . . 166
§ 5. Of Personality 170
§ 6. The primary Facts involved in all Personal Agency . . . 170
§ 7. The Powers and Faculties of the Soul 173
§ 8. Of the original Tendencies of Man's Soul 176
§ 9. Of Conscience 178
§ 10. Of Man's highest Spiritual Capacities 190
Chap. II.—What is the Law of God: What does it require? . . 191
§ 1. Some general Statements as to the Characteristics of the Law . 192
§ 2. The two fundamental Objects or Ends of the Law of God . 194
Chap. III.—The Highest Good. 195
Chap. IV.—The formal Theories of the Nature of Virtue.
§ 1. Virtue is acting according to the Fitness of Things . . . 198
§ 2. Virtue is that which promotes the great End of our Being . 199
§ 3. Virtue is Acting in conformity with the Relations of Things . 199
§ 4. Acting in conformity to the Will of God 200
§ 5. Kant's Theory 203
§ 6. Dr. Hickok's Theory 203
Chap. V.—The Happiness Theories 205
§ 1. The Selfish Scheme. The Ethics of Paley. 206
§ 2. Virtue consists in the Tendency to the greatest Happiness. . 207
§ 3. Subjective Happiness or Self-Love Scheme 210
§ 4. General Remarks on all the Happiness Theories 213
Chap. VI.—The Holy Love Theories 214
Chap. VII.—Some Hints as to a Theory of the Nature of Virtue.
§ 1. Preliminary Statements. 218
§ 2. The Scriptural View of the Nature of True Virtue . . . 220
§ 3. Statement of the Principle of True Virtue in the abstract . 222
§ 4. Arguments for the Definition 225
§ 5. Some Objections to the Theory 227
§ 6. Statement of the general Principle of all Virtue in the concrete . 229
Chap. VIII.—Of Man's Personal Relations to the Law of God . 232
Chap. IX.—Of the Seat of Moral Character. The Will . . 236
§ 1. Of the Idea of the Will. 237
§ 2. Of the Power of the Will 238
§ 3. Of Self-Determination 239
§ 4. Modes of the Will's Action 240
§ 5. Of the Liberty or Freedom of the Will. 242
§ 6. Of the Will and Motives 245
Chap. X.—Of Liberty and Necessity 250
Chap. XI.—Of the primeval Moral State of Man 252
§ 1. The Scriptures teach that there was a primitive State of Innocence 253
§ 2. This original State is described in general Terms as the Divine
Image in Man 253
§ 3. Yet this primitive State was not one of confirmed Holiness but
mutable 255
§ 4. On the different Interpretations of the "Divine Image" . . 255
Chap. XII.—The Destination of Man if he had continued in Obedience.
The Covenant of Life or of Works 258

PART IV.

CHRISTIAN HAMARTOLOGY. THE DOCTRINE RESPECTING SIN.

CHAP. I.—THE FALL HISTORICALLY VIEWED.
§ 1. The Temptation. Is it Historical? 260
§ 2. The Features of the Temptation 261
CHAP. II.—THE PENALTY. THE DEATH THREATENED FOR DISOBEDIENCE . 264
§ 1. As to Spiritual Death 265
§ 2. Temporal Death 266
§ 3. Eternal Death 271
CHAP. III.—THE CONSEQUENCES OF THE FALL TO THE HUMAN RACE . . 273
§ 1. Sin as known by Experience. 274
§ 2. The universal Sinfulness of Man as testified to in Scripture . 275
§ 3. This universal Depravity is set forth in the Scriptures as total, *i. e.*, as affecting the whole Man 276
§ 4. This depraved State is native to Man 277
CHAP. IV.—ORIGINAL SIN. 283
§ 1. General Statements 286
§ 2. The Facts of the Case, in respect to Original Sin, as given in Scripture 291
§ 3. The Facts of the Case as to Original Sin, as argued from Experience, and on other than Scriptural Grounds. 297
CHAP. V.—THE COUNTER REPRESENTATION AS TO SIN AND ITS PUNISHMENT IN SCRIPTURE AND EXPERIENCE 302
CHAP. VI.—THE THEORIES PROPOSED FOR THE SOLUTION OF THE PROBLEM.
§ 1. The Theory of Immediate Imputation 304
§ 2. The Theory of Direct Divine Efficiency, in the way of a Constitution 308
§ 3. The Hypothesis of Physical Depravity. 309
§ 4. The Pelagian and Unitarian View. 312
§ 5. The Hypothesis of Pre-existence 313
CHAP. VII.—OF so-called MEDIATE IMPUTATION 314
CHAP. VIII.—OBJECTIONS TO THE DOCTRINE OF ORIGINAL SIN . . . 323
CHAP. IX.—OF THE BONDAGE OF SIN, ITS POWER OVER THE HUMAN WILL . 326
§ 1. Preliminary Definitions. 327
§ 2. The Power to the Contrary 329
§ 3. The positive Statements as to the Relation of Natural Ability and Moral Inability 331

DIVISION SECOND.

THE REDEMPTION ITSELF. THE PERSON AND WORK OF CHRIST.

PART I.

OF THE INCARNATION IN ITS GENERAL NATURE AND OBJECTS.

CHAP. I.—WHAT IS PRESUPPOSED IN THE INCARNATION.
    § 1. Of the Incarnation in Relation to Sin 343
    § 2. Such a Constitution of the Divine Nature as made an Incarnation possible 352
CHAP. II.—THE INCARNATION PRIMARILY FACT AND NOT DOCTRINE . . 353
CHAP. III.—THE FACT OF THE INCARNATION IN RELATION TO MAN'S MORAL WANTS.
    § 1. It presents us with the Life of a perfect Man as a Model for Imitation, and so meets Need 354
    § 2. The Relation of the Incarnation to Human Wants is seen in its giving to Man the most direct Access to, and Communion with, God 358
    § 3. Incarnation in order to Redemption 360
CHAP. IV.—HOW FAR MAY AN INCARNATION BE SAID TO BE NECESSARY ON THE PART OF GOD? 362
CHAP. V.—THE INCARNATION IN HISTORY 369
CHAP. VI.—OF THE INCARNATION AS CONNECTED WITH THE WHOLE OF THE THEOLOGICAL SYSTEM, AND AS VIEWED BY DIFFERENT PARTIES . 369
CHAP. VII.—OF THE INCARNATION ON PHILOSOPHICAL GROUNDS . . . 373
    § 1. As to the Philosophy of Christianity 373
    § 2. In the Incarnation we have the Means of adjusting the conflict between Christianity and Philosophy 374
CHAP. VIII.—COMPARISON OF THE INCARNATION WITH SOME OTHER FACTS AS GIVING THE CENTRAL IDEAS OF THE CHRISTIAN SYSTEM. . . 377
CHAP. IX.—OF THE INCARNATION AS THE UNFOLDING OF THE POSSIBILITIES OF HUMAN NATURE. THE SECOND ADAM 379

PART II.

OF THE PERSON OF THE MEDIATOR. THE SON OF GOD MANIFEST IN THE FLESH. THE GOD-MAN.

CHAP. I.—THE SCRIPTURAL TEACHINGS RESPECTING THE PERSON OF THE GOD-MAN. 386
    § 1. The general Impression of the Declarations of Scripture on this Point 386
    § 2. The Proof from Scripture of Christ's Divinity 387

§ 3. The Miraculous Conception. 389
§ 4. In the Miraculous Conception the Logos assumed a true and complete Humanity. 392
§ 5. In the Scriptures both the Divine and Human Natures of Christ are often brought under one View 393
§ 6. The various Modes in which what is said of Christ in the Scriptures is to be interpreted in respect to his Person and Natures 393
§ 7. According to the Scriptures, Christ was one Person, and his Personality was from his Divine Nature 394
§ 8. Summary and Conclusions from Scripture Testimony as to the Two Natures and One Person. 395
CHAP. II.—THE EARLY HERETICAL OPINIONS AS TO THE PERSON OF CHRIST. 396
CHAP. III.—LATER DOCTRINAL DIFFERENCES BROUGHT UP IN THE CONTROVERSIES OF THE REFORMATION. 397
CHAP. IV.—THE OBJECTIONS AND DIFFICULTIES URGED AGAINST THE DOCTRINE OF THE PERSON OF CHRIST 399
CHAP. V.—THE ENTIRE RESULT AS TO THE PERSON OF OUR LORD. . . 421

PART III.

THE WORK OF THE MEDIATOR.

CHAP. I.—PRELIMINARY STATEMENTS.
  § 1. The General Object of Christ's Coming 430
  § 2. Munus Triplex. Christ's Offices as Prophet, Priest, and King . 431
CHAP. II.—OF CHRIST'S WORK AS THE ONLY TRUE PRIEST. OF ATONEMENT AND THE NECESSITY FOR ATONEMENT 437
CHAP. III.—OF THE LEADING SCRIPTURAL REPRESENTATION OF THE ATONING WORK OF CHRIST—THAT IT IS A SACRIFICE 442
  § 1. The System of Sacrifices prevalent in the Pagan World . . 443
  § 2. In the Old Testament we find the same essential Elements as in the heathen Sacrifices 445
  § 3. Another Argument for the same Position is derived from the Old Testament Prophecies of Christ 447
  § 4. The New Testament Descriptions of the Sufferings and Death of Christ repeat the same Ideas, give us in more strict Form of Assertion the same Elements 448
  § 5. Consideration of Objections 453
CHAP. IV.—ANALYSIS OF THE SCRIPTURAL STATEMENTS AS TO CHRIST'S SUFFERINGS AND DEATH 461
CHAP. V.—THE THEORY OF THE ATONEMENT 464
  § 1. Theories which define the Atonement ultimately by its Influence on Man, in bringing to a New Life. 464
  § 2. Theories which put the Essence of the Atonement in Satisfaction to Distributive Justice 466
  § 3. Theories which assert that the Atonement consists in the Satisfaction of General Justice 469
  § 4. The Atonement, while it indirectly satisfies Distributive Justice, does not consist in this: it consists in satisfying the demands of Public Justice 470

CHAP. VI.—THE EXTENT OF THE ATONEMENT.
  § 1. Statement of the Question 478
  § 2. Proof of General Atonement. 479
  § 3. Objections to General Atonement. 480
CHAP VII.—THE INTERCESSION OF CHRIST 481

DIVISION THIRD.

THE KINGDOM OF REDEMPTION.

INTRODUCTORY REMARKS 491

PART I.

THE UNION BETWEEN CHRIST AND THE INDIVIDUAL BELIEVER, AS EFFECTED BY THE HOLY SPIRIT.

BOOK I.—PREDESTINATION, ELECTION, THE EFFECTUAL CALL.

CHAP. I.—GENERAL OBSERVATIONS 502
CHAP. II.—ELECTION AND REPROBATION.
  § 1. Statement of the Scriptural Doctrine of Election . . . 505
  § 2. Reprobation 508
  § 3. Objections to the Doctrine of Predestination . . . 509
CHAP. III.—THE GOSPEL CALL.
  § 1. Of the External Call 515
  § 2. The Internal Call 516
  § 3. Under this General Statement, some Questions and Difficulties are raised 516

BOOK II.—OF JUSTIFICATION.

CHAP. I.—PRELIMINARY CONSIDERATIONS 522
CHAP. II.—OF THE TERM AND IDEA: JUSTIFY—JUSTIFICATION; THE GENERAL AND SCRIPTURAL SENSE 526
CHAP. III.—JUSTIFICATION INVOLVES A RIGHTEOUSNESS AS ITS GROUND . . 528
CHAP. IV.—PERSONAL RIGHTEOUSNESS 528
CHAP. V.—THE GROUND OF JUSTIFICATION 529
  § 1. Statements of Scripture as to the Ground of Justification . . 530
  § 2. How Christ can be the Ground of our Justification . . 531
  § 3. In what Way does what Christ has done avail to the Believer through this Union, for his Justification . . . . . as a Righteousness? 538
CHAP. VI.—THE INSTRUMENTAL CAUSE OF JUSTIFICATION.
  § 1. Faith, and Faith alone 539
  § 2. The Idea of Faith 540
  § 3. Some questions in regard to Faith 541

§ 4. Is Man responsible for his Belief—*i. e.*, for his Unbelief? . . 543
§ 5. Why is the High Office assigned to Faith of being the Instrumental Cause of Justification? 544
CHAP. VII.—THE DIFFERENCE BETWEEN THE ROMAN CATHOLIC AND PROTESTANT VIEWS OF JUSTIFICATION 545
CHAP. VIII.—HISTORICAL STATEMENTS RESPECTING THE DIFFERENT THEORIES OF JUSTIFICATION 548
CHAP. IX.—OBJECTIONS TO THE DOCTRINE OF JUSTIFICATION 551

BOOK III.—REGENERATION AND REPENTANCE.
CHAP. I.—INTRODUCTORY STATEMENTS.
    § 1. The Doctrine as held in some of the different Systems . . 553
    § 2. Of the Terms employed 557
    § 3. Connection of the Doctrine of Regeneration with other Truths . 559
CHAP. II.—THE NECESSITY OF REGENERATION 560
CHAP. III.—THE SUBJECTIVE CHARACTERISTICS OF REGENERATION . . . 560
CHAP. IV.—THE AUTHOR OF REGENERATION 563
CHAP. V.—HOW DOES THE SPIRIT REGENERATE THE SOUL? 564
CHAP. VI.—THE MEANS OF REGENERATION.
    § 1. External Providential Means 566
    § 2. Acts of the Sinner as among the Means 566
    § 3. Of the Truth as a means of Regeneration 568
CHAP. VII.—THE EXHORTATION: MAKE TO YOURSELF A NEW HEART. . . 569
CHAP. VIII.—THE CONSCIOUS PROCESSES OF THE SOUL IN REGENERATION . . 570
CHAP. IX.—REPENTANCE 572
    § 1. Some general Statements of the Protestant View . . . 573
    § 2. Repentance should be immediate 574
    § 3. Some special Works and Signs of Repentance 574

BOOK IV.—SANCTIFICATION AND PERFECTION.
CHAP. I.—SANCTIFICATION.
    § 1. The nature of Sanctification according to the Scriptures . . 575
    § 2. The Difference between Justification, Regeneration, and Sanctification 576
    § 3. Of Good Works and Sanctification 576
    § 4. The Means of Sanctification 577
CHAP. II.—PERFECTIONISM 579
    § 1. The older Theories 580
    § 2. The modern View of Perfectionism 581
CHAP. III.—PERSEVERANCE OF THE SAINTS 585
    § 1. Arguments in favor of the Doctrine 586
    § 2. Explanations of the Doctrine 586
    § 3. Objections to the Doctrine 587

PART II.

THE UNION BETWEEN CHRIST AND HIS CHURCH.

    § 1. Of the fundamental and germinant Idea of the Church of the Lord Jesus Christ 590
    § 2. Of the Nature of the Church as seen in the Light of this radical and central Idea 591

PART III.

THE CONSUMMATION OF THE KINGDOM OF REDEMPTION IN TIME AND ETERNITY. THE ESCHATOLOGY.

CHAP. I.—OF DEATH AND IMMORTALITY.
§ 1. Death 598
§ 2. Of Immortality 598
§ 3. Annihilation 600
§ 4. Objections to Immortality 601
CHAP. II.—OF THE INTERMEDIATE STATE 602
§ 1. Historic Facts as to the Doctrine 603
§ 2. PROPOSITION. There is no sufficient Scriptural warrant for such an Intermediate State as described. 604
§ 3. Of Purgatory 606
§ 4. The Sleep of Souls 606
CHAP. III.—THE SECOND ADVENT 608
CHAP. IV.—RESURRECTION OF THE BODY. 610
CHAP. V.—THE LAST JUDGMENT 612
CHAP. VI.—THE AWARDS OF THE LAST DAY 613
§ 1. The Scriptural Testimony as to Endless Punishment . . 614
§ 2. Objections to the Doctrine of Endless Punishment . . 617
§ 3. Of the Restitution of all Things 618
§ 4. Position and Relations of the Doctrine of Future Punishment . 620
§ 5. The Award of Eternal Blessedness to the Righteous . . . 620

DIVISION FIRST.

ANTECEDENTS OF REDEMPTION.

PART I.

THE CHRISTIAN DOCTRINE RESPECTING GOD.

[BOOK I., THE DIVINE NATURE AND ATTRIBUTES; BOOK II., THE TRINITY.]

BOOK I.

THE DIVINE NATURE AND ATTRIBUTES.

CHAPTER I.

THE DIVINE NATURE.

IN Natural Theology[1] we have considered the Being of God as the infinite, absolute, personal Spirit, the ground and cause of all that exists. We are now to consider more fully, *adding the Scriptural proof*, the Divine Nature.

§ 1. *Can God be known?*

The difficulty on this point as it has been discussed, is this: God is an infinite and absolute being; man, on the other hand, is a limited and finite being, of course limited in his power of knowledge. How then can this finite and limited being know the infinite and absolute being? The terms are incommensurable. The whole diameter of being lies between the Creator and the creature. There appears to be no common measure. On the other hand, if God cannot be known, all our idea of Him would be simply equal to zero. It would be an abstract notion without any life. Consequently, both in philosophy and in theology, in heathenism and in Christianity, we have a variety of speculations and statements, ranging from utter skepticism to the height of faith, from the assertion of the absolute impossibility of knowledge to the claim of absolute knowledge.

[1] See "Apologetics," p. 85, and "Introduction to Christian Theology," p. 84.

CLASSIFICATION OF THESE DIFFERENT POSITIONS.

1. *The philosophical positions.* These are chiefly four:—

(*a.*) Many philosophers and schools of philosophy take the position that God in himself cannot be known at all. This is illustrated in Plato's well-known saying (Timæus): "that to find the center and father of all is difficult, and if found it is impossible to talk to all about Him, for He is the highest good, having no essence or existence, but ranging beyond all essence and existence in his worth and power." So Philo says: "God is without any qualities, and we can only ascribe to Him pure being without attributes." This is everywhere the tone of thought in the New Platonic School. Among modern philosophers, Kant teaches that it is impossible for the intellect, "the pure reason," to know God. What we come at under the guidance of reason is a series of contradictions, and what we can know about God is attained not by the pure, but by the practical, reason, by the urgency of our moral wants. Yet these very statements imply some degree of knowledge [1]—*that* He is, if not *what* He is.

(*b.*) The same position is held by many skeptical philosophers, with whom it takes the form of a denial of all piety and of all religion. The highest speculative minds, however, while denying that God can be properly "known," have asserted that our moral nature aspires to Him.

(*c.*) God can be known fully and really, but only in the way of *mystic* contemplation, not in any proper knowledge through the intellect, but only in a knowledge through feeling and devotion. This is an opinion of the ancient school of mystics and also of the modern school.

(*d.*) Counter to all these is the position that God can be absolutely known by the intellect. This is the pantheistic theory, especially as advocated by Spinoza and Hegel. We can know God purely and completely because we are a part of Him. To have the idea of Him is to know Him, and we could not know Him unless we were a part of Him.

2. *Positions held in the Church.* We have the same general

---
[1] See "Apologetics," p. 35.

positions as before, modified by the acceptance of the Christian revelation.

(*a*.) There are those who assert that God can be fully known as we know logic and mathematics. Thus the Arians, in their discussions on the Trinity, claimed that God could be known, and so fully known as to justify the assertion that there could not be any pluri-personality in Him, that He must exist as a single, individual mind.

(*b*.) Others have asserted that God is utterly incomprehensible in himself, that He is above all names. No term can name Him. If we give a name we cannot affix to it any definite conception.

(*c*.) There is also the position that in this life and with the mere understanding God cannot be known, and that He cannot be known by the wicked, those who are alienated from Him by wicked works; but that He may be known so far as He is revealed in Christ, and through this revelation we may attain to a knowledge of Him sufficient for our devotion and direction, but not sufficient to fill up the idea of God.[1]

3. *The Scriptural assertions and statements.* Exodus xxxiii.: the scene in which God appears to Moses. "Show me thy glory," etc. The sense of this gives a key to the whole Scriptural revelation of God. We cannot know God face to face, but we can track Him (Exodus xxxiii. 23) by his revelations.

He cannot be known fully by man: Job xi. 7; Matt. xi. 25; Rom. xi. 34; 1 Tim. vi. 16. These Scriptural representations show us that there is in God that which is to the human intellect incomprehensible and unfathomable.

On the other hand we have statements which show that some knowledge can be had by man: Matt. v. 8; xi. 27; 1 Cor. xiii. 12; Rev. xxii. 4. Particularly do the Scriptures assert that God is known in Christ, as in John xvii. 26. The word *name* here, as frequently, stands for the nature of God.

---

[1] See, in Cudworth's "Intel. Syst.," an admirable discussion of the atheistic positions. Also, Berkeley's "Minute Philosopher." "The Divine Analogy," by Bishop Brown, an opponent of Berkeley, inclines to the position that we must have a revelation in order to gain any knowledge of God.

From these passages of Scripture and from the nature of the case the following results may be obtained—

(*a.*) There is a great difference between the assertion that we can know God without a revelation of Him and that we can know Him through the illuminating influence upon the soul of the Divine Spirit. The finite cannot of itself attain to the infinite. If the finite and the infinite were all and there were no communication between them, the finite could not know the infinite. It is only as the infinite being reveals himself that the finite can know the infinite at all. Otherwise the terms are incommensurable.

(*b.*) It likewise results that God, in his interior essence, cannot be known or fathomed by man. We can know that He is; we cannot know fully what He is. We can know that there must be an infinite Being, the source and ground of all else; we can know that He must be unlimited in all his attributes, but all that is included in his attributes we cannot comprehend, still less can we grasp the essence on which they are based.

(*c.*) It results, that God, in his moral nature, cannot be fully known by the wicked, because they are opposed to Him, and only the loving can know love.

(*d.*) It also results, that God, in his moral nature, may be known by the pure and holy, in proportion to their holiness, their sanctification. In his light we see light; in proportion as we become conformed to his image we know Him. This position is strikingly illustrated in Christian experience in all ages, in an Augustine and Edwards sometimes to such an extent that an enrapturing sense and vision of Deity fills the soul.

(*e.*) It results, that God, in all his fulness of wisdom, love, and grace, is known and can be known only through Christ, only as we know Christ. He is "the Way" of knowledge as well as of redemption. Through Him we attain intellectual views of God as well as knowledge of the divine mercy. So that in one sense *we go through Christology* to Theology, in the way of knowing.

§ 2. *Can God be defined?*

If by definition we mean a complete view, so that the subject can be properly grasped, so that we can understand, and, so to speak, exhaust it, we must all say that we cannot give a definition of Deity. In this sense to define God would be to circumscribe Him. But the word *definition* is used in other senses. There are two chief senses in which we may answer the question in the affirmative. (1) An enumeration of the essential attributes or predicates of any being, substance, or thing. (2) The logical definition, which consists in giving the *genus* and *differentia* of any subject. In both these cases, we may attain at least to a proximate apprehension of what God is. We can enumerate the essential attributes as in the definition of the Shorter Catechism. Or, we can use the other method, the generic idea being spirit, and the *differentia* an enumeration of the attributes of spirit by which He is distinguished from other spiritual beings. God is a spirit, who is infinite, absolute, and perfect in all his attributes. In either of these senses we may be said to give a definition of Deity.

§ 3. *The Mode in which we gain our explicit Conception of Deity.*

There are here two chief modes found in systems of theology. (1) It is said that we can form an explicit conception of God, simply by an analogy of human nature. (2) The general Calvinistic position is that we form our explicit conception of Deity from the analysis of the idea of a perfect being.

Some Statements on both these Points.

1. Is it true that all we can know of the divine nature is from the analogy of human nature?[1] It is sometimes said that our whole idea of God is derived, not from the human spirit, but from the analogy of the human spirit's operations; that we take the human mind which we know by consciousness, and then simply extend the powers and operations of which we are conscious and thus form our idea of God; that this is the way

---

[1] This position has been discussed and defended by Dr. E. Beecher in "Bib. Sac."

in which the idea of God comes up in the human mind; in short, that God is an infinite man in our conception of Him. In regard to this,

(*a.*) Man is made in the divine image, according to the Scriptural representations, as to his essence, his spiritual being, yet he is put under the limitations of time and space. He is made in the divine image morally and also in his spiritual nature and capabilities.

(*b.*) We cannot help transferring to God the essential attributes of spirit as we find them in ourselves. This is a necessity of the mind as soon as we come to think about God. We know these attributes first consciously from our own spirits. Yet,

(*c.*) We do this and can do it and are warranted in doing it only under one condition, that of conceiving these attributes in God as perfect, as unlimited, saying that they are freed from all possible limitations of time and space by which we are confined. It is only on this condition of extending every attribute to infinity that we can make the transfer. Consequently, *besides the analogy of a human spirit, we must have the idea of an infinite and perfect being*, in order that we may make the transfer. The analogy would be false and fatal unless in making it we everywhere extended to infinity and absoluteness every attribute. That we have this idea of God as "native" to us is shown in Natural Theology.[1]

(*d.*) So God is not only like man but He is absolutely different from man, because He is an infinite and perfect Being, and in forming our conception of Deity we have to take these characteristics and add them to the analogy.

2. The other mode of gaining our explicit conception of Deity,—the analysis of the idea of a perfect Being. The older theology says there are three ways in which we do this: the way of Negation, of Causality, and of Eminence. By the way of Negation is meant, removing all imperfection, denying to God any limits or imperfections. By the way of Causality is meant, that what is found in the manifestation or revelation in

---

[1] "Apologetics," p. 76.

the creation, we ascribe to God as the cause, and we ascribe to Him those attributes which are needed to produce the effects in creation. By the way of Eminence is meant, that we ascribe to God in an eminent sense whatever of excellence is in the creature. He has the necessary attributes of spirit, but in an eminent degree. Each of these three ways is to be applied to all the attributes.

§ 4. *Anthropomorphism* and *Anthrqpopathism*. Ascribing to God the form or the passions of man.

This has been done not only by heathen, but by some who have had a light of divine revelation, as the Alexandrian Jews in the time of Philo; Tertullian, in the reaction from the purely ideal speculations of his time; Swedenborg, who says that God exists or is in the form of a man. The tendency of all rude nations is to imagine God as having some definite form and as having passions kindred to human infirmity.

Remarks.

1. All idolatry wherever found comes from the impulse to make an image of God and worship Him as such. The image is first made in the mind, and then carved in wood or stone. The idolatry begins in the soul, it is expressed externally and thus we have polytheism. This is one extreme, that of *superstition*. The image is made and worshiped and does not lead to anything beyond.

2. The other extreme is the thought of God as wholly out of relation with what is human and finite, an abstract deity. This is *irreligion*. This is the essence of the Deistic conception of God. He is supposed to be so distant that we cannot be brought into any relation with Him. Any feeling in Him, it is said, would be an imperfection. The constant tendency of the highly speculative, cold intellect is to this view—a God without feeling.

3. In the Christian system there is an intermediate view. It sets forth that man was made in the divine image, and hence there must be some analogy between God and man, hence there

may be symbols, and in our souls we may find something of God.[1] In the doctrine of the Incarnation, we have the contradictions between these two extremes, idolatry and deism, solved in a higher light. God comes in the form of man, and thus we are justified in attributing to Him human sympathy and love. The Christian faith is thus intermediate between heathenism and deism, in the sense that it exhibits in perfection that which these have felt after, God's nearness to man and his infinite majesty.

§ 5. *Scriptural designations of the Divine Nature.*

In the Scriptures we have a great variety of divine names.[2] They are divided as essential, attributive, and names of the modes in which God works. (*a.*) The essential names are *Jehovah* and *Elohim*. Jehovah is put in the front rank, it was to the Jew the ineffable name. The word is from the Hebrew verb "to be," it designates the pure being of God. Elohim has a more general sense. The relation in which these words stand to each other has been very much discussed. It appears to be proved that in the main Elohim is used of God in his most general characteristics and relations, while Jehovah sets Him forth as the covenant God, the God of his people, the God who manifests himself. This usage can undoubtedly be traced in many parts of the Scriptures.[3]—Another discussion was started some years ago in a work entitled Yah-veh, which urges that the name, as restored to this, its proper form, does not signify the covenant Deity and the pure being of God, but rather "He who is to be," as referring to the future manifestation of Deity in the Person of Christ.—The objections are: that even if the word have the future form, it would not necessarily have a future sense. "Jacob" has the future form, but it means, he supplants, and not, he will supplant. Still further, there is an

[1] Thus in the Old Testament we have representations of God derived from human emotions, as when it is said, "God was angry," "It repented Him of what He had done." So too the form of God is represented as passing before Moses.

[2] See Hävernick's "Introd. to Old Testament," and Hengstenberg's "Authenticity," etc.

[3] At the same time the authenticity of the Pentateuch is not affected if this is not established.

inappropriateness in representing God as revealing himself as one who is to be, merely. The proper revelation in the first stadium would be that of God himself. (*b.*) The attributive designations of God are those which describe Him by certain attributes, as The Almighty, etc. (*c.*) Those which designate Him in relation to his works are such as The Most High, The King, The Lord of Hosts, The Father of all.

§ 6. *Theological Definitions of the Divine Nature.*

The definition of God in the Shorter Catechism is one of the best, considered as a definition from enumeration of the essential attributes. It includes the attributes and the qualities of those attributes. First, He is a Spirit, then, infinite, eternal, and unchangeable, and then these attributes cover all the essential qualities of being, wisdom, power, holiness, justice, goodness, and truth. The highest definition in Pagan antiquity is that of Plato: "God is the eternal mind, the cause of good in nature." Calvin's definition, (and Luther's, nearly the same): "God is an infinite and spiritual essence." This is representative of a class. In the 16th century the Pantheistic discussion had not sprung up. It would do very well then to describe Deity as an infinite and spiritual essence, but it would not do now. In order to save Theism, besides such abstract statements, we must introduce terms which include the personality of God. Another definition very orthodox in its time is that of Wolff: "God is a self-existent being in whom is the ground of the reality of the world." This, if given now, would at once be called pantheistic. In most of the modern definitions the personality is insisted upon. Hase's is a good specimen: "God is the absolute personality who out of free love is the cause of the universe." Hegel's: "God is the absolute spirit," in the mouth of a Christain would mean, a self-conscious spirit, but with Hegel it meant a spirit without consciousness until it becomes conscious in the reason and thoughts of mankind.

A definition intended to combine the different attributes and to ward off Pantheism: "God is a Spirit, absolute, personal, and holy, infinite and eternal in his being and attributes, the ground and cause of the universe." In this definition the following points may be noted: (1) Spirit, which gives the generic idea, in contrast with what is material; (2) Absolute, free from restrictions, not dependent on anything, complete in himself; (3) Personal, to emphasize that characteristic as essential to Deity; (4) Holiness, that holiness which is the sum of his moral perfections, is essential to Him; (5) Infinite and eternal, *i. e.*, his being and attributes are not to be limited by any restraints of time and space; (6) The ground and cause of the universe. The reason of adding this phrase is the fact that as we know God we know Him in part through the universe, ascribing to Him as the cause whatever is found in the universe as an effect.

CHAPTER II.

THE DIVINE ATTRIBUTES.

§ 1. *The Idea of the Divine Attributes.*

In a large sense an attribute may be said to be any conception which is necessary to the explicit idea of God, any distinctive conception which cannot be resolved info any other. We start from the position that there is a divine substance, or essence; and an attribute, in distinction from the substance, is any necessary predicate that can be applied to this essence. The term attribute covers all the generic statements that we can make about God, in respect both to what He is and to his mode of working. Thus the unity of God, though inhering in the essence, is said to be an attribute. God's spirituality is also said to be an attribute, although spirituality belongs to his very essence or nature. Some of the definitions of attribute found in systems of divinity show that it is used in as broad a sense as this, *e. g.*, "Attribute is a quality by which anything is distinguished from any other thing;" "The attributes are the single elements (*momenta*) of the idea of God" (Hahn). In other words attributes are defined as the modes under which we are obliged to conceive of the divine essence, making the attributes simply subjective. Schleiermacher, carrying this to the extreme, says: "The attributes are simply individual relations of the divine perfections, which we conceive of in the fluctuations or changes of our pious feelings." Hegel in common with all pantheists says that the attributes of God are simply our subjective conceptions of God. There is in the divine nature nothing corresponding to them. This suggests the question, the most important one in respect to the attributes, whether there is a real distinction of the attributes in God himself or whether the differences are nominal, related merely to our conceptions. Here comes up the old controversy between the Realists and the Nominalists. The Realist said that in the *divine nature* there were proper distinctions, and the Nominalist that these were merely subjective names for Deity. In respect to this question we remark:

1. The divine attributes do not imply any real distinction in God in this sense, that God is a being composed or made up of distinct attributes. There is no distinction in the sense of composition of parts to make a whole. This can be applied only to a material organization.

2. What we call the attributes expresses our necessary conceptions of God, our analysis of the idea of God, of the most perfect being, and they are the necessary analysis of this idea. This analysis may be imperfect owing to our finiteness. It may include altogether too little; at the same time, it is a necessary analysis. We cannot do otherwise than make it. Otherwise the idea of God is a blank. To hold that the ideas exist merely subjectively in our minds would annul the very idea of a personal God. We cannot conceive of God except as active.

3. The attributes express real distinctions in God so far as this: that no one of them can be resolved into any other, and also so far as this, that all of them cannot be resolved into one idea or one fact about God, except the fact or idea that God is the most perfect being. Take the attributes of love and of omnipotence; you cannot resolve love into power, or power into love. You cannot deduce one from the other. So you

cannot resolve immensity into justice or derive justice from immensity.

4. The attributes describe in part what is essential to God in pure being or existence, and in part what belongs to Him as an active being. Yet,

5. It should ever be held fast that all the attributes are to be taken simply as modes of the being and action of one simple, perfect, spiritual essence. The essence and attributes are not separable. The attributes express the essence, the essence is the ground of the attributes. It is one simple spiritual essence in these different modes.

6. The attributes of God must differ from those of man at least so far as this: In man the faculties or powers act imperfectly, owing to the human finiteness; in God the activity of all the attributes must always concur, there must be a perfect harmony of working of all the attributes. Schleiermacher makes an objection to the whole doctrine of the Divine Attributes on this ground, that these imply limitation, and if so they cannot belong to God, and therefore cannot express anything real in God. As to this we say: (*a.*) What is meant by the attributes is this: certain modes of being or activity of an infinite being. But an infinite being may be infinite in a variety of modes. There is nothing in the nature of infinitude which contradicts the idea that it may be in a variety of modes, and express itself in a variety of ways, and if we say the attribute is a simple mode of being or acting, there is nothing in the nature of infinitude which prevents it. Even Spinoza said that of the infinite substance there were two modes, thought and extension, and one of his propositions is that there may be many others even in an infinite variety. There may be an infinitude of power and also of love, and one does not limit the other, because each of them is infinite. (*b.*) The view of Schleiermacher involves essentially the position that an infinite substance cannot act under finite modes, because it would be limited. This however is contrary even to the pantheistic theory, which claims that the one infinite substance does act or express itself under finite modes and a variety of them. An infinite being need not always act for an

infinite object or end. It may express itself in the finite. Space and time, for example, are boundless, but there is also a limited space and a limited time, and these do not exclude the infinitude of space and time. Then that which is infinite may exist in finite modes; therefore it may be true in respect to God that He can act under finite modes. (*c.*) The position of Schleiermacher amounts to this, that in God there cannot be any distinctions at all, or, in other words, we cannot say anything about God. In respect to Him we cannot have a subject and a predicate together. God is a mere It, blank, vacancy, ultimately zero. With a similar statement Hegel starts, viz., that being and nothing are the same, *i. e.*, being is wholly without distinctions, so that we can say anything about it, and therefore it is the same as nothing.

Concluding definition of a divine attribute: Any simple conception necessary to our analysis of the idea of God, whether in his mode of being or acting.

§ 2. *Classification of the Attributes.*

Various classifications have been proposed. One of the most current is the distinction of the *natural* and *moral* attributes: the natural, meaning the attributes of God in reference to and in contrast with nature; the moral, the attributes of God as our moral governor. (It is not meant, as sometimes interpreted, that the moral attributes are not native to God.) Sometimes the distinction is into *moral* and *metaphysical* attributes, the term metaphysical meaning, beyond the sphere of the physical. Another famous distinction is, the *immanent* and the *transeunt*, the former relating to God as He is in himself, internal, quiescent; the latter, as He is revealed in nature, the attributes in which his energies *pass over* into the external world. Another distinction is into *negative* and *positive:* negative, by which certain limitations are denied; positive, by which certain perfections are expressed. Another: *communicable* and *incommunicable*: those which can be and those which cannot be imparted.

All these modes are liable to the objection that we have to bring in the same attributes under both divisions. Every attribute can be both negative and positive, every one must be both immanent and transeunt, every one must partake of the qualities of natural and moral. Accordingly, there have been various attempts to depart from this merely formal mode and to describe or classify the attributes more from the analogy of man; *e. g.*, Hase and Hahn have a fourfold classification: attributes expressive of the divine essence, those pertaining to the divine understanding, to the divine feeling, the divine will. Undoubtedly there is a degree of truth in this.[1]

It is proposed to consider the divine attributes here under the following general scheme: (1) Of God, as an infinite and spiritual essence, or as pure being, not considered as in action; (2) The attributes of God as the supreme reason or understanding; (3) The attributes of God as moral, as holy.

CHAPTER III.

THE ATTRIBUTES OF GOD AS PURE ESSENCE OR BEING.

Strictly speaking, perhaps these would not be attributes, but they are generally classed as such. They might have been considered under the head of the divine nature, because they are different aspects of the divine substance.

§ 1. *Self-existence.*[2]

This is expressed in barbarous Latin as "*aseitas*," and also in the phrase "*causa sui*," "cause of himself." We could not

---

[1] Dr. Breckinridge has a peculiar classification, fivefold: The primary, essential, natural, moral, and consummate. In this arrangement it is difficult to see where a distinction can be made between the primary, the essential, and the natural. What is primary must be essential, what is essential must be primary, and what is natural must be both essential and primary. The consummate attributes express merely the harmony of the attributes, they are not distinct attributes, but modes in which these exist: fulness of life, majesty, all-sufficiency, and omnipotence. Omnipotence is certainly a primary, natural, essential attribute.

[2] See Sam. Clarke's "Demonstration of the Being and Attributes of God" for an ingenious argument upon this.

now say this in our sense of the word "cause," which implies a priority in time of the cause to the effect. But in the old classical sense it meant also the ground of being, that God has the ground of his being in himself. In other words, God is himself an absolute being, self-existent and complete in and of himself, not dependent on any other being. The proof of this attribute is not deduction, but an analysis of the idea of being. When we come to reflect upon being, as in Clark's demonstration: "Something is, something must always have been, and if something has always been, it must have been self-existent," we find that we are employing, not demonstration or deduction, but analysis. This idea of self-existence is expressed in the word "Jehovah," in the assertion that "the Father hath life in himself" (John v. 26), in the declaration that God is independent of all other beings (Isaiah xl.); Ps. cxiv. is also a description of the same.

§ 2. *Unlimited by Space or Time.*

God is unconditioned and unlimited by space or time. This is defining God in contrast with the finite. The infinitude of God has in it two elements. We define it negatively by denying that the attributes of the finite apply to it, and positively by describing God's being and modes of being. The limitations of the finite being comprehended in the two particulars of time and space, the infinitude of God may be resolved into two points, which are defined and described as two attributes, eternity and immensity.

By the very necessity of our thinking we are obliged to conceive of all that is finite under the limitations of space and time. We cannot define anything except in reference to space and time.

§ 3. *Eternity of God.*

1. The eternity is a necessary inference from the necessary existence. It implies, on the one hand, a negation of the limits of time, and positively, a mode of the being of God in relation to time. One of the old definitions of eternity is: the attribute by which God is freed from all the successions of time and

contains in himself the ground or reason of time. Another definition[1] is: God is the eternal Now. It is paradoxical, but that heightens its force. He is present in all time, as though all time were to Him a *now*. As far as his knowledge of time goes, it is as if past, present, and future time were before Him. Eternity has been defined by the Scholastics as *unicum instans, semper presens et subsistens.*

2. The popular definitions. God exists in the past, present, and future, and this is eternity. Or, that attribute by which God neither begins nor ceases to be. The phrase, God existing in past, present, and future, must be understood with some restrictions. God cannot *exist* in time. If He could, or did, He would be limited by time. The expression is popular, not scientific. The Scripture passages which describe God's eternity are more in the popular than in the scientific sense. Job xxxvi. 26, "The number of his years cannot be searched out;" 2 Pet. iii. 8; Isa. xli. 4; Ps. xc.; Rom. i. 20.

3. Of the relation of Time and Eternity to each other. Time is, properly speaking, according to the common definition, duration measured by succession. The idea of succession is necessary to the time. It is a continuance measured by discrete parts. Eternity, as used in contrast with this, has a two fold sense. It is sometimes used as equivalent to the whole of time, past, present, and future time constituting eternity; and secondly, in the most appropriate and strict sense, it is that which cannot be measured by time, which is not included in time or limited by it; it is the contrast with successions of time, and God as eternal is not in time, but, to use the old phrase, is the "Lord of time," considered as a series of successions. In the origin of our ideas, chronologically the order is time first, but logically eternity is first. Time presupposes the eternity. If it did not, we never could come at it through time, because no succession that we could conceive could make up eternity. It is the same impossibility as deducing the infinite from the finite.

4. In the attribute of eternity is involved the notion of im-

[1] Given by Boethius.

mutability. The two are closely connected in the Scriptures, as respects immutability of being and of the divine purposes. God's relations to man change, his own being never changes.

5. The metaphysical difficulty involved in the doctrine of eternity as applied to God. This arises from the idea of putting the successions of time in the divine mind. If they exist in God, then they have always existed. And as these successions are finite, the finite has always existed. This difficulty is to be removed, so far as we can, by the form of statement that the successions of time are not in God but dependent on God. Time as succession begins with the created universe, when there are beings to whom the succession applies. The successions of time are not in God, although they are present to Him in eternal knowledge. Yet it is granted that there is a difficulty here which we cannot perfectly master.[1]

6. Other points which are raised as to the attribute of eternity.

(a.) As to the Scriptural representation that God repents. Hos. xi. 8; Ex. xxxii. 14; Ps. cvi. 45. How are these declarations of God's repentance reconcilable with his immutability in his eternity? We are to consider that the changes here spoken of are not changes in Him, but in his relation to men. He repents and always meant to. The purpose is immutable. It involves no change in Him.

(b.) A difficulty arises in connection with Christology. If God is immutable, how could He become incarnate? The answer must be found in the position that in the Incarnation there is not a change in the divine nature, but in the divine mode of manifestation. The humanity is assumed by the divinity. The assumption does not change the divinity, which remains. It simply manifests itself in a human form. God can reveal himself in finite forms, and from eternity determines thus to do.

---

[1] There is a remarkable passage in the Principia, which illustrates Newton's metaphysical genius: "God is eternal, infinite, omnipotent, omniscient, i. e., He endures from eternity to eternity and is present from the infinite to the infinite. He is not duration and space, but He endures and is present; i. e., duration and space in their finite measures are not God, although God ever endures and is everywhere present, and by existing always and everywhere He constitutes, He makes duration and space."

§ 4. *The Divine Immensity and Omnipresence.*

By the divine immensity is meant the attribute of God in relation and in contrast with finite and limited space, as eternity is the attribute in relation to successions of time. The attribute in relation to space is expressed by two words, and has thus an advantage over the phraseology which expresses eternity. The two are, immensity and omnipresence. In the attribute relating to successions in time, we have no word corresponding to omnipresence. The immensity of God may be thus defined: the attribute which expresses (gives the point of view) that God is not limited or circumscribed by space, but that on the contrary all finite space is dependent on Him. It has both a negative and positive side: negative, denying all limitations of space; and positive, asserting that God is above space.

This attribute brings God into distinct contrast with all that is material. Matter is in space and is space-filling. Finite spirits have no ubiquity. To every finite spirit there is implied a *here*, which also implies that there is a *there* where it is not. But God by his ubiquity is everywhere, and yet in a certain sense also he is nowhere, in the sense of not being limited. The mode of the divine omnipresence is a question of debate.

1. God is present everywhere in working, in efficiency. There is an operative omnipresence of Deity. He acts in and through all space, He acts with and through every substance and thing.

2. On the other hand, God has also a substantial omnipresence, a presence of his substance or essence everywhere. In what this substantial omnipresence consists it is impossible for us to conceive. The necessity of asserting it comes from the fact that if we do not, we carry in our idea the thought that God is somewhere and works everywhere else, and that is limiting Him at once. The divine spirit must be everywhere in working, and therefore everywhere in essence, but *how* we know not. It is not a difficulty respecting God alone. The case is so in a measure with ourselves. Where we work we are present, but how we are present we know not. We cannot define ourselves with any relation to space whatever; as we can an atom. The

Biblical representations are in the form of description: Job xi. 7, Ps. cxxxix.; Isa. lxvi. 1; Jer. xxiii. 23; 1 Kings viii. 27.[1]

§ 5. *The Divine Spirituality, including the Divine Simplicity.*

These are also enumerated as the attributes of God, although they are but abstract statements for the concrete spirit in its mode of being. The divine spirituality is defined as negative and positive: negatively, materiality is excluded; positively, God is asserted to be essentially spirit or *life*. He is described in Scripture as the living God, as having life in himself, the most perfect life, efficiency, and power. Involved in the divine spirituality is the divine simplicity, the point of view under which God, as He is not allied to matter, so is not susceptible of division, not composite, not capable of being decomposed. Thus God is set forth in the Scriptures in contrast with idols, no graven image can be made to express Him: He is invisible, eternal, spiritual.

§ 6. *The Divine Unity.*

The idea of unity is a simple idea. As applied to God, however, it is not used as it often is in regard to finite things. As applied to these, unity is equivalent to one of a class, as, one man, an individual in comparison with other men, an individual copy of a class. This is not the sense of the doctrine of the unity of God. He is not one of a class. The synonymous word here is not *one* but *only*. God is the *only* God. There is only one infinite, eternal, personal being. God is one in all that concerns absolute divinity. There is but one God.

1. The Scriptural argument for the unity of God. It is at the basis of the whole Scriptures. In the Old Testament, Exod. xx. 3; Deut. iv. 35, vi. 4; Ps. cxxxv. In the New Testament, Mark xii. 29; John xvii. 3; 1 Cor. viii. 4; Eph. iv. 6; 1 Tim. i. 17, ii. 5; Rom. xvi. 27.[2]

[1] In Christian literature some of the most magnificent descriptions of Deity are those of his immensity, as the hymn of Abelard: "Super cuncta, subter cuncta," etc.

[2] Some German writers have endeavored to make out that the Scriptures contain the vestiges of Polytheism, as, *e. g.*, in the word Elohim. Again, in representing God as the God of the heavens, the God of hosts, some find traces of star worship. But star worship is forbidden in the early Scriptures. There is nothing in the Scriptures which has any reference to idolatry except in the way of opposition.

2. The significance of these representations that God is one. It is implied that God is the absolute personality, the absolute causality, the absolute independent being; that He is thus in contrast with idols, that He is the only being to whom these characteristics belong. *Deus solus unicus.* These Scriptural representations are still further opposed to two main errors, Polytheism and Pantheism. The opposition to polytheism is manifest. As against pantheism, the Scripture represents God as a living, personal, conscious being, one in contrast with any mere abstract idea, such as the generic reason or life, as a being having self-consciousness, blessed in himself. All his attributes are in constant life, activity, and energy.

3. Our rational idea of God cannot carry us any further than this, as to the divinity: that God is the absolute personality and causality, and that He is the only being to whom these terms can be applied. Reason does not decide what modifications there may be in the mode of existence of the divine being, as compared with that of creatures. There may be in God modifications of personality and of the attributes, which may make Him unlike the creature. What the Scriptures demand, and our moral nature demands, is one sole being, the object of worship. Scripture and reason both reject the idea of two absolute beings, or two infinite beings. There could not be such. Further than this, however, our reason does not take us.

4. The sense of the divine unity cannot be supposed to be exclusive of the divinity of Christ, as the Unitarians suppose, for the following reasons: (*a.*) Because the assertion of the unity was primarily directed in the Old Testament against idolatry, the worshiping of any beings less than God. (*b.*) Because the sacred writers use such language about Christ as would involve idolatry, if it were understood that the unity of the Godhead excluded the divinity of Christ. (*c.*) The Scriptures would be in contradiction to themselves, if they were interpreted as excluding the divinity of Christ.[1] "In the very exclusion of number from the Godhead, we may find the real significance of the unity

---

[1] In "Bibl. Sacr." 1846, p. 770, there is a very good statement on this point, from Twesten.

of God. By denying to Him all number, we ascribe to Him absolute unity. But this unity is still an immanent attribute of the divine nature." Its meaning is, that the nature of God is not capable of reduplication, is not to be regarded as a generic union, which includes under itself many or several individuals. Unitarians make a great assumption when they call themselves Unitarians, as if they defended the divine unity. The divine unity which many of them maintain is not the Scriptural view; it is the unity of an individual being; God is represented as a single individual, as one compared and contrasted with other individual beings. But this is neither a natural nor a Scriptural view of God. He is the Supreme Intelligence, the one Supreme Personality and Causality, but not one as an individual in the sense in which one man is an individual. If this could be established, the essential Godhead would be destroyed. It is a conception essentially anthropomorphic.

CHAPTER IV.

ATTRIBUTES OF GOD AS THE SUPREME REASON AND UNDERSTANDING.

§ 1. *Proof that God is the most perfect Intelligence.*

This is proved: (1) By the idea of the most perfect being. (2) From the intelligence shown in the world, the course of human history, and also, indirectly, by inference from our own intelligence. "He that made the eye, shall He not see?" (3) The Scriptures assert the divine Intelligence and its perfection, setting forth the omniscience and the wisdom of God: Job xii. 13; Ps. cxxxix.; Luke xvi. 15; Rom. xi. 33; xvi. 27. (4) The divine government proves the divine intelligence. The only basis of certainty in God's government is that He knows what is to occur.

§ 2. *Definition of Omniscience.*

Calvin's is one of the best: "That attribute whereby God knows himself and all other things in one eternal and most simple act." This includes what is omitted in many definitions, the knowledge which God has of himself. The characteristics of the divine knowledge are well given by Dr. Pye Smith: "It is (*a.*) Intuitive: all that God knows He knows by immediate view as we know things by direct inspection; (*b.*) Simultaneous: all that occurs in all times is in the divine knowledge at once; (*c.*) Exact; (*d.*) Infallible." The difference between the divine knowledge and ours is thus summed up in most theological statements: We acquire knowledge, but God knows immediately; we acquire in succession, but God knows simultaneously; we have a knowledge of only a part of time, God has a knowledge of all time; our knowledge is indistinct, God's is clear; ours is fallible, God's is infallible.

§ 3. *The objects of the Divine Knowledge.*

The divine knowledge is further divided in regard to the objects in the divine mind. (1) God knows himself, and in himself all other things, so far as they come from Him. This is the internal knowledge. (2) God truly knows all things as they actually come to be, as past, present, and future. He knows them under their real relations. This knowledge is not conditioned by those relations, but He knows them in those relations. *He makes* those relations. (3) God knows the essences of things, and here is a point where the divine knowledge surpasses any that man can have. Man comes to the barrier when he comes to the essence, but he knows there must be an essence, and it must be an object of knowledge. From our knowing that essences are and our ignorance of what they are, there must be some Being who knows more than we do. This proves that there must be an omniscience. (4) God knows what is possible as well as what is actual. He knows the possibilities of things. In making any human being, He knows how that being might possibly act. He knows how the individual will act under certain circumstances. He adopts a certain action into his plan and this secures a certain occurrence, but He knows also what is possible. This is opposed to the pantheistic view as given by Schleiermacher: "God knows only what is certain, what comes by necessity from his own being, his own nature, and not what is possible." But if God knows only what *is* and not what is possible, his knowledge must be inferior in some respects to that of man, because man can conceive of that which is possible.

§ 4. *Of Scientia Media.*

The authentic definition of this is, the hypothetical knowledge of the conditional future. Make an analysis of this phrase. A conditional future is a future which is dependent on certain conditions or contingencies. A knowledge of a conditional future would imply a certain knowledge of that future with its conditions and contingencies; that though it was contingent there was a certain knowledge of it; but a hypothetical knowledge means that the knowledge is still subject to some doubt. *E. g.*, God creates a certain man and places him in certain circumstances. What he does is dependent upon conditions, upon his surroundings and upon his will. A contingent event is one dependent on will. God knows what the man will do under the circumstances. But the theory of *scientia media* suggests that God's knowledge is not certain but hypothetical. *E. g.*, a man comes to a place where four roads meet. God knows that the man will be there and that four routes will be open to him, knows that he may take either, knows what will happen to him if he takes this, what if he takes that, but does not certainly know which he will take. For each of the contingencies God provides and meets with his own action in government whatever the man may do; He exhausts and provides for all the possibilities of the man's action, but does not know precisely what that action will be. This is the most ingenious theory on the Arminian basis. It aims to leave an uncertainty in respect to human volition and at the same time to secure a certainty of divine arrangement.[1] The form in which the theory is stated above is the one in which it is objectionable. In another form

---

[1] The theory of *scientia media* was first propounded by Fonseca, a Portuguese Jesuit, in the 16th century, and was further developed by Molinos, a Spanish Jesuit, in the 17th century. It was opposed by the Dominicans, by the Jansenists, and by the Protestants generally.

it is given simply as the knowledge of a conditional future,[1] *i. e.*, God knows all that a creature can do, then determines as to what the creature will do, and thus forms his plan. The divine wisdom knows all that is possible, and among all possible things chooses that which it deems best. This is undoubtedly correct and is in harmony with Calvinistic views. But the other view, that God simply provides for all contingencies, confounds two things: the knowledge of all possibilities, which is true; and the assumption that God does not know which of the possibilities will become actual. Against this form of the theory the two objections are: (*a.*) It makes the divine acts dependent on man's choice or will; (*b.*) It annuls the certainty of future knowledge, and if the future knowledge is uncertain, the knowledge is imperfect, there is no omniscience.

§ 5. *The Divine Prescience or Foreknowledge.*

This is commonly divided into knowledge of future necessary things, of future conditional things, and of future contingent things. The future necessary things are those which are in the course of nature connected by physical sequence. The future conditional things are those which will be, under certain conditions. The future contingent things are usually defined as events dependent on free will. The divine foreknowledge was doubted as early as the time of Cicero, who says: "If the acts of man are foreseen, then there is a certain order to them, an order of causation, and if there is an order of causation, then fate is the result." Socinus took the ground that there may be some things which God cannot be said to know in any way. Rothe says that God in creating man free, necessarily relinquished his knowledge of future actions. Dr. Adam Clark and Methodists generally define omniscience as the power to know all things. They deny that God does know all future events, but this is because He does not choose to know. As omnipotence is the power to do all things, so omniscience is the power to know all things, but this does not imply that all things are actually known. But omniscience, if omniscience at all, must be complete in itself,

---

[1] In this form it is carefully stated by Knapp.

it must be the knowledge of all things. Unless God have knowledge of future contingent events, we cannot say that He is omniscient, and in order that there may be any certainty in the divine government, God must know what is to occur in the future.

There are two chief sources of objection to this doctrine, viz., that it is inconsistent with free agency, and that we cannot know how God can know future contingent events. Answer to the first objection: The difficulty is only with those who deny that liberty and certainty can be reconciled. If these are consistent, then God may know how free agents will act. So the question runs over into the other, whether certainty and free agency are inconsistent and contradictory ideas. Even in respect to man, our knowing an event as certain does not prevent its being free. We can predict how some men will act under certain circumstances. If those who know a good deal about man may predict with more certainty, He who knows all about man may know with all certainty. If a tolerable knowledge of certainty with us is consistent with free will, who may say that a total knowledge may not be consistent with free will? The answer to the second objection, that omniscience as implying the knowledge of future contingent events, or events dependent on free will, is inconsistent with free agency, is to be considered more fully in connection with the subject of divine decrees. It may be said here: (*a.*) that the objection seems to rest on the assumption that God in respect to knowledge has a past, present, and future, so that the limitations of time in respect to knowledge apply to Him. This would assume that the whole veil of futurity lies before God as before us. But there cannot be anything future to the divine knowledge any more than there can to the divine being. (*b.*) God may know events in their causes. If He knows all the causes, then He may know all the events. This is a way in which God may know the possible future. Of course we here include in the cause, free will. God who made it may know how it will act under certain circumstances, and may adopt that action into his plan. (*c.*) God also knows the essences of things, and thus has a source of knowledge to us inscrutable, so that although we may not be able to conceive how God knows, yet He may know.

§ 6. *The Divine Reason.*

Not only is God's intelligence or understanding omniscient, knowing all things, but in God is also the primal reason. In God is the source of the ideas and knowledge of all intelligences. In the divine mind are the archetypes of all truth. Others have truth only by gift and derivation. The ideas of all things are ultimately in the divine mind, are eternal. That is the old Patristic view and is the sense and heart of the Realism of the Middle Ages. The Pantheistic view says that the ideas according to which all things are fashioned are extant in the universe; the Theistic view says that they are only in the divine mind.' The ideas of space, time, goodness, etc., exist only in the divine mind. This was the sense of the Logos in the ancient schools, the ideas in the divine mind according to which the world was fashioned. In the school of Philo, Logos means the same as Wisdom in the Book of Proverbs. In Prov. viii. 22 *seq.* Wisdom is personified.

Proof of the divine wisdom: (*a.*) The wisdom of God is asserted in Scripture: Job xii. 6; Proverbs iii. 19; Isa. xl. 13, etc. (*b.*) Besides, it is proved *a priori* from the divine omniscience. It is impossible to conceive that an omniscient and omnipotent and holy God could be other than wise. There is no conceivable reason for God's being other than in perfect and eternal accordance with wisdom. (*c.*) Also there are collateral proofs from the history and order of nature, the whole plan and history of the world, the divine moral government, and especially from the scheme of redemption, where we have the highest wisdom manifest.

Definition of Wisdom: That attribute of God whereby He produces the best possible results with the best possible means. That is wisdom everywhere, and in God it is superlative. The best possible results would of course bring into view the great end of God in creating the universe. Taking that end into view, considering that as decided, wisdom may be defined in another form, bringing out the divine attributes which concur in it, viz., the divine intelligence and love. Then God's wisdom is seen in his using the best means to secure the supremacy of holiness in the universe. Intelligence and love both concur. Wisdom is not merely an attribute of the intellect, but also of the heart.

CHAPTER V.

ATTRIBUTES OF THE DIVINE WILL.

§ 1. *Idea of the Divine Will.*

In some of the discussions in Theology, difficulty is occasioned by the different meanings of the term Will. In respect to God it is used in at least four different senses, viz., (1) As the faculty of self-determination, choice, power of determining self to any given course of action. (2) As significant of what God desires should be, not as expressive of a power but of a desire. This by the Scholastics was called "Velleity." (3) What God determines shall be, what God adopts as a part of his plan. (4) That which expresses the whole moral nature of God, the equivalent to which would be the divine holiness or the divine love, considered as the supreme moral attributes.—These different senses are important in the discussion of two main points: (*a.*) as to the doctrine of decrees, (*b.*) as to the doctrine of virtue.

Definitions of the Divine Will. Gerhard: "The will is the essence of God. It is God willing, *Deus volens.*" Calvin: "The will of God is that attribute whereby God tends to the good recognized by his intellect." The most general idea of will is that power by which one prefers and acts out his preferences. It includes both of these conceptions, both immanent and executive acts. Freedom ought also to be defined so as to include these two conceptions; "doing as one pleases" should not be understood as confining freedom to the executive act; there is freedom in the being pleased as well as in the doing. The divine will may be defined in a comprehensive sense as that capacity of the divine Being whereby He chooses and acts for the highest good. That combines the two senses of will, and states that they have ultimate respect to the highest good. The divine will as thus defined involves radically three notions: (*a.*) Freedom, (*b.*) Power, and (*c.*) Moral preference. The divine will as involving freedom is the absolute freedom of God, as involving power is His divine omnipotence, and as preferring what is best is His divine holiness.

§ 2. *The Distinction of the Divine Will as to its Objects.*

1. There is an internal activity of the divine will which we must conceive of as in God himself under the three points of view named. (*a.*) As freedom. It is the essential freedom of God, the attribute by which He is the author of all his acts. It involves the notion of the highest freedom and the highest moral necessity. (*b.*) As omnipotence. It must be conceived as having an internal sphere, and there it is the perpetual and self-sustaining energy of Deity. (*c.*) In the sense of preference. Here also it has an internal sphere. It is the immanent preference for the highest good.

2. External relation of the divine will. Here it is viewed as omnipotence. (*a.*) As power over possibilities. It is that characteristic whereby what God wills He might not, and what He does not will He might. It lies in his own pleasure to do or to refrain from doing. He might or He might not produce what He does produce in the world. (*b.*) Divine omnipotence as actually exerted in the creation and preservation of the universe. (*c.*) The divine holiness in relation to the creation. This is seen in God's willing and bringing about the highest good, which is the glory of God in the best possible moral system.

NOTE. The divine will can never be considered as arbitrary. The true sense of the expression that He does as He pleases is, that He is independent of the will of His creatures, though having the highest and best reasons for what He does.

§ 3. *Other Distinctions as to the Mode of Manifestation of the Divine Will.*

1. The decretive and preceptive will of God. The decretive is that which has reference to the divine decrees, what God purposes shall take place. The preceptive is that which God commands his creatures to do. These are often confounded by Arminians. God commands all his creatures to be holy. He permits sin. The permission is a part of the divine decree, but God does not enjoin or desire what He thus permits. Example of the decretive will, Isa. xlvi. 11; of the preceptive, the Decalogue.

2. The permissive and efficient will of God. This is the distinction made all through the history of Calvinistic theology down to the time of the Hopkinsian school in New England. God permits the morally evil and effects the good. In respect to sin, He for wise reasons simply determines not to prevent it, all things considered. The efficient will of God has respect to what God directly produces through his own agency. The importance of this distinction is, that we cannot logically or rationally or morally conceive that God would directly produce by his positive efficiency what He forbids. Accordingly we must employ some milder term than efficiency with respect to the relation of God to moral evil, and the term selected is permission. This may not be the best, but it is well to retain it until we get a better.

3. The secret and revealed will of God. This relates to what God keeps in his own counsel, and to what He has communicated: Deut. xxix. 29; Rom xi. 33. The same distinction is signified in somewhat barbarous Latin by the two phrases, "*voluntas signi*" and "*voluntas placiti.*" This distinction used to be much insisted on in the discussion of the divine decrees: 1 Tim. ii. 4; 2 Pet. iii. 9. It was said to be the revealed will of God that all should be saved, the secret will or actual determination in the matter, that some should be. A better point of view for this is found in the distinction between what God desires, in itself considered, and what He determines to bring to pass on the whole. In itself considered, He desires the happiness

of every creature, but on the whole, He may not determine to bring this to pass.

4. Other distinctions have been made, but they are not of much service. (*a.*) The antecedent and consequent will of God. The antecedent, God desires the salvation of all. The consequent, He determines to save some. Here will is used in the two senses of general benevolence and purpose. (*b.*) Absolute and conditional. What God wills without conditions and what is dependent on moral character. He wills sanctification through the truth, but He wills the renewal of the soul without antecedent repentance and faith, because the renewal is in the repentance and faith. (*c.*) The efficacious and inefficacious. That producing by efficiency, and that which does not act directly.

CHAPTER VI.

THE OMNIPOTENCE OF GOD.

This is the attribute of the divine will as power or efficiency.

1. The idea of Power. It is a simple idea in our minds, of force exerted. The origin of it is probably the exercise of our own power of willing or choosing. We get it not so much from external nature, as from the putting forth of energy in our own acts and from the resistance which we encounter.

2. Omnipotence is that attribute by which God is the absolute and highest causality; the absolute, *i. e.*, complete in himself, the highest, *i. e.*, above all other causes. In popular definition omnipotence is said to be that attribute by which God can do whatever He pleases. But this is not a sufficient statement, because it limits the omnipotence to the doing, whereas it is a capacity of doing as well as an actual doing. Philosophical limitation is given to it in another way, that God can do whatever is possible or whatever is an object of *power*.

3. Proof of the divine omnipotence.

(*a.*) Rational proof from God's very nature. We cannot conceive it otherwise than that an infinite and eternal being should be all-powerful.

(*b.*) From the order and existence of the created universe. The act of creation involves an omnipotent energy, if anything does.

(*c.*) Biblical proof. This is various and manifold. Gen. xvii. 1; Job ix. 12; Ps. cxv. 3; Jer. xxxii. 17; Rom. i. 20; Eph. i. 19; Rev. xix. 6.

4. Limits of Omnipotence. This phraseology is hardly strict. The limitations are simply those which arise from the divine nature or the nature of things, and are not any proper limitations of divine power. They relate to points which do not involve power, as, *e. g.*, that which is contradictory cannot be established; in other words, it cannot be an object of power. So God cannot change mathematical relations or make right to be wrong. This simply means that God's power cannot be conceived as manifested except in harmony with and as expressive of his perfect nature. It is not viewed as limited by anything outside of himself. The limitation comes from the perfection of his being.

Here comes up the question whether God can sin. So far as the real act is concerned, the answer must be No. It is inconsistent with his nature. It would destroy his divinity, that holiness or purity which makes the essence of his divinity. If He could sin He would not be God. The question however is discussed on another point, as to the bare, abstract, metaphysical possibility. Has God power enough to sin if He had a mind to? Then the question is absurd. Nobody would contest it.[1]

Another question is whether God can destroy himself. This involves a self-contradiction, the inconceivability of a self-annihilation, in which self both asserts and destroys its energy.

5. Schleiermacher's definition of Omnipotence. He says it is not properly understood as God's power to do what He pleases, but rather that God is the cause of all that is. Also, that there

---

[1] The question has been brought up in connection with "ability." When it is said that a man continuing in his sin can repent but will not, it is said that a parallel case is, God has the power to sin but will not. This certainly does not open much help to the sinful man, for if he should not repent until God sins he would never repent.

is no causality in God other than what is manifested. There is no power of doing but simply a doing. There is no reserved causality in God. The reply is: this is contrary to the very idea of rational, intelligent, and independent being. If God is such a being, his power cannot be limited by what is produced. The hypothesis rests on an essentially pantheistic notion of what God is; that He is simply a substance pouring itself out, and that all that exists is simply an emanation from Him, simply an evolution of his nature.

6. Objects of the divine omnipotence.

These are: (*a.*) Himself, God is self-sustaining. (*b.*) The works of creation, bringing these into being and upholding them. (*c.*) The moral world, omnipotence being directly exerted here in miracles and in the renewal of the soul, while in the ordinary course of nature it is exerted through second causes, making itself thus a regulated, ordinated omnipotence.[1]

CHAPTER VII.

THE DIVINE HOLINESS.

This is the attribute of the Divine Will considered as the immanent preference for the highest moral good or for that which is in itself righteous. This is the positive aspect of the attribute. Negatively, it excludes all moral imperfection and all moral impurity, not only from the Godhead, but as far as may be from the sphere of God's government. The divine holiness, taken in its fullest extent, is applied in a threefold way: (1) As designating the internal operation of Deity; (2) As expressed in the law of God which is holy, just, and good. The law expresses God's holiness in the form of injunction upon others. (3) It has a sphere in demanding moral conformity on the part of others. "Be ye holy, for I am holy."

---

[1] The question whether God could prevent all sin will come up in its proper place.

ANTECEDENTS OF REDEMPTION.   35

As God is holy, so must all moral beings allied with Him be holy. Holiness is sometimes used as equivalent to justice and contrasted with benevolence, holiness having respect to righteousness and benevolence having respect to happiness. But it is better not to use it in so restricted a sense, but rather to employ it to express the sum of God's moral perfections, his internal preference for the highest moral good.[1]

The definitions of the moral attributes of God depend upon the ethical theory which one adopts. Those who take the Utilitarian or Happiness view define all these as having respect to happiness. The same is true when holiness is taken to be the chief good; all the moral attributes being then defined as having ultimate respect to holiness. The various definitions and statements of these attributes form a wilderness. The difficulty arises largely from the fact that theologians are not agreed as to what attribute shall be viewed as the highest in God. In our view, holiness is the best term to use for this, and we frame our definitions in accordance with this usage.

In pagan antiquity the idea of holiness was external. It was simply the separation of the sacred from the profane, and this was largely the idea at the beginning of the spiritual education of the Jews. In no other religion than that of the Old and New Testaments is holiness considered as a distinct moral attribute. There holiness is made supreme in God and made to be binding upon men, and in no system of nature is this the case. Objectors sometimes say that all the precepts of the Bible can be found in pagan creeds, but there is no such precept as "Be ye holy, for I am holy." Neither is there any proof of love being the supreme virtue in any pagan system.

Questions sometimes raised in respect to the Divine Holiness. (1) It is said, we are holy, because conformed to a law; as God is holy, He must be conformed to a law, and therefore there is a law above God. *Reply:* There is no need of supposing a law to which God is subject. God is himself the reality of the law. There is no law above Him. The law is the expression

---

[1] There is one definition of *love* which would correspond with this, as we shall hereafter remark.

of the divine moral excellence, and holiness is the moral excellence itself. The definition of holiness as conformity to a law is inaccurate. Even our own holiness is not found in our accordance with a law. That *describes* holiness, but does not define it. Holiness is not holy because it is conformed to the law, but because it is the best moral state possible. (2) Another point of debate is raised in the statement: God is holy, and in that choice is involved, it is a state of the divine will: then He might not have chosen; and hence, He *might not have been holy.* To this we say: (*a.*) It is a bare, abstract possibility, purely metaphysical. (*b.*) The state of God as holy is spontaneously such or eternally so, by a moral necessity: It is not holy because God first chose to be holy, and then became so. Such a choice is utterly inapplicable to Deity, involving a time when God was not holy. The holiness is the immanent moral state. Wherever there is holiness there is a choice, but holiness is not the product of a choice. A holy state cannot be produced in a creature as a creature moves an arm. Holiness, repentance, faith, love are the choices themselves. So in God holiness was not the result of a choice, but an eternal choice. (3) Another question raised is, Whether God's will as holy is the source of right. *Remarks:* (*a.*) Taking God's will as the source of being to all his creatures, He gives them all, and gives them undoubtedly, the idea of right and of moral law; God's will is the source of right in that sense. (*b.*) Taking God's will as expressing God's moral pleasure or holiness, that will may be said to be the rule and standard of right, because it is supreme moral excellence to which we should be conformed. (*c.*) Taking the question to be whether God's will creates right and wrong, so that it can make right to be wrong and wrong to be right, it becomes absurd. (*d.*) Yet, things morally indifferent may be so commanded that they become right or wrong under the circumstances or relations; not that their nature is changed, but for wise reasons God has chosen thus to command. All external acts are indifferent in themselves and are made right or wrong only by the motive.

CHAPTER VIII.

THE DIVINE LOVE.

§ 1. *Definitions of Divine Love.*

These vary like those of the divine holiness, benevolence, etc. The divine love is taken most truly as equivalent to the divine holiness, in the sense that love is viewed as the subjective feeling, while holiness is the proper term for that as descriptive of its moral character or excellence. "God is love." Love is the interior state. Holiness is its characteristic. Love is the internal affection. Holiness is the purity of that affection.

The best definition is, Love is the attribute by which God delights in and seeks to communicate all good, especially moral good: and as correlative to this, it is implied that God is averse to and must overrule and punish all moral evil. Punishment has a ground in love. If I love moral excellence, I must hate and oppose that which is opposed to moral excellence.

The question arises whether the divine love can be exhausted or fully met within the sphere of the Godhead itself. Love seeks an object to fasten upon. If we say, the object of the divine love is the creature, then until the creature existed, God's love was simply a craving. Accordingly some from the attribute of the divine love deduce the doctrine of the Trinity. Love seeks an object. Divine love is infinite. It seeks an infinite object. Therefore there must be in the Godhead a distinction of persons. Taking this as a demonstration of the Trinity, it is imperfect, but as an illustration it is good.

§ 2. *Proofs of the Divine Love.*

1. From Creation. In the order of creation, love shines through all the hosts of animated beings.

2. From Redemption especially. 1 John iii. 1; iii. 16.

3. The Scriptures abound in descriptions of the divine love, besides those which are given in connection with the plan of redemption. 1 John iv. 16; Matt. v. 45; Rom. v. 8; Luke vi. 35.

§ 3. *Divisions of the Divine Love as to its Objects.*

The divine love has two main objects, the primary, God himself, the secondary, the creature. In the supreme love of God to himself, egoism is excluded by the nature of God. In loving himself most, God loves the embodiment of all that is supreme in excellence.[1] The divine love viewed as having respect to its secondary object, the creature, has two main forms: the love of benevolence and of complacency. The love of benevolence is that disposition of God or that form or modification of the divine love which leads God to desire to communicate happiness to all his sentient creatures, which leads Him to delight in all their happiness. The love of complacency is that element in the divine love which leads God to communicate and delight in the holiness of his creatures. The love of benevolence may be considered as having respect to happiness, the love of complacency to holiness; but both make up the divine love, both together and not one alone. Complacency is taking pleasure in something. Benevolence is disposition to do good to any one.

§ 4. *Other modifications of the Divine Love.*

Mercy and pity. These describe love as exercised towards the wretched, seeking their happiness. Mercy is sometimes used in reference to our needs as sinners. Luke i. 72; here, the term mercy is equivalent to grace, which is the divine love towards the undeserving and sinful.

Patience and long-suffering. Rom. ix. 22, ii. 4; 1 Pet. iii. 20.

Lenity of God, his goodness in mitigating punishment. Rom. xi. 22.

§ 5. *The Divine Benevolence.*

If the divine love as benevolence, or as exercised towards the creature, be taken as the highest moral attribute, it is not properly defined as the communication of happiness apart from holiness. If it be taken as a modification of the highest attribute, it may bear that restricted sense. It has been said that Edwards con-

---

[1] It is not best perhaps to make this prominent in preaching, lest it should be misunderstood; self-love in God being the highest excellence and in the creature the ground of all sin.

sidered benevolence to be the highest moral attribute, made the divine holiness to consist in benevolence and then made the benevolence to have ultimate respect to happiness. But this is not the real view of Edwards.[1] If benevolence be defined as having ultimate respect to happiness, and at the same time be made the highest moral attribute, the following objections lie against the position: (1) The theory presupposes that happiness is the highest good, which is yet to be proved. In the present stage of our inquiries we certainly cannot take this for granted. Rather we must assert that happiness is not the highest good, that holiness is; that being the highest good it involves of course a state of happiness as its accompaniment, but the essence of the highest good is holiness.[2]

2. If happiness be the ultimatum of benevolence, that to which it tends, it is difficult to reconcile with this the existence of so much misery in the world. Misery may be defended in relation to sin, and if holiness is the greatest object to be achieved; but if happiness is the greatest good, it is difficult to see how this can be made consistent with the actual amount and kinds of misery. It is said in reply, "Not all happiness but the highest happiness is the object;" but then what is the highest happiness? If it is happiness essentially then the same difficulty lies against the position; if the "highest happiness" is something more than happiness and includes another element, then that is the thing to be found out. What is that element in the highest happiness which makes it the greatest good, whereas other forms of happiness are not? Now there is happiness or pleasure in sin and there is happiness in virtue, but the difference of happiness is not what makes the difference between sin and virtue, because it would then be simply a difference of degree. Then there must be in the highest happiness an element which is not in the lower, which gives the moral

[1] There are but one or two passages in his treatise which would possibly bear that interpretation and they are not in formal parts of the work. The younger Edwards no doubt made benevolence to have ultimate respect to happiness. The assertion that the elder Edwards did so has been made so positively that it would be well for every one interested in the subject to read his treatise with this question in view.
[2] Happiness is but its glitter.

character; but that element cannot be the happiness, because that is what it has in common with sin. It must be a proper moral element.

§ 6. *Sources of Proof of the Divine Benevolence.*
(1) From the idea of a perfect being. There is no conceivable motive for such a one to be otherwise. (2) From the whole testimony and revelation of God set forth in the Scriptures. (3) From the sentient creation, the millions of sources of happiness found in nature and in man; from the fact that all the functions of animal life and of man in their proper and normal use are accompanied by happiness, and that there is nothing in nature to show a malevolent intent (Paley, Nat. Theol.). (4) From man's whole nature, intellectual, moral, social. (5) From the purpose and plan of Redemption. Here is the revelation of the highest benevolence.

§ 7. *Objections to the Divine Benevolence from the existence of Evil.*
Evil is of two kinds, natural and moral. Natural evil is pain from physical causes, moral evil is sin and its consequent suffering.

1. In respect to natural evil. Natural suffering, *i. e.*, the suffering from physical causes, cannot be shown to be inconsistent with benevolence. It is often warning, it is in different ways subservient to the good of the organism. Much of pain is a means of good in the discipline of the powers of individuals. Pain is not the worst thing in the world. Benevolence may inflict pain and may constitute beings so that they shall suffer pain. A nervous system is given, having high susceptibility to pleasure, and the liability to pain is incidental, often becoming a means of protection. We doubtless exaggerate in regard to the amount and degree of pain which the animal creation endures. In man the moral anticipation and the moral effects are peculiar and are the worst elements of pain. As to death, which is the great article of physical evil, as far as that is limited to the merely animal world, it is consistent with benevolence, taking benevolence to have respect only to the greatest amount of happiness. A succession of animals gives a greater amount of happiness than one animal in continued existence.

2. Moral evil. That suffering which is the consequent or punishment of sin is not inconsistent with benevolence. It is demanded by benevolence. Sin, as the worst thing in the world, must be punished by the next worst, which is pain. Sin is the worst thing, and the only way in which a stigma can be attached to it is to affix the next worst thing to it. Just as happiness in a just administration is connected with virtue as its immediate concomitant, so should suffering be with sin. Such suffering, as it is connected with transgression, has four relations: (*a.*) It is the direct expression of the desert of sin. (*b.*) It is for the highest good, the end of public justice—to sustain the law and the lawgiver. (*c.*) Suffering for sin in a state of probation may be a means of reformation to the sinner. (*d.*) In a state of probation it may be a means of discipline to higher holiness, to those who are already partly sanctified.

3. The real problem or difficulty remains, *the existence of sin itself.* All forms of physical evil can be shown to be consistent with benevolence. But if God might have prevented *sin* in a moral system, how is it consistent with benevolence for Him to allow it? There are several theories on this point.

The first theory. Sin is not an intrinsic evil, but an imperfect state of development. Sin is a necessary result of the finite. It is the imperfect action of the finite, a transition stage only, which is to issue in the highest good. It is a negation, *i. e.*, the sin of any act is what that act falls short of being. It might have been by so much better. A moral being might love God with all his heart, but he only loves his fellow men. He falls short of expanding his love to its full measure, and his sin is that deficiency. All finite beings must sin, and therefore the divine benevolence might allow sin. If a finite world was to be created, sin must be allowed. This is the general view of Leibnitz and his school.—Objections to this theory: (*a.*) It is in conflict with our inherent sense of sin as a moral evil. The disobedience of the divine law is not a partial obedience of that law. Sin is a violation of that which is holy and binding upon us. It is not a negation, it is the strongest affirmation of self. (*b.*) Sin is not merely the choice of a less good, but such a choice as implies the refusal of a greater good. If sin were simply the choice of a less good, the whole animal creation would be sinners, because they choose lower good, and they would be sinners in proportion to their weakness as animals. Sin in act is the choice of the less, knowing the greater. (*c.*) This theory does not show how the existence of sin is consistent with benevolence, but merely shows how the existence of relative imperfection is consistent with benevolence. No one doubts this, and if there are different orders of being, there must be relative imperfections somewhere. It may be consistent with benevolence to inflict pain for the sake of a greater good in the process of education, to stimulate an imperfect being to the proper development of his powers. In order to teach an animal to do something, we inflict pain. And it is benevolence on the whole to do that, if the teaching be worth anything; but that does not show how it is benevolent to make a man morally corrupt for the good of others. (*d.*) Relative imperfection is necessary, but sin is not, and therefore the theory cannot hold.

The second theory. This is the position that sin is the necessary means of the greatest good, though in itself the greatest of evils. This has been attributed to several New England divines of the older Hopkinsian school. It is the result of the divine efficiency scheme. Those who hold it are careful to say that they do not mean that sin is in itself a good or that it is a direct means of good, but that it is overruled to the greater display of the divine goodness. Sin is the necessary means of the greatest good, and therefore it is consistent with benevolence, because benevolence has respect to the highest good. This comes up for discussion afterward in another connection.[1] We mention here only some of the ambiguities in the statement.—What is meant by the greatest good? Is it happiness or holiness, or happiness in holiness? What the purport of the position is, depends very much upon the answer to this question. Then what does the term *necessary* mean? It is used in different senses. It may stand for a metaphysical necessity, so that sin is the necessary stage in the progress toward the greatest good, and in this sense the theory would be the same

[1] Page 147.

as the first. Or, necessary may mean that the highest good cannot be obtained without this, that it is a necessary condition; the sense of the word may be that the end of the moral system could not be attained without sin, that God could not manifest his glory perfectly except by means of, or on occasion of, sin.

The third theory. That sin is in the best system because it is the necessary incident to moral agency. God could not create free agents and prevent all sin in the system. The necessity comes here, not from the relation of sin to the highest good, but from its relation to freedom. Freedom is such a power that it can be exerted in sinning despite omnipotence. God could not prevent all sin in a moral system from the nature of free agency. Prevention of all sin under the circumstances is not an object of omnipotence, any more than altering the relation of the three angles of a triangle to two right angles. We defer the discussion of this theory also.[1]

The fourth statement. The relation of the existence of sin to the divine benevolence is beyond our comprehension. There is clear proof, on the one hand, of the benevolence and even of the grace of God, and on the other, of the existence of sin. We must take the two as matters of fact, and not allow the existence of sin to override the divine benevolence. To solve the problem we would need omniscience.[2]

CHAPTER IX.

THE DIVINE VERACITY.

This is not, strictly speaking, an attribute, but a modification of the attributes of holiness and wisdom. Yet it is often treated as an attribute. Veracity is equivalent to the truthfulness of God, the certainty that He will be true in declaring what He is and what He will do. Truth generally is the conformity of declaration or representation to the reality.

[1] Page 149.
[2] Müller says, that if we could understand sin it would not be sin, for that would imply its rationality, whereas it is irrational.

Proof of the Divine Veracity.

1. There is no cause or motive for error in the Supreme Being.

2. Scriptural Proof: Exod. xxxiv. 6; Num. xxiii. 19; Isa. xxv. 1.

The Scriptural usage of *Truth*, as applied to God, implies three things: (1) That God is the truth, metaphysically, as to his nature. God is that which as God He must be: 1 John v. 20; John xvii. 3. (2) That God is the source and center of all truth. (3) In the sense of the divine veracity or truthfulness. On this point two or three questions are raised: (*a.*) Whether God is sincere in his invitations to sinners who will be lost. The invitations are actually made on practicable conditions, and there is no obstacle to their acceptance but man's depravity. (*b.*) Whether it is consistent with the divine veracity to threaten those who may not ultimately be punished. All such threatenings are to be taken as penalties attached to the violation of law, and if anything can take the place of the execution of penalties, there is nothing inconsistent with veracity in such substitution. The great end to be answered by the penalty of the law is reached in the atonement. The end of the law and of the penalty is not the penalty itself or suffering. If suffering were the great end, then God could not be true and take away the suffering. But the great end is holiness, and the suffering is merely in order to that. (*c.*) Whether it is consistent with the divine truthfulness to say that God repents, etc. This has already been considered.

CHAPTER X.

THE DIVINE JUSTICE.

§ 1. *General Idea of the Justice of God.*

The word justice is one of the disputed terms in the theories of the atonement and of justification. It is used in both a general and a specific sense; in the general sense as equivalent to holiness; in a specific sense, as in distributive justice, for example, where it means, technically, dealing with each according to his deserts. Justice is not benevolence, though benevolence may require it. Benevolence, used in a partial sense, refers to happiness; and justice, used in a partial sense, refers to desert. It is best to carry both up into a higher attribute, public justice, holiness or love. Still, public justice and love differ in this, that love expresses the attribute of God, and public justice its manifestation in a moral government. Holy love induces God to institute a moral system, by which He may show his highest glory and secure the highest good of his creatures. Justice is his mode of administering that system by his moral law, so as to secure its ends, by treating each according to his deserts, yet each in relation to the great ends of the system. We might show by citations from many authors, that this is the established meaning of distributive justice.

§ 2. *Proofs of the Divine Justice.*
1. God as perfect must be just. We cannot conceive otherwise of a moral Governor.
2. The divine justice may be deduced from the other attributes, wisdom, holiness, and love.
3. History abounds in evidences of the divine justice.
4. The Scriptures recognize and assert that God is just 2 Chron. xix. 7; Job viii. 3, xxxvii. 23; Rom. iii. 26.

§ 3. *Distinctions in respect to the Divine Justice.*
1. Legislative, by which is meant, God's holiness in giving a law with sanctions. Its requirements are holy, its sanctions are rewards and punishments.
2. Executive or judicial justice, as seen in God's administering moral government according to moral law, by positive rewards and punishments. There must be in it rewards and punishments in order to distinguish a moral government from a physical, and law from advice. By these God shows his approval of holiness and disapproval of sin, and only thus secures the end of a moral government. This is sometimes called vindicatory justice.

§ 4. *Why does God as a Moral Governor exercise punitive Justice?*

There are four theories: (1) Because sin is essentially ill-deserving. (2) To reform. (3) To deter. (4) From the interests of general justice.

The first theory. Sin is punished because it is essentially ill-deserving. (*a.*) Sin is the worst thing possible, and as such requires to be attended by evil, the next worst thing. (*b.*) Conscience asserts the desert of punishment. In him who sins there is a sense of guilt which is met only by punishment. (*c.*) Our judgments about others attest the same, our indignation, for example, at great injustice or cruelty. The moral emotion is instantaneous, the mind pronounces that the evil act deserves punishment. (*d.*) God as a moral governor must manifest his hatred of sin as the opposite of his own holiness, and to do this He must punish.

The second theory. That the end of punishment is to reform. This is the position of Pelagians, Socinians, and Universalists. It views the punishment in relation to the culprit. There is no doubt that punishment has incidentally this effect. But this cannot be the sole end, for if it were, (*a.*) It would be opposed to the moral convictions of the culprit himself. He feels that punishment is right even though it does not reform him. (*b.*) If this be the end, the end is not answered, there are many cases where punishment does not reform. (*c.*) Punishment could not answer the end of reforming unless it was also felt to be right.

The third theory. That the chief end of punishment is to deter others. This views the punishment in relation to other culprits. Deterring others is also an incidental end of punishment, but is not the chief end, for, (*a.*) It is against our moral convictions as to justice that we should be punished simply to keep others from doing wrong when we do not deserve punishment ourselves. (*b.*) If this is the only end of punishment, it is not attained. Unless the first theory be true, the second and third lose their force.

The fourth theory. That punishment is required by what is called general justice or regard for the general good. This is

ANTECEDENTS OF REDEMPTION.

ambiguous. It is false or true according to the explanation of it. There are three explanations of it. (1) The public good is taken to be happiness. (2) The general good is taken to be more specific—to reform the criminal and to deter others. As thus understood the position comes to be that of the second and third theories. (3) The public good is understood as equivalent to holiness, and thus punishment is necessary as the expression of, and to promote, holiness.

If the public good is taken in the first sense, happiness is made the great end of the divine system, which falls to be considered by and by. If it be said it is the highest happiness which is intended, there is then the doubt as to what the highest happiness means. If the happiness is such as is found only in holiness, another form of the theory is presented.—The third form above is the true statement, viz., punishment is required by public justice, as the expression of, and to promote, holiness. Punishment is needful to express the displeasure of a holy God against sin as ill-deserving, and also to preserve the love of holiness and hatred of sin in others. (*a.*) This unites the two views of the inherent ill-desert of sin and the final ends of the whole system. Sin is punished because it is ill-deserving and also to promote the great end of the system, or holiness. (*b.*) This view does not make the punishment of sin to be the great end of the system, but holiness, the maintenance of the supremacy of righteousness. According to the reasoning of some in respect to the first theory, it would seem that the great end of the system was reached by punishment, but really punishment is inflicted in order that holiness may be maintained. (*c.*) This view will of course allow that punishment may in any case be remitted, if the end can be gained in some other way. Whereas, taking the first view in its strictness, that sin is punished because it is essentially ill-deserving and for that sole reason, then it follows that sin *must* be punished at any rate, and then there can be no atonement, or else it must be a commercial atonement, a *quid pro quo*, an exact equivalent to the same amount of punishment.

BOOK II.

THE TRINITY, OR GOD AS KNOWN IN THE WORK OF REDEMPTION.

"'Εν τριάδι ή θεολογία τελεία ἐστί."—ATHANASIUS.
." Ubi amor, ibi Trinitas."—AUGUSTINE.

PRELIMINARY REMARKS.

1. The specific character of the Christian doctrine respecting God is, that He has become known to man in connection with the work of Redemption, as Father, Son, and Spirit; so that all our knowledge of God may be reduced to the formula: God = Father, Son, and Spirit.

2. The center and source of our knowledge respecting the Trinity is to be found in the Person of Christ, and in his revelation of God to man. His person is set forth as distinct from that of the Father: He also sends the Spirit.

3. The primary Scriptural aspect of the doctrine of the Trinity is not speculative but practical. In the Scriptures it is a great truth, underlying the whole Christian revelation: God as Father, the source of Redemption; God as Son, achieving Redemption; God as the Holy Spirit, applying the Redemption to man. It is not a barren, abstract truth, but vital, interwoven with the whole Christian economy. This holds true, whatever difficulties may be found in the formal statement of the doctrine. The doctrine has always been vital in Christendom, the source of the life and power of Christianity. We find God in the plan, God in the work, God in the carrying into execution of the economy of Redemption. The whole revelation of God *ad extra*, the divine economy *ad extra*, is in this Trinitarian plan.

Nothing can be further from the truth than the representation of the Trinity as a mere abstract doctrine about the interior of God, with no vitality.[1]

4. The doctrine of the unity of God, taken in the sense that God is a single person, like a human person, having a single, circumscribed personality, is no more natural, and no more

---

[1] See Dr. Bushnell, in New Englander, 1854.

rational in itself, than the doctrine of the Trinity. God is the *only* being; there is only one such being—that is the truth, and the whole of the truth on this point. But it is in itself really no easier to conceive of God as one person, single I, than as three persons, and no more rational. It is anthropomorphic as truly as some popular misrepresentations of the Trinity are said to be tritheistic.

5. The doctrine of the Trinity being one respecting the interior economy, as well as the mode of revelation, of the Godhead, we must naturally expect that it will be mysterious, in the sense that we cannot grasp it, conceive of it definitely, as we do of things and beings finite and limited. It is a mystery, not an absurdity; an absurdity is a statement which involves what is self-contradictory to conception. It is a mystery, not an enigma; for an enigma is something that puzzles the ingenuity, of which there is supposed, however, to be a definite solution. A mystery is somewhat, which is partly intelligible and partly unintelligible—intelligible in many of its relations and modes of manifestation, unintelligible in its interior nature. Athanasius hence well says, "this doctrine is not an enigma, but a divine mystery." We may know that it is, but not what it is. A mystery, again, is, in the Scriptural usage, some revealed fact respecting God and the divine agency, which we can comprehend so far as it is revealed—which we can believe on sufficient testimony, but which we cannot grasp with the understanding.

The doctrine does not assert that God is one and three in the same sense, "which one consideration," says Dr. South, "well weighed, will blunt the edge of all assaults against this article." How far we may even find something rational in it, we shall consider.

6. For the Trinity there is a strong preliminary argument in the fact that in some form it has always been confessed by the Christian Church, and that all that has opposed it has been thrown off. When it has been abandoned, other chief articles, as the atonement, regeneration, etc., have almost always followed it, by a logical necessity; as when one draws the wire from a necklace of gems, the gems all fall asunder. It is also

true that it has been the subject of many prolonged controversies and various modes of statement. But the great result of these has been to bring out the doctrine in its various aspects, and especially as interwoven with the scheme of Redemption.

7. The leading formula of the doctrine was adopted to guard against three errors: Tritheism, Sabellianism, Arianism.

Outline of the Course on the Trinity.

PROP. I.—The Scriptures represent God as one, yet they ascribe Divinity to the Father, the Son, and the Holy Ghost.

PROP. II.—The Distinctions of the Godhead set forth here are not confined to the revelation of God, but are internal.

PROP. III.—The existence of such personal distinctions in the Godhead is not contrary to reason, though it involves a mystery.

PROP. IV.—The history of theology and of philosophy tends to confirm the Christian faith in the Trinity.

CHAPTER I.

THE MANIFESTED TRINITY.

First Proposition. While representing God as one, the Scriptures also ascribe divinity to the Father, the Son, and the Holy Spirit.

Course of the Argument.

I.—That God is one—unity is ascribed to God.
II.—That the Father is divine.
III.—That the Son is divine.
IV.—That the Holy Spirit is divine.
V.—That the Father, Son, and Holy Spirit are classed together, separately from all other beings. The Trinitarian texts.

§ 1. *That God is one.*
See discussion of the Divine Unity.
Scripture Proof:
Exodus xx. 3. "Thou shalt have no other gods before me."
Deut. iv. 35. "Unto thee it was shewed, that thou mightest know that the Lord He is God; there is none else beside Him."
Deut. vi. 4. "Hear, O Israel: The Lord our God is one Lord."

Mark xii. 29. "And Jesus answered him, The first of all the commandments is, Hear, O Israel: The Lord our God is one Lord."

1 Cor. viii. 4. "We know that an idol is nothing in the world, and that there is none other God but one." (Referring to Deut. iv. 39. "Know therefore this day, and consider it in thine heart, that the Lord He is God in heaven above, and upon the earth beneath: there is none else.")

Eph. iv. 6. "One God and Father of all, who is above all, and through all, and in you all."

1 Tim. i. 17. "The only [wise] God."

§ 2. *That the Father is divine and a distinct Person.*

This is not contested.

(*a.*) The word Father is used in the Scriptures in a twofold sense and relation in respect to the Godhead: sometimes as equivalent to God, sometimes of the first person in the Trinity.

Of passages where the word is used as equivalent to God, and not implying personal distinctions, there may be mentioned:

In the Lord's prayer: "Our Father which art in heaven."

Deut. xxxii. 6. "Is not He thy father that hath bought thee?"

Isa. lxiii. 16. "Doubtless thou art our Father, though Abraham be ignorant of us. . . . . Thou, O Lord, art our Father, our Redeemer."

Ps. ciii. 13. "Like as a father pitieth his children."

(*b.*) Passages in which the word is applied to God in contrast with Christ, (yet not with direct respect to their personal relations to each other as Father and Son, even in the revelation).

1 Cor. viii. 6. "To us there is but one God, the Father, of whom are all things, and we in Him; and one Lord Jesus Christ, by whom are all things, and we by Him." This is spoken of Christ, not in his internal, but, so to speak, external relation to the Father, (a statement of course not *inconsistent* with the divinity of Christ). The word Father here means not the whole Godhead, but the unrevealed.

Gal. i. 3, 4. "Grace be to you, and peace, from God the

Father and from our Lord Jesus Christ, who gave himself for our sins, ... according to the will of God and our Father." (The latter expression is a Hebraism, *and* for the relative).

John xvii. 3. "That they might know thee the only true God, and Jesus Christ, whom thou hast sent."

Eph. iv. 5, 6. "One Lord, one faith, one baptism, one God and Father of all, who is above all, and through all, and in you all."

(*c.*) There are other passages where the word is used as denoting a special relation to Christ as Son, to Christ in his office of Redeemer.

Rom. xv. 6. "That ye may with one mind and one mouth glorify God, even the Father of our Lord Jesus Christ."

2 Cor. xi. 31. "The God and Father of our Lord Jesus Christ, which is blessed for evermore, knoweth that I lie not."

Eph. i. 3. "Blessed be the God and Father of our Lord Jesus Christ, who hath blessed us with all spiritual blessings in heavenly places in Christ."

John v. 18. The complaint of the Jews because Christ had "said also that God was his Father, making himself equal with God."

John v. 23. Christ's declaration of the design of God, "that all men should honor the Son, even as they honor the Father."

(*d.*) A class of passages may also be referred to, in which a still more intimate relation seems to be implied, (not now to discuss *what* relation, but deferring the question until the *Sonship* is considered).

John xvii. 1. "Father, the hour is come: glorify thy Son, that thy Son also may glorify thee."

John x. 30. "I and my Father are one."

NOTE.—That form of the Sabellian hypothesis, which makes the Father one of the modes of manifestation of the hidden God,[1] has no countenance in Scripture. It is inconceivable. There is no Father manifested; it is God the Father —Father being the perfect equivalent of God.

---

[1] This view says that the hidden, unrevealed, God and the Logos are from eternity, but that the Father, Son, and Spirit are modes of manifestation of that hidden God.

John x. 15. "As the Father knoweth me, and I know the Father."

§ 3. *That the Son is divine and a distinct Person from the Father.*
The argument for this is cumulative, derived from a variety of independent assertions of the Scriptures.

(*A.*) Christ was pre-existent. He existed as a distinct personal being before He came into the world. "Manhood was not his original character."

(*a.*) The following passages have special force, being Christ's own testimony:

John iii. 13. "No man hath ascended up to heaven but He that came down from heaven, even the Son of man," etc.

John vi. 38. "I came down from heaven, not to do my own will."

John vi. 62. "What and if ye shall see the Son of man ascend up where He was before?"

John xvii. 5. "Glorify thou me with thine own self with the glory which I had with thee before the world was."

John viii. 58. "Verily, verily, I say unto you, Before Abraham was, I am." (Socinus would interpret this, Before Abraham can be Abraham, I must be Messiah, *i. e.*, in the decree of God. The Jews interpreted the verse before differently, saying, "Thou art not yet fifty years old, and hast thou seen Abraham?")

(*b.*) Another class of passages embraces such as these:

1 Cor. xv. 47. "The second man is [the Lord] from heaven.'

Gal. iv. 4. "When the fulness of the time was come, God sent forth his Son, made of a woman, made under the law"

Col. i. 17. He is before all things and by Him all things consist."

John i. 1, and 3. "In the beginning was the Word." "All things were made by Him."

(*c.*) There is a class of texts which imply a change in Christ's condition, through his Incarnation.

John i. 14. "The Word was made flesh."

Phil. ii. 6, 7. "Who being in the form of God ..... made

himself of no reputation." (The expression "form of God" proves pre-existence. "Form of God" could not be used for mere endowments.)

(*B.*) Christ was not merely pre-existent (and superangelic, Heb. i. 4, 5, 6; Rev. v. 11), but He was the first of all beings excepting the Father.

John iii. 31. "He that cometh from above is above all."

Col. i. 15. "Who is the image of the invisible God, the firstborn of every creature."

Col. i. 18. "Who is the beginning, the firstborn from the dead; that in all things He might have the pre-eminence."

Rev. i. 5. "The prince of the kings of the earth."

Rev. iii. 14. "The beginning of the creation of God."

Matt. xi. 27. "All things are delivered unto me of my Father."

Matt. xxviii. 18. "All power is given unto me in heaven and in earth."

John x. 15. "As the Father knoweth me, and I know the Father."

Col. i. 15, 17. "Who is the image of the invisible God." "And He is before all things." These and many similar passages show that Christ is the first being in the universe, next the Father.

(*C.*) Christ was not only pre-existent, superangelic, next the Father, but also the Creator of the universe.[1]

John i. 3. "All things were made by Him," $δι΄ αὐτοῦ ἐγένετο$.

Heb. i. 10. "Thou, Lord, in the beginning hast laid the foundation of the earth; and the heavens are the works of thine hands."

Col. i. 16. "For by Him ($ἐν αὐτῷ$) were all things created ($ἐκτίσθη$) . . . . . all things were created by Him and for Him" ($τὰ πάντα δι΄ αὐτοῦ καὶ εἰς αὐτὸν ἔκτισται$).

As to the force of this argument we remark:

1. Creation is an act of omnipotence; it is inconceivable that

---

[1] "The Christian Cosmos: the Son of God the Revealed Creator," by E. W. Grinfield, London, 1857, is full and good on the Biblical teaching, the Testimony of the Church, and the Bearings of the Doctrine.

it should be delegated; if anything implies omnipotence, creation does.

2. Creation is expressly attributed to God, hence Christ is God.

Gen. i. 1. "In the beginning God created."

Isa. xliv. 24. "I am the Lord that maketh all things."

Heb. iii. 4. "For every house is builded by some man, but He that built all things is God."

3. It is no objection that in John i. 3, δι αὐτοῦ is used (in Col. i. 16, it is ἐν αὐτῷ), for in Rom. xi. 36, of God the Father it is said "all things" δι αὐτοῦ; and of Him also in Heb. ii. 10, δι οὗ, "through whom are all things."

4. Nor can an objection be drawn from the passages which ascribe instrumentality to the Son in creation.

Heb. i. 2. "By whom also He made the worlds."

This is not inconsistent with proper divinity: we infer that only through a divine being could such a work be accomplished —for Christ is elsewhere described as divine.

(*D.*) Christ is not only pre-existent, superangelic, next the Father, Creator, but other incommunicable divine attributes (or those we must conceive of as such) are ascribed to Him.

These attributes are not merely such as imply the perfection of any being after his kind, but those which imply divinity.[1]

(*a.*) *Omnipotence.*

Is. ix. 6. "His name shall be called the mighty God."

Phil. iii. 21. "The working whereby He is able to subdue even all things unto himself." (See also 1 Cor. xv. 26. "The last enemy that shall be destroyed is death.")

Heb. i. 3. "Upholding all things by the word of his power."

Rev. i. 8. "I am .... the Almighty."

(*b.*) *Omnipresence.*

Heb. i. 3, see above. (Ubiquity.)

Matt. xxviii. 20. "Lo, I am with you alway."

(*c.*) *Eternity.*

John i. 1. "In the beginning was the Word."

---

[1] The argument is: having divine attributes, He must be divine.

Rev. i. 8. "I am Alpha and Omega."
    17. "I am the first and the last."
    18. "I am He that liveth."
Rev. xxii. 13. "I am Alpha and Omega."

Compare Is. xliv. 6. "I am the first and the last: and beside me there is no God."

(*d.*) *Omniscience.*

As to Christ's superhuman knowledge:

Compare Luke ii. 47: "And all that heard Him were astonished at his understanding and answers," with Isa. xl. 2: "And the Spirit of the Lord shall rest upon Him, the spirit of wisdom and understanding."

John ii. 24. "He knew all men"—"what was in man."

Matt. xi. 27. "Neither knoweth any man the Father save the Son."

John xxi. 17. "Lord, thou knowest all things."

Rev. ii. 23. "I am He which searcheth the reins and hearts." (Compare Jer. xvii. 10. "I the Lord search the heart, I try the reins." Acts i. 24. "Thou, Lord, which knowest the hearts of all men.")

Two confirmatory grounds of argument as to Christ's possession of divine attributes.

1. From his working of miracles—in a peculiar way: (*a.*) As proof of his messiahship, and Messiah is divine; (*b.*) In his own name and for his own glory—different from the disciples, who wrought in the name of Christ, and by power received from Him.

2. The last judgment is to be conducted by Christ, which implies a divine position and authority together with the attribute of omniscience.[1]

(*E.*) Christ is not merely pre-existent, above all, Creator, possessor of divine attributes, but the divine name is applied to Him as to no other being in the Scriptures, excepting the Father, and in a way which implies supreme divinity.

---

[1] In the Christ. Exam., Nov. '57, the judgment is resolved into the idea of retribution as centering in Christ. The older Unitarians did not allow that the Scriptures taught these things of Christ, but the younger allow them and say they are metaphorical.

The passages in which Christ is called God:
Ps. xlv. 8; Ps. cii. 24, 25, compared with Heb. i. 8, 10; Acts xx. 28; Rom. ix. 5; Eph. v. 5; 2 Thess. i. 12; Titus ii. 13; 2 Pet. i 1; John i. 1; 1 John v. 20.

A general objection to the whole argument under this head is that there are cases where the name "God" is applied to inferiors. As Exod. vii. 1, "Jehovah said to Moses, See, I have made thee a god (Elohim) to Pharaoh"; Ps. lxxxii. 6, "I have said ye are gods, and all of you children of the Most High" (Elohim used of magistrates).

But, in these cases the context decides. Besides the term is Elohim (the appellation rather than the most proper name of God), while "Jehovah" is expressly applied to Christ.

(a.) The first class of passages, showing the *direct* use of the name, God.

(The consideration of John i. 1 is postponed.)

1 John v. 20. "This is the true God and eternal life." The passage has immediate reference to Christ. "The eternal life," in John's usage, relates to Christ, and the reference here is the same for the true God as for the eternal life.

Rom. ix. 5. "Whose are the fathers, and of whom as concerning the flesh Christ came, who is over all, God blessed forever." All the MSS. and ancient versions have it thus; in the latter part of the last century, it was proposed to alter to: "Who is over all: God be blessed forever." But (1) this was never heard of until so late; (2) in the Greek, in all regular doxologies, "blessed" comes first; (3) we might, by punctuation, alter any other passage just as well.

Heb. i. 8, 9. "But unto the Son He saith, Thy throne, O God, is for ever and ever . . . therefore God, even thy God, hath anointed thee." (Cf. Ps. xlv. 6, 7.) Some render: "God is thy throne," but against usage and destroying the argument, for it supposes "the throne" to be used as a support, which is not warranted. "*Thy* God" brings to view the relation of the Son to the Father, either as official or internal.

John xx. 28. "Thomas said . . . My Lord and my God." *Not* "mere excitement of feeling."

Acts xx. 28. "The church of God which He hath purchased with his own blood."

John i. 18. For "the only begotten Son" it is most probable "the only begotten God" should be read.

1 Pet. iii. 15. "Sanctify the Lord Christ" (instead of "the Lord *God*") "in your hearts." Cf. Is. viii. 13, "Sanctify the Lord of hosts himself."

(*b*.) The second class of passages: those in which the name of the supreme deity in the Old Testament is ascribed to Christ in the New Testament.

Is. vi. 1. "In the year that King Uzziah died I saw also the Lord .... high and lifted up, and his train filled the temple."

John xii. 37–41. "These things said Esaias, when (because) he saw his glory, (*i. e.*, Christ's, see verse 37, and *seq.*,) and spake of Him."

Ps. cii. 25. "Of old hast thou ("My God," [Eli] verse 24,) laid the foundation of the earth: and the heavens are the work of thy hands."

Heb. i. 10. "And, thou, Lord (verse 8, "unto the Son He saith") "in the beginning hast laid," etc.

Is. vii. 14. "Behold, a virgin shall conceive, and bear a son, and shall call his name Immanuel" (El).

Matt. i. 21. "And she shall bring forth a son, and thou shalt call his name JESUS; for He shall save his people from their sins."

Is. ix. 6. "For unto us a child is born .... and his name shall be called .... the mighty God" (El).

That the New Testament ascribes the whole of what is said in Is. ix. 1–7 to Christ is seen by comparing Is. ix. 1, 2, with Matt. iv. 16, Eph. v. 8, 14; Is. ix. 6, first clause, with Luke ii. 11, second clause with John iii. 16, last clause with Eph. ii. 14, and the expression "the mighty God" with Titus ii. 13: "Looking for that blessed hope, and the glorious appearing of the great God and our Saviour Jesus Christ."

Is. xl. 3. "The voice of one crying in the wilderness, Prepare ye the way of the Lord" (Jehovah).

John i. 23. "He said, I am the voice of one crying in the

wilderness, Make straight the way of the Lord, as said the prophet Esaias." (Cf. John iii. 28, and Mal. iii. 1. "The Lord whom ye seek.")

(c.) The third class of passages: those in which there is an indirect use of the name of God, or of expressions which imply entire divinity. These heighten the incidental effect of the argument.

Phil. ii. 6–8. "Who, being in the form ($μορφῇ$) of God." The form of God ($μορφή$, in distinction from $σχῆμα$, or the outward and changing) means, the real nature, the divine attributes, the aggregate of the "distinctive qualities,"—so from Aristotle down; $ἁρπαγμός$ is not "robbery" (which would directly affirm Christ's divinity), but$=τὸ\ ἅρπαγμα=$ "a prize" ("spoil")—*i. e.*, a treasure to be seized. Still it implies divinity, for (Lightfoot, Comm. on Phil., 1868,) "How could it be a sign of humility in our Lord not to assert his equality with God, if He were not divine?"[1]

Heb. i. 3. "Who being the brightness of his glory and the express image of his person."

John v. 18. "Because he had not only broken the Sabbath, but said also that God was his Father, making himself equal with God."

(It is objected that verse 19 reads: "The Son can do nothing of himself, but what He seeth the Father do:" but the meaning is, Not apart from or independently of God, but in perfect concurrence with and "subordination" to Him).

John x. 33. "For a good work we stone thee not; but for blasphemy; and because that thou, being a man, makest thyself God."

John xix. 7. "We have a law, and by our law he ought to die, because he made himself the Son of God."

Upon the three passages last cited this remark is to be

---

[1] So Dorner (Jahrb. f. d. Theol.): "Though in and of himself having the divine form, he yet did not look at equality with God (such as his whole person was destined for or to) [with a view to] robbery (as to be gained by violence) but He humbled himself," etc.

made: "If Jesus was not God, he *was* guilty of blasphemy, and the Jews were right in seeking to put Him to death."

(*d.*) There are passages, implying Christ's entire community of action and purpose with God, which are best explained by the Saviour's divinity.

John v. 19. "The Son can do nothing of himself." (See above.)

John xvii. 10. "And all mine are thine, and thine are mine."

·John v. 17. "My Father worketh hitherto and I work."

John x. 30. "I and my Father are one."

(*e.*) There are passages such as those which follow, in which the term "God" is, on *the basis of the previous citations*, most naturally applied to Christ.

Eph. v. 5. "Nor covetous man, who is an idolater, hath any inheritance in the kingdom of Christ and of God" (where "even of God" is most natural).

Tit. ii. 13. "The glorious appearing of the great God and our Saviour (there should be a comma after Saviour, "appearing of our great God and Saviour",) Jesus Christ."

2 Pet. i. 1. "Through the righteousness of God and (even) our Saviour (Saviour,) Jesus Christ."

2 Tim. iv. 1. "I charge thee therefore before God, and the Lord Jesus Christ" (before God even Christ Jesus).

Luke i. 16. "And many of the children of Israel shall He turn to the Lord their God." (Proof; verse 17, "And he shall go before *Him*.")

Col. ii. 9. "For in Him dwelleth all the fulness of the Godhead bodily."

(*F.*) Christ is exhibited in the Scriptures not merely as pre-existent, above all, Creator, possessor of divine attributes, and bearer of the divine names, but also as the object of religious worship.

The force of this additional argument is seen from a comparison of passages.

Worship is to be paid only to God: the Son is worshiped.

ANTECEDENTS OF REDEMPTION. 61

Matt. iv. 10. "Thou shalt worship the Lord thy God, and Him only shalt thou serve."

Heb. i. 6. "Let all the angels of God worship Him."

Exod. xx. 3. "Thou shalt have no other gods before me."

John v. 23. "That all men should honor the Son, even as they honor the Father."

Is. xlv. 5. "No God beside me."

Heb. i. 8. "Thy throne, O God, is for ever and ever."

Is. xliv. 8. "Is there a God beside me? yea, there is no God."

John i. 1. "The Word was God."

Result of such comparisons, (Waterland): (1) From divine worship all beings are to be excluded excepting God; (2) Christ not being excluded, must be God.

Other passages:

Heb. i. 6. "Let all the angels of God worship Him." The word for "worship" is προσκυνησάτωσαν; but it is the same as in Matt. iv. 10, "Thou shalt worship (προσκυνήσεις) the Lord thy God." (In Ps. xcvii. 7, to which Heb. i. 6 probably refers, the command "worship Him all ye gods" [Elohim] is preceded by the denunciation: "Confounded be all they that serve graven images, that boast themselves of idols.")

Phil. ii. 10. "That at the name of Jesus every knee should bow . . . . and every tongue confess," etc. Here He is worshiped by the adoring universe.

2 Tim. iv. 18. "To whom be glory for ever and ever."

2 Pet. iii. 18. "To Him be glory both now and for ever."

Rev. v. 13. "And every creature . . . . . . heard I saying, Blessing and honor and glory and power be unto Him that sitteth upon the throne, and unto the Lamb for ever and ever."

The apostles and primitive martyrs worshiped Christ.

Luke xxiv. 51, 52. "He was parted from them, and carried up into heaven, And they worshiped Him."

Acts vii. 59, 60. "And they stoned Stephen, calling upon [the Lord], and saying, Lord Jesus receive my spirit. . . . . . Lord, lay not this sin to their charge."

2 Cor. xii. 8. "For this thing I besought the Lord thrice

that it might depart from me." Who "the Lord" is, is seen in the next verse: "Most gladly therefore will I rather glory in my infirmities, that the power of Christ may rest upon me."

1 Thess. iii. 11, 12. "Now God himself and our Father, and our Lord Jesus (Christ), direct our way unto you. And the Lord make you to increase and abound," etc.

Here there is distinction between Christ and the Father, yet Christ is equally with the Father the object of the prayer.

2 Thess. ii. 16, 17. "Now our Lord Jesus Christ himself" (reverse order from that in the passage just cited, Christ being named first) "and God, even our Father, which hath loved us, ... comfort your hearts and stablish you in every good word and work."

Confirmatory passages:

1 Cor. i. 2. "With all that in every place call upon the name (τοῖς ἐπικαλουμένοις τὸ ὄνομα; compare 1 Peter i. 17, "and if ye call on the Father," εἰ πατέρα ἐπικαλεῖσθε) of Jesus Christ our Lord, both theirs and ours."

This shows that "calling upon" Christ was the trait of Christians everywhere.

John xiv. 14. "If ye shall ask anything in my name I will do it."

When, now, we compare with such declarations and statements of fact, passages such as, Isaiah xlv. 22: "Look unto me and be ye saved, all the ends of the earth; for I am God, and there is none else;" and as, Jeremiah xvii. 5: "Thus saith the Lord, cursed be the man that trusteth in man and that maketh flesh his arm," and see here, how praise and glory and honor, etc., are given to Christ, then we meet this dilemma: Either the Scriptures are self-contradictory or Christ is divine: Either the Scriptures recognize more gods than one, or Christ is divine: Either God gives his glory to another, or Christ is truly divine. The only way of saving the unity of God, consistent with the Scriptures, is by admitting the divinity of Christ.

(The objection that the name "God" is given to other beings than the Supreme Deity has already been considered. It is needful to add only: (*a.*) It is never given to any other as it is to Christ. (*b.*) The argument for his divinity is not drawn from the name alone, but in connection with divine attributes and works which are ascribed to Him, and in the greatest variety of terms.)

(*G.*) The argument is confirmed by the fact, that Christ is the Redeemer and Saviour: we are to look to Him directly, believe Him, trust in Him wholly for our highest spiritual needs.

There is always war here with Christian experience, on the part of those who refuse the divinity of Christ. Such love and trust as arise in Christian experience can be rendered only to a divine being. Christian experience is in harmony only with the doctrine of Christ's divinity.

Thus the proposition is established. The Son is (1) divine and (2) a distinct person from the Father. (The word Son is used here as a general term: for the whole of Christ; his Sonship as such not having been yet considered.)

§ 4. *Objections to the proof of the Divinity of Christ on the ground of the Arian hypothesis.*

The Arian hypothesis grants the pre-existence of Christ, but asserts that God the Father created Him (that He is a product of the divine will), and communicated to Him omnipotence, omniscience, holiness, etc., made Him an object of worship, and allowed Him to be called God and the Son of God.

The general position in regard to this hypothesis is: Passages which imply inferiority can be explained in harmony with the passages which express divinity—but not the converse.

The passages which are cited in support of the Arian hypothesis are those in which the inferiority and subordination of the Son are asserted.

Thus (*a*) works are ascribed to the Father which are not to the Son.

1 Cor. i. 21. "Now He which stablisheth us with you in Christ, and hath anointed us, is God."

Gal. i. 1. "An apostle . . . . . by Jesus Christ, and God the Father, who raised Him from the dead."

Acts v. 30. "The God of our fathers raised up Jesus, whom ye slew."

But compare:

John ii. 19. "Jesus answered, ... destroy this temple, and in three days I will raise it up."

The Father has, as Father, special works: He sends the Son, for example; but those works do not necessarily imply greater power than, e. g., creation, which is ascribed to the Son.

(b.) Omniscience, it is said, is not in Christ.

Matt. xxiv. 36. "But of that day and hour knoweth no man, no, not the angels of heaven, but my Father only."

Mark xiii. 32. "Not the angels . . . . . neither the Son, but the Father."

There are two ways of understanding this:[1]

1. Though the Son as Logos knows, as incarnate, He does not:

2. The Logos, as incarnate, parts with the exercise of his divine powers.

(c.) It is said, that the worship paid to Christ is mere invocation.

See above, under the passages cited.

(d.) Jesus prays to God, as subordinate and doing his will. Matt. xxvi. 39; Mark xiv. 36; Luke xxiii. 46; John xii. 27.

This, however, is in his official relation. It is not inconsistent with his divinity. For prayer is the inmost communion of the soul with God. Christ as incarnate must commune with the Father.

(e.) He calls God his God, and in so doing places himself on common ground with his disciples.

John xvii. 3. "That they might know thee, the only true God, and Jesus Christ, whom thou hast sent."

But compare 1 John v. 20. "This is the true God and eternal life."

To make out the Arian view, John xvii. 3 must be held to mean: know thee the only true God in contrast with me, not God. But the contrast is with idols.

---

[1] This is considered more fully in connection with the doctrine of the Person of Christ.

John xx. 17. "Touch me not... I ascend to my Father and your Father, to my God and your God." The sense probably is, "Do not thus lay hold of me as if you feared to lose me. I go to my Father who is also your Father, to my God who is also your God." This same remark applies to Eph. i. 17, "The God of our Lord Jesus Christ, the Father of glory;" 1 Cor. xi. 3, "The head of Christ is God;" 1 Cor. xv. 28, "The Son shall be subject to Him that put all things under Him."

(*f.*) It is said that there are passages in which the absolute inferiority and derivation of Christ are asserted.

John xiv. 28. "My Father is greater than I." The Father has a greater *office* than the Son, by the very nature of the relation.

John v. 26. "Even so hath He given to the Son to have life in himself." Observe: to have life *in himself*, not to direct the quickening energies which abide in the Father. The resurrection is to be the result of the exertion of the Son's own power, which as Son He has by gift and covenant of the Father, *in himself*.

Col. i. 15. "The first born of every creature. For by Him (ἐν αὐτῷ) were all things created, (ἐκτίσθη) that are in heaven and that are in earth." Evidently, here, Christ is placed, in antagonism with the creation, on the side of God. Moreover, the first *born* (πρωτότοκος) not *created*, the apostle calls Him. See also Heb. i. 8 (from Ps. xlv. 7): "But unto the *Son* (=first born) he saith, thy throne, O GOD, is for ever and ever." Also Rev. i. 5: "And from Jesus Christ, who is the faithful witness, and the *first begotten* of the dead," in connection with verse 8, or 11, "I am Alpha and Omega, the first and the last;" or vs. 17, "I am the first and the last" (compared with Isa. xli. 4, xliv. 6, xlviii. 12), or verse 18, where Christ says He is from eternity, the ever-living.

§ 5. *That the Holy Spirit is divine and a distinct Person from the Father and the Son.*

(*a.*) General usage of the terms which designate the Holy Spirit.

"Holy Spirit" and "Spirit of God" are sometimes used in

an impersonal sense, as denoting a general divine influence or mode of operation.

But we may distinguish (as has been well stated by Ebrard), three distinct modes or relations in which He is spoken of, (1) In the Old Testament, God gives his Spirit to the prophets, or the Spirit speaks in or to them. (2) In the New Testament, converting, regenerating influence is ascribed to Him; He leads to Christ and applies Christ's work. 1 Cor. xii. 3: "No man speaking by the Spirit of God calleth Jesus accursed: and that no man can say that Jesus is the Lord, but by the Holy Ghost." Rom. viii. 14: "For as many as are led by the Spirit of God, they are the Sons of God." John iii. 5: "Except a man be born of water and of the Spirit, he cannot enter into the kingdom of God." Luke xi. 13: "How much more shall your heavenly Father give the Holy Spirit to them that ask Him?" (3) He exerts a special miraculous agency. Acts ii.: the Pentecost. (Fulfilment of the promise, John xiv. 16, 26.) (Cf. John xvi. 7: "For if I go not away, the Comforter will not come unto you.") The Apostles were "filled with the Holy Ghost." In 1 Cor. xii. and xiv., the *charismata*, the extraordinary and also the permanent gifts for the Church, are ascribed to the Holy Spirit. The extraordinary are also mentioned in Acts iv. 8: "Then Peter, filled with the Holy Ghost, said unto them, Ye rulers of the people and elders of Israel," etc. (Compare Luke xxi. 14: "Settle it therefore in your hearts, not to meditate before what ye shall answer" . . . . ["when brought before kings and rulers for my name's sake;"] . . . . "for I will give you a mouth and wisdom.")

Hence, says Ebrard, the work of the Spirit is (1) prophetic, (2) regenerating, (3) Church-building, and this (*a.*) as founding the Church with miraculous accompaniments or (*b.*) sustaining it with permanent gifts.

That these all are from one and the same Spirit, is seen from the comparison of Joel ii. 28-32 with Acts ii. 16, and from the explicit declaration of the Apostle Peter.

In the Old Testament, the Holy Spirit is also the source of converting grace.

A difficulty may seem to be presented by John xiv. 16, 26. "He shall give you another Comforter." "But the Comforter .... whom the Father will send in my name, He shall teach you all things."

But these are to be understood as promising a special mode of the Holy Spirit's operation, for a new stage in the divine economy of redemption.

(b.) The Holy Spirit is divine.

This is generally conceded. He is called the Spirit of the Father, of the Son, the Holy Spirit, the Spirit of truth, the Spirit of life.

1 Cor. iii. 16. "Know ye not that ye are the temple of God, and that the Spirit of God dwelleth in you?" The temple of *God*, by reason of the indwelling of the Spirit of God: the assertion implies the absolute divine holiness of the Spirit, at least. To the same effect is 1 Cor. vi. 19.

Acts v. 3, 4. "Why hath Satan filled thine heart to lie unto the Holy Ghost? .... thou hast not lied unto men but unto God." The offence was not against the Spirit of God as dwelling in the heart—but as objective, the Spirit which rules in the Church. Hence, as present and ruling in the whole Church, He is divine.

The Holy Spirit has the attributes of absolute truth and wisdom. What God says the Holy Spirit says—and interchangeably.

Acts xxviii. 25. "Well spake the Holy Ghost by Esaias the prophet unto our fathers," and

Isa. vi. 8. "Also I heard the voice of the Lord, saying," etc.

Heb. x. 15. "Whereof the Holy Ghost also is a witness to us: for after that He had said before, This is the covenant that I will make with them after those days, saith the Lord," and

Jer. xxxi. 33. "But this shall be the covenant ..... saith the Lord." Also xxx. 1.

The regenerating power and influence of the Holy Spirit are such as could not be exercised by any created energy.

His action within the divine nature is inconsistent with any supposition save his divinity.

1 Cor. ii. 10, 11. "For the Spirit searcheth all things, yea the deep things of God."

(c.) The Holy Spirit is distinct from the Father and the Son, and is personal: is not the mere activity of God.

Matt. xxviii. 19. "Baptizing them in (εἰς) the name of the Father, and of the Son, and of the Holy Ghost." Neither a creature nor a mode of agency could be so spoken of.

2 Cor. xiii. 14. "The grace of the Lord Jesus Christ, and the love of God, and the communion of the Holy Ghost, be with you all." The Holy Spirit must be as distinguishable from the Father as from the Son.

The same fact was symbolized at Christ's baptism (Matt. iii. 16, Mark i. 10), Luke iii. 22. "And the Holy Ghost descended in bodily shape, like a dove upon Him, *and* a voice came from heaven," etc. Here the symbol of the Spirit is distinguished from the voice of the Father.

Rom. viii. 16. "The Spirit himself beareth witness with our spirit."

Rom. viii. 26, 27. "The Spirit himself maketh intercession.... And he that searcheth the hearts knoweth what is the mind of the Spirit."

Eph. iv. 30. "And grieve not the Holy Spirit of God." This is not intelligible, if the Spirit is not personal: a mode of divine agency cannot be grieved.

1 Cor. xii. 11. "But all these worketh that one and the self-same Spirit, dividing to every man severally as He will" (βούλεται).

1 Cor. xii. 4–11. In this passage the Holy Spirit is distinguished from the gifts of the Church; in the fifth verse He is distinguished from Christ, and in the sixth, from God.

1 Cor. ii. 10, 11. "The Spirit searcheth all things, yea, the deep things of God."

Matt. xii. 31, 32. Blasphemy against the Holy Spirit is distinguished from that against Christ.

Masculine, not neuter, forms are employed to designate the Spirit. John xiv. 16, ἄλλον παράκλητον, 26, ὁ δὲ παράκλητος, xv. 26, ὁ παράκλητος, ὅν, xvi. 13, ὅταν δὲ ἔλθῃ ἐκεῖνος, τὸ πνεῦμα τῆς ἀληθείας. (ἐκεῖνος alone would not be conclusive as referring to ὁ παράκλητος, but it is decisive, as referring to τὸ πνεῦμα). See also John xvi. 14. ἐκεῖνος ἐμὲ δοξάσει.

ANTECEDENTS OF REDEMPTION. 69

Personal acts are ascribed to the Spirit. He teaches, testifies, speaks, convinces.

All this is inconsistent with *personification* merely.

Acts xiii. 2, 4. "The Holy Ghost said, Separate me Barnabas and Saul.... So they, being sent forth by the Holy Ghost," etc.

Acts xv. 28. "For it seemed good to the Holy Ghost, and to us."

Gal. iv. 4–6. "God sent forth his Son.... that we might receive the adoption of sons. And because ye are sons, God hath sent forth the Spirit of his Son into our hearts, crying, Abba, Father." Here the sending of the Son and of the Spirit are described in the same terms.

1 Pet. i. 12.—"them that have preached the gospel unto you with the Holy Ghost sent down from heaven."

(*d.*) Objections to the distinct personality of the Spirit.

First Objection: There are passages which speak of Christ dwelling in us, in the same way as the Spirit of God and of Christ is said to dwell in us, *e. g.*, Rom. viii. 9, 10, 11; Gal. ii. 20; Cf. Rom. viii. 14; Eph. iii. 17; Cf. Gal. iv. 6.

Yet the Scriptures speak distinctly of the continued difference of the Son and the Spirit.

Acts ii. 33. "He (Christ) hath shed forth this" (the outpouring of the Spirit). Acts iii. 21: (Jesus Christ) "Whom the heaven must receive until the times of restitution of all things." So through John xiv., the same difference is shown: the Paraclete is to take the place of Christ.

1 John iii. 2. The Spirit transforms us into the image of Christ when at last we see Him as He is.

Rom. viii. 16, 26. The Spirit gives assurance of adoption, but, Heb. vii. 25, Christ in heaven intercedes.

1 Cor. iii. 16. The Spirit dwells in us as a temple, but, Eph. v. 23, Christ is the head of the body.

Acts xix. 2. ($εἰ\ πνεῦμα\ ἅγιον\ ἐλάβετε\ πιστεύσαντες$) "Did ye receive the Holy Ghost when ye believed?"

Second Objection:

In John vii. 38, 39 it is said, "For the Holy Ghost was not yet [given]; because that Jesus was not yet glorified"; as if the existence of the Spirit began with the glorification of Christ.

But Christ had the Spirit before, as prophet; Acts x. 38, "How God anointed Jesus of Nazareth with the Holy Ghost." Christ had received the Spirit at his baptism; Matt. iv. 16, and parallels.

The prophets of the Old Testament were enlightened by the Spirit: 1 Pet. i. 11; Cf. Ps. li. 12, cxliii. 10; Isa. lxiii. 10, 11.

In the Old Testament the Spirit is promised to Christ as Messiah.

Isa. xi. 2. "And the Spirit of the Lord shall rest upon Him" (upon "the rod out of the stem of Jesse ").

Isa. xlii. 1. "Behold my servant, whom I uphold; . . . . . I have put my Spirit upon Him."

Isa. lxi. 1. "The Spirit of the Lord God is upon me." (Cf. Luke iv. 18; John iii. 34—"not the Spirit by measure.")

Isa. lxv. 2. "I have spread out my hands all the day unto a rebellious people," etc. Cf. Acts vii. 51. "Ye stiffnecked and uncircumcised in heart and ears, ye do always resist the Holy Ghost;" and Rom. x. 21.

Hence, it is the same Spirit that speaks in the Old Testament and in the New.

Third Objection:

That the Spirit is the Spirit of Christ, or, Christ coming again to men, as Spirit. The Lord is τὸ πνεῦμα, 2 Cor. iii. 17.

Against this (1) is the fact that Christ promises his disciples that the Spirit should come in his stead: John xiv. 18, xvi. 16, 22.

The return of Christ is to be "in glory"—not at his resurrection—not at the Pentecost: John xiv. 3, "I will come again and receive you unto myself, that where I am, there ye may be also;" this refers to a coming in which He will receive the Church permanently, having previously prepared "a place" for it.

This whole mode of statement, that Christ would depart,

send in his stead the Comforter and again himself return, is utterly inconsistent with the view that He himself returns simply as spirit.

(2) As to passage cited (2 Cor. iii. 17), the apostle goes on to say, " and where the Spirit of the Lord is, there is liberty." The contrast is between the Spirit of Christ and the law of Moses: the sense, he that has the Lord (in contrast with, he that has Moses), has the Spirit.

A fourth objection, from John iv. 24. God is Spirit ($\pi\nu\epsilon\tilde{\upsilon}\mu\alpha$ ὁ θεός).

But this cannot mean, Spirit is equivalent to God: we cannot say the Spirit of Christ is equivalent to the spiritual nature of God. The meaning is, God is Spirit, in contrast with the world.

§ 6. *The Father, Son, and Spirit are classed together, separately from all other beings, as divine.* (The Trinitarian texts.)

It is a conceded point that no other beings or names than these, through the whole Scriptures, are so represented, with divine powers and attributes. That these three are thus represented, *separately*, we have already seen.

But, besides these separate passages, there are also such as combine the three together—in a peculiar way, as no others are thus combined. Having shown the divine names, attributes and personality of each, the Scriptures bind them together in one, and in a peculiar manner.

2 Cor. xiii. 14. "The grace of the Lord Jesus Christ, and the love of God, and the communion of the Holy Ghost, be with you all."

1 Pet. i. 2. "Elect according to the foreknowledge of God the Father, through sanctification of the Spirit, unto obedience and sprinkling of the blood of Jesus Christ."

John xiv. 16. (The Trinity hinted at.) "*I* will pray *the Father*, and He shall give you *another Comforter.*"

1 Cor. viii. 6. "But to us there is one God, the Father, of whom are all things, and we in Him; and one Lord Jesus Christ, by whom are all things, and we by Him." Compare with

1 Cor. xii. 3–6. "No man can say Jesus is the Lord but by the Holy Ghost. Now there are diversities of gifts, but the same Spirit. And there are differences of administration, but the same Lord. And there are diversities of operations, but it is the same God which worketh all in all."

Matt. xxviii. 19. "Baptizing them in the name of the Father, and of the Son, and of the Holy Ghost."

The baptized person is represented here as brought into the same relation to the Holy Spirit, as elsewhere to the Father and Son.

(At the Baptism of Christ, Matt. iii. 16, the voice of the Father is accompanied by the descent of the Holy Spirit.)

§ 7. *Result of the Biblical Evidence in respect to the divinity of the Father, the Son, and the Holy Spirit.*

1. That the Father, Son, and Holy Spirit are personally distinguished from each other. There is recognized throughout a personal relation of the Father and Son to each other. So of the Holy Spirit to both.

2. They each have divine names and attributes.

3. Yet there is only one God.

NOTE. These distinctions are not restricted to Christ's formally appearing in the world, or to the giving of the Holy Spirit; but continue still. Any other view than this would destroy our whole Christian experience. Christ is still the personal object of faith and love, distinct from the Father.

If the distinction is not immanent, yet it is permanent.

We apply what the Scriptures say of the distinction of persons still; we separate between Him to whom we are reconciled, the Father; Him by whom we are reconciled, the Son; and Him through whom, the Holy Spirit.

The Trinity, at any rate, is in the whole economy of redemption, as permanent. From the Trinity in the economy we pass to the second point, THE ESSENTIAL TRINITY.

CHAPTER II.

THE ESSENTIAL TRINITY.

The Second Proposition: That the Distinctions here proved are not restricted to the economy, the manifestation, or revelation of God *ad extra,* but are internal.

Order of discussion:
1. That they are internal.
2. That they are appropriately designated as personal distinctions. Sense of "Person."
3. In what way, as personal distinctions, they exist in the Godhead. How to be conceived of—if at all.
4. Of the "Sonship."

§ 1. *That the distinctions of the Godhead are represented in the Scriptures as internal.*

The question here is a simple one: on Biblical grounds, whether what is asserted in Scripture, of the Father, Son, and Spirit is spoken simply and solely with respect to the modes of manifestation, or, so as to imply, necessarily, internal modes of subsistence.

This is primarily a question of Scriptural interpretation. It is a question with respect to Sabellianism. Sabellianism, as contrasted with Arianism, says: The Son in his nature is divine, but *not eternally personal;* He became, in the Incarnation, a distinct person from the Father. (1) In the man Jesus the infinite God appears, personally; the divine nature is in Him. (2) God from eternity decreed this. (3) As preexistent in God Jesus is the Logos.

Sabellianism has two forms: (1) God, revealed as Father, Son, and Spirit; (2) God the Father, revealed as Son and Spirit. Strict Sabellianism says: The Logos is the medium of the revelation. It is called Modalism.

As compared with Arianism, Sabellianism is more profound; it is congruent with the divine nature of Christ; it explains the passages which speak of that nature, and also of the relative subordination. The relation of Arianism and Sabellianism is this: what Sabellianism urges for the inherent divinity of Christ refutes Arianism; what Arianism urges for the distinct pre-existent personality of the Son refutes Sabellianism. Sabellianism, says Athanasius, is refuted by the idea of the Son, Arianism by the idea of the Father (Ath. cont. Ar. iv. 2. 3.)

The simple primary question is this: Do the Scriptures restrict the personal distinctions to the sphere of the manifestation, or do they demand that we conceive of them as eternal in the Godhead.

(a.) Passages which speak clearly of a personal pre-existence of the Son, before the Incarnation.

John viii. 58. "Before Abraham was, I am." This can not be interpreted as setting forth an impersonal pre-existence in the mind of God, as idea. Also John viii. 42. "I proceeded forth and came from God."

John xvii. 5. "Glorify thou me with thine own self ($\pi\alpha\rho\grave{\alpha}$ $\delta\epsilon\alpha\upsilon\tau\tilde{\omega}$) with the glory which I had with thee, before the world was" ($\tilde{\eta}$ $\epsilon\tilde{\iota}\chi o\nu$ $\pi\rho\grave{o}$ $\tau o\tilde{\upsilon}$ $\tau\grave{o}\nu$ $\kappa\acute{o}\delta\mu o\nu$ $\epsilon\tilde{\iota}\nu\alpha\iota$ $\pi\alpha\rho\grave{\alpha}$ $\delta o\acute{\iota}$): a state which was once, and is to be again: it is to be again, as personal; therefore it was personal.

Phil. ii. 6-8. "Who being in the form of God . . . . took the form of a servant: and being found in fashion as a man," etc. . . . . The "form of man" was personal: so, "the form of God."

John xvi. 28. "I came forth from the Father, and am come into the world."

John vi. 62. "What and if ye shall see the Son of man ascend up where He was before?"

John i. 1-14. The doctrine of the Logos.

Logos must be either reason or word: the latter is the New Testament and Septuagint usage. Reason (Wisdom) as creative is expressed by $\delta o\varphi\iota\alpha$ in the Bible and Apocrypha.

The "beginning" spoken of must be before creation: for, verse 3, "all things were made by Him." He was *with* God, intimate, yet separate. "The Word became flesh and dwelt among us, and we beheld his glory." Before this the Word was either a person or a personification: it could not be the latter, for it is the same being after the Incarnation as before. The Logos is not a mere activity of God. "Word" is inconsistent with that. It is an internal modification. It is an activity, in the sense of an eternal speech, word of God, as a modification of the Deity—such that thereby He makes the world and becomes incarnate.

The great acts of God *ad extra* are two: creation and incarnation, and these are both referred to the Logos.

Even if ἐν ἀρχῇ is to be taken as the beginning of the world, it was the beginning of what is temporal: what is before is eternal.

πρὸς τὸν θεόν designates a living relation.[1]

Col. i. 15. "Who is the image of the invisible God, the firstborn of every creature."

Heb. i. 3. "Who being the brightness of his glory and the express image of his person."

The expression "firstborn of every creature" refers to his ante-temporal condition, also including his superior excellence. Whatever else may be questioned in this passage, it must be admitted that his origin is a *begetting*; not a creating.

(*b.*) Passages which imply such pre-existence (not yielding the strictest proof of it, but not naturally interpreted without it).

John iii. 16. "That He gave his only-begotten Son."

John vi. 33, 38. "The bread of God is that which cometh down from heaven . . . . For I came down from heaven, not to do mine own will."

John xii. 49. "But the Father, which sent me, He gave me a commandment."

This use of the word Father, showing that Christ speaks as Son, and the reference to himself as "sent," presuppose a previous personal relation.

Such passages as these are to be also noted:

Gal. iv. 4. "But when the fulness of the time was come,

---

[1] The historical genesis of the idea of the Logos confirms this. Wisdom, Logos of Philo, Angel of God, Glory of God, Name of God, etc., become concentrated in the doctrine of the Logos. And this proves a pre-existent hypostasis.

God sent forth his Son, made of a woman, made under the law." Observe that before He was sent, He was viewed as the Son.

John xvi. 28. "I came forth from the Father, and am come into the world."

John iii. 31. "He that cometh from above is above all." Cf. verse 11, "and testify that we have seen."

1 Cor. x. 4. "They drank of that spiritual Rock that followed them: and that Rock was Christ."

(c.) The assertion of Scripture that Christ created the world, is inconsistent with all the forms of Sabellianism. Sabellianism supposes that Christ was a person only in relation to the redemption of the world.

(d.) The Old Testament in speaking of Jehovah and the Messiah, the Wisdom, the Angel of the Covenant, etc., confirms the view that the relations of the Father and Son are internal.

Isa. xl. 3, 9, and especially 10. "Behold the Lord God will come with strong hand."

Zech. ii. 10. "Sing and rejoice, O daughter of Zion: for lo, I come, and I will dwell in the midst of thee, saith the Lord." John i. 14. "And the Word was made flesh and dwelt among us." The perfect fulfilment: Rev. xxii. 7. "Behold I come quickly."

(e.) The continued personal being and relation to us of the Son, is also against the Sabellian position.

He is to remain forever in this relation.

Rom. i. 4.—"declared to be the Son of God with power . . . . . by the resurrection from the dead."

Heb. xiii. 8. "Jesus Christ, the same yesterday, to-day, and forever."

Rom. vi. 9, 10. "Christ being raised from the dead dieth no more . . . . . in that He liveth, He liveth unto God."

Acts ii. 33. "Therefore being by the right hand of God exalted . . . . He hath shed forth this, which ye now see and hear."

ANTECEDENTS OF REDEMPTION. 77

§ 2. *Remarks on Sabellianism.*

The general result of the Sabellian hypothesis, on the basis of the Scriptural evidence for the pre-existence of Christ, and that He is the Creator.

Sabellianism wants to show that the personal distinctions belong to the revealed and not to the immanent Godhead—that they arise in the revelation *ad extra* and only for the purpose of a revelation, and have no essential being in the divine nature.

But the passages cited prove:

1. Personal pre-existence before Incarnation, so that *that form* of Sabellianism which makes the personality of Christ begin then is effectually ruled out.

2. They also show that Christ as pre-existent, created the worlds, all things in heaven and earth, so that the personal distinction *had* a being before anything created was, and did not *come* into being for the exigencies of the divine manifestation.

3. The only resort then for Sabellianism, consistent with these passages is to say: God as Son existed personally before Creation and Incarnation—was a distinct personal agent before time began; but if this is said, then the Son did not come into being as a person with special reference to any revelation of God: the utmost that can be said is, He came into being as a person, antecedently, because the world was to be made and redeemed by Him. But his distinct existence as a person is thrown back into the nature of God, into eternity.

And when this is said, we have really either Arianism, or what is equivalent to an eternal generation of the Son. Supposing Arianism to be refuted, the only question that remains in respect to Sabellianism would be this: does God, from a necessity of his nature, exist internally as Father, Son, and Spirit—or, do these personal distinctions in God exist in Him from all eternity, with respect to a future revelation of himself. The eternal existence being conceded, this question is an unimportant one; and there is no ground in Scripture or reason for saying that the existence of these personal distinctions is conditioned by the possible future existence of the world and of redemption.

NOTE.—That form of Sabellianism which makes it to be, that the same God assumed these different characters, viz., as Father, the character of Creator, as Son, of Redeemer, as Holy Spirit, of Sanctifier—is utterly irreconcilable with the patent fact of the distinct personal being of the Son.

Further Remarks on the Sabellian Hypothesis.

1. That the Father, Son, and Spirit are simply manifestations, is inconsistent with the doctrine respecting the Father, as already expounded.

2. If these are taken strictly, as modes of manifestation, following on each other and receding, we lose the abiding personalities.

3. We have still three (if not four) divine persons to worship. We have the inconvenience which is supposed to inhere in the orthodox view, without the firmness of personalities which that gives.

4. The Sabellian view leads logically to the idea of a change in God in his mode of being, a change in time.

After the Incarnation, God exists as, *is*, a triad—a three-fold personality; He was not so before. Hence a change must have occurred in his mode of being, and the view conflicts with the divine unchangeableness. This also leads to the pantheistic view—that the Incarnation is an essential mode of the manifestation of Deity, a process of self-evolution.

Either this must be admitted, or else the personalities must be viewed as fleeting and unsubstantial.

5. Logically, there must be some ground in the Deity why He is revealed as a three-fold personality. Either, there is a creative power, so that the person of Christ is produced by divine efficiency, or there is a mode of subsistence in God himself, corresponding to the manifestation, so that the latter is but the expression of the former. We must apply either the category of cause and effect or that of ground and manifestation. The first cannot be applied; for then Christ would be a created being, and the passages which speak of pre-existence (to refer to no others) are against this. If the second is applied, then

we must recognize a specific mode of subsistence in the Deity corresponding to the manifestations.

The Sabellian idea of God is that of the abstract unity allowing no differences. It is a transference to God of the idea of a human individual personality. Of old it was accused of Judaistic tendencies; it has also pantheistic tendencies.

6. The Sabellian hypothesis, instead of simplifying, does only confuse our relation to God.

We have, as Christians, a direct personal relation to Christ, also to the Father, also to the Spirit. This presupposes a personal relation (objective) between the Father, Son, and Spirit. If it does not, we are in a two-fold relation to God: to God as revealed, and to God as He is in himself. We cannot make this clear, cannot extricate ourselves from an inevitable confusion.

It is taking the subjective side of revelation to the exclusion of the objective—a part of the process which ends in the denial of the objective validity of the Christian revelation.

7. By logical consequence, it leads to the pantheistic view: the Father is God, in his abstract, unfathomable, impersonal unity; the Son is the world, creation—this abstract divinity realized, coming to personality in man; the Holy Spirit is the process by which all things return back to the original condition.

8. The humanity of Christ is lost, on this view. It has no abiding worth. This, if not a necessary, is a natural consequence.

§ 3. *That these Distinctions in the Godhead are appropriately designated as Personal Distinctions—Hypostases,*[1] *in the present Usage.*

The Father is not the Son, nor the Son the Father, the Holy Spirit is neither. They are distinguished from each other, while they are all termed divine.

We express what is common in them by saying, they have the same divine nature (essence) and attributes: the same identical nature and attributes.

They differ, in this, from three men, having the same human

[1] Ἀλλὰ τοῦτό ἐστι τὸ ποιοῦν τοῖς αἱρετικοῖς τὴν πλάνην, τὸ ταὐτὸ λέγειν τὴν φύσιν καὶ τὴν ὑπόστασιν. Joh. Damasc. *De Fide Orth.* lib. i. c. iii.

nature: in the latter case there is not an identity of substance. But in God the same numerical substance belongs equally to Father, Son, and Spirit.

How, now, shall that in which they differ be expressed? It is all expressed in common usage, in the three distinct terms, Father, Son, and Spirit. Another mode of expressing it is by the term *Person*: the first, second, and third persons in the Godhead. The doubts about this are: (1) It is a word not used in the Scriptures for this purpose, (2) It seems to convey too definite an idea, as of three human persons. Some have preferred to say, " three distinctions."

What, then, are the definitions of person, as distinguished from substance or essence? Substance is that which is common, person that in which they differ.

The old Scholastic definition of person is, "ipsa essentia divina certo charactere hypostatico insignita, ac proprio subsistendi modo a reliquis distincta." Each person is a mode of subsistence of the same divine essence. In common usage a person is one who can say *I*: who can be addressed by the personal pronouns. Self-consciousness is then the distinctive attribute of personality —it is that by which we specifically know personality. Each of the persons of the Trinity must, then, be supposed by us to have a self-consciousness: this is the least that can be said, maintaining anything like discrimination. If we do not say this, we deny any *conceivable* distinctions in the Godhead—we must say "three distinctions," three modes of self-consciousness in the Deity.

§ 4. *The ecclesiastical Statements as to the distinctive Characteristics of the Persons.*

How are we to conceive of these immanent personal distinctions? Not how they *came to be*; but, how they *are*—how the persons are distinguishable from each other.

There are two forms of statement here: The persons are distinguishable (1) as Father, Son, and Holy Spirit, (2) As, first person, second person, and third person, of the Godhead.

ANTECEDENTS OF REDEMPTION. 81

Statements of the Westminster Standards:
"Conf." ch. ii. § 3. "In the unity of the Godhead there be three persons of one substance, power, and eternity; God the Father, God the Son, and God the Holy Ghost. The Father is of none, neither begotten nor proceeding; the Son is eternally begotten of the Father; the Holy Ghost eternally proceeding from the Father and the Son."

"Larg. Cat." Ans. to Q. 9. "There be three persons in the Godhead, the Father, the Son, and the Holy Ghost; and these three are one true, eternal God, the same in substance, equal in power and glory: although distinguished by their personal properties." Q. 10. "What are the personal properties of the three persons in the Godhead?" Ans. "It is proper to the Father to beget the Son, and to the Son to be begotten of the Father, and to the Holy Ghost to proceed from the Father and the Son, from all eternity."

NOTE.—The expression, "equal in power and glory" is sometimes interpreted, incorrectly, as if the power and glory were numerically distinguishable.

The Significance of these "Personal Properties."
Without them, the doctrine is reduced to indefiniteness.

The received statements about the Trinity in most of the orthodox expositions, may be here appropriately adduced to illustrate the sense of these distinctions. These statements are given under the three heads: (1) Unity, (2) Difference, (3) Mutual Relation.

1. *Unity.* This lies in the essence, οὐσία, or substance. The earlier mode of conceiving the matter placed this unity in the Father as the fountain and source of the other personalities; but this was abandoned after Augustine's time. It has since been commonly held that the one divine essence is common to all the three, and that each has the totality thereof.

What is this divine essence? It is absolute spirituality, all divine perfections and attributes—those of the understanding and of the will. Thomasius: "The absolute personality is common, the same for the three persons." God, as essence, is not dead, but living: "actus purissimus."

2. *The Difference, or Distinction of Persons.*[1] In the one essence there are different "modes of subsistence," not nominal, nor essential, but *real.* Each one of the three "Persons" has an appropriate mode of subsistence, peculiar to himself, whereby He is distinguished from the others—as a person. The properties of these persons are partly internal acts and partly the personal properties thence resulting. The act of the Father is generation—his characteristic then is, paternity. The act of the Father and Son is *spiratio.* Or, "Generation" is the eternal production of the Son from the Father—"God of God." *Spiratio*—procession—is the eternal proceeding of the Holy Spirit from the Father and the Son.

These acts are different from creation, as being eternal acts and as not being the production from nothing. They are also acts differing from each other, each produces a different person, but what they are is unfathomable.

The personal properties resulting from these personal acts are: the distinctive traits of the three persons, viz., paternity, sonship, procession. The Father is unbegotten, the Son begotten, the Holy Spirit proceeding,—eternally.

The procession of the Holy Spirit is equally from the Father and the Son, not as distinct, but so far as they have the same divine essence. "Fatendum est, patrem et filium principia esse Spiritus Sancti, non ut duo principia, sed ut unum principium." Augustine, de Trin. v. 14.

3. *The relation of the Persons to the Unity.* The three are related to the same divine essence, not as parts, but as modes of subsistence. The divine essence is not before, nor external to, but in the persons eternally. This must be held, otherwise we should have four persons instead of three. The difference is not in the eternity, nor in any divine attribute, but in the order of subsistence. The Father is first in order (not in time), the unbegotten;

---

[1] The derivation of *persona* from πρόσωπον (=πρὸς τοὺς ὦπας) is not sustained. Thomas Aquinas, "Summa," p. 1, qu. 29, art. 4, says "persona dicitur quasi per se una." In the tract "De Persona," ascribed to Boethius, it is said, "Persona dicta est a personando." This is the true derivation, to sound through a mask (larva histrionalis).

the Son is second, the begotten: the Son has the principle (not the cause) of his subsistence in the Father; the Holy Spirit in both. If we say, first, second, and third persons, we indicate, still, an *order* of subsistence.

Aquinas (p. 1, q. 31, art. 1, ad 4^m): "Cum ergo dicimus trinitatem in unitate, non ponimus numerum in unitate essentiæ, quasi sit ter una; sed personas numeratas ponimus in unitate naturæ, sicut supposita alicujus naturæ dicuntur esse in natura illa."

Questions:

(*a.*) Is the Father the cause of the being of the Son and Spirit?

No—not cause—the ground.

(*b.*) Does the Son exist by the will of the Father?

Not as the product of that will: but free activity.

(*c.*) If activity is stated as the ground, then before that the Son was not?

No, the activity was eternal.

(*d.*) Is all subordination inconsistent with divinity?

Yes, if it involves anything *ad extra*—or any want of the divine perfections.

(*e.*) Is not derived being inconsistent with divinity?

Yes: if the relations of time are introduced.

REMARK. The whole conception is in accordance with this canon: "Principium missionis in tempore est principium missionis in æternitate."

§ 5. *Is the term Son used in the Scriptures in reference to Christ's immanent relation to the Father?*

Positions in respect to "Sonship."

1. The term is not used for the mere humanity of Christ.

2. It is certainly used for his whole office as Redeemer.

3. There are passages which seem to imply that it includes his whole relation to God.

4. There are passages which cannot without constraint exclude divinity.

The question is not of the highest theological importance. It has its chief dogmatic importance in connection with the difficulties on two points: an inherent subordination of the Son, and the doctrine of eternal generation. Apart from these points, it is a question of philology and Scriptural usage of the term. As a question of philology and Scriptural usage, it reduces itself to this: Is the term Son applied to Christ, or the term Father to the Father in relation to Christ, solely from his human or official manifestation—or is it applied, when this is not in view? Both sides allow, that now as a matter of fact, it may be applied to the whole divine-human personality of Christ. Those who say it is derived from the human manifestation originally, allow it afterwards to be applied to the whole undivided person. The others say, it is applicable to Christ's original relation to Deity, and that the human and official usage is but a manifestation, a revelation in a lower sphere, of an antecedent relation.

Christ designates himself in Scripture, by four terms:— (1) Man, (2) Son of Man, (by which not his lowliness but his headship of men is indicated), (3) Messiah—Christ, (4) Son of God. The question, then, comes to this: when He calls himself the Son of God, or when He speaks of God as his Father, does He mean the same thing, or refer to the same relation that is designated by either of the other terms—man, Son of man, Messiah; or, does He express another intimate, pre-existent, essential relation?

A preliminary argument for the latter position may be derived from this consideration: He calls God his Father, the Father calls Him Son. Now, who is the *He*, that is thus called? It is the person, Jesus Christ. God is not the Father of Christ's mere bodily humanity; nor of Him as bearing an office, but is the Father of the Son, of that person who is the Son. Now, that person, as a personal being and agent, pre-existed. He did not begin to be a person when He came into the world; He pre-existed as a distinct person from the Father, and when He came into the world He simply assumed humanity. When, now, God is called his Father, it designates, in many cases, the intimate personal relation of the two to each other. It is not the relation of the mere outward humanity, nor of the office to God; but of the person of Christ to the person of the Father.

(a.) The term Son of God (and the correlative, Father) is not used in Scripture in reference to Christ merely as a man.[1]

Luke i. 35. "The angel answered and said unto her, The Holy Ghost shall come upon thee, and the power of the Highest shall overshadow thee: therefore also that holy thing which shall be born of thee shall be called the Son of God."

Because He was born of God, He was to be called the Son of God: He was born of God in a special sense. It is used as a designation of a special relation to God. That relation might have pre-existed in another form: the human (temporal) manifestation may have been merely the revelation of it in time. The passage merely says, that because generated by a direct and special divine influence, He shall be called the Son of God. He is not made the Son of God thereby, but called such. His miraculous conception should lead men to acknowledge Him as the Son of God:, thus He would be known to be Immanuel, Isa. vii. 14.

Besides, to interpret this name, Son of God, with respect to his being born into the world is contradictory to other passages, in which it is applied to Him under other aspects, e. g., the quotations of the passage in,

Ps. ii. 7. "Thou art my Son, this day have I begotten thee" (where יְלִדְתִּיךָ may be, "have I so declared thee," i. e. to be my Son):

Acts xiii. 33, "God hath fulfilled the same . . . . . as it is also written in the second psalm, Thou art my Son," etc. (here the supposition that the "declaration" refers to the resurrection is highly doubtful: it is rather to his whole manifestation that the quotation is applied).

Heb. i. 5, 6. "For unto which of the angels said He at any time, Thou art my Son . . . . . And again when He bringeth the first-begotten into the world."

---

[1] Episcopius (Theol. Inst.) on the Person of Christ says, there are four grounds for Christ's being called Son: (1) Conception, (2) Mediation, (3) Resurrection, (4) Ascension. Another "divine filiation" is not necessary to be believed. Bishop Bull met these assertions in his "Judicium Eccl. Cath." 1694—his second great work.

Heb. v. 5. "Christ glorified not himself to be made an high priest; but He that said unto Him, Thou art my Son," etc.

In these passages, the Sonship is referred to Christ's whole manifestation and work in the world.

The sense is, Christ is declared or proved to be the Son of God, by his whole work, here. He is not made to be such by his Incarnation, his humanity.

(*b.*) Jesus as the Messiah—Christ—is called the Son of God: but it is not asserted that the title Son of God is given Him because He is the Messiah. By his works and words He is proved to be the Son of God; but it is not proved, that that is the reason for so calling Him.

Instances: John vi. 69; Matt. xvi. 16; John xi. 29, and many others.

(*c.*) There are passages in which the term Son seems to be applied to Christ in his divine nature; in his direct personal relation to the Father; or, in respect to which it is at least doubtful whether it be not so applied.

John i. 14. "And we beheld his glory, the glory as of the only begotten of the Father."

This "only begotten of the Father" is undoubtedly the Logos.

John i. 18. "The only begotten Son, which is in the bosom of the Father, He hath revealed Him."

John v. 17. "My Father worketh hitherto and I work."

Jesus here calls God his Father, with respect to his higher nature. The Jews so understood Him.

Rom. viii. 32. "He that spared not His own Son," etc. (John v. 18, Christ "said also that God was his [own] Father.")

Matt. xvi. 16. "Thou art the Christ, the Son of the living God."

John iii. 16. "For God so loved the world that He gave his only begotten Son."

Gal. iv. 4. "When the fulness of the time was come God sent forth his Son."

John xx. 17. "I ascend unto my Father, and your Father" (not "our Father").

Matt. xxviii. 19. The baptismal formula.

(*d.*) The term Son is so used in respect to Christ that we cannot say it excludes, but most naturally say, it includes, his divine nature, his intimate personal relation to the Father."[1]

And even if we get rid of the application of the term Son to his personal relation to God, yet the same kind of relation is hinted at by other terms and phrases, which are applied to Him in respect (probably) to his pre-existent state.

The Logos, the Word, is that which expresses or reveals: that in a being whereby it is revealed. "The image of the invisible God, the firstborn of every creature." If the first clause relates to the historical Christ, the second points to a different origin from the creation, and leads most naturally to the internal relation of the Godhead which is intimated in other Scriptures.

So, the Son is "in the form of God" and "the brightness of his glory and ($\chi\alpha\rho\alpha\kappa\tau\eta\rho$ $\tau\tilde{\eta}s$ $\dot{\upsilon}\pi o\sigma\tau\acute{\alpha}\sigma\epsilon\omega s$) the impression of his essence."

The relation of speech to the mind, of the first (and peculiarly) begotten to the Father, of the brightness to the glory, of the impression to the seal, discovers something of the same relation as is designated by the terms Son and Father: *i. e.*, the same substance or essence in different forms.

§ 6. *How now are we to conceive this relation as an internal one in the Godhead?*

Here is the question and the difficulty; and here is seen the arbitrary character of many theories.

The relation of Sonship is figurative. It cannot be taken literally, or after the mode of human fatherhood and sonship.

---

[1] If we deny any definite internal relation of dependence of the Son on the Father—a certain inequality (yet wholly immanent), we are led to an arbitrary interpretation of some passages of Scripture. What is said about the whole person of Christ and his total relation to the Father, by himself and others, is referred to Him as a man exclusively. "My Father is greater than I"; "I and my Father are one"; if the former of these is spoken of Christ's humanity, or official state alone, so must the latter be. It seems to be forgotten often that it is the same person who is speaking in the different passages; and that what is true of Him as a person, in His personal relation to God, must be abiding.

The relation among men denotes (*a.*) priority of being in the father to the son, in point of time, (*b.*) communication of nature from the one to the other, in the relation of antecedent cause to a subsequent effect, (*c.*) consequently an absolute dependence for being of the son on the father. The literal application of the analogy would draw after it, then, a denial of the independent being, of the self-divinity of the Son. It is an analogy—the best among human relations; and to hold what must be held of the eternity and independence of Christ we must say, it is an analogy which applies only to the *relation* itself, not to the mode in which this relation *came to be.*

It expresses the relation—and of the same general kind as the term Logos; there are two persons, their relation to each other is like that of the son to the father, of speech to the mind.

To arrive at a more definite conception or form of statement of this relation, we may regard it, (1) Negatively, (2) Positively.

1. Negatively: Statements not authorized:

(*a.*) The most common is, that the Father communicates the divine essence to the Son. John v. 26, "Even so hath he given to the Son to have life in himself," is commonly adduced. But this gift does not probably refer to the divine mode of being.

"The communication of the divine essence" seems to suppose that the Father is before the Son; though the relation is not that of a created being, yet it is not eternal.

(*b.*) The view which makes the relation to be that of emanation, as a ray from the sun. The old objection is valid; it implies a division or possibility of division, in the divine essence.

2. Positively:

(*a.*) God is not a single individual person, like an individual man, alongside of other men.

(*b.*) God is perpetual activity—*actus purissimus*; and his eternal activity is not merely that of attributes ever working, but is that of a three-fold, internal, personal relationship, as Father, Son, and Spirit, or as the first, second, and third persons of the Godhead.

(*c.*) In the order of interdependence, though not of time, there is a dependence of the second person, the Son, upon the first person, the Father, and of the third person upon both the Father and the Son; yet not so that the Son is really dependent upon the Father any more than is the Father upon the Son. It is an order of subsistence, an internal relation. The same divine essence and attributes exist eternally in this personal relationship. Any view of the Trinity must concede a *difference* in Father, Son, and Spirit, in the first, second, and third persons; in short an *ordo subsistendi*—a certain inequality. Only in some such mode of representation can we keep clear of annulling the personal distinctions in the Godhead, of reducing them to *three distinctions.*

(*d.*) There is an eternal generation, meaning the relation in which the Father and the Son *are,* not how they *came to be.*

By this, too, we discern in the Godhead the same relationship internally as that which is externally revealed.

The ground is in the divinity itself, why it must be revealed as Father, Son, and Spirit; as it is revealed, so it is, abstracting from it the limitations of time and space. This is the fact with regard to everything else: so by analogy with the Godhead. There *is* the same relation eternally, which in the manifestation is revealed.[1]

---

[1] Pascal, in a letter to his sister (cited in Vinet, "Etudes sur Pascal," pp. 78-9) speaks thus: Referring to a peculiarity in retaining the knowledge of spiritual things, not by memory—"though we can as easily remember an Epistle of St. Paul as a Book of Virgil"—but in things of grace—"Il faut que la même grâce, qui peut seule en donner la première intelligence, la continue et la rende toujours présente en la retraçant sans cesse dans le cœur des fidèles, pour la faire toujours vivre; comme dans les bien heureux Dieu renouvelle continuellement leur beatitude, qui est un effet et une suite de la grâce: comme aussi l'église tient que le Père *produit continuellement* le Fils, et maintient l'éternité de son essence par *une effusion de sa substance,* qui est *sans interruption* aussi bien que sans fin."

Dr. R. S. Candlish (in Introduction to "The Eternal Sonship," by Jas. Kidd, D.D., 1st ed., 1822, London, 1872, p. xlix.) says: "The Trinity is a revealed fact, ... but is there nothing in the laws of intelligent thought, in the essential constitution of the thinking mind, that responds to and closes with the doctrine or fact when presented to it, so as to facilitate the acceptance of it by the understanding, and give it a place *behind or beyond the understanding in the deeper region of the soul's intuitional perceptions.*" Then he goes on to say, substantially: Before creation God was infinite and alone, He was of infinite intelligence and moral excellencies, which latter are essentially communicative—seeking objects of fellowship. If only one being existed in all eternity, it must be assumed that "all these attributes existed in a state contrary to their very nature: a state of sheer passivity, or rather potentiality: under the category rather of the *posse* than of the *esse*." *E. g.*, Love is under "a necessity of communicating itself in grace and glory to some one to whom it may say, I and Thou—I GIVING, THOU RECEIVING." .... "The life of God is love. He lives in loving ... And his love cannot be without an object." .... "Here is the precise difficulty which the doctrine of the Trinity is fitted to solve" (p. lix.)

PART II.

CHRISTIAN COSMOLOGY.

We have considered the proof of the Being and Attributes of God; also God as revealed in and by the system of Redemption, as Triune, the immanent Trinity as the basis of the economic, which latter is found in the whole subsequent work of God. We are now to pass from God in himself to God in his works, the mirror of himself; his eternal power and Godhead are understood by the things that are made (Rom. i. 20), and of course are in them.

The general title here is Christian Cosmology, or, The World viewed as a Divine Cosmos or Order, manifesting the divine glory: The immanent glory as seen in the declarative glory of the Godhead. The subject of consideration here is the Cosmos, not as seen in itself, as science studies it, in detail, by induction and generalization, but as seen in its relations to God, to Redemption, to the Christian system, to eternal life. For the Cosmos is essentially the manifestation of God in time and in its progress towards eternity. It comes from the eternal God, it finishes its course and returns to its source, perfected, transformed into an eternal kingdom of grace and glory. In God himself there is infinite fulness, but that He might manifest his glory He brought into existence a universe, material, moral. In this creation God is revealed, his attributes co-working to produce the highest result for infinite wisdom and infinite love.

CHAPTER I.

CREATOR AND CREATION.

God is set forth in Scripture as the author and creator of the world as well as the Being who sustains and carries it on. The world is to fulfil a good end, the manifestation of the divine fulness so far as this is possible in the forms of space and time.

§ 1. *The Scripture represents God as the Creator of the World.*

It represents Him as the cause of being, to all that exists *ad extra*. The ground and source of all life are in God. This is frequently declared in the Scriptures: Gen. i. 1; Acts vii. 50; Rom. xi. 36; 1 Cor. viii. 6; Eph. iii. 9; Heb. i. 12; Rev. iv. 11. The creation of particular parts of the world is ascribed to the divine power: Acts iv. 15; Heb. i. 10; Rev. x. 6.

§ 2. *The Scripture represents the Son of God as the Medium by whom the World was brought into being.*

Col. i. 15; John i. 3; Heb. i. 2.—The Socinian explanation of such passages is that they refer to the spiritual creation of the kingdom of God, but the passages far surpass such interpretation. See Grinfield's "Christian Cosmos, or The Son of God the Revealed Creator."[1]

§ 3. *God created freely and not by necessity.*

No external or internal necessity for creation can be supposed, certainly no external, for all that is external is the product of the divine act; nor any internal, excepting a necessity from the divine love, which is moral, and not physical or natural. God is described in the Scripture as blessed and sufficient to himself: Acts xvii. 25; 1 Tim. i. 11.—This is shown also by the nature of the case, if God be an infinite and absolute Spirit. In the Scripture, Creation is ascribed to the will of God, of course implying voluntariness: Ps. xxxiii. 6; Eph. i. 11; Heb. xi. 3; Rev. iv. 11.

§ 4. *Creation is not from any previously extant substance.*

It was not a modification of an eternal material. An apocryphal book, Wisd. xi. 17, speaks of creation as "from formless matter," but in the Scriptures God is represented as the only cause, producing by a word and not from extant material. All things are said to be from Him, which implies that there can be no co-eternal system. See Heb. xi. 3, the purport of which is that the visible universe is not a mere manifestation of what is in-

---

[1] He perhaps goes too far in saying that this idea has almost vanished from evangelical preaching; still it is not enough insisted upon.

visible but is the product of divine power. Rom. iv. 17 contains a strongly corroborative expression: Who calls what is not into being as if it were.[1]

Some of the Theories held on this Subject.

The old theologians distinguished between the first and second act of creation: the first, the creation from nothing, indicated in Gen. i. 1, with the result in the second verse; the second, the work of the six days, bringing all into shape and order and implying, what is perhaps correct, a distinction between the creation of the prime material and its specific arrangement and organization. This is found also in some of the heathen cosmogonies, although it is a matter of doubt whether they held matter to be eternal. In Plato this is disputed. The New Platonists were dualists, holding to the eternity of matter. As the question is now raised there are several theories.

The first theory. That there was a primitive or original matter having its laws, which is developed into the worlds and all the orders of life in them, through the gradations of gas, fire, etc., the forces of the planets and their rotation, the geological stadia of the earth's progress, and then the orders of plants and animals up to man—all developed out of an original matter.— The questions which this theory does not answer are: Whence the matter and whence its laws? Whence is the order of creation, and what is it? There cannot be anything in the effect which is not in the cause. If from the cause sprang life, instinct, organization, intelligence, reason, person, and personal being, then in the cause there must have been at least as much, and therefore the primitive matter must have been a matter having intelligence and personality, which is an extraordinary kind of matter.

The second theory. Spirit and not matter is primitive; spirit, not as conscious, intelligent spirit, but in a generalized abstract sense, as containing all the laws and ideas out of which matter is developed. This becomes external to itself, and is developed into all the forms of the created universe. This theory may be either pantheistic or pantheistico-theistic, ac-

[1] Compare this with 2 Macc. vii. 28.

cording as spirit is viewed as having self-consciousness or not. If viewed pantheistically the prime objection to it is that we cannot derive from it any explanation of the mind in the universe. How can the abstract produce the concrete? How can an idea bring into being an animal, by its own force as an idea? If it cannot, the theory will not explain the works of creation. The other form, that spirit is primitive and all else is an emanation from it, is pantheistico-theistic. It allows that the intelligence which is disclosed in nature is divine, but says that there is likewise in the divine Being a kind of material out of which the worlds were formed, the mode of development, however, never having been explained. This is the emanation theory of some German philosophers, and it is akin to the theory next to be mentioned.

The third theory. That God is a self-conscious Being, having an antagonism in himself, which is called "the nature in God." This develops itself in the forms of the finite and material. Space and time, in their finite measures, existed as really for God as for ourselves. In God there is a kind of finite material out of which the worlds were made.

The fourth theory. That which alone is primitive is God, the infinite, absolute, and personal Spirit, and all that is in being is the product of his power. In Him, however, in his being and attributes, there was always the possibility of the existence of a finite and dependent universe. In his love lies the impulse to producing such a universe; in his will, the power of bringing it into being. That which was previous to creation in God was the possibility of its existence and also the idea of the world or the plan of the whole world from eternity. That was the archetype of the world, and it is this ideal world which is realized in a created universe. In creation God brings into being that which was not, as far as force or material are concerned. Although this was always in the divine mind, and in that sense eternal, yet as actually existing it came into being through the divine will. The purport of this theory, in relation to the others, may be shown by two or three considerations. (*a.*) It implies that the substance of the created universe is not that of the divine nature. The substance of the created universe as material is radically different from the divine essence; in the qualities of impenetrability and attractive force, in the qualities which make the atom and form the play of forces, neither of which can be supposed to be existing in a spiritual and eternal essence; and therefore the universe must be absolutely different from God. We must distinguish in creation between the matter (the element or atoms) and the forces. Both of these are entirely distinct from anything that can be in Deity. Thus, that which is absolutely new in creation, which was not there before, is the existing of these material atoms and forces, in the forms of space and time.

§ 5. *The Relation of God as Creator to what He has created.*

The Scripture view is that God is exalted above the world, yet present in it by his works, is both transcendent and immanent, far surpassing the universe, yet dwelling and working in it. He exists in one way in nature, and in another in man; is related in one way to the heathen, and in another to his people the Israelites; is revealed in one method in the Old Testament, and in a closer relation in the New. He dwells among his people and sets his tabernacle among them. The humble and contrite heart He will not despise. Those who love Him become the temple of the Holy Ghost. These different relations are in accordance with the different characteristics of the objects which He has brought into being. Especially is God's relation different to the good and to the bad. Heaven is his peculiar place of blessing. In the realm of despair, He works only in punishing. The omnipresence of God of course extends to the bounds of space and time, but the presence of God, in his special workings, is according to the nature of the objects which He works upon.

§ 6. *The Scripture represents Creation as a Plan and not as a Development.*

Creation is not a development in the sense of the " Vestiges of Creation." It is a plan in which all the parts are connected.

All of it is to reveal the divine glory. The great end of God is the manifestation of his fulness, his wisdom and power, in a created world, and all the universe is made upon one plan with reference to that, with its regular orders and stages: which are set forth even in the first account of creation, that of the six days, where there is a regular and philosophical order in which the objects are brought into being, beginning with the lowest in the scale, and ascending to man. We have first, the elements, secondly, the vegetable kingdom, thirdly, the animal kingdom, ending fourthly, in man; but this is not an order or plan which has a development, in such a sense that the higher springs out of the lower. The unity of the plan is made by its being one in the divine mind. There is no evidence that there can be a passage from a lower to a higher order, or from the inanimate to the animate.

CHAPTER II.

OF THE CREATED UNIVERSE AS SET FORTH IN SCRIPTURE.

It is designated by different names: the Creation, as having its origin in God; the Cosmos, as exhibiting a fair order; the Æons, as having its being in time. It is described as having a real being of its own, not a mere seeming, as held by some philosophers. The finite universe is not a perpetual creation, but consists of proper second causes: Heb. iv. 3. Each particular order has its proper functions and office, its distinct character: 1 Cor. xv. 38, "To each seed its own body," implies a distinction in the natural characteristics. While Scripture represents that there are different spheres of creation, different parts of the universe, it represents them as all having respect to the kingdom of God. Heaven, earth, and hell are the chief divisions, and all are named and described as being a part of one plan, the whole object of which is to illustrate the divine glory.

ANTECEDENTS OF REDEMPTION.

Under this point of view the Scriptural representation is much higher than that of natural science. The conception of unity given here is much higher than the sciences have been able to attain. The two parts of the world, in the general description of them given in Scripture, are the heavens and the earth, the relation of above and below being that which is generally implied: the heavens being the invisible, and the earth the visible (Col. i. 16); the earth being for a time, the heavens for eternity. Yet the earth is to become heaven (Rev. xxi.): they are separated now for a time in order to a reunion, against the time when the Bride shall be prepared to meet the Bridegroom at his coming. Earthly things thus become an image of heavenly things. (*a.*) Heaven is the place in which the kingdom of God is fully realized, where unfallen and redeemed spirits abide and in which God dwells and is perfectly revealed: the Father's house in which are many mansions, with which the name of God as our heavenly Father accords. The kingdom of God is called the kingdom of heaven in reference to its moral character and also to its ultimate destination; Christ is spoken of as having dwelt in heaven and as having returned thither. In it are different degrees or mansions. Christ has ascended above all the heavens. Paul speaks of having been caught up to the third heaven. (*b.*) Earth is that portion of the universe in which fallen humanity dwells, and where the kingdom of God is not yet fully realized. It is to be transformed, and the seeds of heaven are found even here: Heb. vi. 5: "The powers of the world (or age) to come" are already at work. The earth is to pass through a process of change and redemption. Such a process is probably set forth in Rom. viii. 20, 21. The word "creature" here appears to mean the whole physical universe, and this is described as in sympathy with redemption and destined to share in the redemption when completed. 2 Pet. iii. 10 gives further indications of the same destiny. (*c.*) The other grand portion of the universe is the under-world, Hades, the world of departed spirits. This is represented as being under the earth. There are two main divisions of it: Paradise (Luke xxiii. 43), a place for the departed good, called also Abraham's bosom (Luke xvi.

27); and the prison (1 Pet. iii. 19), the place where the evil are kept, which at last becomes the Gehenna,[1] the hell, the lake of fire, denoting the place of final torment to which the wicked are condemned along with the devil and his angels.

CHAPTER III.

OF THE DIFFERENT ORDERS OF CREATED BEINGS.

The creation is represented as having different orders of animated beings, not a series in development, but a series in a plan, constantly ascending to man, the highest. Between man and God there are other orders of beings. The Scriptures reveal the existence of angels, making another scale of ascents. These are sometimes called the sons of God. As far as any distinct revelation guides us, we are constrained to think of these as spiritual beings. If they have any body at all, it must be what is termed a spiritual body, not partaking of flesh and blood; and apparently they are not so far subject to the restrictions of space and time as men are. There is no evidence that they belong to any order of beings that grows from small to large. It appears that what they are at creation, that they remain. Their power is superior to that of human beings, yet subordinate to that of God; working through second causes and not above them; and it is doubtful whether they can have any immediate influence upon human souls: at any rate this is not directly asserted. Probably their influence is limited to working through and by second causes, and thus they must work according to established laws. They are described as appearing for the most part at the great epochs of the world; at the creation, the giving of the law, the Incarnation, and the scenes of the final judgment. That there are some orders

---

[1] Dr. Campbell, in his "Introd. to the Four Gospels," has one of the best essays in respect to the Jewish views as to Gehenna, etc.

among them is implied in Col. ii. 10, and other passages, but we have nothing more definite than the general designations, "principalities and powers," "thrones and dominions." A few names of angels are given. The good angels are described as angels of light, as employed in the service of God, as ministering in some respects to man, and in one passage as having some particular relation to children (Matt. xviii. 10).

As to the evil angels. (1) If there are angels, there may be evil angels. If there may be spiritual beings of purity, there may be spiritual beings impure, sinful, and evil. The evidence that such beings do exist, rests solely, of course, on the testimony of the Bible. From *a priori* reasoning we could make no inference except the possibility of their existence. The fact of their existence is revealed to us in the Scriptures. Specimens of the Scripture testimony are 1 Tim. iii. 16; Jude 6; 2 Pet. ii. 4. It appears from the passages cited that these angels were not originally evil. They became such.[1] (2) The Scripture representation of the character of the evil angels. The love of evil is rooted in them. They rejoice in the destruction of others. 1 Pet. v. 8. Works of deceit, fraud, temptation to sin, and malignity are ascribed to them, as seen in the names, Adversary, Accuser, The Evil One, The Destroyer. In them probably evil has reached its height, so that the love of sin is paramount even when it is known to be folly. (3) The Scripture represents that the evil angels together form a kingdom or organization: Eph. ii. 2; vi. 12. Elsewhere, the prince of demons, of the power of the air, the devil with his angels, is spoken of, so that in such designations we have the intimations of an order. (4) The power of these evil spirits is described as extending to spiritual solicitations and also to influences upon the body. Satan binds the mind and ensnares. "The Devilish wisdom" is spoken of; this power is controlled, but it is a power appealing to men's evil passions and moving them by wicked motives. The power over the

---

[1] The "sons of God," in Gen. vi. 2, are most probably the purer part of mankind, and not angels as some writers would suggest.

body comes out in the Demoniacal Possessions. The reality of these possessions cannot be given up without giving up the historical verity of Scripture. That there are forms of disease now something like these is undoubtedly true, such as lunacy and epilepsy, but this does not show that all these phenomena are connected solely with bodily causes. Epilepsy may be the result of a violent conflict of passion. The phenomena of epilepsy and lunacy may have occurred in connection with demoniacal possessions. That they did rests solely upon Scriptural evidence. We cannot now show that there are cases of possession, and science is unable to prove them impossible. It may be that our Saviour's great work in subduing them was such that the power of these possessions should be paralyzed for the future. That there was a conflict with the power of evil, and that Christ broke that power, is evident from Scripture, and it may be that this was one of the cases.

The chief objections to this doctrine of the reality of evil spirits are presented by Schleiermacher. He objects to the whole doctrine of the Devil as inconceivable, as not to be thought consistently, and therefore reduces it to a personification, placing it among the mythical elements of Scripture, on the following grounds:

1. That the fall of Satan and his host, whether they fell together or separately, is inconceivable, because no motive can be assigned which would not presuppose the fall already accomplished. *Reply.* This lies against the case of every first sin in every creature, and would prove that there could not be any first sin.

2. It is impossible to conceive of the fall of Satan in connection with such high intellectual endowments and knowledge as must be assigned to him! *Reply.* We do not know how much Satan knew. We know that he was not omniscient. We do not know whether he himself knew all the consequences of sin. But even if he did know, that is no reason why he might not have fallen. In every creature the knowledge of the evil consequences of sin is such that

if that knowledge were followed there would be no sin. Human beings know that when they sin they are exposing themselves to wretchedness, and yet they sin. No one can say but that there might have been such knowledge as Satan had, and still he would have fallen.

3. It is inconceivable that Satan should have parted with this knowledge by an act of the will; that the will in surrendering itself to sin should be the means of blinding the intellect. *Reply.* It is of the very nature of all sin and evil that they carry the soul away in opposition to light and knowledge. The knowledge may exist, and the will be still perverse. The reply under the second head applies here also.

4. Some fall while others do not.—This is no real objection.

5. Such a being could not hope to relieve his misery by constant hostility to God, and yet he engages in such hostility knowing that it will only increase his wretchedness. *Reply.* Satan in this respect is like all who sin. Every sinner knows that in the end he must succumb, and yet he sins. All sin is folly in its very nature.[1]

Another objection may be mentioned, viz., that the Scriptural representations of the Devil's power are dangerous: that it is dangerous in a public teacher to say much about this.—If this be true, and the Scriptures are truly from God, it is wonderful that they should contain such representations. There cannot be any danger in using Scriptural revelations in the Scriptural sense. The chief danger has been not in taking Scripture, but rather Milton's "Paradise Lost," as our standard. Whatever be the amount of Satan's power, it is all subject to God's power, and Satan can never overcome the soul that trusts in God.

Observation. We should guard ourselves against teaching the ubiquity of Satan. There may be evil influences widely dispersed, but that the Devil has ubiquity is not contained in the Scripture.—Also we should note the difference between Scripture and other pretended sources in regard to details of the spiritual world. The Scriptures give simply intimations, while fanatics and pretenders enter into minute particulars.

[1] See Twesten's "Doct. of Angels," Bib. Sac. I. 792.

CHAPTER IV.

THE PRESERVATION OF CREATION.

By preservation is meant a continuance in being by God's omnipresent agency of what has been brought into being by God's omnipotence, including of course the preservation of the substance and the qualities and the powers of each individual thing. There are various theories of the Preservation. Some represent it as a continued creation. Others view it as mechanical continuance. A mechanic makes a machine, and leaves it to work through its own properties; preservation here is simply non-interference. Limborch, the chief Arminian theologian, says that preservation is simply not annihilating. Others represent it as a continual influx of God, by a substantial omnipresence, so that God is in everything by his essence. Calvin has some strong expressions upon this subject: he says, God is everywhere present by illapse and influx, terms which would be understood now as having almost a pantheistic sense.

§ 1. *Sources of the Proof of the Doctrine.*

From the divine attributes in their necessary working, Preservation might be inferred. Omnipresence, Omnipotence, and Wisdom, exerted in reference to a world brought into being, involve a divine energy continuing it in existence. It may also be said that the world being the product of divine omnipotence must be continued in being by the same power or fall into annihilation. Otherwise the world would have the principle of its being in itself. Again, God having produced the world, his wisdom and love would of course prompt Him to continue it in existence. The Scriptures set forth God's preservation of what He has made in passages such as the following: Acts xvii. 28; Ps. xxxvi. 6; Neh. ix. 6; Ps. lxvi. 9. Christ is revealed as the Preserver as well as Creator: Col. i. 17; Heb. i. 3.

§ 2. *The Purport of the Doctrine.*

1. It recognizes what is true in the other theories, the theory of continual creation and the mechanical theory, without im-

plying the denial which is implied in them, viz., in the one case, of proper second causes, and in the other, of a continued dependence of the world upon its author.

2. This doctrine further maintains and insists upon the real presence of God in all his works, operative, upholding, and guiding all things for his own purpose and plan. It asserts a real operative presence, and does not deny a substantial presence.

3. The proper theory of preservation also allows the real existence of second causes, while still insisting that these are kept in being and upheld by the great First Cause. They are proper causes in themselves, and have a proper mode of activity and being, but not as separate from God. All experience proves the existence of these causes. They are not modes of action of the great First Cause, but proper second causes sustained by the First Cause. This view alone is consistent with God's making real responsible agents, who must yet recognize their dependence on God.

§ 3. *Theory of continued Creation.*

This theory asserts that the same divine creative power which was at work in the first instance is ever at work, producing all things by an omnipotent energy at each instant. It of course involves a denial of any real subsistence in the things themselves. It is the creative omnipotence which is the upholding omnipotence.

That the creative omnipotence does uphold is undeniable, but that the creative and upholding omnipotence are the same, rests on no valid ground of evidence. This position has been taken by some of the New England divines of the strictest Hopkinsian cast, suggested no doubt by the speculations of Berkeley, who held that the external world had no real proper being, but consisted of ideas, which were constantly produced by the divine power, and had their origin only in the divine mind. This involves of course the position that there is no real substance behind the phenomena.[1]

---

[1] The Divine Efficiency scheme of Dr. Emmons is but a modification of the same Berkeleian position, being Berkeley's principle applied to the inner acts of the mind as well as to the ideas of what is outward.

The Objections to this Theory.

1. It is against our native belief in the existence, external to us, of real, proper substances. This is a belief of which we cannot divest ourselves.

2. If carried out logically, the theory would lead to the position that God is the only real being, and that all besides has merely phenomenal being without reality; and so we should be brought to pantheism.

3. In the same manner the theory runs athwart another of our beliefs, that of a proper causal action, the connection of cause and effect, which is certified by reason. It asserts that God is the only causality. Second causes are denied.

4. It is against the tone and general representations of Scripture, which represents creation as completed: Gen ii. 1, 2; Heb. iv. 3.

§ 4. *A Modification of the Theory of continued Creation.*

This modification is found among the Scholastics, in Thomas Aquinas, and in some of the Reformed and Lutheran divines. Acknowledging the real existence of finite substances, that there is a real proper substance beneath the phenomena, the theory denies any efficiency to this, tracing the efficiency to God. It confesses that there is an underlying substratum which is the ground of the phenomena, but all the activity of the phenomena is ascribed to a divine influence. Newton, in one of his speculations, comes nearly to this, saying that the laws of the material universe are the stated modes of the divine operations. All who deny proper second causes stand here.[1] This same general view is found in the Cartesian philosophy, and is there called Occasionalism, which represents God as producing the activities of body and soul correlatively to each other.

The Objections to this Theory.

1. Like the previous one it contradicts our experience, our native belief—not now in the existence of substance, but—in the existence of causes in nature. What we perceive in nature, according to this view, must be not the phenomena of matter, but

[1] Dr. Woods borders on this. Works, Vol. ii. 20.

the phenomena of God, God working. In thus resolving all activity into a mode of Divine operation the theory tends to a pantheistic conclusion.

2. As applied to mind and moral agency, the theory is in conflict with our conviction that we are proper causes, the proper authors of our own acts, which we know by immediate consciousness, if we know anything. We know that we choose and decide, and do it by our proper power, and yet this theory would compel us to say that these acts are modes of the Divine agency, and would thus annul moral agency.

3. In doing this it would of course lead to the conclusion that God is the author of sin, because all causality is traced back to Him, and this annuls the idea of God as a holy being.

4. While there is no evidence that there are not second causes, there is very much evidence that there are such. They are not independent of Deity, but have a proper sphere of their own. The theory rests on the underlying notion that there is only one cause; but if there is only one cause there is only one substance, and pantheism is the only theory.

§ 5. *The Mechanical Theory of Preservation.*

This is, that God has brought into being the world and all that is in it, and then sustains it without any constant agency or personal direction and care. This was the general view of the Arminians, also of the Deists in England and on the Continent.

The objections are: (1) It makes the creation to be virtually independent of God. After his works are once brought into being, they subsist by their own power, work by their own efficiency. Thus this view is opposed to the truth of God's omnipresence, and it is also opposed to the doctrine of God's Providence, which comes presently to be considered. (2) If the view be carried through and acted upon consistently, there cannot be any prayer. Religion expressing desire in prayer would be impossible, and thus the theory runs counter to the Scriptures and to Christian consciousness.

CHAPTER V.

DIVINE PROVIDENCE.

§ 1. *General Statements in respect to the Doctrine.*

The "Westminster Confession," Chapter V., gives the main points of the doctrine in a full and clear manner, viz., (§ 1) "God, the great Creator of all things, doth uphold, direct, dispose and govern all creatures, actions and things, from the greatest even to the least, by his most wise and holy providence, according to his infallible foreknowledge, and the free and immutable counsel of his own will, to the praise of the glory of his wisdom, power, justice, goodness and mercy." (§ 2) "Although . . . . all things come to pass immutably and infallibly; yet, by the same providence, He ordereth them to fall out according to the nature of second causes, either necessarily, freely or contingently." This providence extends likewise to sin, (§ 4) ". . . . not by a bare permission, but such as hath joined with it a most wise and powerful bounding, and otherwise ordering and governing of them [his creatures], in a manifold dispensation, to his own holy ends; yet so as the sinfulness thereof proceedeth only from the creature, and not from God; who being most holy and righteous, neither is nor can be the author or approver of sin."

The acts of Divine Providence are divided by theologians into *immanent and transeunt*, the immanent being the foreknowledge and purpose of God, and the transeunt the execution of this purpose through and by his creatures. Providence is divided also in respect to its objects, into general, as having respect to all; special, having respect to man and his destiny; and most special, having respect to the good or to the bringing about the supremacy of holiness in the divine dominion.

The doctrine of Divine Providence includes the following particulars:

1. It supposes or presupposes the carrying into execution of a divine purpose or plan in the world, which God has brought

into being. God's agency in the world is in order that his providence or plans may be consummated. This is the *terminus ad quem*, and in doing this all the divine attributes concur. God's power, wisdom, holiness, justice, goodness, and truth are all involved in his bringing about this end by his providence.

2. The doctrine further asserts that to promote and execute this plan, God's government extends to each and all. Everything in the world may be viewed in reference to this end, all being subordinate means to this general purpose.

3. The doctrine further asserts that God governs each thing and all things that He has made, according to their respective natures: that the Providence in respect to the animal and vegetable kingdom is one thing, and in respect to moral agents is another, is a moral government carried out in God's direction of his moral creatures.

4. It still further implies that God treats men as moral agents, governs and guides them according to their character as good or bad; that the divine providence is different in the good from what it is in the evil, *i. e.*, that it acts in a different mode.

5. Moreover, by the very statement of the doctrine it is implied that the natural world is in order to the moral; that God directs the ends of nature not to subserve natural results but to promote the divine plans, and thus nature is ever subordinate to the divine kingdom.

6. It is involved in this that in the regular order of nature God may interpose in the midst of physical causes by special act or by miraculous intervention, acting against and interrupting second causes, producing that which second causes cannot produce. Yet this interposition, this miraculous intervention, are all part of the plan, as much involved in it as second causes are.

As thus stated the doctrine is opposed to the doctrine of Fate, because there is a wise end and a wise author, and equally and for the same reasons to the doctrine of Chance.[1]

[1] James Douglass: "There are but three alternatives for the sum of existence, Chance, Fate, or Deity. With Chance there would be variety without uniformity, with Fate uniformity without variety, but variety in uniformity is the demonstration of primal design and the seal of the creative mind. In the world as it exists there is infinite variety and amazing uniformity."

§ 2. *Proof of the Doctrine of Providence.*

I.—The Scriptural Argument.

1. The Scriptures prove that the divine providence is universal, extending to and embracing the whole world and the whole of human history: Ps. cxxxv. 6; Eph. i. 11, last clause; Ps. ciii. 19; Dan. iv. 34, 35. Here also is to be produced in proof the general tone of the prophecies, which set forth everything as arranged with reference to the divine purpose: Ezek. xxi. 27; Isa. x. 5; Acts xvii. 26; Rom. ix.; xiii. 1.

2. This providence is further declared in Scripture to embrace the natural and animal world, the whole physical sphere: Matt. vi. 26; Ps. civ. 27; Acts xvii. 25, xiv. 17; Job xxxviii.-xli.

3. Individuals also in their destiny are under the divine guidance and providence. This, which is implied in the whole of Scripture, is declared in such passages as the following: Prov. xvi. 9; Isa. xlv. 5; 1 Sam. ii. 7. So in all passages which trace disease and health to the divine guidance, and represent man as in his temporal destiny under the guardianship of God.

4. Still further, the Scriptures represent the actions of men as under the control and government of divine providence: Prov. xxi. 1; xvi. 1. Every opportunity that we enjoy, every capacity, every blessing, is traced to this divine guidance. Success or failure in our enterprises is in the hands of God.

5. Sin also is included in the divine government. God permits and controls it, the permission being such and only such as involves control. It exists not without divine permission, but God overrules it. This is implied in the reasoning of the Apostle in Rom. ix., where he speaks of the hardening of Pharaoh's heart and the blinding of men's eyes. Also, Ps. lxxvi. 10; Rom. xi. 32; Acts ii. 23. Such passages prove more than simple providence, they set forth a predestination, but as a matter of course they involve the doctrine of providence. Yet the Scriptures never represent God as the author of sin. They positively assert the contrary: 1 John ii. 16; James i. 13.

II.—Proof from the divine attributes, their character and characteristics. If God's wisdom be such as we have seen, He would not create a universe and then leave it. His attributes must be in constant activity, and the exercise of these, omnipotence, omniscience, goodness, etc., *is* the exercise of divine providence.

III.—Another argument is from the fact that God is a moral ruler, and as such has a proper end in the creation which He has made, and He must so govern and direct it that the end shall be accomplished.

IV.—From History. The Biblical history is the history of the divine providence, the only history that ever was written from the truest, highest, and broadest point of view; and in this God appears at work in all the events recorded, among the heathen as well as the Jews, directing everything for his purposes. The highest point of view for treating all history would be this.[1] Divine providence is clearly seen in the lives depicted in the Scriptures. Moreover, the general course of history, when regarded from its highest point of view, demonstrates a divine agency, working towards an end. The old world, the mediæval and the modern times unite in one plan, tending towards the consummation of the Messiah's kingdom. No unity can be given to history on any other plan. No other central point of view can be found. History without this is chaotic. The only views that can make any pretence to compete with this are the Positivist and the Hegelian theories: the former asserting that human history is intended to develop the social and material welfare of mankind; the latter, that history is tending towards the illustration and development of human freedom, particularly as that is found in a well-ordered state.[2] But each of these theories narrows the view and cannot take in all the facts.

V.—From the order, harmony, and adaptation of nature. God is everywhere, intelligently acting, directing the different orders of creation, putting them in their just relations, making one subserve the other, the inorganic to contribute to the organic, and the different orders of the organic to each other, until man is reached, the head and crown of all.

[1] See the author's Introd. to Christian Theol., page 174.
[2] [This is well criticised in Flint's Phil. of Hist. in France and Germany, p. 534.]

VI.—From the nature and necessity of faith, piety, and religion. Without belief in God's providence, religion is an impossibility. All prayer, all sense of dependence upon God, involve the belief that God works through his providence.

§ 3. *Distinction as to general and particular Providence.*

General providence is God's control over the whole; particular, his care over each in relation to the whole. There are not two kinds of providence, but the same providence is exercised in two relations. The phrase, special providence, is sometimes used to denote a different aspect of the subject, *i. e.*, to describe God's providence as it appears in its relation to us, to designate some special combinations, as in a special answer to prayer or a relief in an emergency, and in fact in all instances where grace and help come in critical circumstances. There is doubtless a special character in these, involving as they do an unusual combination of incidents in order that a petition may be answered or a particular purpose be accomplished. There is understood to be an ordering of the ordinary course of things particularly to some high moral end.[1]

The proof of such particular or special providence is derived: (1) From the fact that general providence cannot be carried out without this. All great events are somewhere small. The destiny of nations turns at some points on very slight circumstances. (2) From Scripture. In all parts of Scripture it is presupposed that God directs and guides individuals and has a care for their life. Appeals and exhortations are made on this ground: 1 Pet. v. 7; Luke xii. 6; Prov. xvi. 33. (3) From individual experience, particularly of all Christians, who have found that the more they presented to God their cares, the more they were

---

[1] The rule for the due interpretation of special providences is to be taken from their bearing on our spiritual state. Have they made us more spiritual or humble? Probably the "providence" is imaginary when it does not minister to the Christian graces, but fosters pride. Especially should caution be used when matters concern a wide sphere of interest, as, *e. g.*, a nation or political party or church. We may be kept from much error in the interpretation of special providences by observing the condition referred to, viz., in its true idea a special providence is a providence having respect to the spiritual growth or welfare of individuals.

guided and blessed. Such trust in God's providence exercises a healthful influence upon all who love Him. It is particularly necessary to belief in the doctrine of the renewal of God's children. Without a most special providence this is inconceivable. An objection to such special providence is sometimes made on the ground that it represents God as interposing at points which are unworthy of his greatness. This is to be met, if it needs to be met at all, by a consideration of the relation of the little to the great. The objection moreover proves too much. It would bear as directly against God's bringing little things into being, as against his sustaining and guiding them.

§ 4. *Modes of the Divine Providence.*
1. God by his providence governs the whole universe in all its parts, each and all, and each for all.
2. He does this for one comprehensive end, in respect to which we do not yet inquire what it may be.
3. He governs not by suppressing second causes, but in harmony with them. Here comes up the chief point of discussion and controversy on the relation of providence to second causes. From the views and arguments already advanced, it is evident that the government of second causes is not to be taken as a mode of direct divine efficiency. Second causes are not modes of operation of the one great cause. What then the mode of the direction of second causes is, is the topic of discussion. The theological term by which the divine agency in connection with second causes is designated is, *Concursus*, and what we have to consider is *the theory of the concursus.* That there is a co-agency or co-operation is implied in all the Scripture.

The first theory. This co-agency is general. God acts upon and through all, but He does not determine the specific nature of the activity of each second cause. So, *e. g.*, the sun excites all sorts of seeds to activity, but the seeds grow according to their specific nature, and the office of the sun is simply that of general excitation. It stirs equally all sorts of seeds, and then its work ceases, the specific activity of each seed being determined by the nature of the seed. This is the way in which the co-agency of God in man's spiritual quickening and life is interpreted by the Remonstrants and the Jesuits.

The second theory. A more specific statement is made by the main body of the Roman theologians, including Aquinas, and by the greater part of Protestant teachers. It is that besides such a general exciting agency on the part of God, there is an immediate and simultaneous co-operation, a joint agency in every effect, *i. e.*, the divine agency extends to all and each. The agency of the sun upon the seed and plant is outside, is superficial simply, is exerted in the way of general excitation. But the agency of God as omnipotent, omnipresent, exerted in conformity with the idea of the divine co-operation, must enter into the interior as well as arouse the surface. It must go along with every motion, every activity which is found, there must be a joint simultaneous activity of God with the trembling of every nerve, with the particular or specific growth of each plant, so that a divine power shapes and works along with the seed itself, with the secret agencies as well as the external products. And so with the human soul. The divine power must enter into the soul itself, and sustain each second cause in working according to the particular end of that second cause, must sustain and direct it in every movement so that the concursus shall be perfect throughout, as if there were a twofold activity perfectly parallel in every act. But this raises

The third question. How then can this view be reconciled with the sinful activities of certain second causes? In meeting this difficulty almost all Roman Catholic and Protestant divines insist upon the distinction between an act and its moral character, and put the sin, as far as the divine agency is concerned, in defect. God's agency thus extends to sin not as sin, but simply as an act of the creature. Augustine illustrated it thus: the power which causes a lame man to walk is not the cause of his limping: the striking of an instrument which is out of tune is not the cause of the discord. The cause of the limping is not in the agency of God, it is in the structure of the limb, so that there can be co-agency in the whole limping, while yet the co-agent does not produce the limping and is not responsible for it. As to the musical instrument, the influence acting upon it is not the source of the discord. This is in the structure of the instrument, and there may be a co-agency in the production of the sound, the player being responsible only for the striking and the instrument for the discord. So in respect to sin. God's agency may extend to every act and activity, while yet He is not responsible for sin, because this comes not from his agency, but from the state of the heart of the individual with whom He co-operates.—These illustrations are not perfect, but perhaps they are as good as can be found.

A fourth position. God in his providence so governs that the natural world is subordinate to the moral world. He governs the natural in order to the moral. Some naturalists oppose this view, urging that there are two entirely different spheres, the one physical, the other moral, and that the whole physical sphere proceeds without reference to the moral, that the physical realm comprises cases of mere necessity, and that these never can be modified or diverted for moral ends.[1] The doctrine of Divine Providence maintains the general position that although the spheres are different, and though physical and moral laws are different, yet both spheres are a part of one plan and make one whole, and that in the divine plan the natural is in order to the moral, and is upheld and guided for moral ends. In both God is equally a sovereign. The natural laws are seen chiefly in the preservation and in all the agencies and effects of our natural powers. The moral order is God's government of moral beings to secure the highest moral ends. This may be illustrated by the following considerations.

1. As a matter of fact, in the divine government, the natural is made to subserve the moral. This is in the ordinary course of God's providence. Natural pains or pleasures are directly

---

[1] One writer says, they can no more be turned aside than the ball coming from the mouth of a cannon, that both systems of laws must go on, and that the physical cannot bend to the moral. See Prof. Chase in Bib. Sac.

connected with the violation of, or obedience to, moral laws. The course of nature thus works for God's government.

2. Also in the course of nature, besides these connections in the ordinary course of providence, there may be and are, on the part of God, interpositions for high moral ends and purposes. "Seek ye first the kingdom of God and his righteousness, and all these things shall be added unto you." God so directs the course of nature as to make it subserve the interests of his moral government. Obedience to his divine laws in the long run is seen to issue in greater temporal well-being. There is no violation of natural law in this, but there is direction of natural law in it. God so arranges the whole complexus of physical laws that in the long run the physical follow in the wake of the moral, and tend to uphold the moral. God turns the physical law into the current of his moral government. This is illustrated in the prosperity and destiny of nations.

3. God likewise acts above the course of nature, as in the renewal and sanctification of the soul, and as in the Incarnation of his Son.

4. God may and does interrupt the course of nature, as in miracles.

5. God so governs moral beings that they are free. Moreover, his efficiency is not the same in sinful as in holy acts.

6. God governs in different modes of interference according to the exigency.

7. God knows the causes and essences of things, and hence He may and doubtless does work in ways which we cannot fathom.

CHAPTER VI.

THE DECREES OF GOD.[1]

The relation of the decrees of God to his providence is simply this: the whole course and order of divine providence are the

[1] The subjects of the Order of the Decrees, Election, etc., belong in the third division of theology.

result of a decree and purpose. God as a sovereign has foreordained the course and order of providence. He has purposed that things should be and take place as they are and do actually occur. In other words, the doctrine of the divine decrees is the doctrine of divine providence referred back to the divine sovereignty. The doctrine asserts that all that is in the natural and moral world, including the kingdom of grace, takes place in consequence of a fixed and unchangeable and eternal purpose of God. (In some systems of theology the doctrine of decrees is treated before that of providence, which is the logical order, but the natural order is rather to consider the divine providence first.)

§ 1. *Preliminary Statements.*

I.—In his decree God is a sovereign. The doctrine of divine decrees is simply and ultimately that God is the sovereign ruler of the universe which He has created, and that He does as He pleases, according to the counsel of his own will and wisdom, not in an arbitrary sense, but in such a sense that He needs not to take counsel of his creatures. The argument for this is from various sources.[1] (1) The doctrine of the divine sovereignty results from the divine nature and attributes in relation to a dependent universe. (2) It is best that a Being of infinite power and wisdom should be the sovereign of the universe, and that it should not be left to the contingency and change of inferior creatures. (3) Our deepest religious convictions show us the need of the doctrine for our renewal and sanctification. We cannot rest on any created power, but must cast ourselves on the arm of a sovereign. As is often said, Arminians are Calvinists when they pray. (4) The Scripture argument. Ps. cxv. 3; cxxxv. 6; Rom. xi. 36; Eph. i. 5; i. 11; Phil. ii. 13.

II.—This sovereignty is not a bare omnipotence, although that is involved in it, but it includes the activity of all God's attributes and powers. Sovereignty is often taken as equiva-

[1] See especially Dr. Woods's Lectures, Vol. I, and Dr. Balmer in Brown's Theol. Tracts, Vol. III.

lent to arbitrary power, but the doctrine is not that God has no reason for his action; He has the best of reasons for all that He does; He has a rational, wise, holy end ever in view, and the doctrine is that God brings this wise and holy end to its consummation.

III.—God's decrees are one decree, one plan, in which each is for all and all for each.

IV.—God's decrees or purpose simply determine this: that all things are to be as they occur. The order and plan of the universe, both natural and moral, are in divine fore-ordination just what they are in fact—nothing more nor less. Whatever anything is in itself, in its internal and external relations, so it was decreed to be. The decrees refer to all things, results, and means, just as they occur in the course of divine providence. If there are contingent events in providence, there are contingent events in decrees; if there are free acts in providence, there are free acts in decrees; if there are sinful and guilty acts in providence, so there are in decrees. The doctrine of decrees or sovereignty is a comprehensive doctrine. Most objections spring from taking isolated facts by themselves, as if God purposed each event by itself, as if, *e. g.*, He determined to condemn a certain individual to eternal death without any regard to anything else, when the true statement is, that if, in point of fact, the condemnation comes as the issue of a sinful career, so it was in the divine purpose. On this ground we may meet the common objection, that if an action is decreed we cannot be responsible for it. The objection supposes that the action is decreed in circumstances which prevent responsibility, whereas the consciousness of the individual is that he is responsible, and that consciousness is as much decreed as the act is. If there is a sinful act it was decreed as the act of a man and as his own act.

V.—In short, the doctrine declares in substance, that the present system of the universe in all its parts, as it was, is, and is to be, is an eternal plan, or purpose, or idea in the divine mind.

§ 2. *Of the Terms used to denote the Doctrine.*

The term purpose is equivalent to the term decrees. The word decree is in some respects unfortunate, because misunderstood so frequently. Decree is used ordinarily, and in Scripture, in the sense of edict or law, that which God commands. But the theological usage takes the word not in the sense of command or approbation on God's part, but of what He permits or determines to be done as a whole plan. It does not imply moral approval on the side of God, or fate or necessity on the side of the act, but it does imply certainty. Of the general decree of God, predestination is a part. The decree of God embraces all that occurs; predestination is technically a part of the divine decree, and is used of that which relates to moral beings, and especially to their final condition (although predestination really applies to every event of their history as well as to their final destiny). As thus used it implies that man's final state is involved in God's plan, yet never without respect to what has gone before, rather as being the sum of what has gone before. Predestination contains the end only as containing the sum total of what has gone before.

§ 3. *Characteristics of the Divine Decree or Decrees.*

I.—They are sovereign, expressing the good pleasure of God, and so in many respects must be unsearchable to man.

II.—They are unconditional. They are not dependent on anything which is not a part or parcel of the divine decree itself. This does not mean that the decrees themselves are not mutually dependent, but that nothing in the plan is conditioned by anything which is not in the decree itself.[1]

III.—They are eternal. They must be so on the consideration that otherwise there would be a change in the divine plan or appointment: Eph. i. 4; 2 Tim. i. 9; 1 Pet. i. 20. When the Scriptures speak of one decree as preceding another, the order is in the unfolding of the decrees, and not in the formation of them.

---

[1] Yet the phrase *unconditional decree* is usually understood to mean an arbitrary purpose. This is the sense in which it is taken by Supralapsarianism. But that theory, since the Synod of Dort, has scarcely dared to lift its head.

IV.—They are immutable. This is involved in their eternity Ps. xxxiii. 11; Isa. xlvi. 11.

V.—They involve the certain occurrence of that which is decreed. This is the meaning of the word efficacious as applied to the divine decrees, *i. e.*, what is contained in them is sure, certain, the decree is effectual, a purpose which is carried into effect. Not that the decree itself is efficacious, or that God by a direct efficiency carries each decree into operation. The reasons for this are: (1) If it were not so there would be no certainty to divine government. This might be overthrown or set aside. The fulfillment of prophecy may depend upon a million of minute particulars whose occurrence must be secured. (2) The divine attributes prove the position. (3) The Scriptures assert it. All the prophecies establish it: Isa. xiv. 27. Also all passages which declare the divine sovereignty.

VI.—The divine decrees, as including all events, include sin also. The controversy between the Supra- and Sub-lapsarians is not on account of this point, whether the decree of God includes sin as certain, but it is in respect to the order of the divine decrees. The Supralapsarian says that the divine purpose in respect to sin or the permission of sin in the world was subsequent to the divine purpose for salvation and punishment, *i. e.*, in the order of divine decrees, the logical order, the first decree is that God will set forth his glory, the second, that He will do this by saving some and condemning others, and the third is the decree of the fall, the Lapsus. The Sublapsarian says that in the order of the divine decrees, there is first the decree to create, then the permission of the fall, and then election and redemption, or redemption and election. There appears to be good reason for asserting the sublapsarian position as against the supralapsarian, though it is to be acknowledged that the whole subject of the order of the divine decrees is above man's comprehension. But it appears absurd to speak of redemption unless there was a fall in the order of thought, or of a punishment unless there was sin to be punished. Irrespective of supra- or sub-lapsarian speculations, it is necessary to consider that in the whole divine plan sin somehow has its place. It is taken into the plan, not under God's approval nor as the means of good, but as a fact. The arguments for this position are: (1) If sin be excluded from the divine decree or purpose, then that on which the whole economy of grace rests is not contained in the divine purpose. (2) If sin is excluded, much the larger part of the history of mankind is excluded. How much of human history is there which is not sin or of sin? To exclude it would be to throw the divine plan out of the world. (3) As all events are connected, and sin belongs in the line of cause and effect, to exclude sin from the decree would annul the possibility of providence and a divine government. Sin is ever interlocked with good. It is the overruling of sin which produces the highest good.[1] (4) The relation to sin in which the Scriptures exhibit God is that of permitting and overruling it, but at the same time they imply that it is included in his general purpose: Rom. v. 20; ix. 18; xi. 8; xi. 32; Gal. iii. 19; iii. 22.

NOTE.—The question between Calvinists and Arminians is this: whether the decrees depend on foreknowledge. Does the divine decree depend upon God's foreseeing that such and such a thing will be? Is it decreed simply because God foresaw it would come to pass? In relation to this: (1) In one sense the foreknowledge must be the ground of the decree, *i. e.*, God does not decree anything which he does not know, He must know what He is going to decree. God knows what is possible, what is best to be in a certain plan, knows what belongs to all the parts of the plan, knows all this in the order of thought before He determines that the plan shall take effect, and in this general sense the foreknowledge is the logical and intellectual condition of the purpose. But this is not the real question. The real question is, Is the foreknowledge that such and such an event will be, the ground of the determination that it shall be? The Arminian says that God foresees that Peter will do a wrong act, and foreseeing that he will, God determines to allow it. In regard to this, (*a.*) God may undoubtedly foresee that a free agent in such and such circumstances will act in such and such a way, and may determine to place him so and so, and in doing that may virtually determine the action, and here God's determination is simply not to prevent the doing of what He foresees will be done. This is a supposable case, and here of course there would be no interference with the freedom of the individual. (*b.*) But the ground of the certainty of the event that Peter will do a wrong act, is not the divine foreknowledge, but the divine purpose, *i. e.*, the purpose of God to permit the act, to take it into the whole divine plan is the ground of the certain occurrence of the event. God foresaw that Peter would do so and so, but that is not all. That Peter would do so and so is also certain, for it is included in the divine plan. What is the ground of that certainty? Is it that God foresaw that Peter would thus act? No.

---

[1] Nominal Calvinists and Arminians protest against the doctrine of decrees, because they insist upon putting a foreign sense upon the word decree.

Because all which that would bring with it is, that if Peter is placed so and so, he will do so and so. But it is that God has determined that that event with all its circumstances shall be, and it has been adopted into his plan. (*c.*) Unless the event or act was adopted into the divine plan, there could not be a certainty of its occurrence. It would only be possible. Thus there is both foreknowledge and certainty in regard to an event, but the certainty of an event as future rests in the purpose and not in the foreknowledge. The purpose is the ground of the foreknowledge, and not the foreknowledge the ground of the purpose.[1] (*d.*) In respect to the Scripture testimony, see passages cited above. The passage Rom. viii. 29 is brought into the controversy. "For whom He foreknew, He also foreordained (or predestinated) to be conformed to the image of his Son." Even supposing that $\pi\rho o \acute{\epsilon} \gamma \nu \omega$ (foreknew) means solely to foreknow, the Arminian interpretation would not follow; because all that the passage can be said to assert is, Whom God did foreknow (*i. e.*, Christians) He did also predetermine should be conformed to the image of his Son. But the better interpretation is that of taking foreknew as equivalent to predetermine, and to understand the passage as declaring, Whom He predetermined to be Christians He also did appoint to be conformed to the image of his Son.

§ 4. *Proof of the Doctrine of Decrees.*

I.—There is a strong analogical argument from the doctrine of providence. There is the same God working in natural and moral government. There are designs and ends in nature: why not the same in God's providential dispensations? The designs in nature were planned beforehand: why not in the moral sphere? If in the less, why not in the greater? If in the natural, *a fortiori* in the moral, as being more important.

II.—There is also a rational argument on the general position that it is best that all events should be embraced in one plan of a wise and holy, omniscient and omnipresent sovereign.

III.—The various divine attributes imply and demand the doctrine. (1) The attribute of omniscience implies the divine decree.[2] Omniscience cannot know events unless they are objects of knowledge. If they are known as certain, the quality of certainty must have been imparted to them. Anything can be made certain only in one of two ways; either by an internal necessity or by a divine purpose. Free acts are not rendered certain by necessity, consequently if they are certain they can only have become so through the divine purpose. That they are certain is shown by prophecy and providence. If it be said that

---

[1] Edwards on the Will, Part ii. § 12.
[2] Fully argued in Edwards on the Will.

God foreknows them as certain through the laws and processes by which they are made certain, yet it must be acknowledged that He made these laws and established them in their goings, and fixed the conjunction under which they work at any particular point. (2) The immutability of God is a proof of the doctrine of decrees. It is sometimes said that the proper statement is, If men will do *so*, then God will do so, and that is the posture of things in God's government; He changes his conduct when man changes. To which the sufficient reply is, that He does this undoubtedly, changing his relation to men as they change, and that He always meant to do this, and this is the doctrine of the divine purposes; and if He did not always mean to, then something comes upon Him unawares in the course of his providence. It is also said that the decree of redemption was dependent on the fall, and before the fall this decree could not have been formed. In the order of time it is true that redemption is brought in in connection with the fall, and in the logical arrangement of the decrees it is true that the decree of redemption is subsequent to the notion of the fall, but that is simply an order of the divine purposes and not a dependence of those purposes upon anything that is to occur by and by. (3) God's holiness is a proof of his decrees. It must be the purpose of a Holy Being that holiness shall be triumphant, and this can only be by a plan to make it triumphant, and that is the doctrine of decrees, viz., a plan by which God makes everything to work so that holiness shall triumph. In the same way God's benevolence and all his moral attributes may be adduced in proof. Everything must be provided for, otherwise God would commit the fortunes of the universe to an uncertain system. (4) The Scriptural proof. (*a.*) Some direct and pregnant assertions: Is. xlvi. 10, 11; Eph. i. 9, i. 11. (*b.*) From prophecy. The whole of prophecy proves decrees. Christ was delivered by the determinate counsel and foreknowledge of God. It was before announced that He should come. (*c.*) The doctrine of decrees is involved in the doctrine of a special providence as derived from Scripture (see above). (*d.*) From the Scriptural representation that man's destiny for life and death is in the hands of God. "He giveth to all life and breath and all things." Job xiv. 5:—"his days are determined." (*c.*) As far as sin is concerned, the Scriptures represent that as embraced in the divine purpose: Acts ii. 23, iv. 27. (*f.*) The doctrine of election also involves the truth of the divine purpose.

§ 5. *Objections to the Doctrine of the Divine Decrees.*
I.—It is said that the doctrine involves fatalism.

Fatalism is an indefinite term, and the different senses which it has need to be carefully distinguished. (1) The chief doctrine of fatalism is that which makes everything that is produced in the world to be the result of matter and motion. In this sense the doctrine of decrees is not fatalistic. (2) Pantheistic fatalism makes everything to be the result of a blind necessity, and although the original source may be conceived as spirit rather than matter, yet it is a blind unconscious force, and not an intelligence which is at work.—These are the two strict systems of fatalism. (3) The Stoical system of fatalism of ancient times and the system of strict necessity of modern times assert that all things are bound together by a series and concatenation of causes, make God to be merely the necessary First Cause and deny human freedom. The human will is declared to be subject to the law of cause and effect, its freedom not being allowed as one of the causes in the continual connection. This system has been repudiated by Calvinistic divines in the statement that the divine purpose embraces freedom.—Hence, in no proper sense of fatalism can the doctrine of the divine purpose be said to come under it. For the doctrine of divine decrees simply asserts that all things are foreknown and predetermined by a wise, omniscient, and omnipotent being and conscious intelligence, and that in the plan everything is provided for just as it occurs in fact.

II.—Kindred to the objection just considered is that which asserts that the doctrine of divine decrees is a doctrine of necessity.

The word necessity is used in a variety of senses. (1) Metaphysical necessity, by which is meant the impossibility of the opposite. It is impossible that at the same time a thing should be and not be,—that there should be an event without a cause. Wherever there is that in the nature of the case which makes the contrary view impossible, there is metaphysical necessity. In this sense the doctrine of decrees is of course not the doctrine of necessity. (2) Logical necessity, by which is meant the logical impossibility of the opposite. Given the premises, and such a conclusion is the logical result, so that any other logical conclusion is an impossibility. (3) Physical necessity, which is what is ordinarily meant in the objection. This is a necessity which is based on the uniformity of natural laws, a necessity in which the terms conjoined are physical, in which with a certain physical cause a given physical effect must result. The assertion that physical necessity must rule if the doctrine of divine decrees is true, rests on the position that the laws of nature are uniform in their action, and that these imply in their relation to the will, coercion, that they simply force the will. The position implies that the result will come although the opposition of the will may be put forth.—In this sense the doctrine of divine decrees is not a doctrine of necessity, because it does not assert or imply that the decrees take effect in man in spite of his will, or that they coerce man by a physical force which he cannot resist, or that the terms conjoined are simply physical. (4) Moral necessity, by which is meant[1] the certainty that they will be and take place as they are and do. . It is equivalent to certainty. In this sense of moral necessity the opposition of the will is not conceivable. The concurrence of the will is embraced in the necessity. In other words, moral necessity is the conjunction of moral causes and effects, as physical necessity is the conjunction of physical causes and effects. The laws of cause and effect are at work in both moral and physical necessity, but in cases of moral necessity the causes are inclination, motives, desire, etc., which do not force the will. With this understanding of the term necessity, as a combination of moral antecedents and consequents, the doctrine of decrees may be said to involve it, in the sense of there being a certainty of action, certainty not under physical, but under

[1] As explained by both the older and younger Edwards.

moral, laws. The term necessity is an unfortunate one. Certainty is better.[1]

III.—It is sometimes objected to the doctrine of decrees that it is the result of a speculative tendency; that it is the introduction of a philosophical thesis into theology, and has not a religious source. As a matter of fact this is false. All the great advocates of decrees have been influenced not by a philosophical but by a religious view of things.[2]

IV.—Objection is made on the score of human freedom, with which the doctrine of decrees is said to be inconsistent.[3]—But if decrees are inconsistent with human freedom, it must be from something in the nature of the decree, or something in the nature of freedom, which is inconsistent with the decree. The general answer is that there is nothing in the nature of the decree which is inconsistent with human freedom, because what the decree secures is certainty; and there is nothing in the nature of human freedom which is inconsistent with the decree, because freedom is consistent with certainty: *i. e.*, the middle term here is certainty. The decree secures certainty, and freedom is consistent

---

[1] On the position of the younger Edwards some further remarks will be made under the head of Liberty and Necessity. We cannot agree with the limitation which he puts upon the action of the will, especially in seeming to imply that in the case of moral agency we have a given volition or choice, and that what is the cause of that choice is simply and solely the motive, and not the man. In order to save the doctrine of liberty in the causality of any choice, we must put in human freedom, the will as well as the motive. Any given choice or volition considered as a result, is the product of two factors, of the motive on the one hand and the choosing on the other, and the result of the choosing is the choice. The difficulty arises from not distinguishing between the choosing and the choice, between the man willing and the volition which is the result. If we make the whole cause to be in the motive and desires, and the whole effect to be in the volition, and do not put in an act of choice as also included, it becomes impossible to assert the freedom of the will except in mere words. See Pres. Day's Review of Edwards on the Will, which is one of the best expositions of the subject.

[2] See Julius Müller in *Studien und Kritiken*, 1856. He goes through the literature of the subject, and shows that the belief of both Calvin and Luther was connected with their views of justification, and with the general position that man is in such a moral state that he cannot rely upon himself for salvation.

[3] This is the chief argument of Bledsoe in his Theodicy, on the whole the ablest work in this country against the Calvinistic system. He is obliged to take refuge in an absolute self-determining power of the will, ultimately in the sense that that which determines the will to any particular course of action is nothing, that all that can be said is that the will determines itself.

with this. The chief point to be considered is the assertion that *certainty is consistent with freedom.* On this it is to be said:

1. There is nothing in the nature of the decree which is in itself inconsistent with human freedom. The decree says events are certain as they take place, and if they take place freely through choice this is included in the decree. Whether we are able to state fully how this is or not is a secondary question; it is enough to save the doctrine, that the sense in which we hold it is one which includes human freedom in the field covered by the decree.

2. Nor can it be alleged that in the execution of the decrees there are proceedings which are inconsistent with human freedom. The execution of the decrees, as they are actually carried out in regeneration, and so in all cases of sin, takes place without interference with free agency. There is nothing in man's consciousness which is at variance with his acts, his activity from beginning to end proceeds according to his free and responsible nature, and yet his acts are the results of the decree.

3. For each fact, the fact of the divine decree and the fact of human freedom, there is sufficient independent proof, and there we might rest. There is enough proof for decrees on rational and Scriptural grounds, and enough for freedom in consciousness; and if we state the two so that they are consistent with each other, we have done all that is required. They could be so stated as to involve a contradiction; *e. g.,* the decrees as bringing the human will under physical necessity, or freedom as consisting in the power of arbitrary choice or determination of the will, without or in spite of motives. But if we view the decree as that which secures certainty, and freedom as the power of choice under motives, which is consistent with certainty, then so far as the form of statement is concerned there is no objection to be made. And if we cannot find all the links, the points of connection between the certainty which is secured by the divine decree and the freedom which is attested by consciousness, we may simply say that we are under no obligation to do this.

4. Moreover, there are positive facts which show that certainty is not inconsistent with freedom. God's acts are doubt-

less all certain, and they are unquestionably all free. And if freedom and certainty can co-exist in God, the omnipotent, much more may they in man the creature. It is certain that all the divine acts will be holy; it is certain that they are perfectly free. So in respect to Christ, it was certain that He would continue to be holy, harmless, and undefiled, and yet all his acts were voluntary, free. Scripture asserts that the saints will persevere in holiness to the end, yet in the whole course of their perseverance they are conscious of freedom. In all cases of regeneration, we believe that the renewal is effected by the Spirit of God. All Arminians confess this. And yet, in all that we can trace as belonging to the regeneration, we know that we are free, we act "most freely" under that divine influence which secures the certain renewal of the soul. Further, all cases of sin in the sinner's conscious experience illustrate the fact that certainty and freedom are reconcilable with one another. It is certain that sinners will go on to destruction unless grace intervene, and yet in all their course they are free and are conscious of freedom. We ourselves can foresee with tolerable certainty how men will act under certain circumstances; and if we with our imperfect knowledge may have a degree of certainty in regard, why may not God have entire certainty in respect, to them?

CHAPTER VII.

THE END OF GOD IN CREATION.

References: Edwards, vol. ii., also in Brown's Theol. Tracts, vol. 2, "God made all things for the most perfect gratification of his infinitely benevolent mind"; Dr. Spring: "God the end of all things," Princeton Repos., 1832, Princeton Essays, vol. ii., an unsatisfactory discussion; Pres. Day, on Benevolence and Selfishness, Bib. Repos., 1843: "There are several ultimate ends, since an end is a good in itself;" Rev. W. C. Wisner, Bib. Repos., July, 1850: "The end is happiness in holiness,"—against Edwards;

Burton, Essays, pp. 286 seq.; Dwight, Sermon XXV., "The chief end of man"; Dr. Samuel Austin, Worcester, 1826: "that God could not be in any sense His own end—He could not gain anything by creation": so Wisner, for substance; Dr. Harris, in Man Primeval: ch. i., The great reason why God must be his own Last End, ch. ii., The divine all-sufficiency, last end of creation; Hopkins, System, i. 90–92; Bretschneider, Dogmatik, I.; Strauss, Glaubenslehre I., § 47; Ebrard, Dogmatik, I., § 273, pp. 355–8; Twesten, Glaubenslehre, II., pp. 88, 89; Kant, Kritik d. Urtheilskraft (Werke vii.) p. 311 seq.; Schweizer, Glaubenslehre, I., 137–143; The Glory of God the great End of Moral Action, John Martin, D.D., Brown's Theol. Tracts, vol. iii.; Quenstedt: The last end is the glory of God, glory of his goodness, power, and wisdom. "Finis intermedius est hominum salus. Omnia enim Deus fecit propter hominem, hominem autem propter se ipsum."

In the discussion of this subject the following points are assumed on the ground of what has gone before:

That God is the author of creation;

That He is a wise, holy, and benevolent Being;

That the creation is something distinct from himself;

That there is an end, an object, to be attained by it.

§ 1. *Meaning and Statement of the Question.*

The meaning of the phrase, "End of God in creation," is, the final object for which the world was made, the result which God intends to bring about, to consummate in the created universe, the last end, the chief end. Some have discriminated between the chief and the last end, but this can hardly be done, as they run into one another.[1] It is said that the chief end is holiness and the last end is happiness; but this is a forced distinction.

The inquiry is still further after the last end of *God* in creation, not the last end for the creatures simply, though that may be included in it, but the end of the divine manifestations.

It is an inquiry, too, about *one* such last end, to which all others may be referred and subordinated. If there be several

---

[1] See Bib. Sac., Oct. 1853, article on Edwards's Nature of Virtue, where ultimate is made to mean last in order of time.

ends, the problem is, to refer them to one which shall include, in their integrity, all the others.

The inquiry is also for the last end of God in *creation;* and by creation is meant, here, all of the universe which is not God, and which He brings into being for an end.

The last end of anything, Kant truly says, is that end or object which does not need anything beyond it as the condition of its existence. Distinctions have been made as to ends, and differences in theories arise partly from neglect of these distinctions. (*a.*) Subordinate and ultimate ends: subordinate, one that is sought for with reference to an ultimate end.[1] (*b.*) Inferior and chief. These terms relate to a comparison of different ends —whether subordinate or ultimate—as to their respective value and worth. (*c.*) Objective and subjective, in respect to creation. Subjective means, that which moved the mind of the author, his pleasure in the act; objective, the end to be realized in creation, the object in view, *that in which* the pleasure is found. This distinction brings up one of the main differences in the theories. With the distinction as here made, nobody would deny that God's subjective end in creation is his pleasure, his happiness in it. "For thy pleasure they are and were created." But that is not what God intended to realize; our inquiry is not for this subjective end in itself—*that we know;*—but it is for that objective end in view of which this divine joy arises.[2] (*d.*) Original and consequential. Edwards (ii. 197) distinguishes between ultimate[3] ends as original and independent—and consequential or dependent. *E. g.*, God loves to do justice to men as a good in itself: but this could not be an original end with Him in creation, for it is consequential or dependent on their existence. So God loves to make his

---

[1] In this sense ultimate ends may be as various as our specific duties and aims, natural or moral.

[2] Objective and subjective ends are also found in the creation itself; subjective meaning man's happiness, and the delight and happiness of all sentient beings, and objective meaning that manifestation of the divine operations which is to moral beings the source of their highest blessedness. By this usage the terms are much intermingled and confused.

[3] In his use of "ultimate" Edwards is sometimes perplexing. He ought always to have used *supreme* or *last* end.

creatures happy; this is an *end*, yet consequential and dependent upon their existence.

The purpose of the inquiry. In asking, What is the end of God in creation, we mean to inquire for his original, ultimate, objective end in all his works of creation. We mean by *original*, that which needs nothing besides as the condition of its being, which is not to be conceived as derived from a higher end; by *ultimate*, not simply that which is last in time but also that which is supreme in value; by *objective*, that which is extant in the creation itself, and as such is found and rejoiced in by God.

§ 2. *Conditions of the Solution of the Problem—if possible.*

1. The end must be one, and as such, sufficiently general to include in one form of statement a great variety of inferior, subordinate ends. Nobody doubts that there is such a variety, and the question is as to the reduction of all these under one. The problem is virtually given up as insoluble, when several original ultimate ends are stated.

2. These subordinate or inferior ends must be so included in the one that all shall be seen to be parts of that one end, that they all can be referred to it fairly, as expressive thereof. If they cannot be, that one cannot be the end, because there is something which it does not include. This is one of the strictest tests of any theory.[1] God and man must be both concerned in this end.

3. Hence, this end must be one which includes in itself all that is in creation, according to the measure and degree of each part: it must be found and exemplified, more or less, in the whole of creation, natural, moral, and spiritual. The sum of all the works and ways of God is in the natural world with its moral ordering, in providence and in the kingdom of God's grace—what is his end in *all* these, is the question: it is necessary to comprise them all under some object to which they all refer.

4. This end, while it is to be fully realized only at the end or consummation of all things, yet must also be contained, in its

---

[1] In our view one of the strongest objections to any form of the happiness theory is made by the application of this test.

proper measure and degree, in creation as it is, and in the whole past history of creation.[1] It must not be inconsistent with what already is, but be illustrated by it: it must be an end which is future in the sense of complete realization, but present in the sense of partial realization, at each point in the historic course. And hence, it may be possible for us to find the end.

§ 3. *Statement of the Theories.*

Here as elsewhere there are two antagonistic views sharply in opposition, and the question is as to their respective rights. The fundamental contrast is in the statements: the ultimate, objective end is God himself, God makes himself the end; or that end is man, the happiness of the creature.[2] The different theories are formed either by taking one of these to the exclusion of the other, or by attempting to reconcile them.

1. The end is the happiness of man. In its best form of statement, this theory says that God could not make himself the end of creation, because He is sufficient unto himself, and could need nothing. And if He could not make himself the end, then that can be found only in the creature, and ultimately in the happiness of the creature—taking happiness very comprehensively.

2. The end is God himself. The divine glory is the ultimate end: in man there is no ultimate end, only means to the end. Divine glory is used in different senses: some making it equivalent to God himself, others making it to be the objective manifestation of God, while the pleasure of God in this is the subjective ground for the creation.

3. An attempt at reconciling the two: that the good of man is an ultimate and yet intermediate end, while the glory of God is the ultimate objective end.

4. Another attempt at reconciliation: that the end is the glory of God as seen in the highest good of the creature, and that this last is the objective end.

---

[1] Wisner, p. 434, says the end must be "future."

[2] These respectively form theology and ethics: they constitute two great tendencies, the one making God to be all in all, the other making the good of creatures to be the ultimate end. The problem is, their reconciliation.

5. That neither alone is the end, but that the two are identical: the highest good is the divine glory, the divine glory is the highest good. The mediation is through love.[1] Some seem to put the end in happiness in two forms: God's delight in doing good, and the happiness of the creature.

6. The ends are various, as much so as the whole manifestation of the divine attributes in the divine works. This is to say that no solution is possible; there is no last end.

§ 4. *The Scriptural Argument.*

This is elaborated by President Edwards in his " End of God in Creation." He has given it fully: we shall give only a summary. In regard to this Scriptural argument one thing is certain: *either* the ends are various or the divine glory is the end. There is no passage of Scripture which asserts that happiness is the end: there are numerous passages to show that the divine glory is such.

1. A class of passages, which decide only that God in some way—God and not the creature—as He is the source, is also the end of all: Rev. iv. 11; Rom. xi. 36; Heb. ii. 10; Col. i. 16; Prov. xvi. 4. These passages do not say *what* the end is, but do go to prove that that end is in God.

2. Passages which more specifically declare that the divine glory is the end. Scripture sets forth in a variety of ways that this is the end of external nature. It is to be remembered that the glory of God is sometimes designated by the term *name*, which is equivalent to nature or essence: Ps. viii. 1; Isa xliii. 7; lx. 9.

3. Passages which show that the end of the *creature* is in glorifying God. These, as against the so-called happiness theories, are decisive, for if the end of the creature were the creature, then he must be exhorted to seek his own good as ultimate; but if he is exhorted to seek something beyond himself, then the good of the creature himself cannot be the end: 1 Cor. x. 31; vi. 20; John xv. 8. Also such passages as Ps. cxxxvi. 1-9; cxxxviii. 5.

4. Those passages which set forth in the same strain that

---

[1] So Twesten, Vol. ii. p. 89: and so perhaps the younger Edwards.

the holy obedience of the creature is not the ultimate end, that even this redounds to the divine glory. If all that God had in view was to insure the holiness of the creation, then Scripture would naturally stop short with that, but such holiness is said to reach beyond, and to redound to the glory of God. Isa. lxi. 3, where the glorifying of God is not made the means of the holiness of his people, but the converse is stated; Eph. i. 5, where we have the subjective end in the creature or the creature's subjective end, "the being adopted as children," the subjective divine end, "the good pleasure of his will," and the objective divine end, "the praise of the glory of his grace." 2 Thess. i. 10; Phil. i. 10, 11; 2 Cor. i. 20, "unto the glory of God *by* [or through] *us*."

5. Passages which show the end of Christ's work to be the glory of God. John xii. 28; xvii. 4; Phil. ii. 6–11.

The result of the Scriptural teaching then is, that this world is a revelation of the divine glory, and that God's being glorified by it is its chief end.[1]

§ 5. *The supreme End of Creation is the Declarative Glory of God.*

By the declarative glory of God is meant, the manifestation of the internal divine glory. The word glory is used in the Scriptures, in reference to God, in several distinct senses: (*a.*) For the divine internal perfections, the inherent excellency of God's nature and attributes; (*b.*) In the sense of the manifestation of this inherent excellency, of the internal made external or "extant"; (*c.*) For the rendering of praise to God on both accounts, for his internal and external glory; as when we give

---

[1] Edwards, ii. 242, says, "*an* ultimate end of God is the communication of good to his creatures as something not merely subordinately agreeable," yet this is "not what he delights in simply and ultimately." John xvii. 19; Isa. liii. 11; and in short, all the Scriptures which set forth God's goodness, mercy, grace, that He desireth not the death of any, rejoices in his people, delights in doing good, etc. There is no question that the communication of good to creatures, is *an* ultimate end, in the sense of being *a* good in itself.

Such passages as the following are sometimes brought to support the position that the highest good of creatures is *the* ultimate end. Ps. civ. viii. 5; cxix. 64; Acts xiv. 17; xvii. 24. These prove simply the reality of God's goodness.

glory to God. [Another sometimes given as (*d.*), The glory which God has in his creatures, comes properly under (*b.*).] The second is the sense intended in the proposition here maintained: the first is the ground and the third is the result of the second. The second is the true end. (Christ is also called the glory of God, and the Shechinah is perhaps a form or radiance symbolical of all the declarative glory.)

I.—To explain the proposition negatively:

1. It does not mean that this glory is separable, *in re*, from other ends subordinate to this and included in it. It is seen in those other ends, in the good and the happiness of the creature.

2. Nor does the proposition mean that the receiving glory from others is the end. The receiving of glory is an end, included in the supreme end, but is not itself the supreme. God did not create *in order* to receive glory, but to make his glory extant and manifest.

3. Nor is it meant that God had ultimate respect to himself (subjectively) in such manifestation of himself, that his joy in the manifestation was the final cause thereof. This is the subjective happiness scheme as applied to God. He undoubtedly does rejoice in his work, but we cannot say that He did it in order to rejoice in it. Some have taken this view,[1] but this representation of the matter is the chief reason why it is argued that the making the divine glory the chief end of creation is a selfish proceeding.[2] We prefer the statement that the joy of God in his work was the ultimate subjective end in his mind, but was not the objective motive for the creation itself.

4. Nor does the proposition mean that in creation God had not *a* true and *an* ultimate regard to the highest good of his creatures. He must, as a God of love, as a God who delights in what is best, have had such a regard. The creature is not to be sacrificed, the good of the creature is to be estimated at its proper value, but it must also be maintained that the supreme

---

[1] So Dr. Spring. See President Day on the connection between this and the self-love theory of morals.

[2] Edwards, ch. i. § 3, Works, ii. 207-11, explains "making himself the end" as meaning the communication to others of himself, the impulse of and pleasure in self-communication: " a disposition to diffuse and communicate himself."

end is as much larger than the creature, as God is larger. God the infinite Being cannot have ultimate respect to finite beings and their happiness. There is no inconsistency between the two views, that in creation God had respect to his own glory as ultimate, and that He regards also as a real good, and desires for its own sake, the highest welfare of his creatures.[1]

II.—Meaning of the proposition stated affirmatively.

The objective end of God in the whole created universe, *i. e.*, the end which He had as objective to himself, was to manifest, in the most complete way, the sum of the divine perfections or the internal divine glory, in such a way as to ensure as a subordinate end the highest good of his creatures, by their participation in this manifestation. (This is shown to be a subordinate end by the fact that the highest good of the creature is found in glorifying God.) Creation is the mirror of Deity, and *as such* it is the objective end of God. We mean of course by creation, all that is not God. It is the whole system that is the objective end of God. The end is not in individuals or their state, but in these, as parts of the whole plan, in relation and subordination thereto. The whole system, as reflecting God, is the end.

1. In what does the internal divine glory consist, which we here declare to be set forth in creation? It is the radiant sum of all the divine perfections. These may be viewed as consisting of four chief excellences: (*a.*) The infinitude of God's Being, including his power, his resources; (*b.*) The perfection of his wisdom; (*c.*) His absolute holiness; (*d.*) His perfect love.

2. The declarative glory consists in setting forth these perfections, in manifesting them, making them to be extant, which is the objective end of the Creation. And this may be said to be done:

(*a.*) As regards the infinitude of the divine being, comprising the immensity and eternity of God, in the existence of in-

---

[1] Dwight, Sermon XXV., holds that it is God's end to glorify himself: "the manifestation of his inherent glory" is what is intended by the glorifying of God. "To show his own character, to unfold his power, knowledge, and goodness to beings capable of understanding them, was the supreme object He had in view." But Dr. Dwight makes all to culminate in benevolence.

finite space and unending time, which are the conditions of all finite existence. These mirror forth the divine immensity and eternity.[1] The power of God is also mirrored in the energies which act through the creation.

(*b.*) The perfect wisdom of God is set forth in the whole order of creation, and in the plan which is there found, running through all the orders of existence and culminating in man and in human history, where God's divinest purpose is seen in the imparting the knowledge of himself to his creatures.

(*c.*) God's absolute holiness is revealed in the giving of his law, and making rational creatures capable of knowing it as holy, and further in making all that is transacted in history to show the supremacy and triumph of his holiness. The holiness of God is the consent of his will and his wisdom, constituting his supreme moral excellence. This holiness is his essential goodness—love in the broadest sense.

(*d.*) God's perfect love—love in the narrower sense as the attribute which prompts Him to communicate to others—is poured forth and exemplified, in imparting good to all his creatures, and so that He himself is the supreme object in which that good is found, as He is the real source of it, the highest good and joy of creatures being found in glorifying Him. This is seen most fully in his gracious purpose of redemption.

These are the several particulars into which the divine glory both as internal and external may be distributed. The enumeration is not exhaustive, but it is sufficient for our purpose.

The sense in which God makes himself his end[2] is, then,

---

[1] [Of course the question is here raised whether space and time belong to the creation. The following hints of the author's view of this are gathered from his papers:—Certainly, absolute immensity and eternity do not belong to the creation, but time as successive and finite, and as indefinite in duration, and space as limited and indefinite in extent, *do*.—It is a false view that God exists in all space and time; his eternity and immensity precisely are—his *not* existing in space and time.—Space and time are not attributes of the infinite, they are not substances or entities, they are not relations; but if they were any of these it would hold true that they cannot belong to the uncreated or the unconstituted, for then that which is finite—in its parts, though immeasurable as a whole—would be uncreated. Conceive them as merely subjective phenomena, and even then they come into being as such phenomena, with finite existences.]

[2] Undoubtedly there is a sense in which God (as no creature can) makes himself his end.

simply this: that He delights most in that system which best sets forth his own perfection.[1]

§ 6. *Arguments in Favor of this Position.*
1. It is most accordant with the Scriptures. See above.
2. It is the highest conceivable end for God himself. In respect to his creation, nothing more comprehensive or complete can be conceived of than this: that it should mirror forth the divine perfections, so far as this can be done by what is limited and finite. This is the idea of the world, the divine plan of things. All things here are from God and for God. The splendor of his glory irradiates them, is seen through them.[2] If there is any shining, it is the glory of Deity.[3] And this which is a positive result is a higher result than doing good to sentient creatures, than benevolent activity: for that is only a part of God's ways; it is an integral part, an ultimate end, but the highest result must be the highest end.

It is sometimes said, in the way of objection, that this seems to argue a display of the divine perfections for the sake of display. The answer is plain: It is not display, in any evil interpretation, for the sake of the glory accruing, or for any outward sake; it is such a display as everything that has fulness of life is prompted to by its very fulness. It is such a display as is that of the acorn in becoming an oak. It is such a manifestation as a poet makes of himself, when he pours out the fulness of his soul in an epic or drama. The end for which the true genius makes the epic or the sys-

---

[1] In this system we find several *ultimate* ends in the sense of results good in themselves. The divine wisdom, in the plan and order of creation; the divine holiness, in the moral constitution and ordering; the divine love, in providence; the divine grace, where holiness and love are concurrent, in the work of redemption; and happiness occurring in and by each and all of these. The grand objective end is God's union with man through Christ in a divine kingdom. Here the glory of wisdom, holiness, and love all concur. Here the material (in the new heavens and earth), the moral, the spiritual or gracious, all find their unity of ends.

[2] Hegel says that the great end of his primitive substance is, to become objective to itself, and he declares this the ultimate statement in philosophy; so that here Pantheism is compelled to do a sort of homage to old Orthodoxy.

[3] The positive philosophy has given us as the alternative: "The heavens declare no glory save that of Kepler and Newton."

tem of philosophy is, to satisfy the longings of his being for a full expression of itself. So God sets forth himself in his works; in the universal epic of all nature, in the grand drama of history, in the whole system of things which is ensouled by himself; his archetypal ideas are expressed and symbolized in all nature and history. And what higher divine end can we conceive?

3. A third argument is that the end here assigned is alone sufficiently comprehensive to be the true end of all God's ways in creation.[1] It has the advantage of comprising in subordination other ultimate ends, subsuming them under this one. For example, the great end of the material creation is included here. "The heavens declare the glory of God." It is very difficult to bring what we find in nature under the idea of happiness as the chief end. For what end were the hosts of heaven made? To fill the beholders with sublimity, it may be said: but this gives us use for a small part only of the heavens, and gives us an inadequate end even then. How late were the discoveries in astronomy! How impossible to bring under the idea of happiness many of the discoveries in science! We find order, wisdom, manifestation of mind. Doing good to sentient and intelligent creatures can be included under the one supreme end of manifesting the divine perfections, for in all his works of goodness the glory of the divine love is manifested. So also the maintenance of holiness in the universe is a revelation of God's essential holiness, and the blessedness which He gives in redemption is a joy in himself, in the sum of his own divine perfections.

It is objected that the end here stated is too general; but what we are seeking is, a sufficiently comprehensive view to include the whole range of the divine manifestations. If the end were so indefinite as not to allow of being distributed, as not to include fairly all the other ends as subordinate to itself, the objection would be valid. But its value is, that it is a general statement under which all the others may be brought; and therefore we remark, as our next argument,

[1] This alone agrees with the definition of "end" given by Kant.

4. It is also an end which, while fully realized only at the consummation of all things, is found going on and illustrated in all that has been and is. This glory of God, consisting in making himself extant to his creatures, began with creation, when the morning stars sang together; it is illustrated in all the tribes and orders of creation; it is seen in Paradise with its primeval goodness; it looks out upon us through the whole course of human history; it descended incarnate in the person of our Lord; through the centuries since his coming it has been growing more and more radiant; and the full carrying out of the divine idea in the future history of the earth will bring about its consummation, even to the ushering in of that day when Christ shall give up the dominion to the Father, that God may be all in all.

And thus are all the conditions which we proposed of a right solution of the problem met in this most comprehensive statement of the end of God in creation. To this we might add

5. That no other view does meet these conditions; but as there is confessedly only one other view, we defer consideration of that until we come to speak of the Greatest Happiness scheme.

§ 7. *Consideration of Objections.*

1. It is said that a selfish scheme of the universe is presented when the end of creation is made to be the glory of God.[1] Here we might concede that to say simply and without qualification that God made everything for himself, for his glory, is to use language which is liable to be misunderstood. Such forms of expression may not convey the real truth which we hold. In reply to the objection, we say,

(*a.*) Even if God "made himself" the end, He could not be selfish in this. Even if it were strictly true that God made all things for himself, yet his love to himself, as Edwards remarks, cannot be a selfish love, a preference of the individual to the universal, of the narrow to the general; for in loving himself He "in effect" loves all, and in acting for himself He in effect

---

[1] Pres. Day even seems to argue that this view gives support to the self-love theory of morals. But read Edwards, ii. 215, etc.

acts for the universe; for in displaying himself, what does He do but simply bring the universe and all the good and glory and happiness of it into being? *

But (b.) God does *not* make himself the end as alleged. He made the universe, not in order to gratify himself as the great end, although He does delight therein, but to manifest himself, for the sake of his declarative glory. That is the objective reason; the subjective delight therein is not the rational ground, the final cause and end of the creation. And this consideration does away with, or rather puts in its true light, the main objection.

2. It is also objected that this scheme leads to the inference that God created some men in order to damn them, in order that, by their perdition, the awfulness of the divine justice might be glorified. Such a representation may have been favored by the incautious language of some writers. But the fact is, that the punishment of the individual sinner or of all sinners is not truly and properly to be called an ultimate end, that is, a good in itself. The punishment when inflicted does doubtless illustrate the terrible splendor of the divine holiness, but the end of the divine holiness even is not punishment. That the punishment of the transgressor is not an ultimate end is proved by the fact of an atonement, by pardon on the ground of an atonement. If it were an ultimate end, a good in itself, there could not be transfer; Christ could not suffer in the place of the transgressor. God did not create any man in order to punish him.[1]

3. It is asked, which is better, a system in which God's glory is the means of the creature's good, or one in which the creature's good is the means of God's glory? and it is argued that that is better in which God's whole aim is to do good to his creatures, rather than a system in which the creature is—relatively—sac-

---

[1] [No more, says the author, than He made the race-horse, which was driven one hundred miles in eight hours and died at the end, for such inhuman sport of man. If there is perversion of his work and this is visited with his holy displeasure, this does not prove that He did his work in order that it might be perverted. The same argument would seem to apply in reference to Darwin's question, whether divine intelligence made the bull-dog *in order that* brutal men might delight in its ferocity.]

rificed to the divine glory. This comes to be more fully considered elsewhere; here we only say, that that is the best system which puts the two, man and God, in their just relations to each other. And a system which, while it allows that God does all good to his creatures according to the promptings of his infinite love and the dictates of his infinite wisdom, yet asserts that He does also more than this, is a higher and better system than one which restricts the whole agency of God to a single form of activity. If we distinguish between the objective end of the system and its subjective end in relation to creatures,[1] we have ample grounds of comparison and judgment. The objective end of creation is the making extant of the divine perfections; the subjective end of that same system is the promotion of the highest good—not happiness merely—of creatures. And this subjective end of the system is found in creatures becoming participants of, finding their highest good—and therewith their highest happiness—in, the objective end of the system: in the fact that man's chief end is to glorify God; and thus these two ends are in the last result one end.[2]

§ 8. *The Happiness Theory.*

The other system, that which puts the end of God in creation in the happiness of the creature, or in the greatest happiness of the whole system, is comparatively imperfect and narrow in several points. Full discussion of it would come up later, under the head of The Nature of True Virtue; here we only consider:

1. There cannot be subordinated to this end all that is

---

[1] ["Subjective" here has a different meaning from what it has in the distinction made between God's objective and "subjective" end in creation. It means now, the sense which intelligent creatures have of the excellency of God's objective end in creation.]

[2] Compare Edwards, ii. 219. "God and the creature in this affair of the emanation [it must be remembered that in Edwards's time Pantheists had not appropriated this word as they have now; otherwise he doubtless would not have used it] of the divine fulness are not properly set in opposition, or made opposite parts of a disjunction. Nor ought God's glory and the creature's good to be spoken of as if they were properly and entirely distinct, as they are in the objection." "God in seeking his glory, therein seeks the good of his creatures. Because the emanation of his glory (which He seeks and delights in as He delights in himself, his own eternal glory) implies the communicated happiness and excellency of his creatures." " God *is* their good."

found in the creation. All that is, cannot be explained in relation to happiness, still less to human happiness. The vastness and sublimity of the creation are degraded when they are considered simply in regard to the emotions they may excite. Their adequate end is found in their exemplifying the wisdom of God, thus manifesting his glory; while the happiness which they confer is subordinate and resulting.

2. This scheme does not account for the creation, but only for God's conduct to a creation already in being. Creatures existing, God may be said to delight in doing them good; but this does not answer the question, Why did God create them? He created them for a variety of purposes, one of which was that He might do good to them, but this was not the whole. The doing good to them supposes them *to be*, and therefore it could not be the ground of their being brought into existence.[1]

3. This theory begs the question (at least for us at present) upon the most important ethical question, viz., whether happiness be the highest good. If the affirmative of that question cannot be held, the theory cannot be maintained.

4. When framed to accord with the "subjective happiness" view of the nature of virtue, the theory leads to the inference: If God's highest end be the creature's happiness, then the creature should seek his own happiness in all that he does, as the supreme end; thus giving a most vicious ethical theory.

5. When happiness is taken in a larger sense, the term becomes indefinite and the theory that happiness is the end of the creation becomes vague. If the word happiness be made to take in all happiness, including the divine blessedness, and to include a peculiar kind of happiness, that arising from holiness, *i. e.*, to take in all that is good in the system, all that can be appreciated and be the ground of satisfaction to God and to finite intelligences, then of course we simply come out upon the statement that the subjective end of creation is commensurate with its objective end. God created the universe to manifest his own perfections, and in the manifestation He has his own subjective joy and intends that his creatures shall have theirs. But that which *is* highest and

[1] Compare Edwards, ii. 206.

best in the system is distinct from the appreciation and love of what is highest and best, which is the source of the truest happiness. If the highest happiness is made synonymous with the highest good of the whole system, we have one of two things: either a restatement of the subjective happiness view or a vague use of language. If the meaning be, that the end of the whole system is the highest happiness of individual beings, we come back to the inference that the individual should seek his own happiness as his highest end; if it be said that what is meant by the highest happiness is, that which constitutes the goodness of the system taken as a whole, this leaves the question open, what does constitute such goodness of the whole system: its reflection of the divine glory or its power of producing happiness? If the meaning be, that the great end of the system is the sum of good which is in it, all of which is appreciable and capable of producing happiness either in God or in man or in both, then there is no objection to the view, but it would seem best to keep to the common use of terms, and not confound the happiness with the good from which it arises.

In fact, the happiness scheme *if consistently carried out*, would lead to the position that the glory of God in the whole system is the great end in creation. All the happiness of all the good, taking it in its largest sense, is derived from God, is only a participation on their part of what God gives. What God reveals in the system is the objective ground or source of the happiness: the creature's happiness is found in having part in that; and if we could suppose the creature's happiness so great as to be co-extensive with this, still it would be dependent upon this manifestation or revelation of God, and thus the happiness will be merely the accruing good.

§ 9. *The Connection between the View of the End of God in Creation and the Theory of the Nature of Virtue.*

1. That which is the great end of God's work in creation must be the *summum bonum* to his creatures also; for their highest good can only be found in subjection to or harmony with the great end for which all is made.

2. This end, as we have seen, is the whole system of things, considered as declarative of God's inherent perfections, terminating in redemption and the union of himself with man; all of which declare his glory.

3. Man's chief end must then be found in his harmony with this system; in glorifying God and enjoying Him forever.

4. The subjective condition of man's doing this is, his love to the whole system of things as declarative of God, or to God as declared in the whole system.

5. Ultimately then, in the last analysis, love to God as being 'in effect" all being, is the root and ground of all true virtue.

§ 10. *Some historical Statements as to Theories of God's End in Creation.*

Justin Martyr: πρὸς ἔνδειξιν τῆς θείας αὐτοῦ δυνάμεως.

Origen, de Princ. ii. 9, 6: "[Deus] nullam habuit aliam creandi causam, nisi propter se ipsum, id est, bonitatem suam."

Greg. Naz. Orat. xxxviii.: "God's goodness was not content with the purely immanent activity of self-contemplation, but would pour itself out and multiply itself externally."

Aquinas, Summa I. Q. 44, iv.: "Communicare suam perfectionem, quæ est ejus bonitas."

Bonaventura: "The honor of God, *i. e.*, to reveal and impart his glory, and thus at the same time to promote the highest good of creatures."

The Calvinistic theologians who have been led by the very nature of their system to dwell much on this subject, have adopted the general position of Augustine; the glory of God is the end of creation.

Zwingle, iv. 81: ".... ita bona sunt, ut ab illo bono sunt, ut in illo bono sunt et ut ad illius boni gloriam sunt."

Calvin, Inst. I. v. 5: "Mundus in spectaculum gloriæ Dei conditus est."

A common representation is, that the glory of God consists in the manifestation of his love in salvation, and of his justice in condemnation, and that these together make up the glory of the divine holiness, which is to be taken as the ultimate end. The supralapsarian theology emphasized the statement, that God decreed the creation of a reprobate portion of mankind in order that He might show forth the glory of his justice.

The general Calvinistic view is: The objective end is the divine glory; the subjective, the good of creatures. All that is, is from God and for God—a self-revelation or manifestation of God. "The highest end is the manifestation of God—finis objectivus, ultimus, est gloria Dei: the subordinate end"—*our* chief end—"is the glorifying of God in our salvation—finis subjectivus, subordinatus, est salus nostra" (Cf. Schweizer, I. 135).

Stapfer, I. 122: "Finis existentiæ hujus mundi est manifestatio gloriæ divinæ."

Wendelin, 3: "Finis—est glorificatio Dei et nostra salus; hic finis proximus, ille finis summus."

The school of Kant urges that the harmony of virtue and happiness is the highest good, and so the chief end of all things. (But this confines the end to the sphere of the rational and moral.)

Bretschneider, I. 670–1 (for substance): "The last ground of creation, which is also its last end, cannot be objective, but must be subjective, and is to be sought in God himself. (God's independence obliges us to seek the ground of all his purposes in himself.) But we do not fully know what it is. . . . . So much we know: it must be an expression of the divine ideas, a revelation of God, a mirror and image of his perfection. Its immensity corresponds with omnipotence; its order to the divine wisdom; its well-being to God's goodness; to his holiness and justice, rational [moral] beings. The revelation of his majesty to rational beings is a subordinate end; the revelation of his perfection, for its own sake, must be the highest end."

Ebrard, Dogm. I. 358: "The last end for which the world was made must be the glorifying of the moral attributes of God, *i. e.*, of God as holy, blessed, and wise. And since it is personal beings (men and angels) in whom these moral attributes are glorified —and that in the way of their blessedness—it follows that the glorifying of the ethico-Trinitarian nature of God in the blessing of finite subjects, is the last end to which the providence of God is directed."

Edwards. The following seems to be, for substance, the view of Pres. Edwards, especially as unfolded in his last section: Other ultimate ends (*i. e.*, results good in themselves) are instances, exemplifications, all of them of the one end, *i. e.*, the manifestation of the internal divine glory—are different modes and degrees of this manifestation; not means to that end, strictly, so that they are sacrificed to it—but higher and lower modes of realizing it. And the highest mode, within the creation, in respect to the creatures, is, the communication of the divine love, in the form of grace, reuniting man with God. This is the highest, brightest manifestation of the divine love, in respect to the creatures. But this is still, in respect to God's end or total plan, a form or mode of the divine declarative glory.—Some of President Edwards's statements, as when he argues, ii. 207–11, that God makes himself the end, might at first sight seem inconsistent with this, but a careful study of that in connection with the last section shows, that he could not have meant it in any sense which implied a supreme regard to himself *as self;* though on this point he is not always entirely consistent.

The younger Edwards thus represents his father's views (Cf. Remarks on Improvements, I. 481): "The declarative glory of God *is* the creation, taken not distributively but collectively, as a system raised to a high degree of happiness. The creation thus raised and preserved is the declarative glory of God. In other words it is the exhibition of his essential glory." This, though in form a reconciliation of the two theories as to God's end in creation, is in fact a sacrificing of the divine glory as an independent ultimate end; the glory is put *in* the happiness. It is *not* his father's theory, which expressly subordinates the happiness to the glory.

CHAPTER VIII.

THE THEODICY. THE QUESTION OF THE BEST SYSTEM.

The word Theodicy is used in the sense of Vindication of God in the work of creation, especially as to the existence of sin.

The Best System means, not the best conceivable in the abstract, but the best in relation to its materials and objects; that which is best on the whole, in a world of matter, for a race, destined to have a history,—a race of personal, free, and moral beings, capable of sin or holiness, and made for fellowship with God.

The sum of what is intimated in the Scriptures on this subject is that God has special regard to redemption in the permission of sin, and so has regard to the special manifestation of his own attributes: Rom. xi. 32, 33; Acts xvii. 30, 31; Eph. iv. 13; 2 Cor. iii. 18; 1 John iii. 2; especially the argument of Paul, Rom. v. 12-21.

The problem is, to reconcile the existence of sin with the divine character, or, in other words, to reconcile the existence of a system in which sin is, with the position that it is from the hand of an omnipotent, wise and holy author. The fact of sin is conceded. Those who believe that God is holy, wise, and omnipotent, of course believe that the reconciliation may be made even though they cannot effect it. The existence of sin being conceded, and the belief in a holy, wise, and omnipotent God being taken for granted, the different theories are the attempts to account for sin. We come here upon the old dilemma which was put even in pagan times:[1] God either wishes to take away

---

[1] The argument of Epicurus as given by Lactantius, "De Ira Dei," xiii.: "Deus aut vult tollere mala et non potest; aut potest et non vult; aut neque vult neque potest. Si vult et non potest, imbecillis est; quod in Deum non cadit. Si potest et non vult, invidus; quod æque alienum a Deo. Si neque vult neque potest, et invidus et imbecillis est; ideo, neque Deus. Si et vult et potest, quod solum Deo convenit, unde sunt mala? aut cur illa non tollit?"

The dilemma is here carried further than is necessary. It is sufficient to say: either will and cannot, so denying omnipotence, or can and will not, denying benevolence.

evil and cannot, or He can and will not. In the one case He lacks omnipotence, in the other benevolence. There are two main theories in the Theodicy corresponding to the parts of the dilemma: It is said on the one side, It is not against omnipotence to allow sin, *because sin could not be prevented in a moral system;* on the other side it is said, It is not against benevolence to admit sin, *because sin is the necessary means of the greatest good.*

§ 1. *Is Sin the necessary Means of the greatest Good?*

Is it a solution of the problem of moral evil to affirm this? Does that reconcile the existence of sin with the divine character, so that God is still seen to be benevolent, because sin is the necessary means of the greatest good?

There are two chief subdivisions of this theory: I. The philosophical or metaphysical; II. The theological or orthodox.

I.—The philosophical form of the theory. This has been stated and considered under Part I., Book i., § 7, p. 40.

II.—The theological form of the theory. This was found chiefly among the New England divines of the strictest efficiency school, Hopkins, West, etc. It affirms that sin is an inherent evil, yet is the necessary means of the greatest good; in the sense, not that sin is a good or the direct means of good, but that the highest good, such as the complete manifestation of the divine perfections, cannot be reached except by overruling sin.

Is it a solution of the problem to say, that sin is a necessary means of the greatest good? To say the least, the phraseology is objectionable. The only real scheme of this sort is the pantheistic, that sin, from the nature of the finite, is a necessary stage in progress.

1. The theory is liable to the objection that it seems to impose a necessity on God to produce sin, in a moral system; since, from the nature of things, He could not produce the best system without sin. Consequently there is a necessity for the existence of sin, even to God. So that thus the scheme is carried over into the scheme of necessity.

2. If the sense of "the greatest good" be happiness, then it is difficult to see how sin, which is and produces wretched-

ness, is necessary to the highest happiness; for just so far as sin exists, it is so much taken from the sum of happiness.

3. If, on the other hand, we define the greatest good as holiness, the same difficulty remains. Sin is the opposite of holiness, and if so, how can it be the necessary means of holiness? Just so far as it exists, there is a deficiency of holiness in the universe. We might as well say, Darkness is the necessary means of light, whereas just so far as there is darkness, there is a want of light.

4. If the greatest good be defined as the declarative glory of the divine perfections, then the theory is, that sin is necessary to the fullest illustration of these. To this there are objections:

(*a.*) It is difficult to see why, taking the divine attributes separately, the divine wisdom, love, holiness, may not have been perfectly manifested without sin. Why could we not have had, *e. g.*, a perfect manifestation of the divine wisdom, without sin?

(*b.*) In respect to the Godhead itself, the Trinity and the Incarnation of God, why might there not have been a manifestation of God in his triune being or an incarnation, without sin? As a matter of fact, the Incarnation was connected with sin, but we do not see that it was necessarily so.

(*c.*) The only difference in the manifestation of divine attributes which sin has occasioned, that can be conceived or stated, is in respect to two points: Without sin the divine benevolence in redemption could not have been manifested, nor could the divine holiness in punishing. Then this is the theory: Sin is the necessary means of the greatest good, because without sin God could not redeem or punish. This is what the theory must logically come to. It is not all the divine attributes which are here supposed to be fully exhibited, but only those which are concerned in redemption and in the punishment of sin. In respect to this: (1) As to punishment. If we say, sin is the necessary means of the greatest good, because God could not otherwise manifest his glory in punishing, that is to make the punishment an end and object for which God acts as ultimate, which, as we have seen, could not be the case. In consistency with his attributes, He could not bring into being persons with the object of punishing them. (2) As to redemption. If it be said that sin is the necessary means of the greatest good, because without it there could not be Redemption, and in Redemption God's greatest grace is seen, this is to assume that Redemption is the highest good, whereas it is not: it is the highest good for sinners, but holiness is the highest good absolutely. Redemption is not ultimate; it is in order to holiness. The system of the Gospel is a *method*. We cannot then meet the real question in the Theodicy, from this point: we cannot, *i. e.*, say that the simple object of the manifestation of the divine glory in redemption is sufficient, alone, to justify God in introducing sin and misery,— though, being introduced for other reasons or grounds, they do serve to illustrate the divine glory in redemption. Certainly, so far as the present system of the world is concerned, we may say, as a matter of fact, though not of moral necessity, that in the system of Redemption we have the highest glory of God revealed. As far as this scheme is concerned, then, the arguments to prove that sin is strictly necessary to the greatest good, are insufficient, do not reach to the point. All the scheme gives us is, the fact, but *not the fact as a necessity*.

§ 2. *Does the Nature of Free-Agency account for Sin?*

Is it a solution of the problem to say, that from the nature of free-agency God could not prevent all sin in a moral system?

In New England theology this position was taken in opposition to the divine-efficiency or necessary-means-of-the-greatest-good scheme. The position is most precisely given in Dr. N. W. Taylor's Lectures on Moral Gov., ii. 309: "What, then, is the impossibility of God's preventing all sin in moral beings, which it is now supposed may exist? I answer, It is an impossibility, the supposition of which involves a *contradiction in the nature of the case*. It is the impossibility of God's preventing moral beings from sinning, by anything which He can do, when beings who can sin in despite of God do in this respect what they can do."[1]
Yet he says, ii. 340: "[We do] not affirm that God could not

---

[1] Cf. also, Lects. on Moral Gov., i. 321-2; ii. 366; notice that nevertheless he argues, ii. 313-15, "that the moral acts of men and of God may be certain"; ii. 342; ii. 357. In i. 309, it is said that "the power of the creature to sin is superior to God's power."

prevent all sin in a moral system; but simply that its prevention in such a system *may be* impossible to Him."[1]—The position at the root of this scheme is, that a free agent is a being who can and may sin at any rate, in spite of all conceivable or possible agency, even of God. Choice is essentially the power to the contrary, and the power to the contrary always involves a possibility of a different choice and possibility of sin, and even omnipotence cannot control it.[2]—Now, is this position a vindication of the divine government in respect to sin? Does it give us a sufficient reason and account of the present system?

Remarks:

1. This theory at the utmost gives us only the possibility of sin, not its certainty, not its actuality. God in making a free agent, gave him power to the contrary, made it possible for him to sin. The theory accounts for the possibility, not for the fact, of sin.

---

[1] This is an important point in the theory. So Leibnitz, Theod., p. 158, says: "Bayle demands too much: he would have us shew *how* evil is bound up with the best possible plan of the creation, which would be a perfect explanation of the phenomenon: but this we do not undertake to give, nor are we obliged to do so: it would be impossible in the present state; it is enough that it *may be* true, it may be inevitable, it may be that particular evils are bound up with what is best in general. This is sufficient to answer objections, but not for a comprehension of the thing."

Dr. Taylor wishes to throw the burden of proof on his opponents. He does not say, that God could not prevent all sin in a moral system, but, it cannot be proved that He could. God can exclude sin from *a* moral system, but perhaps not from the *best*, not from *all*. The sin and punishment of the fallen angels may be the means, the *necessary* means of preserving the rest: so of man: so that the fact of the existence of sin in some may be the reason why, in the actually holy, God keeps sin out.—But where *does* the burden of proof lie? It is proved that God is omnipotent, that He can do all that can be done. The presumption, then is, that He can exclude sin, and that He has not allowed it because He lacked power, but for other reasons. This presumption is strengthened by the fact that He has excluded it from one system, and that He can and will keep saints to the end. It is for the negative then to show that *such is the nature of a moral system* that God cannot prevent sin in it. The affirmative might go one step further and say, that the nature of moral agency is such that God can prevent sin in a moral system, for He does and will in some. And since moral powers are the same in all, He can in all; and the reason why He does not is not that He cannot, but is something else.

[2] Compare Whately's Bampton Lectures for 1822, App. II., against Arch. King, who says, "the best system is one of free agents, *liable to wrong.*" There is a fallacy, says W., in the use of "liable to sin." It means only, "in his power, and in that sense *possible*, for him to sin"; does not mean, "may be expected to sin": this begs the question.

2. On this basis, sin could never be certain in the system, and therefore it could never be provided for by any eternal purpose or plan. It might be or might not be. The plan of God in respect to it must always be a plan of possibilities and not certainties; because while it is possible for a creature to sin, it is equally possible that he might not sin, and therefore all the future there could be to God would be one of bare possibility and not certainty.[1] The 'creature might sin, though omnipotence should try to prevent it; he might be holy, notwithstanding all finite inducement to the contrary. The matter would be left *in equilibrio.*—So, of other divine attributes. God could not, if his attributes are such as we have proved, bring such a system of uncertainties into being. The theory regards the finite will as an absolute contingency, in respect to which nothing can be certainly foreseen.

3. This theory derogates also from the divine omnipotence. It puts a limit in the creature to omnipotence. God as a matter of fact *has exercised* his omnipotence in keeping holy angels from sinning, and He has promised to keep renewed men in holiness and to secure their final sanctification.

4. An attempt is sometimes made to meet these difficulties by another form of statement, viz., "that sin is necessarily incidental to the best system." This form of statement does not help the matter. It is true, as all will concede, that as a matter of fact sin is incidental to the best system, but what the word "necessarily" means in connection with the term "incidental," is difficult to decide. Of course the meaning is not that sin is a necessary incident in the best system, and then the only necessity which the phrase attempts to keep in view must be that supposed to inhere in the nature of free agency. And here, as we have seen, we have mere possibility, not necessity. "Necessarily incidental" can amount only to this: that sin is necessarily possible, and that really means (unless there be confusion of terms) nothing more than possible; so that the word

[1] See *Meth. Quarterly*, 1860-1 and Jan. 1862: "God foreseeing how each and every possible free agent in any possible case will freely act, so places all free agents in existence, and so adjusts his own course as that from their free, unnecessitated, undecreed actions He may educe the best possible result."

"necessarily" serves only to make it more difficult to understand the theory.[1]

5. Even if the theory could be freed from its difficulties in relation to omnipotence, it after all would not solve the problem before us. The question is, Why did God choose a system in which it was certain that sin would exist? It is no answer to say, God chose it because it must be a system of free agents, about whom it was wholly uncertain whether they would sin or not. The only object of a theory would be to give a reason why God chose a system in which sin was certain to be, while this only states why He chose a system in which sin might possibly be.

6. The theory is still further no answer to the real question, which is this: Why is the present system the best system? All that the answer amounts to is, that the best system is one in which there are beings who have the power of choice. But their having the power of choice is not what *makes* the system *best;* it is simply an incident, a *sine quâ non.* The bare power of choice—or power of sinning—is no particular good. That which constitutes the "good" of the system must be found either in happiness or in holiness; and the theory in relation to either happiness or holiness would amount to this: that the highest happiness or holiness could not be insured without the power of choice, which everybody grants; but it does not answer the question at all, Why sin is in such a system?—To state the matter in another form: the only question which can be proposed in respect to vindicating the divine government, and the point to which any theory that attempts to solve the question must come, is this: To show why a holy and benevolent God chose a system in which sin was to be as a matter of fact, and why the existence of sin in that system was a condition of its being the best system. Understanding that to be the question, it may be said that the theory that sin is the necessary means of the greatest good fairly undertakes to meet the question, though it does not

---

[1] The theory is also sometimes supposed to be stated with a modification, thus: God's omnipotence in the case is restrained by his view of what it is best or not for Him to do. He cannot as a wise Being do what is unwise.—But this is a different theory. It puts the solution on a very different ground. It runs into the first theory or a modification of it.

answer it. But the other theory does not *meet* the question. It merely says, that in the best system free agency involves the possibility of sin, and that there cannot be a moral system without free agents.

The theory thus leaves the question and problem wholly undecided. No relief can be found in a scheme which limits divine omnipotence.

As far as we feel constrained to make a dilemma, we seem to be compelled to say: God could exclude sin but would not. "Could" asserts the divine omnipotence as not limited by, but extending over, moral beings and systems; "would not" of course does not mean that God ever approves sin from any point of view, but simply that He allows it *for some good and sufficient reason* which we may or may not be able to state.

§ 3. *We cannot state all the Reasons for the Permission of Sin.*

The true position is, that we do not know the ultimate or metaphysical reason why God allows sin to exist, and so cannot give a theoretical solution of the problem before us, while yet the Christian system gives a sufficient practical solution, so that they are without excuse who reject the redemption offered in Christ.

The two preceding theories attempt demonstrative solutions, they undertake to give the ultimate reason for the existence of sin—and fail.

In saying that we cannot give the final reason in the case, it is not meant that we cannot give some important reasons, in certain aspects and relations of the matter, but only that we do not know the ultimate reason in the divine mind, or the reason which is the complete vindication of Deity.

The preceding theories may afford a measure of help in meeting difficulties and objections, and clearing the subject in certain relations.

1. The state of the question. We prove that God is a holy, wise, omnipotent, and benevolent Being, on independent grounds and with certain evidence. The proof as far·as we go is sufficient. Then, objection is made to the proof for this one rea-

son: the existence of moral evil or sin, with its consequences. (The existence of natural evils, and of suffering as the just desert of sin, can be left out of account here, as the pressure of the problem is not on these grounds.) That objection is supposed to be sufficient to undermine the whole sum of the evidence derived from other sources, that God is omnipotent, wise, holy, and good. Then the state of the question is this. Is it a valid and sufficient objection to the proof that we have of the divine wisdom and benevolence, that sin should exist in the world? Or although sin exists, may we still hold fast to that proof? In meeting this question, there are two classes to be argued with, on different grounds:—infidels, with whom the whole argument from natural theology is to be urged, with the proofs given there of the divine wisdom and love; and believers in God, with whom the question comes as to the grounds on which we can reconcile the two positions.

2. Points on which the parties in dispute are agreed, as the question has been discussed in this country: (*a*) That the actual system is the best system on the whole, for some reason or other; (*b*) That sin is in it; (*c*) That sin in its nature is evil and only evil, and hence it cannot be in the system for its own sake; God did not put it in the system because it was a good or the direct means of good; (*d*) That it is in the system as the act and guilt of the creature. With agreement on these points, the differences come out in the two theories already considered.

3. Some reasons why this may be the best system, though sin is in it. There is a difficulty about the phrase, "best system." Defining it that no better system can possibly be conceived, involves us at once in a difficulty; because we can imagine a system in which there should be no sin, and that would be better than the system in which we now are. But the best system is defined by Leibnitz as the system which answers the great end the best; we mean by the phrase, not one that we could not conceive to be better, but the system which answers best, or as well as any system we could conceive, the great end: the manifestation of God and the good of the creature.

ANTECEDENTS OF REDEMPTION.

Without pretending to give the *ultimate* grounds or reasons, the divine government may be vindicated on the following grounds, which give points of relief and rebut objections (as that God is not both omnipotent and benevolent, if He allows sin, etc.), in connection with the Incarnation, the Atonement, the Redemptive system.

(*a.*) The divine benevolence, which we have taken as the highest divine attribute, is not a mere and ultimate regard to happiness, but to holiness. The divine benevolence has for its main object to secure the supremacy of holiness in God's moral system. That must be the great object to which God looks: a moral system in which holiness shall be supreme, —not a moral system in which holiness shall be implanted in every creature, but in which holiness shall be triumphant.

(*b.*) Such a moral system can only exist with and by free agents. It is inconceivable that there could be holy beings without freedom, and in that freedom there is of course given the possibility of sin as well as of holiness. This does not make sin certain but possible. The possibility is not a necessity, and if sin ever becomes actual, it will be through a free act for which the actor is responsible.

(*c.*) Now, having got a system in which holiness is to be the end, and a system of free agency in whose free agents there was a possibility of sinning, we advance to the statement that God might allow the possibility of sin to become actual, for two main reasons. For two reasons, God as a benevolent Being having ultimate regard to holiness, might permit the creature to sin. (1) From the consideration that if God should prevent sin by omnipotence or exclude it wholly, this might diminish the capabilities of holiness (and of course of happiness also) in the system. He *could* do it, because omnipotence can do all that can be done, and it could control a free agent. But if God should exercise his omnipotence in that way throughout the whole creation, it might require such an exercise of omnipotence as would diminish the capabilities of holiness and happiness. (2) From the consideration that the system of which sin is a part allows a special manifestation of the divine attribute of benevolence or love, in Redemption. We repeat that these reasons are suggested, not as solving the problem ultimately, but as showing that God in his omnipotence might, in consistency with his benevolence, still permit the existence of sin.

(*d.*) The reasons why God may have permitted sin may also be reasons for his not suppressing it finally in the system, *i. e.*, for allowing some to go to eternal condemnation.

(*e.*) As Chalmers says, for aught we know, it may be better for each individual to be in a system where there is a common sin and a common redemption, than for each to be in a system where he might sin and where there was no redemption provided.—As far as the whole system of the world is concerned, it seems plain that the vindication of the divine government is ultimately in the scheme of Redemption. God chose the system, as far as his own agency was concerned, for the sake of the Redemption in it, and not because He was obliged to take it with its possibilities of evil for the sake of free agency. If there had not been a Redemption, there would not have been a race of sinners, probably. God would have cut off the race at the root, if it had not been in his purpose to provide a scheme of Redemption, and a scheme co-extensive in its provisions with the extent of the apostasy. So far as God's own motive or agency was concerned, a general Redemption set over against a general ruin was the reason why he allowed sin to go on, a Redemption which will ultimately no doubt embrace by far the great majority of the race.

(*f.*) God is more than benevolent, He is gracious. Man is ultimately condemned for rejecting grace. (As to those who know not the gospel, we need not fear to assert that God will deal with them, too, benevolently as well as justly.)

Summary. Concluding Statement: God might, by omnipotence, have excluded sin; yet we must say: for wise and good reasons, some of which we can see, others not, He chose not to exert his omnipotence in the way of its suppression.

For aught that appears, the present system answers its end, *i. e.*, the manifestation of the declarative glory of God and the ensuring the triumph of holiness through free agents, as completely as any can, in which both these elements are to be conjoined. Both of them are to be taken into account in estimating the system.

The full Theodicy could be known only by knowing the universe; for evil began in angelic natures, and has its full issue only in eternity. This world gives us but a part; the Theodicy is to be framed with reserves and suspense of judgment as to what is ultimate; but so far as we do frame it, we are to avoid naturalistic grounds, and put ourselves on the basis of the Redemptive scheme. The problem of evil brings us and leaves us face to face with the offer of Redemption, and that is the most we can do with it: to make opposers concede that the existence of sin is explained as far as may be in the Redemption, and then ask them themselves to taste and see that the Lord is gracious. The practical solution of the problem is and ever must be found in the personal acceptance of the offers of grace.

NOTE.—Some additional statements not incorporated by the author in his lectures.

I.—Attempts to prove *a priori* the metaphysical necessity of sin in the best system fail, if sin be held to *be* sin. The only consistent statement here is the pantheistic: sin is a stage of development.

II.—The proof from free will, motives, etc., fails in showing more than liability, possibility. It does not show how God could choose a system involving the actuality of sin.

III.—The position, This is the best system—sin is in it—therefore, etc., is analysis and not proof.

IV.—Sin the necessary means of the greatest good, fails too.

V.—Yet we have enough to answer objections and difficulties so as to leave us face to face with the system of Redemption. *This is all that can be rationally asked in a Christian Theodicy.*

VI.—We should remember that the moral system of which we are a part, embraces the angelic as well as the Adamic world. Sin is far reaching; it reaches back into the past eternity and forward into the future. Hence the more need of caution the less the probability that we can see or know the whole.[1]

VII.—We should recollect, also, that as far as this world is concerned, it is a system, not of individuals, but for a race; with common characteristics, and a moral government for the whole as well as for each individual. In such a system there may be elements which would not be found in one of pure individualism. *E. g.*, It might be better for each individual to be in a system with sin for all and a common redemption, than in one where each came into the world to stand or fall for himself alone. More might be saved, on the whole, by such a system than by one of individual action and penalty. God would make a race; individuals to be generated; there must then be body and soul; this gave occasion for sin—and also for Redemption. The fact of Redemption is connected uniformly, in the Bible, with Incarnation. No redemption for angels is intimated.

VIII.—Recollect also, the necessary constituents of a moral system. The best system is that which secures the highest glory of God, through and by the acts of free moral agents. There are two elements in it: the declarative glory of the divine perfections, and the agency of the creature: or, the supremacy of holiness as the end, and the freedom of the creature in relation to that end. Such a system of course implies that men are free moral agents; yet also, that God through and by their free agency will secure the end of his system.

IX.—1. The Ideal: God—a perfect world—man, free, holy—collection of individuals like angels—immortal bliss in obedience to the holy law for each.

2. The Actual: God—a sinful world—man in bondage to sin—common ruin—violated law—uncertain or dismal future.

---

[1] As to the fall of Angels, see Birks, Difficulties of Belief, ch. v. (1) A moral system was first set forth in creation, in the simplest way; in angelic hosts and orders; individuals; all favorable to stability. (2) The Fall, through pride, before the Adamic. (3) The system passing over to a mixed one: a new trial, in the human race; sinful angels still connected with it. (Angels not at once cast down to the lowest hell, as is inferred from 2 Pet. ii. 4; Jude 6, 7. This last refers [probably too the first] to the sin of angels with the race, a second apostasy.) "A later fall of Satan in the Garden, in connection with the Adamic."

3. The Union of the Two: Christianity—Man a race—with common sinfulness: Christ a Redeemer—common provision of Redemption—the world a probation—eternity unveiled.

The difficulties of natural religion solved by the Christian religion.

X.—Consider the attitude of God in respect to sin and its consequences. The general maxim here: "Deus concurrit ad materiale, non ad formale actionis liberæ." God is to overrule, bound, control sin. God could not prevent sin, from regard to his plan; could, *per se.* Consider that metaphysical evil is not really such; in gradation there is no real evil. Misery and death are in the world for the sin of the race; they are not necessary; are to pass away: Rom. viii. 21; viii. 18–25; Rev. vii. 16, 17; xxi. 4. Evil still attends sin: Rom. v. 12; vi. 23. Evil serves the glory of God: John ix. 3; xi. 4; Rom. viii. 28; James i. 2–4.

XI.—Such a permission of sin in this race allows a peculiar manifestation of the divine love, in this system of Redemption, where the highest divine glories shine. In its results in saving, it will doubtless reach far beyond our common thoughts and ways of estimating.—Infants.—Who knows what a millennial period may be?—some conjecture three hundred and sixty thousand years (year of thousands). We need not fear to make this statement broad and strong.

PART III.

CHRISTIAN ANTHROPOLOGY. THE DOCTRINE RESPECTING MAN.

This Third Part of the First Division treats of man, in his original endowments, his moral relations, and his original moral state. It differs from Psychology (which considers man in his isolation—a mind—an intelligence) in taking the broadest and highest view of man, treating the whole doctrine respecting man in his relations to God,[1] and as a subject of God's moral government.

Under this title we include the discussion of the much-debated questions as to the nature of moral agency and of holiness and sin, which are to be applied in respect to all the doctrines, both in Anthropology (with Hamartology) and, in the Third Division, the Application of Redemption. We have here to consider the nature of free agency, of conscience, of true virtue; all of which go to exhibit the true nature of God's moral government.

The general subject of the prime constituents of human nature, or of man's endowments and relations as a moral being, can be considered under these points of view: I. What is man as a moral being? II. What is the law for which as a moral being he is made? III. What is man's relation to the law (synthesis between I. and II.)—man's destination as a moral being?— In what is conformity to this law found?[2]

---

[1] [The author sometimes made Anthropology include the Doctrine of Human Nature—I. in Itself; II. as Fallen; III. as capable nevertheless of Redemption. The first head would treat of the prime constituents of human nature and its chief moral relations; the second, of the condition into which man as a race has fallen, and of the penalty and power of sin in men as individuals; and the third, of the need on man's part of deliverance from without and above, and of the possibility of receiving deliverance which still survives in human nature. But on the whole the division of the subject into Part III. Anthropology, and Part IV. Hamartology, suits his treatment best.]

[2] [This is the question of "the nature of true virtue." The above scheme is not strictly followed, yet it governs more than any other in the ensuing discussions.]

CHAPTER I.

WHAT IS MAN AS A MORAL BEING?

In order to know what man is as a moral being, we must consider the relations in which he stands, his endowments and capacities.

§ 1. *Of Man in his most General Relations.*

(*a.*) Man in his relation to the Creator, which is his highest and chief relation, is finite and dependent. His fundamental relation is that of a creature of God, dependent upon Him for life and breath and all things: Gen. i. 26; Acts xvii. 28; Rev. iv. 11. As a creature, man falls under the general condition of finite existence, limitation by space and time. As a creature of God he is made for God, having the destination of glorifying God, so that that is his chief end; and in nothing that he does can he be independent of the divine government, as exercised in the way o general providence, ordering all things with omnipotence and wisdom, for the highest ends of such a government.

(*b.*) In relation to the rest of the material creation man is the crown and head thereof.[1] One aspect of the world viewed by itself is, that it was made for man; it culminates and is centralized in him. This is foreshadowed in the order of creation given in the book of Genesis: man was made last and to have dominion over all.[2] It is proved also by science, which shows that everything in the lower orders of animals points to man.[3] The order is: inorganic; organic with life—vegetables; organic with souls (in broad sense)—animals: man has all these elements in his constitution, and

(*c.*) He has not only what allies him with and makes him the recapitulation of the order of creation, but he has also what

---

[1] "Man is not an animal whose mind is agitated with animal sympathies and passions, but a calm, deep sea, in which the heavens with the sun and stars are mirrored" (Herder).

[2] Here religion and theology have anticipated science.

[3] Especially the investigations into the stages of embryo life.

puts him above all other natural beings, a spiritual subsistence. He is made up of both nature and spirit. The two realms meet in him. The angels are spirits without bodies, and the lower orders have a material constitution without a rational soul. Man is the union of both. This combination assigns him his place in the whole creation. The difference between nature and spirit: (1) General: we cannot ascribe the qualities of the one to the other; (2) Matter is defined by its relations to space: spirit, not; (3) Matter is moved by foreign agency: spirit is self-active,[1] is essentially free; (4) "Spirit has its center in itself: matter, not" (Hegel).

(d.) Man is not only thus related to God and to nature, but each individual man is also one of a race: he is an individual example of a race. What he is as a member of the race is the substratum of what he is as an individual, personal being. The unity of the race as a whole underlies the idea of the individual. In each individual the constituent elements of human nature are individualized. The individual has all the common properties, relations, tendencies, qualities, attributes—or whatever they may be called—of the race of which he is a part and an individual copy. The unity and "solidarity" of the race is at the basis of the doctrines of sin and of redemption. As a whole, as well as in each individual, it is the object of the divine government: Gen. i. 27, 28; Acts xvii. 24-26; Rom. v. 12. The race is in idea before the individual: the whole is in idea before the part: for the part has essential respect to the whole.[2] Hence, men cannot be considered as isolated beings. We cannot understand the human body except in its relations to nature, which it was made to act in. We cannot understand a human affection except as it is related to other beings. The very idea of man is that of an individual being or agent in such leading relations as have been named. His capacities and powers have respect to these. And,

(e.) In all these relations man is a moral being. In them all

[1] In a broad sense we must admit a spiritual principle in animals: they are self-active.
[2] Aristotle, Pol. 1, 2: "Manifestly the state is by nature before the family and before each individual. For the whole must needs be earlier than the part."

he is to live as a moral agent. He is such a being, he has such a constitution that he can and must be in *moral* relations with all, can and must act in a moral way, in respect to all. As consisting of body and soul, as related to nature, to his fellow-beings and to God, he is to act morally, in accordance with a moral law, for a moral end. This is his fundamental destination: to be morally at one with himself, with nature, with other rational beings, and with God.

And he has such *endowments* that he can do this. Man is made a moral being: having such capacities and powers, in such a state, that he can and must act in a moral way, under a moral law. And this leads us to consider—

§ 2. *What constitutes the Individuality of each Man? What are the specific Characteristics of each Man as an Individual Person?*

The most general statement: Man is a personal agent, having capacities or powers and tendencies corresponding to all the relations in which he is placed and for which he was made.

The order of discussion: I. Man as made up of body and soul; II. Personality; III. Faculties; IV. Tendencies; V. Conscience. Man is primarily constituted of body and spirit, and is thus connected with the natural and spiritual sphere; his body has a central principle of life, which is not the result of, but the living center of unity to, all his organism; his personality presides over and expresses itself in all that he does; he has powers or faculties; he has tendencies towards the various objects to which he is related; and in respect to all, he has the power of moral discernment, feeling, and self-determination, and of moral judgment upon himself and upon all that comes within the moral sphere.

§ 3. *Of the union of Body and Soul in Man.*

I.—The dichotomy in man. Man is *animal rationale*, the center between nature and spirit, made up of both; his material portion we call his body: his spiritual substance, his soul. This union is the most wonderful and mysterious fact in our organic frame. Various theories have been proposed to explain or illustrate it. The theories rest upon one of two assumptions: that body and soul are one substance originally, or that there is an essential duality of matter and spirit. On the first assumption we may have (*a.*) Materialism, which affirms that this primitive substance is matter which takes the form of spirit; or (*b.*) Idealism, affirming that the primitive substance is spirit which becomes objective to itself in what is called matter.[1] The difficulty in either of these cases is that things so different as body and soul cannot be deduced the one from the other. We cannot bring one under the other; we can only superadd the qualities of spirit to those of matter, or the qualities of matter to those of spirit. The second assumption, that matter and spirit are dual, essentially distinct, may be carried to the extreme of asserting that they are entirely disparate, giving rise to the three chief theories as to their mode of acting upon each other. (*a.*) The union is made in the sensorium: the nerves carry impressions thither, and then the soul receives them. But when we have got to the sensorium and the nervous action and the spirit awaiting the reception of the nervous influence, we still have to explain the nature of this union as much as before; and therefore some have imagined a nervous fluid intermediate between matter and spirit, which is so vague that it may be taken to be matter or spirit, or both.[2] This theory really materializes the soul, while it leaves the problem unsolved, and simply removes the difficulty to parts unknown. (*b.*) The theory of occasionalism—Cartesian. This started with the position that matter works by its particular laws, and spirit by laws peculiar to itself, and that these are so different that there is no possibility of a mutual action. Then, to explain what appears to be the mutual action, it was said that God, on the occasion of the action of the one, produces by his direct agency a corresponding action in the other. (*c.*) The theory of pre-established harmony, suggested by Leibnitz. This also rests on the assumption that there is no direct interaction between

---

[1] To say, the primitive substance is *neither* matter nor spirit, as in Cudworth's "plastic soul of nature," etc., (so Morell) is to make a union in statement merely, not in any definite conception.

[2] "Physical influx" designates a similar theory.

the material and spiritual, but it hesitates to say that God produces the actions by continual interference; and says in distinction that He made the soul and body in a perfect correspondence the one with the other, so that, e. g., when a motion took place in the body there should be a motion in the soul, not by the direct act of God, but by the action of the spirit itself, according to a pre-established harmony. These three theories have been illustrated by the instance of two watches keeping the same time, which might be taken under three points of view: they keep time together, (1), because they act on each other; (2), because the maker of the watches acts directly upon both; (3), because both watches were made so perfect at the first that they correspond in movement at every point.

The simple facts, however, to which we must come back are: that body and soul are distinct; that they do interact; and that the mode of their interaction surpasses human scrutiny. We must accept the fact as ultimate and a mystery. We may say that the soul is prior; takes to itself a material form; and that in this union neither is understood without the other.[1] "The soul is the entelechy of the body." The whole body is the seat of the soul. Both soul and body are in constant union and mutual action. The body is the organ for the manifestation of the soul, and the medium of its communication with the material world and beings. The union of body and soul is through and by— not bare matter, but—the forces of matter, or through matter as force. There is force in the action of all the organism: mechanical, chemical, vital; there is force also in the soul. Force is common to both body and soul, and here, in some way, is the point of union. The soul shapes, forms the body; and because it does this, it is susceptible to all its motions. This does not explain, so that we can comprehend, the union: but it determines the relations of the body to the soul.

After all, body and soul, while essentially distinct, are perhaps not so disparate as we traditionally imagine.

[1] Compare The Theory of the Soul, by Rev. J. B. Dalgairns. He vindicates, against the Cartesian dualism, the Aristotelian view of the soul as "entelechy." He says, "Man is one complete being made up of body and soul, in the sense that the intellectual soul is by itself the true and immediate form of the body."

II.—Does the dichotomy (body and soul) in man include also a trichotomy (body, soul, and spirit)? Those who affirm that it does, rely upon two passages of Scripture: 1 Thess. v. 23, rendering this "May you remain, be preserved entire, in all your parts, body, soul, and spirit, blameless," etc.—It seems better, however, to understand it: May you in all your spheres, all your relations, be blameless: in Spirit, *i. e.*, in relation to the new spiritual life; in soul, in all your individual traits; and in body. The other passage adduced is Heb. iv. 12; where "piercing to the separation, or the dividing, of soul and spirit" is taken to imply a difference in substance between soul and spirit, or at least a difference in the whole mode of existence and manifestation.—But the passage appears to refer not to two distinct compartments of the spiritual Christian man, but to two different relations: a relation to the whole spiritual sphere and to the natural, both of which are searched to the very joints and marrow of them by the Word of God.[1]

If spirit and soul were two distinct substances, then, (*a.*) death could not be described as the giving up of the *soul* (Gen. xxxv. 18; 1 Kings xvii. 21; Acts xv. 26, Cf. xx. 10, 11), and again as the giving up of the *spirit* (Ps. xxxi. 5; Luke xxiii. 46; Acts vii. 59; Cf. Luke viii. 55); (*b.*) "souls" and "spirits" of the dead could not mean the same (1 Pet. iii. 19; Heb. xii. 23; Rev. vi. 9; xx. 4); (*c.*) we should not find the Scriptural formula for man to be sometimes "body and soul" (Ps. lxxiii. 26; Matt. vi. 25; x. 28), and sometimes "body and spirit" (Eccl. xii. 7; 1 Cor. v. 3, 5).

§ 4. *Of the origin of Souls (after the Creation of the first Soul).*
While it is agreed that the first members of the human race were the immediate objects of the divine power, and that their souls were immediately created like their bodies,[2] on the question how the souls of their descendants come into being there are three chief theories: Pre-existence, Creationism, Traducianism.

[1] The words, "spirit" and "soul" designate, the former, the life as proceeding from God; the latter, the life as that of the individual. This is the only general view that can be carried out.

[2] [With those who do not agree to this, the author's plan was to conduct discussion under the head of Apologetics.]

ANTECEDENTS OF REDEMPTION. 167

I.—Pre-existence: God created originally (on "the first day," some have said, some, on "the sixth,") all the souls of the human race that ever should exist. (The view of the Rabbins was, that these souls were kept in a heavenly treasury until conception took place, and that then the soul was introduced into and united with the new body.) Some have supposed that there is an allusion to this in John ix. 2. If the man did sin, of course he pre-existed, it is said. The phrase, however, is colloquial and not metaphysical. Ps. cxxxix. 15 is also cited, but this is doubtless an allusion to the formation in the womb.[1]

Plato, Philo, Justin Martyr, Theodoretus, Origen, Synesius, Prudentius, taught pre-existence; some holding that the souls were in the ether and came freely, the Church Fathers for the most part teaching that they were brought into the body as a punishment and with the benevolent intent of giving them the opportunity of redemption. Against it were Tertullian, Gregory of Nyssa, Cyril, Augustine, Leo the Great; at a synod under Justinian (Mansi, IX. 396) it was condemned.

II.—Creationism: Each soul is created by the divine power, and united with the fœtus, which alone is propagated. The soul is supposed to be created pure, and united with a depraved body. This view was held by Hilary, Pelagius, Theodoretus, Gennadius, Ambrose, Jerome, by the Scholastics, by Melanchthon, and most of the Reformers. It has been the view of most Roman Catholic divines, and of many Calvinists. Lutheran theologians are for the most part against it, though Luther himself was not decided. Pelagius used it against the doctrine of original sin, urging that God would not create a soul impure. Augustine was not decided. Against it are usually cited: Gen. i. 26; ii. 2; for it, such passages as Heb. xii. 9, "Father of spirits." The chief objections to it are: (a.) It is difficult to see how God could create a perfectly pure spirit, and unite it with a depraved organization; (b.) It puts man out of analogy with all the other living beings in the world; in these the entire vitality is allowed

---

[1] Other citations are: Isa. xlii. 5; Job xii. 10; 1 Pet. iii. 18. The following have been quoted to show that the souls of children are in Hades before birth: Job i. 21; Ps. cxxxix. 14, 15; Ps. xxii. 30.

to be propagated, including all that goes to the animal soul, the degree of intelligence, traits, etc.; (*c.*) It tends to destroy the organic unity of the race.[1]

III.—Traducianism. ("Tradux," the vine shoot, brought over to become a new branch.) This theory, which on the whole has been the most widely approved, accounts for the genesis of souls from the first pair, by the position that the soul is propagated with the body.

Certain passages of Scripture are believed to be most in accordance with this view, though they cannot be said to be absolutely decisive. Heb. vii. 10; Gen. v. 3,—the "likeness" to himself in which Adam begat a son can scarcely be restricted to the body, and if it was also in the soul, then that was included in the begetting; Ps. li. 5,—this certainly cannot refer to the body alone, but to the depravity in the soul. If the Psalmist has not in view his own sinfulness, what could he have had in view? he was not speaking of the guilt of his mother; John iii. 6,—"the flesh" here means, all the natural constitution of man, all that is not the effect of a special divine influence; Rom. v. 12 seq., where the reasoning seems to presuppose transmission of the entire human endowment from the first man; and the general Scriptural mode of describing generation as of the whole man: "Adam begat Seth," "Isaac begat Jacob:" it would seem that there is everywhere recognition of the fact that man does not beget mere animals, but persons, or at least personal natures.

Other arguments in favor of the Traducian view are: (*a.*) the analogy of creation already referred to; (*b.*) the slow development of the powers of the mind seems more in harmony with this view than with Creationism; (*c.*) the traits of parents descend to children, peculiarities of intellect, even moral peculiarities, all of which must have their seat in the soul; (*d.*) the doctrine of original sin is best stated in accordance with this view.

The chief objection to Traducianism is the philosophical

---

[1] Lasaulx, Phil. d. Gesch., p. 15: "In all human pro-creation, it is not the individual man and woman that generate, but the race (the generic) in them; humanity generates life: *i. e.*, in the last instance, "the eternally pro-creative nature," springing from "the original and universal prototype," and "the divine creative power dwelling in the protoplast." So Plato, De Leg.

difficulty raised in respect to the simplicity of the soul. It is asked, how can a pure essence be propagated? is it derived from the father or the mother, or both; if from both, must it not be divisible? Propagation seems to imply a division of souls and a reunion, and yet the soul is not composite, but simple. We can only answer such questions as these by asking others. If on account of simplicity of essence we exclude man's soul from the line of propagation, we must also exclude the animal soul, for that too is simple and indivisible, and we must extend the theory of Creationism to animals. Indeed we should hardly know what to say of the principle of life in the vegetable. Must we assume in each seed a new creation? We should not be free from embarrassment in our thoughts of the ultimate forces of nature. These are simple, at least to our thought, and yet they act in a great variety of ways, transmit, incorporate themselves— so to speak—at different points. Take, e. g., electricity. In fact the old assumption, that simplicity prevents difference in modes of action, has been abandoned.

On the whole, Traducianism is the most natural theory, and has fewer difficulties. We are not bound to answer the question, how the soul is propagated. That we do not know. We need only say, that such appears to be the constitution of the race, that *souls are potential in it*, are ultimately from the first father of the race.

Yet this view should not be held so as to exclude the agency of God from the origination of each soul. God does doubtless act in a specific way in producing each human individual. There is a peculiar co-working of divine power, but the mode of that agency need not be asserted to be strictly creative. Martensen, Dogm. 162, 3: "Every individual is the effect of the natural productivity of the race, while the mysterious natural agency is the organ and means of the *individualizing* agency of God." "Both Traducianism and Creationism are true.[1] Traducianism alone would give us the natural side, the copy of the race: Creationism alone would demand absolute purity, which is inconsistent with the sinfulness of the race."

[1] Pre-existence is also of course true, in the sense that souls existed in idea in the divine creative counsels.

§ 5. *Of Personality.*

Man is made up of body and soul, but he is also a personal agent, and personality is the center of unity to the conscious being. The central fact in respect to man as a moral agent is, that he has a distinct personality. Personality is indefinable, because ultimate. Wherever there is consciousness, there are the elements of self and not-self and the union of the two: there is a knowledge of self and of that which is not-self. The equivalent of personality is self, and personality may be described as that in man which enables him to say "I." It is man's self-hood, knowledge of self (not of "the existence of self") directly given in consciousness. The having of personality is what distinguishes man, so far as the central principle in him is concerned, from the brutes. So far as we know, they do not distinguish between the ego and the non-ego. Rudiments and anticipations of personality are found in the plant and animal: they have centers of life and activity. Man is more than a self-active being; each animal is that, self-active in its sphere; man is a personal agent: he has a derived and dependent, but still a real, personal agency;[1] all that he does is an expression, a manifestation of this central personal force, which is inalienable from his very being.[2] This personality gives the possibility of his fellowship with God, in which his glory as a man chiefly consists. There is a degree of vagueness about the use of the terms, person and personality. The word person is usually employed to designate the whole man as apparent, while personality refers rather to the center of that being, to self-hood.

§ 6. *The primary Facts involved in all Personal Agency.*

Personality is the central principle in man; at the basis is the distinction of the me and the not-me, the personal agent and the

[1] Thomasius, Dogm. I. 135: "The divine idea of man is, that the absolute personality is imaged forth in the limits of the finite and created."

[2] Another form of statement: Man is self-active, is a center of force determined by its relations. This is true of plants, of all that is organized. Brutes are subjects (individuals). But man's center is proper personality, essential to which are reason and conscience and affections of a moral nature, with free will as the organ of manifestation. Personality and free will are inseparable; the latter is the expression of the former. In man, germ (as in plants) and individuality (as in brutes) are merged in personality.

objective universe, with which he is placed in relations; for man's powers have respect to all that is objective, and they cannot be conceived as acting except in respect or relation thereto. But this statement gives us only the central fact in human nature, not its full idea. There are certain fundamental elements in all personal action, or essential conditions of it, or primary facts involved in it. These are:

I.—Consciousness. The fundamental form of personal activity is consciousness; by which is not indicated a specific power, but the condition of the exercise of all our powers. Consciousness simply means that the mind knows that it acts. The tree knows not that it grows, but man feels and knows it, thinks and knows it. He is also conscious of the external world. Consciousness may be analyzed as containing the elements: (*a.*) the person, (*b.*) the object, (*c.*) a real connection between the two. All of these make up every act of consciousness. It is not the knowledge of the operations of the person, but of the person himself in his operations. It is given with, not after, each act.[1] Brutes probably have no proper consciousness: they know, but do not know that they know: do not distinguish self and knowledge. So perhaps, very young children do not say "I."

This is the primitive fact lying at the basis of all the mind's faculties; confirming the position that these faculties have respect to the person's relation to other being, to what is objective.

II.—The fact of personal identity. Personal identity is the continued existence of the same self or person, in a variety of states. The knowledge of personal identity can only come upon a comparison of at least two states of mind. The knowledge of self may be given in a single act; personal identity implies a comparison of at least two. One state of consciousness gives us self and an object: another, self, an object, and *the sameness of self* in this diversity of states. This also is a primitive fact in relation to the soul's agency, and is so deeply involved that doubt of it, in a sane person, is a psychological impossibility; the doubt cannot be stated without affirming the fact: the doubt annuls itself. The identity which we

---

[1] Yet "the marvel of consciousness involves the marvel of memory" (Maurice).

know in personal identity is that of the soul, the self, not of the particles of the body. A person may lose the consciousness of his identity, but not the identity itself. Identity is not in consciousness,—though Locke says: "Identity is dependent on consciousness."

III.—The continuity of the mental states. This is the third fact lying at the basis of the mind's operations. This is distinct from identity, though identity is involved in it. The fact is this: the states of the mind are held together by the self or person in the unity of consciousness; they succeed one another in time and are mutually dependent; they serve to produce and reproduce one another. This fact is connected with the existence of the soul in time. Given the identity of the person and the continued existence in time, and the product is, the continuity of states. A part of this fact is what is known in general under the term, association of ideas, but the whole fact is more than that: it is the association of all the states of the mind. It involves memory. There are: (1) successive states; (2) which are also dependent; (3) which are retained after passing; (4) which come up again, as they at first co-existed: (*a*.) some, always together as ideas, etc.; (*b*.) some, as faculties always operating together (Hamilton's Law of Reproduction).

It should be remembered that the above are *facts*, not *faculties*, of the mind.

IV.—In all its operations the mind is an active agent, working for some end or object; it is an efficient cause working for a final cause; and the final cause, or the object, for which it works, exists and must exist in itself, as impulse or motive. This is a universal law or condition of all the mind's practical agency, activity, in relation to what is objective, different from itself. The ultimate ground or reason for the action is in the mind itself: (1) as efficiency, (2) also as the impulse, motive (the objective as subjective).

V.—In all its agency the mind is both active and passive. This is virtually contained in the preceding. It is the necessary result of man's finiteness, that he should be both acted upon and active, receptive and reactive. Even in the animal soul there are spontaneous reactions, and in the lowest spheres of organized being, this law is shown in contractility and expansibility. In respect to the soul, there are influences from without, waking it up, and reactions, by spontaneous power or force, in view of these. There is no conceivable activity of the mind which is not under this law. Still, the mind, when acted on, is only excited to self-agency, to manifest what it is in itself, in the way of re-agency.

§ 7. *The Powers and Faculties of the Soul.*

All of these facts, now, of personality: consciousness, identity, continuity of states, and action for ends, are presupposed in moral agency, are conditions of such agency; they are at the basis of all the operations of the mind; they are the conditions of the exercise of all the faculties. But they are not these faculties or powers themselves. What these are, we are now to inquire. Under the above conditions all man's powers act: what are these powers? The faculties themselves are man's essential powers as a moral agent.

I.—Of the method of determining as to the faculties.

The term, faculty, is variously used. In attempting to define it, we are apt to run into a practical difficulty, which is the division of the mind, more or less after the phrenological method. It is easy to say that we do not mean to divide up the soul, but difficult to get rid practically of the feeling that we have not done so, when we have distinguished its faculties. Many of our reasonings go upon the supposition of a real division, *e. g.*, in ethics and theology, as respects the question whether regeneration is of the will or the affections. If we only can refer it to the will, it seems as though we had made it much clearer than if we say it is in the affections; but we have not, in reality; we have only put the work into another word. In determining the faculties, the following points are to be observed: (*a.*) The mind acts as one indivisible faculty or power, in all that it does. There is one undivided energy in all its operations; and in almost all its acts, all the main faculties work together: man acts as a person, an agent, not as an intellect or emotion; *e. g.*, a person stoops to pick up a stone: he perceives the stone, and here is at work in the intellect; he desires to take it up,—in the emotions; he determines to take it up,—in the will. (*b.*) Our divisions, then, are matters of convenience and classification, and do not imply real divisions in the mind's operations. (*c.*) By faculties or powers, is meant about this: the largest classes of distinguishable operations under which we can consider the mind and its actions; the largest classes of operations in respect to objects under which we can view the mind; intellectual powers having respect to knowledge about objects; sentient, to feeling; will, to choice and action, in regard to them. Or, stating the matter from another point of view: A general faculty is a class of operations having respect to some specific function of the agent, a distinct mode of operation. (There is a difference between power and state, which comes up for consideration later.) (*d.*) The rules for division into faculties: (1) The sum of the divisions must include all the phenomena of the mind: nothing in it must be left unassigned. This is the rule of comprehensiveness. (2) In each division or faculty, there must be one class of phenomena unlike those which are found in the others. If all the phenomena in one division are like those included in any other, there is no line of demarcation. This is the rule of similarity and difference. (3) The ground of the divisions must be sought in the characteristics of the phenomena themselves. We must make the division on the basis of facts found in the phenomena. We must not come from the outside and put a foreign measure upon them. We must not divide by mathematics or metaphysics, but psychologically, by the laws of the phenomena themselves. This is the rule of characteristic qualities as the principle of division.

II.—The divisions themselves.

According to the principles and rules above given, the main faculties of the human mind will be those of Intellect, Feeling, and Will. The old distribution was two-fold:[1] understanding and will, perceptive and active powers. (This, Edwards proceeds upon.) The division almost universally current now is that of Intellect, Sensibilities, and Will: the phenomena of the

---

[1] Yet Aquinas had the three-fold distinction as clearly as any modern writer.

will being separated from those of the desires and affections. There are unquestionably such phenomena, which cannot be brought under either of the other classes without constraint, though there is a constant tendency to give to the will an autonomy which does not belong to it. These three main powers express man's relations to what is objective to himself; they are real powers for these relations. The most general statement in respect to them is this: by the intellect, we know, perceive what is objective; by the sensibilities, we desire, or, more generally, are affected in a feeling way, in regard to what is objective; and by the will—considered as separate from the affections—we decide to act in respect to objective things; and by the will—considered as in union with the affections—we choose, prefer, love them. This act of will as love includes the action of all the faculties: it is the concentrated action of all our powers, of the whole man, in relation to the objects and ends for which he is made.

These three faculties are also described in another way: as expressing differences in nearness of relation to objects. By the intellect, we view what is outside ourselves simply as a matter of contemplation; by the feelings, we are drawn towards the objects and desire them; by the will, we put forth activity in regard to them, and make them our own as far as we can. So that in the will we have the closest conjunction of man with the objects around him. The will marries the man to what he desires and seeks.

1. The Intellect. In the intellect man is contemplated as knowing. (Sensation and perception are commonly brought under the intellect, although in sensation there is also a physical side. In a more correct division of Anthropology, what has respect to the body would be separated and treated by itself as the basis of the activity of the mind. In the senses, there are physical elements, and the intellect is secondary.) Under the intellect are comprised all the processes by which man obtains, retains, and combines knowledge; and all through which the knowledge thus obtained is brought under generalization, suggestion, and memory; the logical processes, inductive and de-

ductive, are included, together with the powers by which we apprehend ideas.[1]

2. *The Sensibilities.* Under the sensibilities are combined all the faculties which have the common element of feeling. Their having this common characteristic is what warrants us in making this common division of them. Though the sensibilities are widely different from one another, yet they all have this common element. There are the desires which are connected with our animal organization; then, the higher emotions in view of the beautiful, etc.; then, our highest moral feelings and affections, which come forth in connection with our relation to other personal agents. Under this head belong all those affections which unite us to nature, to our kind, and to God. The permanent acts and states of the will are referred by many to this division. But the permanent moral states of man are both feeling and will, and cannot be referred to either class by itself.

3. *The Will.* As this comes up again, we only remark here, that the common characteristic by which we set off a certain class of operations of the mind, called the Will, is that of choice or preference. Wherever there is choice there is will. Intellect and feeling are necessary conditions of the choice, but the choice is distinct from both. The act of the will is the simple act of choice or determination, a putting forth of power in relation to some perceived or desired object. And it is always accompanied by the possibility of not putting forth this act, which possibility is grounded in the very nature and definition of the *Will.* The will may not have in distinct view more than one object, but there is the possibility not only of choosing but of refusing that object, so that there are always two objects in fact, though there may be only one in consciousness.

§ 8. *Of the original Tendencies of Man's Soul.*

We have considered the general relations in which man is placed, and then the specific characteristics of the individual; we

---

[1] If the philosophy of the subject were here our chief aim, we should urge that it is undoubtedly better to consider under psychology only the faculties and their operations, and to take up the subject of ideas as another part of philosophy —metaphysics proper.

are now to consider the tendencies of the individual man in respect to these relations. The personal agent, with intellect, affections, and will, is placed in, is an integral part of, the universe; he has thereby certain relations to nature, to his fellow-beings, and to God. And he not only has general faculties and powers, but also implanted, specific tendencies, constituting the bent, bias of his soul in respect to these relations. He has *inherent* relations to nature, man, and God; and to these relations correspond certain implanted, connatural tendencies, which are not his faculties, which cannot be resolved into his faculties, which are the connatural or native biases of his soul.

These tendencies, abstractly considered, are neither right nor wrong. As we find them in actual exercise, out of their proper state of subordination and government, they are wrong; but in themselves, viewed simply as implanted tendencies and connatural dispositions, they are neither right nor wrong:[1] 1 Cor. vi. 13; Mark vii. 15; 1 Tim. iv. 3. There is an aspect of the flesh and of the will of the flesh in which they are necessary constituents of human nature. The antagonism of flesh and spirit, as given in Rom. vii. 22, 23, Gal. v. 17, is not the original, but a degenerate state. The only rule by which to measure the character of these native tendencies or impulses is that of proportion—the lower under the higher—in a strict subordination: if they are not in that state, they have become evil: Luke xvi. 10; Matt. vi. 33; Luke x. 27. All that is lower is to be subordinated to the higher—to the highest—ends. That alone is a normal state in which this is the case: Matt. iv. 4; 1 Cor. iii. 21-23.

Another form of statement: Man is placed in the midst of varied relations, as an integral part of a great whole. Corresponding to these relations, he has specific impulses and desires. There is for him *a good* in the various objects to which he is related, and in which he finds happiness according to the measure of each object and relation.

The leading tendencies may be classified by means of the

[1] They may become, and actually are, in *all* cases of exercise, probably, either right or wrong.

leading relations. (1) Tendencies as impulses, having respect to the preservation of the body, as the love of life, hunger, etc. (2) Those which have respect to the continuance of the species,—sexual love, family affections, etc. (3) Those which have respect to society and the state, our social instincts in a wider sphere; the love of man for his kind; the disposition to unite in social order, which gives rise to the state and ultimately forms government. (4) Moral tendencies (using "moral" in a restricted sense): those which have respect to our specific moral relations to other finite personal agents, giving rise to human "rights"; which tendencies are also to be regarded as specific and implanted. (5) Those which have respect to what is beyond the sphere of time and sense; to a supersensuous and supernatural world, to the proper and highest Supernatural, to the Divine. Man has these as truly as he has the tendencies and relations of the body or of society. Man is made to be religious, and he has a tendency or bias in respect to that implanted in him.[1]

These are the main tendencies, different from the faculties; they are the man in all his relations; they exist more or less in all; they express, according as they are in proper measure or are inordinate, the bias of each individual in view of his relations; and in these tendencies, all the faculties meet and act. There is always involved in them a feeling of conscious want and an impulse towards its realization, so that they may be said to move between the poles of need and desire.

§ 9. *Of Conscience.*

Conscience is a collective term, embracing certain natural operations of the mind in view of what has moral quality, in view of right and wrong, whether this exist in law, states, acts, or relations.

It is often taken in narrower senses. (1) It is sometimes taken as a special faculty, which decides upon single acts imperatively, by a sort of sovereign arbitrament, without respect to anything but the individual act.[2] Hence an objection is some-

---

[1] "Man is a religious—animal" (Edm. Burke).

[2] See an article on Conscience, by Pres. Day, in New Englander, May, 1856 It is a "moral faculty"; its decisions relate to acts and states of a man's own mind, though it may judge also about others; if allowed to be perverted, "we cannot do right either in obeying or disobeying it."

times brought to its very being, from the fact of different decisions by different men and peoples. (2) By others it is taken as chiefly an emotion, as a particular kind of complacency or displacency in view of our acts. (So Brown and Mackintosh. On the other hand, Butler: "We cannot form a notion of this faculty without a judgment.") (3) It is described by others as a law; a transcript of the divine law upon the human soul; God's law in man's soul; the presence of God in the soul, always judging and warning in respect to acts. (So Coleridge.)

All these different statements have a partial truth, presenting different aspects of what is included in the general term. Conscience is better viewed, not as a special faculty, but as that combination of powers by which we judge and feel in respect to moral right and wrong. It embraces operations of the mind in view of what has moral quality, which are partly of the intellect and partly of the feelings. Conscience as a power cannot be brought exclusively under either: it is combined of the mind's operations both in respect to feeling, and to judging of and in respect to moral right and wrong. The term Conscience no more designates a special faculty than the term Religion does.[1] Under religion we comprise all the mind's operations in respect to God; under conscience are comprised all the mind's operations of judging and feeling in view of rectitude.

The elements that belong to it, or the different points in its action, are the following:

1. It discriminates: discerns right and wrong in actions, states, etc.; has a knowledge of moral right and wrong as ultimate. This may be called the intellectual part of conscience.

2. It feels: (*a*.) it has the feeling of obligation, of what Kant calls "the categorical imperative:" when we know the right, we feel that we ought to do it. This is an urgent feeling. (*b*.) Besides the above, there is another emotion: a susceptibility to right and wrong, a capacity of being moved by the excellency of the one and the heinousness of the other.

3. It approves or disapproves: judges morally about the right

[1] Or than the Æsthetic sense.

and wrong in states, conditions of things, conduct, etc., on the ground of conformity to right, or not.

4. It passes sentence: has a sense of the merit of those who do right and of the demerit of those who do wrong. The sense and judgment as to what is due in respect to reward and punishment belong eminently to conscience.[1]

Some definitions: Aquinas, Summa Theol. i. 79, 13, gives—"actualis applicatio scientiæ ad ea quæ agimus." Butler, Serm. i.: "This principle in man by which he approves or disapproves his heart, temper, or actions is *conscience;* for this is the strict sense of the word, though sometimes it is used so as to take in more." Locke: "It is our own judgment of the rectitude or purity of our own actions." Stewart, Act. and Mor. Powers: Conscience "refers to our own conduct alone," while "the moral faculty" includes also judgments on others. But the unity of conscience is not in its being one faculty or in its performing one function, but in its having one *object*, its relation to one idea, viz., *Right.*

Having made these general statements as to the nature and functions of conscience, we proceed to *some special points which arise under it.*

(*A.*) The Scripture Testimony. The Scripture presupposes the existence of conscience in men. In the Old Testament the word conscience is not found; we have the word, "heart," in which moral judgments and feelings are implied throughout. (There are in the Septuagint one or two instances in which the Greek word corresponding to conscience is used. See Die Lehre vom Gewissen nach d. Schrift. Güder in *Stud. u. Krit.*, 1857.) In the New Testament the nature and functions of conscience are developed most distinctly by Paul, who has been called "the Apostle of Conscience."

1. Conscience referred to in the Old Testament: Jer. xx. 9; 1 Kings ii. 44; Prov. vii. 22; Jer. xvii. 1; Job xxvii. 6; 1 Sam. xxiv. 10; Ps. xxxii.; xxxviii.; li.; 1 Kings viii. 38; Hos. vii. 2.

[1] Another statement: Conscience acts: (*a.*) before we act,—as monitor; (*b.*) when and while we act,—as motive; (*c.*) after we act,—as judge, and also, in part as dispenser of the award, as executioner of the doom.

2. Nature of conscience as recognized in the New Testament: Rom. ii. 15; 2 Cor. i. 12; iv. 2; v. 11; 1 Cor. viii. 7, 10, 12; x. 25, 27–29; 1 Pet. ii. 19 (conscience as determined by the previous knowledge of God). These are the chief passages showing how conscience is regarded as to its essence and principal functions.

3. The relation of conscience to the faith and life: 1 Tim. i. 5; i. 19; iii. 9; 1 Pet. iii. 16.

4. The good conscience: Heb. xiii. 18; 2 Cor. i. 12; Acts xxiii. 1; xxiv. 16; Rom. xiii. 5; 2 Cor. iv. 2; v. 11.

5. The weak conscience: 1 Cor. viii. 7, 12.

6. The evil and perverted conscience: 1 Tim. iv. 2; Tit. i. 15; Heb. ix. 14; x. 22.

The sum: The Scriptures set forth that the mind has a native capacity of judgment and feeling in respect to moral subjects; but that this may be enfeebled, darkened, and even perverted, so as to become a source of delusion and a snare.

(*B.*) The existence of conscience proves a moral law above us, for which we were made. It testifies constantly to the grand fact that man is a moral being, made for moral ends. It leads logically to the position that there is a moral Lawgiver: a moral order of the world directed by a moral Governor. This law is universal: Rom. ii. 14. There is not merely an outward law; it is also written on the heart: Rom. ii. 15. Cicero: "Nor does it speak one language at Rome and another at Athens..... but to all nations and ages, deriving its authority from the common sovereign of the universe, and carrying home its sanctions to every heart." Butler, Serm. ii., upon Hum. Nat. (*ad sensum*): "Superintendence is a constituent part of the faculty of conscience, and to govern belongs to it, from the constitution of man."

(*C.*) The existence of conscience thus testifying to a moral law, implies an essential distinction between right and wrong, an immutable morality. It acts in view of Right, which is a simple idea, no more to be resolved than the idea of Beauty.

From this judgment we cannot get rid. We can no more help pronouncing this and that action to be wrong or right, than we can help judging this or that proportion to be true or false. We not only say pleasant or painful, but we are also compelled to say right or wrong: to put one of these words on each of our acts. We may give good or bad reasons for the judgment, but we sum up by saying, right or wrong. The conscience may be perverted so as to say evil is good, and good is evil; but still it says evil *is good*, etc., *i. e.*, it pronounces a moral judgment. And in that judgment each one for himself rests, as final and sufficient. In individuals there are differences in details[1] about particular courses of conduct, but still a moral judgment and decision is applied throughout.

That there is this independent moral judgment, is proved by several considerations.

1. By our constant consciousness. We are invariably pronouncing this judgment on ourselves: it is a concomitant of all our own acts.[2] It is a judgment we are ever passing on others. And its power is seen in the simple fact that it binds us to a law from which we would, as sinners, gladly escape.

2. By the *consensus gentium*, as shown in laws, customs, language, proverbs, literature. The noblest dramatic literature especially runs back into this conviction. The State is a moral body, existing for moral ends: this is the idea of it, though in actual practice, it is often otherwise.

3. By the early and instinctive moral judgments of children. They can be led to a moral judgment as quickly as any. And then in proportion to the progress of men in knowledge and culture, they judge more and more according to the simple standard and rule of right.

4. (though this may be a branch of the 1st): Even when reasoning from expediency, from prudential considerations, we cannot stop with the affirmation "This is expedient": we pass

---

[1] Though differing in details, conscience is generally true in the main principles, *e. g.*, Honesty is always right; Ingratitude is always wrong; Selfishness is sinful; Benevolence is virtuous.

[2] "A guardian angel or an avenging fiend" (Coleridge).

to the further affirmation, "It is right" and therefore binding. And it is an inexplicable fact that after saying anything is for the highest good, we should also say that it is right, if right be not the ultimate ground of decision, the consideration which is simple, ultimate, supreme. This fact no utilitarian scheme can master.

(*D.*) This perception (and feeling) of right and wrong is immediately attended by a feeling of obligation to do the right and refuse the wrong. We are obligated morally to do only what is morally right. No force can morally bind us which is not resolvable into right. This feeling of obligation is definite and peculiar. It is expressed by the word "ought." It enforces a simple and imperative obligation. In calling it the "categorical imperative," Kant frees morals from the happiness scheme. Right and Ought are inseparable: we need no intervening terms. From a simple regard to happiness or the general good we cannot derive this sense of "oughtness"; we can only derive impulse, tendency, desire, not a specific *moral* obligation. On the utilitarian view, the highest idea of obligation is that man should perform that which is for the highest good; but that gives only desirableness. The statement eliminates from the word "ought" its whole force. *Why* "should" I, or "ought" I to seek the highest good? As a means of happiness, it is desirable, but why is it morally binding on me? The only possible answer is, because I feel that it is right and therefore I ought to do it. This *ought* is native to the soul; it comes up before we have any conception or idea of the highest good; children feel its force against all that seems to be pleasant or desirable.

(*E.*) In the operations of conscience there is always involved moral approval or disapproval. We need not dwell on this further than to say that these are emotions arising in view of rectitude or its opposite. *Moral* approval and disapproval cannot be derived from the idea of happiness or good: all we can get from that source is, pleasure and displeasure, satisfaction and discontent.

(*F.*) Of merit and demerit. There is further involved in conscience a special judgment in view of personal accountability. It differs from approval and disapproval, as having special (though perhaps not always exclusive) regard to personal acts and liabilities, or responsibility. The merit of persons is their desert of good on account of right moral action; demerit, their desert of evil, suffering, personal punishment, on account of transgression. This judgment is made with respect to each individual as under the law, as an accountable moral agent; and it is strictly according to each one's personal character, on the basis of personal acts. Hence the judgment of merit or demerit cannot be pronounced until there has been personal choice or action. On the utility scheme, we cannot distinguish between regret and remorse, between the natural consequences and the deserved punishment of transgression.

(*G.*) The domain or sphere of conscience. To what does conscience apply, or what is under its supervision? As a general answer to this question we say: Everything in which there is moral quality; everything in which right and wrong can be found or are exemplified. Subjectively considered, as my conscience, it has special .respect to my moral states and acts. In its fullest exercise, in the use of all its functions—including the ascription of merit and demerit—it is applied only to individual, personal character; but in some of its activities it has a wider scope than personal actions. Conscience is not merely *my* conscience.

1. We pass moral judgments about laws and institutions, etc. Wherever right and wrong can be applied, conscience has its sphere. We say, such a law or enactment is right or wrong: it is conformed or not conformed to a standard. What do we mean by that judgment? Do we refer merely to the motives and character of the men who passed the law? No; for we also say, they were right or wrong in passing it. We refer to its abstract nature, as conformed to the moral standard. The law is not a person or the act of a person. We speak of the divine law as

holy, just, and good, although it is not a person. So the State is a moral body, and we judge its officers not merely as individuals, but as officers of the law. We may pass a moral judgment on a treatise on Ethics, although it has no merit or demerit in a personal sense. Either it is true that conscience has a wider scope than personal acts, or we must say that the judgments about right and wrong do not belong to the conscience, but to the intellect. We should then make conscience to be an emotion.

2. We pass judgments not merely upon laws, institutions, books, etc., but upon dispositions and tendencies, when not acting or antecedent to action. A man asleep has a moral character. Dispositions which underlie action, native tendencies of the mind, are estimated and passed upon from the moral point of view. We do not indeed make such judgments in an individual, personal sense; but we make them in a general and truly moral sense. That we do this is evident from common forms of speech, and from our own consciousness. I cannot help believing and saying that an inordinate self-love, viewed as a disposition, is wrong, and needs to be extirpated by divine grace.

If it be asked whether the law is worthy of punishment, and the disposition, of everlasting condemnation, the answer is, No,[1] but none the less is the law worthy of moral disapprobation, and the disposition also; and we are bound, as moral beings, to oppose the one and eradicate the other. It may be still asked, does not a moral decision always imply desert of reward or punishment? It always does when, and only when, it has respect to the acts of moral beings; it always does when applied in the way of strict personal accountability. *But there is here a new element,* warranting another judgment, viz., that of personal desert.

3. Conscience, in judging of the individual in his personal liabilities and relations, judges of his outward acts as they are presumed to contain personal intentions or moral dispositions.

---

[1] The theological statement that an evil disposition, a native depravity, causes *liability* to eternal condemnation comes up in its proper place.

Conscience does not blame the acts of the body as such, nor executive acts of the will as such, but blames the person for being influenced by wrong emotions in what he does. The executive acts of the will and the external acts of the man are viewed in relation to the right and wrong motive; but even the motive is not what is blamed, but the person for being influenced by the motive.

4. The opposite view is that conscience has only to do with exercises, choices; and has no other function than the personal one. This rests on two assumptions. (*a.*) That conscience designates a special faculty, whose sole province is to decide upon personal acts, instead of designating all the operations of the mind in judging and feeling about what is right and wrong. One difficulty about this view is, that it is contrary to experience. What we know is, that the mind judges and feels in respect to right and wrong, and this *is* conscience. Another difficulty is that this view is logically obliged to confine conscience to the intellect or to the feelings, while at the same time it is obliged to concede that it is both a judgment and a feeling. Then again, if conscience be a special faculty, how can we account for the variety of moral decisions? The only way of bringing unity into our treatment of conscience (and of ethics) is to subsume it all under the general idea of right and wrong. (*b.*) The other assumption is the atomistic view of morals: that which confines, by force of definition, all that is moral, to acts, and ultimately to acts of the will. Of this we shall have to speak later. Here we need only say, that it appears to rest upon a confounding of two entirely distinguishable ideas, viz., those of right (or wrong) and of personal desert. In fact *right* is by some actually *defined* as that which deserves good; and wrong, as that which deserves punishment: a defining by the consequences, and not by the character, of acts.

(*H.*) Is conscience always right in its decisions? Generally, and not universally. It is more generally right than man is in his acts, and perhaps more generally right than even reason is in pronouncing its judgments; but it is not more universally right than man or reason is. If we assert that conscience is universally right, we must also assert that each man having a conscience is universally right. Also, so far as conscience involves reason, that reason is universally right. If man is not infallible, conscience is not. If reason may be darkened, conscience may be. If man having reason may believe what is false to be true, he may also, having conscience, believe what is wrong to be right.

This further appears:

1. From the diversity in moral decisions. Men agree that what is right should be done: but when we come to specific points, differences commence. This is so evident that those who advocate the universal correctness of conscience say, that in these cases it is the intellect that is wrong, and not the conscience: the data are wrong and not the conscience. But this does not help the matter. The decision is a wrong one, and it is the decision of conscience. If it is not, what is a decision of conscience, and what is the sphere of conscience? · This attempt to evade the difficulty rests on the assumption that conscience is an ideal dictator of right and wrong, something apart from or above the man. Whereas we have maintained that it is neither a faculty pronouncing dictatorially on all actions, nor a faculty giving all men right principles of action, but that it is simply the mind judging and feeling in view of right and wrong: it includes all the operations of the mind in view of what has moral quality, except the desires, the choices, and determinations of the will.

2. Scripture speaks of the perverted, seared, evil conscience, the conscience that needs to be purified, etc.

3. Conscience, as much as any power or tendency of the mind, may and ought to be cultivated, educated, enlightened; and if this be so, it is presupposed that unless it is cultivated, it is not universally right. Kant makes conscience to be purely native.[1] He says: "It is not to be attained; it is not a duty to get a conscience, but every man has it by nature;" he describes it as "the consciousness of an internal judgment-seat in man." But

[1] *Rel. innerhalb*, etc., p. 287.

this is a rationalistic position, and is against Scripture. Conscience, in its primitive function, assures us that right is ultimate, and is essentially different from wrong. This is its most distinct, unmistakable, and well-nigh universal utterance; but it does not tell us what the right is, in all its particulars and relations. Conscience, in short, is not of itself alone autonomic, a self-law above all law, or rather dictating all law. This is the ethical against the theological position: it is the rationalistic against the supernaturalistic. Here is the turning-point in many discussions: in discussions, *e. g.*, as to the Scriptures going against conscience; the general abstract statement of the binding nature of the distinction between right and wrong is mixed up with the question as to what is right or wrong in particular cases. Conscience tells us that there is an essential difference between right and wrong, and does this so certainly that if the word of God should seem to reveal what we absolutely knew to be wrong, we could not receive it and be consistent. But the discussion, so far as Scripture is concerned, does not turn upon that point, but rather upon particular cases. It used, *e. g.*, to be frequently said: My conscience tells me that the Scripture, in allowing the continuance of the relation of master and slave, permits what is wrong, and I cannot receive it as the Word of God. A man is apt to say, in such a case, "My conscience tells me so." Now conscience, as a native power, asserts the general distinction between right and wrong, and the necessity of observing it, but does not, as a native faculty, decide upon particular cases. We do not believe that conscience says *directly*, in regard to any external relation, that it is necessarily right or wrong. The assertion must come back to the internal state. Yet we remark:

4. Conscience, when enlightened and educated, is right; and, as is said above, it is generally right in respect to general principles, though not so generally as to details and modes of carrying the principles out.[1] The ideal conscience is of course theoretically always right.

[1] Yet these are the cases in which those who mistake their wills for their consciences always insist most strongly.

NOTE I.—As to the practical question whether an individual ought always to follow his conscience.

The well-known Scholastic maxim is, that a wrong conscience obligates "per accidens et secundum quid," *i. e.*, as to the matter in hand.

Several quite distinct points are involved in the question. (1) Suppose a man so blinded by sin as to say, "Evil, be thou my good," and to believe that it is so, and he appeals to me who knew it to be wrong: shall I encourage him in following his conscience? Assuredly not. Can I tell him he will be without blame? I know that he will be blameworthy, if he is acting on a wrong basis and from wrong motives. So far then as the judgment is influenced by any wrong motive or belief, so far it is a wrong one, and ought not to be followed, but corrected. (2) This is confirmed by experience. Paul says, "I verily thought with myself, that I ought to do many things contrary to the name of Jesus of Nazareth." But when renewed, he confessed his sin and guilt in doing that which at the time he had allowed. This is the case more or less with all sinners and all sin, and in all Christian experience. Before conversion we approve what we afterwards condemn, and we condemn ourselves not for doing it now, but for having done it then, and this although at the time we may have felt justified. (3) Yet there are undoubtedly some cases in which, while we condemn the act, we acquit the person of intentional blame: he may have meant to do right, but lacked the opportunity and the knowledge. Yet even here we must still condemn the act: it was wrong. (4) There is another case under this same head —in the matter of faith. It is said, "It is no matter what one believes, if he is sincere." This is the general practical form of the matter: *i. e.*, the question comes up in reference to faith rather than to moral duties. A person is *sincere* in disbelieving, and we are asked to say that he is as well off before God and man, as a believer. This demands consideration later under the title of Faith, but here we may briefly say: (*a*) Sincerity can never be taken to be the highest moral state. Sincerity is not the chief of virtues, as seems to be assumed. It is nothing more nor less than my personal conviction that I am right in a given course of action or article of faith. But wholly above the question of my personal conviction, is the question whether my principles be really right and my faith correct. Man's great duty is not to be sincere, but to be right: to be so, and not to believe that he is so. (*b.*) Nowhere would this plea be admitted, except in religion or by religious indifferentism. It is not admitted in the state, for holding a wrong opinion in politics: if communism, *e. g.*, be carried out by men who sincerely hold it, the state comes in and checks them. If the Mormons are sincere in their polygamy, we say so much the worse for them and their society. (*c.*) It is a fact that men may be sincere from wrong motives as well as from right ones; so that the sincerity cannot be pleaded as sufficient. (*d.*) It is a fact—a terrible fact —that men may be given over to believe a lie, and be conscientious in iniquity. But this is no evidence of their being blameless, but of the fearful power of iniquity in them, and of their need of being duly enlightened. (*e.*) The position that it is no matter what a man believes if he is sincere, is inconsistent with the ground that the Bible is the standard and rule of duty and life. In its logical results, the position makes conscience and reason supreme, and religion subordinate. It puts ethics above theology, instead of inquiring for the harmony between them.

NOTE II.—The possession of conscience—meaning by it what has been described and defined—does not confer personal righteousness. It is an essential condition of personal righteousness, but not the righteousness itself. Conscience is man judging and feeling about what is right and wrong; but personal character is in the affections and will. Some Unitarians maintain that a person cannot be wholly depraved, because there remains a conscience, a sensibility to right and wrong. But this may only show the greatness of the depravity, having conscience and yet ever disobeying it.

§ 10. *Of Man's highest Spiritual Capacities.*

The outline of treatment [not carried out]: Man is made for God, with an implanted tendency to the eternal and infinite.

"Thou hast set eternity in his heart." This is not a faculty: but Reason, Conscience, Affections and Will, in relation to their goal. There is an intuition of the unseen, a feeling of dependence, a sense of a law above time and the world, the awe of Judgment, the longing for immortality.

REMARK, in the way of transition to Chapter II.
We have thus far gone over the main points under the general head in Chapter I. What is man as a moral being? viz., (1) Man in his most general relations; (2) Man in his specific traits; (3) Man in his native tendencies, in respect to these relations; (4) Man in his conscience, or his judgments and feelings in view of right and wrong. Now, here as (5) might be introduced the doctrine respecting the Will;—but that is so involved with the inquiry respecting the nature and obligation of the law of God, that we shall first discuss this (which will include the question of the nature of virtue) and then in Chapter III., viz., Man's Relations to the Law, take up the question of the Will.

CHAPTER II.

WHAT IS THE LAW OF GOD: WHAT DOES IT REQUIRE?

The "Law of God"[1] is used in two different senses: sometimes for the positive, written law, given to his people: as such it includes the ceremonial laws, the precepts and prohibitions of the old dispensation; again, it is used to signify the moral law, that which God has made and given for the moral government of his creatures, summarily comprehended in the two precepts of love to God and to our neighbor. The Mosaic law was given for God's people then: from Christ the law is given in a more perfect form. It is also revealed in conscience, the natural law. This law, as recorded in the Scriptures, is the norm, the rule for human life and conduct, prescribing what man, as a moral being, ought to be and to do. It rests in the idea of rectitude; this is presupposed in it, not made by it. It commands what is right and holy. It is commanded because it is holy, and not holy be-

[1] One of the best treatises on the Law is Dr. John Smalley's sermon: "Perfection and Usefulness of the Divine Law," in Brown's Theol. Tracts, vol. iii.

cause it is commanded. The majesty of the law is in this, its inherent rectitude. The law of God may then be defined as rectitude embodied in the form of command (both in precept and prohibition).[1] In the form of example, the law is given us perfectly in the life of Christ. Lactantius calls Him the living and present law. Augustine says, "The law of the Lord is He who came to fulfil, not to break the law." 1 Pet. ii. 21-25.

§ 1. *Some general Statements as to the Characteristics of the Law.*

1. The law is holy, essentially good and perfect. It is such as being the expression of the perfect will of a holy and wise Sovereign. It is the expression of the inherent rectitude of God, enforcing a like rectitude on the part of his creatures. "Be ye holy for I am holy:" there is no utterance which gives us a higher conception of the dignity of human nature than that.

2. This law is enforced, not merely by its own inherent rectitude, which gives it a rational power, but also by the authority of the lawgiver. It is the law of God, our Moral Governor, and as such has the force that a person has over and above an idea. The moral law of abstract ethics is moral duty. The law of the Bible is that same law, enforced by a supreme Power.

3. This law is still further enforced by its appropriate sanctions: penal evil for transgressions, and eternal life for obedience. In each case the award is eternal.

4. The law is for the highest good of each and all. It commands what can ensure—what alone can do this—the highest moral ends of the universe. It is not only the expression of rectitude and designed to maintain rectitude, but it has also in view the highest good.

5. In order to ensure the highest good, the law enjoins perfect holiness on the creature, nothing less and nothing else. Holiness is what the law enjoins, and it is that which is to be

---

[1] Müller on Sin, i. 58. Law, in the purity of its idea, is "die Darstellung der sittlichen Idee in der Form der Forderung."

the highest good of the moral universe. Some restrict the law to external legality, to the outward act, and do not extend it to the inward state. Paul sometimes does this, speaking as a Jew, and in respect to his bondage under the law; but in his Christian experience he recognizes it as spiritual: this is what marks his conviction of sin and his feeling of the need of a Saviour.

6. The holiness which the law requires of each man is his personal perfection. It is perfection to the extent, and the full extent, of man's capacities: "all the heart, all the soul, all the mind, all the strength," Matt. xxii. 37, Mark xii. 28–34. Man's natural ability [1] is to be completely expressed, his physical ability to be completely employed in fulfilling the command.

7. The law, as commanding entire holiness, is always obligatory upon all moral beings. It cannot be satisfied in any individual case with anything less than entire conformity. It is unchangeable in its obligations, and is equally binding upon all. It has not one standard for the heathen, another for the Jew, another for the Christian. It does not require of a child that he love God with the power of an angel, because he has not that capacity; but it demands of a child that he love with all his heart. Man insensible to the demands of God's law is not a man: in the most debased there are gleams of its glory.

NOTE I.—The distinction between moral law and physical. Dr. Wayland, in his Moral Science, gives a singular definition of moral law. He defines law generally as a mode of existence or order of sequence, and then moral law as an order of sequence established between the moral quality of actions and their results. But this is reversing all our moral conceptions, and confounding the province of morals with that of physics. Physical law is undoubtedly an order of sequence: the cause and effect make the law, in the sense that the same causes in the same circumstances will work in the same way. If there be an exception in this sphere, the physical law

---

[1] This is the old notion of natural ability, the reach to which our powers could extend if we would. The modern sense of power to the contrary is a new and derivative idea.

is disproved.[1] But law in morals rests upon an entirely different idea: it is that which *ought to be:* it is rectitude commanded: it is no less law, though what it commands may not be fact: it would be eternally binding, though nobody conformed to it. The moral law is not the connection between holiness and happiness. The consequence depends on the law, and not the law on the consequence.

Müller's position. God's law in relation to man is this: God has the idea of man (end of his being) and prescribes this, as law. In man's formal freedom there is the possibility of losing the end, of not realizing the idea: hence the law comes as the objective norm: man needs it in order to begin his moral life and to grow as a moral being:[2] Matt. v. 17-19, the law and the prophets must control until the end of the economy: Gen. ii. 16, 17, the law was given for the state of rectitude, and laws were needed at the beginning; but to the perfect, law (as external) ceases: 1 Tim. i. 9.—Discussion of the German view, that the *law ceases.* [Discussion is not given, only indicated.] Not so. In nature, law determines things absolutely: in man, the law is distinguished from his powers; he is conscious of it as *demand*, and must ever be, so that it cannot "cease." The "end" of the law is to bring man from the undeveloped and indefinite relation to good, to the full reception.

NOTE II.—As to the order of discussion. The following are the chief points: (1) Moral rectitude—its abstract nature; (2) The common principle of all holiness, in beings; (3) Formal statements of the same; (4) Happiness; (5) Love.

§ 2. *The two fundamental Objects or Ends of the Law of God.*

These are: (1) In respect to the whole system of things. The object of the law is to bring out, to realize, the most perfect state and order of God's intelligent moral universe. This is the *highest good:* the law has respect to the highest good of the whole. The ideal end of the law is to make holiness supreme, to secure gen-

---

[1] We hold a miracle to be the effect of the divine will, interposing, and of course that does not disprove physical law.
[2] [Dr. Bushnell's speculations give a different view. The author, without discussing these, intimates his entire dissent from them.]

eral justice or the triumph of holiness, which is the highest good. (2) In relation to each individual moral being. Its object is, to prescribe that rule, by following which, such a state of the universe may be brought about. This is the highest good of the individual, viz., that state of mind, by which he is adapted to produce, in his measure and degree, the highest good of the universe. This is personal holiness, this is virtue. The law commands each individual to have those motives and that state of heart, by which, if every one possessed them, the great end of the universe would be promoted to the highest degree.

We have thus to inquire: I. What is the highest good of the universe? II. What is the highest good of the individual? What is holiness? What is virtue?

CHAPTER III.

THE HIGHEST GOOD.

We have here the question of the *Summum Bonum*, the vexed question, yet fundamental in morals.

The highest good is taken in a two-fold sense: it is taken both objectively and subjectively.

I.—Taken *objectively*. The highest good, thus taken, can only be found in that state of things which is the last and highest result of the divine providence, of God's government of the world. The whole system of things, carried to its highest degree of perfection, is the highest good, objectively considered. It is the final end, the result, the ultimate end of the whole moral government of God: it is the general good, taken comprehensively.

And that consists, as we have seen (End of God in Creation), in God's revelation or manifestation of himself to his creatures, in the communication of himself to them, so that they find their joy, their good in Him. It is the union between God and his creatures carried out so that all things human are conformed to the divine plan and purpose.

The law of God has this for its *ideal* end; obedience to that law would bring about this result; disobedience interferes with it; God—man having disobeyed—interposes on his part to bring about the same result in another way than that of obedience, viz., by an atonement, but still the general object of the atonement is the same as that of the law, to produce holiness. The law of God is sometimes spoken of as if all its bearing was in respect to individuals. Those who define conscience as a faculty which simply individualizes, which has respect only to individual choices and acts, define the law also as having respect simply to the choices and acts of individuals, and ultimately as having respect simply to acts of the will (in the narrower sense), volitions, which volitions are accompanied with full power to the contrary (in the modern sense), and which are deliberate in view of all the consequences. But this gives us conscience as having to do only with the faculties concerned in choice (as volition), and the law of God as dealing only with the same. Thus original sin is excluded; there is no sin except in such choices; there is nothing save these that comes under God's law. The bearing of such a view upon the atonement is evident. It is granted that Christ suffered in our stead, but not under the law; because the law has to do only with personal acts, and these are not transferable; and if that be so, Christ could not suffer under the law for us, and so the atonement is removed from the law entirely.

[What else the author meant to give under this head appears to have been combined with the final statements of the next chapter.]

II.—The highest good taken *subjectively*. The consideration of this leads us to the *general statements* as to the *nature of virtue*. What is the sense of the inquiry as to "the nature of true virtue"?

1. Virtue is here used in a large sense, as the equivalent of holiness, and so as to include even the virtue of the divine mind.[1] This however is a bad form of speech; because the word virtue

---

[1] Aristotle denies moral virtue to God; *i. e.*, God does not, like man, act from a sense of duty; there is no struggle in Him to an end not yet realized; God's perfection *begins* where man's ends.

has acquired such a secondary meaning that we can hardly speak of God's virtue. In common speech the term is used for the separate virtues, but the inquiry here is not for these, in their limited relationships, but for virtue generally.

2. The inquiry is not, as it is sometimes said to be, an inquiry as to the abstract rectitude of our acts. It is not an inquiry whether there be such an idea as Right, and whether that idea be ultimate. It is assumed in the inquiry, that what is virtuous is right, that virtue is a proper moral state, that it is conformable to the idea of rectitude, that we apply that idea to it. Some, when anything more is stated as to the nature of virtue than that it is rectitude or the love of rectitude, are apt to say that a utilitarian view is presented: but this is a confounding of two inquiries. The questions: What is virtue? and, What is right abstractly viewed? are very different. The one inquiry is, Is there an idea of right, ultimate, independent of all other ideas? The other is, What is that in our state and actions which *is* right?

3. Hence, the inquiry is not as to all that is right, as to all that comes under that idea; but as to what that is in a moral being which is truly conformed to the Moral, what state of the affections in such a being it is which is virtuous.

4. There are a great many minor separate virtues: the inquiry is not whether these are right—that is presupposed; but the inquiry is as to the common subjective principle of what is virtuous and holy. In other words, Can all that is holy be reduced to some one common principle, and can that principle be stated? That principle makes the nature or essence, or as some say the foundation, of virtue. The inquiry is, What is that state of mind or heart which is common to and expressed in all virtuous affections and acts? We are grateful; we love parents and friends; we are just, honest; we seek the welfare of our fellows: is there any common principle in all these acts which makes them virtuous, and which alone makes them to be virtuous?

5. It is still further an inquiry after *true* virtue and holiness How can we distinguish the true from the counterfeit? Is all that men call virtuous really so? Does it come from that which is supremely virtuous? President Edwards was led to write his

essay on The Nature of True Virtue by that which came up in his treatise on Sin; because the Arminians held that human nature could not be wholly depraved, inasmuch as it retains more or less of what are commonly deemed virtues: honesty, kindness, temperance, etc. His object is to show, that although there may be virtues in a minor sphere, yet they are not true virtues, because they do not contain the essence of true virtue.

The *Theories* on this subject may be divided into two classes·
(1) Those that measure and define virtue by some formal and external standard, that describe virtue in some other way than by giving a common internal quality which is found in all virtuous acts. A yard stick can measure cotton, woolen, or silk, but it does not tell us anything about the cotton itself or the silk itself. No more from the formal theories of virtue can we get anything as to its distinctive nature. (2) Those that attempt to define virtue by something contained in the virtuous acts themselves; by some quality or qualities of the acts themselves. These are the only theories that attempt to grasp or answer the inquiry. This class is subdivided into (*a.*) *The Happiness Theories* and (*b.*) *The Theories which put Virtue in Holy Love.*

CHAPTER IV.

THE FORMAL THEORIES OF THE NATURE OF VIRTUE.

§ 1. *Virtue is Acting according to the Fitness of Things.*

This is a strictly formal definition. It was employed by many of the Independent Moralists of England, Cudworth, etc. It has its value in contrast with the theory of mere Utility, which is, acting for present good or happiness. A virtuous man will act according to the fitness of things, but that does not tell us in what his virtue consists. We have here a scaffolding description of virtue. Animals, even machines, act according to the fitness of things, as a horse, a locomotive, going safely on the right track. Many of our own actions accord with this definition which are not virtuous. If, to relieve this difficulty, it be said, Virtue is a voluntary acting according to the moral fitness of things, then in the word *moral* the whole question appears and we have to ask, what is the moral fitness of things?

§ 2. *Virtue is that which promotes the great End of our Being.*

Virtue undoubtedly does this, but the defect of the answer is, that it does not answer two other questions: (1) What is the end of our being? (2) What is that in virtue which promotes or produces the end of our being?

§ 3. *Virtue is Acting in conformity with the Relations of Things.*

This is Dr. Wayland's view in part. There are certain relations, he says, in view of which there arises a feeling of moral obligation: in view of the relation, *e. g.*, of parent and child, there is a feeling of obligation to have certain emotions, to do certain things; in view of the relation of the creature to God, arises a feeling of obligation to love and obedience. An act performed in obedience to the obligation to man, is virtuous,—to the obligation to God, is pious.[1]

1. If a man feel as he ought and act as he ought, he is undoubtedly virtuous, and all his acts take in and include his virtuous acts. Everything finite is in relations, and if we act in accordance with all of them, we are virtuous.

2. But there are some relations which a man may act in conformity with, without being virtuous, *e. g.*, the physical relations. The definition is too wide.

3. Then the conformity cannot be to all relations, but to some particular kind of relations. Therefore there is a question behind that of relations: What particular relations are those which call out the sense of moral obligation? Here is the insufficiency of the theory. In view of certain relations we have the feeling of moral obligation; but what peculiarity is there in these relations which gives rise to this feeling in us, when we

---

[1] Moral Science, pp. 44-48, 75-77. Cudworth and Clarke hold that virtue is to act conformably to relations. The "fitness of things" theory runs into this. They supposed the general power of judging of truth and falsehood to be the power which perceives these relations: Wayland, with the later Scottish School, supposes a distinct power, viz., Conscience.

do not have it in other relations? To get at the moral element, we must go behind the mere statement that we are under certain relations.

4. Even supposing that we have ascertained what these relations are, there remains another inquiry: Virtue, we are told, is acting in conformity with, or feeling as we ought in view of, certain relations; what then are those motives and feelings which are such "as we ought" to have, such as constitute the true conformity with the relations?

§ 4. Is it any better explanation of virtue to say that it is *Acting in Conformity to the Will of God*, or that the will of God constitutes virtue? There are four senses in which this theory is held:

(1) God is our superior, our creator, and as such He has a perfect right to us and to our services. His will is our highest law. Our relation to God as creatures draws this after it, and this is the ultimate thing in morals: it would settle, *e. g.*, the questions raised as to the course of the Israelites with the Canaanites, etc. Virtue is obedience to the will of a sovereign. (2) God's revealed will is law to us: and acting according to that is virtue. (3) God's will creates, makes virtue and its opposite. Virtue exists by an act of the divine will as much as the world does, and so that God could make it different if He chose. (4) God's will is taken for the expression of his whole nature, so that what He declares or reveals, the expression of his will, is the expression of what seems to Him wise and good. (This fourth view is closely connected with the second, though it is well to distinguish them.) And our action in conformity with that will (thus understood) is virtue.

As to the *first* position: We grant that such is our relation to God, our natural relation, that it does lay a foundation for obedience. Moral obligation is inseparably connected with our relation to God. This is indisputable. Still the mere perception of power, even of omnipotence, the mere relation of authority, does not constitute the moral relation which exists between us and God. *God being what He is*, it is our duty to obey Him.

But suppose an omnipotent being who is malevolent, would it be virtue to obey him? The very supposition shocks the mind: but that only shows that we connect with the idea of God's power his other attributes. Without these we could not feel moral obligation. Mere omnipotence may control us in a physical sense, and may constrain us to the performance of certain acts, but it can never call forth a moral response. That can be evoked only by what is moral.

As to the *second* position: It is indisputable that God's revealed will *is* law to us. If God commands me to do anything, I am bound to do it. God's revealed will is the *rule* of action: wherever it is revealed, there it is binding. But this does not reach the inquiry as to the nature of virtue, for two reasons: (1) God's revealed will commands us to be holy, to be virtuous. That is a part of the revealed will itself, it is what the commandment has respect to. If we obey, of course we are virtuous, but it is not the command which makes the virtue. The inquiry still remains, What is that holiness which is thus commanded? (2) And why do we yield such unhesitating assent? It is only from our conviction that God's revealed will must be holy and altogether right. Take, for example, the instance of the Israelites commanded to destroy the Canaanites. They were bound to obey, although they might not see all the reasons for the justice of the command. Why were they bound to obey? Because God commanded. But was it because God commanded as a sovereign, or as a holy sovereign? It was because of their conviction that He could not command what was not holy. (3) This second position really means: God's revealed will is a perfect expression of a perfect will. God gives a law: in doing this, (*a.*) He appeals to our moral nature, the sense of right and duty in us. This is before the command, and necessary to its binding force. And (*b.*) We feel that He knows best in all cases where He gives a positive command. It does not follow, that if we do not see the reason, or the full reason, of a command, we are not bound to obey. But in order to feel the obligation, we must have the conviction that the command *is* right. If we have not this, what is our obedience worth?

As to the *third* position: God creates virtue and vice, by the act of his will, as such,—we do not believe that any one can hold this. Could God make benevolence to be sinful, and hatred to be right? If any one should pretend to a revelation which contained such things, we should instinctively reject it. Still further, when carried out, this theory must deny that God has any essential holiness. There must have been a time when He was not holy. He made holiness by an act of will, and then He became holy.

When we say that it is the essential holiness of God that makes virtue, some object that we are putting something *behind* God; but this is not the fact; we are only putting something *in* God. We do not say that virtue was *before* God. Before has no sense here. But we say, holiness is as eternal as God, and necessary to the very conception of His nature. God, if He were not holy from the beginning, would not be God, any more than if He were not omniscient.

It is further said that God has created us, our minds and moral natures, our perception of virtue and feeling of obligation, and in this sense God is the author of virtue, in this sense virtue is dependent on the will of God. This is undoubtedly true. But in giving us such a feeling in regard to virtue, such perceptions of right, and appealing to these always as ultimate; in addressing to us his commands and making us feel the value of virtue for its own sake; in making us so that we can think of *virtue* and *right* without thinking of his commands; in all this, He shows that the independence of virtue is recognized by Him. He created us capable of perceiving virtue, but that does not include the position that He created virtue. He made us capable of perceiving mathematical truth, but He did not make the truth that the three angles of a triangle are equal to two right angles: that truth is eternal.

As to the *fourth* position: This may be accepted, in the sense that all truth, all relations, all ideas, ultimately inhere in the divine mind. All that *is* wise and good appears to Him to be such; all that is true and right is forever apprehended by Him as such; and if his will is taken as the expression of his whole nature, of course his will and what is right, or virtue, will coincide. Yet, after all, this is not the best form of statement in morals any more than in mathematics. Nothing is added to an axiom by saying that it is the will of God; *e. g.*, by saying, Things which are equal to the same thing are equal to one another, and this is the will of God, because all truth inheres in the divine mind. Right is the will of God, but is not the product of the will of God. In order to have an idea of right, we do not need to have an idea of it as first coming from God. It adds immense practical force to the right that it is the will of the holy God, but we do not need this consideration to have the idea of right.

And after all these statements and qualifications, allowing them their utmost weight, they do not reach to the real point of the inquiry as to the nature of virtue, which is, *not*, what is virtue conformed to? not, what is the source of virtue? but, what is the essence of virtue, or what is the common, subjective quality in all virtuous acts?

§ 5. *Kant's Theory.*

It is taken from the New Testament rule: "Do unto others as ye would that they should do unto you." It is: "Act so that the free use of thy will may consist with the freedom of everyone, according to a universal law." Fichte's is somewhat similar: "Let each restrict his freedom by the idea of the freedom of others."

This, again, is a merely formal rule for virtuous *action*, good for outward actions, but not telling us anything of the principle of virtue itself. What is that universal law, according to which we must act and use our freedom? What does it demand? What is the state of mind which it demands? This is a formula, but not a formula into which all our acts can be put, and it does not give the internal quality of the acts themselves.

§ 6. *Dr. Hickok's Theory.*

"When the man sees himself to be just what the spiritual excellency of his being demands that he should be, he has, in the contemplation of this worthiness, at once his virtue and his reward." "This worthiness is no revelation from without, but a necessary truth seen in the spirituality of his own being from within."[1]

This, again, is one of the formal theories of virtue; it gives us an account of it, but not the thing itself. What is it which spiritual excellency demands that a man should be? In spiritual excellency is virtue, is approbation, is happiness: Yes, but what *is* spiritual excellency? And what is the conformity to it which is virtue? The whole inquiry is still before us.

REMARK on all the formal theories:—The common fault of them all is that they give us a description, a general account, of virtue, but do not tell us what it is in itself. They define it by some standard or rule, but they do not give us any *principle* of it, anything inhering in it, any common quality. If a man has it, he might from these descriptions give a pretty good guess as to what was meant by it, and hence the plausibility of such theories. They give us some characteristics and conceptions of virtue, but not the concrete conception of holiness itself. Defining it thus is like defining body as that which occupies space, instead of by its inseparable qualities. It is giving an external objective measure of virtue, but not its internal, real characteristics.

But the class of theories we are next to consider, though widely differing among themselves, have the common characteristic of attempting to answer the question: What is virtue? and to do this by some supposed common, subjective quality of all that can be called virtuous.

Of these theories there are two classes: those which make HAPPINESS, in some form, objective or subjective, to be the spring and end of all virtue; and those which do not, placing it in HOLY LOVE.

[1] The Westm. Rev., Oct. 1853, says, this reads like Cudworth, but in truth is more like Dr. T. Brown's "moral approbation."

CHAPTER V.

THE HAPPINESS THEORIES.

PRELIMINARY INQUIRY: *What is happiness?* The most general notion of happiness is that of the pleasure or gratification of sentient beings, attending or consequent upon their activity. All feeling in the line of law confers happiness. It is a simple term, expressive of a fact known to all sentient beings in their measure and degree. It is found in animal life. It is found in the exercise of all our powers, whether intellectual, sensitive, affective, or voluntary. Future happiness is such pleasure or gratification expected or destined for any in the future; present happiness is the gratification now enjoyed. Happiness is contrasted with conditions of pain, suffering, want, sickness, etc., where the exercise of our powers, whether bodily or mental, is a source of suffering.

Self-love ("self-regarding affections," Bentham) is defined sometimes as the desire of happiness, the instinctive desire of that gratification which attends the exercise of all our powers: the highest happiness being found in the highest exercise of our powers on their highest objects.

Since happiness is ultimate, all we can do is to describe it. It is a simple psychological fact about the exercise of the powers of sentient beings; in the exercise of them they are happy, and happy in proportion to the degree of the exercise and the worthiness of the objects. But still, notwithstanding this difference of degree, all the exercises have a common element, viz., happiness, and this is a real good, it is the only real good, it is that which alone is sought for its own sake. The highest happiness contains the same elements as the lower forms: its *differentia* is in its objects.[1]

[1] The noblest view of such happiness, as the perfect good, is given by Aristotle: "An energy of the soul, or the powers of the soul exerted according to that virtue or excellence which mostly consummates or perfects them" (Hampden's paraphrase). Further, Nic. Eth. Bk. x. 4: "It is doubtful whether we strive for happiness for the sake of life, or for life for the sake of happiness; both are inseparable." This, from a heathen, is a much higher view of Utility (if indeed it can be considered as an Utilitarian view) than is found in some Christian writers.

Of these happiness theories, there are several distinct forms of which we will first speak separately, and then comment on, in reference to their fundamental common assumption, viz., that happiness is the only good, is the ultimate object of desire and action. The question is, Can all virtue be resolved into happiness, in some form?

There are three chief forms of the happiness scheme:

1. The selfish scheme of Paley, which makes the seeking of our own future happiness (or avoiding misery) to be virtue.

2. The objective[1] happiness scheme, making virtue to consist in a tendency to promote the general happiness, or in the love of the general happiness (happiness, not *good*). Not our own future happiness, as Paley has it, but the general happiness.

3. The subjective happiness scheme (as distinguished from the selfish scheme), or the *self-love* scheme, which is perhaps a union of the two above, the substance of which may be thus expressed: My happiness in the general happiness is the spring and sum of virtue. Logically, both the others are to be resolved into this.

There might be added:

4. A scheme which defines benevolence, as primarily a love to general happiness, and ultimately having regard to it, which has been defended as Edwardean.

5. Perhaps also the theory of President Finney: Virtue is the choice of the greatest happiness of God and the universe.

§ 1. *The Selfish Scheme. The Ethics of Paley.*

"Virtue is doing good to mankind in obedience to the will of God for the sake of everlasting happiness." According to this definition, the will of God is the rule, the good of mankind is the subject, and everlasting happiness is the motive, of human virtue. Take in connection with this Paley's statement about happiness, viz., "Pleasures differ in nothing but in continuance and in intensity," and we have a moral system about as bad as

---

[1] John Maclaurin, Philos. Inq. into Nat. of Happiness (written before 1736, first printed in 1773 in Goold's Edition, ii. 491), makes the distinction of *subjective* and *objective* thus: Happiness must have an objective cause and a subjective experience. God is the sufficient objective cause of the highest happiness to man; man is formed for God's glory, etc.

one can be,—inexcusable even in a heathen. It does not even recognize duties towards God: the doing good to mankind is all that it takes into view as the field of virtuous action.

But particularly and specifically, reduced to a proposition, the subjective motive of virtue is said to be one's own future happiness, seeking our own personal future good.

Against this lie considerations such as the following:

1. Common experience tells us that, when we do not think of our happiness, we are the happiest; *e. g.*, in relieving misery. The idea of our own happiness is an intrusion, in religion and benevolence for instance.

2. Mackintosh says: Upon this theory, unless we are thinking of our everlasting happiness, unless we have that as a direct motive before us in all that we do, we cannot be virtuous. We should be—what, then? vicious? Vice must consist in not seeking our happiness. When a man thinks only of doing good, he is sinful.

3. The theory allows no difference in the motives of sinful and holy action. Both have regard more or less to the happiness, real or supposed, of the agent. There is no rule. All men act from self-interest; all men are so far forth virtuous. All that is left is to resolve virtue into the arbitrary will of God, as Paley does.

4. Acting in view of future everlasting rewards and punishments is undoubtedly acting under a right motive, a motive which has its important place. But why are such promises and threatenings made? and to what? They are given to attract and deter, *to* virtue and *from* vice: not to make either virtue or vice. Motives *in respect to* virtue and vice do not constitute the motives of either. The consequences, not the nature of our acts are here shown.—Exhibition of the future consequences of action serves to arouse those who cannot yet feel any higher motive.

In sum, the motive of self-interest has its place in a moral system, but it is not that which makes virtue to be virtue.

§ 2. *Virtue consists in the Tendency to the greatest Happiness.*

The advocates of this scheme say that virtue and tendency to happiness are the same thing. If this be so, then two things follow: (1) Everything which promotes the general happiness is virtuous; all that is useful is virtuous, because virtue is the tendency to promote the general happiness. (2) Nothing can be declared to be virtuous until we can see or prove in some way that it promotes the general happiness.[1]

But we must deny both of these positions.

1. Not all that in any way promotes the happiness of men is virtuous. Many things are useful, are as useful as they can be, promote happiness, promote as much happiness as they can, which nobody thinks of calling virtuous. Many animals are useful: what they do tends to promote the happiness of the community. Steam engines are useful; vegetables are useful; our natural instincts, our involuntary affections, are all useful: they tend to promote happiness and the highest happiness which from their nature they can do.[2] The tendency to happiness is the same in the unintelligent and the intelligent being: this term remains the same: so that it cannot be this which makes the difference—confessed on all sides—between a virtuous act and one which has no moral character. This forces us to the conclusion than an act of man is virtuous, not because it has such and such a tendency, but—for some other reason, which reason is the object of our inquiry.

[1] Wayland discusses the question on the supposition that virtue and the tendency to happiness are different things. His opponents insist that they are the same thing: that if we want to define virtue we must say that it is the tendency to promote happiness. Christian Spect., Dec. 1835, p. 605: "The ideas (*i. e.*, of right and productiveness of happiness) are identical, or rather one is explanatory of the other." "The tendency to produce the greatest amount of happiness is what makes or constitutes a thing right." Dr. Dwight is quoted to the effect that the tendency to produce happiness is "what constitutes the value or excellency (or as Dr. D. uses the word—wrongly—the " foundation ") of virtue."

[2] Dr. Dwight says it is hardly necessary to answer this objection. But why not? He says: "A smattering philosophy knows that *voluntariness* is necessary to virtue." Here we have a new statement. It is not usefulness alone, but voluntary usefulness, which constitutes virtue. But here we must ask, if the tendency of a thing being useful does not make it happiness, how does its becoming voluntary give it a new character? My choosing a thing does not make it right or wrong; it simply brings in accountability. The statement will be reduced to this: Tendency to happiness in a being not moral, is not moral: but in a being who is moral, it is moral. This is acknowledging a difference in the *nature of the act:* it is the moral element in the nature of the act which we are inquiring for; and we must go somewhere else than to the tendency to happiness to find it.

2. If that which makes the essence of virtue be a tendency to happiness, we cannot say that anything is virtuous until we see that it has this tendency. We of course do not deny that we can see that virtuous acts have this tendency to a very great extent; but the question is, whether our judgments that such and such things are right are dependent on our thus seeing. Before I can say that it is right to speak the truth, must I see that my so doing will produce the greatest amount of happiness? Love to God will undoubtedly tend to promote the greatest happiness: but is the seeing of that necessary to the judgment that the love of God is right.[1]

3. This position confounds two things which are entirely distinct: the nature of a thing with its tendencies, the essence with the manifestation. These are everywhere else kept distinct. The tendency of sin is to misery, but misery does not tell us what sin is: it shows us what it deserves, but does not define its nature. The tendency of all matter is to gravitate, but gravitation does not describe the nature or essence of matter. That is only one of its modes of manifestation. So the tendency of all virtue may be, and doubtless is, to promote the greatest good, the highest happiness of the universe: but this very tendency is a result of its excellent nature, and does not constitute that nature. Such is the inherent excellency of a virtuous disposition that it makes him who has it most happy, that it contributes most of all to the general happiness: but this tendency to happiness does not describe the act as it is in itself. The nature and the tendencies are different. We may judge of the nature, to some extent, by the tendencies, but we cannot, without gross confusion, identify them.

[1] Dr. Wayland here is explicit and right. When Utilitarians assert that virtue is the tendency to general happiness, they say that their meaning is not, that we must see beforehand this tendency (as a distinct motive) in order to the virtue of the act: but, that upon inspecting every virtuous act, we find in it (afterwards) this tendency; i. e., the perception of such utility is not necessary to the *subjective* virtue of the act, but we must see (objectively) this tendency to such utility *before we can pronounce*, judge, any act to be virtuous. Examination of Utilitarianism, by the late John Grote, Lond. 1870. Bentham, the extreme Utilitarian: Murder is wrong "because (1) the evil to the murdered man far outweighs the pleasure reaped by the murderer," etc. "Quantity of pleasure being equal, push-pin is as good as poetry." His Deontology repudiated by Mill. See West. Rev., Jan. 1871, defending Mill.

4. This doctrine is further exposed to the difficulty which comes from the following consideration: Its advocates say that virtue is the best thing, and that virtue is tendency to happiness. Then the tendency to happiness is better than happiness itself.

It is allowed on all sides that virtue does tend to produce the highest happiness: the position here taken is that virtue cannot be resolved into a tendency to happiness.

§ 3. *Subjective Happiness* or *Self-Love Scheme.*

This is a scheme of more refined character than those which have been considered, and on that account is often misunderstood. Of the various happiness schemes, we regard this as the only consistent one. It resolves all moral action into the pleasure or happiness which is found in such action.[1] The system allows that benevolent action is the highest good, but it says the reason why any one is benevolent is for the pleasure there is in it—the happiness in it. Our highest pleasure is in loving God, and the reason why we love God is because our highest happiness is found in it. So our highest pleasure is in doing good, and this is the ultimate motive for doing good. There is happiness in obeying conscience, and the reason why we obey is the happiness which is in it. This is a very different theory from the previous one: instead of making happiness objective, and virtue a tendency to promote that happiness, it puts the virtue in the happiness itself, as subjective; yet one will hardly

[1] This scheme is most distinctly advocated by the late Dr. N. W. Taylor. He began the discussion in an essay on Regeneration in the Christian Spectator, 1835. He laid hold of the instinctive desire for happiness as the lever by which a sinner might be renewed with what is in him, and he professed to start from the position or ground of Dr. Dwight, the Utilitarian scheme, that Utility or Productiveness of Happiness is the essence of Virtue. But in the subsequent debate Dr. Taylor was led to take the view that the essence of virtue is not in the production of happiness, but in the happiness found in benevolent action. The ultimate motive in virtuous action is not a regard to one's own future happiness; it is not a regard to the highest good objectively; but it is the pleasure which one experiences in benevolent activity. That pleasure is the ultimate motive and controlling element. The difference between this scheme and Paley's can perhaps be briefly indicated by emphasis: Paley says, *My* happiness is the *object* of virtuous action: this theory, My *happiness* is the *motive* of such action.

find in the discussions a separation between this and the grosser forms of the happiness schemes.

Now in reference to this view, we grant the whole fact alleged: that our happiness is found in benevolence; but we deny the inference: that this happiness is the ultimate motive for right action, or the ultimate basis of an ethical system, and for the following reasons:

1. This theory gives us no radical distinction between right and wrong actions. The difference is simply and only a difference in the greater or less degree of the same thing, *i. e.*, of happiness. In sin there is some happiness, in virtue there is more. In the wicked and the good man there is the same ultimate motive, love of happiness.

We grant the existence of this motive in all men: it is constitutional: but we say, it is not this self-love which gives the difference in our actions as right and wrong. And if it be made the ultimate thing in ethics, the ethics is not founded on any distinct ultimate conception, whereby it is distinguished from any other branch of science. The difference of right and wrong is not explained by this theory, and if anything else is brought in to explain it, then that something else will be the foundation of ethics.

2. Closely connected with the above is another objection to the theory, viz., that it confounds a purely psychological phenomenon with a proper ethical fact or theory. It is a fact that we are happy in, that there is a gratification attending, the exercise of our moral powers: but this fact is not confined to our moral powers. We are happy in the exercise of *all* our faculties. We are happy in reasoning, in eating, in talking, in seeing, in doing anything. A necessary condition of the exercise of all our powers is that there should be pleasure in doing it. Now if this pleasure, this happiness, is what constitutes morality, then there is morality in all our acts in their natural operations. If a distinction is made, and it is said that only certain kinds of such gratification are moral, then we say, what are these kinds, what distinguishes them from others? and the very thing that distinguishes them from others will be the moral ele-

ment. That is, happiness is common both to the instinctive and the moral action of our powers: and therefore, being common to them, it cannot be the thing which distinguishes them; happiness is common both to the virtuous and vicious exercise of our powers, and therefore it cannot be the thing which distinguishes virtue from vice. The difference between black and white is not that they are both colors. This we take to be an absolute refutation of the theory, as an ethical theory.

3. Moreover, such is the nature of virtue that, even if it did not confer happiness, it would be binding on us. The sense of the binding nature of virtue is in no degree connected with the view that it is the means of our happiness. We can abstract the one from the other. And if we did not feel happy in virtue, we should still feel obliged to do right.

4. This theory proposes, as a basis of ethics, that which when fully and fairly presented to the mind is acknowledged to be sinful. This is a singular anomaly in the scheme. If one keeps his own happiness before himself objectively, making it his supreme aim, that is sinful, if anything is: he must keep before himself God, the good of others. The theory says, if one acts simply *in view* of his own happiness, he sins, while yet it says one's own happiness is the ultimate spring and source of all moral action. So that the theory frames for ethics a subjective basis which cannot become objective. It says: All moral action resides in something which is purely spontaneous and voluntary, and something which we cannot use as a simple integral motive, without committing sin.

5. Self-love, in the sense defined, viz., as happiness in the general happiness, cannot be even (as is often alleged in defence) the spring of the motive to our benevolent acts. (*a.*) It cannot exist before the benevolent impulse itself exists: for it is said to be the happiness which is found in that benevolence itself. Hence, the benevolent impulse must be there before the happiness therein can exist, and therefore the happiness cannot be the spring or source of the benevolence. The benevolence must be at least contemporaneous with the happiness. The sun must be there before the shining. (*b.*) The mere general desire

of happiness cannot be the reason for any of our special acts: that is a mere vague abstraction. Edwards:[1] "Whatever a man loves, that thing is grateful or pleasing to him, whether it be his own peculiar happiness or the happiness of others; and if this be all they mean by self-love, no wonder they think all love may be resolved into self-love." This is calling self-love that which is only a general capacity of loving and hating. This may be a general reason why men love or hate anything at all, but it can never be a reason why man's love is placed on such and such objects.[2] (c.) The position involves a vicious circle: An act is virtuous because it gives the highest happiness, and it gives the highest happiness because it is virtuous.

§ 4. *General Remarks on all the Happiness Theories.*
1. It is conceded on all sides that in virtue there is happiness.
2. It is also conceded that just as there is in virtue the highest present conscious happiness, so in like manner virtue tends to the highest objective happiness, and that *only* virtue does this.
3. Happiness, or the highest happiness, is an indefinite phrase· it tells us nothing of the specific character of our acts: it attends all our acts, and is not confined to those which are moral. In no other department, except ethics, would it be used as a means of explaining what the specific characteristics of a subject are. Who would describe the characteristics of the intellectual acts, or of the nerves, or of the passions, or of duties, as different forms or degrees of happiness? What is music? Suppose it defined as that which confers pleasure, and the best music as that which confers the highest pleasure. That would be the statement of a fact, but it would tell us nothing about music. The fallacy is just as great in ethics.
4. As with happiness so with "the highest happiness." This latter phrase, as employed to modify the theory, is indefinite in

---

[1] Nature of Virtue, vol. ii. of Works, p. 278. Edwards had this whole theory before him, and refuted it.
[2] As to the philosophy of love and self-love, Tennyson puts it just right:
"Love took up the harp of Life and smote on all the chords with might;
Smote the chord of Self, that, trembling, passed in music out of sight."

another way. It may mean (and covertly does mean) the same as the whole system of things with its resultant good, and so it constantly includes distinctive moral ends, *i. e.*, it means *the highest good:*[1] the love of that is doubtless virtuous; but the theory assumes that the highest good and the highest happiness are identical, while in fact happiness is subjective and the good is objective.

5. The happiness theories must all ultimately run into the self-love theories. All happiness, in the last analysis, must be a subjective delight or pleasure. When we speak of the highest happiness of God and of the universe, we must mean the sum of all the various forms of happiness that anywhere exist. Happiness is in its ultimate nature subjective. The general good is only the sum of *self-loves*.

CHAPTER VI.

THE HOLY LOVE THEORIES.

The other class of the theories which define virtue not formally, but by some common characteristic of all virtuous acts and states, may be comprised in these two: (1) Virtue is the love of moral excellence; (2) Virtue is love to being, benevolence to being in general.

I.—Virtue is the love of moral excellence. This is the definition given by the Princeton Review and by Dr. Alexander. Against this we think Edwards's objection holds, viz., that it supposes virtue before virtue. What is moral excellence? It is virtue. Then, virtue is the love of moral excellence, is—the love of virtue. Edwards, ii. 263: "If virtue be the beauty of an intelligent being, and virtue consists in love, then it is a plain inconsistence to suppose that virtue primarily consists in any love to its object for its beauty: either in a love of complacence,

---

[1] The proper self-love scheme insists that, in the last analysis, *my* happiness in the general happiness is the greatest good.

which is a delight in a being for his beauty, or in a love of benevolence which has the beauty of its objects for its foundation."

II.—The theory of President Edwards. Virtue is love, is love to being, is love to intelligent beings, is love to intelligent beings according to their worth. The best statement in respect to his school is not found in the writings of his son. He misapprehended his father, saying that his father's theory makes virtue to have respect to the happiness of being. In Bellamy's Works there is a much better statement. In a letter (Introd. to his Works, p. 29) dated Bethel, 1764, he says: "The whole of virtue consists in conformity to the divine law; love is the sum of the virtue required in the divine law; benevolence, complacence, and gratitude are the whole of love; the object of benevolence is being; of complacence, virtue; of gratitude, a benefactor. The divine law [which commands this] is a transcript of the divine nature: and therefore love is the sum of virtue in God as well as in the creature." He grants the objection that this makes the good of being the chief good, but says: "The good of being in general, which is the object of benevolence, is not the partial, but the complete good of being in general, comprising all the good being is capable of, by whatever name called: natural, moral, spiritual; than which there is nothing of greater worth in the universe. Nay, 'tis the sum of ALL GOOD." Bellamy then interprets the theory thus: that virtue has respect to all good, of course including moral and spiritual good, taking these to be, not the whole of what virtue has respect to, but a part, in fact the very height of the good. Love is then the affection of the soul, and all the good of being is the object on which this love fastens: and that is virtue. Edwards's definition is: "that consent, propensity, and union of heart to being in general, which is immediately exercised in a general good-will."[1] He says also, "Virtue is the love of intelligent beings according to their respective worth," and then distinguishes it into two main points: the love of benevolence and the love of complacency.

---

[1] He distinguishes between consent, propensity, union of heart, and—exercises, which is decisive against those who say that he makes virtue consist in exercises.

"The love of benevolence is that which has special respect to the whole; the love of complacency is the highest form of virtue, and which has respect to the virtue of others." Some say that his theory is this: that virtue consists in the love of benevolence, and that that consists in seeking the happiness of creatures, and then complacency does not belong to virtue but is an offshoot. To us it is plain that the theory makes complacency to be just as much a part of virtue as benevolence is, and not only so, but makes it to be the height of "the love of benevolence" and of virtue. Edwards also argues that the highest virtue is love to God, because He has the highest being and beauty; next, virtue is love to men according to their capacity for good and holiness.

There are some objections to this view.[1]

1. It is objected that we cannot have such love to being, as a direct act on our part. But this objection arises from not comprehending clearly what Edwards was aiming at. He is not describing virtue as it exists in our direct consciousness, but is stating it in its abstract form, in the philosophical form, and not in the form of experience. All particular affections come under this general idea, under all particular affections there must be this general love, if the particular affections are virtue: but it is the particular affections which come within the sphere of consciousness, so that we are not conscious of purely abstract love, but only of the forms of this affection. We suppose that Edwards came to this theory in this way: The law of God commands us to love God and to love men, and that is the sum of virtue. Now here are two statements, but it is cumbrous to use both. He asks then for a formal statement which will embrace both. Taking God and man together as including all intelligent being, if we say love to being, we have the statement which comprises both.

2. It is objected that this theory destroys private affections. The answer to this is, that the relations to which these private affections belong are a part of the system of being to which our love has respect. The private affections respond to the demands

[1] The acutest are those of Robert Hall.

for particular degrees and forms of love, and it is not inconsistent with the theory to suppose such response to be made. The relations which call forth the private affections make the particular "worth" of the object.

3. The theory is said to be Utilitarian. It is difficult to know what some people mean by this word. Generally, in philosophical speech, Utilitarianism means, those theories which make virtue culminate in happiness, or in the "general good," viewed as having respect ultimately to happiness either objective or subjective. If Edwards had made virtue to have ultimate respect to happiness, his theory would have been Utilitarian; but as we understand him, this is in no wise the case.

4. It is also objected that the theory does not allow for rectitude being a simple idea, but that it resolves the idea of right into something else. This objection comes from not distinguishing between right and virtue. The idea of right is a much broader idea than that of virtue. All that Edwards says is this: that rectitude, subjective as it is found in moral beings, is this love to being, and that that is what is right in a moral being. The theory *presupposes* that right is a simple idea, and that it can be applied to this love of being.

5. It must be admitted that there are some difficulties in Edwards's mode of stating the theory. (*a.*) The phraseology "love of being" is too abstract: readers, taking from this the notion of this love being independent of God, are likely to run into a pantheistic view: though as respects Edwards himself, this was fully guarded by his idea of God. Concretely and in consciousness, "being" is not the object of love: God must be the object of love. (*b.*) In Edwards's writings, the discussion of the nature of virtue is perhaps not sufficiently connected with the "end of God in creation," or with the plan of God, or with the whole system of things. The objective ground does not seem to be sufficiently stated. (*c.*) Another difficulty arises from difference of usage as to the word "benevolence." In common usage, it is taken for a lower form of virtue: that which has respect to human beings, and to happiness simply as distinguished from holiness. But Edwards defines benevolence for

himself, and means to include holiness in it or to make it equivalent to holiness. If "benevolence" be taken in the lower sense, the statement, the essence of virtue is in benevolence, is liable to very grave objections. The interpretation of Edwards as taking benevolence in the lower sense, making it to have respect to happiness ultimately, is followed up by Dr. Dwight, and leads to what, in our judgment, is the great defect of his system.[1]

[*A later statement than the above by the author*]: The true sense of Edwards's Theory of Virtue. Love, in its extension, has respect to all sentient, intelligent being, seeking its good: this is the love of benevolence. Love, in its intension and concentration, has respect to, seeks, the best good or holiness: this is the love of complacency. These are not two kinds of love: true, genuine love will, must, take these two forms. Cannot the categories of quantity and quality be here applied with advantage?

CHAPTER VII.

SOME HINTS AS TO A THEORY OF THE NATURE OF VIRTUE.

§ 1. *Preliminary Statements.*

1. Limitations and specific sense of the inquiry as to the nature of true virtue or holiness. The inquiry is not as to the whole of rectitude, but as to the prime excellence of a moral being, or as to rectitude, concrete and subjective, rectitude as existing and exemplified in a moral being; and the inquiry is, as stated before, for some common element or principle in all virtuous acts: whether there be any such.

2. Validity of this inquiry. This may be argued: (*a.*) From the analogy of the other sciences: all strive after unity; (*b.*) From the conscious sense of the distinctiveness of the moral sphere: the kingdom of holiness, kingdom of evil; (*c.*) Historically: there have been constant attempts at such theories. The inquiry, are there many virtues or one? is as old as the Greek philosophy: (*d.*) The inquiry after *one* common principle of all that is virtuous,

---

[1] In Remarks on Pres. Edwards's Dissertations, etc., by Rev. Wm. Hart Saybrook, New Haven, 1771, some points are acutely stated.

is also justified by what may be called, *the unity* of our moral consciousness: we are conscious that here is a distinct sphere.[1]

Even if *we* cannot arrive at a satisfactory solution, this should not lead us to deny the validity and possibility of the inquiry.

It is better to pause and say, we cannot meet the inquiry, than to be content with a theory *which undermines our moral convictions*.

3. The special difficulties of the inquiry.

(*a.*) Since almost all terms, expressing moral states and acts, refer to concrete cases, to specific acts, the chief difficulty is in rescuing some terms from their partial signification and giving them a general meaning. *E. g.*, benevolence, as already stated, is commonly used to express mere general good-will, a kind regard to our fellow-beings, a desire of their happiness. Now if this term be taken to express the essence of virtue, it is very likely to be interpreted in a partial sense,—as it often is in Edwards's system, and made to be the basis of a theory at war with the whole spirit of his system. It is even used in the sense of good-will to creatures, not including love to God: and even as implying a regard for happiness *in distinction* from a regard to holiness. So if justice or holiness, love of the general happiness or good, or love of rectitude, be taken to express the fundamental moral state, we have similar difficulties. Any term which is taken to express the common principle of all moral states *must be* somewhat deflected from its partial use for scientific purposes.[2] This is the case in all the sciences.

(*b.*) A second difficulty about the inquiry is this: Common speech makes a specific difference between what is moral and what is religious, so that a man may be "virtuous" without being religious, and it is also alleged, may be religious without being virtuous. Hence the advocates of mere morality as the sum of human duty, are apt to insist upon a definition of virtue

---

[1] Different from what is stated under (*b.*), as that refers to the objective universe, which we view and must view, as issuing in moral "kingdoms." This relates to our subjective necessity of putting all things under a moral point of view.

[2] Virtue was used by the ancients for manly courage; it is used by us for our lower relationships; and if we enlarge its meaning, the word becomes liable to constant misapprehension.

which will allow this sundering. Modern Philanthropy rests very much here, seizing upon a definition of virtue which will only apply to morals, and leave out love to God. But if there be no real difference, so that where religion is not, there cannot be true virtue, there is special need of making this evident. And here, in fact, is one of the fundamental antagonisms of the times, of Christianity with philosophy. If true virtue can be justly defined without bringing in the religious element, there is a vantage-ground for scepticism.[1]

(*c.*) Another difficulty is that if we reduce all that is virtuous to some common principle, there is danger of making it so abstract that one cannot verify it from experience, and it becomes worthless in fact, and not only worthless but mischievous, playing into the hands of infidelity, as, *e. g.*, the pantheist may say: I have such generic love of being as is said to be the essence of virtue, and hence I am truly virtuous.

(*d.*) Another difficulty—akin to the second stated above—may be suggested by the contrast between the terms, holiness and benevolence, as commonly used: holiness being the love of, and delight in, all moral perfection, and benevolence being a general regard to happiness. Now it is said, these two things are so distinct that we cannot reduce them to any common principle. *E. g.*, When we speak of a holy and then of a benevolent God, ideas so different are suggested that we cannot bring them into union under any one conception.[2] The same is the case with the two terms, rectitude and happiness or good. Some insist that in ethics, all that we can do is to say that rectitude is a simple idea, and that the love of rectitude is virtue, and that if the idea of happiness is brought into ethics, it is vitiated, and the radical distinction between virtue and vice is denied.

§ 2. *The Scriptural View of the Nature of True Virtue.*

The Scriptures do not discuss abstract questions of speculation, either metaphysical or ethical; and therefore it might seem irrelevant to refer to them; but we may proceed here precisely

[1] "All morality without piety is as a goodly statue without a head" (Lactantius).
[2] Dr. McCosh, on the ground of this difficulty, holds to both unanalyzed, as ultimate and necessary.

as we do in respect to doctrines, *i. e.*, in the way of deduction and of using Scripture as a test. What cannot be derived from the Bible cannot be a true ethical theory: what cannot be tested by the Bible cannot be a true ethical theory. Scripture does not give us the general abstract form of statement, but it gives the data from which that statement, if it be true, must be derived. And in fact the Scriptures not only enforce all specific duties, but they also give some general summaries, which make the work of deduction and of test comparatively easy. Such a summary is given us in the law; the principle which runs through that, or rather, the principle which secures obedience to that, must be the principle of all true virtue. "How *love* I thy law!" Besides the law in the Old Testament, we have the re-affirmation of it, and the reduction of it to two principles, by Christ, and in other passages of the New Testament which enforce and apply it. The chief passages bearing on the point are the following: Matt. xxii. 37-39 (parallel, Mark xii. 29-31), where love to God and love to men are the sum of the law, and where Christ says of love to God: "This is the first and great commandment"; 1 Pet. i. 16, where holiness is the word used for the sum of moral excellence in the creature; Matt. v. 48;—then in a specific relation, Matt. vii. 12; Gal. v. 14; 1 John iv. 20-21, where it is argued that love to man and to God are the same principle (also in 1 John iii. 17); 1 John iv. 8, where love is set forth as the supreme excellence in God, insomuch that it can be used for God himself; Rom. xiii. 8, 10; 1 Cor. xiii.; Gal. v. 13-15; vi. 2; Col. iii. 14; 1 Tim. i. 5; 1 Pet. ii. 21-25, where following Christ is set forth as the sum of duty.[1]

The General Results from these passages:

1. Love must be the common principle—love to God and love to men.

2. Love must have chief respect to personal beings, God and men, although it would not exclude some regard to animals.

---

[1] Rothe says (i. 196): There are five principles: (1) Likeness to God; (2) "Be ye holy"; (3) Follow Christ; (4) Have love to God and man; (5) "What ye would that men should do," etc. Müller (i. 140) says—and justly: Not so; none of the others, in dignity and importance, are equal to what Christ so solemnly declares in Matt. xxii. 37 (Mark xii. 29).

3. Love to God is and must be the highest form of virtue.

4. Men must be loved under the aspects and for the ends for which God made man.

5. These aspects, or ends, or this end, is: Man's relations to the kingdom which God has revealed in Christ his Son.

6. Hence, Love to God and to God's great end in creation, and to men in their relation to this end, is the comprehensive sense of "Love" in the Bible.

7. This love is essentially the same in God and man: Matt. v. 48; 1 Pet. i. 16. It is also essentially the same in respect both to God and to man. Love to God will bring love to man with it, and true love to man presupposes and involves love to God. Subjectively and objectively (*i. e.*, as respects the "good" on which it fastens) the love is essentially the same in God and man.

8. It should be observed, that love to men is not (*a.*) love to men as holy, primarily; for if this were so, there could be no love of sinners: yet it is love to men as capable of holiness; (*b.*) It is not love to men as capable of happiness alone, *though this is included*; (*c.*) It is such a love to men as leads one to seek their whole good, in the system of things which God has established, and in ultimate relation to the great ends of the system. Love to man, and even to sinners, will view them in respect to God's kingdom, as capable of holiness, although not yet holy, and will lead us to strive for their holiness. (This is another objection to the definition of virtue as the love of moral excellence. It is a love which would lead one to seek the whole good of man.)

9. Love to God is not—love to the divine happiness: it is love to God as the highest and best of beings.

§ 3. *Statement of the Principle of True Virtue in the abstract.*

There are two modes of statement: the abstract and the concrete. The abstract is the mode for the intellect, for science, in the form of general truth, and so as to cover all virtue or holiness, that of God as well as of the creature. The concrete is the *real* mode, the description of virtue in its vivid, living traits, the statement of it as it consciously exists in moral beings, as it is in the real system of things, as it is to be preached and practiced, and specifically, of virtue as it exists *in men*.

1. The principle of all virtue in the abstract must be found in love, that being the highest form of activity of our moral nature. All the powers of the mind concentrate in love. Love is union of heart to other beings, involving delight, and prompting us to seek all their good in the relations in which they are placed.

2. It is not, however, love as a mere internal emotion, as a subjective state alone. The character of love is that it demands an object: it is defined and characterized by its objects, and only thus. The character of holy love can then only be defined by stating its proper objects. All love is not virtuous. There is a doctrine of final causes in ethics. There are instinctive forms of affection, and natural affections which have not the element of true virtue in them. Our affections chiefly have respect to personal beings, to moral beings, beings having moral capacities and ends.

3. The definition of Holy Love or True Virtue. There are various forms of statement, in the way of general description,— the object being to give a general statement which shall embrace *all* the modes of virtuous love.

(*a.*) General and indefinite: True Virtue is love (the highest subjective state) of the highest good (the greatest objective wellbeing). It is described sometimes, as love of the whole system of things, and of each part in its due relation to the whole.

(*b.*) More particular: It is, love of intelligent and sentient beings, in relation to the great ends of the system. Or, it is love of the good of intelligent beings, with ultimate respect to their, and to the, highest good.

(*c.*) A definite statement: True Virtue is, love of all intelligent and sentient beings, according to their respective capacities for good, with chief and ultimate respect to the highest good, or holiness.

We have here: (1) love, the subjective affection; (2) the object of love, intelligent and sentient beings; (3) the variety of love: it varies according to the relative capacities of its objects for good; (4) the main, supreme object of the love, that which is chiefly and ultimately in view, the holiness of beings.

True Virtue has thus respect to all good, and to all beings as capable of good (including capacity for happiness), but in its very nature it has chief respect to the highest good or holiness. According to this, it would follow that virtuous love in reference to *each individual* who may be the object of it, can only consist in loving him according to his place in the system; and this is determined by three considerations: (1) The inherent dignity and capacity of the individual himself; (2) The relation of the individual to the great ends of the system; (3) His special relations to us in our relations to the whole system. (This last point gives the elements which are necessary to vindicate the private affections.) There must not only be capacity of being, but also *relation to the ends of the system.*[1] Satan has more capacity of being than many saints.

(*d.*) Some further explanations. True Virtue is love of the whole system, of all its ends, yet chiefly its highest end. The distinction between the primary and the ultimate object of virtuous love is important. Virtue has respect to all good, to all beings as capable of good, but it has, in its very nature, chief respect to the highest good or to holiness. Virtue regards each one according to his relative dignity and value: it loves most, it must love most, the most excellent of beings; this is also of its nature. Virtue seeks the good of each, all the good, chiefly the holiness, of each, and delights most in holiness. The chief, highest form of virtue is conceded to be the love of holiness, the love of beings for their moral worth, and in proportion to this. Virtue is not the love of moral excellence alone; some forms of virtue are not contained in this.[2] It is not the love of abstract being, but of being as it exists. Virtue is not the love of the Good exclusively (as distinguished from the True and the Beau-

---

[1] This does not appear to have been sufficiently insisted upon by President Edwards.

[2] [The remainder of this paragraph consists of hints which the author appears to have noted down for his future consideration.]

tiful). All *being*, as it is known to, and appeals to, us, may be comprised in the objects of the love which is virtue. Virtue, as the highest subjective moral state, may be said to be the love of the True, the Beautiful, and the Good, according to the respective and relative value of each and all,—being highest in love to God, as the supreme Truth, Beauty, and Goodness. Is it not partial and arbitrary to restrict virtue to the sensibilities, to the love of good as a sensitive state? Is not love of the *truth* equally essential to its nature? It is, love of the True and the Good; also of the Beautiful, in its measure.

§ 4. *Arguments for the above Definition.*

1. It is comprehensive. It is the union of the highest subjective state with all, and with the highest, objective weal.

2. It includes morality and religion both, and puts morality in its proper place as subordinate to religion.

3. Unless virtue be thus defined as having ultimate respect to holiness, the definition is not complete. Any other view of virtue would fail to bring us into relation to the *real end* of God's kingdom, which is, as regards the creature, his holiness in union with himself. Therefore we must include the statement of this.

4. Unless so defined, the definition does not include the very *highest form* of virtue, which is conceded to be the love of holiness. This would not then be shown to belong to the essence of virtue, but would be merely one of its manifestations or productions. Can any love to a moral being be holy, which has not ultimate respect to his holiness, *i. e.*, to his highest and best state as, love to a child? If true virtue have respect to the good of moral beings, it must have chief respect to their highest good: from this there is no escape. And that which true virtue or holy love chiefly seeks must be a product of the very essence of virtue, though it be not the whole thereof. The love may show itself in doing good in a thousand ways, but the highest love must be shown with reference to holiness. No definition of the intellectual operations would be sufficient, which did not

cover their highest exercise, the intuitive discernment of truth. We cannot show that virtue must have supreme regard to holiness, unless in our definition we make it such that it will. If virtue, both primarly and ultimately, is regard to happiness, then there is no reason in its very nature why it delights in holiness.

5. As defined, Virtue includes all the forms of virtue, all the different virtues in their place, and it shows why the virtues of the impenitent are not truly such. (*a.*) It includes the animate tribes, according to their place: although that form of virtue which has respect to the holiness of the object of love is not applicable here, yet that same temper of love which most delights in holiness will have kind regard to their well-being. (To alter all our definition for their sake alone would hardly be wise: something must be understood in every definition.) (*b.*) It includes love to the impenitent, seeking their good, yet ours is not virtuous affection unless it regards their highest good. (*c.*) It includes gratitude, for all good, while it demands the highest gratitude, for the highest good, to our highest Benefactor. (*d.*) It includes self-love, in its proper place, loving ourselves according to our place in the system, yet so that we have chief respect to our holiness: there is no true self-love without that.[1] (*e.*) It includes justice: treating all as conformed or not conformed to the great end of the system; and truthfulness: acting and speaking according to the real relations of things in the spirit of love. (Eph. iv. 25, "Speak ye truth each one with his neighbor: *for we are members one of another.*") (*f.*) It includes the love of rectitude, of all that is right, especially of the highest forms of what is right: the love of complacency in all moral excellence. (*g.*) It includes justice in the form of punishment, as upholding holy ends. It is difficult to get warrant for punishment from theories which make virtue to be the love of happiness; it may be said, Punishment is the infliction of misery on those who are opposing the highest happiness: but how is that right, if virtue has regard only to happiness? (*h.*) It includes faith, which is "nothing without love," and true repentance, which springs from holy love, and is a mode of its manifesta-

[1] Aristotle says: The wicked ought not to love themselves, but the good may.

tion. Thus all the other virtues are included in it. (*i.*) The definition also shows why the virtues of the impenitent are not truly such. It is because they have not the main element of true love, a supreme regard to God and his glory, and the great end of the system.

The form of statement given above for the abstract nature of virtue, is intended to meet the difficulties suggested by the contrasted terms: holiness and benevolence, or rectitude and benevolence (love of happiness.) The tension of the ethical problem is in these two contrasted terms. The real problem is to find a statement of the nature of virtue which shall give its just place to these. This we have attempted.

In all true virtue there must be both holiness and benevolence. But if virtue be made the love of holiness, it is exposed to the objection already recited, that virtue is the cause and effect of itself. Again, if, to avoid this difficulty, we say, virtue is (both primarily and ultimately) the love of beings as capable of happiness, we are exposed to the difficulties attending the happiness theories; we have no real ethical end as the object of virtue. The former seems to banish good-will as a real form of virtue, and the latter to resolve all virtue into good-will.

There is a real difficulty here, as already expounded, and whether it is successfully met in our statement, is the question. In point of fact, when men put all holiness in the love of the highest happiness, do they not really suppose, that in the highest happiness, in that which makes the highest happiness of God and the universe, there is a distinctive moral element or end?

§ 5. *Some Objections to the Theory.*

1. The definition is too abstract. We cannot have such love to all good, or to "being." It has been already granted that this is true, if the definition is understood to imply that we are to have this public affection as a specific, distinct exercise. But in fact we are simply inquiring for the common quality of all our virtuous acts, of our specific exercises.

2. The definition supposes virtue before virtue. This objection lies only against the position that virtue has exclusive re-

gard to moral excellence; that this is its primary ground as well as ultimate end; that virtue not only essentially consists in, but is wholly made up of, love to moral excellence in the concrete: or, in other words, that the whole of virtue is in complacency, or a delight in beings for their holiness. Our statement seeks to avoid this by saying that virtue is love to all good, yet chiefly and ultimately to all *in its relations to the highest good*, to holiness. In other words, virtue has primary reference to beings as capable of good, ultimate, to their highest good. The ultimate object of virtue, that which it ultimately seeks, must be a state of things in which holiness abounds, in which holy love rules all. But virtue includes also the love of other things, of inferior ends and beings, and of all inferior ends and beings in their proper degree and in their due subordinations and relations to the highest end or good. Love chiefly respects: (1) persons; (2) the value of persons; (3) their capacities for good; (4) their highest good or virtue; or: personal being—which has variety and gradation—which in all its gradations has capacities for different kinds of good—and which has in all capacity for the highest good or holiness. As the sentiment of the beautiful has ultimate respect to beauty objectively, so love seeks ultimately to beget love. In short, our definition makes virtue to be, subjective love to an objective system, which includes in itself both happiness and holiness, yet holiness as ultimate. Virtue, abstractly considered, is a generic affection embracing both these.

3. Such a view of virtue, as the definition gives, destroys the private affections. This has been already considered. The fact is, that the definition simply puts the private affections in their place. The natural relation is a part of the capacity or worth of the object.

4. Every definition of virtue is utilitarian, which does not make it to be, strictly and exclusively, the love of rectitude. This also has been considered. The definition of virtue as consisting exclusively in love to moral excellence, if strictly carried out, would leave no room for love to sinners.

5. Resolving virtue, as this definition does, into the love

of all good, makes virtue as compared with vice to be simply a matter of degrees: love to the minor forms of being is sin, and to the highest forms, is virtue. The reply is in the repetition of the theory. Virtue consists in the love of the whole, and the love of each is virtuous, only as it is based upon and expresses this love of the whole. Sin is found in the less love where a greater good ought to have been loved. Sin is the love of the less, and virtue is the love of the whole; and thus the distinction between virtue and vice is not resolved into a matter of degrees. In the love of the whole, there is an element which is not in the particular love.

§ 6. *Statement of the general Principle of all Virtue in the concrete.*

1. The real moral system,[1] that in which we live and act, is a system which has God, a personal being, for its author and end. To live for and to promote the great ends of *that system* is our *real* virtue.

2. Even in this world, our chief if not exclusive relations are with personal beings, in their relations to the great ends of the system, and in respect thereto. Our affections primarily, and of course ultimately, have respect to personal beings. The love of animals, flowers, etc., is transient and subordinate.

3. The highest relation, which we sustain as personal beings in this system, is our relation to a personal God, whether we regard his inherent dignity, or his relation to the whole system and its ends. God's glory is the objective end of the system. That glory is chiefly shown in promoting holiness—holiness in the creature—and in making this supreme.

4. If all virtue, then, consist in love, its fundamental, its highest, its most comprehensive form must be in love to God. This is the *reality* of virtue, virtue as it exists in the concrete.

5. But love to God is not only the chief form of virtue: it may also be said to include in itself all forms of virtue, to be the common, real principle thereof.

All agree that love to God and love to man include all the

[1] Compare Müller on Sin, vol. i., The Real Principle of Holiness.

virtues. The question here is of the reduction of both these to the common principle of love to God. It is favored by the following considerations: (*a.*) "God is in effect being in general" (Edwards); all that is, is from Him and for Him: He is the author and end of the whole system. (*b.*) "The real primary ground of virtuous love to man," as Müller says, is perhaps to be found in the fact that he is made in the divine image. "And this commandment have we from Him, that he who loveth God love his brother also."[1] "Therewith bless we the Lord and Father; and therewith curse we men, which are made after the likeness of God."[2] (*c.*) Holy love to man must have ultimate respect to him in his relations to God, and to his place in the system which God has established. (*d.*) May not all our private affections be brought under this? God has established in his system these relations: of family, of brotherhood, of society, of the state, in which all our lesser affections move. Are any of these virtuous except as they respect the whole end of the system? Is not that end the union of God and men in holy love? Moreover, it is God who has made us capable of loving in these connections, and therefore all love is to be traced to Him. (*e.*) In short, from supreme love to God it will result, necessarily and naturally, that we love the whole system He has ordained, that we shall love all in the system ultimately in its relation to Him, and to the ends which He proposes to produce by means of the system. Love to God is not properly the co-ordinate of love to man, but is the cause of love to man. Loving God, we shall love the system which He has established. Our own holiness is manifested, through doing this: in seeking and doing all things for the sake of God and his kingdom. This is the *reality* of the moral sphere. This gives us the proper end or object, as well as the highest motive: the end, that of God—God himself and the end which He proposes in his system; the motive, love to Him. This at any rate *is* the reality in conscious Christian experience, and not love to any abstract ends. And this best agrees with the position, that all real love moves in the personal sphere, all

---

[1] 1 John iv. 21. [2] James iii. 9.

moral affection moves there. The highest form of it is in love to the highest Person and to his ends and objects.

6. This, which is the highest and most real and philosophical, is also the simplest, form of statement for the reality of virtue. Is there any true virtue which has not its root and ground in love to God? If there be, a pantheist may have real virtue.

7. This best agrees with the Scriptural views of the moral law and of holiness. Our Saviour teaches: "This is the great and first commandment." Holiness in the Bible, is obedience to the divine law, from love to the Lawgiver. The law is from Him; we are to obey from love to Him; He commands this love first of all. Transgression is against God, not against an abstract system. "Against thee, thee only." Retribution is from God's hand.[1]

8. *The real statement*, then, of the fundamental principle of all true virtue would be, that it consists in love to God, and to all other beings in their relations to, and as parts of, the divine system of things.

9. The connection between § 3 and § 6—the deduction or mode of deducing this principle, as the real one—may be stated in this way: The essence of virtue is in "love to being," *i. e.*, is in love to all beings, according to their relative place in the whole system of things, and with ultimate respect to their highest ends. But this system *in its reality*, is from and for God; and its highest ends are, the divine glory in the holiness of the creatures. Hence, true virtue, as real in the system, must be love to God. Or again: Virtue is love to all good, with an ultimate respect to the highest good. But this ..... only in persons, only in a system of personal agents. Virtue then is love to *this system.* But this system is from and for God. Hence, virtue is love to God, essentially. Or, again: Virtue must consist in having the soul accordant with Rectitude. This Rectitude is embodied in *the law:* love to God and man. This law is divinely given, completely in revelation: it is the disclosure of God's Nature, the expression of God's Will. Hence, obedience to the divine law, from love to the Lawgiver, is true virtue.

[1] See Tayler Lewis, Bibl. Ethics, in Bibl. Repos., July, 1848.

CHAPTER VIII.

OF MAN'S PERSONAL RELATIONS TO THE LAW OF GOD.

The subject of consideration now is, MAN AS A MORAL AGENT in a more specific sense. It is, THE SEAT OF MORAL CHARACTER IN MAN: THE WILL AND AFFECTIONS in relation to Moral Character.

We have considered, What Man is in the constituents of his being; what is the Law for which he was made; what it enjoins and has respect to, viz., True Holiness, which we have attempted to describe and define: we come now to consider more particularly, The Relations of Man to this Law.

We come here upon the more difficult subjects of Anthropology, where there has been the greatest diversity of opinion and stress of conflict; and also, as a result of the conflict and to increase the difficulty, the greatest diversity in the usage of terms. We have no doubt that there has been, in point of fact, a greater unity of real belief, among the orthodox, than would appear from their conflicts. In respect to the facts of the case, there has been more harmony than in the use of terms by which the facts are expressed, or in the definitions by which the respective ideas are set forth. The differences are, in many instances, rather philosophical than in matters of real, substantial faith. Although the tendencies of one set of opinions may be to fundamentally false views, yet those who have advocated the opinions may not have been aware of these tendencies.

Remarks as to the Terms used and their Definitions.

1. The terms used in respect to moral government, moral quality, human action, the law of God, the administration of justice under that law, have in common parlance, in theology and in philosophy, a two-fold sense: an abstract and a concrete, a general and a specific, an objective and subjective, (some say, a proper and an improper) sense. We prefer the phraseology, general or specific. The *general* (equivalent to the *abstract*) sense is applied in all our judgments about laws, institutions, govern-

ments, etc., according as these are conformed or not conformed to moral ends or objects, and according as they tend to produce or not to produce a state of things which is truly moral. The standard of judgment here is their conformity or non-conformity to a moral standard viewed in relation to its ends or objects. It is not like a mathematical judgment: it is essentially a judgment as to conformity to a moral idea and a moral end. It differs from an æsthetic judgment, which has respect simply to beauty. On the other hand, the *specific* application is simply to moral beings, considered as the subjects of the divine government, as under the divine law, considered as conformed or not conformed to that law, as their state corresponds or does not correspond with the law, as their state has or has not a tendency to bring about, or a harmony with, the ends of that law.

2. Again: all the terms used in respect to these concrete cases, to this subjective conformity or non-conformity to the law, have at least a three-fold sense and application, in common life, in philosophy, and in theology, which causes the perplexity and difficulty about them, to wit: (*a*.) These moral terms are applied to a disposition, tendency, or bias, which precedes and is the ground of the personal activity, preference, or choice. Some call this a state of the will, and some a state of the affections. (*b*.) They are sometimes applied to a spontaneous outgoing of the soul in respect to moral objects or ends. This again is called by some an act of the will; by others, an act or action of the affections.[1] (*c*.) They are applied to a deliberate choice, where the soul elects between two objects, knowing the two, judging between the two, and deciding "with full power to the contrary choice." This, in the great question of choice between God and an inferior good, is called by some, prime preference, generic choice, governing purpose. (Moral terms are also applied to specific choices, and to external acts even; but, when so applied, it is only, with any tolerable thinker, as the external act and specific choice are supposed to contain and express an antecedent, already existing, general preference or affection of the soul.) Those who hold to the legitimate use of moral terms

[1] Edwards considers this to be of the will.

in the first sense, of course hold to their proper use in the other two senses. A man may hold to their use in the second sense, and deny their proper use in the first, at the same time holding to their proper use in the third; while others may say that their only proper use is in the third sense. *E. g.*, Take the word Sin. Some say that it can be applied to a state which antedates all conscious acts; that there may be a state, properly sinful, of human nature, before even the spontaneous movement of the soul: a sinful state by nature; and they say that the word sin can be properly applied to that state before any action; and that we can apply moral judgments to that state, and can say that it exposes the being having it to the divine, displeasure and renders liable to eternal condemnation. Others say, No; we cannot use the word in reference to any previous state, but it can be applied to the first activity of the soul, although this may be purely spontaneous, although it be an affection or feeling, although there be no deliberate choice, and this first act is a moral act, and is a sinful act. (The old doctrine of Hopkinsianism and of Emmons.) Then, another class say that the word sin is improperly used in reference to a native condition or spontaneous preference. It can be used only where there is deliberate choice, only where the person has before him the two ways, and has full and equal power to decide for the one or the other, and only to such acts can any moral judgment be applied by God or man; and if we apply a moral term to any other cases, we do it by metaphor and not strictly. The word Holiness has similar variations of meaning. Some say holiness may have been concreated in Adam; others say, No; there can only be holiness in activity, either spontaneous or voluntary (this is the old Hopkinsian view); others again say, No; we can only speak of holiness where there has been choice on the part of an individual. Of course those who hold this position cannot consistently hold that holiness is the gift of the Holy Spirit. The same three-fold usage, in respect to moral ends, obtains with the terms, "disposition," "desire," "affection," "feelings," propensity, principle, consent of heart; but the discussions have turned most upon the question as to how man's state before the law of God is to be viewed. The law commands love to God; supreme non-conformity in a moral being is such a state as implies preference for something else, some inferior good, and of course the absence of love to God. Now this state is one of non-conformity to the demands of the law, and taken as a state—of destitution of love to God and preference of something else—it is viewed: (1) as connatural, (2) as spontaneous preference, (3) as deliberate choice, or as the result of such choice.

3. The definitions of the terms relating to moral states differ according to the ultimate points of view taken in making the definition. There are three such current points of view, varying according to what is assumed as the *terminus ad quem*.

(*a.*) Some say that the point to be had in view, or the last standard to which all definitions are to be referred, is Personal Choice, an act of the Will. Nothing is moral, moral predicates can strictly be applied to nothing which is not an act of choice, viz., of choice to conform or not to conform to the requisitions of the law. All that is moral, religious, holy, is *essentially* an act of the will, nothing else can be such. The *ultimate respect* here is to the causality of the state or act: it is caused by choice; its being so makes it *moral*. Whatever—in disposition, tendency, or state—does not come strictly under personal choice, belongs simply to the physical sphere. In this view the two ideas, moral and choice, are inseparable; it is choice—of a moral end—and that alone which confers moral quality. That in this sphere the moral *is found*, nobody denies: the question is, is this its exclusive sphere?[1]

(*b.*) Another point of view is, not the choice as the cause of the state, but the *desert of the choice;* the desert of an act under the law; its worthiness of punishment under the law. For example, sin is defined as that which is worthy of everlasting

---

[1] Assuming the point that all that is moral is in personal choice, and framing all our definitions accordingly,—clean work can be made. There will be strictly no original sin, only a physical state; atonement will be not under the law, strictly; justification will be pardon simply, with a figurative representation attached; God's moral government will be simply over individual, personal agents,—will have no other direct sphere; all else will be sovereignty merely: according to laws and for ends not distinctively moral.

punishment, and if you find anything of moral abnormity which is not worthy of everlasting punishment, it is not sin. This conclusion of course comes because you have limited yourself in the definition.

(c.) The ultimate point of view or standard is taken, not in the sphere of personal choice, or in the desert simply, but from the *internal nature* of the state of a moral being, considered as conformed or not conformed to the ends of the law. This is Edwards's maxim or canon: "The virtue or vice of a disposition of the mind lies not in its cause but in its nature." Holiness is holiness, not because I produce it by an act of the will, nor because God produces it, but because of its inherent excellency, and its tending to produce the highest good of the universe. Sin is sin, not because it exists through my volition, but from its own nature, and because it runs counter to, and if left to itself would annihilate, God's moral government. Therefore we should define sin and holiness, not by what produces them nor by what they produce, but by their own nature.

CHAPTER IX.

OF THE SEAT OF MORAL CHARACTER. THE WILL.

General Proposition. What is moral in man, as a subject of the divine government, is not found in his external actions, primarily or strictly; nor in his instinctive desires and affections, considered in and by themselves in respect to their appropriate objects. Nor is it found in his intellectual activities exercised on their appropriate objects. Nor, again, is it found ultimately in the executive acts of the will considered as the choice of means to an ultimate end; nor in any single native disposition, which does not imply a respect to a single ultimate end.

All of these acts and dispositions may be exercised in a moral way; they may become moral; *perhaps* they are never exercised when there is not a moral aim included in them, determining them: but they are not by themselves moral; the seat of the moral quality is not in them. What is moral in man is only to be found in the affections or the will, or both, considered as conformed or not, to some one ultimate end, to the highest good.[1] (*E. g.*, I give: there is the external act,—not moral; the perception of the object, an intellectual act,—not moral;—from natural sympathy, as impulse,—not moral;—from choice to give, the act being determined upon from this impulse,—not the ultimate seat of what is moral in the proceeding;—from love to man,—if it stops there, no true virtue;—from a love to man which is expressive of a general love to all good and ultimately to the best good,—this is "true virtue.")

In moral states and actions giving rise to moral character, the soul, the man, or the person, is considered as having relation to moral ends, to *the* ultimate moral end. All the soul is brought under view; what is moral resides in that which is and must be a *central*, definite tendency or act; all of the power of the soul must be in it, converging upon it. What is moral in man is, in short, the condition of a moral being, in relation to the *great end* of his being, as conformed or not conformed thereto; and that condition must be in the affections or the will, one or both.

§ 1. *Of the Idea of the Will.*

The position of the Will, psychologically, in man is this: There is (*a.*) human nature, (*b.*) with its state, its general condition, its generic biases and tendencies: or, (1) the endowments of reason, feeling, conscience, and affections, (2) in a certain connatural condition, *i. e.*, having a constituted relation to certain ends (the "tendencies" of man), (3) centering in a distinct individuality or person—an ego. This person, now, with these general constituents, which he has in common with the race, considered as having capacity of choice, or as putting forth power especially in the form of choice or choosing, is what we mean by *Will*, in its most general sense. ("The conative powers," Ham-

---

[1] Query. Is the seat of moral quality in the affections?
 Is the seat of personal responsibility in the will?
In Immanent preference there is union of will and affections.

ilton.) The man choosing, the person choosing—is Will. The will is not anything distinct from the person;[1] it *is* the person himself, considered as acting or as having the power of acting in a certain way, the way of choosing. The distinctive and only function of the will is choice. Where there is choice there is will, and where there is not there is no will. Choice is a simple ultimate fact, like feeling. We cannot resolve it into anything simpler: if we could, the will would not be a distinct faculty. It implies always some object or end, and of course the object or end chosen is always distinct from objects or ends not chosen. There is always in that sense an alternative. It does not seem to be necessary that there should be conscious knowledge of any other object. The choice may be distinct and perfect with only one object in view. We need not have two objects in view in order to choose God, but might choose Him directly from a perception of his glorious character. But the choice of God implies that we do not choose an inferior object, and, as far as the power of choice goes, it implies that there was something else which might have been chosen, or, at least, it implies the capacity for choosing something else.

§ 2. *Of the Power of the Will.*

Man, acting as will, choosing, is an efficient cause; among second causes in this world, the chief: a dependent, but real, cause. There is a proper causal efficiency in every act of choice.[2] Power is an attribute of cause: it is the distinctive attribute of an efficient cause: it is that in the cause which gives it its efficiency in respect to any particular end or object. A man wills to move his foot, and there is an efficiency in the choice. The power of the will is not distinct from the power of the man: but

---

[1] It is a great misconception, that the will only acts after the other powers: it acts in and through them, putting forth energy. The mistake here arises from the arrangement of topics in popular text-books. See Archb. Manning, Contemp. Rev., Jan. 1871, on the Relation of Will to Thought, in fixing the mind, attention, etc. He conducts the argument against materialists.

[2] Pres. Day, in discussing this point, which is urged by some Arminians against Edwards, says, that nobody denies that a man is the author of his own acts. Edwards, the same. There is an article in the Princeton Review, Jan. 1857, showing that the highest Calvinistic view is not inconsistent with this position.

through the will the power of the man is exerted, so far as power is involved in choice. Power is seen in all conscious energy: attention, fixed feeling, as well as in choice.

§ 3. *Of Self-determination.*

This is one of the points in debate between Calvinists and Arminians. Edwards discusses it fully, and with particular reference to the Arminian definitions of his day.

I.—The self-determining power of the will. By this is meant, a power in the will to determine itself by its own act alone. This is a fiction, an absurdity, involving the contradiction that it at the same time is and is not. Edwards argues against it, showing that if it could be at all, it must be in one of two ways, both of which involve absurdities: (1) By choosing to choose, which implies always a choice before a choice, and requires the assumption of an infinite series of choices. All that the will does is, to choose. The will does not "determine itself by its own acts": it simply determines; or (2) The will is determined by nothing at all, and here we have an equal absurdity: pure "liberty of contingence," without motives.[1]

II.—There is another sense in which the phrase, Self-determining Power or Self-determination is used (with which the first is often confounded), in which it expresses a real fact, viz., that the self or person, through and by his choice, is determined, is in a state of determination, to some ultimate end. This is expressive of a fact about the mind which is always true and real. So far as consciousness extends, we know ourselves to be in such a state, in such a moral condition of self-determination (not speaking now of how it came to be, or of how it may come to be, but simply of the fact). There are two forms of such *ultimate* self-determination of a moral being, viz., for evil or for good,

---

[1] [See Prof. Smith's Review of Whedon on the Will, in the volume, Faith and Philosophy, p. 369. "We do not contest that motives are the occasional and final, and not the efficient causes of volition."

Also, p. 368. "Freedom (as defined by some modern Arminians) consists in . . . . the 'unrestricted power' of 'putting forth a different volition.' And this power is not merely the 'natural ability' conceded by the school of Edwards, but . . . . a creative energy. Arminianism, ... is coming to represent the will's action as that of pure causality in the form of a creative act."]

for God or against God, for the ends of the law or against those ends. These are our highest moral states.

§ 4. *Modes of the Will's Action.*

Not to mention others, there are two chief modes: (1) Its agency in the form of single volitions or executive acts; (2) In the form of ultimate preference, or immanent preference, which is internal.

I.—Of the will as the power of single volitions. In all such cases, the character of the act is this: the will as cause, by its act, which is a single volition, produces an effect outside of, and distinct from, itself. These are executive acts of the will, in relation to something to be done or not done, in relation to one external object or end rather than another; and such executive acts are the common sphere of freedom—of all civil and religious liberty; the term freedom is usually employed with reference to such acts. The liberty of the will here consists in the power of doing as one pleases, the power of carrying out unhindered what one purposes, in freedom from coaction and from necessity. Deliberate and imperative acts terminate in some action, which we believe to be in our power. This is not the best part of freedom, or true spiritual freedom, but it is the full sense of freedom in regard to the executive acts of the will.[1] It appears to be a defect in Edwards's treatise that he makes this the whole of freedom. Aristotle (Eth. iii. 2, translated here by Archb. Manning) says: "Deliberate preference appears to be voluntary, but not to be the same as *the* voluntary, for voluntary is more extensive; because both children and other beings share the voluntary, but not deliberate choice."

II.—The will's action as Immanent Preference. Müller: "As I am, so I will, and as I will, so I am." This is the immanent preference, the wholly internal mode of the will's action: in which direct respect is not had to objects, to doing or not doing, but to some ultimate moral end or object, which is *preferred*. Im-

---

[1] See Dr. Richards's Lectures on the Will, for the distinction between executive and immanent,—upon the whole the best statement. Dr. Woods, in his Lectures, uses will almost wholly in the sense of executive volition, and puts into the sphere of the affections the immanent preference.

manent preference is the choice of some ultimate supreme moral end. In it the choice and the motive blend. We cannot say here that the motive is the cause and the choice is the effect, nor that the choice is the cause and the state of preference is the effect,—the one to the exclusion of the other. They are concurrent and inseparable: the motive becomes the choice. *E. g.*, God is before the soul, and the soul chooses God. The motive is what is in God: the soul by its immanent preference chooses God, and that motive becomes its controlling principle in and by the choice. This is the sphere of love, of moral love, the love of some moral end. This action of the will, in distinction from executive acts, has not reference to anything external. It does not produce an effect distinct from itself. The choice becomes the state of the will. Such a preference is free in its very nature, free because it is a choice, free as every one who has it knows. This is the sphere of the spontaneity of the will in its moral acts. The choice here becomes a permanent state of the will. In an executive act, the choice passes away with the end gained. In immanent preference, the choice stays, and is the character: it is the highest freedom, internal freedom. The will, as bare power of choice, cannot beget such a state.[1]

Some further differences between the immanent preference and executive acts are: In the immanent preference are virtue and vice: it is their seat; in the executive acts, virtue and vice are found only derivatively; the immanent preference is spontaneous, the executive acts are deliberate; the immanent preference includes the affections, the executive acts express the affections, are prompted by them.

There is both freedom *to* choose and freedom *in* choice. The former is the *liberum arbitrium.* The latter is the real freedom, *voluntas.* "We must not merely will to be good, we must have a good will" (Müller). The analysis is ultimate: Immanent preference is love: in the love both the motive and the choice are included. Immanent preference is a state of the will: the will can be and is in a state of permanent choice.

[1] See later, under the head of Motives.

§ 5. *Of the Liberty or Freedom of the Will.*

I.—The General Notion of Freedom. Freedom is an attribute of the will, essential to it. External freedom is the liberty to do as one pleases; internal or true freedom is found in choice, and in nothing else or less. This freedom is simple, ultimate, and indefinable. It implies freedom to an act, freedom from an act (need not do it), freedom in an act,—exemption and choice, both. Wherever there is choice there is freedom. Choice cannot be forced, though the external compliance may be. Freedom *in* choice is the fact: this is much neglected by Arminians, in their statements as to the will. This freedom is not found in power to the contrary, though we do not say that freedom does not involve this in some important sense, does not imply some residuary power. Freedom is not found in anything we do not do, in any power we do not exert, but simply in the power we do exert in choosing. Those who *define* freedom as power to the contrary fall into the singular anomaly of implying that freedom is in a power that is never exerted; and of course nobody can know anything about it. As soon as it is exerted, it ceases to be; it is then the power which is exercised.

II.—This freedom [in reference to what is external, objective, *outside*,[1]] implies always the possibility of election between different objects, deliberate choice. We do not mean to say that this is all upon which the election depends, but as far as the will goes the freedom is the possibility of a different election. Of this we suppose men are distinctly conscious, and it is only on this supposition that there is the possibility of a change in our moral character, of the regeneration of the soul. Real freedom is attained on the basis of this formal freedom.

III.—This freedom does not imply what has been called the liberty of indifference, in its technical sense: by which is meant that the will, in order to be free, must be balanced entirely between the two opposite poles of choice, with an absence of any previous inclination. It has been said that the will is like the pivot in the scale-beam, perfectly even between the two scales. But will is different from the pivot, because it is the will which

[1][In some statements by the author the clause in brackets is omitted.]

moves. The will goes down the scale. Some[1] assert that there is no such influence in existence as that of motives, and when we ask " What then determines the will?" the reply is "Nothing at all. It begins to be and it comes to pass, and that is all we can say about it." Against such liberty of indifference Edwards argues, showing that on such a supposition all free action is taken at random and becomes hap-hazard,[2] and that an act could have no possible moral value if we were indifferent.

IV.—Nor does liberty involve the contingency of volitions. An event is said to be contingent, (1) when it depends as an effect upon its cause, so that if the cause be absent, the effect will not exist, but in this sense nobody would deny the contingency of a volition; (2) in reference to our knowledge and ignorance, but this sense is not in the discussion; (3) when there is a real uncertainty in the nature of the case, and this is the sense in which the contingency of volitions is affirmed by Arminians[3] and denied by Calvinists. We have already considered this under Divine Providence.

V.—The distinction between formal and real freedom (Müller on Sin, ii. ch. 1). Formal freedom is that freedom which one has as endued with the capacity of bare choice, with the possibility of electing between two or more objects. This is given in the abstract nature, in the very idea, of choice, or of the will, as power of choice. It is inalienable from the will; it cannot be destroyed without destroying will. Power of choice implies that *so far as the will goes*,[4] in the presence of two or more objects, there is the possibility of selecting the one or the other. Real freedom is found in the choice itself; in any given choice my freedom is actualized; in the choice, the thing chosen, I am free.

But in respect to this there is another fact to be noticed, viz., that not in all moral choices is there real conscious freedom. It

---

[1] As Bledsoe.

[2] ["Choice for reasons lies between caprice and fatalism; it is in contrast with chance, rather than cognate with necessity." Faith and Philosophy, 378.]

[3] Some endeavor to make a fourth meaning for "contingent," viz., that which may take place without a cause. When the West. Conf. says, "the contingency of second causes is not thereby taken away," etc., contingency is used in the second sense in the above enumeration, as is shown by the proof-text cited.

[4] It may not be able to go so far as to procure or attain the objects.

is a part of inward experience that we feel ourselves *really free* ("free indeed," John viii. 36), only in loving and serving God, only in *love*. So, gifted men are "free" in the productions of genius, in acting out the inmost self; still higher is the freedom of true love. The choice of sin is a bondage. This is undoubtedly the Scriptural position. If there is no higher freedom than formal, all our religious *states*, our highest moral states, are excluded from its sphere, and all character.

Yet, formal freedom always remains. It is not exhausted in, or restricted to, any one preference, any immanent preference, though the immanent preference may be so strong that we never think of the formal freedom.

VI.—Of the limits of human freedom. Man's freedom is not absolute: the freedom of none but God can be. As man is dependent, his freedom must be consistent with dependence, it must be the freedom of a dependent being. As man is under laws, his freedom must be limited by, and consistent with, that fact. It must be consistent with the divine government and purposes, with the certainty of election, regeneration, perseverance, through the influence of the Holy Spirit, with the Divine Sovereignty in all its modes. We are free from all physical necessity in the mode of the mind's action; but we are not free from the regular laws of the mind's action: we are free *in* these. We are not free from moral causes and effects, though we may be free in them.

Another statement of the limits of the power of the will.

It is not infinite nor absolute. It is not disconnected from the other powers of the mind, nor from God, nor from nature. The will acts in, with, and by all these. More particularly—

1. It cannot act without a motive.

2. It cannot choose two contrary or incompatible things at once.

3. In one sense of "power"—possibility, it may choose either; in another sense—energy, it may be that it may not.

4. It must always act within the laws of the world, of the body, etc.

5. It cannot directly control or change the emotions.

6. Its freedom must be consistent with the prevalence of law,

and with the certainty of moral acts, and also with the sovereignty and prescience of God.

7. Its freedom must be consistent with the fact of its always choosing that which in the view of the mind is most desirable.

§ 6. *Of the Will and Motives.*

The position that the will acts according to motives is no other than the position that man acts according to laws; if man does, the will does: for the will is the instrument of all human activity. On this general basis is maintained the *proposition*—That the will in its choice, or—better—the man in his choice is effectually influenced by motives.

I.—The sources of proof of this proposition.

1. If it were not true, there could be no possibility of human government. Human laws, with their rewards and penalties, imply it. It is implied in the whole action and working of human society.

2. We judge others upon this basis. We ask, why did a man do so and so? We always state some ground, reason, or motive for the action, and when we want men to take a certain course, we ply them with motives, and knowing what motives influence men, we can sometimes predict what they will do.

3. The appeals of the gospel presuppose that the mind is effectually influenced by motives.

4. It is evident from the doctrines of the divine providence and foreknowledge. These imply a plan and regular order of God which is carried on by human agents, which could not be unless they acted according to some general order in the divine plan. Foreknowledge is inconceivable without certainty in the mode of human action.

5. We not only believe this of others, but believe it of ourselves. When we want to give a reason for any action, we go back to the motive, the inducement; and we are conscious that we have thus ever been influenced by motives. We have the direct witness of consciousness.

6. We cannot conceive it to be otherwise. We cannot conceive of an action without a motive. Such an action is a mere

abstraction. It is an action without an object, bare action, bare purpose, and nothing purposed; for if there is anything purposed, that is the motive.

From these considerations we reach the general conclusion that the will is influenced by motives.[1] The question still remains, how far?

II. What is a Motive? Motives are divided generally into two classes, internal and external: all the objects without, which have relation to us, which we can know or desire as a good, and all the responses within. Ultimately, however, all motives are internal. They are motives only as they influence some internal susceptibility. Edwards: "Motive is the whole of that which causes, excites, incites the mind, to volition." Hamilton: "Motive abstractly considered, is no other than end or final cause, that for which, or in view of which, the mind acts. But a motive in its concrete reality is nothing apart from the mind itself. It is a mental tendency." A motive thus in relation to this discussion—to bring it down to the point for which we wish to use the word—may be defined: The final state of the man in the indivisible instant before choice, having relation to that choice.

III. Are motives in this sense the efficient cause of volition? Edwards in discussing this point says: "An appearing most agreeable to the mind or pleasing to the mind and the mind's preferring and choosing seem hardly to be distinct." In our view, this is the least satisfactory passage in Edwards's treatise on the Will.[2] In this view the motive would be the efficient and not merely the occasional cause of volition. The real relation of the two is, that the motive is the proper occasional, and the

---

[1] "If to break loose from the conduct of reason be liberty, true liberty, madmen and fools are the only freemen; but yet, I think, nobody would choose to be mad for the sake of such liberty, but he that is mad already." Locke, Essay, ii. 21, 50. Hamilton: "The determination by motive cannot, to our understanding, escape from necessitation." "How the will can possibly be free, must remain to us, under the present limitation of our faculties, wholly inconceivable." "How moral liberty is possible in man or God, we are utterly unable speculatively to understand." Descartes also thought that a solution of this difficulty lies beyond the reach of the human faculty.

[2] Compare Pres. Day's exposition, pp. 25, 77.

will is the efficient, cause. If the motive is made the efficient cause, it seems impossible to save freedom.

IV. Do motives determine the will? To say that motives determine the will, is a different thing from saying that the motive is the efficient cause of the mind's choices. Edwards puts the question in this shape. By "determination of the will" he means, "determining the will to be one way rather than another," "causing that the act of choice should be thus and not otherwise," "determining to one act among various acts." Determination, as here used, is direction and not efficiency. Motive is not that which causes the choice, but is that which determines the direction of the choice. The general reason why the mind determines, is that it is an agent: why the mind chooses, is that it has the power of choice; but the reason why the mind chooses one way rather than another, this thing rather than that, is different. We must distinguish here, the efficient, the final, and the occasional cause. The agent, the mind choosing, is the efficient; the final cause is the end or object in view of the mind; and the occasional cause perhaps may be said to be, that object as it influences the desires, etc., before the act of choice. The algebraic expression here would be: Will+Motive=Volition or Choice.

V.—In this sense of the determination of the will, is it a law of the will's action, that it always acts according to the stronger or strongest motive? By law here is meant, general fact, fact of induction, not an *a priori* necessity. The question here is one of fact, and not of mere theory. What is the strongest motive? It is not that which is intrinsically the strongest, because then virtue would always be the strongest motive; but that was never meant in this discussion.[1] But the strongest motive is that which appears most desirable to the mind at the instant preceding actual choice. Not that which is the strongest objectively, in itself, but in itself in relation to us and our state. Again: the assertion is not that the strongest motive *must* carry the will, but simply, that it *does*. It is not an asser-

[1] Yet this objection has been often made, *e. g.*, by Dr. Bushnell in Nature and The Supernatural.

tion as to what it is possible for the will to do, or whether the will as an abstract possibility might make a different choice, but as to what the will actually does.

Arguments for this position.

1. Consciousness. We cannot recall any actual choice which we did not make according to the strongest immediate inducement.

2. In the rational view of choice, in conceiving it as a rational act, this law is necessary. Leibnitz: "To suppose a man acting from the weaker and against the stronger motive, is to suppose a man acting against himself."

3. If this be not so, then, so far as we can conceive, there is no certainty of action, there is no conceivable mode of the divine government. We do not say that God could not govern without this, but that we cannot see how He could govern rational beings, unless through this general law. This is the main argument of Edwards. God cannot foreknow what is not certain. Arminianism says: We do not know how God knows. True; but if an event in space and time is wholly fortuitous, by the very mode of statement the divine knowledge is excluded.

Objections to the position:

1. Such is the variety of motives that we cannot compare them, so as to say, one is stronger than another. There are motives, *e. g.*, drawn from the sphere of obligation; and others, from the sphere of desire: and these we cannot compare, as there is no common term. We cannot say that the one is stronger, for it is in a different sphere. The reply is in the consideration that all motives assume the form, the general form, of desire: *i. e.*, all motives affect the sensibilities and therefore they may be compared. This objection[1] is merely an evasion of the statement that, as matter of fact, the will is as the strongest motive.

2. The will is not under the law of cause and effect, is out of space and time. The reply is that neither part of this objection is true: the latter is most certainly not true. To our view, the former is inconceivable. Every event or change of existence im-

---

[1] It is much dwelt upon by Upham and others.

plies a cause: that is an ultimate, rational truth. The will is not under the law of cause and effect, in the sense of physical cause and effect: no one pretends this; but the law of cause and effect must run through the will, because the law covers every change of existence in time: it declares that every such change *must* have a cause. This is not saying what the cause is, not that it is all in the motives or all elsewhere. That all the cause of its action is not outside of itself, is true.

3. The position is said to involve reasoning in a circle: the motive is called the strongest, because it prevails: and it prevails, because it is the strongest. The reply is, that the objection does not lie against the argument from consciousness, where we put the force of the proof. Consciousness tells us that the motive prevails because it is the strongest. We find out, to be sure, that it prevails by prevailing. But what we find out by consciousness is, that it is the strongest.

4. It is said that the position is fatalism. We have already considered this. In fatalism, all actions are (*a.*) under a blind necessity, (*b.*) are determined by a natural necessity, and (*c.*) ultimately by external necessity. Here (*a.*) actions are determined by a rational law: choice-from-motives; (*b.*) they occur under a moral certainty; (*c.*) they have an internal cause. That is fatalism in which the action is determined without choice, but here in every case, it is by and through choice. Until it can be shown that man in choosing from the strongest motives does not choose, the objection from fatalism will not hold.

5. Instances are alleged against the position. *E. g.*, Adam and his fall; the Angels and their lapse. Here, it is said, the strongest motive was not the inducement. It is to be said in reply, that certainly it was not the strongest intrinsically, but Adam must have been less wise than he is reputed, if he sinned for what seemed to him less desirable than something else. It makes, however, no difference whether we deal with this objection in one way or another: because first sins cannot be explained on any theory.

This is true about the strongest motive: we cannot decide beforehand which is the strongest motive always in view of the mind. A slight circumstance may decide, as far as the mind goes, and it is often in a state where it is nearly equally balanced, and where the mind is not fixed on the strongest motive.[1] The strongest motive is the indivisible state before the choice. There is often not time to think of this: but we see that it was so on looking back.

CHAPTER X.

OF LIBERTY AND NECESSITY.

The whole question here has reference to the application of the law of cause and effect to the Will. Ought it to be applied, and if so, in what way?[2]

I.—Of the terms used. Natural Necessity means the connection between events as found in the ordinary course of nature, the connection of cause and effect in physical events. Here there is in the phenomena invariable antecedence and consequence, and our minds compel us to conclude that there is in connection with the antecedent a *power* adequate to produce the consequent.

Moral Necessity is the real and certain connection between moral acts and their causes. This phrase Edwards uses, throughout his treatise, in the sense of certainty, and says that the word necessity is applied to it improperly.

Metaphysical or Philosophical Necessity is used in the same sense as Moral. Edwards (Inq., Pt. i. § 3): "It is *nothing different* from *certainty:* I speak not now of the certainty of

---

[1] Whether intrinsically strongest, or what proves strongest actually.
[2] The chief passages in the Westminster Confession, bearing on this subject: Chap III., in reference to the Divine foreordination, "nor is violence done to the will of the creature"; Chap. IX., "God hath endued the will of man with that natural liberty that it is neither forced, nor by any absolute necessity of nature determined, to good or evil." The confession does not directly decide the question. It is not strictly a scheme of philosophical necessity. It can be interpreted in consistency with philosophical necessity, and perhaps better in consistency with that than with any other scheme. It is decidedly opposed to pure self-determination of the will.

knowledge, but the certainty there is in things themselves which is the *foundation* of the certainty of the knowledge of them: or that wherein lies the ground of the infallibility of the proposition which affirms them."[1]

The term necessity is rather an unfortunate one to use, but, being used, we ought to know in what sense it is employed.

II.—Statements of the Points in the Case. Schelling says, "That freedom which men try to find in empirical actions is as little real freedom, as that truth which they find in empirical knowledge is real truth. There is no freedom which is not consistent with necessity." Schleiermacher: "Freedom is personality itself. To ascribe sin to freedom means to reckon to each one his own acts." Hegel says: The connection between necessity and freedom is the most difficult subject in the whole of speculation. He gives the following: (1) Essence and properties go together. In the properties we find the essence, and in the essence the properties. (2) Substances act on each other. There is a reciprocal action. Each substance is a cause in relation to the other and an effect. Each is active and passive in this reciprocal action. (3) So in respect to necessity and freedom. In the case of man the substance determines as well as is determined. There is the activity of the free will and also that which determines the activity—the motive object or end in view of which the mind acts. The necessity consists in the fact that that something, in view of which the mind acts, is something given, and not originated, and that these data are as necessary as the power of choice itself. (4) The net result of the whole is, that the causal relation does not exclude freedom, when it is considered as reciprocal action. There may be a causal relation and freedom also. What is given, or the influences around us, constitute motives; then the mind, thus acted upon reacts; thus solicited, chooses; but it cannot choose beyond the metes and bounds of the influences brought to bear upon it, *i. e.*, it cannot originate the substance of its choice, but only the fact of its choice. It can give the formula of the choice, but it cannot

---

[1] The younger Edwards puts it still more sharply, and leaves still less place for a definite act of the will besides the motive.

fill up the formula. Hamilton: Both "are incomprehensible, as beyond the limits of legitimate thought. Though freedom cannot be speculatively proved, so neither can it be speculatively disproved; while we may claim for it as a *fact* of real actuality, though of inconceivable possibility, the testimony of consciousness, that we are morally free as we are morally accountable for our actions."

III.—Conclusion upon the Question. Volition is an effect. As an effect, it is under the law of cause and effect. As an effect, it must of course be produced by its appropriate cause or causes. This cause or these causes are what immediately precedes the volition. That which immediately precedes the volition is, choosing in view of motives, and the volition is the result. That is, the choosing and the motives constitute the cause,[1] and the volition as the resultant, constitutes the effect. The motives are the occasional and final cause, the agent—the man choosing—is the efficient cause. In this statement the law of cause and effect, as applied to the will, is allowed and the freedom of the will is saved. Thus in the will there may be a union of "necessity" (of moral necessity, of certainty) and freedom.

[What would be CHAPTER X., OF NATURAL ABILITY AND MORAL INABILITY, will be considered under the head of CHRISTIAN HAMARTOLOGY.]

CHAPTER XI.

OF THE PRIMEVAL MORAL STATE OF MAN.[2]

The main points in man's primitive state are given in the answer to Question 10 of the Westminster Shorter Catechism: "God created man, male and female, after his own image,

---

[1] Edwards does not appear to make this distinction, but Pres. Day thinks that he did not intend to question that man is the proper author of his own acts, and that his statement here was merely analytical.

[2] References: Dwight; Müller on Sin, ii. 482; Thomasius, i. 178; Hofmann, Schriftbeweis, i. 241; Hutterus Redivivus, 194; Martensen, 169; Ebrard, i. 250; Bretschneider, i.; B. Tyler's Lectures, i., ii.; Ed. Wm. Grinfield, Scriptural Inquiry into the Image and Likeness of God in Man, Lond., 1837; Bishop Bull's Discourse V.: State of Man before the Fall.

in knowledge, righteousness, and holiness, with dominion over the creatures." Man was created after the other works, as the crown of the creation; all the rest centering in him, and he having dominion. First Adam and then Eve, "male and female created He them:" the beginning and center of unity and source of the whole race was in this one pair. Society began, marriage was ordained. The law of God was written on man's heart (Rom. ii. 15). He was placed in the garden with liberty to eat of the fruit of the trees; the creatures were put under his dominion.

§ 1. *The Scriptures teach that there was a primitive State of Innocence.*

1. They do this by describing sin as the consequence of temptation. Therefore man was in a state of innocence before. Gen. iii. is the proof. Also, Rom. v. 12, 15. The expression, "tree of the knowledge of good and evil" (Gen. ii. 17), implies man's innocence at the beginning. He could be in this state only by not knowing evil, and his temptation was to gain this knowledge. All the description of the Paradisaical state confirms this view, implying a state of entire purity. Sensuality was not known (Gen. ii. 25, cf. iii. 7).

2. The Scriptures also make more positive statements. Gen. i. 31, All was "very good," after man's creation; Eccles. vii. 29, the expression "upright" is general.

This state is not that of children, still less that of primitive savagery: it is a state of innocence, of moral purity, of simple childlike communion with God. In order to their having communion with God in a personal way, there must have been a ripe condition of the powers. Gen. i. 28, 29; ii. 16; ii. 19, 20, presuppose more than childhood. Dominion, knowledge of the trees of the garden, power to name the beasts, confirm what is implied in the great fact of communion with God as to the comparative ripeness of man's powers in the primitive state.

§ 2. *This original State is described in general Terms as the Divine Image in Man.*

Gen. i. 26; v. i.

The divine image in man designates both something that is

permanent in human nature and also a state of that nature which was lost by the fall.

(*a.*) What is permanent is referred to in Gen. v. 1, 3, where Adam's likeness to God and Seth's to Adam are brought together, so that we naturally conclude that the divine image remains; Gen. ix. 6; 1 Cor. xi. 7; James iii. 9.

These passages imply that the image remains in man, but the question still might arise, whether they even then refer merely to man's intellectual and moral powers in the abstract, or to what these may *become*, what it is possible for man still to be, his latent possibilities.

(*b.*) What was lost of the original image may be inferred from Eph. iv. 24, where the idea of the "image of God" is expressed by righteousness and holiness; Col. iii. 10, where the image is represented as divine, spiritual knowledge, the term "renewed" implying restoration to a former state. (It is noticeable also that the former state, "after the image," is expressed in language which might be a reminiscence of the Septuagint version of Gen. i. 27.) These passages show that to the full moral image of God righteousness and holiness belong.

How now shall we conceive of the divine image under the two points of view of completeness and defectiveness in man? That which is permanent is found in man's personality, his being a spirit, his having intelligence and moral capacities, his having a moral destination and likewise, to some extent, dominion over the creatures. In distinction from this, the part lost was the holy state of these faculties. They were originally not merely potentialities, but were in a state of righteousness and true holiness.

To enforce this distinction still further, there is also a metaphysical proof. Man could not be made in the moral image of God, unless he had been made a spirit like God. Man could not be holy as God is holy, unless he had intelligence, feeling, and will, as far as a creature can have them like God. His *capacity of being like God* remains, although the actual moral likeness was lost by the fall.

§ 3. *Yet this primitive State was not one of confirmed Holiness but mutable.*

The primitive state is to be conceived as one of comparatively unconscious goodness, rather than of goodness which has been developed and come to full self-possession in conflict with temptation. The tree of the knowledge of good and evil was to be the test, the means of bringing man to a full consciousness of the difference between good and evil. It might be to him a source of blessing, by confirming him in holiness. Full, conscious freedom in good might be the result. We may conceive in Adam, of a spontaneous direction of his powers to God, in love, and yet one not tried, not so high a state as that in which they would be after temptation, if he had successfully resisted it. Besides what we gather from the Scriptures on this subject, ("Blessed is the man that endureth temptation or trial," etc.,) there is an argument of rational probability, from what we might suppose God would do: if He created, He would create what in its measure is perfect, the best. As far as we can conceive of this primitive state in which Adam must have been, it was either: (1) one of total indifference to good and evil, with no knowledge or susceptibilities in respect to either, with capacities only; or (2) one of positive inclination to sense, gradually to come to reason; or (3) one of positive inclination to holiness or good. The latter is the more rational, as well as the Scriptural, position.

§ 4. *On the different Interpretations of the "Divine Image."*

The Greek Fathers put the divine image[1] in man's general endowments, in reason and freedom, which had an original perfection, were active in communion with God, with the Logos, constituting the vision of God, a life in God.

The Western Church, especially as is seen in Augustine, construe the primitive condition as one of righteousness, dwelling upon the state of man's will. Man was not made with merely the possibility of a good will (Pelagianism), but with the ac-

[1] They often make a distinction between "image" (the capacities) and "likeness" (the moral resemblance), which cannot be exegetically carried out.

tuality. But though created with a good will, yet not complete, as even Augustine allows,—not in the highest state. He says the image both is lost and remains: there is possibility of restoration only because something of the divine image is still left: he finds in man an image of the Trinity: memory, intelligence, will.

Through the Middle Ages, there was a constant tendency to make the divine image in man to consist merely in the rational powers, and any positive goodness which was in him at creation to be, not a state of his faculties, but a supernatural endowment: the former being often viewed as the "image," the latter as the "similitude" of God. It may be said that this has become the Roman Catholic theory of grace: Righteousness is something superadded to the faculties of man, rather than a state of the faculties.

In the Reformation, this original state of righteousness was one of the sharp points of contest. The Roman Catholic view, as fully developed at that time, was: In man at birth there are simply *pura naturalia* without any specific tendency. The tendency to good, which Adam had, did not belong to human nature, but was a supernatural endowment, and was lost by the fall, and this grace is that which is restored by the church in baptism. The Protestants took the view that the integrity of human nature, in a moral sense, was lost by the *fall*, and they ran perhaps into the other extreme of making the whole image to be moral likeness, not emphasizing the permanent likeness which man has as a personal spirit, etc. The main point in the view was, that man had not merely capacities for goodness, but that these capacities were in a holy state, having a holy bias or tendency in them. The Protestant Reformers generally would say, that holiness was concreated in man, that there was an original righteousness. Almost all the Reformed symbols, Lutheran and Calvinist, have this view. The divine *image* is the whole of the primitive perfections, original *justice* (or righteousness), the special ethical relations in man: they differ as the whole and the part: the whole man is the image, his moral tendencies (wisdom, love, etc.,) the justice. The Roman Catholic objected, that on this view the loss of the divine image was the loss of religious and moral endowments: the reply was, Not so, —only of the original state or tendency of the endowments. But this state or tendency was primeval. This is a much profounder view than the Roman Catholic, which makes grace *external*. The wisdom and holiness, however, were not a perfect state of the soul, but rather predisposition, tendency, etc. The state was one of probation, with consummation over against it. This is the general position and usage of language in our American theology. Edwards (sometimes said to have held that all holiness is in exercises) says: " Human nature must be created with some dispositions . . . . . otherwise it must be without any such thing as inclination or will;" "the notion of Adam's being created without a principle of holiness in his heart is inconsistent with the account in Genesis." By principle he means, "a foundation laid in nature, either old or new, for any particular kind or manner of exercises of the soul, or a natural habit." Bellamy: "As there was a holy principle in Adam before the first holy act, so there is in the regenerate." Smalley [1]: "Adam was created with an active principle of holiness." Hopkins [2]: "He was made in the moral image of God, with a good discerning taste or disposition, a rectitude of mind and will, or heart, by which he was perfectly conformed to the rule of his duty, or the moral law." Dwight (i. 346): "Adam possessed a sanctified or virtuous mind at his creation;" (i. 347): "The affections of his soul at his creation were virtuous;" (i. 394): "Man was created holy without any mixture of sinful affections." [3]

Rationalists view the primitive state as one of savagery, out of which man emerges by gradual cultivation; *Pantheists* say: Spirit begins in nature, and is gradually developed to reason and goodness: *Pelagians* argue for a total moral indifference as the primitive state; *Arminians* find the image of God mainly in man's immortality and dominion over the brutes: *The General*

---

[1] Works, ii. 400. [2] Works, i. 196.
[3] Emmons says: "It is agreeable to the *nature* of virtue or holiness to be created." Moral exercises "are virtuous or vicious in *their own nature*, without the least regard to the *cause* by which they are produced." But he does not recognize in man any power of action before or in distinction from action. His position was overthrown by Dr. N. W. Taylor.

Orthodox view is: The image consisted in the entire spiritual capacities and powers of man, which were in a state of positive proclivity to holiness and to divine wisdom (or the enlightenment from God), which state was to undergo a trial in order to become confirmed. While doubtless there has been much exaggeration as to Adam, the substantial truth, nevertheless, is expressed in this last position. To the questions, Could holiness be created? Can it be created in me? perhaps the only answer that need be given is that man may be so created—and new-created—that the spontaneous bent of his soul is towards a holy end. Sartorius speaks of the original righteousness in relation to man's whole being, as his *health* in relation to the body. As health is not different from the bodily powers, and is not a special substance, but only a normal condition of the members, from which the well-being of the body results: so grace is not a special substance in man, but the normal, unperverted nature of the whole faculties of man in all his impulses, in which is also contained an untried blessedness.

CHAPTER XII.

THE DESTINATION OF MAN IF HE HAD CONTINUED IN OBEDIENCE. THE COVENANT OF LIFE OR OF WORKS.

By the Covenant of Life is meant God's destination of man to "life," if he had not fallen, which is declared or intimated in the prohibition with the penalty, Gen. ii. 17. The term "covenant" is not understood here as implying an actual transaction, a compact distinctly made and entered into by two parties. What is meant to be set forth by the term is, that if man had continued in his state of original rectitude, if he had stood the trial, the test, he would have had what is here called *life*, as the reward of his obedience. Or, in other words, if man had continued in his original state, had not transgressed the law, he would have reached the great end of his being; his destination under the divine government would have been complete. What that destination was, may be gathered partly from what we know about the nature and capacities of man, but chiefly by reasoning back from what we know to be accomplished by the redemption through Christ, to wit:

1. He would have come to a state of confirmed holiness and perfect wisdom and communion with God.

2. It is possible that the natural body, in the course of its development and growth, would have come to be what is called in Scripture the spiritual body of the resurrection,—although this is only a speculation from the analogy of what is and is to be done in Christ and his people (his own resurrection and ascension and 1 Thess. iv. 17). How this would have been attained without death, we of course do not know,—perhaps as the butterfly from the chrysalis. There is nothing in the so-called laws of nature to forbid the possibility. The resurrection proves that death, as we now know it, is an unnatural state.[1]

3. With Adam would have begun a kingdom of God on earth, and the laws of marriage and increase of population would have been laws of increase to that kingdom on earth.

4. To man would have been given dominion over the world, subduing it unto himself in the service of God. Man was made to be prophet, priest, and king here on earth. He lost his right by the Fall, and Christ came to be prophet, priest, and king, in order that, standing in man's stead, He might restore what was lost in the fall.

---

[1] As to the "tree of life," whether through its inherent virtue or by divine grace, the immortality was to be conferred, is not decided. Augustine calls it a "sacrament." Hengstenberg (Rev. ii. 35) takes it to be a tree of life, "not as conferring, but symbolizing, life."

PART IV.

CHRISTIAN HAMARTOLOGY. THE DOCTRINE RESPECTING SIN.

CHAPTER I.

THE FALL HISTORICALLY VIEWED.[1]

Westminster Shorter Catechism, answer to Ques. 13: "Our first parents, being left to the freedom of their own will, fell from the estate wherein they were created by sinning against God."

§ 1. *The Temptation: is it Historical?*

Position: The New Testament treats it as such, and draws doctrinal consequences from its facts: Rom. v. 14; 1 Cor. xv. 22; 1 Tim. ii. 13.

It is said that Moses could not have known it as a history: but he might have known it by tradition, and what he did not know in that way, he might have obtained by revelation.

It is also said that the *form* of the narrative is allegorical. The form is rather natural, in conformity with man's condition. It is to be interpreted, we suppose, in the way of a real temptation, though we would concede that Satan may be here represented in the form of a serpent, so that "serpent" here means, is *the name of*, Satan, and that name being taken as the equivalent of Satan, the narrative goes under that similitude; and that is all the symbolical element which need be supposed to be in the narrative; the curse being not literally a curse on the serpent, but on Satan, and being represented as a curse on the serpent. It is not necessary to assert that Satan took the form

[1] Edwards on Original Sin; Hopkins, i. 8, a very able development; Julius Müller, The Christian Doctrine of Sin, the great work of our century.

of a serpent, though we think it is probable that the Tempter did appear in *some* form.[1]

To those in the condition of our first parents, God would not probably have given an abstract law, but a specific command. It was the easiest of commands, apparently; and as the obedience was easier, the ill-desert of failure was much greater. In short, if the race were to be tried again, the circumstances of man's condition as here given are as natural[2] as any other supposable circumstances, and as favorable to man as any could be.

So that the temptation is suitable to the *condition* of our first parents. If that condition was an historical fact, there is no reason why the temptation should not have been. The objection that it is unreasonable to suppose that so much could be made dependent on beings in such a state, is to be met by pointing out that the state was as good a one as we can suppose.

Furthermore, the connection in this world between sin and evil spirits, as the Scriptures describe it, is historical fact, and hence the beginning of this connection—in the temptation—is to be viewed as historical. The conflict between Christ and Satan was real, the conflict is real between Christ's kingdom and Satan's. Christ met and conquered Satan and all his host for us, in a struggle of which we have only a partial revelation and a dim conception. It would appear that the power of Satan in the world reached its culminating point in the time of Christ, and has been less ever since. If Christ's temptation by Satan and victory over him were historical events, there seems to be no ground for supposing that the first temptation was not an historical event.

§ 2. *The Features of the Temptation.*

1. Man, as we have said, was in circumstances which were highly favorable to him. In the profuse bounty of the earth only one point was forbidden. The prohibition made a real,

---

[1] The Serpent of Eden from the Point of View of Advanced Science, by Rev. John Duns, D.D. (Free Church of Scotland), in Bib. Sac., Jan. '64. De Bow's Rev., '60: "The original tempter a black man,—the gardener."

[2] Everything is in *concrete* form, with depths of truth, such as myths alone could never have.

practical test, but one where obedience was easy. Dwight (i. 398): "No metaphysical or philosophical discussion was demanded or admitted." The reward of obedience was to be great, and the penalty of disobedience great, more so than they then knew, but it was sufficiently known: they knew that a divine command was given, with a penalty attached.

2. The temptation was subtle, corresponding to the character of the tempter and suitable to that of the woman. The first question excited curiosity, the next assertion aroused pride. The heart of the temptation is in the desire to know, and not in the sensual gratification. Knowledge, independence, likeness to the higher beings, were to be gained. First there is suggested the doubt of God, whether He could be trusted, then there is the appeal to pride, the spirit of "affecting deity," which had perhaps first prevailed with the tempter himself,[1] then a solicitation through the senses.

3. As to the Possibility of the Fall. What is here in question is, the psychological possibility of the fall. Man was made mutable. In his primitive state, he loved God spontaneously. Would he love Him in spite of temptation? He knew good in direct feeling: he knew his relation, and God's rightful command. The temptation does not give the necessity of sinning, but it gives the necessity of deciding between good and evil, God and the world. The state of the case, as far as we can enter into Adam's experience, is this: Before the command there was the state of love without the thought of the opposite: a knowledge of good only, a yet unconscious goodness: there was also the knowledge that the eating of the fruit was against the divine command. The temptation aroused pride: the yielding to that was the evil. Taking the fruit was not the sin essentially, the yielding to pride was the sin. The change was there The change was not in the choice as an executive act, nor in the result of that act—the eating, but in the choice of supreme love to the world and self, rather than supreme devotion to God. It was an immanent preference of the world,—not a love of the world following upon the choice, but a love of the world which is the choice itself.

[1] Tim. iii. 6.

We cannot account for Adam's fall, psychologically. In saying this we mean: It is inexplicable by anything outside of itself. We must receive the fact as ultimate, and rest there. Of course we do not mean that it was not in accordance with the laws of moral agency,—that it was a violation of those laws: but only that we do not see the mode, that we cannot construct it for ourselves in a rational way. It differs from all other similar cases of ultimate preference *which we know;*[1] viz., the sinner's immanent preference of the world, where we know there is an antecedent ground in the bias to sin, and the Christian's regeneration, or immanent preference of God, where we know there is an influence from without, the working of the Holy Spirit.

Of course we do not mean that we may not make suppositions enough to account for it, both in respect to man's soul and to God's agency. But then the difficulty is only transferred to the suppositions, and remains just as great; and it is better to leave it with the simple fact—as ultimate in the case—of an immanent preference, free, accountable.

Examples of such suppositions: (*a.*) That the Divine Spirit left Adam before his choice. This would seemingly account for the fall: but then the difficulty arises, as to the taking away of the Spirit, which we naturally suppose to be the consequence, and not the antecedent occasion of the fall; and if the Spirit remained in Adam, how could he have fallen? (*b.*) God arranged events so that Adam would certainly fall, yet he fell by his own free choice.[2] But this too drives us to choice, as ultimate. (*c.*) Natural susceptibility explains the fall: Adam desired the food, had his ambition aroused, and, under such influences, chose

---

[1] The phrase in the Catechism, "being left to the freedom of their own will," is not intended as a psychological explanation of the fall. It guards against the Supralapsarian view, and also against Necessitarian views. The Supralapsarian says that God decreed the fall after He had decreed election: the Sublapsarian says (in the form preferred by us), that God decreed to permit the fall, and then, in view of his purpose of providing Redemption for the race, elected out of fallen men a people to his praise.

[2] Dr. Emmons has a theory which is certainly not lacking in boldness, the theory of direct divine efficiency. "Satan placed certain motives before his [Adam's] mind, which, by a divine energy, took hold of his heart and led him into sin." "His first sin was a free, voluntary exercise, produced by a divine operation in the view of motives." Works, iv. 356.

freely, which was undoubtedly the case. But here is no explanation. This is merely a statement of the circumstances, without accounting for them. This choice was made while Adam was still loving God: how then could it have been made? (*d.*) He chose because he had the power of contrary choice. This also is leaving it an anomalous case, the only case extant, and impossible at that. (*e.*) If it be said, Pride rose to a certain height, and under its influence man chose to eat, then the pride is the immanent preference itself: if it be said, the pride was merely natural, had no character, and got a character by choice added to it, then pride was chosen,—then that choice of pride was an immanent preference or not: if it was not, we have not reached any character: if it was, we have still an immanent preference to account for.

We must leave the whole question with the immanent preference standing forth as the ultimate fact in the case, which is not to be constructed philosophically, as far as the processes of Adam's soul are concerned: we must regard that immanent preference as both a choice and an affection, not an affection the result of a choice, not a choice which is the consequence of an affection, but both together.[1] As to the divine agency in the case, that simply runs into the general question of the permission of sin, which we have already considered.

CHAPTER II.

THE PENALTY. THE DEATH THREATENED FOR DISOBEDIENCE.

In consequence of the transgression, sentence was pronounced on all who were concerned in it: on the tempter, the woman, and the man. Gen. iii. 14–19. Of the specific term, the death threatened, nothing is directly said, except "dust thou art and unto dust shalt thou return:" but the evils which were included in the original threat are brought out in the more special assign-

---

[1] And this is the ultimate analysis of the psychology of the case in every change of moral character. Here is the mystery of the will's action, and this is the sphere of moral quality, moral accountability.

ments: to the woman, pain and sorrow in childbirth and subjection to man: to man, a condition of toil and sorrow closing in literal death. (The literal sentence on Satan is in accordance with his assumed character: enmity between thee and the woman, thy seed and her seed: you seem to have a triumph, it shall prove a discomfiture.) It would seem that we must give such an interpretation to the whole sentence as shall show that it began to be at once fulfilled.

Death is usually distributed into a three-fold form: as death spiritual, temporal, and eternal; and almost all expositors agree that "death" here includes these three points. It is questioned, however, whether some of these are not to be considered rather the consequence than the strict penalty of sin. The difficulties are as to temporal and spiritual death; there is no question that eternal death is included in the sentence. The objection to including spiritual death is that it "makes sin to be the punishment of sin:" to including temporal death, that it brings a penalty upon infants, *e. g.*, as members of the race simply, and so assigns a "penalty" for something which is not strict personal transgression; also, that Christ has taken away all that really belonged to the original curse, but temporal death is certainly not taken away; and again, on grounds of physiology and modern science, in which death is viewed as a purely natural event. On the other hand, if we say eternal death is all that was included, we are driven to say that there is then no instance of the proper penalty of the law being inflicted in this life, and hence there is no moral government which employs punishment, here. The general, the almost universal, interpretation includes all the three forms: the exceptions are very few.

§ 1. *As to Spiritual Death.*

By this is meant, the loss of communion with God, the withdrawal of the Divine Spirit, the supremacy of worldly and selfish affections—and consequent "moral inability"—with whatever misery comes in connection with these. By spiritual death is not meant merely sin in its formal mode of being, as an act or affection, but sin *as involving* separation from God, the withdrawal of the divine life, and as involving in its very nature misery, wretchedness, pain. Now undoubtedly sin cannot be punished by sin, but a part of its *judicial* consequences may be in bringing with itself, from its very nature, loss of the divine communion, wretchedness and pain. Every passion as it is indulged, not only becomes more sinful, but adds to our estrangement and misery. It is of the nature of all sinful desires that as they increase in intensity and pass beyond certain limits, as they are sure to do, they give pain, not pleasure. In this sense, the sentence of the law begins at once to be fulfilled. We may say, this is only a consequence of sin, but it is a *just* and an ordained consequence of sin, and *only of sin*, under God's moral government; and so it is a part of the punishment of sin, unless we arbitrarily limit the term, punishment. All usage is in favor of this view. All in the soul which we mean by spiritual death: the cutting off from the source of life and from our true happiness which is in holiness, and the power of worldly appetites: these all are a proper part of the penalty. So too with remorse, which comes in the soul as a part of the spiritual death, and which may be said to be the most significant part of the penalty. If the pangs the sinner feels do not belong to his punishment, what does belong to it?

This spiritual death is referred to in the Scriptures, in a variety of strong and vivid representations. Rom. i. 24, where a deeper death in sin is the judicial consequence of certain forms and degrees of transgression; Rom. vii., where we suppose spiritual death is described most fully; Rom. viii. 6; 2 Cor. ii. 16, "a savour of [or from] death" (spiritual) "unto death" (eternal). Eph. ii. 1, where the "death" is distinct from the "trespasses and sins"; Col. ii. 13; 1 John iii. 14.

§ 2. *Temporal Death.*

The question as to the connection of temporal death with sin brings us into the comparatively uninvestigated region of the relation of the moral to the physical, the relations of sin and redemption to our bodily constitution: of sin to death, and of redemption to a resurrection. The fact that the resurrection is a part of redemption leads by inference to the position that the death of the body is a part of the evil or penalty which was the consequence of sin, and from which redemption is to deliver us. There is a spiritualizing of sin and holiness which abstracts them from all relations with the body, from all our natural ties, giving over the whole of physics to natural science. But the Scriptures do undoubtedly maintain a connection between sin and the death of the body, on the one hand, and between redemption and the glorified body, on the other hand. A mechanical view of nature, and a merely abstract spiritualizing and reasoning about sin and redemption, have led to attempts to explain punishment and redemption as if they had nothing, or little, to do with our physical constitution. But sin infects and affects the whole man, soul and body: redemption is also equally extensive,—for the whole man, soul and body. Thus only is the full idea of the Christian redemption realized. Through sin came disorder in the fleshly appetites (Gen. iii. 7); the law of death is at work in our members; and in this respect, also, the sentence began to be fulfilled at once. As to the connection of sin with death: Death is undoubtedly natural for the brutes, who have no proper spiritual being, each animal being only one example of his species, with no spiritual powers and aspirations, no personal being. It is not so with man. Death is not natural for man, considering him from his spiritual side: it is unnatural: immortality is his proper attribute. The separation of soul and body, as we know it, see it, with its pain, sorrow, suffering, is an anomaly, a mystery, an enigma in our being. We would not say that if there were no sin there would be no separation of soul and body; but it is certainly supposable that the transition to another state might be made, without anything of that which now goes to make up the terribleness of death. Then tho power of death over the sinner is another illustration. It is clad in fearfulness to him, and it is natural to consider it as a consequence of transgression. Man's body, of course, in a natural sense could have died like that of other animals, but we cannot say that it *must* have died.[1] The position that temporal death

---

[1] The "hypothetical" (posse non mori) and "absolute" (non posse mori) immunity from death: distinction asserted against Pelagianism.

is a penal consequence of sin is confirmed by the fact that redemption contemplates the resurrection, the restoration of the body. This fact serves to make it seem stranger still, more unnatural, that there should be a separation of the two at the end of our present being: why separated, if to be reunited? It seems —as Müller among others forcibly says—that the only explanation of this anomaly is to be found in the fact revealed in Scripture, that the death of the body is a direct consequence and punishment of transgression. This makes the whole Scriptural representation harmonious. Temporal death is not the whole or a chief part of the penalty of transgression, but still it is a part of the same, under certain aspects and in certain relations.

The passages of Scripture[1] which show that this temporal death is included in the sentence, and is a consequence and the evidence of the existence of sin, are such as follow: Gen. iii. 22; Job iv. 18, 19; xiv. 1-4; Rom. v. 12 seq.; vi. 23; 1 Cor. xv. 21 seq.; xv. 56; 2 Cor. v. 2, 4, cf. Rom. vii. 24; Eph. ii. 4; Col. i. 22; ii. 11; 2 Tim. i. 10. There is an implied reference to this death also (though not exclusively to this) in John viii. 21; xi. 26. In fact, while in the Scriptures "death" is applied to the penalty in the future life, yet, in its primitive meaning, it refers to the dissolution of the body. For Christians this death loses its terrors: it is to be conquered finally by the resurrection to life: yet such is the state and power of sin in them, so deeply has it penetrated their whole nature, that they must still die. The evil is changed into a means of blessing through the grace that is in Christ. Redemption extends not only to pardon, not only to deliverance from the second death and the sense of condemnation, but it also embraces and renovates our whole being. It is to be noted that this death is not merely the separation of soul and body, but includes pain and suffering. It therefore includes whatever may hasten and aggravate the temporal death.

Objections:

1. Is all evil and suffering in this life penalty for sin?— Most unquestionably not. But that does not touch the real

---

[1] See Stier, Words of the Lord Jesus, on John viii. 44. Krabbe on Sin: "There is no passage in Scripture in which there is not a lingering allusion to temporal death."

point, which is, that there *are* evils, sufferings, pains, here, which under God's moral government are punishments for sin. Those are such, and only those, which in Scripture or providence, are seen to be connected with sin, naturally or by infliction. And still further, many pains and evils are to one a punishment, because he is a sinner, and are to another not a punishment, because he is a servant of God. Thus, to the Christian, what was punishment is now chastening: his regeneration transforms it into a remedial influence. So far as sin is in him, too, evil and suffering have the nature of punishment; they are just inflictions for his remaining sin: but still, triumphant over them is the power of grace, making them a final blessing. Death itself comes, and still with solemn terrors, for sin still dwells within him, yet also deprived of its sting, for grace triumphs.

2. The exclusive penalty of the law is eternal death, and consequently temporal death is no part of the penalty. The motives for this objection are two. One is, its bearing on original sin. One argument for the reality of a morally evil condition of every human being at birth, which condition in an important sense is properly to be called sinful, is the death of the body: if men die, they are under the curse of the law: if human beings, as such, are liable to death from the beginning of their existence, then they are also under a judgment for sin or sinfulness. In order to get rid of this conclusion, it is denied that temporal death is any part of the penalty for sin. It is held to be consequence, but not penalty: for, in that case, infants suffering penalty would have a part in the sin which cleaves to the human race. The other motive for the objection is that Christ has removed the penalty of transgression, has taken away the curse: and if so, nothing which the Christian endures here can be a part of the penalty. Otherwise Christ did not endure it all. Moreover, it is involved in the objection, that nothing which sinners endure *here* can be part of the strict penalty for transgression. The position is then, that the penalty is eternal death and only that, and that there is no proper penalty inflicted in this life for the violation of the divine law.

Remarks on Objection 2.

(*a.*) What is meant here by eternal death, it is somewhat difficult to state. It appears to mean: those sufferings which come after the final judgment in execution of the sentence. This involves, of course, the position that at the last judgment will occur the first pronouncing and infliction of the real sentence upon the sinner. Whereas, we understand that every sinner is now under the sentence. The great object of the judgment is not the pronouncing of the sentence, but the winding up of the present course of things, and the vindication of the divine government.

(*b.*) We must note the logical consequences of the position that the only penalty of transgression is eternal death. Then there is no instance of penalty or punishment in this life. All that we suffer here comes under the physical point of view,—it is the appointment of the divine sovereignty,—it comes in the way of consequence: it does not come under the moral point of view, as a just coupling of evil with sin. To carry out the principle, it must be said that remorse is no part of the penalty of sin (while it must be admitted that remorse *is* a principal part of eternal death); and if remorse is no part of the penalty of sin, what is it, and what can be penalty? Moreover, under the strict application of this principle, we could not find an instance of God's moral government in the whole history of mankind: and how is this to be reconciled with God's punishments of men and nations, his threatenings and fulfilment of calamities, his visiting of iniquities, etc., which are broadcast through the Scriptures and in providence? We shall be compelled to say that there are two kinds of divine punishment: one for the violation of the law, and another for—something else. The position that the whole penalty of sin is future, if strictly enforced, would drive God's moral government out of the earth for the sake of getting rid of the proof of original sin.[1]

[1] Or, is a distinction to be made between God's moral and his legal government? ...... If any concede, however, that these other evils are *just* "consequences" of transgression under the divine moral government, concede them to be moral and not merely physical—not merely cases of arbitrary sovereignty and yet prefer to reserve the word "penalty" for the second, for eternal, death,

(*c.*) The difficulty on the ground of the Atonement, as having taken away the whole condemnation of the law, is removed by considering that the object of the atonement is not simply to give pardon and relief from future condemnation, but to deliver from all the just consequences of sin—though these may not all be taken away at once, on account of the evil state remaining. The atonement not only provides for pardon, but for the removal of spiritual death, and also for taking away the chief evils of temporal death. It gives us, moreover, the resurrection of the body. This is a part of the effect of Christ's work. The difficulty has come from restricting the atonement to a mere provision for pardon.

(*d.*) The physical philosophers resolve all punishment into the natural consequences of transgression: some theologians resolve it all into an external infliction, granting that all the momentous "consequences" are out of the sphere of punishment. The true view combines both. The *continuation of a system* in which evils were ordained to be peculiarly "consequent" upon sin, and in which by divine providence such consequences are often specially combined and directed in token of the divine displeasure at transgressions, is a visitation of penalties in the proper sense upon offences.[1]

§ 3. *Eternal Death.*

The third form of the death is eternal. This is also called, the second death, Rev. ii. 11; xx. 6; xxi. 8. The term, second death, is significant: it refers back to a death already existing; it is an intensified form of what already exists; it is not the only penalty, but is the intense and final form of the penalty. By eternal death we understand this: a continuation through eternity of the evils, sufferings, and pains which are the just consequence of sin. These are heightened, of course, by all the

---

so as to have a more precise usage for this definite case (which certainly has its special circumstances): though they depart from the general usage, yet it may be allowed, perhaps, as a mere definition for one class of cases.

[1] Denial of this gives a great advantage to such writers as Combe. Temporal evils are made to be only natural consequences of sin, and the *moral* is banished from the present sphere.

circumstances of the then existing state, by the fact that mercy is lost, that hope is forever excluded, etc. This second death or final condemnation is represented in Scripture as inflicted only in view of actual transgression, and it is there represented not only as punishment for violation of law, but also for the rejection of the gospel. There is a liability or exposedness to it in all the members of Adam's race, but the reality of it comes only to those who are condemned on account of their works. James i. 15; Rom. vi. 21; vii. 6; 1 John v. 16.

As has been already said, we cannot regard this eternal, or second, death as a new, an absolutely distinct form of the penalty of sin, so that it may be said to be that penalty in the strict sense, while the other forms are not. The elements of eternity, of hopelessness, of intensified evil, are added, but the very epithet, eternal, implies that it is death *continued* through eternity. Still further, if the temporal evils can all be regarded as only the consequence of transgression, eternal death might equally be regarded as a consequence: and if the eternal death is a penalty, then the temporal death may be a penalty. We cannot conceive of an element in the eternal penalty, of which there is not an analogy or beginning in our temporal lot. The contrary persuasion seems to us to rest on a merely external theory of punishment, taken by figure from human justice.

Summary.

Death, in its most general idea, as the penalty of the law, includes all the evils and sufferings which come upon us, justly, under God's moral government, in consequence of the transgression of the divine law. The object of the penalty is to give sanction to the law, testifying to God's displeasure at sin. In a state of probation, these evils may also be means of trial, and may even become only chastisements. They may be internal or external: remorse and pain of soul, or sufferings and death of the body. The loss of the divine favor and of the Divine Spirit is also amongst them. In short, the general notion of death is separation from God and from all good, on the one hand, and on the other, suffering; as the consequences, the penal consequences, of transgression. It corresponds to "life," which includes all good, and as the expression of divine approbation, as the award to obedience. More specifically, death is (*a.*) spiritual, the forfeiture of the Spirit, moral inability, the internal legitimate consequence of sin—perhaps including remorse; (*b.*) Evils and pains—perhaps including here remorse—closing in death of the body; (*c.*) Most specifically, death, as the full penalty of sin, is eternal: it is hopeless misery, all the consequences of sin and wretchedness inflicted in various ways in God's providence, enduring forever. This, in the highest sense, is the penalty of the law. As to Adam, when he sinned, he came at once to a state of spiritual death, the curse of temporal death began to work (we may *suppose* that the withdrawal of the Spirit gave such supremacy to the bodily appetites that they began to derange the bodily constitution, making it certain that death would ensue), and he was justly exposed to eternal death, from which only grace could rescue him.

CHAPTER III.

THE CONSEQUENCES OF THE FALL TO THE HUMAN RACE.

Answer to Q. 17, Westm. Shorter Catech.: "The fall brought *mankind* into an estate of sin and misery;"—to Q. 16, "The covenant being made with Adam, not only for himself, but for all his posterity, all *mankind*, descending from him by ordinary generation, sinned in him, and fell with him in his first transgression."

The emphasis here is on *mankind*: the fall affected man as man, every man as a member of the human race. The divine dealing was with Adam, not only for himself, but as "a public person": all mankind, *descending from him by ordinary generation,* are involved in his first act of disobedience. No personal presence of individuals is intended to be asserted. The idea is this: Adam is not only the individual man Adam, but the head of the race: all the race is from him by natural descent: he was created innocent, and fell: his transgression involved us, not in a personal sense, or in our personal relations, but so far as we have the common position and liabilities of the whole race under the divine government. In consequence of his first sin, all men come into the world alienated from God, propense to sin, and exposed or liable to eternal death, unless grace interpose. This is the simple fact of the case. It is not so much a theory as the statement of a fact. The Scriptures trace this condition of mankind, this common estate, back to the transgression of Adam. Whether this is viewed as a matter of pure divine sovereignty, or of justice, does not alter the facts of the case. Even if it is sovereignty, it must be in some sense a just sovereignty. The doctrine then does not immediately concern individual responsibility as such, but has to do with the common heritage and condition of humanity. The question about individual responsibility, desert, and destiny, is distinguishable and to be kept distinct. Although the two run into each other, yet we can draw the line, viz., in personal consent to sin and evil. There personal responsibility arises, but whether all that is moral, or all that concerns the divine moral government, begins there—is quite a different question.

§ 1. *Sin as known by Experience.*

All men, even in their natural state, know that they are not as they ought to be; that they are living in a state of alienation from God. A sense of sin and guilt has always attended the human race. But the full power of sin is known only by the redeemed, to whom the law has been a schoolmaster to bring them to Christ. Grace has taught them in respect to sin. Every Christian knows that there is in him by nature, and in him still, a profound depth of sin: he experiences its power in daily conflicts, in the necessity of constant self-denial. He knows sin as the state of alienation from God, and as lust for the world, as the higher and the lower forms of selfishness: the higher being pride, independence of God; and the lower, that which leads us to seek the world. He sees that, in his natural state, his heart's affections are perverted, his understanding is darkened, his will is set in him to do evil. Thus no one feels or fully knows the terrible power of sin, until he is renewed or is in the process of renewal.

This corruption and evil of human nature, reaching to its very depths, the sinner under conviction and the Christian acknowledge and feel to be guilt; it makes the soul guilty before God; God cannot but look upon it with displeasure and abhorrence, and visit it with his judgments.

It is also—this too is a matter of experience—so deeply rooted and grounded in man that he can be delivered from its power only by redemptive grace; he feels the need of atoning blood. He knows that so far as there is in him anything good, it is from grace alone; in all the course, from the beginning to the end, grace leads, enlightens, renews, sanctifies, and grace alone. "It is a striking fact in Scripture, that statements of the depth and power of sin are chiefly from the regenerate." (Thomasius.)

§ 2. *The universal Sinfulness of Men as testified to in Scripture.*
The general position: The whole of the Old and New Testaments rest on the presupposition of the universality of depravity.

I.—The confessions of those who have been renewed. They speak, in Scripture, of their own experience. 1 Kings viii. 46; Job ix. 2; xiv. 4; xv. 14; Ps. li. 6, 7, 10; Eccles. vii. 20; Prov. xx. 9; 1 John i. 8–10; Rom. vii. 15–25,—the two passages Rom. vii. 14–25 and viii. 1–11 exhibit the two sides of regeneration: still the sense is to show the terrible power and depth of sin in us; Gal. v. 17, showing that even in good men the power of sin is so strong that all their goodness is from grace: the conflict in them is between grace and nature.

II.—Passages which speak directly of the universality of sinfulness. Gen. vi. 5, "heart," center of moral life: "imagination" and "thoughts" from that—though this is not to be too strongly urged; Gen. viii. 21; Ps. xiv,—this is the judgment of God on man (Paul cites it in Rom. iii. 10–12) for all, Jews and heathen. "The Old Testament has no passage in which the universality and depth of human corruption is so powerfully depicted" (Hengstenberg); Ps. cxliii. 2; Eccl. ix. 3; Jer. xvii 9; Matt. xv. 19; John iii. 6; Gal. iii. 22.

It is objected that the passages of the Old Testament, particularly Gen. vi. 5, and viii. 21, treat of those times only. But in the New Testament the writers cite similar passages as universally true: e. g., Is. vi. 10 is cited in John xii. 40 (and elsewhere); and Rom. iii. 10–18 contains citations from Ps. v.; x.; xiv.; xxxvi.; cxl.; and Is. lix.

III.—The assertions of Scripture as to the nature and necessity of Regeneration prove the universality of depravity. *Only two states* of men are known or recognized. The two states in contrast: Eph. iv. 22–24; 2 Pet. i. 4. The nature and necessity of regeneration: John iii. 7. The necessity of regeneration: Rom. vii. 14; John iii. 5; Eph. iv. 18; Eph. ii. 1, 5; Col. ii. 13. Compare Matt. xvi. 24; John xii. 25; Rom. vi. 4–6; Gal. v. 24.

IV.—The assertions of Scripture as to the necessity and nature of Redemption show a universal depravity of the human race. (*a*.) If the atonement is general, for all mankind, then all mankind must be in a sinful state. The depravity must be universal, because the atonement is to deliver men from a sinful condition: Rom. v. 18; Heb. ii. 9; 2 Tim. i. 10. (*b*.) Man cannot deliver himself, cannot "live" by the law: Rom. iii. 19; iv. 15; vii. 14; Eph. ii. 15. (*c*.) The gospel is of the forgiveness of sins: Luke xxiv. 47; (*d*.) No one cometh to the Father but through Christ: John xiv. 6; Acts iv. 12; Matt. xvi. 16; John i. 12, 13; iii. 14, 15; Rom. iii. 9, 19, 20, 23; Rom. v. 12–19; Gal. iii. 27.

§ 3. *This universal Depravity is set forth in the Scriptures as total,* i. e., *as affecting the whole Man.*

The proof of this is, to some extent, the same as the proof of the universality of sinfulness, which shows that man is depraved as far as the affections of the heart and the external acts of the will are concerned. As to the influence of depravity on the intellect, the Scriptures have statements such as the following: Eph. iv. 18; 1 Cor. ii. 14, which shows that the gospel first gives true light; Eph. v. 8; 2 Cor. iv. 6; John i. 5; iii. 19; 2 Cor. iii. 18. So, sin is "folly," "blindness," "darkness": Is. xlix. 9; Prov. xiv. 8; Rom. ii. 19; 2 Cor. vi. 14.

By "total depravity" is never meant that men are as bad as they can be; nor that they have not in their natural condition certain amiable qualities; nor that they may not have virtues in a limited sense (*justitia civilis*). But it is meant that depravity, or the sinful condition, of man infects the whole man: intellect, feeling, heart, and will; and that in each unrenewed person some lower affection is supreme, and that each such is destitute of true love to God. On these positions: as to (*a.*) the power of depravity over the *whole* man, we have given proof from Scripture[1]; as to (*b.*) the fact that in every unrenewed man some lower affection is supreme, experience may be always appealed to: men know that their supreme affection is fixed on some lower good—intellect, heart, and will going together in it, or that some form of selfishness is predominant—using selfish in a general sense—self seeking its happiness in some inferior object, giving that its supreme affection; as to (*c.*), that every unrenewed person is without supreme love to God, it is the point which is of greatest force, and is to be urged with the strongest effect, in setting forth the depth and "totality" of man's sinfulness: unrenewed men have not that supreme love to God which is the substance of the first and great command.

§ 4. *This depraved State is native to Men.*

Man has such a nature that he uniformly sins; it is as certain that he will sin as that he will speak or reason. He will

[1] Experience and observation also furnish proof. Aristotle, Eth. vi. 12: "For depravity perverts the vision and causes it to be deceived on the principles of action, so that it is clearly impossible for a person who is not good to be really wise or prudent." Quintilian: "The orator is a good man, skilled in speaking," cited from Cato, and adds: "Goodness in a man is the greater and more important quality." "The pure heart maketh a clear head." Carlyle (on Mirabeau): "The real quality of our insight, how justly and thoroughly we shall comprehend the nature of a thing, especially of a human thing, depends on our patience, our fairness, lovingness, what strength so ever we have; intellect comes from the whole man, as it is the light that enlightens the whole man."

exercise his moral powers in transgression as certainly as he begins to speak or act. "Native" is here used in the general sense of what belongs by nature to the human constitution so that it will be acted out.

I.—The rational grounds for calling this state native or connatural.

1. We cannot trace it back in experience to any deliberate choice, but only to a spontaneous preference.

2. Sin begins to show itself, probably as soon as it can, in all children. As soon as sin *could* be manifested, it is manifested, in all.

3. This has been the case everywhere, with all men, in all ages, under the most varied circumstances. There have been no exceptions, unless where grace may have been bestowed before moral action has commenced.

4. This depravity is such that men come into a different state, as a matter of fact, only through and by divine grace. In every case divine grace has been the source of different action, and divine grace acting against, subduing and renovating the nature.

Now, on rational grounds, it is inconceivable that such should be the state of the case, if there were not a specific bias to what is sinful, somehow, in man as man. There is a determinate reason in man's state, why he should sin, rather than not sin. There is as much proof of a spontaneous out-going of the soul in the way of worldliness and selfishness, as of anything spontaneous in man. This depraved state cannot be accounted for by the mere power of choice: that gives no reason why the acts of choice are sinful and not otherwise.

Objections.

1. Adam sinned once without such predisposition, why not all his descendants?

Answer. (*a.*) That which may be possible in a single case is not probable for a race. (*b.*) The Scriptures make a difference between Adam's case and the case of men in general. He is represented as having begun his course in innocence, and his sin of course implies a fall from that state of innocence. The

ANTECEDENTS OF REDEMPTION.

case is not said to be such with any other member of the human race.[1]

2. Sin may be accounted for by bad example. This is the Pelagian view.

But how are we to account for the universality of the bad example? This is simply using the effect to account for the cause. How happens it that *bad* examples have such universal influence, and why do not good examples—as of pious parents—have an equally good influence?

3. Depravity may be accounted for by the fact that the senses, that man's animal nature is earliest developed. This is the Rationalistic ground.

But in the senses and in man's animal nature *as* animal, there is nothing sinful in and of itself. There is nothing sinful in any animal propensity taken in its proper place. The difficulty still remains. *Why* do the senses and the animal part of man always take this form of selfishness and worldliness? Why are these always supreme? Why is man subject to the world and sense?

4. This doctrine of a connatural depravity supposes a positive principle of evil in the soul as a specific thing, and that implanted by divine power or agency. God must create this principle of sin in the soul.

The common orthodox view is that from the absence of the Divine Spirit, justly withheld, the supremacy of the lower and selfish principles naturally follows, without a specific principle of evil.[2]

5. This doctrine supposes the very *nature* of man to be depraved.

The word, nature, is used in different senses. It is sometimes meant to imply simply the constitutional faculties and endowments. In that sense it is not claimed or said that man's nature is depraved. It is also used in the sense of the bias or bent of human nature, a state of the faculties, their bent, disposition, underlying principle. In this sense the na-

---

[1] See Edwards, Orig. Sin, 261.
[2] On this point Edwards has a noble passage, ii. 477.

ture is depraved; because that bent or bias is the evil principle. Perhaps it is not strictly accurate to call it a depravity of nature because nature is more frequently used in the previous sense. According to Calvinistic theology, depravity is of the accidents and not of the substance of human nature; *i. e.*, it is separable. A renewal of the soul does not suppose a change in the physical constitution, but a change in the moral principle that is in man. "Principle" is defined by Edwards as a foundation laid in human nature for a particular kind of exercises. It is not the faculties themselves, but the direction of those faculties.

II.—Scriptural Proof that depravity is connatural.

1. The strongest proof is found in the Scriptural usage of the word σάρξ, translated flesh. John iii. 6, here "the flesh" includes the natural birth, but "flesh" is not that which is not spiritual, our material frame, but the principle opposite to that which is spiritual: the passage contains birth, sinfulness, and derivation. "The flesh" means that which is native to man. The fact that it also means the bodily constitution makes the proof complete that depravity is native. Our evil desires are traced to the "flesh," as our good desires are traced to the spirit. Rom. vii. 18: Flesh is here not merely the equivalent of sinfulness, but the whole man in his present sinful condition. Sin is spoken of as dwelling in the flesh. Gal. v. 19-21: The inclusion here of *heresies* in the works of the flesh shows that the word is not restricted to the physical sphere. Rom. viii. 6: The *mind* of the flesh. Eph. iv. 18: Here to the flesh is attributed *understanding*. In Gal. v. 17 we also see that the flesh is not a mere state, but an impelling power—ἐπιθυμεῖ. The essential thing in this flesh is, then, according to the Scriptures, not merely a sensual condition, or any overbalance of the senses, but the principle of sin. The word designates the whole natural man, in all his movements of heart, mind and will: it is used to describe man as estranged from God, from life, and subject to sin and death: hence its constant antagonism with spirit.

2. Besides this use of σάρξ, there are other passages of Scripture showing that depravity is traced to a native state. Ps. li. 4: David, in the deepest penitence, is confessing his sin—sin so deep

in him that he traces it to his very birth (as the next verse shows). There are only two possible interpretations: (*a.*) that the sin referred to is that of David's mother. But it is a singular time for him to take to confess his mother's sin. (*b.*) It refers to his own native state, his condition by birth. It means, my state, as I came from my mother's womb, was a state of sinfulness.[1] The only way of escaping this is taking it poetically. Eph. ii. 3: The sense which the term flesh has here has been already defined. The word "nature" is to be considered. Let the connection be noted: "lusts of the flesh"; words which express the native condition and tendencies as fully as any can do, and "were by nature children of wrath" (wrath[2] must mean wrath divine; the attempt of Maurice to render "children of impulse" is without support). Actual transgressions were already expressed, "among whom also we all," etc.; he could have said, on account of these active desires we were children of wrath, but what he does is to add another circumstance to these actual sins, "*and* were by nature," etc.[3] The unemphatic position of φύσει (τέκνα φύσει ὀργῆς) is important. "It is an indirect and therefore more convincing assertion" of original sin.[4] φύσει in Gal. ii. 15, means, transmitted, inborn; in Rom. ii. 14,—inherent; in Gal. iv. 8,—essential, nature. The only interpretation by which this conclusion can be avoided is: "we were by nature such that we became through our own act the children of wrath."[5] But if the apostle had meant this, he could have said so; there is a proper Greek word for "became": the word which is used can only be rendered "were." There may be discussion as to the full extent of the wrath, and the character of the native depravity; but as to the fact of such a depravity and of its being, in some sense, an object of divine displeasure, there can be

---

[1] De Wette's translation: "Behold with a sinful nature was I born, yea, in my mother's womb did I possess it." Tholuck: "David confesses that sin begins with the life of man; that not only his works, but the man himself, is guilty before God."

[2] In thirty-four other places in the New Testament the word has only the usual sense—the punitive justice of God.

[3] See Harless on Ephesians. See also Müller, Sin, ii. 306.

[4] Ellicott.

[5] Dr. Taylor's "Concio ad clerum."

no doubt, from this passage.[1] Job xv. 14, shows that sin is hereditary. It is to be viewed in connection with xiv. 1.

Objections.

1. The Scriptures speak of children as innocent: Matt. xviii. 3; xix. 13; Luke xviii. 17.

These passages undoubtedly imply a relative innocence of children, but they do not do away with the depravity or native propensity to sin in us, because the children are to come to Christ, and Christ is a Saviour. The very fact that they are to come to Him proves that they need a renewal.[2]

2. From certain expressions of Scripture. (*a.*) 1 John iii. 4: This is supposed by some to be the nearest to a definition of sin which the Bible contains. But the rendering should not be "sin is the transgression of the law," but, "sin is non-conformity to the law."[3] This passage is urged to prove that all sin is in exercises, but it rather shows, under strict translation, that sin is a state. (*b.*) James i. 15: This is urged to prove that sin, properly speaking, only exists when it is "brought forth" in conscious activity, but what it really shows is, that "the lust" is that which produces sin, that like begets like. The sin produced shows the sinful disposition. Instead of proving that such a disposition is not sinful, the passage proves the contrary. These passages confirm the general definition of sin given in the Westminster Catechism, which is probably the best that can be given: "Sin is any want of conformity unto, or transgression of, the law of God."

---

[1] Besides these passages, Müller also cites 1 Cor. vii. 14 (ii. 376).

[2] There is a relative innocence. Ps. cvi. 38: The "innocent blood" is the blood, not of children, nor of innocence before God. So, 2 Kings xxiv. 4. Jonah iv. 11 is a proverbial expression. Rom. ix. 11 simply states that moral quality can only attach to moral existence.

[3] [Revised Version: "sin is lawlessness."]

CHAPTER IV.

ORIGINAL SIN.

Thus far we have considered the general facts as to human sinfulness, and have traced them back to a sinful, corrupt inclination or tendency. This only brings us to the verge of the real problem, which is contained in the doctrine of Original Sin.

We have here the question of IMPUTATION. This turns upon the three terms: sin, guilt, and punishment. If we define all these by their relation to personal acts exclusively, we cannot apply them to any native condition or race relation; there can be in no sense a moral oneness of mankind in the sight of God, and no such moral dealing on his part with *mankind* as is intended to be expressed in the term Imputation: in a word, there cannot be any Original Sin. But we should understand that this result is due purely to the definition we have made, and that we have dismissed the problem, not solved it.

An important question as to the statements in the Westminster Confession (Conf. vi. 3, Larger Cat., Q. 25, Shorter Cat., Q. 18) may be here briefly considered. In the three chief articles indicated above, the following statement is reiterated: The sinfulness of man's estate, or, original sin, consists: (*a.*) In the guilt of Adam's first sin, (*b.*) the want of original righteousness, and (*c.*) the corruption of his whole nature. The question is: Are these three statements co-ordinate or successive? Is it meant that the sinfulness of man's estate consists in the guilt of Adam's first sin, which was *followed* by the want of original righteousness and by the corruption of his whole nature? If that is the sense then the strict theory of Immediate Imputation has a foothold in the Confession, but if that is not the sense, then it has not. To us it seems plain that these phrases were intended to be co-ordinate, and that no causal relation between them is meant to be expressed. "Guilt" is liability or exposedness to penal evil. It does not mean exclusively personal ill-desert. It has in theology a well authenticated meaning, though in the modern sense it is applied in strictness only to personal ill-desert. But in the Confession guilt is exposure to punishment. The imputation is not said to be of the sin, but of the guilt of that sin. That is the strict sense. If it were an imputation of sin, then it might be that our natural sinfulness as coming from Adam might be included in the imputation: but as imputation here is exposure to punishment, it cannot be said that our sinfulness is a part of the imputation, unless it be also said that sin is a part of the punishment. In the article in the Confession (vi. 3), the natural relationship of mankind to Adam is put first: "they being the root of all mankind." This fact that all mankind were contained in them as the root appears to be taken as the ground of the procedure of imputation. This is the view taken in Mediate Imputation,[1] *i. e.*, that the natural headship comes first, and that the federal headship is grounded upon it. *It is not said* that the want of the original righteousness, and the death in sin, and the corrupted nature, were a part of the imputation; and this must be said to sustain the strict theory of Immediate Imputation; the corruption must be a part of what is imputed.

Another statement. Immediate Imputation, in its extreme form,[2] is the theory of the federal headship of Adam in distinction from the natural headship. It says, God determined to create a certain number, and He determined that they should fall into sin, and that out of that fallen mass some should be redeemed. As yet it is only a hypothetical possible number of individuals who are thus to fall, and of whom some are to be redeemed. Adam is appointed in the divine purpose to be the federal head of all that come into this world, to stand as their representative. Adam is to stand for all those supposed and supposable individuals who are to live here,—to stand for them as a federal head, as much as a representative in congress stands

---

[1] [In its higher form. There is a form, at least one attributed by opponents, which allows no federal headship to Adam, and makes the corruption *in the individual* the only ground of imputation.]

[2] [In this country the most influential advocates of Immediate Imputation—the Princeton theologians—have not urged it in this form. The supralapsarian elements are disavowed by them. See Dr. Charles Hodge's Systematic Theology and Dr. A. A. Hodge's Outlines.]

for the people of his district. What Adam does is to be reckoned to their account, they as yet being by supposition without any character, but as Adam does, so they are to become. Because he sins, they are likewise to come under the penalty of sin. Then in order that that may be carried out, God makes this Adam (who is hypothetical as yet) to be the head of a race, in order that what he does may be transmitted down to all those individuals for whom he stood. *The natural headship is instituted in order to carry out the federal headship.* And the sinful condition of every member of this race is a punishment for Adam's sin. Each individual is punished for Adam's sin by being made sinful. Adam is said to stand for them all, and what he does is immediately made over to them. The theory of Mediate Imputation on the other hand is, that God makes Adam to be the head of a race: he sins: in consequence of his sin, because he is the head of a race, all his descendants are born in a sinful condition, not as a punishment, but in the way of a natural connection, and the punishment of each is on the ground of the sinful condition of each, including as final punishment his own personal acts and ill-desert. Punishment is always based on sin, and each individual's punishment is based upon what he is as an individual. The infliction of punishment is on the ground of the sinful nature, and just as much in Adam's descendants as in Adam himself.[1] The relation of Adam's transgression to ourselves, according to the statement in the Catechism, is not to be viewed as that of an individual transgressing for us as individuals. Adam is not only the individual Adam, but the head of the race; all

[1] [It should be remembered that the author is here stating what is commonly understood by Immediate and Mediate Imputation, and is not giving his own view. On the whole he favored the theory of Mediate Imputation, yet not precisely in the form as given above. There is a note in his papers which reads thus: "Neither Mediate nor Immediate Imputation is wholly satisfactory." There is no further explanation, but it is probable that one point of the theory of Mediate Imputation as it is sometimes urged, which he found unsatisfactory, was the position stated above: "the punishment of each is [exclusively] on the ground of the sinful condition of each." This fixes the divine regard in the matter of imputation upon the isolated individual, viewed as corrupt before personal action, etc., and leaves out of consideration all race liabilities, which the author elsewhere strongly insists upon. It would seem that he intended to assert a proper federal headship based upon the natural; but it is much to be lamented that this note is the only indication of the final statement which he had in mind.]

the race come from him by natural descent; he was created innocent, and fell; his transgression does not involve us in a personal sense, immediately, but only so far as we have the common liabilities of the whole race under the divine government. In consequence of this, all men come into the world alienated from God, propense to sin, and exposed or liable to eternal death unless grace interpose.

Original Sin means in theology just one thing: not, the first sin of Adam; not, the first sin of each man; but—the general condition of all the members of the race by birth, before actual transgression, into which they are brought in consequence of the fall of Adam, the head of the race. And the great questions in the debate are, whether this general condition is in some true and proper sense sinful, whether there is an imputation of a sinfulness which justly calls forth God's moral displeasure, and whether such imputation is of what truly belongs to mankind in its connection with its natural and federal head.

§ 1. *General Statements.*

I.—No one can apprehend the doctrine of original sin, nor the doctrine of redemption, who insists that the whole moral government of God has respect only to individual desert, in the way of personal obedience and disobedience, who does not allow that the moral government of God, *as* moral, has a wider scope and larger relations, so that God may dispense suffering and happiness on other grounds (in his all-wise and inscrutable providence) than that of personal merit and demerit. The dilemma here is: the facts connected with native depravity and with the redemption through Christ either belong to the moral government of God, or not. If they do, then that government has to do with other considerations than those of personal merit and demerit (since our disabilities in consequence of sin and the grace offered in Christ are not in any sense the result of our personal choice, though we do choose in our relations to both). If they do not belong to the moral government of God, where shall we assign them? To the physical? That certainly cannot be. To the divine sovereignty? But that does not relieve any difficulty;

for the question still remains, Is that sovereignty, as thus exercised, just or unjust? We must take one or the other of these. The whole (of sin and grace) is a mystery of sovereignty—of mere omnipotence, or a proceeding of *moral* sovereignty. The question will arise with respect to grace as well as to sin: How can the theory that all moral government has respect only to the merit or demerit of personal acts, be applied to our justification? If all sin is in sinning with a personal desert of everlasting death, by parity of reasoning, all holiness must consist in a holy choice with personal merit of eternal life.

We say then, generally, that all definitions of sin which mean *a* sin are irrelevant here. Edwards, vol. ii., p. 309, says: "Original sin .... the innate sinful depravity of the heart" includes not only "the depravity of nature, but the imputation of Adam's first sin; or in other words the liableness or exposedness of Adam's posterity, in the divine judgment, to partake of the punishment of that sin." This doctrine of original sin in this general shape has come down from the time of Augustine, through all the Reformed confessions, and is recognized by most of the orthodox schools. Historically, the following points have always been agreed upon:

1. That the distinction is to be made between original sin and actual transgression.

2. That original sin belongs to a man as a member of the race, and as the result of Adam's transgression.

3. That it involves, or is, the corruption of the whole race, in its moral bias.

4. That it exists in the race *in its moral relations* to God, not as a mere physical state, nor as a matter of divine sovereignty excluding God's moral government or outside of the same, but that it has to do with the same moral relations in which redemption is to be viewed. The later German divines, too, reacting from Rationalism, are all on this general ground: Neander, Tholuck, Müller, Ebrard, Thomasius, Twesten, Dorner, etc.

NOTE.—As to whether there is a valid distinction between original sin and actual transgression. The simple facts of the case are to be regarded: (1) Native depravity exists: an immanent preference (not known to be the result of a deliberate choice, but which manifests itself as a choice) beyond and before conscious memory; which we associate with, and which involves, a sense of *guilt;* (2) Which we connect with our condition as members of a sinful race, involving us in the common evils of the race; (3) Which the Scriptures assert to be the consequence of the Adamic transgression.

II.—Original sin is a doctrine not, primarily, respecting individuals, in their individual capacity and responsibilities, in their separate personalities; but it is a doctrine respecting what is common to all men,—their common condition and needs,—what belongs to them as members of the human race. It has its bearings on them as individuals, but it has not *specific* reference to this,—just as in the atonement of Christ, redemption is not provided, primarily, for this or that man, but for the whole human race. The Scholastic maxim has its abiding truth: "In Adam the person corrupted the nature: in us, the nature corrupts the person."

III.—In this doctrine it is not pretended, nor is it necessary to give a solution of the problem of moral evil. This is not what we are after in discussing the doctrine. The object of the doctrine as a doctrine is simply to give the general facts of the case on the ground of which the solution of the problem of moral evil is to be attempted. And as to the solution itself the different ways of viewing human sinfulness do not affect it much. It is no more easy to solve it in connection with the theory of "physical constitution," etc., than with the common orthodox view. The constitution is still to be referred back to God. If we say, there is no bias to sin, but only a world of temptation in which sin is certain for all, yet we must say again, God made the world and man.[1]

IV.—In the matter of original sin there are three problems around whose solution the difficulty turns—

1. The relation of the race to the individual—and of the individual to the race: the old question of the genus and individual, running back into the Realism and Nominalism of the Middle Ages.

2. The relation of our native dispositions to their manifesta-

[1] The theory of pre-existence only drives the solution back a little further.

tions: whether we can reason back from the manifestation to what is in the constitution; whether what is expressed in the manifestation can be ascribed to the constitution; whether the phenomena reveal the substance.

3. The relation of the moral government of God, in its general aims and ends, to that government as exercised over individuals: whether the moral government is only for individuals or is also for the race.

V.—And as there are three problems, so there are three terms in the discussion for which definitions are sought: sin, guilt, and punishment. Can these be attributed, in any valid sense, to God's moral government of men as men, in distinction from the government of each individual? Do they have to do with the native dispositions of men? Does the whole of what is moral, in short, lie in personal choice and personal desert (of happiness or of misery)? If it does, we have only an ethical, moral system as the sum and substance of Christian theology.

VI.—In contrast with this mode of viewing man, as simply an individual standing for himself, it seems plain from Scripture that he is there viewed (not excluding his individual responsibilities and deserts) under two prime relations, wider than this (—in respect to God's moral government,—in respect to both sin and holiness): under the relation to Adam as the head of our fallen humanity and the relation to Christ as the head of our renewed humanity. The headship of Adam and the headship of Christ are the two grand foci of the Scriptural system respecting man. Man's personal responsibilities, liabilities, and deserts are brought under, included within, subordinated to, or grow out of, these more general relations in which he stands.

Running through the Scripture, there are two relations of man, under the aspects both of sin and of redemption: one, general; another, individual. There is the sin of the race—a community in sin; the sin of each individual—his own personal acts and responsibility. There is grace for all in Christ, while the faith and obedience of each are also required. We fail of the Scriptural view when we do not emphasize both. If all is individualized, we make mere ethics: if all is generalized, we make necessary sin, and redemption without personal holiness. Nor can we draw the line in experience and consciousness between the two. The great fact at the basis of the doctrine of original sin is that of the moral unity of the human race: man is one in the estate of sin and misery: there is a common guilt and ruin (as well as individual sin):—the great fact at the basis of the new life is that of a common redemption provided for all.

This same point is further illustrated by the general statement that the Scriptural representation makes the headship of Adam on the one hand and the headship of Christ on the other to be the central points in respect to the ruin on the one side, and the recovery on the other, of the whole family of man. Again,—not without the personal intervention and compliance of each individual—his own participation—in the sin and in the redemption. Putting these two over against each other so prominently: the first and second Adam—death from the one, life from and in the other only: this is the great leading grouping of the *whole* human race, in respect to its ultimate destiny, in the sacred Scriptures. This is the Biblical view. The notion of the *Covenants* may be in form a fiction, but it is in fact a fact. It is partly false and wholly true. This is the basis of the whole *history*, of the Bible,—of its facts, as historic, realized in history. This makes the Scriptural view entirely different from any merely moral view of the human race and of human destiny. Each individual of the race is represented as under the one or the other of these two points of view, either as connected with a race that fell in Adam, or with that race as redeemed by Christ.

Another Statement. There are two points of view about man in the Scripture, on the face of it: one that of personal desert and liabilities, another, that of his condition as *man*, as a member of the race, in his social liabilities, in his relations to the whole government of God. To the former, belong the practical, the personal, the ground of personal adjudication, the sphere of actual transgression: to the latter, viz., man in his general relations and liabilities, belong all facts and statements connected with both the *fall* and *redemption.* Neither of these is primarily for each man personally, but each has respect to the race as a whole, to man as man, though both may be in and for each man also.

There is a sinful condition of the race as such, introduced by the fall: over against this God has set a provision of redemption, for the whole race, covering the whole sphere of sin and its consequences. (Limited Atonement, Particular Redemption *ought* to be held only by those who say, all sin consists in sinning.) These are the two grand primary aspects under which the Bible views man. Now the sphere of personal liability and desert comes in under these conditions and arrangements—of the common sin and the common redemption. That sin in each shows itself as preference (consent): then come his personal liabilities and desert, and *not till then.* To him, in this state, salvation, grace through Christ provided for all, is offered: which he may accept or reject. (This is to all to whom the gospel comes.) Sometimes the doctrine of original sin is represented as implying that each individual is personally worthy of eternal damnation for Adam's sin. This is not true. The conditions of judgment as to personal desert do not exist until personal transgression has occurred.

§ 2. *The Facts of the Case, in respect to Original Sin, as given in Scripture.*

We have thus far reached a native depravity, common to all men, the ground and source of actual transgression. The doctrine of original sin carries us back one step further, viz., to the origin of this depraved condition; original sin refers specifically to that. The inquiry is, What is the connection of the depravity of each individual with the sinfulness of others: what is the origin of our native depravity? We speak here of the facts of the case as *given in Scripture.*

I.—The passages already adduced to prove native depravity imply that this depravity is hereditary: Ps. li. 5; John iii. 6; Rom. viii. 7; Eph. ii. 3; Job xv. 14. Also, Luke i. 35, the Annunciation of Christ's supernatural conception by the Holy Ghost, and the result, Christ's holiness.

II.—The Scriptures view the race of man as one, descending from Adam, having a physical and moral unity. This position is at the foundation of the Scriptural doctrines of sin and of redemption.[1] Acts xvii. 26; Gen. i. 26, 28; The Genealogies of the Old Testament: Gen. v., before the flood; Gen. x., after the flood; Matt. xix. 4; 1 Cor. xv. 45; 2 Cor. xi. 3; 1 Tim. ii. 14; Rom. v. 12–19.

III.—The Scriptures further declare that all men are under sin and exposed to its just consequences. Rom. iii. 9; iii. 19, "that all the world may become" ὑπόδικος τῷ Θεῷ subject to the charge of sin before, or by, God; Gal. iii. 2, 3. These passages do not show the connection with Adam, but the state of man as depraved and subject to the divine judgment.

IV.—The Scripture then carries us one step further. In Rom. v. 12–19, it is distinctly declared that Adam's transgression is the source and root of this guilty, depraved condition. Whether with or without our consent, is not now the question. We have here to consider simply the matter of fact that this passage decides at least this much: that the hereditary depravity, the sinful, guilty condition of the race, is to be traced directly to Adam, the head of the race, as its ground and source.

(a.) This position does not rest on the interpretation of the obscure clause ἐφ' ᾧ in verse 12, for it is much more explicitly asserted in the following verses: 15, "if through the offence of one [the] many were dead" [or, died]; 16, "the judgment is by [of] one unto condemnation;" 17, "by one man's offence death reigned by [the] one;" 18, "through the offence of one [one offence] [the] judgment came upon all men unto condemnation;" 19, "through one man's disobedience [the] many were made sinners." Apart from verse 12, these assertions establish the fact that Adam's transgression was the judicial ground of bringing all men into condemnation. Whatever else the passage does or does not prove, it undoubtedly represents a moral judgment on the basis of Adam's offence on the one hand and of

---

[1] Science just at present, inclines to favor the position that mankind is from one pair. The unity of the race might be argued from the powerful social instinct, the love of the race, which is so deeply implanted in us.

Christ's obedience on the other, as the ground of the death of all and of the eternal life which is offered to all. It is utterly inconsistent with the position that all of God's moral dealings have respect ultimately and solely to individual merit and demerit. It is utterly impossible to interpret this passage as teaching or implying a merely physical relationship. It sets forth a moral judgment. (At the same time this passage does not teach the way in which this was done; through what intermediate stages it is carried out and takes effect; through what personal agency of each individual the moral judgment is consummated; and there is room left for further statements. The passage does not assert, nor necessarily involve, the position taken in the extreme immediate imputation theory, viz., that the sin of Adam is the judicial ground of *making us sinful*, or that our native depravity is the punishment of Adam's sin.) The object of the passage. and particularly of the 12th verse, is undoubtedly the contrast between the ruin through Adam and the recovery through Christ. *As really* as Christ is the ground—and the moral ground—of our restitution—and of our moral restitution, so really is Adam of our ruined condition. The headship of the two is explicit and contrasted. Not that they are in all particulars the same; especially are they different in that the restoration is not merely coincident with the ruin, but ampler,—a superabundance of blessings is given in Christ.[1]

(*b*.) As to the 12th verse. Some would read: "and so death passed upon all men *because* all have sinned" [or did sin]. That is, the reason that death passed upon all men is that all have sinned: death (which on this understanding must be eternal death) is the condemnation for sin, and therefore there is no death as penalty where there is not personal sin. (This view does not say: personal death and the ground in each person of personal sin have passed together unto all: death and corruption are interlinked; that might deserve some careful considera-

---

[1] As men sometimes erect a grander edifice over the ruins of one destroyed, so, it might be said, God has done with the temple of humanity. (See John Howe's Living Temple.) Here, in Rom. v., is the best intimation which has ever been given of the final theodicy, and given by the divine oracle, not by human speculation.

tion.) The advocates of this rendering hesitate or refuse to admit that "death" here includes temporal death (which it certainly does); because then it is necessary to say, that all before they die have actually, personally, sinned, and that involves the assertion of a personal transgression in the case of every infant as the ground or reason for its natural death, and also perhaps of its final condemnation. And in saying that the death is eternal death there is an equal difficulty in the implication that the youngest babes have already so violated the law in personal transgression as to be worthy of eternal death. But even if the force of this 12th verse could be annulled by translating ἐφ' ᾧ "because," and making "sinned" refer to personal transgression exclusively, yet the other passages remain, asserting unmistakably that the judgment is "of one unto condemnation."

In our view, the best interpretation of the 12th verse is that suggested by Tholuck and favored by other exegetes:—"and so death passed unto all men *as is manifest in this* that all have [1] sinned." The sense of the verse is this: Sin and death came into the world by Adam: from him death has passed as a common lot upon all, as is seen in this, or as is proved by this, that all have sinned—who could sin. ἐφ' ᾧ explains what goes before, "so far as all have sinned," *i. e.*, death has passed to all from Adam, only so far as sin is found in all: *inasmuch* as it is found in all, the death is universal.

Another statement as to the interpretation of Rom. v. 12. ἐφ' ᾧ should be rendered: "under which relation." "And so death passed upon all men," under which relation, *i. e.*, of death having passed upon them, all have sinned. It is a clause appended to prove and substantiate the foregoing.

But whether we can reach a satisfactory interpretation of verse 12 or not, the meaning of the whole passage, Rom. v. 12–19, is plain: it is that through one man sin and death have come upon all, and that there is a divine judgment in this. The ultimate ground of the sin and death of all is as much in Adam, as the ultimate ground of the life for all is in Christ.[2]

[1] [The author invariably refuses to accept the strict force of the aorist both here and in the important passage, 2 Cor. v. 14.]
[2] [Dorner, Glaubensl. § 79, Eng. trans., iii. 15, says: "The result, therefore, of

V.—That there is such a sinful condemned condition of the race is still further proved *on Scriptural grounds* from the provisions for redemption and from the need of regeneration. These concern the whole human race.

1. As to the provision for redemption. Rom. v. 18, showing that so far as death reigns, so far redemption is provided; 2 Cor. v. 14, 15, as far as spiritual death[1] even reigns, so far the redemption is provided; Heb. ii. 9; 2 Cor. v. 19. The argument here is simple. The redemption of Christ is a redemption from Sin: if it is for all, then all are in a state to need it. The atonement *is* for all mankind, is for children as a part thereof: else there are two kinds of atonement, one for moral depravity, and the other for physical.

2. So of regeneration. Take only a single passage. John iii. 5, 6 shows that all that are born of the flesh need the regeneration of the Spirit; else they cannot see the kingdom of God. Hence all as born of the flesh are in a sinful condition; for regeneration is a spiritual change. Else there are two kinds of regeneration. Either there is moral ruin, needing a moral remedy, or else physical needing only physical remedy. What is the meaning, too, of baptism as applied to children, if it is not significant of the washing of regeneration? (It is no answer to cite the case of Christ's baptism, for that is always understood as meaning something different.) What things are principally asked for in prayers for infant children? And as to the hope of the salvation of children dying in infancy: which is the best system, one which is able to say outright, Christ died for them, they may be the subjects of renewing grace, or one which is obliged to hesitate and falter on this point? Otherwise, strictly taken, infants are not saved through the atonement of Christ and the renewal of the Holy Ghost.

VI.—This Scriptural argument is confirmed by Scriptural

the Biblical teaching is that all men, from the days of Adam on, stand in need of redemption and that a divine judgment of reprobation rests upon them as sinners, from which Christ alone can set them free. A more intimate explanation of the way and manner in which Adam became a cause of the sinfulness of his posterity, is given neither by Paul nor John."]

[1] ["Then were all dead" is the rendering preferred by the author.]

facts and facts of history in respect to God's moral government here. Under the moral government of God, one man may justly suffer on account of the sins of another. An organic relation of men is regarded in the great judgments of God in history: they are in proportion to the social position of offenders. There is evil which comes upon individuals, not as punishment for their personal sins, but still as suffering which comes under a moral government.[1] The church as a whole has held either natural or spiritual death, or both, to be the just consequences of Adam's sin. The atonement, at the very least, is suffering under a moral government for moral ends, by an innocent person instead of by the guilty; a substitution; not indeed the suffering of the penalty of the law for personal transgression, but still, in the lowest view, a suffering justly under the law for the sake of redemption. We have explicit assertions of God's dealing with men morally in view of their connections in the family order; the descendants of Canaan suffered under the curse pronounced upon their forefather; Reuben's sin affected his tribe; David's misdeeds were visited on the nation; Gehazi's offence was punished in his offspring as well as in his person, 2 Kings v. 27; the sin of Jeroboam involved the ten tribes in its penal consequences; the result of the imprecation, "His blood be on us and on our children," who can measure? What is asserted in the second commandment of the law, is reasserted by the prophets. Jer. xxxii. 18, "Thou showest lovingkindness unto thousands, and recompensest the iniquity of the fathers into the bosom of their children after them."

It may be said, all these are merely "consequences" of family or tribal or national or race relations,—"evil becomes cosmical by reason of fastening on relations which were originally

---

[1] Dr. N. W. Taylor: "The connection with Adam is stated in such a way, by *God's sovereign constitution*, that the sin and just (not actual) condemnation of all men to bear its penalty must be inferred from their connection with Adam as his descendants." But there is no relief in ascribing the evil which comes upon men in their race relations to sovereignty alone, for that leaves the difficulty the same, and adds the element of arbitrariness. Moreover it removes from the moral government of God the most important transactions affecting that government.

adapted to making good cosmical:" but then God's _plan_ must be in the consequences;—a plan administered by a Moral Being, over moral beings, according to moral considerations, and for moral ends: and if that be fully taken into view, the dispute as to "consequences" or punishment becomes a merely verbal one.

§ 3. *The Facts of the Case as to Original Sin, as argued from Experience, and on other than Scriptural Grounds.*

I.—The testimony of many of the wisest and profoundest philosophers is entirely accordant with, and leads to, the Scriptural view. Socrates speaks of a general corruption of the best of nations, and calls it a disease for which no human art had found a remedy. Plato ascribes to children an inward pravity even of nature, for, he says, if they learned evil by example as birds learn to sing, then it would only be necessary to seclude them in order to make them good. Xen. Cyrop., vi. 1, § 4: "It is clear that I have two souls; for surely if it were one, it would not be good and bad at the same time, and inclined to good deeds and evil too, and willing at one time to do certain things and not to do them. But plainly there are two souls, and when the good one gets the upper hand, it does right, and when the evil, it enters on wicked courses." Sophocles, Antigone,[1] 583 seq., 606 seq.:

> "I see the ancient miseries of thy race,
> O Labdacus, arising from the dead
> With fresh despair: nor sires from sons efface
> The curse some angry Power hath riveted
> Forever on thy destined line."

Of Jove:—

> "Spurning the power of age, enthroned in might
> Thou dwell'st mid heaven's broad light.
> This was, in ages past, thy firm decree,
> Is now, and shall, forever, be:
> That none of mortal race, on earth, shall know
> A life of joy serene, a course unmarked by woe."

Seneca, Ep. 52, ad Lucilium: "What is it, Lucilius, that when we set ourselves in one way draws us in another; and

[1] Prof. W. S. Tyler, Bibl. Sacr., Jan. '61, p. 58 seq.

when we desire to avoid any course drives us into it?" . . . . .
"By what means or when shall we be drawn away from this folly? No man is able to emerge from it by his own energy. Another must stretch forth his hand and lead us out." Cicero, Tusc. iii. 1, 2: "Sunt enim ingeniis nostris semina innata virtutum; quæ si adolescere liceret, ipsa nos ad beatam vitam natura perduceret. Nunc autem, simul atque editi in lucem et suscepti sumus, in omni continuo pravitate, et in summa opinionum perversitate versamur." Cicero in Hortensius,[1] speaks of sages, "qui nos ob aliqua scelera suscepta in vita superiore, pœnarum luendarum causa natos esse dixerunt." "These men," continues Cicero, "seem to have had some proper perception (aliquid vidisse videantur); and *that* may be true which we find in Aristotle,[2] that we are punished like those of yore, who fell into the hands of Etruscan robbers, and were slain with elaborate cruelty; their live bodies being tightly bound with corpses placed exactly opposite: thus are our souls linked with our bodies as the living in conjunction with the dead." With these agree the philosophers of modern times. Leibnitz; Kant, rationalist as he was, speaks of the *radical evil* of human nature; Hegel, pantheist as he was, declares that original sin is the nature of every man; every man begins with it.

In point of fact, the whole of logical and even of pantheistic infidelity confesses all that makes up the substance of the orthodox doctrine of original sin: alienation from God, hereditary depravity, constant sinning by all from their youth up:—only they ascribe to it a simple physical character, denying it to be moral; they make it a necessity, and so do not lessen its evil, while they thereby stifle the sense of guilt, and deny the necessity of redemption.[3]

---

[1] There are only fragments of this Hortensius. It helped to lead Augustine to faith.

[2] Brandis says, "Aristotle would have believed in original sin." (See Peip, Trinität, in Herzog's Encycl.)

[3] Coleridge, Lit. Remains, 3, 324: "One of the main ends and results of the doctrine of original sin is to silence and confute the blasphemy that makes God the author of sin, without avoiding it by flying to the almost equal blasphemy against the conscience, that sin in the sense of guilt does not exist."

II.—The hereditary character of the depravity of mankind is also confirmed by the analogies recognized by science and philosophy. The human race is descended from one pair. The descent is by propagation, under the law that like begets like. The law of propagation in the animal kingdom carries down all the peculiarities of the animal, the animal instincts, the animal soul. The same law in the human race brings down national traits, family traits, intellectual peculiarities, strength or weakness of the will, moral traits, special moral peculiarities, pride, envy, jealousy, revenge. That is, this law of propagation carries with it the special peculiarities of all the faculties of the soul, and therefore it carries the soul also; which is also according to the analogy of the animal kingdom. Besides these, it carries with it what belongs to the race as a whole, its general bias, its generic moral condition, in relation to moral ends, and this generic moral condition of the race is—original sin. In all other spheres the law of propagation carries everything else down [1]: *it is according to the analogy* that it should carry the generic moral bias of the human race.

III.—The experience of all men, so far as it can reach back, tends to confirm the doctrine of original sin. We do not mean, of course, that our experience traces it back to Adam, but it does trace back the sin in us so far as this: that we cannot detect its origin in our deliberate choice. No human being is able, in experience, to go back to the time when he first decided consciously and deliberately for self and the world and against God. All men, when moral consciousness is awakened, as a matter of fact, find themselves in the state of immanent preference for some lower good, and this, they all feel and know to be, as it exists in them, a sinful, a guilty condition. This is the solemn and mysterious fact about our experience of sin and our knowl-

---

[1] [The student will find in Dorner's Glaubenslehre some profound observations on the individuality which is not "carried down," but which rather perpetually springs up in the intellectual and moral differentiation of the race, and which Dr. D. is perhaps inclined to ascribe to that *very special divine concursus* which attends the propagation of mankind. There is evidence that the author would have agreed with Dr. D., here.]

edge of its real nature. It is, too, our own sin, our own guilt.[1] This state we find as a preference, a direction, a bias of the will. We may speculate about the time when we first came into this state, but we cannot reach that time in experience. Our sense of personal ill-desert is doubtless connected with, based upon, the fact, that this sinful preference is felt and known to be ours, approved and loved by us, to be our love, our choice. But the universality of such a sinful preference, beyond the sphere even of memory, proves that it has its ground in our very constitution.

Another form of statement.—This state in which we are born is the ground of our first moral choice, of our immanent preference, so that the latter only expresses in the form of choice, of preference, what was before in this state, *in potentia*. And this immanent preference was before any present memory of ours, so that we find ourselves in it—as the whole bent and bias of our being—our inmost, profoundest moral reality. And for this, when the light of the law comes, we feel and know ourselves to be guilty before God: it is a state justly subjecting us to the divine judgments, from which we can be delivered only through regeneration and application of the atoning blood of Christ. And this is the common state of men, as men, as descendants of Adam, under the divine government. *Provided these points be granted*, it becomes a verbal dispute whether we call this state sinful or depraved, or not: the mere term is not worth contending for, because such different definitions may be given of it.

IV.—This is confirmed by Christian experience and by that which usually precedes it: by the light which comes in regeneration, and the deeper convictions about sin through which souls are led to their conversion.

Rom. vii. has here its decisive application. A depth of sin and evil is disclosed in us, a greatness of guilt and ill-desert, of which we before had no conception. vs. 23, "I see another law in my members"—there is a *law* of sin in us. By the law is the knowledge of sin. vs. 7, "I had not known sin, except through the law" (yet, the sin is there). This is the voice of all deep

---

[1] See President Marsh's *Essay on Sin*,—on some aspects of sin the very best Essay that we know of.

and true religious experience. Sin is profounder in us than any depth to which we have reached before the law comes. It exists in an unconscious state, which must be brought out into the light of distinct consciousness. The sinfulness and guilt exists before the consciousness of it. There is a broad distinction between guilt and the sense of guilt. Under the influence of God's Spirit, we become sensible of a pollution, of a guilty, most sinful condition, from which we know that no power or might of our own can deliver us, but only grace, only redeeming grace, only regeneration applying atoning blood. Just here *experience leaves us*. It conducts us to the knowledge of a deep-seated depravity, which we know not that we originated, but which is ours by preference: it expresses itself to us in that form. For that we feel guilty and condemned. *Reason and Scripture* together then lead us one step further—to this point: that before that preference, there was a bias, a propensity thereto, in our native condition. *Scripture* carries us back one step further, viz., to the knowledge that the human race have come into this condition in consequence of the apostasy of our first parents.[1]

In respect to the problem of original sin, such are the facts to be taken into the account, on the one side: they may be thus summed up: In consequence of the sin of Adam, the head and beginning of the race, all men come into the world, in the way of natural descent, in a state of condemnation, not only without holiness, but with a bias or propensity to sin, subject under the divine government to evils, suffering and death, from which condition they can only be delivered through the redemption that is in Christ. And this native state becomes their imma-

---

[1] Every profounder view of human life, human history, human character, is compelled to go behind the individual action to its causes and grounds: its grounds in human nature itself: in the connection of each man with all others. We cannot escape this if we think upon it. All philosophy leads us in this direction. Especially does the whole idea and system of redemption lead to this: our union with Christ, the grace of the Holy Spirit. The ground of our holy acts and of our redemption is not in our own wills. The greatest minds, the best and most life-giving theology of the Christian church, the deepest Christian experience, lead us to view men *ultimately*, not under their individual aspects and responsibilities, but in their connection with the whole race and the whole system of things.

nent preference, as soon as they act morally. And for this they know themselves to be guilty and condemned before God.

Here is *one side* of the problem to be solved: before considering the solutions which have been attempted, we must bring into view other Scriptural and moral positions, in order to have before us all the elements which belong to the question.

CHAPTER V.

THE COUNTER-REPRESENTATION AS TO SIN AND ITS PUNISHMENT IN SCRIPTURE AND EXPERIENCE.

I.—In Scripture. Besides those descriptions and statements, in the Scriptures, about sin and death, in which they are viewed as the heritage of all men, there is another class of passages in which sin and punishment are spoken of under the exclusively personal aspect, in relation to the words and deeds of each individual: and the same is true of redemption and salvation.

There are what we may call the generic and the personal classes of passages, specimens of which may be compared:

Generic:—		*Personal:*—
Exod. xx. 5; Num. xiv. 18,	with	Ezek. xviii. 20; Gal. vi. 5.
Rom. v. 16,	"	Rom. ii. 6.
2 Cor. v. 14,	"	Deut. xxx. 19; Rom. xiv. 12.
Matt. xv. 19,	"	1 John ii. 16.
Rom. vii.,	"	2 Cor. v. 10.
Holiness, too, is from the power of the Holy Spirit, waking the dead to life;		Yet, we are commanded to be holy.
Grace is of God;		Yet, commended to our choice.

Yet it is to be noted that while the Scriptures thus put life in our election, it is not in the form that by obedience to the law any human being can be saved. It is only in the form of accepting a grace offered. They thus presuppose the state of sin and the need of redemption in every human being. They never intimate, they deny, that any member of the race can obtain eternal life by the deeds of the law. Rom. iii. 20; Gal. iii. 21

II.—In experience as interpreted by moral philosophy.

1. It is said, that the testimony of our moral nature is, that nothing can be considered sin in us, or as involving guilt, which is not our own free, personal choice. Inherited propensity, bias to the world and self are conceded: but these are not sinful, and guilt attaches only to free acts. We cannot be held morally responsible for a native state which we could not avoid. Conscience condemns us only for our own deliberate choices. Sin, guilt, and punishment can relate only to what we do, internally or externally. All else belongs not to the sphere of moral responsibility, but to the course of nature and providence, external to the proper moral government.

2. Still further it is said, that justice and right demand that God should not bring new-created beings into a state where the advantages of a safe issue should not be greater than the disadvantages.[1]

Thus, by these antagonisms the question is raised, on the three points already stated: (*a.*) the relation of the ruined condition of the race to our personal guilt; (*b.*) the relation of our native state to our personal acts; (*c.*) the relation of God's government, so far as it respects the whole race, to the demands of justice in respect to each member of the race.

Hence the Problem, in its different aspects, is:

1. To reconcile the fact that through "the one man's disobedience the many were made sinners" (Rom. v. 19), with the position that all men become sinners by their own act.

2. To reconcile the fact that we are born with a propensity to sin, with the position that guilt implies also personal ill-desert, and that all such ill-desert is of our own origination.

3. To reconcile God's justice to each man, as seen in the rev-

---

[1] This is one of the positions of Dr. Edward Beecher, in his "Conflict of Ages." He grants that in the present sphere the disadvantages are undoubtedly greater.

elations of the last judgment, with the fact that He has brought all men—or allowed all men to come—into such a state that they will certainly sin and perish, unless arrested by grace.

The two extreme positions, so far as sin is concerned, may be said to be contained in the two formulas: All men sinned and fell in Adam,—and, All sin consists in sinning. Each of these plants itself on one side of the dilemma, as containing the whole truth: and each of these, taken strictly by itself, is about as true, for the solution of the problem, as the other: for each neglects the other, and leaves unaccounted for about half of the difficulty.

So, as far as the vindication of God's justice is concerned, the two extreme positions may be said to be these: (*a.*) God's justice has to do only with our personal acts; but God's inscrutable benevolence has put us in a condition in which all those acts will certainly be sinful: (*b.*) God's justice has to do both with our generic condition and our individual acts; but his justice is inscrutable.

CHAPTER VI.

THE THEORIES PROPOSED FOR THE SOLUTION OF THE PROBLEM.

§ 1. *The Theory of Immediate Imputation.*

The word impute means, to set to one's account legally; or, to reckon to one's account; or, to treat as if (not, make to be, but, to treat as if). To impute the guilt of a sin is to treat as if guilty of that sin. To impute a righteousness is to treat as if having that righteousness. The word is not used in the sense of a transfer of moral character from Adam to his posterity,[1] or of an infusion of an evil principle into the soul, but, of a sentence of

---

[1] Any objection to immediate imputation on *this* ground is simply an objection to a misapprehension of the theory. The New England interpretation of this imputation, since the younger Edwards, has popularly been, transfer of moral character, which, however, is denied to be possible by both sides.

condemnation passed on all the race for Adam's first sin. Those who hold the position of immediate imputation also hold that there is an innate, human depravity, but they say the innate depravity is not the ground of the condemnation. It is tho consequence of the imputation. The theory of immediate imputation, carried out a little more definitely, is this: Adam is both the federal and natural head of the human race, but the federal headship is first, prior in logic and thought. Adam as the federal head stood, as an individual, for all other individual men, as their immediate representative. This was by a divine arrangement. And when he fell, they were included in the sentence, because he directly represented them. Whatever he did is directly—*immediately*—made over to them. Then the natural headship is the *means of carrying down* the consequences of the imputation to his posterity. And so the corruption of the posterity is the consequence and not the ground of the imputation.[1]

Objections to this view:

1. It is not borne out by Rom. v. 12, which is the great passage cited in its favor. That passage undoubtedly teaches a condemnation of all on the ground of the offence of one, but it does not teach that the condemnation is without respect to the moral condition of Adam's posterity. It asserts the fact, but does not give the *media*, of the condemnation. This theory denies that the exposure of mankind to punishment is made in view of the corruption of their nature, that the corruption forms any essential part of the whole state of facts which comes under the divine regard in the imputation; the passage in Romans does *not* deny this, but is perfectly consistent with it, though it does not explicitly affirm or deny on either side of this particular question.

2. The theory tends to present the whole matter of sin and its punishment in an external, arbitrary, and *merely* forensic manner. It is merely an outside form to the whole real order

---

[1] Among the New England divines, Bellamy comes nearest to this statement, Works, i. 223, 224 (Boston ed.) Hopkins also comes very near to it, but he does not throw out an intermediate depraved nature, as having no consideration in the imputation.

of facts. It is simply a scaffolding around a building, and all the facts of the case are inside.

3. The theory rests upon an unreal and unphilosophical view of the relation of Adam to his posterity: it is a carrying out of the theory of the Covenants in such a way as Scripture does not warrant. The notion is, that Adam, an individual, represents all other individuals, so that his act is representatively their act. The unity of the race, as a moral organic whole, is lost in this theory, just as much as in the extreme theories on the other side. We have only an individual acting for a great many individuals. (Hence, too, the theory of a limited atonement: a provision of salvation for such and such a specific number of individuals, with no *provision*, although an incidental sufficiency, for a *race*.) The theory takes the doctrine of original sin out of its proper place, as the sinful state of the race, and individualizes it.[1]

4. It is also encumbered with all the difficulties of the ordinary view: for *besides* the imputation, it has to concede a real, native corruption, in the way of descent. And it is obliged to view this as a punishment, a punishment without any ground in the individual, without any ground in the race connection of the individual.[2]

5. Nor does it help us in our vindication of the divine government. All the truth there is about it is, that we can, in the way of illustration, so represent the relation between Adam and his posterity. But it gives us a structure outside of the real matter rather than the matter itself: a scaffolding rather than the skeleton. It is claimed for this theory that it "explains" the corruption of the race, while that of Edwards, it is said, simply states the fact: but it would rather appear that the theory of immediate imputation neither states nor explains. There is a question of fact: what is the connection between Adam and man-

---

[1] It also involves creationism as to the origin of individual souls. It is a theory no more true to fact than the "social compact" theory: in fact it is in the same style of thought as that.

[2] [It is doubtful whether any prominent American theologians should be regarded as advocating the position stated in this last clause. A certain element of mediate imputation is often recognized by those who in the main contend for immediate.]

kind as related to human corruption? This theory says: the
connection is primarily one of representation, and secondarily
of race-unity: which does not state the fact. Then there is
another question, viz., How is it just that we should inherit the
corrupt nature of Adam? This justice, it is said, is *shown*, by
the theory of immediate imputation, or representation. But
that is no explanation of the justice: it is simply giving an abstract statement of the fact. The whole question remains: How
is it just that Adam should be our representative? We are at
least helped towards an answer by taking into view our oneness
with him on some real and evident ground.

6. The argument from the imputation of Christ's righteousness does not hold. It is said, the sin of Adam must be imputed
to his posterity, without their participation, and in order to their
participation, because so the righteousness of Christ is imputed
to his people (and if this latter be denied, justification is merged
in sanctification). But, to speak of nothing else here, the argument assumes that because grace is given gratuitously, punishment may equally be.

7. The history of the doctrine, or at least the weight of historic testimony, is against this view of immediate imputation.
Augustine teaches that Adam stood for the whole race, that
the whole was seminally in him, but he does not separate the
imputation from the propagation of the corrupted condition.
The two things go together. With him Adam *was, not, stood
for*, the whole race. Among the Scholastics, in Anselm and
Aquinas, we find the separation first so distinctly made, and
carried out by the Roman Catholic divines, in the service of
their sacramental theory. The "guilt" of sin, it was said, is
taken away in baptism: and here the guilt is separated from,
and made quite external to, the nature, while the concupiscence
admitted to be in the nature and to remain after baptism, is declared not to be sin. Some such position must be taken by the
sacramental system. The earlier Reformers, Calvin, Luther,
Melancthon, in returning to the position that concupiscence is
of the nature of sin, kept the immediate imputation in the background. Turretin teaches it afterwards, distinctly: teaches *reatus*

pœnœ without a *reatus culpœ*, but, as we read him, he also teaches both theories together. The whole of the French school of Saumur reacted from it; Stapfer in Switzerland, who has the ablest discussion on the subject, states the opposite view, which Edwards cites largely; and Edwards has argued the question in the most thorough and philosophical manner. Edwards in this country first distinctly said, that the sin is not ours because it is imputed to us, but it is imputed to us because it is ours.[1]

§ 2. *The Theory of Direct Divine Efficiency, in the Way of a Constitution.*[2]

The theory is: God in his sovereignty established a constitution, in which it was appointed, that by occasion of Adam's sin, all his posterity should be brought into being sinners, or so that they should sin in their first moral acts. The capital phrases here are, "a divine constitution," and "the divine sovereignty." Hopkins (Syst. i. 268) says: "By a divine constitution there is a certain connection between the first sin of Adam and the sinfulness of his posterity, so that as he sinned and fell under condemnation, they in consequence of this become sinful and condemned. Therefore when Adam had sinned, by this the character and state of all his posterity were fixed, and they were, by virtue of a covenant made with Adam, constituted or made sinners like him, and therefore were considered as such before they had actual existence." Then the way in which it comes to us is by our consent to Adam's sin in our first moral act. "This," he says, "is the only rational, consistent, and satisfactory account of this most interesting affair that can be given." But again, "Our sin is not the penalty of Adam's transgression; the sin of Adam is not imputed to us, we being innocent." Adam's posterity are "born in sin," "so as to begin to sin as soon as they begin to exist with a capacity of sinning, as soon as they begin to act as moral agents." "If by their being his [Adam's] children they become corrupt, they must of consequence

---

[1] See Stuart, Scriptural views of Imputation, Bib. Rep. 1836, against the view that Imputation is transfer of character.

[2] Hopkinsianism, especially as carried out by Dr. Emmons.

be corrupt as soon as they exist, or become his children. If it were not so, it would not appear from fact that they became sinful by being the posterity of Adam" (p. 274). As soon as the infant exists, he may have moral corruption in sin. Hence we are not to distinguish between original and actual sin (Note, p. 276). Emmons takes substantially the same position.

Objections to this theory:

1. It is unnatural. It neglects the unity, the vital moral connection of the race, resolving everything into an arbitrary appointment and decree in the most abstract form.

2. It supposes the earliest sinful exercises to be the result of an immediate divine efficiency, making God to be virtually the author of sin.

3. It neglects what undeniably exists, a nature or bias before the motions thereof. It is Berkeleian in its philosophical assumption. It cannot answer the question: What were children who died before a sinful act—were they moral beings, or little animals?

Yet, it was a laboring upon a great problem, in a peculiar and original way. The solution is attained by the virtual denial of one half of the problem—the hereditary descent of the evil nature. God—decrees—volitions: that is the whole scheme. It gives an abstract unreal "constitution."

§ 3. *The Hypothesis of Physical Depravity.*

This says: In consequence of the sin of Adam, all his descendants are born with disordered susceptibilities, with a "constitutional" derangement, which is not sinful or guilty, which has no character, but which is always the certain occasion of sinning. There is no sin until sinning takes place, and this sinning is the just ground of condemnation. The word constitution has here a very different sense from that of the Hopkinsian theory, considered in § 2. This is sometimes represented as Hopkinsianism, but there is a wide difference, there is a different psychology. Neither Hopkins nor Emmons would have admitted a nature, however qualified, as innocent or without character. In the old Hopkinsianism, the word constitution is used for a divine arrangement; in the modern, for what is human, for the physical constitution of man. The older would not grant any soul before act, but the later brings in a soul under the first act, alleging that until it acts it is innocent or neutral. Dr. N. W. Taylor not only reinstated the human soul in its native rights, but he also affirmed the existence of susceptibilities, tendencies, dispositions, antecedent to voluntary action. But as he also held that all that is moral is in voluntary action, he of course said that these tendencies and dispositions have no moral character.[1] Here is a human constitution, the basis of sinful action, securing its certainty, and not a mere divine arrangement. This native state may be called vicious, vitiosity, depravity, anything to imply what is odious, but it has no moral character, and the above terms when applied to it must not be understood as having any moral sense.

The Difficulties of this theory:

1. It virtually resolves the whole doctrine of original sin into a physical condition. It is a proper doctrine of physical depravity.

2. It derives its plausibility from its definition of sin. It defines sin as—an act or exercise, and as that which in its own nature makes the individual worthy of everlasting death. The whole question of original sin is set aside by this definition. With such definitions, all that the theory claims must be conceded.

3. As it is often carried out, it leads to superficial views of depravity, so that all spontaneous feeling, all that is not deliberate choice, is excluded from the sphere of sin (some exclude even the affections, putting all sin in a purpose). When thus carried out, hardly any theory can more surely undermine the foundations of religion—and of ethics. It tends to low views of the Atonement and of Regeneration. Denying the real facts of depravity, it tends to deny some of the essential things in the redemption. It cannot meet, and it cannot do away with, the fact that we feel guilty for our spontaneous preferences, for our nature as acted out.

---

[1] See Faith and Philosophy, 259. There is an acute discussion in Beecher's Conflict of Ages, and in Müller on Sin.

4. The theory makes an unnatural separation between what has no character and what is moral in us. We cannot draw the line of accountability and of guilt by this theory. As soon as we attempt to do it by finding acts in which we have full power to the contrary, we narrow the sphere of our moral acts.

5. There is made a like unnatural and merely theoretical separation between God's moral and his general or providential government. The theory is compelled to exclude from God's moral government all excepting deliberate personal choices. It cannot even allow God's moral government of nations in a distinctive sense. It concedes that if the great facts of human nature are brought under the moral government of God, the theory is indefensible, and so it virtually concedes that God's justice cannot be defended in this matter. But what is gained by this? If God has put the race into this condition, it must be consistent with his justice as well as his benevolence—and in fact, the benevolence is but a part of the justice. The theory is fatal to man's culpability[1]; for, to account for the universality of sinfulness, it makes the liability to sinfulness very great, but in saying that this is not sinful, it diminishes the sense of guilt.

6. The difficulty as to the divine government is in fact only carried back one step. God gives a nature which will certainly lead to sin in every child of Adam. But it is no more easy to reconcile that view with the divine justice than the ordinary view. How early does an infant decide? After a month, or six months, or a year of existence? Can this be reconciled with our views of what justice would demand, more easily than other theories? No real relief is gained in fact, only in terminology: all the advantage is in a word—*sinful*.

7. While the theory gives no real relief on this point, it is embarrassed in respect to the atonement and regeneration, unless it allows to each of these a physical efficacy and physical relations; and if it does allow such efficacy to the atonement and to regeneration, then why not to sin?

8. The scheme of a divine efficiency producing the sinful

[1] See Prof. Fisher, New Englander, Aug. 1860.

volition, in the form of a *constitution*, referred back to divine sovereignty, outrages all our moral conceptions. It is a merciless system. Against this Dr. Taylor protested with vigor and success. But his scheme[1] of a neutral state, neutral yet always producing sin, for which state no regeneration or atonement is, strictly, provided, is inferior in its moral appeals to a system which allows that regeneration and atonement may be provided for *such a state*.

9. As respects the nature of the decision which is the real beginning of sin in us, and which must be "inferred" from our connection with Adam, it is purely hypothetical; it has no known facts to stand upon. That it was with "full power to the contrary" we may assert but can never prove.[2] To lay the whole burden of the vindication of the divine government on the hypothesis of such a power to the contrary in a child six months or a year old is, to say the least, unwise.

§ 4. *The Pelagian and Unitarian View.*

We have here no proper theory for a solution of the problem, but simply a denial that the problem exists. The facts of the universality, the totality, and the native character of sin are set aside. It is claimed that the sin of Adam did not injure his descendants at all, that men are born with a mixture of good and evil, that we cannot use the words depraved, vicious, etc., in respect to the natural condition of men. To each one is transmitted the same nature in kind and condition that Adam had, and each stands and falls as Adam did.[3]

---

[1] Dr. N. W. Taylor, on Rom. v. 12-14. Object to show "that all the posterity of Adam became sinners and subject to temporal death in consequence of his sin, and yet in such a way or mode of connection as not to exclude their individual responsibility for their own sin, nor to imply that temporal death was the legal penalty of sin; but in such a way, by *God's sovereign constitution*, that the *sin*, and just (not actual) condemnation of all men to bear its penalty must be inferred from their connection with Adam as his descendants." "Such is the constitution or nature [of men] that in all the appropriate or natural circumstances of their existence, they will uniformly sin from the commencement of moral agency."

[2] In Hopkins and Emmons the position taken merely amounts to this, that the soul is morally active from the beginning. Emmons at least leaves it an open question whether the activities *are* not the soul.

[3] Rev. Geo. E. Ellis, Chris. Exam., Nov. 1853.

§ 5. *The Hypothesis of Pre-existence.*

In recent times this theory has been brought forward by Julius Müller as a hypothesis to explain the facts of human depravity. (Edward Beecher has also urged it as a means of vindicating the divine government, and showing that God acts according to the principles of honor.) The hypothesis is framed to meet two positions: (*a.*) That all sin is from personal choice; (*b.*) That we are sinful from the beginning of our existence in this life. We suppose that those who maintain the theory do not hold it as a fact, but simply as a hypothesis, just as it is held that there is a diffused ether in space, in order to account for a retardation of the heavenly bodies.

Objections:

1. The theory assumes that there cannot be in man a strictly depraved bias, which is not the product of his own free act. It is true that such a bias becomes our choice, and that we feel guilty for it as such; but the assumption is more than this,— that it must have been produced by our choice.

2. Modern advocates of this theory are inconsequential in conceding also a kind of hereditary depravity, of which the punishment is natural death, and of which we are partakers on account of Adam's transgression. This should have led them to the orthodox view.

3. The theory cannot be reconciled with the account of the Fall in Genesis and the consequent Scriptural representations, nor with Rom. v. 12, etc.[1] We cannot connect our present being with a former state of existence; there is no *evidence;* whereas there *is* evidence of the connection of the race with Adam. Rom. v. 12-19 stands directly in the way of the theory: the state of mankind as ruined is traced directly back to Adam's transgression.

---

[1] Dr. Edward Beecher says this passage "gives a *typical* sequence; *i. e.*, there is a sequence given between Adam and his posterity which is typical, standing for a type of what is true in respect to each individual." But Rom. v. declares—if anything can declare—that through the offence of one condemnation came upon all. So the interpretation of Rom. v. 12, etc., as "apparent and not real causation" is indefensible. The causation, on the very face of the passage, is just as real in reference to Adam as to Christ.

4. It appears to grant that the divine justice is indefensible so far as the present order of things is concerned, without some such unnatural hypothesis. It will not allow us to take refuge in mystery, and trust in God. If an infidel does not receive the hypothesis, then he may say: you grant, what we say, that the present order of things is unrighteous.

5. It gives no explanation as to our sense of guilt for our depravity. We cannot very well feel guilty for an act done in an unconscious, ante-mundane state: while we may—and do—feel guilty for our sinful dispositions.

6. It gives really no solution of the ultimate problem as to moral evil. It simply pushes this back. Some facts in relation to our present experience are supposed to be explained by the theory, but the real difficulty of sin is not touched at all.

7. Those who defend this theory argue against the orthodox view throughout on the ground that it assumes that each of the descendants of Adam is a new created being and is created sinful. But this is not the view of the major part. In this country, the propagation theory is more generally held than that of creationism,—although some have argued as though they believed the latter.

CHAPTER VII.

OF SO-CALLED MEDIATE IMPUTATION.

I.—Statement of mediate imputation.

We have given the leading theories proposed for the solution of the problem of sin, with the difficulties about them. One we have not particularly dwelt upon, not considering it a theory,[1] which we proceed to state.

[1] [In connection with this clause "not considering it a theory," the note already referred to, may be recalled: "Neither immediate nor mediate imputation is wholly satisfactory." Understand by "Mediate Imputation" a full statement of the facts in the case, and the author accepted it; understand by it a theory professing to give the final explanation of the facts, and it was "not wholly satisfactory."]

The only true course is that which undertakes nothing more than to give the facts of the case, on the Scriptural basis, resolving the chief difficulties into the more general problem of the divine permission of sin in the race as a whole. This will establish the federal headship of Adam, making it follow the natural headship.

The facts of the case in their bearings on the problem of original sin, have already been indicated. They may be thus summed up:

1. The human race is not a mere collection of individuals, but an organic whole in the sense of a physical and moral unity: and as such a unity it is considered in the Scriptures, both in respect to sin and to redemption,—in respect to both the first and the second Adam: so that original sin and a general provision for redemption stand or fall together.

2. Adam was by divine appointment the head and beginning of the race: all men were virtually, potentially, or as some say, seminally, in him. Not that they were in him as individuals, not that they all nestled in him, but rather as the acorns that are in the tree were in the acorns that were planted. And this was determined by a divine constitution which made of one blood all the nations of the earth (in this respect the same as to man as in respect to the animal and vegetable world). Adam at the beginning was the race.

3. On this basis of fact, the theory proceeds to the further statement of fact: that the fall brought about in Adam a loss of original righteousness and corruption of nature, so that selfishness and worldliness became supreme. This general moral corruption becomes the heritage of all men by descent, and it shows itself in all men in a twofold way: negatively, in the absence of holy principle and positively, in a propensity to moral evil. Of course this bias to sin is latent before the act, but still it is a reality in every child of Adam, as is proved by the subsequent facts.

4. On account of this innate depravity, all men, mankind as such, are exposed, liable, to evils, to sufferings and death here, and if divine grace do not interpose, to eternal death here-

after; and in such exposure or liability consists the Imputation.[1] The common current phrase in theology is not desert, but liability or exposure. This runs through all Calvinistic formulas. For this native corruption before act, we need not say that the person who is the subject of it will receive, or deserves everlasting death. It is a liability, exposure,—justly such; but not personal desert. The desert of eternal death is a judgment in respect to individuals for their personal acts and preferences. Until such choice there cannot be, metaphysically or ethically, such a judgment. Original sin is a doctrine respecting the moral conditions of human nature as from Adam—generic: and it is not a doctrine respecting personal liabilities and desert. For the latter we need more and other circumstances. Strictly speaking, it is not sin which is deserving, but only the sinner. The ultimate distinction is here: There is a well-grounded difference to be made between personal desert, strictly personal character and liabilities (of each individual under the divine law, as applied specifically, *e. g.*, in the last adjudication), and a generic moral condition—the antecedent ground of such personal character. The distinction, however, is not between what has moral quality and what has not, but between the moral state of each as a member of the race, and his personal liabilities and desert as an individual.

5. This original sin would wear to us only the character of evil and not of sinfulness, were it not for *the fact* that we feel guilty in view of our corruption when it becomes known to us in our own acts. Then there is involved in it not merely a sense of evil and misery, but also a sense of guilt; moreover, redemption is necessary to remove it, which shows that it is a moral state. Here is the point of junction between the two ex-

---

[1] [In this statement also, it is intended to keep to what are believed to be simple facts. "Imputation," viewed as a matter of fact, is a coupling of evils, sufferings, death with a state of moral abnormity; Imputation, viewed as an attempt to state the reasons and *all the reasons* which the divine mind has for treating moral abnormity thus and not otherwise, is theory, and theory which is perhaps beyond our present power of construction.]

treme positions, that we sinned in Adam, and that all sin consists in sinning.

6. The guilt of Adam's sin is—this exposure, this liability on account of such native corruption,—of our having the same nature, in the same moral bias. The guilt of Adam's sin is *not to be separated* from the existence of this evil disposition.[1] And this guilt is what is imputed to us. Here are to be considered the important statements of Edwards (ii. 482, etc.) " The first existing of a corrupt disposition in their hearts is not to be looked upon as sin belonging to them distinct from their participation in Adam's first sin; it is, as it were, the extended pollution of that sin through the whole tree by virtue of the constituted union of the branches with the root." Just before, "I am humbly of the opinion, that if any have supposed the children of Adam to come into the world with a double guilt, one the guilt of Adam's sin, another the guilt arising from their having a corrupt heart, they have not so well considered the matter." And afterwards, "Derivation of evil disposition (or rather co-existence) is in consequence of the union"—but "not properly a consequence of the imputation of his sin; nay, rather antecedent to it, as it was in Adam himself. The first depravity of heart, and the imputation of that sin, are both the consequence of that established union, but yet in such order, that the evil disposition is first, and the charge of guilt consequent, as it was in the case of Adam himself." (He quotes Stapfer: "The Reformed divines do not hold immediate and mediate imputation *separately* but always together.") And still further, ii. 493: "And therefore the sin of the apostasy is not theirs merely because God imputes it to them: but it is truly and properly theirs, and on that ground God imputes it to them."[2]

[1] [The author would no doubt have continued to urge this position, had he written out his system of theology. He always approved the general positions of Edwards given above. But it is a question whether he did not intend to make some final statements which would bring out more distinctly the proper federal headship of Adam *on the basis* of the natural headship. All that is found, however, is the note, "Mediate imputation not wholly satisfactory." There is no evidence that he meditated any retraction of what he gave in his lectures, but he probably had in mind a statement of the whole subject under some larger point of view.]

[2] To the same effect, Dr. John Owen, Works, xii. 249. Dr. Payne (Cong'l Lectures) calls original sin "a loss of chartered blessings." And in fact the so-called

II.—The bearings of this view upon the three problems which have been stated.

1. The relation of the race to the individual: of Adam to his descendants. This is stated in the theory. Adam, by divine constitution, was made the head and source of the human race. They share in the consequences of his transgression. At the same time, from the beginning, over against this, redemption was provided. In the divine purpose the sin was doubtless permitted and allowed to be handed down *with respect* to the redemption: not for its own sake, nor for the sake of the punishment of it, nor for the sake of administering a merely moral system, but—for the sake of the redemption, eternally provided in view of it. Hence "this is *the* condemnation" or judgment (John iii. 19). To all that have known of Christ, the judgment —final—to endless ruin—is for the rejection of Him. Infants are undoubtedly to be considered as included in the covenant of redemption. As to all dying in infancy, and as to the heathen who do not know of Christ, perhaps no better statement has been made than that of the Westminster Confession (Conf., chap. x. §. 3): "Elect[1] infants, dying in infancy" (including all infants dying in infancy according to the almost universally prevalent hope and belief) "are regenerated and saved by Christ through the Spirit, who worketh when, and where, and how he pleaseth. *So also are all other elect persons, who are incapable of being outwardly called by the ministry of the word.*"

2. The relation of the common sinfulness of the race to individual sin. The union between these two points and their harmony is found in the fact of experience to which we have adverted—our sense of guilt in view of this depravity when it becomes known to us, and the "consent" of which we are conscious. This is a fact above all theory.

Covenant is not historically a covenant only, because it is much more than a covenant; a system "not of divine equity merely but of rich sovereign grace:" a plan by which, in and through a human race, good might become "cosmical," as Dorner has put it.

[1] [The author in a certain place of his notes for lectures has referred, with strong approval, to Crawford's statement ("Fatherhood of God," App.): Election comes to this—"that what God does in time He purposed to do from eternity."]

A fuller statement. Question: Is there any common ground to which we may come in the conflict between the two positions—that all men sinned in Adam and that all sin consists in sinning?

(*a.*) The sinning and falling in Adam is not of the individuals of the race—else it were, as has been said, a fall of millions and not of one. It is, that human nature thereby came into a corrupt condition, having a bias and propensity to sin, and exposed to evils and death. This each one has by descent. This is the sin and fall in Adam.

(*b.*) As soon as each individual acts morally, this corrupt nature becomes his own preference, his own immanent bias and preference. It is for this that he feels guilty and condemned. And there is the point of junction in *experience* between these two views. Were it not for this preference, our whole native condition would wear to each one the character of an evil, and not of a strictly guilty, state. This is a fact of universal experience and the ultimate fact in our analysis, the last point in which the two views come together. (This is what Hopkins and Emmons insist upon, though they are led—especially the latter—to insist, that this is the beginning of any moral condition in the descendants of Adam, and is coeval with the existence of each individual.[1]) Here is where *reatus culpæ* and *reatus pœnæ* meet.

The question is fundamentally of the relation of the generic to the individual, a question between *Realism* and *Nominalism*. There is no more difficulty in principle about original sin than about anything that is native. In much of the modern ethics, what is moral is made merely individual; pure individualism is asserted: the existence, the "real"[2] existence of the generic moral

---

[1] *I. e.*, in the relation of the moral abnormity of each individual to the moral abnormity of the race, of the stock from which each springs. As regards the divine view of the condition of the race, which pronounces this to be strictly sinful, the author of course admits difficulty. He inclines to carry back the difficulty of the permitted perpetuation of sin and of God's moral judgment upon this, into the insoluble difficulty of the permission of the existence of sin, and to leave it there.

[2] [An elaborate paper by the author on Realism and Nominalism—elaborate, *i. e.*, as a preparation for a work which never was executed—comes out upon the general position of universalia *in re*, but insists that the universals must be recognized as *realities* as truly as the individuals are.]

is not allowed. Here ethics is in the rear of the advance in the natural sciences.

3.—As to the justice and goodness of God in providing such a constitution for the human race.

The common view, which vindicates God's justice and goodness on the basis of a *scientia media*, is not entirely satisfactory.

The fact is that strictly the question here is not of God's justice in respect to individuals, but to the whole race. Yet *as the question is always argued* with reference to individuals, we will consider it in that relation.

(a.) If there was to be a race at all, existing by descent, it is difficult to see how it could be under any other condition;[1] and it was better to have a race even with such liabilities than not to have a race.

(b.) As to individuals, it is not improbable that it is better for each one to be in a state where there is a common sinfulness and *in which there is a common redemption provided*, than it would be for all the members of the race to stand or fall, each by himself, *without such a provision*.[2] As we now come into the world, it is under a dispensation of grace offered. With such a constitution, there is hereditary depravity:[3] without it there might, there probably would have been, angelic liabilities.

(c.) Yet ultimately we must say: The depths of the divine wisdom and sovereignty we cannot penetrate, on any theory—of justice or of physical law. *The ultimate reason of the existence of sin is not disclosed*, and the question of God's justice and goodness in dealing with mankind as the subjects of original sin runs back into that greater problem—the divine permission of sin.

---

[1] [Any other, *i. e.*, than this, in which advantages and attainments, as well as disadvantages and forfeitures, should be transmitted, and the whole line of transmission, so far as it had moral bearings, should be under the divine moral approval or displeasure.]

[2] Some suggest: Adam was in a better position for deciding than any of his posterity would have been; could we have had a voice, we should have chosen him to decide for us, etc.; but this does not reach to the heart of the difficulty.

[3] [Reference is made with approval to Dr. Charles Hodge (Essays, p. 71): "We believe as fully and joyfully as he [Prof. Stuart] does, that the grace which is in Christ Jesus secures the salvation of all who have no personal sins to answer for."]

Another statement. On the question: If no provision for redemption had been intended, would God have continued the race through Adam, after his fall? Would God, *i. e.*, have brought into existence a race, merely that He might show the glory of his justice in punishing forever all that belonged to it?—It is very possible that a general redemption is only possible where there is a race; that the same constitution which involves liability to generic sin makes a general atonement possible. Christ, in order to redemption, must have part in the race, be consubstantial with man. We are apt to spiritualize both sin and redemption more than the Scripture does. In the Bible, sin is connected with the death of the body, redemption with the resurrection of the body; sin is from Adam to the race, redemption from the second Adam to the race. The physical and the moral are here blended.

The grand relief in respect to the problem of sin is not to be found in the will of man, nor in any real or supposed efficacy of that will against the inroads and might of human sinfulness. Exalt that power as we may, still, all that we can get out of it is a vindication of our feeling of guilt and responsibility in view of the evil and sin that are in us. Its best effect is reached when we have deepened the sense of sin and sharpened the feeling of responsibility. It may thus serve a purpose of vindicating the divine justice in respect to our lot. But farther than this it cannot carry us. It is not a power on which we can *rely* for our moral change; that change is only, in fact, through divine grace, through the redemption that is in Christ Jesus. To have that redemption is absolutely *essential* for pardon.—Nor is that power of the will of any real availability in respect to accounting for our first moral choices in this sphere of being. It only enables us to say they were in some sense avoidable, not necessary, *i. e.*, by a merely physical necessity. But still the broad, terrible fact remains, that there is that in human nature which, in spite of this power, always carries the will, and begets our immanent preferences. The *real* thing in us is this mighty power of sin. To meet speculative difficulties, some such view of the will as that referred to above, has its value: to meet our practical difficulties we need more than this. As a *matter of fact*, to all the human race there is no hope out of the redemption that is in Christ Jesus.—And on the highest question as to God's moral government, the solution must be found *not outside of, but within* the Christian system. The great ultimate ground is this: this world was made, sin was permitted, Christ came, the kingdom of God was established, in view of, and with respect to, Redemption from sin.

Perhaps the only position where we can get any real relief, as far as the divine government is concerned (and it is only partial), is this: Adam sinned; God would at once have condemned to remediless punishment, had He not intended to redeem. Adam would have had no posterity, had it not been for redemption; our coming into being is under the economy of redemption. Our position is between the two economies—the evils of the one, through natural descent—the hope of the other, through grace. We may be saved through Christ. It is better for us to come into being thus than to come, each to be tested for himself. *To all to whom the gospel is offered* the last and great condemnation will be that they have rejected grace provided and offered. Then *as to those who die in infancy*, there is a well-grounded hope that they are of the elect.[1] As to *the heathen*, and those who have never heard of Christ: doubtless they will be judged finally according to the light that they have had: not merely according to and by their nature, but as they have used or not used such opportunities of repentance as have been afforded

---

[1] As to the salvation of infants, Clem. Alex. held that they could not be saved without baptism, Augustine, the same (De Anima, lib. 3, c. xiv.; contra Pel. lib. i. xl.—Pelagius had said: "Quo *non* eant scio, quo eant, *nescio*"); Perrone, in his Manual, defends the proposition: "Infantes ex hac vita sine baptismo decedentes ad æternam salutem pervenire non possunt;" Martin (R. C.) in his La Via Futura (Paris, 1853, pp. 435-455) cites testimony of the Fathers that unbaptized infants in the *Limbus Infantum* suffer deprivation only, not pain; Brownson, Quar. Rev., 1862-3, assigns them to "a state of natural beatitude;"—it is noticeable that Arminius admitted the damnation of infants as possible (Works, iii. 368, ed. of 1853): "I affirm that they rejected the grace of the Gospel in their parents, grandparents, great-grandparents, etc., by which act they deserved to be abandoned of God;" see the debate between Lyman Beecher ("Spirit of the Pilgrims," 1828, i. 42, 78, 95, 149) and Andrews Norton (Chris. Exam., 1827, iv. 431; v. 229, 316, 506); also a good article by H. C. Townley, Chris. Rev., July, 1863, p. 418; [also, article by Dr. Prentiss, Pres. Rev., 1883].

ANTECEDENTS OF REDEMPTION. 323

—and this, too, on the ground of the redemption in Christ, whether they have known it or not.[1] This is not free from difficulties; but it seems to be the utmost that can be said. It makes Redemption enter into the constitution and the final judgment of the world.

CHAPTER VIII.

OBJECTIONS TO THE DOCTRINE OF ORIGINAL SIN.

1. It is said that the doctrine of original sin makes sin to be the cause of sin. But this does not hold properly against the doctrine, because:

(*a.*) According to the doctrine, the cause of all sin in the world is the transgression of Adam: sin is not the cause of sin, but Adam is the cause of sin.

(*b.*) This original sin or native depravity in us is, properly speaking, the source, the ground, the principle of sin rather than the cause. The category to be applied—sin being in the race —is not that of cause and effect, but, of ground and consequence, of source and stream. The objection assumes that all sin is a choice, of a person; but this is not the sense of the doctrine.

(*c.*) The objection proves too much. Sin *may be* the cause of sin. Sinful habits, when formed, are the cause of sin in everyday experience.

2. It is objected that a propensity to sin is not properly sinful. This has been considered already, but the reasons for calling it sinful may be here summed up.

(*a.*) Such is usage. The confining of all terms denoting

---

[1] [In a sermon on the Atonement the author indicates his fear that no man in the heathen world ever did live up to the measure of his light and knowledge, and also, that hope for the masses of adult heathen would be better based upon the almost universally prevalent systems of sacrifice, viewed, amidst all their monstrous perversions, as still containing the confession of sin and the yearning for deliverance; but it would seem that the suggestion was not thought to deserve any place in the theological scheme.]

moral quality to individual acts belongs to a conventional and narrow system of ethics, to the philosophy of individualism.

(*b.*) It is sinful in the sense that it is from sin and leads to sin. It is from sin alone, and leads only to sin.

(*c.*) It is the same disposition in us latent for which we feel guilty and which we know to be sinful when it comes into distinct consciousness. A propensity to sin is a latent, inordinate love of the world and self. All grant that, after choice, the propensity is sinful. How does it now differ from what it was before? It has become a personal, manifested choice, involving personal liabilities. As soon as we define sin by its *real nature*, and not by its liabilities, not by its causes and consequences, we have to bring a propensity to sin under it.

(*d.*) It is sinful because it exposes all the members of the race to divine judgments under the moral government of God, to evil, misery, death.

(*e.*) Because we need regeneration and atonement in order to be delivered from it: and these are moral and not physical remedies.

Yet, while vindicating the propriety of calling it sinful, we would not dispute about a mere word, if the facts of the case are conceded. Native depravity is perhaps a more unobjectionable term than original sin. If people call it native depravity in a moral sense, and say that it comes from Adam, all that is essential is granted.

3. It is objected that the doctrine makes two kinds of sin. Of course it does, if sin is to be defined as actual transgression, as specific volition, as conscious preference. Otherwise not. It makes two forms of sin: one the conscious and the other the unconscious; one the native and the other the active. The objection sometimes is: there cannot be any sin without a knowledge of good: choice of evil, knowing the good, is sin, and only this. But the Apostle Paul says: "I had not known sin but by the law." The sin was there before. The Psalmist prays: "Cleanse thou me from secret faults." There is a great deal of sin in us, in all Christians, which is only brought out in times of temptation and trial.

4. Objection is sometimes made to the *form* which the doctrine takes in mediate imputation. (*a.*) This is said to be "Realism,"[1] involving numerical identity of substance in all the members of the race. But the doctrine does not involve any such speculation. The assertion that the human race is a *reality* as truly as the human individual is, is not "realism" in the sense of this objection. (*b.*) It is said that the doctrine in this form involves an act of a nature,—which is impossible. But this only on the assumption of *universalia ante rem*. *Universalia in re* is consistent with the position, that "in Adam the person corrupted the nature, in us the nature corrupts the person." There *was* a nature to be corrupted by an act: there *is* a nature which furnishes the corrupt ground of the person who becomes corrupt. '(*c.*) For the same reasons, it is said that this form of the doctrine would bring upon us the guilt of all of Adam's sins, and of all the sins of our forefathers. But this would only hold against a form of mediate imputation which should deny the federal headship of Adam, asserting all the evils of sin to be mere consequences of transmission, and denying any righteous judgment of God upon the race as in Adam, the public person, and upon his act, his first sin, as the *source* of all human corruption and transgression. (*d.*) It is said that mediate imputation is no imputation: that "impute" means, to reckon to one what is done by another. Waiving the question[2] whether this is accurate, we assert that any tolerable doctrine of mediate imputation does "reckon to one what is done by another." The mode or *media* of· reckoning may be different in different cases.

In conclusion we say that the definition of sin, which will cover original sin, is our standard definition: "Sin is any want of conformity unto, or transgression of, the law of God."

[1] See Princeton Review, Jan. 1865.
[2] Dr. Charles Hodge, Syst. Theol., ii. 194, says: "So far as the meaning of the word [impute] is concerned, it makes no difference whether the thing imputed be . . . . . our own personally, or the sin or righteousness of another."

CHAPTER IX.

OF THE BONDAGE OF SIN, ITS POWER OVER THE HUMAN WILL.

We have here the question of *Natural Ability* and *Moral Inability*.[1]

The inherent difficulty of the inquiry, and of the right mode of stating the exact truth, comes from the fact that the truth is not a simple, but a relative one. We are in danger of taking one half and neglecting the other, of stating the natural ability without the moral inability, or the moral inability without the natural ability, whereas both together make the truth. Here, too, we have to do with one form of the reconciliation of the great facts of dependence and free-agency, and also, of the certainty of depravity with the existence of accountability. Accordingly, the truth must be so stated as to save both sides. Besides, here the greatest interests are at stake: the divine government on the one hand, and human freedom on the other; while the discussion also bears upon the most solemn and important part of preaching—the grounds for the exhortation of the sinner to repentance.

One way of meeting this difficulty is to assert both truths in an unreconciled way. This is the common sense mode. This is the way in which the truths lie in most minds, each being held to be proved by sufficient evidence, and both being affirmed without the endeavor to reconcile them. God is sovereign, man is free: God's sovereignty extends to all events, man's freedom to all his moral acts. Or, in another point of view, man is depraved and always will sin, and yet he is always free in doing it. This is the sound, practical way of looking at the subject. Many theoretical attempts do not amount to much more than this. And it is better to leave the question in this shape, holding both positions, each by itself, than so to state and enforce either as to cut the nerve of the other. No theory of freedom

---

[1] See Smalley's Sermons, reprinted in Brown's Theol. Tracts, I. Compare also, Dr. Hickok's Science of Mind from Consciousness.

can be true, which interferes with the divine government, in regeneration, election, etc.; and no theory of the divine government can be true, which interferes with, or denies, the proper responsibility and free will of man. And besides, all concede that it is necessary to preach both in order to make a right impression—both certainty and free-agency: now, if it is necessary to preach both, neither is true by itself alone, neither is true in an abstract statement about it, made without respect to the other; no definition of either can be correct which is not made with respect to the other, in view of it, and as balanced by it. An abstract metaphysical inability and an abstract metaphysical ability are both false.

The problem therefore is, how to state the two facts in their relations to, and connections with, each other. The different extreme positions are these: (1) Man has no ability *of any kind* to repent and turn to God; he is utterly disabled to all good, in the proper strict sense of inability and disability. His condition is that of "absolute disability." (2) The counter extreme position is, that man has in the strict sense power to the contrary in all moral acts; *i. e.*, entire adequacy to repentance, full power, all power needful for the act of repentance, is given in the power of contrary choice. The mere fact of power to the contrary choice gives full power to repent, without divine grace. (3) Man has the natural ability to repent, while he is morally unable, and the two are consistent with each other. This is the New England statement, the position of Edwards.

§ 1. *Preliminary Definitions.*

1. Natural Inability. By this is meant a want of powers or power of choice, or of physical advantages and opportunities, *e. g.*, when one lacks the requisite faculties, so that the power of choice cannot apply to the case, as when an impotent man resolves to walk and cannot. This is always applied in connection with the possibility of there being a willing mind. Natural inability means, that one cannot though he will.

2. Natural Ability. By this is meant, having all the faculties and powers of a moral agent, including the power of choice,

—whatsoever is in the possible compass of one's natural capacities, so that, if a man wills to do anything, he can do it, just up to the extent of his natural capacities; *e. g.*, a man wills to jump; his natural ability is the extent to which he can jump if he puts forth all his power. If a man is capable of one hundred and twenty degrees of virtue, and one hundred and twenty-one are demanded, that one hundred and twenty-first is not rightfully demanded of him, because it is not in the compass of his natural capacities. Whatever his physical capacities, all his powers of reason, heart, and will combined, can effect, provided he wills it—that is his natural ability.[1]

3. *Moral Inability.* By this is meant, such a state of the heart or will as makes continued sinful action certain, such, *e. g.*, as makes it certain that the sinner will not repent without divine grace. It means—unwillingness, but unwillingness as implying a state of the will supremely fixed on some end or object, a permanent state or habit of the will, the supreme love of the world. It is sometimes said that the older New England theologians meant by moral inability merely unwillingness, and that is true if the word unwillingness is used in its full meaning, as setting forth the fact that the will is in a permanent state of choice. The word meant such unwillingness as is a real and sufficient obstacle to actual repentance.

4. *Moral Ability.* This means such a state of heart and will as implies a preference for anything, and the ability of doing which *results from the preference.* It means more than the general capacity which is involved in free agency or natural ability, it is intended to designate—entire, immediate adequacy to an end.

Natural Inability is = a man cannot though he will.

Natural Ability is = a man can if he will,—can if he will not,—he has all that is necessary except the will, but the will is needful to the actualizing of the case.

Moral Inability is = a man will not though he can.

Moral Ability is = a man will. It is, the state of the will itself.

---

[1] In later schools of New England theology there has been a curious changing of the meaning of these terms, so as to make natural ability signify only the power to the contrary choice. But it is evident that the sense given above was the meaning originally, from the terms used as equivalent to it, *e. g.*, "physical ability."

Reply to the question: Can a man will? It may mean, Besides and above the will, is there a can? Ans. No; this is volition before volition. It may mean, Can a man will under the appropriate circumstances?[1] Ans. Yea.

§ 2. *The Power to the Contrary.*

This phrase is sometimes used to mean the same as natural ability. It is sometimes employed to designate a distinct power from that which is actually exerted, and such power is regarded as that which constitutes the freedom of the will. But this cannot be. There is only one indivisible power of choice, and the power to the contrary is simply that power of choice viewed in relation to something which is not chosen, but which might have been, had the person preferred. If the will is put on one object, it is metaphysically implied that *the will*—the same will, not a distinct power—might have been put on a different object.

In relation to moral action or agency, the term natural ability is better suited than that of the power to the contrary choice, to express the real facts of the case. It is a matter of consequence here, what our words are: a difference in phraseology may cause the widest difference in our mode of apprehending the facts. The reason of using the phrase, natural ability, rather than the simple general phrase, free agency, was, the reference and contrast in the former to moral inability. It is a phrase which states one of the facts *with reference* to the other, which is what we must do in all discussion of the subject before us.

The Difference between Natural Ability and Power to the Contrary:

1. Natural ability, the power of choice, is exercised in every act—not the whole natural ability, but the capacities according to the degree of them which is demanded—while the power to the contrary is never *exercised*. It cannot be. As soon as it is exercised, it is not the power to the contrary, but the power

---

[1] If by liberty be meant a power of willing and choosing, as exemption from co-action and natural necessity, and power, opportunity, and advantage to execute our own choice; in this sense we hold liberty" (Dr. Edwards, Reply to Dr. West, Works, i. 326). But with the author, "appropriate circumstances" means more than this, it includes "willingness" in the deeper sense.

which is put forth. It is a contradiction in terms to suppose it actually exercised.

2. The assumption of a specific power to the contrary cannot help us in explaining any acts of actual choice. It is said: Adam could not have sinned or repented, unless he had the power to the contrary. It is true, so far as this: unless he could have willed differently from what he did, he could not have sinned; but he did not use the power to the contrary, he left it behind. So when a sinner repents, he does not use the power to the contrary.[1] We *mean* by natural ability, or free agency, all the faculties of a moral agent, including the power of choice, whereby the *possibility* of another than the actual choice is always given. But no new faculties, no new power of choice, no power hitherto unexercised, is necessary, in order to a different result. It is a new *choice, i. e.,* a new exertion of the one indivisible power of choice, that is alone requisite.

3. The word power, as used in the phrase, "power to the contrary," is indefinite. It is sometimes used as though "power" were a simple ultimate idea. But that which is simple is "choice"; power has a variety of modifications. The Greek language gives this distinction in δύναμις and ἐνέργεια: the first is potential power, the second is power in act, power exerted. Now the word, power, in "power to the contrary," means and must mean, that which is potential, a possibility inherent in the nature of the cause. It can never mean, the power exerted. There is a difference between possibility and power: one is that which *may be*, the other is that which not only may be, but is, and is put forth.[2] As far as power of choice goes, which must be exerted in repentance, the sinner has it, and so has the possibility of coming into a different moral state, and if he had not that power, he could not be brought into a state of repentance. But

---

[1] He uses the same power that he formerly used in his course of impenitence, but in a different way, on different objects. The contention is against the existence of any power to the contrary *distinct* from the power which is used.

[2] ["The most elaborate of the Aristotelian distinctions is that between power in possibility and power in act. Man (*in potentia*) may be viewed as a possible cause of either of several effects; but to pass from power to action requires other conditions or causes, which help to constitute the effect" (Faith and Philosophy, p. 372).]

the result depends upon something more than the power of choice; it depends also upon the motive, the end or object of the choice. There must not only be the efficient cause, but the occasional and final cause.[1] So that all that the result depends upon is not given in the power of choice, although an essential element of it is given.

To say, that a man can repent, *actually* do so, without grace, is contrary to experience, to the Scriptures, to the certainty of his sinning until regeneration,—to his moral inability. To grant him all the faculties and powers, including choice, as possibilities, in respect to repentance, is consistent with these—and with the facts of the case.

§ 3. *The positive Statements as to the Relation of Natural Ability and Moral Inability.*

The First Proposition. Though the sinner has the natural ability (in the sense assigned) to repent and believe, yet, on account of his depravity, for the exercise of that ability, he is dependent on divine grace. The whole simple truth is contained in what the Apostle Paul says, Rom. vii. 18, taking his statement in a strict metaphysical sense: "To will is present with me but [how] to perform [I find] is not." This, with the context, gives the facts of the case, in a way to reconcile the two truths of moral inability and natural ability. It assigns the ground of the non-exercise; *i. e.*, *depravity*. That is the reason, and the only reason, why his natural ability will not be exerted. The ground is not put in a want of capacity, or of natural power of the will; but it is put where it belongs—viz., in the depravity. That is the only hindrance, but that is an effectual hindrance to repenting, without grace. The Apostle does not say, merely, that it is *certain* that he will not exercise his natural ability, nor simply

---

[1] President Day: "A man may have some power, but not all power; that is, he may not have all that on which the result depends. . . . . If the word power be used in its broadest sense, as including not only opportunity, knowledge, capacity, but motives of all kinds, it is not true that a man has always equal power to opposite volitions."—The term, power, is simple, but for the exercise of it we need other conditions than its existence. These two points are often confounded.

that he "will" not exert it: but he gives the ground and reason of the certainty that he will not. Moreover it is not "a gracious ability" which is conferred when repentance occurs, but the simple fact is, that an ability is exercised through grace,— with divine aid. The passage agrees with the explanations commonly given of "power to the contrary," viz., "can but will not," but it also gives the grounds of the will not.

And this also suggests the real point of inquiry and doubt, in respect to some of the misapplications and misunderstandings of the theory of natural ability—and shows its limitations. It is asked, What is ability, but a power which may be exerted? True: it may be: it is possible; and the having this power is perfectly consistent with the position that it can only be exerted under certain conditions, and if the hindrance is a sinful one, with our responsibility for the non-exertion. To illustrate. "God cannot lie"; the meaning is, He cannot actually do it; there is only an abstract, metaphysical, not a real, possibility.

Why we assert natural ability: Otherwise there is no obligation, nor even possibility of change of character. This will appear from

The Second Proposition: There is no sufficient ground for going further and saying positively, that a totally depraved being has sufficient power to repent, *without divine aid.* That would be to assert the possession of power in the second sense, in the sense of what one can actually do, in his condition, without God.

1. This is a position which can never be proved by induction; there are no facts on which it can be based: at the best it is but a metaphysical proposition. The facts of the case, the consciousness pleaded in the case, reaches no further than to the possibility of the act: *it does,* in our judgment, *reach to that point,* but not beyond—not to the position that man, in his state, without divine aid, can really, fully, and truly turn to God.

2. Nor does the argument from obligation reach any further

than our statement.[1] The argument from obligation is, "I ought, therefore I can." Whence is the ought in the case? It is based on a sense of right, of duty, which is the simple utterance of conscience. It is my duty: hence I ought to do it. This is primitive and simple. The "ought" is not primarily dependent on the "can," but precedes it. The feeling of obligation is the first and simplest. But it is said: "I ought, therefore I can:" the ability is the condition, though not the ground of the obligation. True so far as this, that the ought cannot exceed the measure of the natural ability—all the heart and soul and mind and strength. But it is a different thing to say, "I ought, therefore I can—actually—do it." For there is a hindrance, in the sinful self; and that is not a natural, but a moral hindrance, one for which I am guilty and responsible.

3. Nor does the command of Repentance imply more than our first proposition. "Man is bound to repent, therefore he can repent." Here we have the "ought" and the "can" brought under the point of view of Repentance. Avoiding the ambiguity in the word "can," we reach the same result as before. (*a*.) It may be remembered that there is no evidence that the command to repent is ever actually given except in a system in which divine aids are also given. But we do not insist upon this, since repentance is obligatory in any case. But we say, (*b*.) The command of repentance is also one on a level with man's natural ability. Man can—if he will. He has the power of choice, the capacity of choice, and that is the condition of the possibility[2] of his repentance. The hindrance is precisely as before, yet it is a real hindrance to *actual* obedience. *Objections:* "God commands us to repent actually, does He not?"—Yes. "Therefore we can actually repent, can we not?"[3] Still as before say, Yes, we have the natural ability actually to repent, and what prevents us from doing it is our own evil hearts, but that does prevent. "Is a man responsible for not obeying the command to repent?" Yes, because the reason for not obeying

---

[1] Müller: "Ich sollte freilich können, aber ich kann nicht."
[2] —condition in which there is the possibility—
[3] [Hints probably of answers to questions put by students in the class-room.]

is simply our preference for sin. And this is a final statement: we cannot get beyond it. "What is the sense of the phrase, 'he can *if he will?*'" "Can the sinner repent—if he will?" Yes, if he choose to do so. He can—if he will: the actual exercise of the will, as power of choice, is necessary to the volition: the doing is dependent on the willing. "Is it the same as when we say, a bird can sing—if it will?" No; there is no comparison to be made between the cases; the bird has not the faculty of Will, it is not a moral agent with such a faculty.

The Third Proposition. The position that a sinful, depraved being can actually repent without grace, involves us, when carried out strictly, in inextricable difficulties.

1. This position sunders in form of statement, what is always united in fact—viz., the divine and human coworking in all our religious acts.[1] Here the two factors are sundered, and then the result is supposed to be achieved by one. In actual human experience, there never has been such a state as religion without grace. Those who take the bold ground here do it in precisely the same sense in which they say that God can sin. The doctrine of power to the contrary is applied in a parallel way in the two cases. And we suppose it is just as true that a man can repent without grace, as that God can sin, and no more true. It is a bare metaphysical possibility given in the power of choosing.

2. Let us carry out the supposition for a moment, and make the hypothesis that a person repents without divine grace. What is the resultant state of mind? Repentance is turning to God, and supposes the divine presence, but by the supposition, God is not really present in the act. All that the act can amount to is this: I have an intellectual conception or idea of God, and I love or turn to that. It is an abstract love to an abstract idea. It is not a religious reality.

3. The position is consistent only with the supposition of the self-determining power of the will.

---

[1] On this all religion depends. It is this which gives the distinction between Religion and Morals. A religious state is one in which a divine influence is felt.

4. It implies self-regeneration, because wherever there is repentance there is a regeneration of the soul. The soul is renewed in and by repentance.

The Fourth Proposition. The Scriptures always conjoin the two truths of natural ability and moral inability, and they should be conjoined in all preaching. Neither by itself is the truth: both are the truth. The great thing is to keep the two truths together. Matt. iii. 2; Phil. ii. 12, 13; John vi. 44; xv. 5; Jer. xiii. 23; Rom. vii. 18; Rom. viii. 7, 8; Gal. iii. 21. The Scriptures give the truth in a concrete form. God is there addressing man. The relation of dependence, of mutual activity, is presupposed. They do not contemplate man as sundered from divine influence, except by sin. The most characteristic invitations, Matt. xii. 20; John vii. 37; Isa. lv. 1, 2; *on the face of them*, imply grace provided. The Scriptures do not know of any repentance, except through and by divine grace. The power which the gospel sets over against the mighty power of sin, is not the might of our own wills, but the power of God's grace through Jesus Christ.

As to Preaching: The best and the only real preaching is that which connects the two truths, natural ability and moral inability. The one cannot be set forth truly without the other. If natural ability is preached without moral inability, then the natural ability in its true sense is not preached, and *vice versa*. Wherever the duty is insisted on without the grace, or the grace without the duty, we are sure to go wrong. The best preaching combines—sovereignty, depravity, and natural ability: all other is jejune and bald. The *practicability of immediate repentance* cannot be urged on any other ground than the two conjoined: power of choice and grace offered. The question is not, Shall the sinner be exhorted to immediate repentance, but—on what grounds? Not—Has the sinner power of choice? but—As to the way of using that power. The obligation is urgent, the duty is full,— *how do it?* The answer: Grace is offered in Christ. Immediate repentance is always to be urged on the ground of the two combined; the power of choice giving the possibility, and grace offered giving encouragement; the duty which springs from man's capacities and relation to God, the obligation which binds the soul while its being lasts: man's helplessness in himself, his need of divine grace, and *that grace offered in Christ*. The two are the perpetual complements of each other. Such preaching has been the source of revivals in this country, in their best form. Even in the acutest essay to vindicate full natural ability which we have,[1] when the author brings the sinner to the point where he suspends his self-love, he makes the Holy Spirit come in and guide, in order to make effectual the choice. And so it must be always, in order to the renewal of the soul. In fact, the most strenuous advocates of unlimited ability say that they preach ability so that a man may feel his duty, try to perform it, find he cannot really do it—so hard is his heart—and then be led to accept the grace offered. But they might as well make the conclusion a part of the theory.

Summary. The great practical points.

1. Man has all the powers—perfectly so, which are necessary to moral agency.

2. All the inability he is under is a sinful inability. This is an unwillingness, which is not merely an act of the will or a lack of action, but is also a state of the will, constituting a real and sufficient obstacle to his actually doing right.

3. He has the ability in will as the power of choice, to accept or reject the grace offered to him, to obey or disobey the calls,—has the efficiency, though not the sufficiency.

4. He is under obligation to immediate repentance: he ought at once to repent and turn to God.

5. Under the offer of the gospel and the command of God, he may comply; no man can say that he has not enough of the influences.

6. This ability is not gracious merely; it is primarily in man's will as power of choice: so that to refuse is the greater sin.

[1] Dr. N. W. Taylor's in Christian Spectator.

CONCLUSION OF THE FIRST DIVISION OF THEOLOGY: THE ANTECEDENTS OF REDEMPTION.

We have considered The Being and Attributes of God; his Works, his End in Creation; Man as made for God, as having endowments to carry out and promote God's great end in creation; Man as fallen, as lying under and exposed to the penalties for sin, and as involved in the bondage of sin. There remains to be considered: The Possibility of Redemption, notwithstanding the sinful, guilty condition of mankind. [This was not treated by the author.] The possibility on God's side is found in the doctrine of the Trinity, which has been considered,—opening to our view personal distinctions in the Godhead, through which the Incarnation and the Redemption may become actual. The possibility on man's side consists: (1) In the divine image remaining in him, in his natural capacities and powers, and his immortal destiny: the groundwork of his nature, as a moral, spiritual, immortal being, remains. (2) In the capacity yet remaining to him, of receiving divine influences, whereby he may be restored.

DIVISION SECOND.

THE REDEMPTION ITSELF. THE PERSON AND WORK OF CHRIST.

DIVISION SECOND.

THE REDEMPTION ITSELF. THE PERSON AND WORK OF CHRIST.

We enter here upon the Second General Division of the System of Christian Theology, which is also the center and key-stone of the whole. The central idea to which all the parts of theology are to be referred, and by which the system is to be made a system, or to be constructed, is what we have termed the Christological or Mediatorial idea, viz., that God was in Christ reconciling the world unto himself. This idea is central,[1] not in the sense that all the other parts of theology are logically deduced from it, but rather that they center in it. The idea is, that of an Incarnation in order to Redemption. This is the central idea of Christianity, as distinguished, or distinguishable, from all other religions, and from all forms of philosophy; and by this, and this alone, are we able to construct the whole system of the Christian faith on its proper grounds. This idea is the proper center of unity to the whole Christian system, as the soul is the center of unity to the body, as the North Pole is to all the magnetic needles. It is so really the center of unity that when we analyze and grasp and apply it, we find that the whole of Christian theology is in it. Thus: the analysis of Incarnation in order to Redemption *presupposes* the doctrine respecting the divine nature, the end of God in his works, the nature of man, and the condition of man as sinful: and this comprised the first division of theology—The Antecedents of Redemption. The same principle, *in its concrete unity*, gives us the doctrines respecting the Person and Work of Christ, which make up this, our second division of the system. And the same principle, *in its applications*, gives us the third division

---

[1] See Introduction to Christian Theology, p. 58.

of the system, embracing regeneration, justification, sanctification, the doctrine respecting the church and the sacraments, and the eschatology.

The general scheme for the Second Division:—

PART I.—The Incarnation in its general nature and objects: on Scriptural, historical, and philosophical grounds.

PART II.—Of the person of the Mediator: God manifest in the flesh.

PART III.—Of the work of the Mediator: in His three offices of Prophet, Priest, and King.

PART I.

OF THE INCARNATION IN ITS GENERAL NATURE AND OBJECTS.

CHAPTER I.

WHAT IS PRESUPPOSED IN THE INCARNATION.

Two things are presupposed: viz.—the fact of sin, and such a constitution of the Godhead as makes the incarnation possible.[1] These we have already considered. In order to redeem man from sin, an incarnate Redeemer, one divine in Himself, having our nature and bearing our sins, was needed. ("Cur Deus Homo?" Why the God-man?)

§ 1. *Of the Incarnation in Relation to Sin.*

We do not mean that we can say that only through an incarnation our deliverance could be effected. But we can say these things: (1) That such a being, one having the divine and the human nature, is eminently adapted to this work. (2) That no one can prove that any other being could have performed such a superhuman work. (3) That there is a more perfect congruity between such a person and such a work, than between such a work and any other person that we can conceive to exist. And we may add (4), that on the inductive method of reasoning from facts to principles, if it be proved historically that such a being has appeared, in the divine administration, for such a work, it is a rational conclusion that such a being was needed

---

[1] [There is a third point,—such a constitution of *human* nature as makes the Incarnation possible, which is considered incidentally. The author did not deny the position of certain eminent German theologians: that God and man are to be viewed as "capable of each other," but he would not affirm it as the leading position in Christology. He prefers to view the Incarnation always in its relation to *sin*.]

for the work. God does nothing in vain. Such a manifestation of glory and suffering, of glory in suffering, would not have been, unless a necessity for it—at least a moral, if not a physical or natural, necessity had existed.

Over against the sin of the world, to redeem men from it, the God-man appeared. This is his position. The fact of sin made it necessary, in the above sense, that he should appear for this object.

And in relation to the human race, He is the second Adam, the Lord from heaven. He assumes the same position in respect to the human race as to its redemption from sin and to eternal life, that the first Adam did in respect to sin and death. This is clearly and fully put by the Apostle Paul, 1 Cor. xv. 46–49,[1]—a wonderful passage: life from Christ as death from Adam, spirit from Christ as soul from Adam. The parallel is complete: the headship of Christ in relation to redemption is set over against the headship of Adam in relation to sin. We may with advantage make some fuller statements here upon this important point. We can have from this position the best survey of theology; in retrospect as to what we have considered—under the headship of Adam, and in prospect of what is before us—under the headship of Christ.

Fuller Statement of the Doctrine of the Two Headships.

In the Scriptures, especially in the two passages, Rom. v. 12–21, and 1 Cor. xv. 45, 47, two contrasted economies, making one divine plan, are presented to us. On the one hand is sin and death, and on the other hand, righteousness and life. Sin and death come to the human race from one man—the first Adam: righteousness and life also come to the race from one, that is, Jesus Christ. Condemnation is by the first, Justification is by the second: we are involved in death by the former, and we obtain resurrection and the reigning in life by the other, that is, by Jesus Christ.

In these positions is disclosed the grand and striking peculi-

---

[1] Compare on this: the relation to Philo, and the difference between Paul and Philo, ("Jour. Class. and Sac. Philology," No. 1, 1854.

arity of the Scriptural mode of viewing human nature and human destiny in relation to God. It is precisely here, on this point, in this way of summing up and stating the matter, that the Gospel of Christ is distinguished from all other schemes and systems, from all theories and speculations of merely human origin, from any merely physical or moral system, that proposes to explain the facts, and to forecast the destiny of the race. It is in the contrasted headship of the first and of the second Adam. For the whole Scriptural doctrine of sin runs back into our natural union with the first Adam by descent; the whole Scriptural doctrine of righteousness runs back into our vital union with the second Adam, which is not of nature but by grace.

I.—The Scriptural view of the relation of the race to the first Adam, is at once simple and complete.

1. The human race is not a mere aggregate of units, but rather a physical and moral unity. There is one family of man it is made up of individuals, each one having his personal rights and personal responsibilities; but these separate individuals are also bound together, by the inflexible law of a common descent; and the unity is as real as the individuality; in fact, the generic, in plan and in idea, precedes the individual. It is not meant, or implied, in this, that there is any mystical identity of substance; but only a real unity, made by the law of propagation and descent, so that we are all truly the children of the first Adam, and have part and lot in his inheritance.

2. On the basis of this physical unity of the race, the Scriptures still further teach us, that there is also a moral unity. The union comes under the rubric of moral government, as well as under the caption of physical connection. In other words, in the technical language of theology—which is a convenient, though not the only, form of stating the truth,—Adam was constituted the federal, as well as the natural, head of the human race. In some way, as a matter-of-fact, if not of *formal* covenant,[1] he stood for us, as our representative, so that what he did might be, and was, made over to his descendants, involving them in the consequences, whether of advantage or of liability,

---

[1] It was more than a covenant—a "charter," v. supra.

of his act. And this was not merely a physical sequence, a matter of divine sovereignty alone: it is also represented as a moral, even as a judicial process, in terms too distinct to be evaded. "As by one man sin entered into the world and death by sin, and so death passed upon all men, for that [or, as is seen in the fact that] all have sinned;" "through the offence of one many be dead;" "by one man's offence death reigned by one;" "by the offence of one, judgment came upon all men to condemnation;" "by one man's disobedience many were made [constituted] sinners." If these statements do not imply a moral union and dependence, a relation not physical, but judicial, it is hardly possible for language to do so. In the technical language of theology, this is represented as the imputation of Adam's first sin to his posterity, that is, as reckoning to their account the penal consequences of his transgression. We sinned in him and fell with him—not as personally present, but through our community of nature.[1]

3. But we are chiefly concerned with the *fact* itself, that in consequence of Adam's sin we come into the world in a state of sin and death, and liable to penal evils here and hereafter, unless divine grace intervene. Here is doubtless a great, an awe-inspiring mystery: but, as Pascal intimates, though it is a great enigma, yet the enigma of man's life would be still greater, and still more insoluble, if this were not so. What we assert is, that this doctrine, with all its fearful shadows, is still only the reading and rendering of *the facts of the case:* it is not a mere theory to explain the facts, it is the facts themselves compendiously summed up and stated.[2] And however we may explain the fact of our com-

---

[1] The older Hopkinsianism of New England, in making the first moral act of all Adam's descendants to be "the consent to Adam's sin," was immeasurably nearer the truth than the more modern Hopkinsianism, which represents our first moral act to be simply our personal violation of the divine law, in full view of the consequences, and with full power to the contrary.

[2] It is a striking fact, that the profoundest infidelity of the age has swept round on this point to the substance of the orthodox view,—substituting fate for God. Materialism confesses that man is by nature engrossed in sense and the world; Pantheism makes original sin to be the very substance of human nature. Both systems grant the fact of alienation from God, and explain it by denying God. Christianity in addition brings the facts under God's moral government,—making them a part of the divine plan in respect to the human race.

mon ruin and sinfulness, it meets us everywhere. No man's conscious experience reaches back to the beginning of sin within him. When we wake up to a sense of our moral position, it is always with a sense of sin, and never of innocence. When we first know the law, it is as a condemning power. We cannot think of saving ourselves by doing the deeds of the law: for by the deeds of the law shall no flesh living be justified. Salvation cannot, for any members of Adam's race, come by the law. The life commended to our choice in the Bible is a life through grace freely offered. We find ourselves exposed daily to penal evils, from our youth up: and the very infant that dies before moral agency is detected, in that death gives evidence to the sentence of the law, and confirms the Biblical statement, that we are by nature the children of wrath. And with this agrees the profoundest spiritual experience of the depth and nature of sin. Its roots run deeper than our volitions; actual transgression is the offspring of original sin. The exercises of the will only reveal the will's immanent state and inmost preference. That which is born of the flesh is flesh; that is, our native state is a sinful state; and the renewing and sanctifying Spirit works beneath the sphere of direct consciousness and volition, and gives to the regenerate a new heart and a right spirit. And in all this work it is not of him that willeth, nor of him that runneth, but of God that showeth mercy.

Such is the headship of Adam in relation to the race, entailing sin and death as the sad consequence of the great, original apostasy.

II.—But over against this headship of Adam, the grace of God has established another economy, centering in another covenant. The headship of Christ is one of life and redemption, as that of Adam was of death and condemnation. The divine plan of redemption from the evil and curse of sin centers in the Person and Work of the God-man, Christ Jesus. The purpose of mercy antedates the fact of sin: for He is the Lamb of God, slain from the foundation of the world. He is the head over all things to the church. There is (Col. i. 19, 20) an intimate relation between Him and all created beings: He is the medium of access for all creatures unto their heavenly Father.

And this headship of the Lord Jesus is on every point parallel, and contrasted, with that of Adam. What Adam is in relation to sin and death, that Christ is in relation to righteousness and life. By man came death, by man came also the resurrection from the dead. As in Adam all die, even so in Christ shall all be made alive,—referring here, too, to the resurrection. The judgment was by one offence to condemnation, the free gift is of many offences unto justification. The eternal Son of God assumed our nature, lived in it his sinless life and in it died his sacrificial death: there is that which is human in the second Adam over against that which is human in the first; there is that which endures and stands to perfection over against that which falls and sinks into corruption; there is that which expiates over against that which incurs; that which satisfies divine justice over against that which calls it forth; that which provides for answering the demands of the divine law in respect to the whole race over against that which brought the whole race under the penal demands of that law. The cross of Christ is the link between earth and heaven, and it is the shield between earth and hell. There converge and commingle the rays of the divine justice and of the divine love—the justice and the love equally satisfied—and thence emerge all these rays only to bless and to save. There the dignity of a divine nature imparts an infinite value to the pangs which only a human nature could endure, and with the cry "It is finished," the second Adam stands forth in the perfection of his obedience and suffering, in the parallel and contrast with the first.

The contrasted parallel between the first and the second Adam is thus complete in all its parts and relations. The first is our natural head, the second is our spiritual head; the first brought in condemnation, the second, justification; the first involved us in spiritual death, the second is the author of spiritual life; the former made the death of the body to be our mortal heritage, the latter makes the resurrection of the body to be our immortal privilege; the first alienates from God, the second reconciles unto God; the first is the progenitor and head of our fallen humanity, the second is the source and head of our renewed humanity; from the former we receive that natural life which contains the seeds of death, from the latter, through the Spirit, we receive that spiritual life which is the ground and pledge of our eternal felicity; the tie that unites us to the one is that of natural descent, the bond that allies us to the other is a union no less real, no less vital, subsisting through faith, and insuring to us all the blessings of the new covenant: for, if by one man's offence, death reigned by one, much more they which receive abundance of grace and of the gift of righteousness shall reign in life by one, Jesus Christ.

Such, set over against one another, are the headship of Adam and the headship of Christ. But they are not only contrasted with each other, they also run into each other. We therefore proceed to state,

III.—That the two form one system, one plan, so that the one cannot be understood without the other. The two together, and not either by itself, embrace the purpose of God in respect to the human race. Human nature and human destiny cannot be explained without reference to both. God's government of the world cannot be explained except as including both. It would else be like explaining the orbit of a planet with only one focus. God's moral government has the two foci of sin and of redemption. It would else be like trying to explain the course of our earth without both the centrifugal and centripetal force: God's moral government includes the centrifugal power of sin as well as the centripetal force of redemption.

Here is found the mistake of many theorizers upon the moral government of God,—reducing it to the level and scope of their own speculations. It is very easy to make out some such scheme with a few simple definitions,—and then to substitute the definitions for the facts. But the facts of the case after all are the solid things. Thus, for example, it is easy to construct a system of natural ethics, to say that the whole of God's government is by a simple rule or law of right with its appropriate sanctions, of reward or punishment. But this position, logically carried out, would exclude the whole system of redemption. So, too, it is easy to say, that the divine benevolence, in the sense of a disposition to confer happiness, is the great principle of all God's acts and dealings; but this reduces holiness to a means of happiness, and resolves the atonement into a mere means of moral impression. So, too, we may set forth, in theory, the whole of the divine influence upon man as a mere moral suasion, like that of man on man; but in doing this we rob regeneration of its vital element. Or yet again, we may represent our whole relation to Adam as merely natural and physical, and not as moral and spiritual, and may define sin as consisting merely in personal choices and volitions, and thus rule out, by definition, the whole doctrine of original sin; but this is plainly incompatible with the inspired statement that by one offence judgment came upon all men unto condemnation: and what we may seem to gain by such definitions in increasing the sense of personal responsibility, is more than counterbalanced by the loss of all profounder views of the depth of our corruption, and of the absolute necessity of divine grace for any spiritual good accompanying salvation.[1]

But the evil of such partial theories and explanations does not end here. The divine plan and system in respect to both Adam and Christ is one and the same in its general principles and bearings. The headship of Adam in relation to sin, and the headship of Christ in relation to redemption, stand and fall together. Any theory which excludes the former, equally excludes the latter, if logically carried out. Or, in other words—to bring the matter to its test on the two central doctrines, where both headships converge—the doctrine of original sin and the doctrine of justification by faith alone, stand or fall together. If we give up the one we cannot save the other in its essential integrity. One way of testing the truth of our theories of sin is to see whether the principles of our theory will leave justification by faith intact and complete,[2] in all its evangelical grace

[1] It has been said, in the way of a taunt against the older theology, that men are very willing to speculate about sinning in Adam, so as to have their attention diverted from the sense of personal guilt. But the whole history of theology bears witness, that those who have believed most fully in our native and strictly moral corruption—as Augustine, Calvin, Edwards—have ever had the deepest sense of their personal demerit. We know the full evil of sin only when we know its roots as well as its fruits.

[2] Yet many adhere firmly to the Scriptural view of justification, who deny all sin but actual transgression.

and fulness. We must define sin and holiness by parallel and harmonious formulas. If there be no sin, but personal ill-desert, there cannot be any holiness but personal merit, and heaven is of debt and not of grace. If there can be no condemnation excepting for personal choices and acts, neither can there be any justification excepting for personal choices and acts. If Adam cannot involve us in sin and ruin, neither can Christ confer upon us righteousness and life. If the sin of Adam cannot be imputed to us for our condemnation, neither can the righteousness of Christ be imputed to us for our salvation. If there cannot be a headship of Adam in respect to our natural death, there cannot be a headship of Christ in respect to our spiritual life.

But if we take such positions, how contrasted our view is with that divine plan, which consists not in theories but in facts—facts centering in persons and in covenants, which may not be so fully and clearly grasped, which have a background of wonder and mystery, but which are also majestic and simple, and give us fixed points and centers for our theology and our faith. Here on the one hand is Adam, made originally in the divine image, the head of the human family, placed in the garden of Eden, in familiar intercourse with his Maker, receiving the paradisiacal command, at once intelligible and fitted to his condition; appointed, if he obeyed, to be the head of a holy society through all time; condemned, if he disobeyed, to return to the dust, and to convey to those who were to come from his loins the same death in sin into which he himself plunged. And over against him, in the divine plan for the race, is the God-man, our Saviour; appointed to suffer and conquer for those who were involved in the wreck and ruin of the fall. We behold Him, hanging upon the cross, his head crowned with thorns, his hands stretched out upon the accursed tree, that He might both suffer and save. We hear his dying words of unutterable anguish, in their very sharpness of love full of unspeakable blessings for our lost humanity: his dying cry is the watchword of our salvation.

And in these two contrasted forms, we read the sum of human destiny—its beginning, its center and its eternal issues; in these two we see the whole of the Law and the whole of the Gospel, the whole of justice and the whole of mercy, blended in one system.

§ 2. The second point presupposed by the Incarnation is *such a constitution of the divine nature as made an Incarnation possible.*

This has been considered in the doctrine of the Trinity: we only refer to it here by way of completeness of systematic view. This constitution is that of the existence of distinct personal agencies in the Godhead, especially of the Son as personally distinct from the Father.

Here again, we would not say that an Incarnation was possible only on the ground of the essential Trinity: *i. e.*, by a metaphysical necessity: for that we do not quite know. Sabellianism is metaphysically possible. But this we may say: (1) The existence of such personal distinctions in the Godhead is most congruous with the fact of the Incarnation, with the personal distinction of Father and Son, as that comes out in the Incarnation. For that such a personal distinction existed when Christ was incarnate, and since then—if Christ still lives —cannot be denied. Nor can it be shown that his personality began with the Incarnation. The contrary can be proved. (2) Any other view makes the personality of Christ at least to *seem* ephemeral. (3) Passages of Scripture take for granted a pre-existing personal relationship. Gal. iv. 4; John iii. 16; xvii. 5: xvii. 24; xvi. 28. (4) We gain a more intelligible view of the economy of redemption on the basis of the Trinity than on any other. We see the different offices of the different persons in the great work: and all, in every stage and part, divine.[1]

Such are the two chief points of the connection of the Incarnation with the whole system of theology. We proceed now to consider the Incarnation in its general nature and objects.

[1] Pascal: "If the world subsisted to teach men of the existence of God, his divinity would be reflected from all parts of it in an incontestable manner; but as it subsists only by Jesus Christ and for Jesus Christ, and to teach men both their corruption and redemption, all in it shines with these two truths. That which there appears marks, neither a total exclusion, nor yet a manifest presence of Deity, but *the presence of a God who hides himself:* all bears this character."

CHAPTER II.

THE INCARNATION PRIMARILY FACT AND NOT DOCTRINE.

The Incarnation is to be viewed primarily as a revealed fact. It is a revelation of God in the form of fact and history, and as such has about it the majesty of fact. It is not a mere speculation, nor a mere doctrine, nor a mere abstract truth: but a truth of fact. It belongs to what we have called the Christian Realism in distinction from Nominalism.[1]

Nor yet again, is it a mere fact of an inspired record: it is not merely a *truth* announced in such a record. So to speak, it lies back of the record, and the record tells us about it. It is an historical manifestation of God in the midst of men. Christ the God-man appears in human history, as a part thereof; becomes a member of the race; lives, suffers and dies for our redemption; and in all this we have a sublime series of facts, of which the Scriptures give us the record. The first point to be aimed at, then, in respect to the doctrine, is the proof of its historical verity, on the basis of evidence; and not the speculative apprehension of it, or an *a priori* deduction of its possibility. This is a far-reaching statement about this truth, and puts it— and this alone puts it—in its just position. This is the way in which it stands in the Bible, as differing from systematic theology. The Scriptures enter into no speculation about the two natures and their union, nor into philosophical objections, but they announce the grand and simple truth that God was in Christ. The Proem to John's Gospel is a narration given by a man who has seen a vision of facts: the first act, Creation, the second, Incarnation.

[1] Introd. to Chris. Theol., p. 5.

CHAPTER III.

THE FACT OF THE INCARNATION IN RELATION TO MAN'S MORAL WANTS.

It may be said to be demanded by man, in the sense in which need implies demand.

§ 1. *It presents us with the Life of a perfect Man as a Model for Imitation, and so meets Need.*

1. Every being who has a conscience has also the image or ideal of a perfect man and a perfect life. Wherever there is any morality, there is a certain standard, not only of abstract, but also of human excellence. There is an innate loyalty of the soul to what is good and great. Nations will have heroes, though they have to invent their most heroic qualities. Children must have models for imitation, though they may be models of imperfect men and women. Thus there is in the human race both the universal desire for a model and a universal defect in the models. And this universal longing is satisfied, this universal defect is supplied, in the life of Jesus.

2. The natural longing of the human heart for the view of moral perfection is not met by promulgating law and sharpening the sense of duty, nor by exalting the ideal of morality. The profoundest minds of every age have given their best thoughts to ethical systems, to codes of righteous laws, to the description of what each man should be as the citizen of a perfect state. And all of us have some vision of personal perfection, some imagination of the harmonious blending and working of our powers, some impulse towards the attainment of purer love and higher holiness. We all have some ideal of excellence. But even though we give to our abstract ideal of excellence the form and features of a man, it does not touch our hearts; it may be as beautiful, but it is as cold as a statue. An imagined excellence is not really human; an ideal man is not a man at all. Ideal virtue has not been diffused through the affections, nor has it

emerged from the will, of a moral being. It has passed through no conflicts, has resisted no temptations, has purified no affection, has not been the basis or the result of any choice; it is neither a moral act nor a moral state of a moral being. And hence it is that it has so light attractions upon the affections of a moral being. All praise virtue in the abstract, but the praise is barren of fruit. The voluptuary may not only pant for an ideal beauty, he may also admire an ideal virtue. It may attract everything within him, but—his affections; may touch all that his nature contains, excepting—his depravity. And even with the best of men it is found that some of the most effectual motives to obedience and a holy life, and especially to the practice of humble and self-denying and daily virtues, are not so much derived from the abstract purity of a holy law, nor yet from the sheer imagination of a possible human excellence, as from some electric excitement of human sympathies, some powerful constraint from the lives and self-sacrificing zeal of one or another around them, from some kindling of holy affections in communion with an unseen friend, and most of all, from some emotion of gratitude or benevolence or love of virtue that has become an effectual motive from the view of the life, the love, the sufferings of the Lord Jesus.

3. The conformity of such a character as that of Christ, to our moral necessities, is still further seen, if we consider some of the special virtues on which our peace and happiness, the welfare of individuals and of society depend. The fact is that these depend on the practice of the humblest virtues. Pride grows by nature, humility thrives only by culture; self-boasting needs to be excluded, self-denial to be excited; wilfulness is born with us, a truly submissive spirit is a new birth of the soul. Natural kindness is often overcome by spleen, soured by disappointment, made fretful by petty cares and trials; and it is hard to ensure its constancy. Justice is more praised than loved; obedience oftener commanded than practised. It is easier to hate foes than to forgive them; it is easier to pray that they may be forgiven than to seek to win their good-will. In the business of life, what evils are there which honesty and a

checking of the inordinate love of wealth would not counteract? Fraud, unjust gains, immense speculations, too great inequality in the distribution of the things of life, the making haste to be rich by which we fall into temptation and a snare: all these and kindred evils can be done away, and can only be done away, by a recurrence to the practice of the simplest, yet hardest virtues. And to suffer shame and reproach on account of the gospel and of truth, to be mild when reviled, to bear the desertion of friends and the scoffs of enemies, to dare to speak the truth in season: these things are not easy of attainment, though most needful in an evil world. To relieve the wretched, to seek out the wanderers, to help the suffering, to reclaim the abandoned, to sympathize in the sorrows of the poor and minister to their consolation, to seek the vicious with love when they repel us with contumely: in short, to live in a sinful world and among evil men as children of the light and of the day, redeeming the time because the days are evil: this is most necessary for the world's welfare, yet difficult even for those who are striving for redemption. Now of all these necessary and neglected virtues Jesus Christ is the most eminent exemplar. It was not necessary that He should be a temporal king, but kings are greatest when they rule their kingdoms as He ruled his spirit. It was not necessary that He should be a statesman, but statesmen are noblest when the favor or frown of the people are to them as they were to Him. (It was not necessary that He should be a husband or a father—this were to degrade his mission, and to class Him with the sons of men—but it is necessary that parents should practise his virtues, and fulfil their duties in the same spirit in which He fulfilled his. It was more needful that He should be a child, that thus to all the race from their earliest years his example might be held up clear and fair.) It was not necessary that He should be to us an example in the virtues which the world loves and honors, for the world rewards its servitors only too liberally, it incites them to wealth and honor only too strongly. But it was needful that He should be an example of self-denial, of humility, of forgiveness of enemies, of daily endeavor to do good, of patience, of submission, of speaking against all evil and sin, while He sought to reclaim the sinful, of meekness and forbearance in the midst of reproaches and persecutions, of seeking to do the will of the Father and of perfect submission to that will. In short, it was necessary that there should be a perfect harmony of all his powers, and a harmony created by their entire subjection to the law of love, to the love of God. It was well, it was needful for all mankind that they should see that the highest human perfection, the most potent human influence, is not found in the objects which are of the highest human esteem, not in wealth, nor in power, not in the senate nor on the field of battle, not in literature nor in science, but in love to God and love to man, in a love which can be shown in poverty as well as in riches, when despised as well as when powerful, in daily life more than in the career of statesmen, in the field of the moral conflicts of the race better than on fields of carnage and of blood. That He might be the pattern of the race in all things, this was needful. That men might be incited to the love and practice of these daily and self-denying virtues, it was fitting that a model should be set before them,—one, a man like themselves, exposed to the same, and to greater temptations and trials than they all, living in the same evil world, finding the same foes to duty, and yet living above the world, and overcoming all its temptations and malice and might—overcoming by yielding to his enemies everything but his virtue, his love to God and love to man. Such an example is Christ to us, to all of us, in all those daily and hourly conflicts we are called to make for the sake of truth and duty.

4. But the whole effect of such an eminent example is not found—perhaps its chief effect is not found—in the single virtues of his noble and ennobling character. *The total impression of such a man, and of such a life, is the grand source of its strong influence upon others.* It is the harmony and completeness of his spiritual character, it is the consistency of his whole life with our highest standard of perfection, it is because we feel that all He did and said flowed from one pure unfailing source, and that the purity of his life was only an expression of

the spotlessness of his soul—it is this total impression of his spirit upon us which moves us most strongly, and which makes Him to be a perfect *model* to us.

§ 2. *The Relation of the Incarnation to Human Wants is seen in its giving to Man the most direct Access to, and Communion with, God.*

1. Man craves such an impersonation of Deity. We may say that his religious instinct leads him to seek some visible and palpable representation of God's attributes. This may be to some extent the effect of sin, but it is also congruous with those infirmities of our finite state which are not sinful. The expression of this desire is most palpable in heathenism. It is indeed there disfigured and distorted. Their idols are an abomination unto the Lord, as are their sacrifices also. But even as their sacrifices show how deeply the sense of guilt and the need of expiation are seated in human nature; and as these feelings are true and necessary, though the mode of their exhibition is false and degrading; so in respect to their idols, it may be asserted that they are evidence of a profound longing in the human mind for some visible manifestation of deity. God and man are at such an infinite distance from each other, that when man would seek God, he will even make an idol that he may thus at least imagine that he has found Him. Between the infinite Spirit and the finite soul there is a space which, when men try to fill, they people with idols; but which God has filled by the person of his Son. So deep-seated is this desire of some visible connection with the invisible God, that even in the church of Christ, when it became Roman Catholic, and when the living sense of a direct personal relation between Christ and his followers had become feeble (and his actual presence was limited to the external order and worship of the church), it was found necessary to accommodate the notions of that church in so far to the wants of man, as to supply the place of the Redeemer who had been hidden from them, by the winning graces and image of his mortal mother, by crowds of saints and by images of glorified spirits. They banished the Saviour from his immediate connection with the hearts of his people; but they

were obliged to find some substitute to satisfy the cravings for an object of worship which should call out human sympathies.—Not only in false or corrupt religions is this want experienced: it is also deeply felt whenever there is an unusual excitement of our religious feelings. We long for a closer walk with God than we can have with a being whom we consider only as infinite in his attributes, "removed from us by the whole diameter of being." Almost unconsciously, we make to ourselves an image even of the invisible Father. We think of a throne and Him that sits upon it. We think of a countenance of terrible majesty, severe in justice, or melting into love. We seem to see an eye, fixed upon our path, noting all our ways; a hand stretched out to rescue us, an arm for our defence. All this is indeed imagery, but it is the natural and necessary imagery of the religious spirit. And the stronger the fervor of the religious spirit, the more do such images crowd upon us. In the Incarnation we learn that all this imagery has become reality. These scattered images drawn from different members are, so to speak, gathered into one matchless and human form.

It has been *objected* that such a craving of the soul for some visible manifestation of the Godhead belongs to an inferior stage of religious culture.—But the fact is, that the more enlarged our views of God are, the more do we need such a help to our worship and love. "The difficulty," says Dr. Whately,[1] "of coming near to God and fixing our affections upon Him is *increased* in proportion as man advances in refinement of notions, in cultivation of intellect, and in habits of profound philosophical reflection. A semi-barbarous people is less likely to think of the vastness and infinity of God, than is a more enlightened age. Hence it is that the religion of those whose speculations respecting the deity have been accounted the most refined and exalted, has always been cold and heartless in its devotion, or rather has been nearly destitute of devotion altogether." To counteract the chilling tendency of our abstract speculations about God, nothing is so adapted as that conception of Him which we reach through the wondrous doctrine of the Incarnation. In the Per-

---

[1] Sermon: God made Man, p. 10.

son of his Son, God's infinite majesty is transformed into a majestic loveliness; his infinite love is made audible and visible; his rebuke and hatred of sin are indeed revealed most clearly to our conceptions, but his love of the sinner, his willingness to pardon and receive him, are manifested in the whole life and in the death of Jesus, as they could be exhibited in no other way.[1]

2. What man thus craves is *more perfectly* given in the Incarnation than in any other conceivable way. God assumes the nature, form, and speech of man; He addresses him as a member of the same race; He becomes united to him by all the ties of brotherhood. This is the perfection of a divine condescension; and it appeals to man more forcibly than can aught else. Consider the difference between Moses and Christ. And all this difference is made by the fact that in Christ we have God Incarnate, the God-man.[2] In the one case, it is an ambassador delivering a message; in the other, it is the King Himself, conversing with the subject, pleading with the rebel. The dignity of the Incarnate God arrests and attracts us.[3]

§ 3. Especially is the need of an Incarnation manifest when we view it *as an Incarnation in order to Redemption*, and as thus meeting man's moral wants as a sinner. Here is a real *moral necessity* for it.

1. The effect of sin is to increase, seemingly to the mind, the remoteness of Deity, separation from Him, and this in three ways: (*a.*) as man's spiritual perception is darkened; (*b.*) as his heart is cold to the call of God's love; (*c.*) as he fears chiefly the judgment of God against him as a sinner. This sense of remoteness is removed in all these respects: (*a.*) since Christ in the most persuasive manner brings spiritual truth, with authority, and so breaks in upon the darkness of the spirit; (*b.*) since He in the fulness of divine-human love appeals to the human heart; (*c.*) since He testifies by words and deeds that He is come, not to condemn, but to save.

---

[1] See a remarkable utterance of Dr. Arnold, Life, p. 212.

[2] "Thus He stood behind the wall, and showed Himself through the lattice" (Leighton).

[3] Chalmers, The Moral Uses of the Doctrine of the Incarnation.

2. This moral necessity of an Incarnation in order to Redemption is seen more clearly in the light of the great fact, that man himself cannot atone for past sin. Such an incarnate Redeemer was needed to make satisfaction: Rom. iii. 20; Gal. ii. 16.

Thus does the Incarnation meet man's needs as a sinner, the facts of his sinful condition. Its force, its power, its urgency, are in this, that "there is none other name given under heaven among men, whereby we must be saved."

3. Moreover there is a moral necessity that the moral attributes of God be seen to be *harmonized* in the pardoning and justifying of sinners. The harmonizing of mercy and justice, of maintenance of law and love of the sinner, is accomplished in the Incarnation in order to Redemption, as it could be in no other way. And Christ suffering, dying in our stead, appeals to the human heart, as does, as can, no other spectacle. Here that manifestation of the divine attributes, which is necessary, is made, and in the mode best fitted to the wants of an apostate world.

Thus, in the Incarnation, we have not only the life of a perfect man (as we have seen in § 2), but we also have a manifestation of God, in a mode adapted to our human necessities. And our Saviour not only revealed God to us, but was Himself the very manifestation of God in the midst of the world. Not only could He point us upward to the Father, but without presumption He could say, he that hath seen Me hath seen the Father.

Another Statement.—Far be it from our thoughts to attempt to penetrate the depths of the divine counsels in this great matter of which a Father of the church says, "Of things in heaven and earth nothing is so wonderful as that God has become incarnate," excepting as these counsels are made known in his word, as they are seen in the history of his church, and as they are felt in the souls of his children. We may not be able to know all the reasons why the Word became flesh: but some of them, and sufficient to engross all our power of thought and feeling, are manifest in the ends actually accomplished, in the revealed and visible and experienced results of the Incarnation.

These actual results may be thus summed up: The first result is to give to our imitation the life of a perfect man; the second is to bring, not only God's attributes, but God Himself near to us; the third result (to be considered by and by) is the entire union of the infinite and the finite, the divine and the human natures, in one Person; and the fourth result, to which all the others converge, is the making a propitiation for our sins and furnishing the headship for that eternal church, in which is our accomplished salvation.

CHAPTER IV.

HOW FAR MAY AN INCARNATION BE SAID TO BE NECESSARY ON THE PART OF GOD?[1]

Here there are different classes of opinions. Some say: An Incarnation on the part of God is absolutely necessary, is demanded by the divine nature, apart from sin. Others: It was absolutely necessary on the part of God, after man had sinned: the divine attributes unconditionally demand Redemption through an Incarnation. Still others: No Incarnation was needed; men might as well have been redeemed by the proclamation of God's grace in other ways.

Really there are only two theories: (1) that of metaphysical necessity: the divine nature demanded an Incarnation as its necessary complement; God is not complete without man; the infinite requires the finite as much (relatively) as the finite the infinite: (2) the theory of a moral necessity; and this is subdivided into: (*a.*) moral necessity, in that all the divine attributes, justice as well as love, demand it; (*b.*)—in that it is demanded by love, though not by justice.[2]

[1] Aug. de Trin.: "Alia multa sunt cogitanda in Christi incarnatione præter absolutionem peccati."

[2] As to the Incarnation of God, apart from sin, see W. Flörke, Luth. Zschrift., 2, 1854. "There is only one passage in antiquity for it, Iren. adv. Hær., v. 16"; "the doctrine of Irenæus and the Fathers is, that Christ became incarnate for sin, and not without, and that there are only casual expressions against this!"

The voice of antiquity is well summed up in Thomasius, Dogmatik, p. 166. The Nicene Creed is against it: "Who for us men and for our salvation," etc. Au-

THE REDEMPTION ITSELF.

I.—The modern Socinian, Unitarian view. No Incarnation at all was needed: we might as well have been redeemed without it, by the proclamation of God's grace in other ways.

This opinion is as bold on the side of denial, as that of absolute necessity is on the side of affirmation. It is a purely ethical, rather than a Christian view. The basis of it is the view that all that is needed for man's culture is, teaching, motives, an ethical training;—and for man's renovation, only a higher and more impressive degree of teaching and class of motives. God, it says, might as well have announced the fact of his gracious designs, have revealed his love in a way to impress us; and for all we can see, the same end would have been answered. But: (*a.*) This is a mere opinion, unsupported by facts. So far as we know, no mere influence of motives is enough. History is against it. (*b.*) From the actual fact of the Incarnation, we may justly conclude, that, whether we can see it or not, there is a fitness, a moral necessity, of such a mode of Redemption as is given in the Incarnation. It is, doubtless, the wisest and best method of restoring fallen man. (*c.*) While philosophy may not affirm the absolute necessity of an Incarnation, it is equally incompetent to affirm that it was not necessary. It may be, that after human nature had become degenerate by the fall, it could

gustine: "Tolle morbos, tolle vulnera, et nulla medecinæ causa." Among the Scholastics, Wessel, Scotus, and the Franciscans favor the position. Aquinas: "Peccato non existente, incarnatio non fuisset." Anselm knows nothing of this view. Servetus favored it. Calvin is against it, Inst. ii. ch. xii. § 4–7. Socinus (under the influence of the Italian philosophy): Christ would have come if there had been no sin, to insure immortality. At present, the position is advocated by Liebner, Dorner, Martensen, Kurtz (who gives it up in one of the later editions of his Bible and Astronomy). Julius Müller is against it, see Deut. Zeits., Oct. 1850. "The Reformers had too deep a sense of sin to accept this." "The whole of Scripture is for the soteriological point of view." "This view makes the death on the cross a mere accessory, incidental event." In Brit. and For. Ev Rev., Jan. '66, Dorner's interpretation of the passage in Irenæus is disputed. Irenæus: "Si non haberet caro salvari, nequaquam verbum Dei caro factus esset." Dorner: "If it had not been possible to restore humanity to its archetypal form—." Review: "If flesh had not required to be saved—." There is a remarkable passage in Aquinas, 3ª. q. iii., art. 8, "Convenientissimum fuit personam Filii incarnari . . . . quia . . . . verbum Dei, quod est æternus conceptus ejus, est similitudo exemplaris totius creaturæ. Et ideo sicut per participationem hujus similitudinis creaturæ sunt in propriis speciebus institutæ, sed mobiliter, ita per unionem Verbi ad creaturam non participatam, sed personalem, conveniens fuit reparari creaturam in ordine ad æternam et immobilem perfectionem."

not become regenerate in all its parts, except through an Incarnation,—*e. g.*, as respects the resurrection of the glorified body through Christ.

II.—The assertion of the absolute necessity of an Incarnation. Here we have the Christian system in the form of metaphysics, without its ethics. The metaphysical is substituted for the ethical. It is said that the divine nature demands an Incarnation, sin or no sin.

1. As to the Biblical basis. The passages cited are the four: Eph. i. 10; Col. i. 15, 16;[1] Eph. iv. 24; Col. iii. 10, 11. It is said that these teach the relation of Christ to all the creation, apart from sin. But, *contra:* (1) The Christ whom Paul had habitually in mind is the Christ appearing for sin.[2] (2) Christ might have had an intimate relation to all created beings as a mediator (in large sense) without sin, and *without an Incarnation.* (3) The Bible explicitly represents sin as the final cause of the Incarnation: Rom. viii. 3; John iii. 16; Gal. iv. 4, 5; Heb. ii. 14–16; 1 Tim. i. 15; 1 John iii. 8; Matt. xx. 28.

2. As to the ontological aspect. This view attempts to support itself by saying that God, for his own completeness, needed to become incarnate: there was a metaphysical need. It is also said that there was a moral need, a need in order to the perfect exercise of love: his love could not be otherwise fully communicated, neither his love to his Son, nor his love to men.

But, (*a.*) It is not to be seen why God might not have fully and spiritually communicated Himself to men without an Incarnation. He probably does to angels,—why not to men?[3] Cf. Heb. ii. 16. Some say: man here is above all angels, greater and higher.

---

[1] This, which is the most important, is considered a little later.

[2] Cf. also, 1 Cor. xv. 45-7; Eph. i. 21-3; 1 Pet. iii. 22.

[3] Dr. Candlish, Lectures on the Fatherhood of God, 1864: Against Incarnation without Fall, but says: even angels are not by nature sons of God: they *became* such through a probation, like man's essentially: the point being, a demand to become subject to the Son of God revealed proleptically as the Word made flesh. (Cf. Jonathan Edwards's view of the Probation and Fall of Angels, and Owen's view of the Recapitulation of all in Christ.) Against: Brit. and For. Ev. Rev., Jan. 1866: "Candlish's view leads to the position that the Incarnation would have occurred, if no sin."

(*b.*) The consequence of this position would be, that the Son of God really came for his own sake, not for ours.

(*c.*) "'The Bible says, God is love: this view, Love is God" (J. Müller).

3. The anthropological side. That for the completion of human nature, to bring it into full union with God, an Incarnation was necessary. "Man cannot obtain perfection but by the Incarnation of the Logos." Christ is the head of humanity: the first Adam presupposes the second.

This appears to commend itself to those whose sense of sin is not deep.[1]

But, (*a.*) This view supposes that in the first Adam the means of obtaining the end of his being did not exist before the Fall. This is against the Scriptures, both in respect to Adam himself and in respect to the restoration of the divine image.

(*b.*) How are we to explain, that Christ came only in the midst of history and not at first?

(*c.*) Moreover, it is a mere assumption: an abstract, logical assertion, destitute of evidence.

(*d.*) All spiritual influences needed might be otherwise bestowed.

(*e.*) This view is defended by saying, if the Logos had not become incarnate, the race would have had no unity, no head: but this supposes that Christ came, not for sin, but for man, that He is the head of the race, not of the redeemed, and so it is against the Scripture, which says that Christ is the head of those only in whom He works by his Spirit: Eph. i. 22; iv. 12; Col. i. 18; ii. 19; 1 Cor. xii. 3. On this view, all men have eternal life in Christ, and thus it runs against the whole soteriology of Scripture. Christ comes, not for human nature in general, but for sinful human nature, to redeem it. He is not the head of humanity, but of redeemed humanity.

III. The third class of opinions. An Incarnation was necessary, on the part of God, after man had sinned. The moral divine attributes demanded it, all the attributes, *i. e.*, on the score

---

[1] Strongly put by Müller, in the article cited above.

of justice.[1] They demand it (*a*) unconditionally; (*b*) conditionally, on the ground of love. There is a truth in this, so far as it does not put a natural, but only a moral necessity in God; and so far as it does not claim that God, on the score of justice, must redeem a fallen world.

(*A.*) The unconditional demand. The substance of this view: Metaphysically, there is no absolute necessity. Yet God, in creating a world, must create it to have its end in himself, for his glory, in the good of creatures. This is the only conceivable end. Hence, if creatures sinned, and so lost the chief end of their being, God, to promote and achieve this end, must provide redemption. He *need not have created*, yet, having created, and for an end, if the creature by sinning is in such a state that the end cannot be attained, there is, on this ground, on the ground of this supposition, a moral necessity of a scheme of redemption. Or, to take the same thing under a different aspect, God, as love, must communicate himself freely to his creatures: if they are closed against it, there is a moral necessity of his providing a way thus to communicate himself.

But, (*a.*) Even granting what is here asserted, it does not follow that in order to communicate himself, there *must* be an Incarnation,

And (*b.*) There is no proof of such an unconditional demand, excepting on the hypothesis of universalism. The view makes it necessary for God to redeem and save all, on the score of justice, and as a matter of strict right.

(*B.*) The conditional demand. The necessity which love is under to realize the end of creation, so far as is consistent with moral government. On the score of divine mercy and love, there is a constraining influence leading to redemption. The question here then returns: How much may be asserted on Biblical and other grounds, respecting the *necessity* of an Incarnation in order to Redemption.

1. Man and perhaps all created intelligences are created for,

[1] See Rothe, Ethik, § 526.

THE REDEMPTION ITSELF. 367

and destined to, union with God, through Christ. The chief passage on this is Col. i. 15-17.[1] Here we have the following points: (*a.*) Man—and all beings—are destined to, created for, union with God through Christ. (*b.*) In order to this *some manifestation* of Christ is needed for and by all. (*c.*) An Incarnation was needed on account of sin and its consequences. (*d.*) Only through such an Incarnation could the end of Redemption be secured, so far as we know. (*e.*) What man thus gains in Christ is much more than what was lost in Adam. (*f*) We come to the general position that man, at any rate, could have reached such glory only through a process; he had it not at first through Adam.

2. This general position is further illustrated by the fact that Christ is the center of unity, the head of the race as redeemed, of the church. The passages in which He is thus set forth refer chiefly to the work of redemption, to Him as head of the church: but *in the church God's great plan for the race is realized:* Col. ii. 10; Eph. i. 10; i. 22, 23; iv. 12, 15, 16; v. 23; Col. i. 18; ii. 19.

3. Accordingly, men—all redeemed men—are really united to Christ, by his Spirit dwelling in them. Through this union, and, so far as we know, only thereby, do men attain to a regenerated state, to the real end of their being. (*a.*) Passages in which this union is spoken of directly: Eph. i. 23; iv. 16; Col. ii. 19 (Cf. Rom. viii. 9; 1 Cor. xii. 3); John xvii. 21, 23, 26. (*b.*) Passages in which the fruits of this union, being like Christ, having his image, living and dwelling in Him, are spoken of: John xiv. 23; xvii. 10, 22, 23, 26; Rom. viii. 29; Gal. iv. 19; ii. 20; 2 Cor. iii. 18; Col. iii. 10.

From the foregoing heads, (1), (2), (3), it is natural to conclude that Christ would have been in some way the mediator to men, even if they had not sinned; that created beings were made with respect to Christ. So we add:

---

[1] Col. i. 19, 20, sets forth the *reconciliation* of all things unto God, through Christ. Calvin thinks it relates to the influence of Christ's work, in confirming angels in their love and obedience; others take it as affirming a relation to all created beings, which is more probable.

4. That it is probable that some manifestation of the Logos is needed by and for all beings, in coming to God.

To all his creatures God must reveal himself that they may know Him. The Logos, so far as we know, is the medium of such revelations. Only by some revelation could the divine nature and attributes be made known. How is it that God reveals his attributes?—We cannot know, no finite being can know, the Infinite One directly: there must be a medium. This may be (*a.*) implanted knowledge, as ideas, in the mind. But this is complete knowledge only intellectually, and not a complete knowledge *of fact*; (*b.*) some finite manifestation of himself —in works—or by persons commissioned—or in personal form. It may be that the Son of God appears, as the image of God, in personal, finite form, to the angelic hosts. Hence we say,

5. The revelation by an Incarnation is imperatively needed, so far as we know, on account of sin and its consequences, if the race can be redeemed. It is needed, not metaphysically, but morally and teleologically, if God is to fulfil the end of creation, viz., the most perfect manifestation of his highest attributes, his declarative glory. The Incarnation was not needed by God, but for man. It was a free act of condescension and grace on God's part. We cannot say that Redemption could have been secured in any other method. Though a free act on God's part, and of grace, we know not but that such an act was necessary both physically[1] and morally, *if* man was to be redeemed. God might have left man to perish, and justly; but, if He would save man, it may be that there is no other way than through an Incarnation. It is very possible that the manifestation of grace to a race of beings, to be redeemed, made up of body and spirit, could be only by an Incarnate Redeemer. (The *ontology* and *physics* of Christianity.)

[1] As relates to the resurrection of the body, *e. g.*

CHAPTER V.

THE INCARNATION IN HISTORY.

The Incarnation on Historical Grounds, including Prophetic. [Only the main positions].

I.—The ancient Pagan world strives to realize the idea, yet without success. This is seen: (1) In the great religious systems—the Oriental and Græco-Roman, (2) In the aspirations of wise and thoughtful men.

II.—The Jewish Scriptures gradually unfold the idea, giving elements, adumbrated, prophetic; so that they are seen to be fulfilled in Christ. The Jewish monotheism might seem to be antagonistic, but running through the whole there is prophecy, promise, pointing to a Deliverer, of the seed of man, yet the Son of God.

III.—Jewish and Pagan elements come *speculatively* together, in the Idea of the Logos. (Philo.)

IV.—Hence, Christianity fulfils the expectation of the whole ancient world, yet in a more perfect way.

V.—All history before Christ can be grouped only as a preparation for his coming.

VI.—The subsequent history of the church and its doctrines is a constant testimony to the reality and central authority of the Incarnation.

CHAPTER VI.

OF THE INCARNATION AS CONNECTED WITH THE WHOLE OF THE THEOLOGICAL SYSTEM, AND AS VIEWED BY DIFFERENT PARTIES.

I.—The lowest view is the Socinian, Humanitarian theory. According to this, the Incarnation, if at all acknowledged, is held to have only the design of giving us an example, or (Socinus) to confer immortality, or, to teach that God is favorable to man, is a Father, and that immortality is a fact. The whole sense and meaning of the Incarnation is ethical, to communicate truth.

II.—The Roman Catholic view. The Son of God became man; through the sacraments we receive Him, as grace; we become partakers of his very body and blood, by the transubstantiation of the elements. Thus we are united with, grow up into, his humanity. (Modification in Consubstantiation.)

III.—The Oxford view. The sacramental system. The sacraments are an extension of the Incarnation, channels of grace. The Holy Spirit is given through them. Neither transubstantiation nor consubstantiation is advocated, but a real, spiritual, mysterious reception of Christ's humanity, as much as we receive humanity from Adam in the way of natural descent.[1]

IV.—The Spiritual Life Theory. Discarding sacramental systems, and holding to the fact of union with Christ, this view is distinguished by the position, that we receive through the Incarnation, directly from Christ, through his Spirit, a new spiritual life. And the communication of such a life is the grand object for which Christ came. The Atonement is merged in the Incarnation. Life, life from Christ, real and true life, is the great fact of the Incarnation. So Coleridge, Bushnell, etc. Redemption is resolved into regeneration.

V.—The Incarnation simply and chiefly has respect to Christ's atoning death. The Arminian View. The Exhibition Theory or Governmental Theory. This view denies the reality of the union with Christ, and of justification on the ground of this union. It resolves the union into a metaphor. It says substantially this: The real truth in the case is, that we become like Christ by choosing the same end as He did, the glory of God and the good of man. We become like Him morally, in having the same states of heart and will. This is all the union

---

[1] Tracts for the Day. "The Eucharist is the complement of the Incarnation, which began in the union of God with man's nature, and culminates in the union of individual men with God." In the Eucharist there is a "union between the Person of Christ and the elements of bread and wine; so that it may be said, without a metaphor, that there is a renewal or continuation of the Incarnation" (No. 59, Tracts for the Day). "*The sacrifice of Christ is not once for all and complete, but continuous.*" Neither Transubstantiation nor Consubstantiation is accepted, for these seem to *define* the work.

that exists. His atonement removed an obstacle out of the way; we rely on that atonement—not on Him, but on the atonement, and thereupon God pardons us. Justification is this: God accepts us as holy, so far as we are; and justifies us because He foresees or has determined that we shall become perfectly so, by and by. All the relation of the Incarnation to us is, that it excites feelings, susceptibilities, more than anything else could well do, and thus incites us to choose right. It presents to us an affecting exhibition of God's love of us and hatred of sin, and so moves us to come to Him in penitence and faith.

VI.—The general Protestant view. Union with Christ as the ground of our Justification and Sanctification. By faith, through the operation of the Holy Spirit, we are united to Christ (the mystical union), whereby we are both justified and renewed, all through the direct operation of the Holy Spirit. The great fact in objective Christianity is the Incarnation of a Redeemer: the great fact in subjective Christianity is our union with Him by and through his Spirit. Sacraments are expressions, primarily, not vehicles of grace. To the new life the Incarnation has the same relation that Creation has to the old: it is the second great act of the Logos, the center of his spiritual kingdom, for which the whole of the old creation groaneth and travaileth in pain. And the Redemption in Christ has the same relation to our renewed state that the Fall in Adam has to our depraved state. The Incarnation has the same position in Revealed, that Creation has in Natural, Theology.

VII.—Outside of specific Christianity. The Incarnation is true in idea, *i. e.*, the union of the divine and human, but this union is not in one Person, but in the whole race.[1] Divinity and humanity are different aspects of the same substance, the absolute substance. God comes to consciousness in men. Men at death are resolved into this universal substance.

---

[1] Sometimes put in this form: "The divine ideas which had wandered up and down the world, till oftentimes they had forgotten themselves and their origin, did at length clothe themselves in flesh and blood; they became incarnate with the Incarnation of the Son of God. In his life and person, the idea and fact at length kissed each other, and were henceforth wedded for evermore."

Remarks on these different theories as to the place and purpose of the Incarnation.

Every theological system must meet the questions raised by the Incarnation, somewhere and somehow, and must show that it is a necessary constituent of the system. For all religion has respect to the relation between God and man; its ultimate problems and questions are in this relation, are on this point. And especially must every system meet the question as to this relation between God and man so far as it is affected by sin, and every system must find its center in the point, how the relations between God and a sinful world are to be restored, to be readjusted. In other words, religion being essentially union between God and man, the central inquiry of theology is this: how is the lost communion between God and man to be restored, how is the reunion to be accomplished. And the different views, as above presented, as found in the different and chief theological systems, say in substance (adopting a little different order of statement), as follows, in reply to this inquiry. In order to this restoration:

1. It is enough for God to come and teach men his goodness, and assure them of immortality;

2. Man is to be restored, only as he partakes of the very flesh and blood of Christ, through the transubstantiated elements;

3. —only as he partakes of the divine humanity of Christ (not his literal flesh and blood) through the sacraments;

4. —only by partaking of the life of Christ, not necessarily through the intervention of the sacraments;

5. —only through justification before God as a Moral Governor, on the ground of Christ's atonement, of which justification by faith is the instrument, uniting the believer to Christ, which faith is the regenerating gift of God's Spirit;

6. —only (as above) on the ground of our justification, which justification is, however, = pardon, which justification also, does not include a real union with Christ. The Incarnation, in this view, is to *exhibit* God's hatred of sin and love of the sinner, and not to effect a real union between God and man.

(We do not dwell on the naturalistic and pantheistic hypotheses here, because they are out of the pale of Christian theology.)

CHAPTER VII.

OF THE INCARNATION ON PHILOSOPHICAL GROUNDS, AS RELATED TO THE PHILOSOPHY OF RELIGION, AND TO THE CONFLICT BETWEEN CHRISTIANITY AND PHILOSOPHY.

In the question, Has the Son of God become Incarnate for the Redemption of the world, the whole of the Christian system centers. Upon the decision of this question rests the fate of Christianity, as a distinctive religious system, as the absolute and perfect religion, *i. e.*, of Christianity as compared with all other systems of faith, and also its fate, as compared with philosophy.

Two propositions are to be maintained here:

I. The question comes up in relation to the philosophy of Christianity, where it is to be shown that the Christian is the perfect form of religion, because it centers and culminates in the Incarnation, *i. e.*, in the position that in the Person of Christ we have an Incarnation of the Son of God for the redemption of the race.

II. —in relation to the conflict between Philosophy and Faith. The superiority of Christianity to any system of mere philosophy is also found in the same position, since, in Christ and his work, we have a system more complete, better adapted to man's moral, spiritual, and intellectual wants than philosophy, without it, can possibly offer.

The Christian Religion is the most perfect religion.

It also contains the highest philosophy.

§ 1. *As to the Philosophy of Christianity.*

The Incarnation gives us the Philosophy of Christianity, as the most perfect religion. The proof of this position is to be conducted on two grounds: historical and comparative.

1. Historical. It is to be shown, in the way of historical testimony, on the basis of the history of religions, (*a.*) that the Christian system, under the divine plan, has always existed in

its elements, as type, etc., in human history; (*b.*) also, on the same historical ground, that the other religions, under the divine guidance, so far as human history has advanced, have been tending towards, have led to, Christianity, to the Incarnation for Redemption, as their historic consummation.

2. *The Comparative line of argument.* To show (as in Comparative Philology, etc.,) (*a.*) that Christianity contains all the truth which is felt after in other religions, (*b.*) in a more perfect form, (*c.*) and other, most needed, facts and truths, which cannot be found in any other form of religion; and, that these are found in the Person and work of Christ, where the superiority of the Christian system is alone fully manifested.[1]

NOTE.—For the completion of the Philosophy of Christianity, there would also be needed a comparison of the different systems of Christian theology, in the different sects, etc., in order to find which one of them was most complete, most Scriptural and most practical, and so best fitted to attain the ends of the Christian system, the subjugation of man to the service of Christ. The Augustinian-Calvinistic-Edwardean.

§ 2. *In the Incarnation we have the Means of adjusting the Conflict between Christianity and Philosophy.*

A different question comes up when we come to the conflict between philosophy and faith, between Philosophy and Christianity. It is no longer a comparison of Religions among themselves, as in the Philosophy *of* Christianity, but it is a comparison of the whole of Christianity with the whole of Philosophy, in order to show that the Christian system not only is the highest form of faith, but also contains the highest form of philosophy, that *the philosophy of Christianity is the highest philosophy.* The question here is: Where shall we find the ultimate and complete system, adapted to all man's wants and needs, for time and for eternity,—*philosophy as the guide of life?*

As between philosophy and religion in general, the question reduces itself to that between philosophy and Christianity.

[1] See Introduction to Christian Theology: Philosophical Apologetics.

As between philosophy and Christianity, it is really, ultimately, a question between Christianity and Pantheism, "Christ or Spinoza." Deism, atheism, and other forms of infidelity are swallowed up in pantheism. The present tendency is to an alliance between pantheistic philosophy, extreme democracy, and infidel socialism against the whole Christian system,—fully developed in Europe, rapidly approximating in this country.

1. The preliminary questions, in speculative thought, between Christianity and Pantheism.

(*a.*) The fact of sin, as a moral evil, in opposition to the pantheistic view, that sin is to be resolved into a mere natural necessity, a stage in the progress of the race.

(*b.*) The fact of the being of a personal deity, the intelligent and moral governor of the universe.

(*c.*) The possibility and the fact of a supernatural revelation, through teachers, authenticated by miracles, and recorded.

(*d.*) The fact that in Jesus Christ, divinity and humanity are united, and the world's redemption is achieved.

(*e.*) The fact of immortality—that man is to exist hereafter as well as here—that the kingdom of heaven is not to be realized here on earth.

These are the chief points. In establishing these it is necessary to show—as is proved by fact: (1) That the common orthodox view on these points is the only one which will be of any avail against pantheism: Deism, Pelagianism, Unitarianism, cannot make headway against the philosophic vigor and completeness of the pantheistic system; (2) and, that the orthodox view of these points gives us a system, centering in the Person and Work of Christ, more rational, more complete, more adapted to man's wants, than any to which the pantheistic philosophy can pretend.

2. Superiority of Christianity to Pantheism.

The Incarnation, on philosophical grounds, gives us the highest possible system, one higher than any which philosophy can pretend to. This is to be shown in the following particulars:

(*a.*) As to the fundamental problem of all religion and of all philosophy, viz., how can divinity and humanity be united, the

Christian system gives us, in the Person of Christ, that union in a more perfect form than can be found elsewhere. Pantheism gives us only the union in idea, of something divine with something human. Christianity gives us the union in fact and complete, in a personal form—the best and highest. And through faith in Christ men also are made participants in this union. Such is the philosophical value of the Incarnation.

(*b.*) As to the fundamental moral problem, the highest we can conceive, viz., how can a sinful being be reconciled to a holy God, how can a sinful nature be changed: Christianity, in the work of Christ, as applied, gives us the solution of this in the most perfect way (justification and regeneration); meets and solves the problem; and Christianity alone does this; while the Pantheistic system is obliged to ignore the problem, and resolve sin into a necessary stage of development, thus annulling the dictates of our moral nature; and reconciliation into the mere reconciliation between man and nature, or man and his fellow-beings, so that selfishness is lost in good-will.

(*c.*) As to the highest question about man as a social being, as made for social fellowship and communion, it may be shown in the same way, that the Christian system gives us the most complete view, in the idea of the Kingdom of God, established in the world for its redemption, centering in Christ as its Head and Lord. The question raised by all thinkers, giving rise to schemes of republics, to utopias, to socialism, etc., is met and answered in the Christian system, as in no other, wherein men are not merely united with each other, but with God, through Christ, in his kingdom—a moral kingdom, where love reigns. To the possibility and actuality of such a kingdom, the Incarnation has intimate and necessary relations.

(*d.*) As to the final question, in all philosophy as well as in all religion: What is the destiny of each man and of the race? here, too, Christianity evinces its inherent superiority. The kingdom which it discloses is an eternal kingdom, begun here, perfected hereafter: our aspirations and hopes of immortality are encouraged and fortified, and a future is held out in the endless progression of this kingdom of God in Christ, such as naught else can offer. And this too centers in the truth of Incarnation in order to Redemption.

Every system of philosophy must meet and solve these four problems: they are fundamental in respect to man and to the universe. Every system must give some answer to the questions which these four raise. The most perfect system is that which gives the completest and most satisfactory answer.

Our position then is this: that as the Christian system, in its doctrine of the Incarnation in order to Redemption, meets and answers all these four problems, in the most satisfactory manner, it is thereby proved to contain the highest system of philosophy as well as to be the most perfect form of religion.

CHAPTER VIII.

COMPARISON OF THE INCARNATION WITH SOME OTHER FACTS AS GIVING THE CENTRAL IDEAS OF THE CHRISTIAN SYSTEM.

I.—Comparison of Divine Sovereignty and The Incarnation as central principles.

Calvinistic theology has had—unconsciously for the most part—two germinant principles: Sovereignty and The Covenants; the former the older, the latter more narrow, but with some advantages. In the Confessions we often see an unconscious union of the two. Sovereignty tends to run into supralapsarianism and the assertion of the exclusive divine efficiency: Will is made to be all; the ethical is obscured. The objections to it are: (*a.*) It is too abstract; (*b.*) It is liable to perversion, to the construction that God is all Will; (*c.*) If it is taken concretely, *i. e.*, if the Sovereignty is understood to stand for Plan, it comes to much the same with our principle: Incarnation in order to Redemption *is* God's Plan.

II.—Comparison of The Incarnation and The Covenants, as the central principles.

1. The original usage of The Covenant, in theology, as set-

ting forth an arrangement, an ordering, on the part of God, is allowable and true.

2. As applied in the Covenant of Works: "This do and thou shalt live," we may say, It is *as if there was* such a covenant.

3. As applied in the Covenant of Redemption, that between the Father and the Son, it sets forth clearly, for popular representation, that in the divine plan, Christ performs conditions and his people are given to Him in consequence. (Only in this Covenant there should be included all that Christ's work accomplished: Propitiation for the sins of the whole world and the General Offer of Salvation as well as the Provision for the Elect.)

4. Applied as the central, constitutive principle of theology, it is hardly satisfactory. (*a.*) In respect to the Covenant of Works, there is a lack of historical foundation for anything beyond the divine announcement and pledge in respect to the consequences of obedience and disobedience. (*b.*) In respect to The Covenant of Redemption (between the Father and the Son), it easily degenerates into the semblance of a commercial transaction. (*c.*) In respect to The Covenant of Grace (the Covenant of God with his people), it is not really directly with them, but with them in Christ. (*d.*) In respect to both these last, there is a difficulty on account of the confusion resulting; we have to use "conditions" in a different sense in the two: in The Covenant of Redemption, Christ's sacrifice is the condition of the promise; in The Covenant of Grace, faith and obedience are the conditions, but in the latter the sense of "conditions" is not the same as in the former: in the former the sense of "condition" is—the procuring, meritorious cause, in the latter, it is—the occasional cause, merely a *sine qua non*, not meritorious.

5. It is better for theology to state as its central principle, the essential and fundamental fact of the case.

CHAPTER IX.

OF THE INCARNATION AS THE UNFOLDING OF THE POSSIBILITIES OF HUMAN NATURE. THE SECOND ADAM.

"The secret of Man is the secret of the Messiah." [1]
"The measure of the stature of the fulness of Christ" [2]
"Complete in Him." [3]

Man's nature, need, and destiny are, so to speak, wrapped up in Christ. The secrets of our own inmost being, the enigmas of our destiny, are revealed to us in Christ and in Him alone. Life is a maze; and we do not find the clue to guide us safely through until we find Christ. Life is an enigma, and the word that solves the enigma is Christ, the Word of God. When we know Christ we know what we are, and are made to be; and out of Him we grope in darkness and conjectures. When Christ is revealed to us, we are also revealed to ourselves. Only in Him can we unveil the secret and scan the end of our destiny. We are complete in Him.

I.—We know ourselves only as we know the end of our being, and this knowledge is given to us chiefly in and through Jesus Christ.

Socrates was thought to have received from the gods the immortal and searching precept, "Know thyself." He awakened the inquisitive Athenians to self-reflection and moral consciousness. But he could not probe the depths of human nature, because he had no definite conception of the great end for which man was made—to glorify God and enjoy Him forever in a divine kingdom. He inculcated at the best only a kind of intellectual morality and sincerity: he could not pierce the sky and see the Father of all, nor unveil the future to descry the destiny of man. And so, he could not lead to the highest self-knowledge, because he had not the instruments and truths with which to ply the soul, and extract all its secrets. If we are to have the true estimate of life, we must know the true end of life.

[1] Jewish Proverb.   [2] Eph. iv. 13.   [3] Col. ii. 10.

And this the great Teacher of our race, and He alone, was able to declare unto us. For he came forth from the Father, and abode in tabernacles of clay, that He might disclose to us the way of coming to eternal life. He revealed God to a sinful, doubting, despairing race as "our Father who art in Heaven." He taught us to pray to Him in those hallowed words which children learn by heart and sages cannot fathom. He told in His own words and taught by his own example, how the sufferings, trials, and woes of time may at last but enhance the joys, the peace, and the blessed rest of eternity. He led us to see that this earth is our pilgrimage and heaven our home. And by thus setting before us, in the simplest terms, the greatest end of life, He has taught us the real meaning of life. And in disclosing to us this blessed reality He made us to know ourselves. For no man knows himself until he knows what He may attain unto. The glories of heaven instruct us about the things of earth; only in the light of eternity do we rightly read the events of time.

II.—We know ourselves only as we know the law for which we were made. This knowledge is given to us most fully in Christ. He is not only the living Gospel: He is also the living Law. He republished the Law of God in all its purity and sanctity, and taught us its inmost meaning by His own perfect obedience to it. He came not to destroy, but to fulfil. He unfolded the law in its length and breadth, in its letter and its spirit, in its rewards and its penalties—up to the judgment of the last assize. And He so interpreted that law to the human conscience and the human heart, and He so exemplified it in His whole incarnate life, that it really, in and through Him, became fully known to the human race as the law of life.

And when this perfect law was unfolded before the vision of the human race, it was like a deeper moral consciousness, penetrating below the surface of our common thoughts and aims, and disclosing to us our inner, even our inmost selves. For when man comes to know the law aright, then he also knows himself aright; he sees what he ought to be: that he ought to be holy in all his desires and thoughts and acts, and that as long as he is not thus pure he has failed of attaining the great end for which he was made. For the law is made for man's soul as much as light is made for man's eyes; and to let the light of the law upon the soul is a revelation no less clear and distinct than to let the light of the visible sun in upon eyes that may long have had a film gathering over them.

Our blessed Lord gave us the law, not only in words, but also in His life. He was the embodied law, because He was love incarnate, obedient even unto death. *His perfect example was an example of perfect obedience.* And thus, in giving to man the law in its highest interpretation, and exemplifying its spirit in His own matchless and perfect obedience, He has revealed to us what we are and ought to be; He has set before us a pattern to show us what it is to be a perfect man; He has taught us to measure ourselves by the measure of the stature of the fulness of Christ.

III.—We cannot know ourselves truly until we know the misery and guilt of sin, of which we are all partakers. And Christ has also taught us to read this lesson, that He may become our great Deliverer. Human misery and guilt were not indeed first disclosed by the Messiah; for the experience of that misery and the consciousness of that guilt are the common heritage of all the race. But the knowledge of our wretchedness, which is given by nature, is a knowledge without hope, tending to recklessness or despair. While the knowledge which Christ imparts pierces and troubles the soul that it may purge and purify it.

One striking fact about human misery and wretchedness, brought out by the Gospel as by no other agency, is, that the sense of our wretchedness is almost always accompanied by a sense of the dignity and grandeur of our nature. "Our grief is but our grandeur in disguise." Along with the consciousness of our sinful condition, giving to it its sharpest stings, is an inalienable conviction that this is not our real self, that though it be our common heritage, it is not the end of our being. Brutes may suffer and die, without remorse, without hope, without despair. But so it cannot be with man; he has remorse for the past, and fear or hope for the future. And this is because, made originally in the image of God, that image is still and ever before the eye of reason and of conscience, though the heart and will be fixed on inferior and transient delights. Man is a sinner, condemned to death; and the condemnation is so terrible because he was made not to die, but to live forever; though he might aspire to a throne, he walks to a scaffold, and the scaffold becomes awful because it has such a regal victim; awful even though, yea because, the condemnation is just.

And when the divine law, as *interpreted and applied by Christ reaches to the very depths* of man's consciousness of sin; when it sets before him its inviolable sanctity and its irreversible obligations; when it forces him against his will to test himself by its solemn and searching light; when it reveals the depths of his sin and guilt, far below the careless, worldly thoughts and feelings that usually engross and blind the soul: when sin by the commandment becomes exceeding sinful, and is pictured in all its blackness upon the vivid stainless background of this imperial rule of rectitude; then it is that man comes *to know himself*, to know himself as a sinner, as a sinner not only against a holy law, but also against a holy God, to know the terrible power of his depravity as clinging to the very roots of his being.

(This certainly is not the only way in which Christ reads to us the lesson of our woe, and of our guilt. We have to look forward to the subject not yet considered, His atoning work, to see where it is that He impresses this lesson most vividly upon the soul. If man, at the cross of Christ, will not see his wretchedness and his doom, then on that cross he cannot see his pardon and his peace. There is no redemption, if there be no condemnation. We must know ourselves to be sinners, if we would know Christ as a Saviour).

And so, in the mystery of sin is revealed to us the mystery of our being. In an eminent sense it holds true that the secret of man is the secret of the Messiah.[1]

---

[1] It is related of Pascal, that he always carried with him a paper on which were written these simple and broken words: "God of Abraham, of Isaac, and of Jacob, not of philosophers and the learned. Certainty, certainty, feeling [sentiment],

IV. The same holds true, of course, of the final perfection of our human nature, in its completed and glorified state. The destiny of man in Christ is to come to the measure of the stature of his fulness. Christ is the very ideal of humanity realized. Even in a human point of view, He is the consummate flower of the human race, a character unique in wisdom, love, and holiness.[1]

V. Not only in the individual life and individual perfection does this relation subsist between man and Christ, but it also holds of man as a whole, of the collective race, of man in history. We are *all* to come into the unity of the faith and knowledge of the Son of God.

That which enables us to explain history must be the soul and life of history. History, the life of our race, is also the great problem and enigma of our race. What is the meaning of this mysterious birth of the human race upon the shores of time? What is to be its future destiny here on earth and in the inaccessible night of eternity? Here is the question of profoundest import to all the members of our race. And to this question the only reasonable and satisfying answer is given us in the revelation of God in Christ. Infidel writers are not able to find any other center to human history than the life and death of Christ. In point of fact, the whole of the ancient Jewish history, in type, symbol, and prophecy, pointed to the Messiah, while ancient secular history was prepared by Providence for his advent. And since He came, his kingdom has given the law to all other kingdoms; his church has gone on conquering and to conquer. And here is an incomparable and irrefragable

joy, peace, God of Jesus Christ." And then followed this significant phrase: "Grandeur of the human soul!"—And indeed, what must be the inherent dignity of a nature for which God himself puts forth all the resources of his mighty love, for which the Son of God could die upon the cross of Calvary? What must have been the guilt that demanded such a sacrifice; what must be the blessedness that could warrant such a sacrifice?

[1] This is confessed even by those who deny Him to be anything more than man. Thus Renan cannot withhold the confession that "He is the incomparable man, to whom the universal conscience has decreed the title of the Son of God, and this too with justice. . . . . Every one of us owes to him that which is best in himself!" Weigh those last words, and make the necessary inferences. Faith in Christ becomes our highest need, life in Him our highest blessedness.

argument for the dignity of the Redeemer. He who gives the law to history is the lawgiver of the race. In Him, and in Him alone, the secrets of humanity are hid, its enigmas resolved, its salvation insured. He who redeems the race must be the Head and Lord of the race. The whole human family finds its center, its crown, its peace, in Him. "Christianity," says one of the Apostolic Fathers,[1] "is not a work of silence, but of grandeur," and its grandeur is seen in the fact that Christ is the center of history.

Hence, it appears, that to know ourselves, we must know Christ, and that to know Christ is to know ourselves. Just as one born a poet does not know the full stores of his own imagination until he has read Homer, Dante, Milton, and Shakespeare; just as the sculptor does not know his gift in art until he has gazed entranced upon the matchless products of Greek and Roman statuary; just as the young Roman painter, when standing before the breathing canvas that revealed to him all the power of the pencil, cried out in wonder "I too am a painter"; —so the human soul may gaze on all other forms, linger on all other impersonations of thought and feeling, and explore all art and science, but until it stands face to face with the Lord of the race, the Saviour of the lost, it knows not, it cannot know, it feels not, it cannot feel, all the height and depth of human woe and of human love, all the soul's boundless capacities, its supreme destiny. The hour when Christ is revealed in untroubled splendor to the heart and mind, is the hour when it realizes what it is and may become. In the knowledge of the Son of God, it sees that it may arrive at the perfection of manhood, that it may attain to the measure of the stature of his fulness.

[1] Ignatius. Compare our own Edwards: The work of Redemption is a work carried on in two respects: "(1) in its effect on the souls of the redeemed; this remains the same: (2) as it has respect to the grand design in general, as it respects the universal subject and end: this is carried on from the fall of man to the end of the world in a different manner, not merely by repeating or renewing the same effects in the different subjects of it, but by many successive works and dispensations of God, all tending to one great end and effect, all united as the several parts of a scheme, and all together making up one great work."

PART II.

OF THE PERSON OF THE MEDIATOR. THE SON OF GOD MANIFEST IN THE FLESH. THE GOD-MAN.

"The Word——was made [became] flesh."—JOHN i. 14.

The subject of this Part of the Second Division is, The Doctrine respecting the Person of Christ. The Proposition: The Mediator was the God-man. Or, In Christ as One Person there is the Union of Two Natures, the Divine and Human.

There is a full and careful statement of the doctrine in the Savoy Confession of Faith adopted by the Synods held in Boston in 1680, and at Saybrook, Conn., in 1708. This is the same as the Westminster statement: "The Son of God, the Second Person in the Trinity, being very and eternal God, of one substance, and equal with the Father, did, when the fulness of time was come, take upon Him man's nature, with all the essential properties and common infirmities thereof, yet without sin: being conceived of the power of the Holy Ghost in the womb of the Virgin Mary, of her substance. So that two whole, perfect, and distinct natures, the Godhead and the manhood, were inseparably joined together in one person, without conversion, composition or confusion. Which person is very God and very man, yet one Christ, the only mediator between God and man."

See West. Conf., c. viii. § 2; Larg. Cat., Q. 36–40; Shorter Cat., Q. 21, 22.

It is a fact which here comes into view, viz.: The Second Person of the Trinity assumed human nature, and by this assumption became the God-man, uniting both the divine and human natures in his sacred person.

These points are essential: I. Christ is both human and divine; II. Christ is one person; III. This Person is the Second Person of the Trinity.

Scheme.

CHAP. I.—The Teachings of Scripture respecting the Person of the God-man.
CHAP. II.—The Partial and Conflicting Representations: Earlier and Later.
CHAP. III.—The Objections and Difficulties urged.
CHAP. IV.—The Result as to the Entire Person of our Lord.

CHAPTER I.

THE SCRIPTURAL TEACHINGS RESPECTING THE PERSON OF THE GOD-MAN.

§ 1. *The general Impression of the Declarations of Scripture on this Point.*

In the Scriptures Christ is described by a series of the most amazing contrasts. He is called the Son of David—yet David calls Him Lord; He was understood to claim equality with the Father—as man He had not where to lay his head; He took part with flesh and blood—yet thought it not robbery to be equal with God; He took the form of a servant—yet his proper form was the form of God; He tabernacled in the flesh—yet came down from heaven; He said that He could of his own self do nothing—yet He is said to be the Lord of all; His mother is called Mary—yet He is over all, God blessed forever; He was born under the law and fulfilled the law—and yet in his own name gave a new and more perfect law, and brought in a new and everlasting righteousness; He was received into heaven out of the sight of his disciples—yet He is still with them, with any two or three of them, always, and even to the ends of the earth; He was found in fashion as a man—and yet is the image of the invisible God; He hid not his face from shame and spitting—though He be the very brightness of the Father's glory; He increased in wisdom—yet knew the Father even as the Father knew Him; He increased in stature—yet is the same, yesterday, to-day, and forever; He died at the mandate of a Roman governor—yet is the Prince of the kings of the earth; He could say, The Father is greater than I—yet also say, I and my Father are one, he that hath seen Me hath seen the Father; He said in the time of his temptation unto Satan, It is written, Thou shalt worship the Lord thy God, and Him *only* shalt thou serve—yet He also declared that all men should honor the Son even as they honor the Father, and of Him it is asserted that every knee should bow to Him and every tongue confess that He is Lord to the glory of God the Father.

It is the total impression derived from the amplitude and variety of such expressions as these, which brings the surest and truest conviction to the mind. One and another of the terms may be explained away, but the difficulty is—we have to keep explaining away one, and another, and yet another. The Bible was meant for and is adapted to the average understanding and religious wants of men. It is fertile and varied in its mode of bringing out the same truth. And the natural and total impression left by the perusal of it will inevitably be —that Jesus Christ is a complex personage, that He was a man, yet is an object of religious worship.

§ 2. *The Proof from Scripture of Christ's Divinity.*—This has been already given in the discussion of the doctrine of the Trinity. It is referred to here only as it bears upon the union of the two natures in his person.

1. That such a Saviour, Redeemer (*a.*) was to come and (*b.*) did come, is the substance of the Gospel-message; it *is* τὸ εὐαγγέλιον.

"The first annunciation of the New Testament, Luke i. 16, 17, was in reference to the highest and last prophecy of the Old Testament, Mal. iv. 5, 6" (Ebrard).

The second annunciation—to Mary—is in reference to the old Messianic prophecy given to David by Nathan, Luke i. 32, "and the Lord God shall give unto Him the throne of his father David"; 2 Sam. vii. 12, 13, "and I will establish the throne of his kingdom forever."

The general announcement—to Joseph—Matt. i. 21, "and thou shalt call his name JESUS: for He shall save his people from their sins."

And as here the wonderful office is set forth, so immediately following is the evangelist's declaration respecting the wonderful person, as the fulfilment of prophecy, Matt. i. 22, 23. This is presented on the Old Testament basis. Both humanity ("the Virgin shall bring forth") and divinity ("shall call his name Immanuel") are in the Old Testament; as elements—as we have already seen. (Lectures on the Trinity.)

2. Titles and Comprehensive Statements as to the Gospel.

Mark i. 1. "The beginning of the gospel of Jesus Christ, the Son of God."

John i. 1–14. Especially, vs. 14, "And the Word became flesh."

Rom. i. 1, 3, 4. Especially, vs. 4.

3. The appellation, Son of Man,[1] originating in the Old Testament, adopted by Christ as the designation of his Messiahship, involving both in the Old Testament and the New, divinity. Meyer: By Son of Man "Jesus means to designate himself as Messiah,—not referring probably to Ps. viii., but to Dan. vii. 13." His divinity as the Son of Man is shown in his coming to judgment in the clouds of heaven.

4. More specifically as to the Old Testament representations of the Messiah.

(*a.*) Certainly one peculiarity of the Old Testament religion was its (apparently) almost exclusive *national* character. The covenant with Abraham; covenant at Sinai; the Theocracy for the Israelites.[2] But

(*b.*) It had, equally, *a universal character*. The idea of God as One; the thoroughly ethical conditions between Israel and God; especially the view and scope of prophecy.

(*c.*) The union of these two is the *essence* of the Old Testament as compared with any other ancient religion. It is characterized by Nationality *and* Universality.

(*d.*) This appears most clearly in the fact that the Messiah is predicted not as a national king merely, but as the king ruling from Zion over all nations, and again, not as such a king merely, but also as the prophet and priest for all mankind: Isa. ii. 3; xi.; liii.; Ps. xl.; cx.; Gen. iii. 15; xxii. 8; xlix. 10; Deut. xviii. 18; Mic. v. 2; Hag. ii. 7; Mal. iii. 1; iv. 5, 6.

---

[1] Keil's Daniel, p. 273, Not, mere humanity. The phrase is used only by Jesus of himself, while on earth. So Bengel on Matt. xvi. 13, "Nemo nisi solus Christus, a*nemine dum ipse in terra ambularet, nisi a semetipso, appellatus est filius hominis." Acts vii. 56; Rev. i. 13; xiv. 14; are passages outside the gospels, and borrowed from Dan. vii. 13.

[2] See Dr. C. von Orelli, Der nationale Charakter der alt-test. Religion. Zürich, 1871.

5. The Old Testament as authoritatively interpreted in the New, in respect to this point.

(*a.*) Christ himself asserts that He was foretold as Messiah: Matt. xx. 18; xxvi. 54; Mark ix. 12; Luke xviii. 31; xxii. 37; xxiv 27; John v. 39; v. 46; and especially the great office and work predicted for the "Son of Man," Matt. xxvi. 64, and for "The King" and "Son of Man," Matt. xxv. 31–46.

(*b.*) The Apostles declare the same: Acts ii. 16; ii. 25; iii. 18; xiii. 27, 32; xxvi. 22; 1 Pet. i. 11; 2 Pet. i. 19.

Hence,—From the Old Testament itself, and from the interpretation of it by the New, we learn that the Saviour was to be divine and also of the house of David,—a man, yet of prophetic, priestly, and regal power, beyond all that mere humanity could aspire to or wield. *This is fulfilled* in

§ 3. *The Miraculous Conception.*

(In theological usage, "Miraculous Conception" refers to Christ, "Immaculate Conception" to Mary.)

I.—The carefulness of Scripture and of the best creed-statements, here.

John i. 14, "The word *was made*—became—flesh." Heb. ii. 14, "Forasmuch then as the children are partakers of flesh and blood, He also himself likewise *took part* of the same;" Matt. i. 18,—"she was found with child of the Holy Ghost;" Luke i. 35, "The Holy Ghost shall come upon thee, and the power of the Highest shall overshadow thee: wherefore also that holy thing which shall be born shall be called the Son of God."

Reflected in the creed-statements: West. Shorter Cat., Q 22, "Christ, the Son of God, became man, by taking to himself a true body and a reasonable soul, being conceived by the power of the Holy Ghost, in the womb of the Virgin Mary, and born of her, yet without sin." Articles of the Church of England, Art. ii.: "The Son . . . . took man's *nature* in the womb of the blessed Virgin."

How must we think of this conception?

The Saviour must be sinless, free from all taint of original sin. Hence, (*a.*) No generation in the ordinary sense. The

Second Person of the Trinity assumed human nature in the womb of the virgin; (*b.*) The passivity of the mother, and assumption of human nature within the womb entirely by the power of the Most High; (*c.*) A miraculous proceeding, in the highest degree. The Holy Spirit not in the place of an earthly father; the assumption not to be brought *in any way* under the ordinary laws of the production of a human being, but to be left in its mystery, as a new creative work of the Logos enacted through the Holy Spirit.

II.—As to the Question, Would not Christ have had stain from the mother, if she also had not been miraculously rendered pure?[1] The question of the Immaculate Conception. The question is, Was the Virgin Mary herself conceived without the taint of original sin? Was she "sancta, non sanctificata"? Gonzalez (Span. Jesuit, 17th cent.): "The conception of Mary had *three* parts: (*a.*) material, before the infusion of the soul, (*b.*) natural, the *infusio animæ* superadded, (*c.*) the spiritual conception, caused by the *infusio sanctificationis.* So that, the Virgin, in the second part, might have for an instant have been under the power of original sin." But Perrone and modern writers say: there were only two parts: (*a.*) *conceptio activa*, the marital act, (*b.*)—*passiva*, the union of the soul with the seed, which was co-instantaneous with the bestowal of grace.

The question then is, Can it be dogmatically defined that the virgin Mary was holy as soon as she had a soul? The Roman Catholic Church decided this in the affirmative by the decree of Dec. 8, 1854.

Remarks. (1) The consent of the church cannot be pleaded to this dogmatic decision. This is shown (*a.*) from the fact that the Fathers know nothing of immaculate conception. Tertullian, Athanasius, Augustine, John of Damascus, teach that all are under sin; (*b.*) from the fact that the Mediævals were against it. Bernard's (1140) doctrine is, that Mary was freed from sins, by

---

[1] Schleiermacher says: "We must suppose a supernatural, sanctifying influence in the embryo." Müller's suggestion is better: "Sinfulness is through the propagation, not of the embryo, but of the person, the individual: this not by generation in Christ's case. This holy person would repel all impurity from the very start."

grace, after conception: "sanctificata in utero," like Jeremiah and John the Baptist, and so for a time under original sin. The church of Spain followed him. Peter Lombard (1150) was against it: "grace to conquer sin" [received by Mary]. Alex. Hales, (13th cent.), a chief authority, teaches that she was "sanctified"; Bonaventura (13th cent.), "Mary needed redemption"; Aquinas, The festival of 8th Dec. [introduced in 1140 by canons of Lyons, as the Festival of her Conception] is for the "sanctification," and not for the "conception" of the virgin; Mary was "sanctified," when, we do not know.[1]

2. No proof whatever is offered. Perrone cites Gen. iii. 15 (Vulgate: "*She* shall bruise"), and Luke i. 28, "Hail, highly favored!" He grants that there is no decisive proof for the doctrine in the Bible; says there is no proof from the Bible against it. But, the passages of Scripture which speak of original sin and the universality of redemption, allow of no exception.

3. The argument from consent—even of Papal authorities—fails. Launoy (Jansenist, 1731) gives thirteen citations from seven Popes against the doctrine. At Trent, a decision could not be obtained.[2]

4. As to the theological argument. (*a*.) The position, "Only a sinless being could beget [conceive] a sinless," would prove the sinlessness of Mary's parents: (*b*.) The argument from fitness[3]—God would make Mary most fitting for her office, as "the mother of God," as "the bride of the Holy Spirit"—asserts more than we can know, except by revelation. It could not establish fact, but, at the most, only show possibility.

5. Arguments against the doctrine: Luke i. 47; ii. 43; John ii. 3; 1 Cor. xv. 22; Eph. ii. 3; Rom. v. 12.

6. The position taken by the church of Rome in this decision of 1854. (*a.*) Deciding by "infallibility" what has against it a large consent of her greatest teachers—thus sacrificing "tradition" to infallibility. (*b.*) Deciding a point of faith by papal

---

[1] Perrone's explanation of Aquinas and Bernard: "The division of parts;' "They refer only to the animal conception, before the infusion of soul, when they speak of original sin."

[2] Cf. Perrone, p. 113.   [3] Ibid, pp. 102-111, 148.

decree—the ultramontane theory, of infallibility in the Papacy, carried out as never before so clearly. (*c.*) Deciding by "infallibility," on the ground of mere human consent, a matter of fact, which only omniscience could know—thus stretching infallibility to its utmost. (*d.*) Carrying to a still higher extent the adoration of the creature, making the virgin to have a prerogative which, of all human beings, Christ only can claim; exalting her worship, and thus becoming more idolatrous, and departing further from the faith. (*e.*) Giving itself up yet more completely to the control of the Jesuit influence—the most baleful form of Romanism.

§ 4. *In the miraculous Conception the Logos assumed a true and complete Humanity.*

Our Saviour was a proper man, possessing a "true body and a reasonable soul."

I.—A true body. Proved, (*a.*) From his conception and birth, Matt. i. 25; Luke i. 35; ii. 7; (*b.*) His growth like other children, Luke ii. 52; (*c.*) Hunger, weariness, infirmities: need of rest, sleep, Luke iv. 2; xxii. 44; John iv. 6; (*d.*) Pain, suffering, wounds, John xi. 33, 35; xix. 34; Luke xxii. 44; Matt. xxvi. 37; John xx. 27; (*e.*) Flesh and bones, Luke xxiv. 39, 40; (*f.*) Crucifixion, death, and burial, Luke xxiv. 39; Heb. ii. 14.

II.—A reasonable human soul. (*a.*) Growth in wisdom, declaration of "ignorance," Luke ii. 40, 52; Mark xiii. 32; Matt. xvi. 21; xxiv. 36; (*b.*) Temptation, Matt. iv. 1; Luke xxii. 42; Heb. iv. 15; v. 2, 8; (*c.*) Sorrow and sympathies, Matt. xxvi. 37; Luke xix. 41; John xi. 35. (*d.*) Dependence on God, Prayer,[1] Matt. xiv. 19; John xi. 41; (*e.*) Acts ii. 31. (*f.*) To Christ a human πνεῦμα belongs, John xi. 33, 38; xiii. 21; xix. 30; Matt. xxvii. 50; Mark ii. 8; Luke ii. 40; x. 21; xxiii. 46; 1 Pet. iii. 18; (*g.*) To Christ a human ψυχή belongs; John xii. 27; Matt. xxvi. 38; Mark xiv. 34.

III.—The indispensableness of holding the complete humanity of Christ. Denied by Docetæ, not truly held by Arians,

[1] The Prayers of Christ illustrative of his Humanity, Jour. Sac. Lit. and Bib. Record, Oct. 1861.

undervalued by Sabellians—"we want only God," they say, "not man." The church has always confessed the need and want of the God-*man* for redemption. (*a.*) It is important in connection with the interpretation of Scripture. Christ, on the face of the Gospels, is man—proper, true, real—if any ever was. Man is not man without the human soul with all its endowments of "spirit"—is only animal. An interpretation which expels the humanity undermines all correct interpretation. (*b.*) It is important as regards the power and efficacy of his example. We are to be like Him. (*c.*) In regard to his position as the second Adam. (*d.*) Most of all, in connection with redemption. According to the Scriptures, the Redeemer must be of the nature of the redeemed: Heb. ii. 17, 16, 14; Gal. iv. 4. (*e.*) Atonement must be effected through his human nature, the divine could not suffer. The roots of the Scriptural doctrine of redemption are cut off, if we deny the proper humanity of Christ.

§ 5. *In the Scriptures both the Divine and Human Natures of Christ are often brought under one View, are referred to in their connection.* Rom. ix. 5; John i. 1-14, (*a.*) The Word with God, was God, and the first great divine act—creation—ascribed to Him: (*b.*) The Word became flesh, dwelt among us, and we beheld his glory; 1 John i. 1, 2; Phil. ii. 6, 11; Rom. i. 3, 4; Heb. i.; ii.; 1 Tim. iii. 16; John i. 18.[1]

§ 6. *The various Modes in which what is said of Christ in the Scriptures is to be interpreted in respect to his Person and Natures.*

Whenever we speak of any whole which is made up of different elements, we use the same subject with different predicates, which may be applied, which must be applied, to this or that element. The following are the various modes in which Christ is spoken of: (*a.*) The human nature gives the designation of the subject while the predicates belong to the divine nature. Instances: "As concerning the flesh Christ came, *who*—is God

---

[1] "Only-begotten *God*," as read by some. See Ezra Abbott, Bibl. Sac., Oct. 1861.

over all," Rom. ix. 5; "See the Son of man ascend up where *He*—was before," John vi. 62.

(*b.*) The converse of the foregoing. Passages in which the person is designated from the divinity, while the acts are of the humanity. Instances: Rom. viii. 32; 1 Cor. ii. 8; 1 Cor. xv. 47.

(*c.*) The whole person the subject with divine predicates: John viii. 58.

(*d.*) The whole person the subject with human predicates: "I—thirst."

(*e.*) The whole person the subject with predicates of both the natures. All the passages just cited in § 5 are instances.[1]

§ 7. *According to the Scriptures, Christ was one Person, and his Personality was from his Divine Nature.*

I.—One Person. There is nothing in Scripture to show anything like a two-fold personality—two Christs, a man and a God; but the same undivided person is, as to his humanity, from David—the Son of David; and as to his divinity, the Logos—the Son of God. The Scripture asserts this, or rather, rests on this unity of the person. In his primeval estate of glory, in his appearance in the world, in his resurrection and consequent glorification, He is the same—the same yesterday, to-day, and forever. There is as much evidence, and of the same kind, that He is one person, as there is in regard to any being or man in history. There are two ways of showing this: (*a.*) He always uses the first personal pronoun: "Before Abraham was, I am," "The glory which I had with thee before the world was," "I am with you always"; He is also addressed as "Thou," and is spoken of as He, Him, etc. (*b.*) He is never spoken of as if the man and the God in Him had personal relations or converse with each other (as is the case with the "Persons" of the Trinity).

II.—This one Person had its personality from the divine nature.[2] It is otherwise logically inconceivable. There was not

---

[1] Illustrative Parallel. (*a.*) Man—is a religious animal, (*b.*) Man—is spiritual and sleeps, (*c.*) Shakespeare—is a genius, (*d.*) Chatham—suffers pain, (*e.*) Burke—delivered an oration.

[2] Usage of person and personality. Person, usually broader: the whole outward manifestation, the same being in all his attributes. Personality, the central point of the person, the indefinable I, Ego.

a human personality, there was a human *nature*, perhaps impersonal, or the personality merged in the divine person. "Christ was not a human person with a divine nature, but a divine person with a human nature." Another view: There may be supposed an embryo, with human personality, yet never coming to distinct being, lost, merged in the divine personality. It is difficult to conceive human nature without potential personality. Some say, personality is in consciousness alone.

[Some fuller statements on this point are given in Chap. V.]

§ 8. *Summary and Conclusion from Scripture Testimony as to the Two Natures and One Person.*

Generally. Christ is very God and very man, yet one Person, the God-man. The induction of these points is not from a few expressions, but from, and giving the final expression to, the greatest variety of utterances concerning Him. Omitting either of these points puts us in a false position, suppresses some Scriptural statement.

Analytically. (*a.*) Christ is one Person, (*b.*) A perfect divine nature, (*c.*) United to an entire human nature, (*d.*) In this the divine nature is active, the human nature passive, (*e.*) The act is called "personal unition;" the result, personal or hypostatic union, ἐνανϑρώπησις. (*f.*) So Christ is the God-man, ϑεάνϑρωπος,[1] and so abides. (*g.*) In this union the natures are not confounded or commingled. (*h.*) Nor is the Person divided. There is in the one person a *communio naturarum*, so that the properties of either nature may be ascribed to the one person, and there is "one theandric energy."[2]

The Proof. (*a.*) It is inconceivable that it should be otherwise. (*b.*) The reasons for the union always remain.[3] (*c.*) The

---

[1] First in Origen.
[2] [But see further on, and especially in Chap. V., for the sense in which this statement is made.]
[3] 1 Cor. xv. 24, 28, urged against this. But according to that passage "the Son" remains, only the mediatorial scepter is laid down. The position [advocated by Dr. Hickok?] that when Christ gives up the kingdom, the Man remains Head of the Church, while the Logos goes back to God, is not consistent with such passages as are cited under (*c.*).

Scriptural assertions. The eternal reign, Dan. ii. 44, vii. 14, 18; Luke i. 33; Rev. xi. 15; The eternal relation to the church, and to the redeemed soul, Rev. vii. 16, 17; xxi. 22, 23; xxii. 1, 3; Heb. vii. 25, 16, 21, 28; vi. 20.

CHAPTER II.

THE EARLY HERETICAL OPINIONS AS TO THE PERSON OF CHRIST.

This belongs to the History of Dogmas. Here only a sketch is to be given.

I.—Scheme of the Possibilities. The Scriptural elements as we have seen are—Christ is one Person, having a divine nature and a human nature, and his original and essential personality is that of the divine nature. Then the following views are possible:

(*a.*) Taking the Person as basis and denying the reality of one or the other of the natures, denying the divine nature—Ebionitism:—the human nature, Docetism.

(*b.*) Denying—not the human nature, but the integrity of it—Apollinaris.

(*c.*) Allowing the two natures in their integrity, but asserting (virtually) two Persons—Nestorianism.

(*d.*) Affirming one nature and one person and that divine—Eutyches, Monophysites.

(*e.*) Affirming one nature from the two, with one will—Monothelites.

(*f.*) Affirming one person, two natures, with differences upon the question of the two wills—The general orthodox position.

II.—Definitions. (*a.*) Nature, οὐσία: what belongs to the essence or substance. (*b.*) Person: substantia individua quæ nec alterius pars est, nec in altera sustentatur.[1] (*c.*) Personality: suppositum intelligens per se subsistens.

[1] Chemnitz.

III.—Statement. The human nature of Christ never existed out of union with his divine nature, and so has no *distinct* personality. Yet it lacks nothing of complete human personality. The ultimate question here is, Did the two natures manifest themselves as two? Monothelites said: There are two natures but only one will—one manifestation. Orthodoxy inclines, with reservations, to the position of two manifestations. "One theandric energy," proposed by the Emperor Heraclius, 633. [The author declares neither for nor against this. Would "two manifestations *of* one theandric energy" indicate his view? See Chap. V.]

CHAPTER III.

LATER DOCTRINAL DIFFERENCES BROUGHT UP IN THE CONTROVERSIES OF THE REFORMATION.

I.—The Calvinistic bodies have stood on the old foundation.

II.—The Socinians renewed Ebionitism or Arianism.

III.—The Lutherans affirmed communicatio idiomatum, that one nature partakes of the attributes of the other. The communication is of the divine to the human—not the converse. "Finitum capax infiniti." This applied especially to the Lord's Supper. Ubiquity is the word which expresses the most essential thing in the theory.

Objections of the Reformed: (*a.*) Christ's body, then, is present everywhere as much as in the sacramental bread. (*b.*) How can a human nature become omniscient and yet remain ignorant, etc? How can this be affirmed without strict logical contradiction? (*c.*) The theory would result in a monophysitic view, annulling the real humanity. (*d.*) It ought to teach that the divine partakes in the human, which it does not. (*e.*) Generally: transference of properties would annul nature—infinite to finite, finite to infinite.

IV.—The doctrine of Kenosis.[1] Phil. ii. 7, ἑαυτὸν ἐκένωσε μορφὴν δούλου λαβών. The Incarnation was a self-emptying act of the Logos, the laying aside, for a time, of divine powers and prerogatives.

Objections:

(*a.*) This would involve a change, for thirty years, in the Divine Trinity.

(*b.*) It is inconceivable that the Godhead should thus become naught. Gess and Reubelt[2] say, If Christ has life in himself, He may annul it of himself. But the act ascribed to Christ in Phil. ii. 7 is best understood as a humiliation, a taking of new conditions—not as an annulling of his divinity.

(*c.*) It is argued that God the Father might effect the Kenosis, as He gave life to the Son. But (*a.*) Phil. ii. 7 says *Christ* did whatever was done; (*b.*) The Father could not annul the divine being of the Son any more than his own; (*c.*) if He could, the Son would not be equally divine; (*d.*) The doctrine leads over into the position of the entire dependence of the Son for nature, being (as well as Sonship) on the Father.[3]

V.—Philosophical views. Schelling: The essence of the Incarnation is in the principle of Identity—the union of opposites. Hegelians: The second Person is the world. Schleiermacher: The truth is that of Divine Humanity; in Christ is found the ideal union, of which we partake. Christ was not personally pre-existent. Dorner: Divinity and Humanity are not diverse. See Hodge.[4]

---

[1] For it, Thomasius, Liebner, v. Hofmann, etc. Dorner against it (Glaubensl.).

[2] Prof. J. A. Reubelt. Two articles in Bib. Sac., 1870–71. Also, Transl. of Gess, Script. Doct. of Person of Christ, Andover, 1870.

[3] Gess says, "Aseity is to be ascribed to the Father only."

[4] [The reference is doubtless to Dr. Charles Hodge's Systematic Theology, and seems to indicate that the author agrees in the main with his strictures.]

CHAPTER IV.

THE OBJECTIONS AND DIFFICULTIES URGED AGAINST THE DOCTRINE OF THE PERSON OF CHRIST.

Preparatory Considerations.

All great truths, like all great men, pass through a protracted struggle before their victory is secure. Though not contrary to reason, they are above it, and reason will assail them. They are above common sense, and common sense will take offence at them. They are revealed to faith, but all men have not faith. They are given to meet our spiritual wants, but sin deadens our sense of the greatness of these wants. They show the relations and reconcile the opposition between God and man, heaven and earth, but many who live on the earth care not for heaven, and many men have little sense of the greatness and the wonderful works of God. They unfold the mysteries of the divine nature, but some can hardly see the difference between a mystery and an imagination.

The greatest truths, too, are those that reconcile the greatest antagonisms, but many do not understand, and many explain away the fearful antagonism there is between a holy God and a sinful world; the great gulf is for them only a narrow stream which they may readily leap over at any time; the vast mountain, seen in the distance, seems so like a mole-hill that it appears not at all necessary for God to come down to earth to enable us to surmount it.

But if we might expect the great truths connected with our redemption to be assailed by man, no less may we expect that they would be defended and made triumphant by the power of God. And so it comes to pass. From conflict they emerge with higher luster, purified and exalted. The attack sharpens the defence. The truth becomes more clear and definite, is reduced to more precise statements, is guarded against perversion, is seen in its connection with other truths, is adjusted in the great system which sets forth God's dealings with man, is illumined and not consumed by the fire sent down to devour it. Thus has it been, pre-eminently, with the doctrine respecting the Person of Christ. No truth has been more fiercely debated, through longer ages; none has experienced greater opposition from all sorts and conditions of men; none has received more precise and accurate definitions; none has asserted its triumphant claims more successfully against the wit and wisdom of this world. In the early church the doctrine respecting Christ's Person even took the precedence of the doctrine respecting his atoning sacrifice. With a humble and direct faith, men came to Him, clung to Him, loved Him with a deep personal affection, saw in Him the object of all praise and glory. They believed in Him heartily, before they began to reflect upon their faith. And the first subjects of doctrinal discussion were those that grew out of his complex nature. One sect exalted the humanity, another the divinity: the respective attributes of each nature were defined. Council after council, through six centuries, was called, to rebut heresies, or establish and define the faith. Let some see in all this only the jarring disputes of theologians: let them also see that they were disputing about what formed the central object of their faith and spiritual life. Far from seeing in these controversies an evidence against, we may derive from them the strongest evidence for, the existence of the most striking elements of contrast in the person of Him to whom all parties equally looked as the engrossing center of their faith.—And where in modern times this doctrine has been assailed with the greatest vehemence, it has come forth again from the assault with greater luster. In the land most boastful of its philosophy, philosophy even came to pay its homage to Jesus Christ. The problems which the church held as articles of faith have come to be most vehemently discussed as questions of philosophy. Around the person of Christ their hosts have gathered, they have assaulted Him with their fiercest questionings, they have been baffled by his wondrous person, and even when they do not bow to his person, they yet confess that the doctrine respecting Him is the sublimest doctrine to which man has attained; they have taken it and placed it in the very center of their systems, and proclaimed that the union between what is divine and what is human is the great central and reconciling truth to which all the facts of history and all the speculations of philosophy must bring men's minds.

And in our own New England, when many wavered in their belief in the divinity of Christ, when most of its literature, its culture, its honored names in church and state, and the predominant influences of refined society were all enlisted in favor of a system which denied the more excellent, though it glorified the more humble, nature of our Lord, how was it that such a cause, with every prestige of success, was suddenly checked in its advancing course? It was not by argument alone, it was not alone by showing its inconsistency with Scripture, but it was also because there was a new outpouring of the Spirit of God, giving a deeper sense of sin, a more thorough longing for salvation; it was because men's souls were deeply stirred, and came to grapple with the great problems of their destiny; because they saw their helplessness and sinfulness, and felt the need of an Almighty Deliverer: it was because by the exercise of simple and hearty faith in Him, as the giver of spiritual life, they saw the fitness of such a Redeemer to all their wants, and experienced the full sense of pardon and peace only when leaning on the arm of this gracious Deliverer. And all this was and must have been a wonder to those who felt not the burden of sin, and realized not the full meaning of the law of God, and whose religious feelings were not quickened, so that they could cry out, my heart and flesh long for the living God. But they who sought the living God, perfect in holiness and abounding in mercy, found Him in the person of Jesus Christ, and bowed in adoration before Him as the Lord and giver of their spiritual life. Very like a living power has been the cause of Jesus Christ through the history and changes of his church; very like a living influence is that which still draws men to Him from the depths of sin, from the heights of human reason; very like a living Being does He still and ever present Himself to the eyes of our faith; a secret and unseen agency still draws in every clime men's hearts towards Him; they love Him as they cannot love a man who has gone to his grave; men oppose Him as they do not oppose a Luther or a Calvin: even when they try to prove that He is not divine, they do it because there is so much to show that He is divine; they never try to prove that Paul was a mere man, or that John was not a God: they reason against Christ's divinity as they reason against nothing that is unsubstantial and imaginary—not as men reason against a chimæra, but as they contend against a power which the force of the contest shows really to exist.

Such has been the living course of Christ, as the Head and Leader of his church, through its conflicts in this world. No one doctrine has been more impugned, or has maintained its ground more firmly, than that respecting his Person. In the course of the controversy the greatest variety of objections have been made. Some of the chief of these we now proceed to consider.

I.—It is said that we can explain all that the Bible says about the Person of Christ, without assuming his divinity. Some few texts, it is said, do seem to have a halo of divinity about them, but when we come to examine them closely, the halo is not so distinctly visible. This brings up the subject of

The right Mode of Interpreting Scripture. [The observations which follow would have been in place in the Introduction, as giving the point of view from which the author would regard the Scriptures in reference to every main doctrine. But the general statements could not well be sundered from the special references to the doctrine now under consideration. Their importance with reference to the whole theological system will be the explanation of their being inserted here at such length.]

There is a strong tendency in men's minds, when dealing with a difficult subject, to banish all difficulties by simply denying them. Many prefer to receive the half of a truth by the understanding, to taking the whole of it by faith, especially where the truth seems to involve both something mysterious and something intelligible; we are very apt to grasp the intelligible half, and let the mysterious remainder evanesce. Thus, in explaining God's moral government, it is much easier to think out a system made up wholly of divine purposes, or to think out one made up wholly of free agency, than it is to combine both these parts of the system into one orderly and consistent whole. So it is not difficult to understand that Jesus was a man—this is simple, there have been many very wonderful men in the world —but to say that He is also God introduces a profound mystery, a somewhat that is quite unfathomable. If now the Bible could be interpreted so as to be consistent with the intelligible half of what is said of Jesus, that would relieve us of a great mystery, and to relieve the soul of mysteries is thought by some to be the great end of all interpretation and reflection—one evidence of the advance of knowledge and culture. And at the worst—or best—though some difficult passages should remain, it is thought to be better to leave some uncertainty about their interpretation, than to leave anything inexplicable in the nature of Christ. And besides, it is very well known that words are used in a great variety of senses, and if the highest sense of a word be mysterious, the lowest sense may be level to our understandings; if the highest sense involves in difficulties, the lowest makes all plain. And the great aim in interpreting the Bible is to remove all difficulties. Figurative language also abounds: the Orientals were famous for the use of it; and the Bible was written in Oriental parts. They were not so careful to distinguish between what was divine and what was human as we are.

A series of rules for the interpretation of Scripture might in this way be easily made out. Prove first, that Christ was a man; assert next, that He could not be both God and man, that this involves an absurdity; and explain all the Scripture by this rule. Another formula would be, Take any word applied to Christ, which has been interpreted of his divine nature, reduce it to its lowest terms, and show that it can possibly mean something less than absolute divinity; show this of each of the terms so used, and the result will be, that whatever words in whatever variety have been used to unfold the higher nature of Jesus, they could not by any possibility prove that He had that nature—because it is impossible at the outset. All the difficulties will in this way disappear. For what is difficult can be explained by what is easy, and what is mysterious by what is natural, and what crosses our feelings by what suits our feelings, and we may make a very perfect man out of one who is called God, a very clear system of natural religion out of an obscure system of revealed truth, an easy system of morals out of a hard system of divinity; and we shall become versed in all the easy parts of Scripture and easy in all the difficult parts; and if we do not understand God's ways with man, we shall at least see clearly what are man's ways with God and with his revelation.

But against all this we urge the position, that precisely where and when the Bible speaks of the mysteries of the divine nature, if it be indeed the Word of God, we are bound in critical justice to be most guarded and reverential in our interpretations. Far from seeking to diminish or explain away the words which announce to us such a wonderful manifestation, we should rather seek to give them their greatest intensity of meaning, and should let them be invested with something of the sacredness and awfulness of the subject which they are meant to announce. In their very best estate, human language and human thoughts are all too poor and meagre to declare to us the immensity and wonderful works of Jehovah. All language bends beneath the weight of such supernatural themes. What folly, then, in the wisdom which will take all the words and phrases of the Scripture that have been selected to describe God's wonderful manifestations of himself, and give to them their smallest possible amount of significancy, which will take a figurative expression, and give the lowest meaning to the figure—when it would seem as if even natural reason might teach us, that any figure of *human* language, when applied to the divine works, must be taken in its most eminent and daring sense, in order to conform to the nature of the subject which it is intended to describe.

We may interpret historical facts in the Bible by the laws which govern us in the interpretation of history; we may write the lives of the great and good men who are there described to us as we would write the lives of other great and good men; we may interpret poetry as poetry, and prose as prose, and many things according to the religious culture and national habits of the chief actors in them—in short, we may interpret the things that belong to men by the standard of men, but we must also interpret what relates to God in a manner conformable to the mysteriousness of his Being and the wonderfulness of his works. And when He unfolds to us, so to speak, his hidden nature, when He unveils his glories to our gaze, and lets us catch a glimpse of the interior economy of the very Godhead; and when He unfolds this in connection with the greatest work in which we can conceive even God to engage, the redemption of an apostate world; what reverence can be too great, what caution unwise, that we do not misunderstand or diminish the full sense of the majestic truths so graciously delivered to us!

Against the attempt to show that the language respecting Christ's higher nature can be interpreted in a lower sense we urge again—what has been said in another connection—that the conviction respecting his divinity does not result from isolated phrases, is not determined by the interpretation of particular words, but is formed from the total representation given of Him in the inspired record. In almost every variety of phrase and image are his wonderful glories depicted. In his relations to God and in his relations to man, both natures are implied, implied when not directly asserted, most naturally inferred when not expressly stated. Hence the process of trying not to find his divinity is one of constant explaining, if not of explaining away. The Person of Jesus Christ, so to speak, is inwrought into the very texture of revelation. Give the New Testament a living form, and the form it takes is that of the God-man, the mediator between heaven and earth, equally allied to both God and man. Now we do not deny but that a skilful anatomist may dissect this book, and not find the divinity of Christ which animates it: but the very process of dissection has killed the living spirit, which of course eludes all his future research.

In interpreting the Bible, something more is needed than critical skill,—a humble acceptance and belief of God's revelation to us—an expectation of finding, when God condescends to unfold his nature, what may surpass our understanding, though it may claim our faith—a sense and feeling that God is there revealed in his Word, as nowhere else—and a reverential interpretation, and a thankful acceptance, and an implicit belief, of all that is declared respecting the person of Him, whose is the only name given under heaven amongst men whereby we must be saved. And if Christ be really the God-man, if his state of humanity was a state of humiliation, of humiliation for our redemption, what ingratitude to transform all that shows the greatness of his condescension into an argument to disprove the greatness of his majesty, what shame to make his human sympathy and suffering the ground for denying his antecedent and eternal glory!

In respect, then, to the objection under consideration, we grant fully, that it is *possible* to explain the whole of Scripture without proving Christ to be the God-man. This *can* be done, it has been done. But how? On principles which undermine every rational theory of interpretation; on principles which assert that it is possible for a person to be called God, to have divine attributes ascribed to Him, to have divine works (as creation) ascribed to Him, to be worshipped, to be an object of our highest trust and love, and yet not to be divine. On such principles Scripture can be interpreted so as to do away with the proof of Christ's divinity, and *only* on such.

II.—A second objection which is brought against the doctrine that in the Person of Jesus Christ two natures are combined in One Person, is, that the doctrine, in this form, is not found in the Bible, and therefore cannot be an Article of Faith.

This objection, however, brings up to our minds a peculiarity of the Bible in respect to its mode of revealing truth, and also a remarkable fact in the history of the church as to the mode of developing truth. The Bible is not a book of dry, dogmatical statements; it contains no Confession of Faith; it gives us no system or summary of doctrine. It is altogether a different book from what a mere man would have written. Its words are spirit and life. It is a book for all times. It states the same truth in a great variety of ways. It involves one truth in another. It is somewhat like the book of nature, where all things seem most strangely blended, in the greatest variety—the larger animals, birds, insects, trees, shrubs, earths, all existing together without any sign of regular classification. Now when any one begins to study nature, he systematizes, he describes accurately, he reproduces, in another form, what he finds scattered so profusely around him: he does not mean to make it over again, or to make a better system, but only to describe what actually is—and that is more than he has ever done yet—and it is a necessary course for him to take in order to get fully acquainted with the laws and harmony of nature.

So it is in respect to the Bible and to human systems framed upon it. Men will think about the Bible: it was meant that they should; and they will set forth what they think: and they may not think to good purpose—but still they think. They cannot produce anything half so living as the Bible; they cannot exhaust it; it always remains the only source of infallibility, the chief source of sanctifying truth. But as men think about the doctrines there contained, and think more and more, they attain a profounder sense of its wonderful depth and consistency. The doctrines are developed from age to age in new harmony. One set of doctrines after another is taken up by the church and discussed—often vehemently, seen in all their bearings, brought into a definite and consistent whole: and then another series is begun upon: and so the treasures of the Bible are successively poured over into men's minds; but it still remains an exhaustless fountain.

If this is true as a general fact, much more will it be found to be true respecting the doctrine of the Person of Christ. He is revealed in the Scriptures as a living Person, full of majesty and grace. God did not reveal to us a doctrine, He sent his Son: He does not proclaim a system, which men are simply to understand and assent to, He sets before our eyes a Being, a living Person whom we may love and trust. But we not only believe in Christ, we think about Him. And now if any one in telling his thoughts about Christ should say, He is a mere man—to meet this statement we may, first of all, quote some texts which show Him to be divine. It will be said in reply, they do not prove that He is divine, and then comes a controversy. And the very substance of the controversy is this, whether what the Bible says about Christ shows Him to have one nature or two natures. No simpler mode of stating it can be framed. And in this statement, He has two natures, we express our faith. Now it is objected, this statement is not found in the Bible. We grant it, but also say that we are compelled to make it, to refute a notion which has been advanced, which is also not found in the Bible, viz., that Christ is only a created being. Had that assertion not been made, we had probably not made ours. Had some others not expressed their belief about what Christ is, in a way different from that of the Bible, neither had we done so. And it is a most extraordinary piece of irrelevancy, after others have led the way, by saying something about Christ which is not contained in so many words in the Scripture, and which we believe to be inconsistent with the Scripture, to find fault with us for doing the same thing. But yet we can thank them for it. Even such objections are not without benefit. They lead us to study more closely the character and person of our Redeemer. To refute the objections, we have had to penetrate more fully into the sense of the inspired word, and to dwell more intently upon the nature of Him who is its living center. We have thus got to clearer views and more enlarged conceptions of what He is in all his relations. And thus it is that heresy sharpens and deepens faith.

III.—This same objection, for the substance thereof, is found in the statement that the doctrine of two natures and one person was not held by the early church. We grant that the early Christians had not this exact form of stating their faith, but they had for the most part, what was better—the faith itself, whole and undivided. They were filled with a living sense of their union with Christ: they loved Him so earnestly, and believed in Him so undoubtingly, and served Him so zealously, that they stayed not to analyze what He was, in logical phrases.

But when his complex nature was questioned, when doubts were raised and queries put, then the defence was as vigorous as the assault, then the answers were given, always in the form best fitted to meet the objection. Had you asked an early Christian, Was Jesus Christ a man, he would have been astonished at your simplicity: did He not appear upon the earth, and have not these apostles seen Him? Had you asked him, Was Christ very God?— he would have said, There is also God the Father. But, Is Christ *divine* in his *nature?*—the word "nature" in this connection would have been new to him, and he would have thought somewhat further. Well, was He a created being?—Assuredly not. May you worship Him?—We do so every day in hymns and doxologies. Do you love Him with your whole heart?—Yea, and try to show this love every day of my life. Do you love Him and trust in Him as much as you can do in any being, in God Himself?—With a countenance full of joy, he would have answered, All I have and all I am, all my faith and all my love, are his now and for evermore.

And if all this would not substantially prove that he really believed that Christ was a being who united the human and divine natures in One Person, it is hard to see what can prove it.

IV.—A fourth objection that if Christ be held to be divine his *veracity* is impeached, would hardly be worth noticing, had it not been put forth with some pretensions, by a certain sort of reasoners. Thus one says, "this doctrine attributes to Jesus deceit, equivocation, and falsehood." And he adds, "we cannot endure to have the name of Jesus, even by supposition, coupled with fraud and dishonesty." "We hold a belief of his integrity among our fondest persuasions, and this belief nothing would tempt us to resign." But he then goes on to show that this belief which *nothing* would tempt him to resign, he must inevitably give up if Christ were omnipotent and yet said, I can of mine own self do nothing: if infinitely good, and said, There is none good but one, that is God: if omniscient, and yet asserted, Of that day and hour knoweth no man, neither the Son, but the Father.

Eager and unskilful disputants are often earnest to resolve

every question they discuss, if possible, into a question about personal veracity or the moral character of the individuals who are the subjects of controversy. This is an easy way of seeming to settle a difficult subject, which requires from its very nature a prolonged and careful investigation. The question in the case before us is thus transferred from critical to moral grounds; from being a question about natures and persons, difficult to understand, into being a question about the truthfulness of Jesus Christ. The argument might be good for one side, if it had not the unfortunate quality of being just as applicable, with a wider extension, on the other.

This Being of perfect veracity and unimpeached openness *did* so speak, that He was understood to claim equality with God. He who prayed to the Father, did claim that the Son should be honored even as the Father. He asserted virtual omnipresence, when He told his disciples that He would be with them even to the ends of the earth. While He said that He knew not the day nor the hour, He also said that He knew the Father even as the Father knew Him. While He asserts that He can of his own self do nothing, to Him is also ascribed all power, even creative power—and if the fact of creation does not involve the idea of omnipotence, we confess that it is not in the power of our thoughts to form any conception of it. If creative power can be given to a creature, then the prime distinction between a creator and a creature is at once subverted. If omnipotence and omniscience can be imparted to a being who is by nature finite in power and knowledge, all distinction between the attributes of God and those of his creatures must at once be done away.

And if the question of Christ's veracity is to be raised in connection with the discussion respecting his natures, we may boldly assert that it is more seriously impeached on the supposition that He was not divine than in any other way. His character receives its darkest shade when we try to conceive how a being only derived and dependent could ever use words which even seemed to imply an equality in any sense with the Almighty Father: how such a one could place Himself in the midst between heaven and earth, and claim to fill up all the space between, and say in the most unqualified terms, no man cometh unto the Father but by me: how one who was finite in his knowledge could say, or how it could be said of Him, that He was to be the final Judge of the character and destiny of all who have lived here on the earth. Here is not merely a want of veracity, here is such pride as astounds, such arrogance as confounds us, unless there be such divinity as may claim our homage. We must turn from Him as a usurper, if we do not bow to Him as a Lord.

V:—Another objection which has been somewhat strenuously urged against the doctrine of The Two Natures in the One Person is, that it is derived from Gnostic or heathen sources; that the pure, original faith was perverted by foreign elements, the pure fire was mingled with strange fire brought from heathen altars, a dependent being was deified, and idolatry was introduced into God's own church.

Now the deification of a man is one of the grossest forms of heathenism: there is no idolatry worse than this. At the same time as a historical fact it is undeniable that Christ has been honored as a divine being in the Church from the earliest ages, and that the number of those who have refused their homage has always been inconsiderable. If this be idolatry, several things follow. It follows that the Jewish religion as a whole was much purer than the Christian, for the Jews worshipped God alone. It follows that Mohammedanism, in its doctrine respecting God, has been on the whole superior to Christianity. It follows that in respect to the essential point of all religion, viz., whom and what we shall worship, the church has been in a fatal error or delusion, and that not for a few centuries but in every century of its course. It follows that Christianity conquered heathenism only by yielding to heathenism, for it adopted one of its grossest superstitions. It follows that what has been taught with the largest and longest consent may yet be only a pernicious error. It follows that the church of Christ has erred, fatally erred, not in a matter of outward form, not in a point of secondary and derived significancy, but in a point of vital importance, involving the very substance of its faith;

has erred, not now and then, but always, through all its centuries; that it is in fact heathen and not Christian.

Does not such a position as this go as far as any can to undermine our faith in Christianity itself, and to leave us without any standard of truth, without any settled conviction in the reality of God's government and guidance of his church? It may all be consistent with the position that it is human to err, it is hardly so consistent with Christ's promise that He would give to his followers the Spirit of Truth. It is more in harmony with the notion that a few men in these later times have gained an infallible reason, than it is with the idea that there is infallibility in the body of Christ, taken as a whole.

But yet, it is said, it cannot be denied that the heathen had incarnations and deifications, and that heathen became Christians—and what more natural than that they should bring over some of their old faith with them? But what if they had some presentiment of the truth, some troubled and distorted images, some scattered rays: and what if they found in the Christian faith and in the Person of Christ the reality of that which had so long haunted them like a vision, the perfection of what they strove vainly and idolatrously to depict, the full, concentrated brightness of what they had before known only in fitful gleams? What if there was, after all, something of truth even in Paganism? Is this so impossible to be believed? If an Egyptian had ever gone from his temples, where grotesque images were piled together in every variety of incongruity and deformity, into a Grecian temple where statues that realized the ideal of majesty and beauty met his gaze, might he not at once have felt that here was the visible representation of that which his own misshapen deities only caricatured? Might he not have forsaken his hateful gods to worship at the shrine of these miracles of art? May it not have been somewhat thus with the Christian Incarnation in its relation to the heathen deifications? What they grossly imagined was here perfectly realized. What was in them idolatry was purified in the Christian faith into the most perfect form of worship. When Satan cannot create a lie, he caricatures the truth. Error is best overcome by showing the highest and perfect form of the truth with which it is commingled. The heathen bowed before the Person of Jesus, and for Him renounced their idols, because they saw, that what they ignorantly worshipped was here declared unto them.

In respect to this objection, then, we say, that the doctrine respecting the Person of Christ was not derived from heathen sources, but that it is the perfect form of expressing a truth dimly apprehended by heathen superstitions. No heathen religion ever contained such a sublime truth as that the human and divine natures were perfectly united in one Person, although there was in heathenism a preparation for such a truth.

And, besides, we do not find that those who make such an objection are always consistent with themselves. When they would prove the being or the unity of God, the immortality of the soul, a future state of rewards and punishments, they derive some confirmation to their faith in these truths from the general consent of men, from the dim light of heathenism. What then if we call these also heathen doctrines? The reply would be, Yes, but Christian also, clearer and purer in Christianity. But if this argument be of weight in these cases—as it assuredly is—it is still more weighty in respect to the Incarnation. For here is a truth more generally anticipated, most grossly defiled, which arises in the fullest purity and splendor, and commands the homage of the world. In the Incarnation of the Eternal Word, in this union of perfect divinity and perfect humanity, divinity is brought down to earth, and humanity is raised to heaven, humanity is ennobled and divinity is made apparent.

This charge of approximation to heathenism does not lie against the position of those who hold that God became man, but it does lie against the view of those who, while asserting the intrinsic inferiority of Christ to the Father, do yet not scruple to say that he has become an object of rightful worship. This *is* deification, this is the making of a god, this is the theory of the person of Jesus which is strictly allied to the notions of heathenism: for to worship any being less than God is idolatry.

VI.—The last objection we shall notice that is brought against the received doctrine of the God-man is, that it involves contradictions. It is said that what we assert of Him either will force us to acknowledge two persons—and this would destroy our doctrine—or, if we hold to One Person, then that person is made up of such contradictory traits that He becomes an absurdity, an absolute impossibility.

It should be observed that this same difficulty, or the substance of it, lies against any scheme which allows to Christ any other than a mere human nature. If we allow a pre-existent and super-angelic state, in which Christ ever derivatively had another nature or other powers than those he had as a man, the same difficulty presses upon us. It is a difficulty which vanishes only with the more difficult assumption of the mere humanity of our Saviour.

It should also be asked, whether we really know just what a person is, whether we know it so far as to be able to decide just what variety of qualities and attributes any being must have in order that he remain one person and do not become two persons. We know that man is mortal and immortal, spiritual and material, that his whole character is made up of contrasts—selfishness and benevolence, pride and humility, thought and feeling, freedom and dependence, that he may be spiritual and worldly, sinful and holy. And the higher we ascend in the scale of being the more do contrasts accumulate. Do these things destroy, or in the least impair, the unity of man's person? Does not his very superiority to the brutes consist in his uniting in one person a great variety of different and almost opposite traits? Is not the unity of his person found in the harmonious operation of the respective powers of a spiritual soul and a material body? And in the highest point of view, this finite creature, this mortal man can become, is bound to become, a temple for the Holy Ghost, to be in some sense a partaker of the divine nature. And the more completely his finite and imperfect nature is filled with the Spirit of God, the higher is our idea of him as a person. True, we cannot understand how God's Spirit acts upon and in man's soul, but we do know that it does not in the least impair the unity of his person, although it acts in direct and constant opposition to many of his natural tendencies and aims.

Such a view even of human nature might lead us to be careful in our assertions as to what may and what may not destroy the unity of a person. And when we come to think of a divine Person, and to endeavor to conceive the possibility of his uniting in himself a two-fold nature, it is at least befitting our ignorance that our statements should be most cautious. Who can tell what are the possibilities of deity? We can know them only as they are revealed. If a human being can unite in himself such opposite traits as we know that we do, who will dare set limits to the capacity of a divine being, and to set the limits in such a way as to assert the absolute impossibility of his becoming man?

The objection we are considering is one that is meant to destroy the very possibility of the doctrine of the God-man, to destroy the possibility of the existence of a doctrine which has been held, age after age, with the firmest faith, by the church of Christ. It is a bold thing to say that anything, not contradictory nor sinful in its nature, is impossible with God. We should rather naturally expect that when God engaged in his greatest work, He would manifest himself in a manner beyond our common thoughts. But philosophy and reason here come in and say, that one particular mode of manifestation is an impossibility, that a God-man cannot be.

Now we conceive that in the idea of Person there is nothing, so far as we know it, which has any bearing upon the objection. A person is—the same conscious being, the same individual, the being who can say I, under every variety of circumstances. The definition of person has nothing to do with the greater or less variety of attributes or qualities which the person may possess. The person is—the same subject under all conditions. This is what we affirm of Christ: He was the same identical Person in heaven, on earth, and in his glorified state. He is the same yesterday, to-day, and forever. He was the same being in different states. And why may not the same person assume a different nature without loss of identity—who will show it to be impossible?

But, it is said, that when we assert that Christ assumed a human nature, and united it with a divine, we assert that He united not merely *opposite*, but *contradictory* qualities in the same Person. But this is what we deny. A contradiction is to be proved only when it is said that the same assertion is both true and not true in respect to the same thing in the same sense. If a man says that any act of his is both sinful and holy in the same sense, or that any act of his was both free and necessary in the same sense, here is a contradiction. But if a man says of himself that he is white, he is not understood, even by those who interpret everything most figuratively, as meaning to say that his soul is white. When a man says he thinks, he does not mean that his body thinks. This assertion that he thinks cannot be interpreted of the *whole* of his complex nature, and yet it is a person who has a complex nature that does think, and yet again, it is only a person who has a spiritual nature that can say that he thinks. So Christ may say that He is weak and dependent and suffering, and He may pray to God, and yet He cannot be understood as affirming what is contradictory to his omnipotence and divinity, unless it be said that He means to affirm that his omnipotence was weak, and his divine bliss was suffering, and his uncreated nature was praying to itself. The two natures, the divine and human, are not *contradictory* to one another. There is no contradiction between the finite and the infinite: if there were, God could not create anything. They are in startling contrast to each other: they are opposites, but they are not contraries. If there were a contradiction between a divine nature and a human nature, we should have an impassable gulf between us and God. And if these are not contradictory, who shall say that they may not be united in one Person?

But let us narrow the objection down to its directest application. It is said, the doctrine of the Person of Christ requires the assertion that Christ in the same mental act was conscious of opposite states: that when He was suffering on the cross, He was conscious of the intense felicity of heaven: that when

He prayed, He was at the same instant conscious of omnipotence that when He said He knew not the day, He was also conscious at the same instant that He did know the day: that when He was a slumbering infant, He was conscious of being the Lord of all: that while He grew in knowledge, He was conscious of omniscience: and a consciousness of contradictions is no consciousness at all. Reduced to its last terms, the objection resolves itself into the dilemma, that He either had a two-fold consciousness, and so was two persons, or was conscious of entirely opposite things at the same time in the same act.

Now what if there be a difficulty here which we cannot perfectly explain? It is a difficulty like to that we find in respect to other truths, which we are still compelled to admit. For example, in the act of regeneration God's Spirit works in man, and man is free: and both the operation of the Spirit and freedom are involved in the same mental act. We cannot see *how* this can be, yet we know that it *must* be so. And man, when under the highest influence of this Spirit—an influence opposed to his natural tendencies—remains still the same individual person, and has only a single consciousness. Man may be in as opposite states as those of sin and holiness, and yet have only one consciousness.

But, it is said, man has after all only one nature: but Christ is affirmed to have had two natures.—Does then a two-fold nature demand a two-fold consciousness? We are spiritual and we are material, and have only one consciousness, but that consciousness may be at different times of things as opposite as matter and spirit. This consciousness of opposite things does not destroy the unity of the consciousness itself. And so it is of Christ, in respect to most of the points alleged. He was conscious that so far as He was human He was weak, and so far as divine, was omnipotent. He was not conscious that as human He was omnipotent, or as divine, was a sufferer. This would be a contradiction.

The strongest case is that in respect to his ignorance of the day and hour of judgment. He said that He knew it not. And the inference made is, that if He knew it in any way at all, whether as divine or human, it was a contradiction for Him to say that He knew it not. Two things may be suggested here. (1) What if He did not know, as He then was in his state not only of humanity but of humiliation—does this invalidate in the least the evidence of his divine nature? What if his assumption of human nature made it impossible for Him to exercise his divine prerogatives, what if his human body did not and could not permit Him to be at the same time and at all times conscious of omnipotence and omniscience, deprived Him of the constant sense of divine bliss and perfections,—would this prove that they were not his, or would it only prove that when He came into the flesh, He submitted to all the conditions of the flesh?[1] There are states of the human body in which we cannot and do not exercise the powers and knowledge which we undeniably possess. Is it said that an undying consciousness of perfect power, knowledge, and happiness is the prerogative of divinity?—it is granted—but that does not prove that it is essential to divinity, when divinity is united to humanity. So thought and feeling are essential to the idea of spirit, but there is little thought in an infant, and often no thought at all in sleep. It is said that here there is something which no one can understand? That is granted: it is a mystery, but a mystery is not a contradiction. And all that the objection really amounts to is this: that we do not know the exact conditions upon which the divine and human natures may be united. And what the objection asserts is, that there must have been at every instant in the soul of Christ here upon the earth an equal consciousness of his divine attributes and of his human acts. But this assertion is totally without proof: it is an assumption: it is a conclusion which we deny to be legitimate from the doctrine of the two natures; because we can really conceive that it was, if we cannot prove that it must have been, otherwise.

(2) But there is a second consideration, which is this: A contradiction cannot be made out even on the supposition that Christ did know of the day as God, and was ignorant of it as a

---

[1] [This suggestion is drawn from a source which was not included in the author's lectures on theology. In these lectures he rejects the entire doctrine of Kenosis. Perhaps, if he had revised what is given above, he would have made some modifications.]

man. A contradiction can be established only when it is affirmed that in the same state of mind, He both knew it and did not know it. But if his mind existed in successive states—and if He was a man, it could not be otherwise—one state may have been that of the predominance of the human, and another state that of the predominance of the divine nature: one state may have been that in which the future was hidden, and another state that in which the future was clear: one state may have been that in which He spoke to his disciples, and another that in which He had held direct intercourse with the Father. And the full expression of his state of soul at that moment, when the weakness and ignorance of humanity predominated, may have been—of that day and hour knoweth no man, no, not the Son, but the Father only. Perhaps the very attempt to analyze the consciousness of Christ demonstrates that the task is beyond our powers: the only reason for attempting it is to show that no such contradiction can be proved to exist as would destroy all possibility of proving the existence of a complex nature in our Saviour.

We cannot dismiss this objection without remarking that in the highest point of view, so far from being an objection to, it may even become an argument for, our faith. The highest truths are those which reconcile the greatest contradictions. The best system is not one made up of one idea. Wherever we look we find apparent contradictions, but real harmony. In all great doctrines there is something which to the superficial view seems contradictory. A comprehensive theology combines these opposite elements, and tries to show their consistency. Even where we cannot understand how opposite truths can co-exist, we cannot deny but that they have an equal claim to existence and assent. Predestination is not really, though it may be seemingly, inconsistent with free will. A system which denies the divine purposes is a system without a God, a system which denies free agency is a system without a man. Even in our own minds there is something of the same sort. Nothing is so free, nothing is so constraining as love. We find our highest freedom in our most perfect submission. The power of law is greatest in the freest countries. Calvinists have been most zealous for political and religious liberty. We cannot understand our own acts without bringing in a divine agency. When God acts in the world He employs a secondary agency. We cannot understand history unless we combine a knowledge of the deeds of man and of the providence of God. Even sin itself must be brought into a direct relation with the divine purposes, and has been the occasion of the highest manifestation of divine love.

Perhaps, if our philosophy could reach so high, we should see that when sin had separated between God and man, when divinity and humanity had been sundered, not only by a difference in nature but also in character, it was impossible for a reunion to be effected by any other person than a God-man. That this was absolutely necessary, it were presumption to assert: it were greater presumption to deny that it was necessary. That such a Person alone fitted Him for such a work, we dare not say: that He is eminently fitted for this work, we can even see, and that there is a greater harmony between such a work and such a person than between such a work and any other person whom we can conceive to exist. We *may* venture to affirm: the God-man, by his two-fold nature, was better fitted to make an atonement, than God alone, than man alone, than any angel or archangel, or than any of the seraphic or cherubic host, or than all the hosts of heaven combined.

How deeply the doctrine of the Incarnation is involved in the whole Christian system is evident from the fact that the denial of this doctrine leads to the denial, one after one, of all the distinguishing doctrines of the Christian faith. A system without this doctrine ceases to urge the doctrines of grace. It loses its hold on the strongest feelings of the conscience and of the heart. It relapses into the commonplaces of the most meagre divinity. It refuses to grapple with the great questions of theology. It praises the moral virtues: it wonders at all zeal. It has lost the feeling of the constant presence of that Captain of our Salvation, who has inspired the faith, quickened the ardor, aroused the intellect, and led forth the hosts of Christendom. "Its relation to Christ," as has been well said, "is a past, a dead relation," and so they eulogize him as they do a hero, and venerate him as they do a saint; but such eulogy and such veneration are faint and heartless when compared with the living energy of the faith of Paul, or with the devoted love and absorbing contemplation of the beloved disciple who ever spake and lived as in the presence of a living Lord. As a matter of fact it is true, that the greatest earnestness, the loftiest faith, the deepest religious experience, the most heavenly spirituality, the most profound systems of theology, the most awful sense of God's majesty, and the most affectionate reliance upon his love have been found in connection with the belief in an Incarnate God. And surely if anything can arouse all our powers, awaken our intensest love, make us self-sacrificing, fill us with the holiest zeal and the purest enthusiasm, and satisfy perfectly all our wants, it is living faith in such a Lord, who is not only a Lord, but a brother also: in whom all that we can venerate as divine and all that we can love as human are combined in perfect harmony.

CHAPTER V.

THE ENTIRE RESULT AS TO THE PERSON OF OUR LORD.

The Statement. In Him the two natures were united in one Person. *The Analysis.* (*a.*) The natures are to be distinguished. (*b.*) The natures are to be connected. We are to consider Christ not only as having the two natures, but as having them in entire union. (*c.*) Each nature remains perfect in the union: The Godhead is perfect, the manhood is perfect. (*d.*) The union between them is perfect. (*e.*) The Godhead is that of the Second Person in the Trinity: the manhood consists of a body and a reasonable soul. The Godhead existed from all eternity, consubstantial with the Father: the manhood was assumed in the body of the virgin Mary. (*f.*) Thus, the two natures, united, constitute the One Person of Christ.

Observations.

1. We are driven to the position of the One Person in our Saviour in the same way as to the recognition of the two natures. The Bible always speaks of Jesus Christ as the same identical subject—whether in his primeval state, or in his earthly manifestation, or in his future glory. He who lived on earth as a man was the same being that existed in the bosom of the Father before the world was; and He who came forth from heaven is the one who also ascended to heaven: He who left the eternal glory for a season, entered into it again for eternity. There is one person, and one only, yet in wholly different states, presented to us in the volume of our Faith.

And if He was the same Person when in the world, that He was before He came into the world, this necessarily leads to the conclusion that it was the Eternal Word that constituted the Person—that it was He who was, so to speak, the formative principle, it was He who formed and actuated and gave its personal character to this new combination. He is the same person in the world, as before He came into the world. It is the One Person of the Logos in whom the two natures co-exist. If He existed before He came into the world, when He came, He did not part with what He was: He only assumed what he had not before. He took to himself another nature. The Eternal Word was not changed into a man—but He was found in fashion as a man—which of course implies that his fashion as a man was not all of himself.

2. There was no change in the character of either nature. The divinity remained entire, the humanity remained entire. The humanity, as is most clearly seen from many utterances of Scripture, had the soul as well as the body. The body of man is the smallest part of man. Christ's connection with the race would indeed have been superficial, were He like them only in outward form, but not in the passions and affections of the soul. All that we are required to abstract from our total conception of man, in order to have a just and consistent view of the God-man, is a merely human personality. The personal element or character was given to the God-man by the Eternal

Word. But the *whole* nature of man was taken up into this union—not excluding even the Will, if we take that in as indefinite a sense as it was taken by the Council which decided that in Christ there were two wills—or energies.[1]

3. The union thus effected must also be conceived of as real, substantial, and permanent—like to nothing else, yet most like among things we know of, to the union between soul and body. There are different kinds of union. There is a mechanical union, as when two distinct things are brought into external relations. There is a magical union—existing only in imagination. There is a union by absorption, as when one substance passes over wholly into another substance. There is a chemical union, as when out of two substances a third different from either is formed. There is a natural union, as we may call that between our souls and our bodies. There is a union between God and man, as when his Spirit dwells in man: and this may be of two kinds—extraordinary, as in his prophets and chosen messengers, where knowledge and power were supernaturally communicated —or, ordinary, in the operations of his Spirit in the souls of believers. But the union of the two natures in Christ was not mechanical, for their relations were not external,—the natures were not kept separate, as Nestorianism asserted; nor was it magical, as if by some arbitrary assertion of power or some miraculous transformation, as Cyril asserted; it was not natural, as if occurring in the usual course of things; nor unnatural, as if a prodigy were produced; it was not effected, as some pretend, only when the Spirit descended upon Him at his baptism, but began with the beginning of his human existence; it was not like that in the prophets and inspired men, for this was temporary and "came and went"; nor was it like the union between the believer and God's Spirit, for this does not impart divinity, but only divine aid and grace. But this wonderful union, so far as we can describe it positively and not merely negatively, was real, was supernatural, and remains eternal. It is like to nothing else in the heavens or on the earth, yet it may be im-

---

[1] That same Council was careful to assert that the human will was always subordinate to the divine in all the acts of this complex person.

aged by a union of the heavens and the earth. It is not like to anything we can conceive of God in his infinite and independent existence, nor of man, in his purely human nature—but it is a wondrous harmony and combination of the two, such as may well fill our souls with adoring love!

It is like nothing else we know of, yet is most like the union between soul and body. For, as in the union of soul and body, neither loses its distinctive character and both conspire to the same ends and form one person, and each part is developed in perfect harmony and fitness with the other, the body not limiting the soul's thoughts and affections, and the soul not acting—in a healthful state—with such intensity as to mar even the most delicate and sensitive of the nerves with which it comes in contact; as the one is attempered to the other in most perfect fitness, so that the soul does not unfold its powers too rapidly for the body to bear their intense activity, and so unfolds them as to heighten and enliven the material organization in which it is enveloped:—so, we may without irreverence and without detriment conceive it to have been in the Person of Jesus Christ.

4. Combining together the whole of the Scriptural representations, we may, perhaps, go one step further in this analogy, and say, that as in the soul and body there is a process of *development*, so in a limited sense it may be asserted in respect to the Person of our Lord, that the union was complete at the beginning, yet there was a process constantly going on before the perfect divinity was united to the perfected humanity, and so much only of the divinity was imparted at each stage as was necessary for Christ's mission at that particular stage. There may be a difficulty here, lest we seem to infringe upon the divinity; but there is also another difficulty, lest we represent Christ differently from the view given of Him in the Scriptures.

We are warranted, it would appear, in distinguishing three distinct states of being of our Lord: his primeval glory, his state upon earth as a man, his present glorified condition. In the second of these states, by becoming united to human nature, He put Himself under another law, under the law which regulates the development of human nature. He came into a condition of humiliation and ignorance, and infirmity and suffering. It was indeed the Eternal Word, the equal of God the Father, who came into this state, but yet it is equally true, that into this state He did come, and submit Himself to the change. There is indeed a mystery here, and so we might be content to leave it: but the mystery may be one of two things, and there may be a choice between them. Either,—that as a child, a youth, a man, He was all the time conscious of being also an infinite, omnipotent, and omniscient being, and so united in Himself a double consciousness; or, on the other hand—the mystery may be this: how an omnipotent and omniscient being could for a time part with the constant exercise and conscious possession of his divine attributes, and resume them in their fulness only after his humiliation was completed. Between these two forms of stating the mystery it has always been held allowable to make one's choice, and neither of them impairs either the divinity or the humanity, or the union between them.

There is a difficulty in understanding how a being who is really divine could part with the exercise of any divine attribute, could denude Himself of omnipotence and omniscience.[1] This may be impossible, yet our ignorance might[2] prevent us from denying its possibility. We may perhaps say, that his divine nature was put under the law of human development, was exercised more and more in its growth and progress as it was needed —upheld Him oftentimes—often gleamed through in transient rays of brightness—was remembered rather than directly exercised—was sometimes increased in its power, as when the Spirit descended upon Him at his baptism—and was expected by him-

---

[1] [This difficulty seems to have been more deeply felt by the author as he considered it in the later years of his theological teaching. He pronounces emphatically against every form of Kenosis. Yet what is given above is, so far as can be found, nowhere retracted.]

[2] [It ought to be said, that these paragraphs form no part of the author's mature theological system. It is thought that readers will have an interest in seeing what turn his speculation took on this point. Moreover, what follows is perhaps the only sketch we have from him to indicate how he would have written a "Life of Christ." It can only be said that the view which follows was neither sanctioned nor repudiated in any later utterances.]

self to be finally and perfectly resumed, only after the travail of his soul had been fully experienced, only after He had triumphed over death, hell, and the grave, and through his humiliation and sufferings purchased our redemption—through his mediatorial cross come to his mediatorial crown. Most certainly this much may be averred—that his divinity was not so fully *manifested* as to be recognized and believed in until the very close of his earthly career. His disciples did not worship Him until they saw Him ascending to the Heavens. However it may have been in his own soul, whatever may have been the state of his consciousness (and it is perhaps impossible for us to get any clear conception of what this really was)—it still remains on the face of the record of his life, that the divine nature was not in any degree so united with the human, did not so affect it as to prevent the God-man from being hungry and weary and weak, from bearing all our infirmities, from suffering the intensest sorrow, from asserting his ignorance, from growing in knowledge, from undergoing real and not apparent death. And all this, too, after the union had taken place: for the union occurred with the commencement of the human existence. As a union, it was then perfect and entire, although there was a process of growth on the part of the human being, and a gradual imparting of the resources of divinity, according to the progressive power of the humanity to endure them.

When we compare the Evangelists with the Epistles, we find confirmation of this view. Considered historically, as of an historical personage, we cannot fail to see how the representation runs much as though a human being were advanced, through successive stages, even to divine honor and glory. And the corrective to any idea as though a man were deified is found in the constant assertion of his pre-existent state, as the Eternal Word, the Creator of all things. Here is the efficient cause and the only source of the divinity which was ascribed to Him. Unless He had been divine by nature, He could not have become so by any sufferings as a man, or even by any gift of God to a creature.

But when He assumed our nature He submitted to all its

conditions. When his divinity entered into its alliance with humanity, it became conformed to its unparalleled condition. Gentle must have been the contact between the Eternal Word and the infant child, feeble the assimilation between such a glorious being and such a frail tabernacle. He assumed, yet consumed not, our nature. Flesh and blood could not abide the full pressure and intense effulgence of the undimmed brightness of the Son of God It was a part of the lowly estate which our Redeemer chose that He should become a very child, an infant in the weakness of its powers, an infant whom its mortal mother might press to her bosom, and love with a most motherly though most hallowed affection. The Eternal Word became a child without speech, who was yet to learn to call Mary, blessed among women, by the name of *mother*, who had yet to learn to speak the language of men, though He had through eternity spoken face to face with God the Father as his co-equal Son.

And under the care of this loving mother and of his Eternal Father, Jesus grew to man's estate, distinguished, we may well believe, for every human excellence, yet not manifesting his divine glory, except as a perfect youth and man is all that even God could be when He became man. He felt the greatness of his work; He knew his mission—what it was—yet entered not upon it—his divine nature fitted not his human nature to enter upon it until he reached the years in which the maturity of manhood has begun—when the body combines freshness and strength, and has by nature the matured harmony and unison of its powers. Then it was that the Spirit of God descended upon Him; that his miraculous powers were exerted; that He spake as one having authority; that He began to unfold truth after truth to his chosen followers, leading them gradually on, step after step, through the recognition of his mediatorship, to a knowledge of his divinity. Then it was that by a word and a look He exercised such gentle and constraining influence upon all with whom He lived. We may well believe that there was that in Him which awed the vicious, and which attracted those who were seeking after the kingdom of heaven; that a mild yet powerful influence went out from Him to the hearts of all susceptible of such impressions. Almost might we echo the words of the most eloquent orator of the Oriental church, "that the heavenly Father poured upon Him in full streams that corporeal grace, which is distilled drop by drop upon mortal man." But yet, even among his nearest disciples, He was known only as a perfect man. They were slow to discern his divinity. Sometimes it seems to break through the veil, like a hardly suppressed fire, like a light flashing in the darkness,—but it is only in broken words, in sentences that sounded enigmatical, which were best preserved and most fondly pondered by his beloved disciple. And He ever seems to speak of his divine glory as something He remembered, or as something He was still to attain unto, rather than as an object of present and conscious possession. Once, and only once, did it break through the veil of his flesh and irradiate Him wholly—when He was transfigured before the gaze of three of his disciples, and a supernatural brightness environed Him. But at other times few, if any, with whom He came in contact were led to say that He was divine, unless indeed they might infer that none but a divine being could be such a perfect man in the midst of a sinful world. And as Jesus Christ comes ever nearer to the termination of his earthly mission, He seems on the one hand to have had a constantly increasing sense of his intimate fellowship with God, yet on the other to feel more and more the burden which He must bear all alone. In proportion to his necessities must the resources of his divine nature have been developed—to sustain Him—but, though thus sustained, the agony He endured was beyond all expression. Through suffering was He to be perfected; by passing through death was his humanity to be perfectly united with his divinity: this was the struggle that awaited Him—this the terrific conflict through which He passed, and when He had passed through it, then was the union between them perfected. It is after his resurrection that his disciples seem to have come to a believing acknowledgment that He was divine. It was when He led them forth at early morning, and gave to them his last words and vanished from their sight, his hands extended over them in a parting benediction, that they knelt down and worshipped

Him. The sense and full perception of His divinity had now taken possession of their hearts. He led them on, step by step; his nature was unfolded to them, degree by degree, until the most incredulous no longer doubted, until they were brought to address to Him their prayers, and look to Him for present and constant aid. They remember Him as a man, they refuse not to call Him God. And while in the Evangelists, who tell the story of his earthly career, the humanity is most apparent, and the divine nature rather hinted at than disclosed; in the Epistles, it is the reverse: there He appears in glory and blessedness, as the Mediator between God and man, as the Head of the church, as the Life of the believer, as the object of direct faith, as the Being in whom all things in heaven and on the earth are brought together and united. There he appears—and is revealed to us—as sitting at the right hand of the Father, as worshipped by angels, as the giver of eternal life, as the Lord of all. There He appears, still having in inseparable union his divinity and his humanity, still the Being in whom all of God and all of man are combined in perfect union, but in whom human nature has become perfected and glorified; in whom the human nature, in its glorified state, is no hindrance to the perfect manifestation of all his divine attributes. No longer, as when He walked the earth, is it a veil to hidden glories: it is a transparent medium by which the glories are attempered to the gaze of those who cannot bear the full splendor of unmitigated divinity. Thus we are permitted to represent Him to us—still a man, ever divine. In Him is the perfect union of all that is divine and all that is human. All things in heaven and all on earth are concentrated in Him. He the center and the sun: there is no need of the light of the sun, for He is the light of the heavenly places as He was the light of this our darkened earth; He who was the central object in earth's history, the source of earth's redemption, is also the center of heaven's glory, and the source of such blessedness as only the redeemed can know.

PART III.

THE WORK OF THE MEDIATOR.

CHAPTER I.

PRELIMINARY STATEMENTS.

§ 1. *The General Object of Christ's coming.*

The Scriptures declare that Jesus Christ appeared in the last great dispensation to put away sin; by the sacrifice which He made for its expiation.[1] This was the great end and purpose of the manifestation of Christ in the flesh. This is the culminating point of the Incarnation. The Son of God assumed our nature that He might bear our sins. Other purposes might be and were answered by his appearing: He may have come to give us the model of a perfect man for our daily imitation; He may thus have manifested the moral attributes of God more clearly to man than they could otherwise have been exhibited; He may have thus presented to our adoring love the perfect union of divinity and humanity in one wondrous Person; but the chief reason why He was apparelled in the flesh and dwelt here upon the earth was that He might suffer and die for our redemption. To this the prophets give witness; and evangelists and apostles conspire in representing this as the one great end of the Incarnation. The Prince of glory came to be humbled; the Son of God came to be dishonored; the Lord of life came to be slain. He lived his sinless life, and so was as a Lamb without spot and blemish prepared for the altar; He revealed God to us more perfectly, but chiefly as a God who had determined to manifest, in the saving of a lost world, the highest of his attributes in their harmonious action; He united in himself the two natures, so that the awful dignity of his Person might

---

[1] See especially Heb. ix. 26.

give its full efficacy and value to the work of atonement which He wrought out.

§ 2. *Munus Triplex.* *Christ's Offices as Prophet, Priest, and King.*
I.—Idea of this mode of representing his offices as Mediator. *Office* is, all that one is and does in a legitimate public relation; *Function*: the chief or any special object in a public office. Christ's office as Mediator embraces all that He was and did in his public relations as Mediator between God and man.

The idea of the Three-fold Office: The whole work of Christ is the Redemption of a sinful world: prefaced by instruction (Prophet), effected by atonement (Priest), carried to completion in the course and consummation of his kingdom (King).

II.—History of this mode of representation.

The Jewish Rabbins and Cabbalists ascribed to the Messiah a three-fold dignity: "the crown of the Law, the crown of the Priesthood, and the crown of the Kingdom."[1]

Three passages in the Old Testament are guiding lights: Deut. xviii. 15; Ps. cx. 4; Zech. vi. 13.[2]

The church historian, Eusebius, speaks of it as a common view in the early part of the fourth century.[3]

It is referred to by Chrysostom and Theodoretus: less frequently employed by the Scholastics, it was used by Calvin in his Institutes,[4] and has entered into the current catechisms[5] and common modes of thought of the Reformed churches.

The German rationalists gave it up as tropical.

Later Germans have readopted it. Schleiermacher, Nitzsch, Hase, Rothe, Julius Müller, all approve it.[6]

III.—Reasons for retaining it.

1. It must be conceded to have strong claims on the score of giving a living impression of Christ's whole work, in a form

---

[1] Schœttgen, Horæ Heb. et Talm., Dresden, 1742, ii. 107, 228.
[2] Or, Ps. lxxii. 8.   [3] H. E., i. 3.   [4] Lib. ii. chap. xv.
[5] Geneva Cat. (1545), Heidelb. (1562), Westm. Assembly's, Ques. 23, Shorter Cat.—Even Racov. Cat. has it.
[6] Ebrard, Herz. Encycl., Jes. Christi. dreifaches Amt.—Martensen, Dogmatik, p. 332, has some admirable statements.—Krummacher, Prophetenthum, u. s. w., Deutsche Ztschft., 1856.—Diestel, Jahrb. f. d. Theol., 1862.

at once adapted to popular use and sufficiently comprehensive. It calls up vivid images of the whole of the Mediator's functions. We seem to see Him as the Great Teacher, imparting words of heavenly truth; as the High Priest, suffering upon the cross; and as our Prince and King, ruling in divine majesty.

2. But we are disposed to go still further in urging the claims of these ancient symbols of the wisdom, sacrifice, and power of our Redeemer. They are valid not merely in figure, but also in fact. The real Mediator must be all these: Prophet, Priest, and King; He could not be a full Mediator unless He bore these three offices; by them all his work is defined; in them all his work is comprehended.

3. To illustrate the sense and need of these three offices, we may refer to the fact that among the most developed, cultivated nations, both before and since Christ's advent, we find them in existence. No mighty people is known in which there are not classes of teachers, priests, and rulers. The instinct of human nature, in relation to its highest wants, seems to demand this three-fold form of the highest functions. Even in the midst of all the sinfulness and degradation of heathenism, there is this prophetic and typical imaging forth of the grand characteristics of the Messiah. They must have prophets to teach and to foretell, though their words were double-tongued; they must have priests to minister at the bloody altars, though no real expiation followed the sacrifice; and in the mighty despotisms of Babylon, of Assyria, of Egypt, in Alexander's power and Cæsar's sway, the regal authority reached its height of worldly pre-eminence. These three, and only these three, are found throughout heathenism, as the highest forms of official rank. They point, in symbol, to the great offices of the Messiah.

4. As among the heathen, so also among the people of God, his chosen race, we find the same three offices, yet in a higher and purer form. The whole of the Old Testament is a preparation for the New, its divine type, its historical root; and in the whole of the Old Testament are the institutions of prophecy, priesthood, and royal dominion, divinely established and set forth. The glory of the Israelites was in these three offices. Abraham was taught,

and did himself teach, the name of Jehovah; as a priest he entered into covenant with God; and as a prince he ruled his patriarchal house. The whole history of the Israelites centers into these three words: Moses and the prophets; Aaron and the priesthood; David and the royal house. Here were the grand institutes of the theocracy. For a thousand years, inspired prophets were commissioned to teach, to rebuke, to encourage, to warn, in the name of the Lord. In the most degenerate times of Israel they spake with the greatest boldness; in its lordliest periods they held up visions of brighter days to come. A whole tribe was set apart to the office of the priesthood: the shadow and symbol of the Great High Priest. Kings, also, Saul, David, and Solomon, ruled in majesty, yet were only types of one who was to come of the stock of David. The history of the Jewish people, in short, can only be understood in the light of the three words: Prophet, Priest, and King.

5. The wide bearings of this three-fold office are further seen in the fact that the Messiah promised to the Jews from the beginning was foretold under the same grand imagery. As the Anointed One, He was to be clothed with these three offices and none other: He was to be anointed to preach the Gospel to the poor;[1] as King, He was to be anointed with the oil of gladness above his fellows;[2] his priesthood was to be through an unction from above,[3] not after the law of a carnal commandment, but after the power of an endless life. The whole of the last part of the prophecy of Isaiah represents Christ as the servant of God, who was to teach, to suffer and die, and to rule at last in majesty. Not David, but his root and offspring, was to sit upon the throne in universal dominion.[4] He was to be a priest forever after the order of Melchisedec. He was to bear our griefs; He was to be led as a lamb to the slaughter. He was to teach all nations: to bring in everlasting righteousness; and of the increase of His government there was to be no end. The heathen were to be his inheritance: from sea to sea, from the river to the uttermost parts of the earth, was to be his do-

---

[1] Luke iv. 18.
[2] Heb. i. 8; Ps. xlv; Isa. lxi. 1.
[3] Heb. v. 4, 5; vii. 16, 17.
[4] 2 Sam. vii.

minion. In such exalted strains did the prophetic word depict the coming glories of the Messiah, and the sum of all this is: Prophet, Priest, and King.

6. In the New Testament, also, we find complete warrant for this three-fold view of the offices of the Mediator. The testimony here becomes, if possible, more full and distinctive. The three offices, separated among the Jews, are united in One Person. The carnal Jewish mind expected only a temporal prince attended with the pomp of earthly magnificence; but their true king, anointed of old, came first in lowly garb, appeared as a simple teacher, suffered indignity and death—yet showed his regal power by conquering death. He disappointed every earthly hope, and fulfilled every divine prediction. (*a.*) He was a prophet, acknowledged as such;[1] He spake as never man spake; He foretold his own death, the destruction of Jerusalem, the victories of his kingdom; He reveals God; He is the very Word of God; He is at once the living Law and the living Gospel: the Law appears in Him as an example, and the Gospel as the truth. His words are life; they are never to pass away. Never was the law spoken in such purity, never was grace declared with such fulness. He speaks in the name of God; He knows and teaches all the divine will. He reveals new truths; the new and perfect revelation has come to the world in his teachings. He declares the future; the vision of the whole course of things is drawn by Him in bold outlines. His words abide ever true and powerful; they are sources of undying life and joy. (*b.*) That the New Testament also describes the Mediator as priest, the Great High Priest—*priest and sacrifice in one*—the only true priest, the only real sacrifice, we do not stay to argue here. He offered himself without spot, unto God, through the eternal Spirit. All other oblations are vain and ineffectual. The whole of the Epistle to the Hebrews is one grand proof, not only that Jesus Christ is High Priest and Sacrifice, but that He alone is such; all others are but types and shadows. (*c.*) And the same Epistle, too, connects his kingly with his priestly functions. We have such an high priest, who is set on

---

[1] Heb. i. 1; John iii. 2; Luke xxiv. 19.

the right hand of the throne of the majesty in the heavens. John, in the Apocalypse, sees the four and twenty elders cast their crowns before his throne. "Worthy is the Lamb that was slain" is the song of heaven, "to receive power—." His crown of thorns becomes an imperial diadem. He works the works of his Father; He declares to Pilate that He is a King; God highly exalted Him and gave Him a name that is above every name. All things are put under his feet; He is the Head over all things to the church.

Thus these three offices are ascribed to Christ in the New Testament as well as foretold in the Old. And our Lord himself, in that most wonderful high-priestly prayer (John xvii.), brings them all together; for He says, that He has manifested (as a Prophet) to his disciples the name of God: (as Priest) He intercedes for them in his bitter suffering and tender love: (as King) He claims them as his own, for He has kept them: ending, I declared unto them Thy name, and will declare it; that the love wherewith Thou lovedst me may be in them and I in them.

7. Other titles applied to Christ, *e. g.*, Head, Surety, Pastor, do not so distinctly designate different offices, and are not used with such constancy throughout all the Scriptures.[1]

8. There is an inherent propriety in having these, and only these three, as the offices of the Mediator. If man is to be fully redeemed, his Mediator must have these three functions and none others. For Redemption from sin must include these three things: it must give knowledge of God's plan in the way of revelation; it must provide an atonement for sin; and it must deliver from the power and consequences of sin, in an eternal kingdom. And these three points are the ones met, and precisely met, in the three offices of our Lord. As a prophet He reveals; as a priest He atones; as a king He subdues us unto himself.[2]

[1] See Note in Ridgeley's Divinity, i. p. 494.
[2] It might perhaps be also argued that these three offices correspond to the three great faculties of the human mind: to the intellect, the feelings, and the will. As Mediator between God and man, Christ must address and be adapted to the whole man. As a teacher, Christ addresses our intellect; as a sacrifice, He appeals to the deepest moral wants of the heart and conscience; and as a king, He guides and rules our wills, making them conform to his will.

9. The essential and almost organic quality of these three offices in the Christian system is shown in the fact that they are necessary to each other: just as much as intellect, heart, and will are necessary to each other as well as to man. To feel, one must know; and to will, one must both know and feel. Even so, Christ could not be a priest, unless He were a prophet; nor could He rule in a kingdom of redemption, unless He were also both prophet and priest. His teachings must prepare and guide his disciples to know the meaning of his atoning death; and his sacrificial death is the basis of his claim to our supreme love as our Head in his mediatorial kingdom.

10. It is only by viewing Christ in all these offices, that we can be saved from one-sided and partial notions of his work as a Redeemer. It is true, indeed, that He appears chiefly as a prophet during his life; chiefly as a priest in the agony of death; chiefly as king, when ascended to the right hand of the Father. But as a prophet, He teaches us even upon the cross, and still and ever, by his Spirit, though He dwells in heaven. His whole life as well as his death, was in his priestly character, suffering shame and humiliation. And He exercised his kingly functions while on earth, yea, in the very grave, conquering death and hell by his mighty power, as truly as He now subdues his other foes. And the grand error, among all who do not receive Christ in his fulness, is that they take one of his offices, as if that were the whole, neglecting the rest. They hold to Christ in one or another of his names, but not in the fulness of his character. Thus some take Christ only as the Teacher; others dwell most fondly on his atoning death; and others again view Him chiefly as the Lord of spiritual life. But He is each and all. And we do not know Him fully, nor truly, until we know Him in all his offices—as our Prophet to teach us—our Priest who atones—our King to rule over and in us.

CHAPTER II.

OF CHRIST'S WORK AS THE ONLY TRUE PRIEST. OF ATONEMENT AND THE NECESSITY FOR ATONEMENT.

The Priestly Office of Christ is that office in both natures whereby He makes an atonement. In the same priestly office and in virtue of his atoning work his Intercession is maintained. Intercession belongs to Christ as priest: it includes his constant application of his sacrifice; or, generally, all his agency in redeeming mankind, in his glorified state.[1] Of the two parts of Christ's work as Priest—Atonement and Intercession—we speak here only of *The Atonement*.

I.—Usage of the word, and of certain terms which cluster about it.

1. Of the terms Redemption and Atonement. Redemption implies the complete deliverance from the penalty, power, and all the consequences of sin: Atonement is used in the sense of the sacrificial work, whereby the redemption from the condemning power of the law was insured.

2. Of the terms Reconciliation and Atonement. Reconciliation sets forth what is to be done: Atonement, in its current theological sense, likewise involves the idea of the way, the mode, in which the reconciliation is effected—that is, by a sacrifice for sin.[2]

---

[1] This is treated by the author under the Third Division of Theology; as the priestly side of Christ's office as King.

[2] A writer who became prominent as a controversialist on this subject, wrote, some years ago: "Every tyro in theology knows or ought to know that atonement means nothing more than at-one-ment, that is, the reconciliation of opposing parties." But none but a tyro in theology knows that this is its only sense. Even admitting the correctness of this etymology, it must be said that this way of reducing the large import of language to the smallest possible dimensions, by means of etymology alone, and of deciding theological controversies by an appeal to the primitive sense of words before they had gained their full signification is one unworthy of the scholar and the theologian. All the etymology in the world would never be sufficient to show that atonement means only reconciliation—for the very plain reason, that for hundreds of years it has borne in the English language an additional sense, that is, it includes a designation of the mode in which the reconciliation was effected. (Atonement=reconciliation, in Sir Thos. More, Shake-

3. Of the terms Satisfaction, Vicarious, Expiation, Propitiation

(*a.*) Satisfaction. This is the most specific term, in reference to the relations between Christ's sufferings and the demands of the law upon sinners as *condemning* them: Christ satisfied, by his work, the demands of the divine law.—The word may be used in a wider sense: Christ satisfied also the divine love and all the divine perfections; but the *specific* sense is: He so satisfied the claims of the divine law, in respect to sinners, that these, through faith, are freed from its condemnation.

(*b.*) Vicarious. The term to designate substitution. Christ's sufferings were substituted for ours: He suffered in our stead: what He did is accepted as if we did it.—Here, too, there is a wider sense, in which "vicarious" is understood as meaning merely in our behalf, for our benefit. Socinians would make this the only sense. But specifically the word is used to set forth that Christ was a substitute, as sacrificial victims were.

(*c.*) Expiation. The act or means of atoning for a crime, so that in respect to the law its guilt is cancelled. The sense is: *removing guilt*, removing the *reatus:* not, the moral defilement, but the exposure and obligation to punishment. Expiation, used in relation to the criminal, "denotes that which is an adequate reason for exemption from penalty" (J. Pye Smith). An expiated offence does not demand punishment: the "guilt," *i. e.*, the obligation to suffer penalty, is removed.

(*d.*) Propitiation. This "relates to the ruler, and designates that which has the effect of causing Him to accept the expiating transaction." The offender is expiated, God is propitiated: not that any change in God's essential mercifulness is effected, but that his holiness no longer demands punishment.

4. Sacrifice. Here too we find the wider and the specific sense.[1] This most important term is reserved for another chapter.

II.—Of the Necessity of the Atonement.

The necessity of the atonement (not a natural, physical, or metaphysical necessity) is affirmed most specifically in opposition

speare, Beaumont and Fletcher, Bps. Hall and Taylor; =expiation, in Milton, Swift, and Cowper. Waterland (Disc. of Fundamentals, v. p. 82):—"the doctrine of expiation, atonement, or satisfaction, made by Christ in his blood.")

[1] "The Scriptural Idea of Sacrifice," by Alfred Cave.

to two views: (*a.*) that mere mercy on God's part, and (*b.*) mere repentance on man's, suffices to meet all the exigencies of the case.

1. The necessity may be argued on rational grounds.

(*a.*) God is holy, man is sinful: man's sin is the opposite of the divine holiness: to bring God and man together, some satisfaction to the divine holiness is needed.

(*b.*) Another form: Sin deserves condemnation: that it may be pardoned, there is needed some mode of removing the condemnation, of taking away the guilt of the transgressor.

This mode cannot be the repentance and reformation of the sinner alone: for (1) if he could become holy, his guilt and desert of condemnation would remain; (2) in order to his becoming holy, or returning to God, a knowledge of God's righteous favor or holy mercifulness is requisite. The mode cannot be that of mere forgiveness: for this would satisfy neither the claims of the divine holiness nor the necessities of a moral government. It would show that the law was not law—moral law—but only a sequence.[1]

Hence, on rational grounds, presupposing God's holiness and man's sin, there is need of some other way—need of an atonement for sin.

2. This necessity may be argued on the grounds of man's moral nature: an atonement is eminently adapted to man's convictions and needs as a moral being.

(*a.*) Man's conscience assures him of the supremacy, the absolute supremacy, of righteousness—of holiness, and not of mere happiness—of that holiness which *is* the highest happiness. This conviction is not responded to by the mere forgiveness of the sinner. If happiness were the greatest good, then a forgiveness insuring happiness would meet all of man's wants. But if holiness be the chief good, then, in the pardon of sin, God must appear as holy, righteous, answering the highest ends of his moral government—in order to meet our highest wants.

---

[1] "Mercy is not itself, that oft looks so;
Pardon is still the nurse of second woe."
Measure for Measure, Act II.; Scene I.

(*b.*) Man's conscience leads Him to feel the necessity, under a moral government, of punishment or a *moral* equivalent; not always the necessity of the punishment of the offender, but always the necessity of that or a substitute which will answer the same moral end.

(*c.*) The satisfaction of man's moral nature in an atoning sacrifice proves the fitness of it to his moral wants.

3. The nature of the divine law proves the necessity of an atonement—of a sacrifice for sin.

(*a.*) Law implies, necessarily, sanctions, the punishment of transgressors, or an equivalent, under it. A law without a penalty is no law. Penalty is not the final end of law, but it is a means to that end. Hence there must be for transgression either penalty or what answers the same end—which end is the maintenance of holiness in all its glory. Hence, law from its very nature demands something which will answer this end as well as would the specific punishment of the transgressor. Christ said, "One jot or one tittle shall in no wise pass from the law." He magnified the law in his teachings and death. Mere pardon virtually annuls the law—sets it aside—declares it needless—says: no law.

b. Another form. Sin always deserves, merits punishment. The inflicting of this is, the distributive justice of God: rendering to every man according to his deeds. Holiness, or public justice, demands this or an equivalent, and an equivalent is that which will equally satisfy holiness or general justice. An equivalent cannot be something of a totally different nature, looking to a totally different end, providing for happiness in stead of holiness.

4. The necessity of an atonement is seen in the fact that it has actually been made.

(*a.*) If such a sacrifice had not been necessary, it would not have been made.

(*b.*) The necessity is directly asserted in Scripture: Mark viii. 31; Luke xxiv. 46; John iii. 14, 15; Acts xvii. 2, 3; Heb. viii. 3; ix. 22.

5. An argument for the necessity of the atonement may also

be derived from the general consent of mankind: everywhere there are systems of sacrifices.

The prevalence of sacrifices for sins is one of the most wonderful facts in the moral history of mankind. It is an article of natural religion more universally held than the unity of God or even than immortality. This universality proves the following points, as the moral conviction of mankind: (*a.*) That mere repentance is not enough, according to the *natural* conscience; (*b.*) That some expiation for sin is needed; (*c.*) That this must be effected by the offering up of sacrifice—in suffering and blood —instead of, to take the place of, the deserved punishment of the guilty.[1]

6. The grounds of this necessity, under God's moral government, stated in sum.

(*a.*) The ultimate ground of the necessity must be in God himself: there is that in the divine perfections which requires the atonement. What is it?

(*b.*) The object of the atonement is to reconcile sinful man with the holy God, under law; or, to remove the penalty from, and restore favor to, transgressors. Then the necessity must be this: God as a moral governor could not otherwise pardon and justify (=be reconciled).

(*c.*) Why could He not otherwise? Because the end which would have been answered by the punishment of the real culprit must be in some other way attained.

(*d.*) What is that end? Not the punishment of the culprit itself, for its own sake, as a good: but the punishment as a means of showing the divine abhorrence of sin and sustaining the honor of God and his law.

(*e.*) The atonement, then, has its necessity in this: that the divine holiness—justice (not distributive but general) could not otherwise be satisfied in the pardon of sinners.

---

[1] Cf. Bib. Sac. vol. i., p. 368 seq., von Lasaulx.—John Dav. Michaelis: "Almost all nations have been unanimous in the idea of bringing to the Deity offerings, particularly with the shedding of blood, as the means of obtaining pardon of sin and a restoration to favor. This awful idea, which is the almost universal impression of the human race, even seems to be a product of what the Romans call *sensus communis*—a natural dictate of the sound understanding of man."

(*f.*) An inquiry. Is the divine justice in the way of the pardon of sinners? (1) Justice is—distributive, commutative (not brought into consideration here), and public (or general). (2) If distributive justice be taken as the whole of justice, or as the great end of the system, and as requiring the punishment of the identical offender—his specific punishment, then justice would absolutely forbid pardon. There is no place for mercy. (3) But distributive justice is subordinate to general justice: it is for general justice. General justice demands that the honor of the law be maintained; that the fact that sin deserves suffering be made manifest; that the great end of the system—the manifestation of the divine glory chiefly as a supreme regard to holiness—should be attained. If this end be gained, then distributive justice is not in the way.[1]

CHAPTER III.

OF THE LEADING SCRIPTURAL REPRESENTATION OF THE ATONING WORK OF CHRIST—THAT IT IS A SACRIFICE.

Preliminary. Terms most frequently used in Scripture to describe Christ's work.

Redemption—as means of deliverance, and not as an accomplished work: Eph. i. 14.

Ransom: Matt. xx. 28; 1 Tim. ii. 6.

Purchase: Acts xx. 28; 1 Cor. vi. 20; vii. 23.

Offering: Heb. x. 14.

Propitiation: Rom. iii. 25; 1 John ii. 2.

Such expressions, figurative as to means, are *real as to re-*

---

[1] Upon the question, Is the divine veracity in threatening punishment, in the way of the pardon of sinners? Dr. Charles Hodge says: threatenings "are not what shall be, but what most justly may be."—This resolves itself really into the above. The divine veracity is pledged, not to strict distributive, but to complete general justice. "It was not only the divine mind that had to be dealt with, but also that expression of the divine mind which was contained in God's making death the wages of sin." Cave, Script. Doct. of Sacrifice, pp. 361, 362.

sults, that is, as to deliverance from the demands of law upon transgressors.

Proposition. The grand representation of the work of Christ is that it is a SACRIFICE—a sacrifice for sin—a sacrifice in our stead. This gives us not merely the result of the atoning work, but the means, viz.—by his death as a sacrifice for us.

To know the sense of Sacrifice, we must *go to history.* There alone do we get the ideas. The Scriptures also give us history; the facts which they set forth are part of what has occurred; the terms in which these facts are described have a proper historical sense; such terms are related more or less to the facts and views which stood within the general experience and knowledge of mankind. Hence, in order to deal fairly with this great subject, we must consult four sources. The questions are: What elements were involved in a sacrifice? and, What are the constituent elements of the sacrifice which Christ made? The sources from which these elements may be derived, from which—if we are to reason historically—they must be derived, are these: (1) The system of sacrifices prevalent in the Pagan world; (2) The system appointed for the Jewish worship; (3) The prophecies respecting the work our Saviour was to accomplish; and (4) The mode in which Christ's sufferings and death are everywhere spoken of in the New Testament. If all these different sources of evidence conspire in representing the same leading ideas, then it would be indeed presumptuous to deny the validity of these ideas, to deny that they are involved in the very notion of a sacrifice.

§ 1. *The System of Sacrifices prevalent in the Pagan World.*

The evidence derived from this source is preparatory and presumptive. The sacrifices of the heathen in the form which they always took, and in the reliance put upon them, were indeed an abomination. But if, as some hold, the origin of these heathen systems is to be traced to an original divine appointment, then even in their perversion and decay we may trace some vestiges of the divine original: or, if we do not trace them back to God, but suppose them to be prompted by the instinctive religious sentiments of mankind, when feeling its guilt and sinfulness, still they may be of importance in showing us what ideas the race have always held, as to the mode in which they might become acceptable to their offended deities.

The propriety of deriving an argument from this source may be still further evinced by the fact, that one reason why the gospel made such progress was, that by the systems already prevailing men were in a certain sense prepared for the prevalence of the Gospel. These false religions, in their corruption, were unable to satisfy men, and therefore they welcomed a new; but it is also true that some of the ideas which were at the foundation of their false systems were seen fully realized and purified in the religion of the gospel. They recognized the sacrifice of Christ as a true sacrifice, because they saw in it the perfect form of what they had so grotesquely mimicked and superstitiously believed in their own forms of worship. They were ready to receive a sacrifice for sin, because they had always believed in sacrifices for sin.[1]

Such being the state of things, the question now comes up, what were the leading ideas which these ancient nations always connected with the sacrifices they offered.

The basis of the sacrifice was the fact of their sinfulness. They lived under the constant sense of their being in a state of feud with their gods, and of the necessity of appeasing the wrath of those terrible beings who had the rule over them. The sacrifice was the means which they made use of, which they supposed effectual, in averting from them the wrath of their deities, and in procuring pardon and favor.

And the sacrifice which they offered for this object contained, and was designed to express, the following leading elements. In the first place, it was a *substitution* of the sufferings of one being

---

[1] It is noticeable that just those persons who are most ready to derive an argument from the *consent of nations* for the being of God or the soul's immortality are the ones who assert of the systems of sacrifice prevalent in all the world, that they are simply the product of superstition and priestcraft. To say this, however, is to avoid, and not to meet, a difficulty: for the question still remains, Why did superstition uniformly take *this* form; why was it that priests found the system of sacrifices the most effectual way of binding the hearts and consciences of the people?

for the sufferings due to another; in the second place, it was a substitution of the sufferings of a being comparatively *innocent* for one that was sinful; and in the third place, this substitution of the sufferings of the innocent, instead of the deserved sufferings of the guilty, was supposed to have the efficacy of making an *expiation*, an atonement to the gods for the sins committed—was supposed to be of such virtue that the deserved punishment might be averted.

No one at all acquainted with the horrible rites of heathenism, whether in ancient or modern times, will doubt the existence of all these elements in all their bloody sacrifices. And when we find in almost all the heathen nations not only the sacrifice of animals but of human victims also, in offering whom all natural feeling must have been suppressed, who can fail to see, even in this frantic excess of heathenism, that there must have been a mighty power which held them so entranced, that there was at the basis of the whole system an unconquerable conviction of the necessity and efficacy of sacrifices? However abhorrent such a conclusion may be to the so-called system of natural religion, yet in all the actual natural religions of the world we find a sacrifice for sin believed in and offered. It is not argued that these sacrifices were right or in any way acceptable, but it is argued that we may show from them what means were considered necessary to win the favor of the deities.

§ 2. *In the Old Testament, in the System of Sacrifices appointed for God's chosen People, we find the same Essential Elements as in the heathen Sacrifices.*

The Jews were to be a distinct people, and yet they retained the rites of heathenism. Well has it been said, that "Moses, zealous as he was to separate his people in all respects from Paganism, still retained those sacrifices which made the most prominent part of pagan worship." The very parts of the old dispensation, too, which were typical of the new, are to be found in the victims laid upon the altar. Here are the bloody sacrifices which give purification. They remind one of heathenism—they look forward to Christianity.

With this system of sacrifices, which had been divinely ordained, the Jews connected the same ideas which we have already found in Pagan systems. The sacrifice was *vicarious*. In the expiatory sacrifices, the animal was considered as having become unclean, and its remains were to be burned without the camp, and this, as is expressly declared,[1] because it was a sin-offering. When a man was slain, and it was not known who had committed the crime, a sacrifice must still be offered, and by the washing of the hands the guilt was transferred to the victim.[2] The idea of *innocence* or ceremonial purity was also involved in the whole transaction. The priests who offered it were not only a separate class, but they must be especially purified before they could present the offering. The animal offered must be without blemish. The paschal-offering was a lamb—the chosen symbol of innocence. But in these sacrifices was the third element—that of an *expiation* for sin—also contained? It was contained, yet symbolically and typically, rather than actually. The peculiarity of the Jewish system is just this, that it did not permit its votaries to rest in the rites themselves, but ever bade them look forward to the time of their Great High Priest. Expiation for sin *was* in these sacrifices, though only symbolically. The solemn rites of the yearly festival of expiation show this: for, while the goat that was killed was the sin-offering, by which the sin was represented as expiated, the sin was laid upon the other, the scape-goat, to make a visible yet symbolical manifestation of the taking away of the guilt. Equally applicable to the same point are the words which, it is supposed, contain the key to the whole system of Jewish sacrifices—the words addressed by Jehovah to Moses, Lev. xvii. 11: "For the life of the flesh is in the blood; and I have given it to you upon the altar to make an atonement for your souls: for the blood maketh an atonement for [or "by means of"] the soul." The idea of an expiation for sin could not be more fully expressed than in these words. In all the statutes by which atonement was to be made for sin, we find confirmation of the fact that Substitution—of the Innocent—in order to Expiation—are necessary elements of the religious

---

[1] Exod. xxix. 14. [2] Deut. xxi. 1-9.

faith of a people which had transgressed the law of God, and would become reconciled to Him. Under the whole of the Old Testament economy, sin was not forgiven except as its desert was exhibited, and its expiation insured, by means of a vicarious sacrifice.

§ 3. *Another Argument for the same Position is derived from the Old Testament Prophecies of Christ.*

A *distinct* argument is drawn from this source, for two reasons. (*a.*) The prophets often seem to speak against sacrifices, to reprobate the reliance placed upon them; but if they foretold another sacrifice, then they reprobated only the carnal reliance put upon those which but prefigured the true expiation. (*b.*) The prophets stand, as it were, in the transition stage between the law and the gospel. They spake of a perfect redemption which was to appear. And now if they represent the new dispensation which was to bring in an everlasting righteousness as containing the same essential elements with that which was to pass away, then they form, as it were, the second premise in the syllogism of which the law is the first, and the New Testament the conclusion. What the ceremonies and rites of the law expressed in symbols, that the prophets expressed in words; and both equally referred to Jesus Christ, who was the substance which the law foreshadowed and the visible fulfilment of the prophecies, and who thus fulfilled both the law and the prophets.

Language cannot express the elements which we have found to be contained in the very nature of a sacrifice more distinctly than we find them in Isa. liii., and to this, for the sake of distinctness and conciseness, we confine our illustrations. There is first the *vicarious* suffering: Surely He hath borne our griefs and carried our sorrows; He was wounded for our transgressions, He was bruised for our iniquities; the chastisement of our peace was upon Him, and with his stripes we are healed; all we like sheep have gone astray, and the Lord hath laid on Him the iniquity of us all; He bare the sin of many. There is the *innocence* of the sufferer: He was brought as a lamb to the slaughter, and as a sheep before her shearers is dumb, so He opened not his mouth; for the transgression of my people (not his own) was He stricken; He had done no violence, neither was any deceit in his mouth. And the sufferings of this innocent victim procured the *expiation* of the sins of his people: He shall see of the travail of his soul, and shall be satisfied; by his knowledge shall my righteous servant justify many; for He shall bear their iniquities; when thou shalt make his soul (or, when his soul shall make) an offering for sin, He shall see his seed, He shall prolong his days, and the pleasure of the Lord shall prosper in his hand. Thus spake prophets of the coming Redeemer. They described Him in terms taken from the sacrifices appointed under the law. They described Him as they would have described a victim offered upon the altar—only making the victim a mighty Saviour instead of an animal without blemish—only speaking of the substitution, the innocence, and the expiation as *real*, and not as merely symbolical or typical.

§ 4. *The New Testament Descriptions of the Sufferings and Death of Christ repeat the same Ideas, give us in more strict Form of Assertion the same Elements.*

We have seen what were the religious ideas prevailing throughout the world at the time that the Redeemer came— ideas in which Gentile as well as Jew participated. Everywhere men believed in the necessity and efficacy of sacrifices. Such was the preparation which God, in his providential government of the heathen nations, and in his special revelation to his chosen people, had made for the reception of his Son, when He should be sent in the fulness of times to gather together all things in one, and to draw all men unto himself. The sense of sin, the need of deliverance, the belief in a deliverance only through propitiatory sacrifices—these are the deepest religious feelings which we find impressed upon the whole ancient world—in these men all agreed. Every altar proclaimed them, every victim renewed them. Daily as were the sacrifices, so, every day these ideas were brought before men's minds, in the blood of dying victims, in the agonies of departing life.

A strange preparation this, for an economy which was to do away with and deny all these things, for a dispensation which, as some suppose, not only overturned the altars, but destroyed all the ideas connected with them. Whether it was so or not, remains to be considered. Whether the essential elements of the ancient religion were abrogated or confirmed in the religion which was to supersede all other forms of faith, we are now to inquire.

Did Christianity abolish, or did it confirm, the sentiments we have found existing as to the mode in which a fallen world could become reconciled to its God? Did it destroy the law and the prophets, or did it fulfil them? Did it take up the religious sentiments of the race and purify them, or did it introduce entirely new conceptions as to the way in which man was to be justified before God? Did it go to a Jew and say, All the ideas you have had as to the way of pardon must be entirely erased from your mind, and you must accept a scheme which in its essential features is wholly different from that which God gave your fathers by the prophets,—or did it present him with the perfect realization of what was at best but imperfectly exhibited in all the ceremonies of the law and the rites of the altar? Did it go to the heathen, and while it bade him quit his false gods and atrocious rites, also preach to him that he was to look for no sacrifice and quit all hope of a proper expiation, that he need do nothing but amend his life and trust in a mercy which accepted him without a propitiation? Did it, in presenting Jesus Christ as the way and the truth and the life, and his sufferings and death as the ground of acceptance, carefully abstain from all expressions which would recall the long-cherished views, both of heathen and Jew, as to the efficacy of sacrifices,—or did·it describe Christ and his death in such a way as involved all the elements which they believed to belong to a vicarious expiation? Did it alter in any essential particulars the views universally prevailing as to the nature of a sacrifice, on the ground of which deity was to be made propitious,—or did it describe the superiority of Christ's sacrifice as consisting precisely in this, that it perfectly realized all that it was believed a sacrifice must be and could effect, and that, therefore, all other sacrifices were vain and worthless?

To state the case, to one who is familiar with the mode in which the New Testament speaks of Christ, is almost to prove it. It is hardly an exaggeration, when a distinguished apologist for Christianity[1] asserts—"that Christ suffered and died as an atonement for the sins of the world is a doctrine so constantly infused through the New Testament that whoever will seriously peruse these writings and deny that it is there, may with as much reason and truth, after reading the works of Thucydides and Livy, assert that in them no mention is made of any facts in relation to the history of Greece and Rome."

Are the sufferings and death of Christ, then, represented as endured in the place of others, as a *substitution*, as vicarious? —What else can our Saviour mean when He says that He gave his life a ransom for many,[2] and that He lays down his life for the sheep[3]? What does Paul mean when he writes to the Galatians,[4] Christ hath redeemed us from the curse of the law, being made a curse for us? Why does the Epistle to the Hebrews declare that Christ was once offered to bear the sins of many?[5] Why does Peter preach Christ as the one who his own self bare our sins in his own body on the tree,[6] and also declare that Christ suffered for sins once, the just for the unjust?[7] (The words used, for, instead of, bearing the sin of others, and the like, express substitution, if any words can do it; and the variety of phrases, all of which concur in the same vicarious significancy, forbids us to suppose it was accidental. Had there been only one word or form of expression for it, it were easier to interpret it otherwise: but the variety of the forms of expression forbids such a violence.) Why are these and similar declarations respecting Christ's sufferings constantly introduced by the Apostles, when they addressed both Jew and Gentile, if they did not mean to teach them the necessity and efficacy of vicarious sufferings? If on this point their previous views had been

---

[1] Soame Jenyns. [2] Matt. xx. 28. [3] John x. 15.
[4] Gal. iii. 13. [5] Heb. ix. 28. [6] 1 Pet. ii. 24.
[7] 1 Pet. iii. 18.

erroneous, would such descriptions of the death of Christ have any other effect than to confirm them in their error?

The second element in the idea of a sacrifice is, the *innocence* of the victim: it must be the fairest of the herd, the gentlest of the flock. We are told that such an High Priest became us, who is holy, harmless, undefiled.[1] The Apostle Peter speaks of Him as a lamb without blemish and without spot.[2] And Paul concurs in this, when He asserts that God hath made Him to be sin for us, who knew no sin.[3] The attribute of blamelessness, which the sacrifice must have, was perfectly realized only in the Lamb of God. His alone was moral guiltlessness; and this was one reason why his alone was the acceptable sacrifice. An animal could only symbolize or typify; it could not possess that moral purity which was necessary in order that the sacrifice might be available and acceptable, might be a true expiation. And this is one of the points in which the sacrifice of Christ, and that alone, realized the full import of the word and the thing.

These vicarious sufferings of an innocent victim were designed to make *expiation* for sin—to make God propitious, and as a consequence to free man from the overburdening sense of guilt and fear of punishment: for both these particulars are involved in a real propitiation. And in this, in which resides the very vitality of a sacrifice, Christ's alone fulfilled the office. While it was ever held as essential to the idea of a sacrifice, yet it was never realized, whether on Pagan or Jewish altars. It was symbolized by the one, and both symbolized and typified by the other. With Christ came the reality, and this is what chiefly makes his to be the only, the real, the proper sacrifice, beside which none other may be named. Of all the offerings ever made his alone was accepted; others were available only as they spake of his. All others neither purchased the favor of God, nor brought true peace to man: Christ's did both, and was therefore an expiation for sin, in the only legitimate, and the most perfect sense of the words. The sacrifice of Christ, and that alone, satisfied God, and brought peace to the conscience.

[1] Heb. vii. 26.   [2] 1 Pet. i. 19.   [3] 1 Cor. v. 21.

—Testimony on these points crowds upon us—text after text, evangelists and apostles, eager to be heard, while they speak in exulting faith of Him, who hath washed us from our sins in his own blood;[1] in whom we have redemption through his blood, the forgiveness of sins;[2] whose blood cleanseth from all sin;[3] through whom God declares his righteousness in the passing over of sins;[4] in whom God was, reconciling the world unto himself.[5] The whole testimony is summed up in a wonderful passage, which connects the old and new economy, giving the chief defect of the old and superiority of the new, and which contains all the elements of a sacrifice and the whole virtue of an argument: For if the blood of bulls and goats, and the ashes of a heifer, sprinkling the unclean, sanctifieth to the purifying of the flesh; how much more shall the blood of Christ, who through the eternal Spirit offered himself without spot to God, purge your conscience from dead works to serve the living God?[6]

The conclusion to which we are irresistibly led from such passages as those we have cited—and the number of them might be greatly multiplied—can be nothing less than this: that the sufferings and death of Jesus are represented as containing all the elements of a sacrifice for sin, and are so spoken of in writings addressed to people who had always believed in the necessity and efficacy of sacrifice; and, consequently, that we must either give up in despair the chief canon for interpreting language aright, *i. e.*, the sense it would naturally carry to those to whom it was addressed, or we must admit that the Apostles meant to teach an expiation for sin, in the boldest sense of the words. To this dilemma we are reduced: either we cannot find out the meaning of Scripture, or it means to teach expiation; and consequently, either we believe it and receive the atonement, or, if we reject the atonement, we reject inspiration also. Archbishop Magee says:[7] "The atonement by the sacrifice of Christ was more strictly vicarious than that by the Mosaic sacrifices whereby it was typified." And the substance of this remark may be

---

[1] Rev. i. 5.   [2] Eph. i. 7.   [3] 1 John i. 7.
[4] Rom. iii. 25.   [5] 2 Cor. v. 19.   [6] Heb. ix. 13, 14.
[7] On the Atonement. No. LXXIII.

still further applied. All the elements which enter into the very nature of a sacrifice are represented as more fully exhibited in the death and sufferings of Jesus Christ, than they are found anywhere else. Instead of these elements being any of them weakened, they are all confirmed in strength and emphasis, when applied to the death of Jesus. The vicarious suffering was more strictly vicarious,—it was a more real substitution; the substitution of one moral being for another; the innocence of the sacrifice is in Him alone perfectly realized,—all others were at the best only physically blameless, He alone was morally pure; and as to the propitiation which was intended to be effected by means of a vicarious death, his alone effects that propitiation, his alone gives boldness of access to the very throne of the Eternal. We say, then, still further, that not only are we obliged to admit that Christ's death is a proper sacrifice, but that we are forced to confess that his is *the only* proper sacrifice, and that if no other had ever been known, if men had never heard of the propitiatory sufferings of the innocent for the guilty, yet they would have been obliged, if they received the Scriptures of the New Testament, to concede that it was there found and most distinctly expressed. If the points enumerated do indeed constitute the elements of a real sacrifice, then does Christ's death, and that alone, correspond thereto. Not only may it be so interpreted, but it must be so interpreted; not only does history lead us so to view it, but without history, though we knew of no heathen rites, though we had read of no Jewish altar, we must still confess that the sufferings and death of the Son of God were endured instead of ours; were endured by One wholly spotless; and were of such virtue that they purchased the remission of sins and purged the unclean conscience.[1]

§ 5. *Consideration of Objections.*

Obj. I.—Why may we not interpret all that is said about the sacrifice of Christ just as we should interpret the language when

---

[1] "And this I am sure," says Dr. South, "is spoke so plain and loud by the universal voice of the whole Book of God, that Scripture must be crucified as well as Christ, to give any other tolerable sense of it."

it is said that one man suffers for another, a mother for a child, a patriot for his country and such like—where all that we mean is, that by the suffering some outward good was attained, or some evil averted—some peril warded off? This would make the doctrine more intelligible, level to our present associations, analogous to what is daily seen in God's providence.

But what special temporal good *was* purchased by Christ for his followers: what special temporal evil did his death avert from them? None—absolutely none. Such an explanation, instead of making the Scriptural representations intelligible, makes them wholly unintelligible. The good He purchased was a spiritual good, a freedom from the condemnation for sin and the sense of guilt. Outward good might follow the inward; but the inward was first. The good He purchased for us had relation to human sin, and not chiefly to the evils which beset humanity. He was a propitiation for our sins, and not for ours only but also for the sins of the whole world. One man may die for another man: but how can the death of the one procure from God the pardon of the sins of the other? Here the analogy utterly fails.

And besides, this sense of sacrifice so current amongst us, is a derived sense, and not the direct Scriptural sense,—is one which has respect to human relations and not to the relations of man to God. Had the Apostles designed to convey this meaning clearly, the Greek language offered them abundant facilities, without their resorting to terms taken from the altar and its victims. If we would faithfully interpret the New Testament according to the sense of the times in which it was written—times, be it well remembered, in which not only animal but human sacrifices were offered in almost every nation—there remains but the choice between these two things: that when the Apostles represented the death of Jesus Christ as a proper sacrifice, they would either be understood as meaning to assert that He was a *human* sacrifice, and thus have perpetuated in their teachings that direct abomination of heathenism; or else, that they ascribed to the death of Jesus such efficacy as no death of a mere man could ever possess. To interpret the language in the way in which we now speak of one man's being a sacrifice for another, is forbidden by the whole spirit of antiquity. To interpret it as meaning a proper sacrifice, makes it either to be a human sacrifice—the most atrocious of abominations,—or forces us to attribute to it some peculiar value in consequence of the dignity and relations of the sufferer.

Obj. II.—Another mode in which this doctrine is sometimes drawn down from its high elevation, and left in an indefinite vagueness, is by saying: it is enough for any man to believe in the sufferings and death of Christ, to trust to that, and leave all theories about expiation and propitiation to the care of disputants. Christ suffered and died, and for us: so much is plain; here we can all unite. This is plain fact, revealed fact, but theories about the atonement are not so plain.

The sense of this is, that the position that Christ's death was expiatory is a theory, a philosophical explanation of the fact, and that all we need to believe in is the fact that his death was for us. But if the investigation we have instituted be of any worth, if it have taught us one thing more than another, it is this: that the very nature and essence of the sufferings and death of Christ is, that they are an expiation for sin. This is the very idea of a sacrifice. It is its exhaustive definition: it is the thing itself, and not a deduction or inference from it. This *is* the fact and not a theory about it. If one does not believe in the expiation, he does not believe in the sacrifice. We have the shell and not the kernel; we have death and sufferings and not life and peace. The expiation cannot be separated from the death without destroying the life that is in the death. We may form theories about the sacrifice of Jesus, in its relations to the moral government of the world, or to the wants of the human soul: but the very essence of the thing about which we are to form our theory is that it was an expiation for sin. And to represent this as a theory instead of being *the* fact, is to confound the whole relation between theory and fact. To require us to believe in the necessity of the death of an Incarnate God for our redemption, without making that death to be a propitiation for our sins, is to require us to believe in the most startling of facts, and to close our eyes to any reason or availability of it, is not only to demand an historical faith, but a faith for which no sufficient reason can be assigned—in a fact at once monstrous and enigmatical.

Obj. III.—It is difficult, if not impossible, to see how one being can bear the penalty which others have deserved, how Christ's vicarious sufferings could procure for us exemption from condemnation.—We suppose that those who press this objection will desire to use care in presenting it, so as not to cut off all hope or possibility of salvation from every son and daughter of Adam. If every soul must bear its own sins and penalty, and if it be a true saying that the soul that sinneth it shall die, and if conscience alone is to decide the case, we see not but that conscience demands that the penalty should be carried into full execution.—We also suppose that care will be used not to make the objection so positive as to conflict with the ordinary providential dealings of God, where a kind of substitution is to be seen. It is hard to contest the facts, that the father does suffer for the son and the son for the father, and one generation of men for those that come after. Almost all the civil and religious rights we enjoy have been purchased by the blood of others. Sins are visited upon children. It is possible to carry this individualism of sin and penalty so far as to conflict with the plainest facts in God's every day government, and in man's commonest relations.

But after all care has been exercised in relation to these points, the objection cannot be conceded to be valid. If the objection means, that we cannot see how the literal penalty of the law can be inflicted on any but its transgressor,—this is doubtless true: but the doctrine of a sacrifice for sin does not involve this necessarily: it says only, that the sufferings and death of Christ were instead of this penalty. Of course the objection does not mean that there can never be any vicariousness of suffering: for this would run counter to plain facts in the ordinary providence of God. If it is meant, however, that we can not see just how the sufferings and death of Christ are the procuring cause of the pardon of our sin, then we say, that it is not necessary that this should be seen in order to a living faith in Christ as our Redeemer. We do not believe in a bare abstract plan of atonement, which we can see through and round: we believe in Jesus Christ, our High Priest, our Sacrifice. And in his sacrifice *there is doubtless a mystery, unfathomable to mortal penetration.*

Then in respect to this objection, we say:

1. Here, as elsewhere in theology, mystery is to be admitted, while facts are to be accepted on their proper evidence; and the suitableness of the facts to illustrate the glory of God and to meet the wants of men is to be fully recognized. Mystery invests all reality. It is no objection to a divine proceeding, a divine provision, that while it comes largely within our apprehension, it also goes largely beyond. If there were no mystery here, we might suspect that there was no divine reality. It would *be* an objection to the atonement if there were no objections to it.

2. On the ground of uniform Christian experience we are warranted in asserting, that it is a fact of man's spiritual history, as abundantly confirmed as any fact can be, that faith in the atoning death of Christ is the constant and only source of the glad feeling of reconciliation with God; that this is the procuring cause of the feeling of redemption from the penalty and power of sin, as much as sin is the procuring cause of guilt, as much as right is the source of the sense of obligation. If this be a fact verified by constant experience, then as a fact it stands, whether we can penetrate to all its grounds and reasons or not.

3. But further, this objection runs counter, not only to the religious experience of Christians, but to the religious convictions of the human race. The assertion that there can be no vicarious sacrifice for sin attacks the religious faith of entire humanity. It is not modern orthodoxy alone that is thus attacked,—the uniform consent of the church of Christ is assaulted; it is not the doctrine of the church alone that is assailed,—it is the whole tenor of the New Testament: it is not the New Testa-

ment only,—it is the whole sacrificial system and the great prophetic burden of the Old Testament; it is not only the old dispensation and the new which is undermined,—it is the belief of every nation, where forms of worship have existed. If we can prove anything from what has always, everywhere, and by all been received, we can certainly prove the necessity of a sacrifice for sin. The heathen altar, the Jewish law, the Christian cross equally proclaim it. It has in respect to the universality of belief an evidence for itself far above any that can be alleged to exist for any one of the articles of the so-called system of Natural Religion. How dim the anticipations of immortality among the heathen!—how floating their notion of a divine unity!—how constant their victims on the altar!—how plain their faith in substitution!

4. While admitting that the objection is made to that relation of the atonement which is veiled in mystery, we assert that we can see, nevertheless, the fitness of such a mode of reconciliation as the sacrifice of Christ, on the one hand to God's character and government, and on the other hand to the wants of men.

(a.) The expiatory sufferings of Christ are on the one hand conformable to what we know of God's character and government, as a provision for the pardon of the sins of his creatures. They are thus fitted because they make the most perfect display of the moral attributes of God, showing us his love as it is nowhere else exhibited, and his justice in its unchangeable perfection. The atonement shows how his justice can be immutable, and yet grace abound. It shows how the apparently conflicting claims of God's justice and love can both be met, and the being who is the object of a just condemnation can become the subject of a redeeming love. Nowhere else are these attributes so perfectly manifested as in the work of our Saviour. This alone gives it a surpassing glory, and would be sufficient to vindicate it from every objection. How can the love of God be bestowed in its fulness upon any creature, in respect to whom his justice speaks only of condemnation? The justice of God must be satisfied, else his love cannot be imparted. Such satisfaction the atonement of Jesus bestows. As the representative of the race He kept the law, He suffered in our stead its extremest penalties—not the same in kind, as, *e. g.*, remorse and eternal death—but all those which a substituted sinless being could suffer: his infinite nature qualified Him to stand for the race, and made his sufferings available. And all that are united with Him by faith receive the benefits of his sacrifice: God looks upon Him who is their shield, and remembers the face of his anointed, and for his sake spares and adopts them. His justice is here exhibited, satisfaction is made, the sinner is pardoned, and the glory of the redemption is shared by Him who through love gave his Son to die for us, and by the Son who purchased us with his own most precious blood. This satisfaction to the divine justice is involved in the work of atonement, and is necessary; yet it should ever be carefully distinguished from the work itself. The work consists in the expiatory sufferings of Jesus, and it is these which do satisfy the divine justice, though it is sometimes represented otherwise, as though the atonement itself consisted in such a satisfaction.—Not only are God's attributes thus more perfectly and harmoniously displayed: his moral government also is upheld, his authority as a lawgiver is fully maintained by it. And here again we say that the maintenance of this authority does not constitute the substance or matter of the atonement: but rather, that the atonement has this for one of its effects, for one of its relations—an important and necessary relation—but still not itself the chief end or ultimate purpose of the atonement. That chief end is, the salvation of the sinner. The sinner must be saved, if at all, in such a way as is *consistent* with the moral government of God,—as will uphold the authority of the law: but still the virtue of the saving act will consist, not in the upholding of the law, but in the expiatory sufferings by which the ransom is effected. Beyond and above all analogies drawn from the relations of men, and the maintaining of a human law, are the awful expiatory sufferings of our Great High Priest. Not the son of a king suffering instead of rebels, not a royal father, having the light of one of his own eyes extinguished, that one of his son's eyes might be left unhurt, can fully illustrate the relation of our Redeemer's sufferings to the inviolability of God's law. The force and impressiveness, and we may add, the logical accuracy of the whole representation is rather weakened than strengthened by resort to such imperfect analogies. We should rather lay the stress upon the fact that Christ by his very nature, by his natural relations to God and his assumed relations to humanity was fitted to be the Mediator, to fulfil the *whole* law and make it honorable, and *thus* to maintain its dignity in the eyes of the universe.

(*b.*) This atoning work of Christ, on the other hand, is no less fitted to man's nature and wants, than it is to God's character. To represent the atonement as designed only to affect man, and not—so to speak—to influence the divine mind, to describe it as a moral spectacle, exhibited chiefly to enlist and arouse the feelings of man, his sense of sin, and his need of redemption—is assuredly unscriptural and defective: yet that it has this effect is scriptural and undeniable. It represents to man the justice of God in the clearest light, and this meets his own sense of justice; and the love of God in its highest form, and this is fitted to awaken a responsive affection. It is adapted to his conscience, so far as it upholds the law, and to all his deeper, tenderer feelings, since nothing appeals to them so strongly.

In sum, then, we say, with reference to Objection III., viz., *how* can the sacrifice of Christ procure the pardon of sin—what is the rationale, what are the ultimate grounds of the system which centers here: that there is room for a variety of explanations, and *here is where the theories of the atonement come in.* But we should be careful to draw the line between the facts and the theories. We have endeavored to bring out the great revealed, Scriptural fact about Christ and his sacrifice, in its simplicity and in its integrity. That fact we suppose to be embraced in the statement, that the death of Christ was a proper sacrifice for our sins. We suppose that this is revealed in so distinct a manner that it is a part of the *facts* of the Gospel. When we say that the death of Christ was instead of our punishment, and that it made expiation for our sins, we are not stating theories, but revealed facts. We suppose that in this fact is contained an answer to the question, how can a sinner be pardoned, and that answer is, by faith in Christ as the sacrifice for our sins: by a belief in his sufferings and death, instead of ours. We do not suppose that anything which can properly be called a theory is involved in any one of the points that we have presented in respect to the doctrine of sacrifices. Theories of the atonement have for their object to show how this fact, viz., that the expiatory death of Christ is the means of pardon to the guilty, is to be understood in its entire relations to what we know from other sources about the attributes and the moral government of God, and the wants and needs of man. It would be a sufficient answer to the objection to show that the fact is proved by evidence which cannot be invalidated; it is a further answer, that the atonement throws a light upon God's character and government, and meets the wants of man as nothing else does: to show *precisely* how God construes this greatest and most far-reaching of transactions, and to give an account of the *whole* of its effect upon the divine mind and the divine government, is a task which we do not undertake.

CHAPTER IV.

ANALYSIS OF THE SCRIPTURAL STATEMENTS AS TO CHRIST'S SUFFERINGS AND DEATH.

I.—The height of Christ's atoning work, its center, was in his sufferings and death. These are the matter of the atonement. Isa. liii. *Death:* Heb. ii. 9, 14; ix. 15; Rom. v. 10; Phil. ii. 8; Rev. v. 6, 9, 12. *Cross:* 1 Cor. i. 23; Gal. iii. 1; Eph. ii. 16; Col. i. 20; Gal. vi. 14. *Sufferings:* Luke xxiv. 26; Acts iii. 18; 1 Pet. ii. 21; iii. 18; Matt. xx. 28. *Blood:* Matt. xxvi. 28 (Mark xiv. 24; Luke xxii. 20); Eph. ii. 13; i. 7; Col. i. 14; 1 John i. 7; Rev. i. 5; v. 9.

II.—Christ suffered and died for others.
Isa. liii. 5, 6; Matt. xxvi. 28; Rom. v. 6; Gal. iii. 13, 14; 2 Cor. v. 14, 15.

III.—Christ died for sin and sinners.

Isa. liii. 6, 8; John i. 29; Rom. iii. 25; v. 8; vi. 10; viii. 3; 1 Cor. xv. 3; 2 Cor. v. 21; Gal. iii. 13; Heb. ix. 28; 1 Pet. ii. 24; iii. 18; Rev. i. 5.

IV.—As to the necessity of such a sacrifice.

Luke xxiv. 26; Gal ii. 21; iii. 21; Heb. ii. 10.

V.—That in what Christ thus did and suffered, He was a sacrifice for sins—*was really* what was symbolized under this form in the Old Testament.

(*a.*) He was Priest, High Priest: Heb. ii. 17; iii. 1; iv. 14; v. 1, 6, 10; vii. 11, 15, 26; viii. 1; x. 21.

(*b.*) He was also the pure offering. *Lamb:* John i. 29; 1 Pet. i. 19; Rev. v. 12; vii. 14; xiii. 8. *Sacrifice:* 1 Cor. v. 7; Eph. v. 2; Heb. ix. 26; x. 12. *Offering:* Heb. ix. 14, 25, 28; x. 10, 14. *Propitiation:* Rom. iii. 25; 1 John ii. 2; iv. 10.

VI.—That Christ is the only sacrifice: He alone makes an atonement for sin.

Rom. iii. 20-28; Acts iv. 12; Heb. i. 3; ix. 28; x. 10, 12, 14, 26. 1 Pet. iii. 18; Forgiveness only through Him; Reconciliation through Him alone; Faith upon Him enjoined.

VII.—That Christ's sacrifice was voluntary.

John x. 17, 18; Gal. ii. 20; Eph. v. 2; Heb. ix. 14; x. 7-9.

VIII.—As to the relations of his atonement to the race.

(*a.*) He died to save his own people: John x. 11; xv. 13; Rom. v. 8; Eph. v. 25; Heb. ii. 13, 14; 1 John iii. 16.

(*b.*) For many: Matt. xx. 28; xxvi. 28; Heb. ix. 28.

(*c.*) To save the lost: Mark ii. 17; Matt. ix. 13; xviii. 11; Luke v. 32; xix. 10.

(*d.*) For all, for the world. John i. 29; iii. 16; vi. 51; xii. 47; 2 Cor. v. 14, 15; 1 Tim. ii. 6; Heb. ii. 9; 1 John ii. 2.

IX.—That what Christ did and suffered for us was under the law—in some sense, for some object—to meet its claims.

1. He is represented as a sacrifice: this has no meaning unless under or in direct relation to demands of law.

2. He is represented as bearing the curse of the law: Gal. iii. 13. What is the curse of the law but its penalty?

3. He is represented as bearing sins: as bearing iniquity and

sin: the measure of these is the law; if Christ bore sin, it could only be under the law: Isa. liii. 6, 12; 2 Cor. v. 21; Heb. ix. 28; 1 Pet. ii. 24. It is not enough to say, "Christ bore suffering in consequence of sin:" this is not hermeneutically just.

4. That Christ's redeeming work was under the law is expressly asserted in Gal. iv. 4, 5.

5. His obedience was a fulfilling of the law: Rom. v. 18, 19; x. 4; Phil. ii. 8; Heb. v. 8; Matt. v. 17 (where πληρῶσαι means not "to complete,", but "to fulfil").

X.—Effect of what Christ did in relation to man.

1. Generally: He came as a Saviour, Deliverer, Redeemer: Matt. i. 21; xviii. 11; John iii. 17; xii. 47; Acts iv. 12; Gal. iii. 13; Tit. ii. 13; 1 John iv. 14.

2. He took away sin: Matt. xxvi. 28; John i. 29; Acts v. 31; xiii. 38; Col. i. 14; Eph. i. 7; Heb. i. 3; 1 John iii. 5.

3. Propitiation for sin: Rom. iii. 25; 1 John ii. 2; iv. 10.

4. Cleansing from sin: Eph. v. 25; Heb. xiii. 12; 1 John i. 7; Rev. vii. 14.

5. Reconciliation: Heb. ii 17.

6. Justification: Acts xiii. 39; Rom. iii. 24; v. 9; Gal. ii. 17; 1 Cor. vi. 11.

7. The source of blessings to the universe: John xiv. 13; Heb. ix. 15.

XI.—In relation to God.

1. God's love is the ground: John iii. 16.

2. God's purpose—plan—in it: John iii. 17; Acts ii. 23; Rom. iii. 25; viii. 32; 2 Cor. v. 21; Heb. x. 5–9.

3. The righteousness of God in it: Rom. iii. 25; 2 Cor. v. 21.

4. God gives Him as an offering: Isa. liii. 10; 2 Cor. v. 21.

5. Christ gives Himself as an offering: Eph. v. 2.

6. God reconciles us to himself through Christ: Rom. v. 11 (through whom we have now received the reconciliation); 2 Cor. v. 18, 19.

XII.—Summary from this Scriptural analysis.

This gives us the revealed facts as to the nature and relations of Christ's atoning work—no theory, no hypothesis—only an arrangement and array of the chief Scriptural assertions.

And it amounts to this, viz., that in Christ's death as a sacrifice for our sins, He

1. Suffered and died for sin, in our stead, as a proper sacrifice: that his were the vicarious, substituted sufferings of a representative;

2. —under the law, to answer the ends of the law, in some way, in our stead;

3. —in order to remove its curse from us;

4. —which was done by his substituted sufferings, death, obedience;

5. —and which had further the effect of a propitiation, declaring God's righteousness and reconciling man to God.

CHAPTER V.

THE THEORY OF THE ATONEMENT.

PROPOSITION. The different (imperfect) theories of Christ's atoning work give different aspects and relations of that work, and are true in these aspects, while false in the implication or assertion that these give the only or the ultimate point of view.

Classes of Theories.

1. Those which define the atonement ultimately by its influence in bringing man into a new, a regenerate state.

2. Those which affirm that the essence of the atonement consists in the direct satisfaction of distributive justice.

3. The governmental theory: The atonement is a satisfaction of general justice—in the sense of expediency and Utilitarianism—having respect to happiness.

4. Those which affirm that it consists in the satisfaction of general justice—as holiness—and that it incidentally satisfies distributive justice.

§ 1. *Theories which define the Atonement ultimately by its Influence on Man, in bringing to a New Life.*

I.—Christ's atonement consists in so setting forth, by example and instructions, the purity and excellency of the law, that sinners are thereby moved to repentance and obedience.

Christ did this: this was necessary to the atonement: a high moral end was answered by it. But the atonement did not consist in this.

1. This fails to account for the emphasis laid on Christ's death and sufferings.

2. It is inconsistent with the representation of his dying for us, in our stead and for our sins: in short, with the idea of sacrifice.

3. It is inconsistent with the included idea, that forgiveness of sins is procured by and through Christ.

4. Christ's example and instruction are never said to redeem and save us: Christ himself saves us by his atoning work: the stress of Scripture is not on that, but on this: Scripture says less of his life than of his death, in this relation.

II.—The theory that the atonement is a symbolical, outward exhibition of what occurs in each man, in turning to God. (Kant, McLeod Campbell, in part.)

III.—Christ's atonement is defined ultimately with respect to regeneration, and it consisted in this: by his Incarnation, He brought in a new life—a divine-humanity—which is imparted to believers in regeneration. Suffering is incidental, and a necessary incident to, an Incarnation of a holy being in a sinful world. The world is arrayed against Him, and He suffers in soul and in body, because it could not be otherwise with such antagonisms. So Coleridge[1] and others substantially.

[1] Robertson resolves the Atonement into a work of love. This law of life and love was adopted consciously by Christ. Christ became voluntarily submissive to this law of suffering. What Christ suffered was the suffering inflicted on Him by sin because He was opposing it. Bushnell says, Christ by the law of love was bound to do what He did. Coleridge, however, asserts a Godward as well as a manward aspect, says that the Godward side is the essence of the Atonement, but that it "is a spiritual and transcendent mystery which passeth all understanding." Manward, the effect is, regeneration, being born anew: Christ is a quickening, lifegiving Spirit: there are four *metaphors* of this (compare Bushnell's "altar-forms"): sin-offering, reconciliation, debt, ransom; all of which describe the effect, not the nature, of the Atonement. McLeod Campbell: The Atonement is "the vicarious confession of sins:" "To Christ alone Death had its perfect meaning as the wages of sin—for in Him alone was there full entrance into the mind of God towards sin." Rothe has a peculiar theory.

1. This theory is true in respect to one effect of the Incarnation, viz., regeneration.

2. It is false, in denying the whole sacrificial character of Christ's mediation.

3. It is false, in making the death and sufferings of Christ merely incidental. Scripture makes these necessary and the height of his work.

4. It is false, in making the source of these sufferings to be the sinfulness and rage of man: Scripture represents them, in part, as from God.

5. The theory thus fails to explain the Scriptural positions exhibited in the preceding chapter.

6. It is not a theory of the Atonement, but of regeneration as connected with the Incarnation: it resolves the proper work of the Spirit into the work of Christ; explains the nature of that work by one of its remote effects—as if one should explain the sun's rays by the processes of germination through heat.

§ 2. *Theories which put the Essence of the Atonement in Satisfaction to Distributive Justice.*

I.—The Mercantile or *Quid pro quo* Theory. The fundamental image here is that of a debt and its satisfaction. The theory asserts the strictest personal substitution. It embraces the following points:

1. Christ is the federal Head of the elect.

2. He took their law-place, their place under the law.

3. Sometimes it is said that He became really and personally a sinner.

4. He paid the debt of the elect, by suffering just what distributive justice demanded of them.

5. He obeyed, in the same personal, distributive sense, the law, for the elect.

6. So that the merits of his active and passive obedience are directly imputed to the elect, over whom the law has no claims.

Remarks.

(*a.*) Very few hold the theory in this extreme form.

(*b.*) It is thoroughly antinomian.

(c.) It is inconsistent with proper pardon and grace. All is legal.

(d.) Such a substitution in the way of strict distributive justice is morally impossible.

(e.) Christ did not and could not suffer the penalty as a sinner does, for He was not a sinner, and could not have remorse, neither did He undergo eternal death.

(f.) Upon this theory, the Atonement is not something *substituted* for the deserved penalty of the individual, but simply the suffering of that penalty by another.[1]

II.—The modified satisfaction theory. This is the satisfaction theory with its objectionable features removed. It reduces to general statements what is particular in the mercantile theory. It disregards the distinction between distributive and public justice. It insists, most properly, that the atonement is a proceeding under the divine law: not a device outside of the law, to exert moral influence, or uphold the authority of government. It has respect to law and to the ethical nature of God, which is the source of law, and so it meets the needs of the ethical nature of man.

This theory maintains that Christ's satisfaction was

1. Legal: rendered to the law and justice of God.

2. Complete, adequate: it had an intrinsic value and sufficiency to the end, *i. e.*, to the propitiation of the ethical nature of God, and meeting the law's demands.

3. That it consisted in the perfect obedience and the sufferings of his whole life.

4. That it was strictly vicarious for us and our redemption —was not at any point exclusively for himself.

---

[1] Anselm was the chief advocate of the satisfaction theory. He considered the last ground of the Atonement to be the divine justice requiring an infinite equivalent for the infinite guilt of sin,—that there was a necessity for it founded in the infinite nature of God. Abelard, on the other hand, maintained that the Atonement exhibits the free grace of God, which, by kindling love in the breast of man, blots out sin, and with sin its guilt. Baur, Versöhnungsl. 195. His view, as expounded by Aquinas in contrast with Duns Scotus (Redemption not connected with the sufferings of Christ ex insito valore, sed ex divina *acceptilatione*), was maintained by the Reformers, and afterwards the mercantile form of the theory was developed.

5. But the penalty of the law cannot be met as its preceptive demands can. What we owed to the precept was of debt, and it makes no difference who pays a debt, whether the debtor or some one else,—no difference whether we obeyed or Christ for us. What his obedience merited, viewed as rendering what the law demands in respect to conformity, is paid. But the penalty for disobedience cannot be settled by anybody. Distributive justice forbids. The demand is not only for a penalty, but that the guilty person shall bear it. How then are we to bring Christ's substituted sufferings under the strictest idea of distributive justice, and show that the law is satisfied in its demand for the execution of the penalty? The theory virtually says, This cannot be done: there must be here a relaxation of the law. The Sovereign Lawgiver can graciously accept what He sees[1] to be of equivalent value to the honor of the law and the satisfaction of his own ethical nature. Thus antinomianism is avoided. As the Lawgiver is not bound to accept the substitute for penalty as He would be the payment for debt, He may prescribe what terms of acceptance He pleases. The claim of law is not satisfied until the conditions on which the Lawgiver accepts substitution are complied with: hence, not until faith and repentance. Moreover, upon faith and repentance pardon is given, and the believer is brought into a justified state.

Remark:

It is doubtful whether the forms of statement of the mercantile or extreme satisfaction theory should be retained when so much of its substance has been abandoned. The theory insists that Christ made satisfaction to the law or justice of God, fulfilling in our behalf all that the law required in order to acceptance; further, that it is necessary to punish sin in the person of the offender; and says that this is the *only* view of divine justice which can be held. Yet it also adopts the statement that penalty does not designate either the nature or degree of sufferings, but the kind, and explains that it is the *design* of the suf-

---

[1] He does see the equivalent value. Dr. A. A. Hodge, Outlines (Rev. Ed.), 414, gives a careful statement: Christ "suffered precisely that kind and degree and duration of pain which divine wisdom, interpreting divine justice, required in a divine person suffering vicariously the penalty of human sin."

ferings—their relation to the law of God—which makes them penal. In this the theory is right, but in putting the matter thus, it makes God's justice to be something other than what is strictly distributive. It brings into view the *ends* of the law, the *design* of the penalty. In securing that through the substituted death of Christ, the design of the death denounced by the law upon sinners shall be fully attained, God's essential justice is satisfied; but the strictest distributive justice is not satisfied, seeing that as regards that, "the law is relaxed." The theory is involved in a degree of confusion by insisting that there are only two positions with regard to the divine justice, that of distributive justice and the governmental view—which is made to have respect to expediency, to happiness. Thus it is said, or implied, that the *whole* of real, essential justice is seen in distributive justice.

§ 3. *Theories which assert that the Atonement consists in the Satisfaction of General Justice,* viewing this as having reference to happiness or expediency, in maintaining the authority of the divine government.

The peculiarity of this class of theories is, the assertion that the Atonement meets certain exigencies of moral government, in distinction from satisfying *law.* Law is understood in the individual, personal sense, exclusively.

I.—The atonement is designed to produce a moral impression, not on each individual, but on the universe,—to be a substitute for punishment,—to honor, not satisfy, the law,—to set forth the truths that God is holy and must manifest his holiness,—to exhibit his holiness and hatred of sin. In Grotius, *De Satisfactione,* against Socinus, the Atonement is viewed as designed to secure certain governmental—not legal—ends.[1] The Arminian position: The Atonement is designed to make it consistent to offer salvation on easier terms—terms of "evangelical obedience"—there is no proper satisfaction.

This is usually, now, associated with the expediency or happiness theories of ethics. (See II.)

[1] Cf. in Bib. Sac., April, '52, from Baur. Grotius retains orthodox phraseology, but is claimed on the Socinian side (Bib. Fr. Pol.).

Remarks:

1. The theory denies: (*a.*) That satisfaction is rendered to, or made under, the divine law, in any form or way; (*b.*) That sin deserves punishment.[1]

2. The theory fails: (*a.*) To give a legitimate sense to Priesthood, Sacrifice: says, they are figurative; (*b.*) To show *how* Christ's sufferings and death manifest God's love of holiness and hatred of sin; (*c.*) To give a satisfactory account of justification.

3. It is not a theory: it is a mere assertion of the facts of the case, in an unsatisfactory form.

II.—The proper governmental theory.[2]

"Justice . . . is . . . a benevolent disposition on his [God's] part to maintain, by the requisite means, his authority as the necessary condition of the highest happiness of his kingdom."[3] "Atoning justice" "involves a particular disposition to maintain his authority by means of an atonement."[4]

Remarks:

1. This rests on the happiness, expediency theory of morals.

2. God's authority, as the Moral Governor, is maintained by legal sanctions: but *how* that authority is maintained by an Atonement is not shown.

3. The atonement, upon this view, has respect to others, but not to God; it is designed to maintain authority for the good, *i. e.*, the happiness, of the universe.

§ 4. *The Atonement, while it indirectly satisfies Distributive Justice, does not consist in this: it consists in satisfying the Demands of Public Justice,* meaning by that the divine holiness or the holiness of the law, *i. e.*, what the divine holiness sets before itself as the chief end of the universe, or that which is the end of the requirement of the law.

In the statements which follow, it is not proposed to give a

---

[1] Not that it is not intrinsically odious and ill-deserving, but if governmental reasons do not require its punishment, there is no necessity of punishing.

[2] *I. e.*, as that term has been employed in the theological controversies of this country.

[3] Dr. N. W. Taylor, Lectures, ii. 282.

[4] Ib., ii. 283.

complete theory of the Atonement, but to offer some hints which may show what the extreme theories are, and which may suggest some points of agreement.

I.—Moral Government and Moral Law cannot properly be sundered here.

In the popular and even in the scholastic discussions, the Law of God is often taken and defined, solely from and in view of its relations to, and its demands on, individuals, and their personal merit and demerit—that is, its whole scope is said to be fulfilled, its end reached, by the infliction of penalty on the disobedient, or the conferring of reward on the obedient. The law—taken in this sense—it is said, must be fulfilled to the letter. On this basis, and with these definitions, many have said, In the Atonement the demands of law are not and cannot be satisfied strictly: the Atonement is not a *legal* transaction. Then, because it is seen that if the whole of moral government and moral law is simply the carrying out of distributive justice, the Atonement, which is substitutionary, cannot be brought under such government and law, ground has often been taken which logically results in the position that the Atonement is *not* under moral government or law at all. Adhering to the position that the whole of moral government is in and by moral law, addressed to each individual's conscience and will, many who would be classed with the "New Schools" of American theology have involved themselves in the position, that while the atonement is an expedient of moral government, while it manifests God's holiness and hatred of sin, it is nevertheless a transaction out of the strictly moral administration of God. It has been said that "the satisfaction of divine justice is merely an established phrase," and that the whole theory of the Atonement is that "it satisfies general justice," in the sense that it is the expression of, and provides for giving realization to, God's disposition to secure the highest and purest happiness of the universe.

In opposition to this the points to be maintained are: (*a*.) The Atonement *is* under moral government and under moral law. (*b*.) A moral government is one which is administered by moral law. Moral government *is* government by moral law. (*c.*) As there is no procedure on the part of God in his dealings with his intelligent universe that does not come within his moral government—least of all would the greatest of transactions, the Atoning Sacrifice of his Son. (*d.*) His moral law, which is the expression of what his holiness demands, both in the universe as a whole and in each individual, is in force at every point of his government, and must be met and " satisfied " in its requirements.

II.—But Moral Law has two main ends.

1. To secure the supremacy of holiness—of holy love [1]—in the universe; this is the generic end.

2. To furnish the rule for individuals—moral agents—exacting conformity to that generic end.[2] This rule is carried out in distributive justice, in rendering to each according to his deeds. Here, only personal obedience with the accompaniment of reward, and disobedience, with penalty, can be considered. If it is insisted that the Atonement satisfies, *directly*, the law and justice of God, in this sense, we are driven either to Antinomianism or to " a relaxation " of the demands of law, such as we have in the modified satisfaction theory.

3. Distributive Justice is subservient to General or Public Justice: only it must always be understood that general justice is the real, essential justice of God, that which requires the supremacy of holiness in the universe, and not merely that which seeks to procure the greatest happiness.

4. Hence, if General Justice is fully, directly, gloriously satisfied, Distributive Justice is really and entirely, though incidentally, satisfied.

III.—Of the Divine Holiness as related to the Divine Law.

1. The divine law is an expression of the divine holiness: the securing and maintaining of that holiness is the end of the divine government; the law is given to secure that end: all other divine procedures tend to that end.

Divine holiness is a mode of the divine love: viz., Love

---

[1] See Lectures on the Nature of True Virtue.
[2] " Be ye holy, for I am holy."

seeks to communicate all good: holiness is, and seeks the highest moral good=rectitude, of moral beings. Divine love is, supremely, love of holiness—God's own and that of all others.

2. To secure this end, viz., manifesting and establishing the divine holiness, the law has its sanctions, chiefly rewards and penalties. *These are not its ends*, but means to its end. To establish and maintain holiness—moral rectitude—is the final end or object of the divine law, is its grand, ultimate end. In this *is* the highest good of rational and moral beings.

The law demands personal obedience, and punishes disobedience, *in order to* holiness. The punishment of the individual cannot be the *final object* of the divine government, the divine holiness: it is final in the case of the impenitent, as far as their destiny is concerned, but in relation to God, it is not an absolute end, but a mode of manifesting the divine holiness.

3. Hence, in this discussion, holiness, moral government, and law are three modes of the same thing: the law having a two-fold end in view, or, as we may say, the same end under a two-fold aspect: the first great end, to manifest and establish the divine holiness; the second, a subordinate means thereto, the personal demands on individuals—of their obedience, with reward—or if disobedient, of their righteous punishment.

4. Hence, too, the justice which is satisfied in the Atonement cannot be of a different kind from justice in general: it is the true, holy justice of God, that which requires the maintenance of the supremacy of holiness. It cannot be resolved into expediency, nor into Utilitarianism, nor into the good of the whole (as happiness); but it is that justice which the Law is designed to enthrone.

IV.—The Relation of Christ's Atonement to the End of the Law.

1. Atonement rests generally on the idea of mediation: its most general aspect is that of a mediation between God and man. The whole mystery of the Incarnation is involved.

2. It rests on the idea of substitution—in a moral sense:

under God's *moral* government, one, such a One, may stand and transact for, instead of, others. Here is the mystery of Redemption by God. If it is not a transaction under moral government, there is no sense in it: if it is not essentially moral, a part of moral administration—then what is it? And if the whole of moral government be in and by law, then the Atonement must be under the law. And if the whole of moral government is not by and through law—what is moral government?[1]

3. The Atonement being thus a substitution, from the very nature of the case it is something done and secured under the law—something which is instead of, which takes the place of, what the sinner deserved. This is the very idea of substitution, that not the thing itself is presented, but something else—something which answers the same purpose.

As soon, therefore, as terms are defined, it is impossible to call the Atonement a matter of pure distributive justice, because that has respect ultimately and solely to personal desert—merit and demerit. (Yet, as we have urged, distributive justice is satisfied in the sense that all the ends which it was intended to secure are met: for the believer, all penal claims are cancelled.)

But it does not follow from this that the Atonement is not a proper transaction under the divine moral government, under moral law, a manifestation of the demands of the divine holiness and justice—unless all these terms are restricted to the narrow sense of distributive justice.

That the Atonement is under God's moral government no one will contest, however some may take positions which might lead logically to the denial of it. That moral government is in and by moral law, is certainly true and undeniable. So the Atonement must be under the law, and that, too, has been

---

[1][There is, however, this statement made elsewhere by the author: Moral government is to be taken not in the sense of an administration by pure law, but in the sense of—all the means and instrumentalities which are used to secure the ends of that government. "Pure law," here, evidently means: law as the published rule of action with its sanctions, issuing in strict distributive justice. In the text, "law" rather means: the whole requirement of the divine holiness, covering all procedures in God's moral government.]

proved from Scripture. That it was not under the law in the sense of distributive justice, seems plain: it cannot be, if the standard definitions of that justice be adhered to. What remains then? It is necessary to say—either, that it is out of the moral sphere altogether—or else, that it is a transaction which answers the same grand ends as are intended to be answered by distributive justice, but in a different way.

4. What, then, are the ends answered by distributive justice, and how does the sacrifice made by Christ secure these ends?

(*a.*) The ends answered by distributive justice are: the sustaining and showing God's supreme regard to holiness, which He does by demanding the obedience, and punishing the disobedience, of each and all his moral subjects. Punishment, *i. e.*, suffering for transgression, is demanded on two grounds: (1) as the just desert of personal transgression; (2) to answer the ends of public justice: penalty relates to *both*: Atonement has respect not to the first, but to the second.

(*b.*) Christ, in his atoning work, answers these same ends: (1) As He is our Mediator—as by his Incarnation, life, and death, He stands and is in our stead, instead of the whole race; (2) More specifically, as, standing in our stead, in our place, under the law, for us, He obeyed and suffered in our stead; (3) Still more specifically, as his obedience and death in our stead answer the ends of public justice—show God's supreme love of holiness and hatred of sin—since it is thus manifest that only a perfect obedience and suffering for disobedience can answer the ends of the divine government. That is, the obedience of each and all individuals is demanded, in order to the satisfaction of the divine holiness. Instead of this, we having failed in obedience, and being subject to penalty, Christ in our stead, in stead of the demands on each and all, does and suffers what answers the same, the identical ends. What He did and suffered is not the same in kind or degree, but the same in essence, nature, and in its relation to the end or design of the divine government or law.—Are Christ's sufferings penalty, then?—Not in the sense that distributive justice was meted out to Him, but in the wider sense, in which penalty includes suffering under the law, to show God's displeasure at sin—in the sense in which suffering is demanded to answer the ends of public justice, which is holiness.

V.—Yet while making these statements as demanded by the Scriptures, and as not against reason, we must still say, that there is a background of mystery in the Atonement, as well as in the Incarnation, and in the Atonement in connection with the Incarnation, which no man can fully fathom, which has not been, and was not meant to be, fully revealed.

The view given above answers the question, what is the relation between what Christ did and the demands of holiness, which the mere governmental view does not: it does not answer the ultimate metaphysical question, *how?*

So to speak, the whole ontology and physiology of the system of Redemption is not disclosed. It is a theological rather than an ethical system: it is religious—a system of divine realities—up to which our theories of moral government do not reach. It is not a *merely* moral government at all;[1] it is that, and more, profoundly more.

VI.—In general we may say this: Partial theories of the Atonement give different aspects of the comprehensive truth.

1. The Atonement of Christ does produce the highest subjective moral impression: but the ground of the impression is, that we see in it our guilt and the divine holiness; this is the source of the impressiveness.

2. It also has one of its ends in our regeneration: but it shows how, in regeneration, sin and guilt are taken away, and God's favor is insured. Regeneration is grounded in our union with Christ. The giving of new life is grounded in the Incarnation and the Atonement.

---

[1] [The author elsewhere gives it as his judgment, that an ethical system like that which Edwards had in view, covering all the points of the revealed system, would make ethics and theology to be identical, and he asserts, as is seen in this discussion, that in such a large sense, the divine government is moral throughout. The statement in the text must be taken to mean, that the divine government is not to be measured and judged in all its scope by any human theory of ethics: that it all comes, in a divinely perfect way, under the ultimate idea of Right, would be strenuously asserted by him.]

3. It also symbolizes the inward transaction—the death to sin and living unto God—in affecting and eloquent language: but the essence of that transaction is in the reconciliation of the soul, its pardon, justification; and that the Atonement sets forth.

4. A moral impression is made upon the universe, by what Christ does, which God accepts: but the Atonement gives also the means by which this impression is produced.

5. The Atonement "renders it consistent for God to pardon sin and bestow infinite blessings upon those who had committed sin." It "satisfies general justice" in the sense of benevolence: it secures the highest "good" of the universe, viewed as true happiness as well as holiness. But the true theory points out the specific mode: it shows the ligament between the two things —sacrifice and pardon.

6. Also, the view we have indicated shows that God's justice is satisfied. Moreover, all his other attributes are satisfied, in the sense of having here the most glorious exercise and manifestation. The view shows how distributive justice is satisfied, while it lets grace abound.

7. It allows fully, for pardon, for grace, to each. Grace provided the way. Each sinner who comes to Christ is pardoned in and through grace. Distributive justice might still take its course: to all out of Christ, it does: it is satisfied only for those in Christ.

8. It is a view reconcilable with the offers of salvation to all.

9. It does not make it obligatory to save any but believers, and the obligation to them is of grace.[1]

10. Universalism is not in it: for the simple reason, that it makes union with Christ necessary to salvation.

NOTE.—The real difference between the two chief parties to the controversy on this matter is on these points: (1) Is distributive justice the whole of the justice, the law, the holiness, the moral government of God, in relation to man? (2) Is the end of the divine government holiness or happiness? Or, is it holiness or —something else? In other words, Does general justice (= public justice, real, essential justice) have ultimate respect to holiness or happiness? If general justice is taken to be, essentially, holiness, and to have supreme respect to that, there is no need of controversy.

---

[1] The obligation is contracted through grace: the covenant is a gracious "promise suspended upon conditions."

CHAPTER VI.

THE EXTENT OF THE ATONEMENT.

§ 1. *Statement of the Question.*
It is: Did Christ die for all men or only for the elect? Some who contend for the latter position differ among themselves: a part insisting that the sufficiency and efficiency of the Atonement are identical, that Christ suffered what the elect deserved and only that: others taking the ground that the Atonement is sufficient for all, yet made only for the elect, that only the provision for them was in God's *design*, that the sufficiency for others is simply incidental. There are also differences among the advocates of a General Atonement. Lutherans: Christ died to make such satisfaction that God could offer salvation to all. Election is denied. Arminians: that God might offer salvation to all on the ground of a less strict obedience. This also denies election. Others: to prevent the evils of mere pardon, to sustain the authority of a beneficent government. This allows election.

There may be points of agreement:
(1) As to the nature of the Atonement; (2) As to its sufficiency and universal applicability; (3) As to its actual application—to believers only, or, leaving out of view Lutherans and Arminians,—to the elect only.

To the question, then, Did Christ come into the world, suffer and die, solely for the elect? the theory of Limited Atonement replies: That was the sole design: all other objects effected thereby are not of the design, but incidental; the truth of General Atonement says: The Atonement made by Christ is made for all mankind, is such in nature *and design*, that God can save all men, consistently with the demands of holiness, on condition of faith and repentance.

Explanations:
1. The distinction is to be made between Atonement and Redemption. Atonement is the provision.
2. The design of the Atonement *was* to save the elect, but not

merely to save them; it was also designed to impart some blessings to the whole world, and to make the offer of salvation and the duty of accepting Christ urgent upon all who hear.

3. Not that it was actually designed to be applied to all, but to some.

4. Not that it is consistent with all the interests of the divine government for God actually to save all, but—consistent with the demands of penal justice.

5. The Atonement, as such, does not save any.

§ 2. *Proof of General Atonement.*

1. The key-passage is 1 Tim. iv. 10.

2. God offers salvation to all men: therefore it has been provided for all.

Isa. xlv. 22; lv. 1–3; Matt. xi. 28–30; Rev. iii. 20; xxii. 17. It is sometimes said that the meaning is: "Some among all classes" or "in all lands." But (*a.*) this is an unscriptural distinction; (*b.*) we do not know that the offer, in the sense of "effectual calling," is made to "some in all" these cases: (*c.*) the sincerity of God is here at stake: He offers to all a salvation which He has not provided for all.

3. Special guilt is ascribed to those who reject the atonement. Matt. xxiii. 37; Luke xiv. 17; John iii. 19; Acts vii. 51.

4. Scripture declares the Atonement to be for all.

John i. 29; iii. 17; xii. 47; 1 Tim. ii. 6; 2 Cor. v. 14, 15; Heb. ii. 9; 1 John ii. 2.

5. All men receive some benefits from the atonement.

(*a.*) The offer of eternal life, to many non-elect.

(*b.*) The knowledge of the divine plan and ways.

(*c.*) The continuance of probation and many temporal blessings.

6. There is an argument for General Atonement—*ex concessis*.

It is conceded to be "sufficient" for all: then it was designed to be so: then, it is consistent for God to offer—and if to offer, then to grant, on conditions. To the question, "Is it sufficient then for fallen angels?" the obvious reply is, Christ did not come for them.

7. Some special arguments.

(1) The parallel between Adam and Christ, Rom. v. 18

(2) Christ lays down His life for some not saved. Rom. xiv. 15; 1 Cor. viii. 11; Heb. x. 29; 2 Pet. ii. 1.

(3) From the connection of truths. (*a.*) From the view it gives of the glorious character of the divine government. God, the God of grace. (*b.*) From the effects of the doctrine on men —the high moral influence. (*c.*) From the view it gives of the final condemnation of the lost. God's mercy provided a way: they refuse: their condemnation is just—resisting grace. (*d.*) Christ's relations to the universe are consistent only with General Atonement.

§ 3. *Objections to General Atonement.*

1. It supposes different and inconsistent purposes in God.

—Not so: one purpose is, to make the salvation of all possible; another is, to save some; what inconsistency?

2. God makes provision for an end, which He determines never to effect.

—Not so: God makes provision to make the salvation of all men possible.

3. It is inconsistent with the doctrine of election.

—Not, if election is on this basis. The condemnation at least of some non-elect is, in part, on the ground of refusal.

4. The divine holiness demands the salvation of all for whom provision is made.

—Not if other good reasons forbid.

5. The Scripture says, Christ died to save his people.

—It also says, Christ died for the whole world. Christ's special design does not exclude a more general design. To say, Christ came to save, redeem, deliver, sanctify his people, is most certainly true, but is, in this argument, a *petitio principii;* it assumes that Christ in his work had only one design. The doctrine of General Atonement does not assert that the purpose of God in Christ's death had equal respect to the elect and the non-elect, in the sense that God intended to apply it equally.

6. From the union of Christ and his people. All that Christ

did, it is said, He did for those who are united to Him by faith.

This is most true, but is irrelevant here. The doctrine of General Atonement does not assert that all that Christ did *and does*, He does for all mankind.

CHAPTER VII.

THE INTERCESSION OF CHRIST

Here we make the transition to the Third main Division of Theology. The Intercession of Christ has both a Priestly and a Royal side.

I.—The general view: the super-historical[1] relation of Christ to the world.

When earthly heroes, patriots, statesmen, poets, orators, philosophers, philanthropists, and even saints pass away, from the scenes of their wars, their sacrifices, their counsels, their eloquence, their wisdom, their beneficence, or their spiritual conflicts, they leave behind them, it may be, a lasting memory and an imperishable renown; but they themselves are taken away from all conscious and direct and living intercourse even with their dearest friends and their most devoted adherents. Imagination and memory may linger upon their words; their praises may be rehearsed in eulogies and song; their image may be recalled by sculpture, by painting, and in poetry; their deeds may be transmitted from sire to son in a long and grateful tradition; their lives may even be depicted as an embodiment and summary of the whole century in which they lived, and thus handed down from generation to generation. But their living, personal presence is neither felt nor known, unless it be in the mere fancy of some materializing spiritualist, confounding the fiction of a disordered imagination with the facts of a supernatural sphere.

[1] See Martensen, Dogm., p. 365.

But in startling contrast with all others, we find that a belief in the real and living presence of Christ, after his departure from the world, remains the constant heritage of his church. We come to Him daily, as to a Personal Friend, for succor, for wisdom, and for strength. His Presence, at the right hand of the Majesty on high, greets the eye of faith, as it looks upward. In the hour of contest, of anguish, of death, we see that loving eye, we lean upon that mighty arm. We have not an High Priest who cannot be touched with the feeling of our infirmities. Our Advocate is not deaf to our petitions. If any man sin, we have an Advocate, a Paraclete, with the Father. In that He suffered being tempted, He is able to succor them that are tempted. He is able to save to the uttermost all that come unto God by Him, seeing that He ever liveth to make intercession for them. Between the Christian and death—the wages of sin—is the divine Deliverer: between the Christian and God is the divine Mediator: and who then shall lay anything to the charge of God's elect, seeing it is Christ who maketh intercession for them?

It is this loving care and presence of the God-man, this constant activity for his kingdom, which is denoted in Scripture and handed down in the faith of the church, as his Intercession. His work of Intercession is that of a King to whom our souls have been committed, as well as that of a Priest by whom our sins have been expiated.

II.—The Qualifications of Christ for this work.

His nature is allied to God and knit with ours in inseparable bonds.

His sacrifice alone is the basis of his moving petitions.

His dignity gives them their authority.

By his rights they are made effectual.

Only He is qualified so to intercede, that his intercession shall be always effectual, and for all, and for each thing that He may ask. He alone, the only-begotten Son who is in the bosom of the Father, knows the very mind of God, and knows the Father as the Father knoweth Him.

He, the High Priest, holy, harmless, and undefiled, can intercede with perfect holiness, so that no earthly desire shall mar the purity of his request.

He can stand before the eternal, holy Majesty, as Sponsor and Advocate, having satisfied the divine justice, and thus transferred the sovereignty of justice into a sovereignty of love.

His work of intercession can be coextensive with the race and with the utmost stretch of history. He can intercede for all men, in all times, for barbarian and Scythian, bond and free, for the lettered and the rude, for the prince on his throne, for the savage in his forest, for the patriarchs and prophets of the old dispensation, for the apostles, martyrs, and heralds of the new. His intercession is as eternal and unchangeable as the priesthood on which it is based, and as the kingdom in which his regal petitions are the sum of all other prayers, and give their virtue to all other forms of interceding. He ever liveth to make intercession.

There arises from all parts of the world, at the morning and the evening, and through the labors of the day, a perpetual incense of adoration and of petition; it contains the sum of the deepest wants of the human race, in its fears and hopes, its anguish and thankfulness; it is laden with sighs, with tears, with penitence, with faith, with submission; the broken heart, the bruised spirit, the stifled murmur, the ardent hope, the haunting fear, the mother's darling wish, the child's simple prayer: all the burdens of the soul, all wants and desires, nowhere else uttered, meet together in that sound of many voices, which ascends into the ears of the Lord God of hosts. And mingled with all these cravings and utterances is one other voice, one other prayer, their symphony, their melody, their accord—deeper than all these, tenderer than all these, mightier than all these—the tones of One who knows us better than we know ourselves, and who loves us better than we love ourselves—and who brings all these myriad fragile petitions into one prevalent intercession, purified by his own holiness, and the hallowing power of his work.

III.—In what does his Intercession consist?

1. His Intercession, in its largest sense, may be said to con-

sist—in all his agency, at the right hand of the Father, for the final and complete redemption of man. Whatever He does, on the basis of his sacrifice, now and ever, in the way of mediation between God and man, is comprised in this intercession, taken in its fullest scope. It consists not in words alone, but also in deeds: his succor, his pity, his care, his love for each and all his followers; his guardianship in the hour of temptation, his aid in our spiritual conflicts, his grace imparted according to our need, the balm of his consolation, his strength in our weakness, the answers to all prayers put up in his name: all belong to, and make a part of, his intercession.

2. We need not be embarrassed by the suggestion, that because He is one with God, therefore to talk of intercession is as if we spoke of a man's interceding with himself. For even between the divine Persons of the Trinity, there is doubtless converse as well as community; communion as well as oneness; converse in thought and reciprocity in love. Moreover, all these acts of intercession are in Christ's human nature and in his mediatorial office; they belong to Him as the God-man, and the federal head of the race; so that there is no more difficulty about conceiving of the Intercession, than of the Incarnation, in connection with the Divinity of Christ.

3. From its very nature the Intercession has a two-fold aspect and relation; it looks both Godward and manward; it is for us and is unto God. It embraces in its comprehensive scope whatever pertains to the application of redemption.[1] Thereby our imperfect prayers are made perfect; our daily transgressions pardoned; our penitence is made available; our feeble desires for holiness are enlivened; our faith is emboldened; our weakness is strengthened; our darkness illumined; our righteousness made blameless; our sanctification insured. And so, in this Intercession, we have a constant and living access to the Father, by that new and living way. The mere sense of duty disquiets us as we think of our sins; the power of philosophy reaches

---

[1] Schneckenburger, Christologie, pp. 124, 129, thinks it would not embrace, strictly speaking, the regeneration itself, but all that belongs to the perseverance and sanctification of the children of God.

chiefly to the discipline of the intellect; we may strive even for sanctification, and if it is in our strength, the striving reveals to us chiefly our sinfulness and weakness. But when we think of Christ as a living and personal Intercessor, duty in Him becomes persuasive, truth vivid to the heart, and sanctification a reality and a power; we know then what He meant when He said, For their sakes I sanctify myself, that they also may be sanctified through the truth.

IV.—How is Christ's Intercession conducted?

1. According to Heb. viii. 1, and ix. 24, the eternal reality of Christ's sacrifice is found in the procedures in heaven, and not merely in the transactions of earth. As a Priest, He offers the sacrifice in the outer court, on this foot-stool of earth, and then goes within, to the Holiest, into heaven itself, there to appear in our behalf before the face of the Father; and this is his Intercession. There is one sacrifice, once for all; yet also a constant Interceder.

2. He intercedes as our High Priest, and therefore still clothed upon with his human nature. In that very human nature which allies Him with all of us, making Him our elder brother, and the consummation and crown of humanity,—in that human nature, spotless though fiercely tempted, holy though weighed down by the burden of others' sins, victorious though crushed by Jewish hatred and Pagan power and the devil's malice and wiles, most glorious when wearing the crown of thorns, most triumphant when nailed to the accursed tree—in that very nature, raised from the dead and ascended to the right hand of the Majesty on high, He appears as our Advocate before the Father's throne—the Lamb slain from the foundation of the world, making intercession for us. He is an everliving High Priest, though exalted to rule and to reign.

3. The representation of Him as an Advocate is taken from the forms of human tribunals, where the accused appears by his attorney, who, it is supposed, can plead his cause better than He can himself. We have an example of his Intercession in John xvii., where we see the objects which are sought, the grounds on which they are asked for, and the confidence with which the pleas

are made. The plea reaches its culmination in the utterance, Father, I *will*[1] that they also whom thou hast given me be with me where I am. Here the right which He has acquired and which is most freely accorded in fulfilment of the eternal counsel of the Father, comes into view; and here, too, He touches the deepest and loftiest aspiration of the redeemed soul: to be with Christ, to see his glory, to gaze upon the reality—the archetypes —of all our hopes, the substance of our faith, the Person of our Lord.

4. Does He, then, plead and ask in words, in speech—as we do one to another? The only answer that can be given is that He pleads in celestial places and with celestial speech. If it is not like our speech, it is because it is better and truer; if it is not in mortal tones, it is with immortal meaning: if not articulate in the air, it is articulated in the very plan of God; if not expressed in sentences, it is wrought into the counsels of the Father of all.

5. Does He plead minutely, for each and every need and gracious blessing? We might ask in reply: Does God's providence feed the ravens; does divine beauty clothe the lilies; does infinite wisdom number the very hairs of our head? And is grace less careful than providence? Does redemption extend to the whole man, and the whole life—to body, soul, and spirit; who then will put limits to the prayers of our Great Advocate?

6. Is his prayer limited by ours, repeating only what we utter? This is to ask, Does Christ know us, only as we know ourselves? Alas for us if this be so. He asks for what we need, and not for what we vainly wish. We ask for prosperity, and our Advocate asks that we may have prosperity through adversity. We ask for more light, and He interprets our petition aright and implores that we may be refined in the fire. We ask for day while it is yet midnight, and He gives us not yet day but songs in the night.

V.—The Fruits of his Intercession.

These are to be considered in the Third Division of Theology. They consist of Justification, Rom. viii. 33, 34; the Adoption of

[1] John xvii. 24, θέλω.

sons, Rom. viii. 15; the boldness of access to the throne of a holy God, Heb. x. 19; the daily cleansing from sin, 1 John ii. 2; and the whole direction of our affairs unto sanctification and complete redemption, 1 Cor. i. 30.

SUMMARY OF THE SECOND DIVISION AND TRANSITION TO THE THIRD.

We have seen in this Division, that the ancient history of our race pointed to Christ, and the modern has received its law from Him; that the insignia of divine power and the best human influence attended his earthly career; that He has enlarged and purified our views both of human nature and of God, and of the intimate alliance between the two; that He was fitted as God-man for the solution of the greatest problem of our destiny, and by his death reconciled us to God; that, having conquered death, He now, in his glorified humanity, gives the most blessed and sure hopes to all who trust in Him, that they too shall be like Him, and thus robs death of its sting and eternity of its awful forebodings, delivering us from the fear even of our last enemy. Jesus Christ, the God-man, is the center of a grand and real economy which is within the world, and above the world, and reaches out beyond the world; all the great points in the history and destiny of the race are made to converge in Him, so that the central truth of his Person is seen to be the center of the whole divine economy. And thus it appears that the Incarnation in its practical bearings is as wonderful as it is in its inherent sublimity: for the most comprehensive of purposes is thus seen to be vitally connected with the most comprehensive of doctrines. These practical bearings are now to be considered in the Third Division of the system.

DIVISION THIRD.
THE KINGDOM OF REDEMPTION.

DIVISION THIRD.

THE KINGDOM OF REDEMPTION.

We have divided Christian theology into three parts: The Antecedents of Redemption; The Redemption Itself; The Consequents of Redemption. But there is a better, a more Scriptural, title for this last part, which we here adopt. And before proceeding to the outlines of discussion on the topics which belong to this Division, we shall bring together some statements as to the general nature of that KINGDOM OF GOD which Christ is carrying forward according to the counsel and will of the Eternal Father, and through the immediate agency of the Divine Spirit. In this last part of theology, we are especially to emphasize the Work of Christ *applied by the Holy Spirit* in bringing man anew into the union with God which he has forfeited by sin. This part contemplates God in Christ as renewing and sanctifying man and bringing him into a new kingdom, through the work of the Holy Spirit. The general underlying idea of this part of the system of theology is that of a union between Christ and the believer, through the work of the Holy Spirit. By the supernatural influences of the Divine Spirit, man is united to Christ and through Christ to God. The union between Christ and the believer is the fundamental conception.

The whole of this Third Division would comprise three main parts: I. The Union between Christ and the believer as effected by the Holy Spirit; II. The Union between Christ and the Church. The Doctrine of the Church and the Sacraments. III. The Consummation of the Kingdom of Redemption in time and eternity; or The Eschatology of the system.

Here we have come to the proper place for giving to the

Kingdom of God a fuller consideration than it has previously had in these lectures.

This general position is to be affirmed and illustrated, in any system of theology which undertakes to meet the wants and questions of our times, viz.,—that the Christian system gives us the noblest and most complete and most animating view of what man is and is to be; and that in that system, and not out of it, the great problems of human destiny are to find their solution. And it does this in what is sublimely called the kingdom of God, a kingdom in which the divine purposes of wisdom and love are to be fulfilled, in which God and man are reconciled, in which the true basis and bonds of a real brotherhood are found, a kingdom in which all men are to be reconciled with each other, by being united to the Father, through the Son and by the Holy Spirit, so that heaven and earth are joined in entire fellowship.

In contrast with schemes of human device, which look mainly at the temporal, the social, and the political welfare of mankind, this kingdom, while favorable to all these and intended to promote them, puts them also in their just relations.[1]

I.—The fact that Christianity, in its very nature, looks forward to the realization of such a kingdom, is one of the striking and grand peculiarities of the Christian revelation.

1. The lowest view which any religious mind can take of Christianity is, that it is a grand scheme designed to give him personal happiness, to give him hope for the future. The idea of such a one is, that he is in a lost condition, is converted by God's grace, is to go on trying to improve his heart, is to live that others may be brought into the same condition, and is at last to be transferred to the eternal mansions, where he shall be forever blessed: and *that* is what religion is given for, for *that* Christ came into the world. Now this may all be right, as far as it goes; religion is good for this, but—this is not the measure of its real good. There is something that is worthy of regard besides our own salvation. When we become Christians, we

---

[1] This is in accordance with the spirit of Christ's promise: "Seek ye first the kingdom of God, and his righteousness; and all these things shall be added unto you."

enter into a divine kingdom, where the highest wisdom and the grandest thoughts and the most far-reaching purposes of God Himself are concentrated: we are translated into a sphere in which all our thoughts and purposes are to find full employ in their largest measure, and out of which they cannot find such employ.

2. Nor is the true idea of Christianity exhausted when we conceive of it as limited to our churches and denominations, and working in them for the spiritual building up of their members. Many stop here. They make the church quite separate from the world, having only external points of contact with it. Its object is to cultivate right internal affections, to indoctrinate, and to gather new members for the same object. And meanwhile all the other interests of society move on independently. The church *has* one object, to convert men and prepare them for heaven: but there are other and almost independent objects in the world likewise. There is not only religion, there are politics and trade and the sciences and the arts and reforms of all kinds, and each one of these makes a separate battalion in the march and progress of our race. The main care is the prudential one, not to have them jostle against each other. And what all these separate organizations are for, and whether, and how, they are to unite together, are unvexed or deferred inquiries.

3. To one having such an idea of Christianity there comes some speculative reformer, who propounds a scheme in which, he says, all these different interests are combined and harmonized, and that he can so adjust the desires and passions and aims of man as to make them all concurrent; and though he may neglect man's eternal interests, yet he tries to systematize all his present interests: and though he may not satisfy the intellect, yet he inflames the imagination; and though he may not beget the conviction that his scheme is sufficient, yet he may weaken the confidence of those who give to Christianity only an intellectual assent in the sufficiency of a system which holds itself aloof from such general views of society and the social state.

But such a view of the nature and intent of Christianity is essentially erroneous, and such human speculations are in reality only feeble imitations of that more comprehensive view of human nature, interests, and destiny which was prophesied in the Scriptures of the Old Testament, and limned with a divine hand in the perfected revelation of the New, and which is to be consummated in the Kingdom of God. It constitutes one of the most striking peculiarities of the Christian faith.

It is a wonderful fact that, while the wisest men, as Plato and Aristotle, among the most cultivated nations of ancient times, in their conceptions of the true condition of man, never rose above the idea of a single state or community, the Jewish people so unlettered and remote, looked forward under prophetic guidance to a divine kingdom, centering in a glorious Head; into which all nations were to flow, and in which all strifes and conflicts were to be adjusted. Their prophets dwelt upon this hallowed vision with inspired exultation—with faces not turned backward to a golden age already past, nor forward only to a ruinous catastrophe—but backward to read the promise made from the beginning, and forward to see its fulfilment in Him who was to bring in a time of freedom and joy, of reconciliation between man and God, and man and man, and who was to gather unto himself all the nations of the earth.

In the apostolic church, the signs and powers of this kingdom of God become still more marked; for here are its conflicts and victories, its establishment and progress among the mightiest nations and to the remotest climes. A few men went forth, and what they did was to preach the words of this kingdom and to seal their testimony with their sufferings: they proclaimed the advent of a realm which was to subdue all nations unto itself; the weapons of their warfare were not carnal, but spiritual; they prophesied the downfall of states—and states have fallen; they proclaimed that the kingdoms of this world were to become the kingdoms of our Lord—and this proclamation, so daring, so visionary, so utterly unknown to all other nations has been in a course of constant fulfilment even until now. Nation after nation has since perished, not one which then had an historic influence now remains: but that kingdom continues, wider spread, more diffused in its influence, more penetrating in its power, with every century; and all the changes of its outward form are only illustrations of its inherent spiritual might, are only signs of the expansive and resistless energy of the Spirit that dwells within it. It has subdued nations, reformed institutions, overturned philosophies, changed the current and the objects of human thought, given to mankind the highest notions of justice and feelings of benevolence, been at the foundation of their contests for civil and social rights—and this in a continuous and progressive course. If anything true and real is to be learned from human history; if permanence in spite of the greatest obstacles, if victory over the mightiest foes, can give any assurance of divine vitality in that which thus endures and conquers; then has this kingdom of God unrivaled claims upon our faith.

It is not only the fact that in the idea of such a kingdom the Christian religion stands alone—no other religious system knowing anything about it. But the idea which it contains is more comprehensive and satisfactory than any other scheme— than even those which have borrowed from it their impulse, when not their outlines.

II.—The contrast of the way in which human nature and destiny are spoken of in this divinely revealed kingdom with that presented by the most ambitious theorists who neglect or would supersede the Christian faith.

1. They differ in their radical conception of human nature. The Utopias and Republics of human invention take human nature as it is, and show, not the necessity of a renewal, but the need of an adjustment of human passions. One passion is to check another passion, and the passions of one man the passions of others. While the theorist himself acts in daily life just as really on the supposition that men are depraved, as do those who do not hesitate to avow it, yet when he speculates about man's nature and destiny, he becomes unwilling to lift the veil. For were the extent of the evil fully recognized then were also seen the need of a divine aid, of which nothing but an avowed revelation can give to man any assurance. This neg-

lect of the great fact of human depravity, and the consequent reliance on natural powers and agencies, is a fatal defect in any system, in its adaptation to human wants. Man's general condition is one of selfishness and hostility, of alienation from God. To reconcile man with God, in any rational view, must be the first great object. To counteract depravity is the first great necessity. To organize human passions is not to correct human nature. There is not here a force sufficient for the emergency. To put the body in a decent posture does not stay the progress of corruption. But—in contrast with this—in the kingdom of God the depths and nature of our evil are fully disclosed, and the first great object proposed is the reconciliation of man with God.

2. Equally contrasted are the respective systems in the means to which men's thoughts are directed as the efficient agencies of reform. In the one our attention is first turned to education or the deliberate re-organization of society; in the other, while the influence of human wisdom and education and of all right methods and organizations is not neglected, they are made to be wholly secondary to those spiritual and internal influences which are the gift of God, in answer to prayer, through the energy of the Holy Spirit. The intercourse of the soul with God—this, in the kingdom of God, is the cardinal means of renovation and growth. To work from within outward is the law of God's kingdom; to work from without inward is the weakness of human schemes. To feed upon eternal and spiritual truths is the first aim of the Christian: to make eternal and spiritual things seem shadowy and distant is the bane of mere human reforms.

3. The sense of this contrast will be still further increased, if we look at the ends which they respectively propose, as well as at their means of efficiency. The kingdom of God views men primarily as immortal beings, subject to an immutable law, and having an eternal destiny. And so it makes prominent just what in human plans is kept subordinate,[1] and it keeps sub-

---

[1] Chalmers calls that "the grand practical delusion, the bane and bewilderment of our species, whereby eternity stands before us in the character of time, and time wears the aspect of eternity, whereby the substance appears to be the shadow, and the shadow the substance."

ordinate that which man naturally exalts. Nothing is more striking in the history of the best human speculations upon the destiny of man than the limited sphere which is assigned to it. To regulate the material interests of society, the production and exchange of wealth, to bring justice into our social and political relations, to educate in useful knowledge, in sciences and the arts, in short, to promote temporal well-being—these are their highest aims. And they are noble and worthy aims, but not the highest or best. And never can they be pursued with a fitting earnestness, never so without extravagance, and never so without danger, as when they are viewed only as subordinate parts of a grander and more comprehensive economy, by which man is to be carried through the changing scenes of life to the unfolding of all his capacities and the attainment of his enduring well-being in that perfected kingdom of God, of which this life is but the preparatory theater. That which is the very fruit and blossom of human Utopias is but a subordinate scene, an initial act in the sublime unfolding of the kingdom of God.

4. This divergence in their respective views about human nature, and the means of its advancement, and the ends which are held before it, has its ground in a still more fundamental difference between the two schemes, viz., in their professed origin. The kingdom of God is revealed to us as grounded in the direct purposes of the Most High, and as containing the counsels of infinite wisdom for the Redemption of a lost world. Its origin and efficiency are from above. It has not its basis in our physical constitution, as has the family, nor like the state is it for the establishment and protection of natural rights, of property, and of temporal justice; but it is established upon the word of God, and upon the deeds of the God-man. It looks at man not as a denizen of this planet, but as an heir of immortal treasures, as subject to a law which shall never pass away. Human systems, on the contrary, profess to be only the result of human speculation, and are restricted to our temporal interests. Whether they put our social condition, or our freedom, or science, or art, as the great end and object—and under all these four points of view speculations have been framed—still, they are for this world

and for this alone, for the seen and temporal, and not for the unseen and eternal. And the origin of these systems is sufficiently attested by the very shape in which they are brought forward. They contain deliberate plans of reorganization, carried out in all their minutiæ. But something more than a speculation or a plan is needed for the reform of the race. That something more is given us in those sublime facts and realities which lie at the basis of the kingdom of God; for this kingdom is revealed to us, not as a theory or speculation, but in just the simplest way, in just the most unpretending form, as something which God has done and is doing. This simplicity in the announcement of the kingdom of God is one of its most sublime characteristics: just as nature is most unobtrusive in her greatest works, just as great men are most simple in that which constitutes their greatness. The kingdom of God came in simple words and energetic deeds. There was much less speculation about it than there is about many a modern plan for reforming the nations. To really reform mankind, we need the deepest conviction that the mind of no man has fashioned the scheme, and that the power of One more than man is enlisted for its accomplishment: that the ends which it proposes are eternal, and that the means it has at its command can reach and rectify the heart of our disorders, and combine all our interests in one harmonious and perpetual kingdom.

III.—Some of the more prominent characteristics of the kingdom of God, both as to what it is, and what it is to be.

1. The most striking fact in respect to it is, that this kingdom is described as established and gathered together—centralized as we might say—in One Person, the person of Jesus Christ. It is one of its prime glories that it has for its head and center a being in whose wonderful person are united the attributes both of divinity and humanity, and who is thus fitted to be the Mediator between God and man; a person who laid the foundations of this kingdom in the most stupendous sacrifice, by which the highest moral problem of the race was solved; a being fitted to all our human wants—our wants as sinners—so near and gracious that the vilest and lowliest may come to Him,

and so majestic and mighty that He can welcome and save *all* that come unto Him; a being beyond the glories of whose person and the wonder of whose work, human thought in its largest speculations has never reached, and to whom human love in all its tenderness and trust may ever turn, and who is nearest to us with his richest blessings when our misery is most real and our needs most urgent. Faith in Him is the beginning of the new creation, and glory with Him is its consummation. In such a person is the kingdom of God centralized and knit together.

2. Another of its peculiar characteristics is, that the truths which center in Christ are described as applied to the human heart by a subtle, mighty, and persuasive influence—that of the Holy Spirit, whose power reaches to the very thoughts and intents of the heart, and who subdues our sinfulness by implanting new and higher principles of action, and who so acts upon the soul that its freedom is not impaired, but enlarged. Thus at the very foundation of this kingdom we have the agency and working of God, in his three-fold personality, as Father, Son, and Spirit, and from them go forth the influences which give it shape and perpetuity. The anatomy of this kingdom is found in the Triune Godhead.

3. This kingdom is one which, from its very nature, is adapted to enter into and remould all other institutions in the highest and best conceivable manner. It does this by its spiritual nature, making the laws and principles of all other institutions gradually submissive to its own higher spirit and laws, giving to all that is lower its fitting place and its moral worth. It is able to do this, as is nothing else. When the lower prevails over the higher, it is oppression; when the higher prevails over the lower, it is law. The kingdom has already done this in countless instances; it is still doing it, in such an increasing extent that, were we not familiar with it, and did we judge it as we judge other things, we could only wonder at it. There is no doctrine of philosophy, no scheme of man, no other organized influence, which has gone as has the kingdom of God, to all men of every name and degree—from the most brutish to the most civilized—

and found entrance and made conquest. And this is because its principles and influences and teachings are not only most sublime but also most simple, simple in the sense of being directly adapted to human nature and human wants, for this is the only real test of the simplicity of a doctrine.

4. Not only is it thus adapted to man's most urgent wants, but it also affords the most efficient means for developing the whole of human nature, giving to all our powers their highest energy and noblest motives. It ennobles love and dignifies the very love of self; it opens to the deepest and most luminous knowledge, it gives the strongest incentives to increase in wisdom. It brings the highest motives to bear upon the performance of all our social and political duties, and to all the virtues of the character it adds grace and strength.

5. That it is thus fitted to all our relations and institutions, and gives them their highest character, is proved by the fact that a Christian family, a Christian community, and a Christian commonwealth are felt to be the highest forms which the family, society, and the state can assume.

6. When we would labor for the reform of the race, what teachings can we put in the very van of the contest in preference to the Christian view of the equality and brotherhood of mankind, of the evils of the inordinate love of wealth, of the terribleness of war, of the necessity of justice, and to its exhortations to the love of our neighbor and our brethren. All true reforms can only be the carrying out of the spirit and the injunctions of the kingdom of God. Moreover, the safety of reforms is best argued on the ground of the permanence and victories of that kingdom. And patience in the midst of discouragement and defeat is made more serene by our conviction that this kingdom must finally prevail, that the triumphs of sin and the maxims of expediency are for the day and the hour only, while the triumphs of truth and righteousness are for eternity.

7. Philosophy, science, and art, in their deepest and truest principles, are in harmony with God's kingdom, are advanced by it, and approximate to their perfect form as they receive and enthrone its truths.

8. That view of our future destiny, which is contained in sure promise and definite description only in the kingdom of God, is the only view which answers perfectly to all man's most enlarged and developed capacities, and to his highest and most hallowed aspirations.

9. It is for this kingdom that God has been ever laboring, it is his great, his grandest work, it contains the wealth of His wisdom, the crown of his purposes.[1] It will be the very embodiment of what is most grand and glorious in divinity, so far as it can be revealed to man. And in it man too has his part. Human achievement in carrying out divine purposes will have its eternal fruit and reward in this kingdom.

10. How far it will be perfectly realized upon the earth is a question of secondary importance. It is a kingdom the very idea of which when once embraced can stimulate human powers to their highest energy, human love to its noblest self-sacrifice, even to forgetfulness of self. That it will go on until the fulness of the seas is gathered in, until on the tops of the mountains the Lord's house shall be established, until every kingdom shall become Christ's, until all war and oppression and unrighteousness shall cease, until the very glory and fulness of the nations shall be given to Immanuel—this we know, for it has been declared. Whether its fullest glories are to be revealed on the very theater where sin has so long reigned, or in another sphere —that we know not fully. And whether we know it or not is of little moment compared with what we do know, and that is, that this kingdom of God will be perfectly consummated in glory and beauty somewhere and at some time.

[1] In this light the doctrine of Election should be viewed.

PART I.

THE UNION BETWEEN CHRIST AND THE INDIVIDUAL BELIEVER, AS EFFECTED BY THE HOLY SPIRIT.

This embraces the subjects of Justification, Regeneration, and Sanctification; with the underlying topic, which comes first to be considered, Election.

BOOK I.

PREDESTINATION, ELECTION, THE EFFECTUAL CALL.

CHAPTER I.

GENERAL OBSERVATIONS.

I.—The topics now coming up are known as the doctrines of grace. Grace, in its widest sense, means, any favor bestowed by a superior on an inferior. All our gifts in this sense are grace. But it is here used in a specific sense as favor bestowed upon the individual, fallen man, through the influence of the Holy Ghost. Man's entire sinfulness is presupposed, and Christ's atoning work, and here we consider the operation of the Holy Spirit.

II.—This operation must be traced back to the purpose of God, as part of the decrees of God. These have been already considered in part. It was stated that they included all events in Providence, as they take place. As events are in fact, so they are eternally in the purpose of God. The doctrine of decrees is simply that of divine providence considered as an eternal plan in the counsels of God. Any objection to decrees is an objection to the course of Providence. These decrees form one decree, one plan. All are connected with the main decree, or the great end for which God made and governs the world. That portion of the divine decrees which has respect to the final condition and destiny of moral beings, especially of man, is called Predestination.

III.—The doctrine of Predestination has to do simply with God's purpose or plan, as that includes the final condition of each individual, just as it comes to be. It contemplates the final condition of each individual as a part of the divine decree; not of course without respect to what has gone before, but including the whole life of the individuals, of which this end is the consummation.

IV.—In further elucidation of what is meant by Predestination, we make the following statements:

1. Predestination is not fatalism. Fatalism views all events and all actions as a mere matter of necessity, springing from natural causes and ultimately from blind causes. But Predestination refers all events ultimately to the purpose of a wise and holy God.

2. The doctrine of predestination is not to be confounded with supralapsarianism. In many objections to it, it is so confounded. Supralapsarianism views the fall of the human race as directly decreed on the part of God, in order to the divine glory. The sublapsarian view is, that evil was permitted and not efficiently produced, and that in the order of decrees the permission of evil goes before the decree for redemption.

3. Predestination is not the same as the doctrine of the divine efficiency. This latter doctrine, when carried out strictly, says that each event has for its cause a direct divine agency,—that God by immediate power brings into being every act of moral agents,—that his action in the matter of sin is as distinct as in the matter of holiness. The doctrine does not give heed to the distinction between what is decreed as part of a plan, and what is decreed by itself.

4. Those who hold to predestination are not the only persons who hold to the eternity of God's decrees. Many Arminians hold a doctrine of eternal decrees, while they deny predestination. Those who, believing in regeneration, believe also that man's free will goes before, while God assists, can also believe that from all eternity God determined to assist, and therefore they can hold to eternal divine decrees.

5. Predestination is not arbitrary, in the common usage of

the word arbitrary. The doctrine implies that all the divine purposes have wise and holy reasons. Predestination is arbitrary in the sense that God is not dependent on any will but his own for his purposes and plans; in the sense that He acts from mere will and mere power, it is not arbitrary. We may not be able to see the reasons: these are for the divine will and not for ours; but God would forfeit his rational nature if He ordained anything without a good and sufficient reason.

6. The theological systems which include predestination do not differ from other systems, *e. g.*, the Arminian system in its modifications, in respect to the grounds of God's final judgment upon men as to their final condition. In both cases the ground is wholly moral. It is the relation to Christ, involving the good or bad character of respective individuals, in regard to which this destiny is fixed.

7. The systems which include predestination differ from the Arminian systems in their view of the nature of divine grace, and of the way in which that grace operates. The latter say, and must say ultimately, that grace only assists, and is dependent on the human will for its use,—grace aids human volitions. The former say that grace ever precedes and directs the human will, while the will is free. The term in Arminianism is—assists: in Calvinism—grace precedes and directs. This is sometimes expressed in the formula: Grace is irresistible. This term is not to be approved, because it suggests an idea which is not intended to be conveyed. Irresistible, usually means, that which cannot be resisted or overcome even if the will be opposed to it, *e. g.*, in the case of natural force: but this cannot be the meaning in this case, because the divine purpose always carries the will with it.

8. The ultimate principles on which the assertion of the divine predestination rests are two: (*a.*) All events must have a sufficient cause; (*b.*) Of all true religious life God is the cause. The doctrine of original sin is presupposed, which makes the need of God's causative energy in the new life still stronger and more imperative.

CHAPTER II

ELECTION AND REPROBATION.

The doctrine of Predestination runs into the doctrine of Election. Election is a part of Predestination. Election is the expression of God's infinite love towards the human race, redeeming man from sin through Christ, and by the Holy Spirit bringing him into this state of redemption, so far as it is consistent with the interests of God's great and final kingdom. It is the divine love in its most concrete and triumphant form. It is called in Scripture the riches of divine grace.

§ 1. *Statement of the Scriptural Doctrine of Election.*
Westm. Shorter Cat., Q. 20. In Larger Cat., Q. 13, more particular statements are given: that the election is in Christ—that it is eternal—and includes the means thereof.

1. Election may be said to be: God's eternal purpose, as a part of his whole plan, to save some of the human race, in and by Jesus Christ. Election to eternal life is the end of all the divine purposes, including the means. The order of time is in the execution of the decree, and not in the decree itself. The following statements form no part of the doctrine of Election: That God created some men to damn them: That Christ died only for the elect; That the elect will be saved, let them do what they will; That the non-elect cannot be saved, let them do what they can; That the non-elect cannot comply with the conditions of salvation through natural inability. These positions we have considered elsewhere: whether in themselves they are true or false is not in question now: what we here say is, they form no part of the doctrine of Election.

2. The Scriptural statements.

(*a.*) The fullest passage is Eph. i. 4, 5, which gives the doctrine in its connections.

(*b.*) Election has reference to individuals and not to nations or classes. Luke xiii. 23: "Few" is individualizing, and so in the verses which follow. Mark xiii. 20; Rom. viii. 20-30: "Foreknew" includes a purpose as well as a knowledge. It is not a mere vision of knowledge. John xv. 16: "Ye" must mean individuals: John vi. 36-39; Acts xiii. 48; Rom. ix. 11.

(c.) It is to eternal life. The object of the whole plan of redemption is to bestow eternal life upon the lost: Acts xiii. 48; 1 Thess. v. 9, 10; 2 Thess. ii. 13; John xvii. 2. So that it is not a call to external privileges.

(d.) It is not of works. Although it is through and by the gracious acts of the individual. The works are the election itself in its carrying out. They are not the basis of it, but a part of it: 2 Tim. i. 9; Rom. ix. 11; xi. 6; Eph. i. 4, 5; 1 Pet. i. 2. In short, the election is *to* faith and holiness, and is not of persons as holy.

(e.) The election is ultimately to be referred to God: Matt. xi. 26; Rom. viii. 29; ix. 11; Eph. i. 11; Rom. xi. 5.

(f.) The election is in Christ: Eph. i. 4; John xvii. 2.

(g.) The election is eternal and unchangeable: Eph i. 4; Rom. viii. 29; John vi. 37; 2 Thess. ii. 13; Rev. xiii. 8.

3. Proof of the doctrine from other doctrines.

(a.) It results from the doctrine of the divine sovereignty.

(b.) It results from the fact that salvation is of grace: Eph. ii. 5, 8.

(c.) It results from the doctrines of depravity and original sin. By nature we are in such a state that only divine grace can rescue us.

(d.) It results from the doctrine of regeneration.

(e.) It is confirmed by the experience of believers. They all confess that the new life within them is of grace.

4. Theories of Election.

I.—The theory of Nationalism. This is, that nations are elected; God sends the gospel to certain peoples; Election is not to eternal life, but is a national call. It is, living among a people where God's grace is proclaimed. Some non-elect in this sense may finally be saved: in nations where the gospel is not preached, some may be saved through an accidental hearing of the word, or through a special calling of divine providence.

Remarks:

(*a.*) This theory concedes the principle. God may make a discrimination in regard to nations on a large scale, and be just and benevolent in doing it.

(*b.*) It is impossible to see or show how God can elect nations without electing individuals. The general demands the specific, the universal the particular. In the order of thought the generic comes first and the specific next, but in the order of history the specific comes first and the general afterwards.

(*c.*) The argument of the apostle in Rom. ix., which is relied upon, is against the theory. He has before shown (chaps. v., vi., vii., viii.) that in Christ alone are justification and sanctification: then he encounters the objection from the Jew as being the seed of Abraham: the promise to Abraham, he says, is not frustrated by the calling of the Gentiles, leaving Jews to perish: God has always thus shown his sovereignty: Isaac only was called, 7-9; Esau and Jacob are instanced, 10-14; Pharaoh, verses 15-18. This is not unjust to those whom He condemns on account of their sins. Israel is passed by because they sought righteousness not by faith but by the works of the law. Verse 22, vessels of wrath fitted to destruction, gives the substance of the doctrine of Reprobation.

(*d.*) The arguments already given to show that Election is of individuals, and that it is to eternal life, disprove this theory.

II.—The theory of Ecclesiastical Individualism: God calls individuals, but only to the external privileges of his church.

This is advocated by many of the divines in the Episcopal Church, in order to unite Arminianism with their theory of the church. As many of them interpret "regenerated" in the baptismal service as meaning, united with the church in an external way, so election is understood as election to the external privileges of the church.

Remarks:

(*a.*) The theory is true as far as it goes.

(*b.*) It includes the principle of election. If God discriminates externally, He may internally.

(*c.*) It excludes the divine agency from the most important part of the whole work—the internal and spiritual.

(*d.*) Scripture testifies to the election of individuals to faith, holiness, and salvation.

III.—The Arminian, and in part the Lutheran, and in part the Pelagian, theory.

This asserts that election is not external, nor national, but—is election to salvation: it is, however, an election of those who repent and believe—not of individuals, but of that *class* of persons who repent and believe. It is of all those who comply with the conditions. God foresees that such and such will accept the conditions, and therefore elects them—on the basis of his seeing that they will of themselves repent and believe. Pelagians say that one man repents and believes and another does not, and election and reprobation are based upon these facts. Arminians say that God has given to all men sufficient grace,—that there is no urgency of that grace, no specific efficiency of it, but one accepts it and another does not.

Remarks:

(*a.*) This makes God's agency to be dependent on that of man. Man chooses God first, and then God chooses him to blessedness. The Scriptures say: According as He chose us in Him . . . . that we should be holy and without blemish before Him in love, Eph. i. 4.

(*b.*) The doctrines of sin and grace show that there is a moral inability in man which only God's grace can or does overcome.

(*c.*) The theory is against Christian experience. No Arminian or Pelagian can pray according to this doctrine, however much he may preach it.

§ 2. *Reprobation.*

This includes two parts, Præterition and Reprobation (Final Condemnation). The Præterition is a sovereign act; the Reprobation is a judicial act. The predestination in this case does not refer to the sinful state as coming from God (the supralapsarian view), but to the divine act which is consequent upon the sinful state. In the præterition, the divine agency is simply negative—a not interfering. The reprobation is judicial and in that sense positive. If any are finally lost, there must of necessity be a divine purpose in respect to the loss: otherwise there is that in the fact which was not taken into the plan. It is not Calvinistic to say that God created men to damn them, or that He made them on purpose to condemn them, in order to show his justice. That position has never been accepted in this country, and in the school of Edwards it was effectually demolished. The end of God in creation is not to illustrate his justice in condemning some to eternal torment. The condemnation is simply incidental to the great end of the divine government, which is the securing of the supremacy and triumph of holiness. In regard to those who do not submit to that government, this end is attained, as far as it can be, by their destruction; but that destruction is not the end or object. The chief objections to this part of the doctrine of Predestination almost all arise from viewing reprobation as something by itself, and not as a part of God's whole plan. The representation often made is that God chose the punishment as though He delighted in it,—but God delights in holiness. Another objection comes from supposing reprobation to be without reference to character or desert: but it is the final condemnation on account of the desert.

1. The Scriptural proof.

(*a.*) The doctrine of Election involves Præterition.

(*b.*) All passages that prove the final condemnation of some imply the doctrine of Reprobation. More particularly, Rom. xi. 18; 1 Cor. i. 26; 1 Pet. ii. 8; Jude 15.

§ 3. *Objections to the Doctrine of Predestination.*

First Class. Objections on philosophical grounds.[1] The objections are to the two main statements: Every event must have a cause, God is the cause of all spiritual life.

Obj. I.—The more consistent Arminians object that the law of causality does not apply to the production of our religious states. They assert that the law of causality does not apply to all events in time,—that events produced by the power of the

---

[1] Well stated in Bledsoe's Theodicy and Mozley's Predestination.

human will are not under the law of causality, as respects their origination in the will.

Remarks:

1. The law of causality is not, in any consistent thinking, understood to be that for every event there is wholly an external cause. This notion of it is derived from the sphere of mechanics and dynamics, and not from the sphere of life, still less from psychology. A stone cannot move without an external power acting upon it, but everything having life, besides the external agencies which bear upon it, has also an internal energy. So it is in the human soul. There is a principle of spontaneity, of origination. That however does not exclude causality. It is a proper causal power or energy. The law still applies, only we have here a new causal power given in the will itself. Unquestionably there is such spontaneous force or power in man, so that he is the proper author of his own acts. He is not the sole author, but he is the proper author, and the law of causality covers this spontaneous energy as much as it does the external influences.

2. But, besides this internal force of the will, there must be some object in view of which the will is exerted; else there can be no choice. Mere will cannot of itself produce choice. Choice implies an end or object, which is as necessary to the choice as the possession of will. It enters into the choice as a part of the whole effect. Volition is made up of two elements: the action of the will and the thing chosen. These two together make up the cause of the volition, as the effect.¹

Obj. II.—(Mozley.) It is not to be affirmed that God is the *proper* cause or source of all religious life, because if God be such,

¹ [The above is found only in students' notes. The fuller view is given in Faith and Philosophy, p. 359 seq. Perhaps the author's statements might be thus summed up: Into choices there must perforce enter, not merely the *form* of personal agency but also its vital substance. The feelings and affections can no more be kept out of the will than out of the man. Self-determination is essential to freedom, but self-determination is a procedure of the man, and not of the will viewed as mere capacity of choice. What is *in* the man—as affection, etc., as well as what he reaches out to—as object of desire, etc., goes to the self-determination, and hence it is vain to say that human spontaneity is not covered by the law of causality. Like everything else in the successions of time, the originations of the human will have their limitations, their processes, and *their laws*]

there cannot then be first, *i. e.*, proper and real, causes of the religious life in the action of the human soul.

Remarks:

1. There may be good and sufficient second causes working under the first, and having their proper sphere—not absolute, but relative—not independent, but dependent—yet still proper causes, not mere modifications of the first cause, but having force of themselves.

2. The very notion of God makes Him to be the author of all religious acts. Religion is inconceivable without divine influence. There may be morality without divine influence, but not religion.

3. All the more is such influence necessary in the case of depraved beings, where the moral power is lost. If God must be the source of holiness in the angels, He must be the source of it in human beings where the soul is alienated from Him.

4. The Scriptures expressly refer holy acts and states to God: Eph. ii. 10; Phil. ii. 13; Rom. xii. 3; John vi. 44.

5. The Scriptures make a difference in respect to the divine agency as to sin, and as to holiness: making it direct in regard to holiness, and permissive in regard to sin.

The Second Class of Objections. Objections brought against the divine justice and benevolence in Predestination.

Obj. III.—God is unjust, or at least not benevolent, towards the non-elect.

Remarks:

1. We have the apostle's reply, in Rom. ix. There is that in the divine dealings which is inscrutable, in this as in other matters.

2. The objection is one against actual facts; because God does actually bring some to eternal life, while He passes by others, and must have purposed to do what He actually does.

3. The objection involves the assumption that God ought to treat all men alike, which would apply against discrimination in providence as well as in grace.

4. If the non-elect are sinners, it is just to treat them as sinners. Sinners cannot establish a *claim* upon God for the

highest measures of grace. If they are and continue to be sinners, they deserve punishment as a simple matter of justice

5. But—is it benevolent to pass them by? It is, we must say, the procedure of a benevolent being: of course we do not argue that the benevolence is illustrated in the præterition. (*a.*) If we cannot see how the benevolence is consistent with the præterition, still we must admit both the facts; God is infinitely benevolent, and there are some whom He does not bring to eternal life; inasmuch as each is established by its own evidence. (*b.*) Benevolence, in its highest sense, has supreme regard to holiness, and not to happiness. Holiness is the ultimate term with God even as a benevolent being. (*c.*) If it is right for God to leave any to perish as sinners, it is right for Him to purpose to do so, because this is simply the same thing over again. (*d.*) God shows his benevolence to all men, in various ways. The sparing of their lives in a state of probation, the provision of an atonement for the whole world, the offers of eternal life under the sound of the gospel, are all proofs of benevolence. (*e.*) Perhaps some weight is to be allowed to the suggestion of Bishop Butler,[1] that the election of all might be hazardous to the interests of the divine government. The belief of Universalism certainly has no tendency to keep men from sin. (*f.*) For aught that we know, the amount and kind of divine influence necessary to secure the salvation of all men might be inconsistent with God's moral government.

Obj. IV.—From the effect of the doctrine upon those who are not yet Christians, *i. e.*, those who cannot be said to be nonelect, their case being not yet decided. The doctrine of election is said to be formidable to them.

But, (*a.*) The doctrine of election and præterition concerns the final state of men, which no man can absolutely know beforehand. A man cannot know so that the doctrine shall deter him. (*b.*) The doctrine of election is, still further, that men are elect in Christ. It is on account of a general atonement, of a provision for all men. What a man has to do is not to determine who are the elect, but to come to Christ. (*c*) The divine

---

[1] The suggestion is approved by Chalmers.

purpose of election runs through the human will, and it is with the conscious action of this that man has to do. The question of salvation comes up in the form, Will a man accept or reject Christ? (*d.*) Election comprehends the means as well as the end, and not the end without the means. It is the whole of God's plan in respect to each individual. Almost all the objections against the doctrine of predestination rest on the hypothesis that God, by a merely arbitrary choice, has consigned individuals to a final state. That is not the doctrine. The objections also rest upon the hypothesis that an individual can and may know that he belongs to one or the other class. But even the elect cannot certainly know their election, or at all events, not until they come to assurance, which is the gift of God in their highest sanctification.

Obj. V.—The effect of this doctrine on those who suppose themselves to be of the elect must be to make them presumptuous.

But, (*a.*) It is the *saints'* perseverance which is set forth in the doctrine of election. If any are living in presumptuous sins, they cannot claim that they are in the course of such perseverance. The elect are those, too, who *persevere*. The objection rests on the notion that one can be assured of election without holy exercises, while the doctrine is that he can be assured only in such exercises. The objection assumes that the end may be known without the means; the doctrine is that the end can be attained only by and through the means, and the certainty of the attainment can be judged of only in the light of the means of the attainment. A kindred form of the objection is that the elect are led to believe that they may be saved whatever they do. The answer is that the doctrine has respect to God's purpose about the final state of believers. No man can know anything about the divine purpose regarding his salvation, except as he is practicing the Christian virtues.

Obj. VI.—God cannot sincerely make the offer of life to all, when He knows that there are some who will not accept.

The marks of sincerity in any offer are the following: (*a.*) That the blessing offered is in existence and at the disposal of the one who offers it. (*b.*) That he is willing that it should be accepted. (*c.*) That it is offered on terms that can be complied with by the individual to whom it is offered, so that all that is needed on his part is willingness.

Such is the case with respect to the offer of salvation to all men in the gospel. It is a blessing which really exists, because a general atonement has been made; it is a blessing which God is willing to bestow; He is not willing that any should perish. It is within the compass of man's natural capacities to comply. No addition needs to be made to his powers and faculties, to enable him to comply. Acceptance or rejection is the action of his own voluntary nature.

There is an ambiguity in the discussions of this subject in the different uses of the word *will*. It is used sometimes in the sense of a general desire, sometimes of a specific purpose. (*a.*) It is undeniable on the ground of Scripture that God desires the salvation of every man as, in itself considered, the best thing for him. He offers salvation to all, and pleads with them to accept it. He offers that which is provided, and which they may accept, and urges it importunately. (*b.*) God's decree of præterition is not that some shall not believe, but is simply not to use certain means of moving them to belief. All things considered, He has chosen to pursue his purpose of having a people to his praise, to the extent of insuring belief in some instances, but not in all. (*c.*) All of God's reasons for this course we do not know. Some reasons are intimated. Blindness of mind, hardness of heart, resistance of light, of grace offered, of the influences of the Spirit, are given as characteristics of many of those who are not included in God's purpose of election. It may be that many of the finally impenitent resist more light than many who are saved.

CHAPTER III.

THE GOSPEL CALL.

Election is carried out through the proclamation of grace, through the call to repentance and faith, issuing in the effectual calling of those who are finally saved. This call is both external and internal. The external is in the preaching of the gospel, and the internal is the call to the spirit or soul. This internal call, considered in its results on the elect, is called efficacious or effectual grace. The election results in the call, both external and internal, and in the formation of the elect into the church. Some of those who are opposed to the doctrine of election, *e. g.*, the Lutherans, make the call to be universal, and make it to consist in the whole of divine providence towards all nations. The Lutheran formula asserts very strongly that a special call addressed by the Divine Spirit to the soul must be maintained to be universal, even though experience seems to run counter to it.

§ 1. *Of the External Call.*

This is an invitation on the part of divine grace to sinners to accept through grace the blessings offered to them in Christ, addressed generally through the preaching of the word, although it may also be by the printed page or personal conversation. It is as wide as the proclamation of·the gospel in any form. It includes the announcement of the fact of salvation in Christ, an invitation to accept that salvation, an invitation which rises to a command, including a promise and a threat—John iii. 16, 18. This external call is to be addressed to all. It is part of the function of the church to see that it is addressed to all men—Rom. x. 14, 15. Still further, this call, as thus addressed, is binding upon all men. Men are bound to accept this gracious invitation. Not to comply is the great sin. In a state of ruin, invited to accept of everlasting life, their guilt is heightened if they reject. It is not addressed to the *elect* alone, but is addressed to and binding upon all men.[1] This external call has for its characteristics—that it is sincere on the part of God—that it may be resisted—and that it is adapted to lead to conversion.

§ 2. *The Internal Call.*

The internal call of God to eternal life is a call of divine grace made by the word, applied by the Spirit, in part by his direct agency, upon the soul. This divine influence upon the soul is not exercised upon one of its faculties, but upon all the faculties of the mind, illuminating the understanding, rousing the feelings, and leading to right acts of the will. Still further, this call is made under these influences in view of two grand facts: on the one hand, the condemnation of law and knowledge of sin under the law; on the other hand, the presentation of Christ as the Redeemer from sin.

§ 3. *Under this general Statement, some Questions and Difficulties are raised.*

I.—Is the knowledge of the word, the Scripture, the revealed truth, of Christ as the center and source of salvation, always *necessary* in order to salvation?

The extreme positions: (1) Except as Christ is known the soul cannot be included in the electing love of God; there is no salvation except through and by a distinct and explicit knowledge of Christ. (2) Under the light of nature alone and without Christ, men may be saved by complying with the demands made in conscience and by reason.

Observations:—(1) It is a matter of fact that the knowledge of Christ *is* given and is *necessary* to be given where men are saved. There is, humanly speaking, no probability of salvation apart from such knowledge. (2) It is equally undeniable that such a knowledge of Christ is necessary to full, explicit, confident trust. There cannot be the peace of believing, or a full knowledge of salvation, a personal conviction in the case full and

---

[1] This is one of the great points in the controversy against the Antinomian position. See Fuller's "Gospel Worthy of all Acceptation" and Bellamy's "True Religion Delineated." It was such preaching as this against a dead orthodoxy which led to many precious results in revivals.

round, unless there be such knowledge of Christ. Without this there must always be doubt in the individual's personal experience. (3) Yet there may be, under the influence of the Holy Spirit, renewal of the soul without this explicit knowledge. That follows from the secret nature of the divine agency, and from the position that infants dying before actual transgression are of the elect. (4) Yet such internal renewal, if it be genuine, will always lead to a belief in Christ as the only Saviour, when He is made known. The test of the reality of the new birth would be, that as soon as Christ is presented the soul will welcome Him. This is in conformity with the position in the Westminster Confession, chap. x., § 3.

II.—Are the Scriptures the only efficacious means of such a renewal? The purport of this question is: whether the Scriptures considered as light and illuminating influence, as addressed only to the intellect—excluding the direct operation of the Holy Spirit on the soul—are the only efficacious means of salvation; or whether, besides the Scriptures there is in the case of renewal a direct influence of the Holy Spirit, which is not restricted to the word, which is not simply by and through the word. Whether the entire efficacious influence is the Scriptures *and* the Holy Spirit, or the Holy Spirit *in and through* the Scriptures.

The various forms of opinion: (1) The Pelagian view. Mere truth, a vivid presentation of the truth is enough, and is the only means about which we can know anything definitely. It has been said by some one, that if he was as eloquent as the Holy Spirit, he could so preach as to convert souls. (2) Another opinion. That in some way, to us unknown, the word of God as preached is made clear and mighty by the Spirit, and becomes an effectual motive—yet without the direct operation of the Spirit on the soul. The Spirit operates through the word, so that the word forms the influence and motive, and the Spirit in the word gives it efficacy. The word is the sword, and the Spirit wields the sword. (3) The third view is, that besides the truth and the Spirit in the truth, there is also a direct operation of the Holy Spirit upon the soul.

As to the first opinion.—It is conceded by this that the Spirit is the author of the truth, that the gospel truth is the highest kind of truth, but it is said that there is no other operation of the Spirit than that which is given in the word through the truth.

We say: (1) This revealed truth is ordinarily necessary and essential. (2) It is the instrumental cause. (3) But the question remains, Why is this truth so much clearer and brighter at some times than at others? Why are the feelings roused so strongly by the truth on certain occasions, and left dead at others? This must be attributed to the influence of the Holy Spirit. (4) It is difficult if not impossible to conceive of an operation of the truth without an operation on the soul. Here are the words of Scripture: at one time they are without influence, at another they become effectual. The Holy Spirit is said to work through the truth, but how can He do so without affecting the soul? (5) The Scriptures distinctly recognize a direct operation of the Spirit.

As to the second opinion.—This asserts that the truth is made clear and potent by some unknown efficacy of the Spirit, yet the operation of the Spirit is confined to this, and is not a direct influence upon the affections and the will. The Holy Ghost is necessary, wherever the word is uttered, to give it influence, yet through the word alone does He operate on the affections and will. A modification of this view is seen in the doctrine of moral suasion—that the Spirit operates on men as men do upon each other.

Remarks:

(1) The truth is doubtless the instrumental cause, ordinarily. We are begotten—or brought forth—by the word of truth (James i. 18). (2) The truth is brought to bear upon us in greater light and power through the influence of the Spirit, in a supernatural way—by an operation kindred to moral suasion. (3) But unless the feelings are also enlisted by influencing them, how can the truth affect them? The sensibilities to religious impressions are dormant through depravity. They are to be excited and roused, in order that the truth may be felt. Through

this excitation of the feelings, the truth becomes clearer and more efficacious, and only through this. A supernatural influence must be conceded here. (4) Nobody can deny that there are other kinds of operation besides that through the truth. It is natural from what we know of God's working, that there should be other modes through which the Holy Spirit shall influence the soul. God works in all and through all. In the sphere of divine providence, the divine energy attends the working of all second causes. Much more in the sphere of grace. The divine agency doubtless attends as much the operations of the feelings as the intellect, and as much those of the will as the feelings. It is impossible, in any rational view of the divine agency, to exclude it from any part of the work. The view under consideration excludes it from every part except the intellect. The fact that we do not know the mode of the Spirit's operations should admonish us not to limit them.

As to the third position.—This is, that besides all that can be put under the head of moral suasion and of supernatural influence through the truth, there is in the renewal of the soul, according to Scripture, a divine, secret, and direct influence. This is shown by the following considerations: (1) The Scriptures distinguish between the two, and assert the need of both: 1 Thess. i. 5, 6; 2 Thess. ii. 13, 14; John vi. 44. (2) The Scriptures also speak of the inward working of the Holy Spirit: Phil. ii. 13; Heb. xiii. 21; Acts xvi. 14. (3) The descriptions of regeneration imply this. It is spoken of as a new creation and a resurrection to life. The working of the Spirit is compared for its might with the working in Christ when He was raised from the dead: Eph. i. 19, 20. (4) The Scriptural view of depravity, of man's natural state and need, makes such an internal working of the Spirit needful: 1 Cor. ii. 14. Depravity leaves the affections dormant. The spiritual affections are asleep. They need to be roused most of all. The most powerful outward means are resisted until God brings the soul into subjection. (5) Prayer implies more than an operation of the word. We ask God for grace not only to understand the truth but to sanctify the soul, purify the affections, guide the will, and change the will. In the struggles of renewal, every soul feels that divine grace working within, and working mightily, can alone save it. We have examples of this in the prayers in Scripture: Col. i. 9-11. To this may be added the good effects of the doctrine, the ascribing to God our holiness, and the cleansing and purifying of the affections and dispositions, and the constant sense of our dependence on divine grace for all advances in sanctification.

III.—Is there a common, as well as effectual, grace? The affirmative is the correct reply, on the following grounds:

1. From the experience of the impenitent, and of ourselves while impenitent. The influence of the Holy Spirit is much wider than we are apt to suppose. Probably there is always more or less influence of the Spirit by and with the word. Belief in such common grace is the strength and confidence of the preacher, and it is very probable that all moral good in the world is ultimately to be ascribed to this, even in the lower spheres of humanity, i. e., to the influence of God's grace in the course of his providence. It is much more scriptural and much safer to extend the sphere of the Spirit's influence than to extend the scope of human ability. The influence is so wide that probably we cannot extend it too far, i. e., in respect to the common methods in which it is exerted.

2. The Bible speaks of a resistance of the Spirit, a grieving of the Spirit, which implies that there is a common grace as well as that which effects the conversion of the soul. All that precedes the renewal of the soul—the conviction of sin, any feeling or desire leading towards renewal or a better life, is properly to be ascribed to the influence of the Holy Spirit in the way of common grace.

3. This common grace passes over into effectual grace in proportion as the sinner yields to the divine influence,—so that the work is God's, not man's.

IV.—How does effectual differ from common grace?

1. Effectual grace is the grace which effects that which common grace tends to effect.

2. Its efficacy, in the last analysis, is owing to the divine

influence. It is God's sovereign power, and is applied according to his purpose to save the elect. The pressure of the divine influence is what causes the efficacy. All that man does in the case is removing the hindrance.

3. In consciousness, psychologically, we cannot distinguish the difference between the two: we can ascertain it only from results. We cannot distinguish the divine grace from the good produced by it, or our own act, because it is only in our act that *that* divine grace is known. That which is immediately presented to the soul is its own acts, feelings, and thoughts. That these come from God, we say on the ground of Scriptural testimony, and because they are leading to that which is well pleasing to God—renewal and sanctification of the soul. We are conscious of the reality of the influence only after the act.

4. This effectual grace is irresistible in the sense that it carries the will and affections with it. No counter influence is supposable in the case, because what it does is to engross the affections and change the will. The word irresistible was applied to it first by the opponents of Calvinism, but is explained by Calvinists in this sense—that the will goes with the divine will and influence, and there is no thought of resistance.

BOOK II.

OF JUSTIFICATION.[1]

CHAPTER I.

PRELIMINARY CONSIDERATIONS.

1. If considered in the historical order, the order of time, the justification of the sinner before God comes after regeneration. Our discussions tend to it naturally here. But regeneration, in the Christian sense, presupposes a possible justification; it includes justification as possible and actual, in the case of each regenerated person. When regenerated, believers are, for Christ's sake, justified. Regeneration is not a mere change of inward state, but of external relations, through union with Christ. Being freely justified for Christ's sake, man is brought into a state of pardon and acceptance with God. The law no longer condemns—the sinner is justified.

2. The question, How can man be just with God? is at the heart of all religions. The Pagan systems abound in mortifications, etc., by which a justification is sought.

3. In the doctrine of justification, the gospel is most radically distinguished from a merely legal system, and from any moral system which rests on merely legal ideas. These make personal obedience, conformity to the law, to be the only ground of acceptance. In justification, acceptance is on the ground of what Christ has done, of his merits,—of what another has done for us, in our stead. The doctrine of justification is a central one; it modifies all the rest; according to the view taken of this, the entire system is distinguished.

4. Views of the atonement determine the views on justifica

---

[1] References. Owen, one of the ablest treatises in the English literature. The view of the Anglican Church is in Bishop Bull's work on the Harmony between Paul and James. There is a good exposition of the Scholastic view in Dr. Hampden's Bampton Lecture, V. One of the best expositions of the subject is in Dr. Richards' Lectures.

tion, if logical sequence is observed. We have to do here, not with views of natural justice, but with divine methods.[1]

5. Justification by Faith alone is the distinguishing article of the Reformers' position against the Roman Catholic system. Romanists make justification and sanctification to go hand in hand, personal holiness to be the ground or reason of justification, and hence works are mixed up with grace. The Reformers insist on the direct relation to Christ, justification for his sake, union with Him, trust in Him. It is "the gift of the giver, and not the reward of the worker."

6. Nor are justification and pardon the same in Scripture. The view of Emmons (Works, vol. v.) is: that justification "is no more nor less than pardon," that " God rewards men for their own and not Christ's obedience."

(*a.*) But the words as used in common life relate to wholly different things.[2] If a man is "declared just" by a human tribunal, he is not pardoned, he is acquitted, his own inherent righteousness as respects the charge against him is recognized and declared.

The Gospel proclaims both pardon and justification. There is no significance in the use of the word "justify," if pardon be all that is intended.

(*b.*) Certain expressions of Scripture are opposed to the view that justification is simply pardon: Rom. v. 1, 2, 17, 18, 21; 1 Cor. i. 30.

(*c.*) Justification involves what pardon does not, a righteousness which is the ground of the acquittal and favor; not the mere favor of the sovereign but the merit of Christ, is at the basis,—the righteousness which is of God. The ends of the law are so far satisfied by what Christ has done, that the sinner can be pardoned. The law is not merely set aside, but its great ends are answered by what Christ has done in our behalf. God might pardon as a sovereign, from mere benevolence (as regard to hap-

---

[1] If we regard the atonement simply as answering the ends of a governmental scheme, our view must be that justification merely removes an obstacle, and the end of it is only pardon and not eternal life.

[2] See on this point a sermon on Justification by J. F. Stearns, D.D., before the Synod of New York and New Jersey, 1853.

piness), but in the gospel He does more—He pardons in consistency with his holiness—upholding that as the main end of all his dealings and works.

(*d.*) Justification involves acquittal from all the penalty of the law and the inheritance of all the blessings of the redeemed state. The penalty of the law: spiritual, temporal, eternal death, is all taken away, and the opposite blessings are conferred in and through Christ: the resurrection to blessedness, the gift of the Spirit, and eternal life.

(*e.*) If justification is forgiveness simply, it applies only to the *past*. If it is also a title to life, it includes the future condition of the soul. The latter alone is consistent with the plan and decrees of God respecting Redemption—his seeing the end from the beginning.[1]

7. Justification is not a merely governmental provision, as it must be on any scheme which denies that Christ's work has direct respect to the ends of the law.

Neither does it find its ground, where some extreme Protestant views would place it, in our internal state of repentance, faith, or love, or any inward works (this being made the distinction from the Roman Catholic ground—external works), as the meritorious basis of our acceptance. That ground is Christ, what Christ has done—faith is the instrument. An internal change is always a *sine qua non* of justification, but not its meritorious ground.

8. Union with Christ is the capital idea here. Edwards: "What is real in the relation between Christ and the believer is the foundation of what is legal." Dorner (his own summary of his doctrine in Neue Evang. Kirchenzeitung, 1867, p. 744): (*a.*) The *Actus Forensis* in God becomes also transeunt,—seen in the "Friedensruf Gottes," in the believing soul; (*b.*) By this, peace and joy flow into the soul; (*c.*) From the consciousness of the forgiveness of

---

[1] The reason why justification has been taken as pardon is two-fold. (*a.*) It *does* involve pardon: this is its negative side, while it has a positive side also—the title to eternal life. (*b.*) The tendency to resolve the Gospel into an ethical system. Only our acts of choice as meritorious could procure a title to favor, a positive reward. Christ might remove the obstacle, but the title to heaven is derived only from what we ourselves do.

sins, and the blessedness given therewith, are developed the desire and love of the good; (*d.*) Man becomes partaker of that peace and joy, and conscious of his justification, in that Christ is laid hold of by faith, and thus the *union* or the marriage of God and man is completed; (*e.*) The renewed man, even in his sanctification, can never derive (deduce) his gracious estate from the sanctification, but only and always the sanctification from the grace.

9. The statement of the doctrine in the Confession, Q. 33, Shorter Cat.: "Justification is an act of God's free grace, wherein He pardoneth all our sins, and accepteth us as righteous in his sight, only for the righteousness of Christ imputed to us, and received by faith alone."

Observations:

"Imputation" means, reckoning to one's account that which he has not—treating one as if he were that which he is not. It does not mean, transferring of personal righteousness.

The relation to *God* consists in his exercise of "free grace," his "pardoning" and "accepting as righteous."

The relation to *Christ* is seen, in his righteousness being that "for the sake" of which the justification is made. The righteousness is "imputed," what is his is set to our account. And it is "righteousness" which is imputed: the transaction is a moral one.

The relation of justification to *ourselves* is seen, in the fact that it is received by "faith alone." ("Yet is it not alone in the person justified, but is ever accompanied with all other saving graces." Confession, chap. xi. § 2.) Faith is the instrument by which justification is received, and it is the only instrument.

A further statement in the Confession of Faith, chap. xi. § 4: "God did, from all eternity, decree to justify all the elect; . . . nevertheless, they are not justified until the Holy Spirit doth, in due time, actually apply Christ unto them."

CHAPTER II.

OF THE TERM AND IDEA: JUSTIFY—JUSTIFICATION; THE GENERAL AND SCRIPTURAL SENSE.

1. The general term δικαιοσύνη, righteousness, means, (*a.*) The righteousness which the law demands, holiness. It applies to the internal state. It is, the state of man as corresponding to the divine law—not merely the outward relation, but also the internal state. This is not justification. But the Scriptures distinguish—(*b.*) That righteousness which is the ground of our justification, not of works, but of God, through faith: Rom. i. 17; iii. 21, 22, 26; iv. 3, 5, 6, 9; Gal. iii. 6.

The classic sense of δικαιοσύνη is, state of righteousness, justice (without reference to what is due to a personal God), whereas the general Christian sense of the word is, the state of a man corresponding to the divine will (or law).

Δικαιοσύνη is the general term for conformity to law: the property of those who belong to the kingdom of God. It is, their whole state as conformed to the divine law; it is susceptible of degrees; it also includes sanctification. (That it includes the internal state as well as the objective relation is seen from Rom. ix. 30; Gal. v. 5; Rom. vi. 16; xiii. 1 seq.; xiv. 17; 1 Cor. i. 30; Gal. iii. 21; Cf. Gal. v. 5.)

Λογίζεσθαι εἰς δικαιοσύνην (Rom. iv. 3, 5, 6, 9, 22; Gal. iii. 6; James ii. 23, all from Gen. xv. 6) designates the contrast to the personal δικαιοσύνη (that ἐξ ἔργων): and means that righteousness which, without merit of ours, is declared to be ours by God, for Christ's sake.

2. The terms δικαιόω, δικαίωσις, are always used of the *actus forensis*, the declaration of righteousness, whether made in view of the present state or of the future, of δικαιοσύνη τοῦ Θεοῦ, or of full personal righteousness. They set forth Justification in distinction from Sanctification. (The only exception is Rev. xxii. 11, "He that is righteous, let him *be* righteous still," δικαιωθήτω ἔτι; but the best reading is, δικαιοσύνην ποιησάτω ἔτι. Which-

ever be adopted, the variation shows that δικαιωθήτω in the sense of: let him *make himself* or continue *to be* righteous, was "intolerable to a Greek ear.")

δικαίωμα is used in both senses: as a righteous deed, Rom. v. 18 (= τῆς ὑπακοῆς, v. 19); and as a justifying act, Rom. v. 16 (where it is opposed to κατάκριμα).

3. The whole question about the Scriptural terms rendered "justify," "justification" is—do they mean, declare righteous, or, make righteous.

(*a.*) In common speech, to justify one's self, to justify God, etc., is not—to make just. "Ye are they which justify yourselves before men" (Luke xvi. 15) is, Ye are they which assert your righteousness before men; "he, willing to justify himself" (Luke x. 29) is, wishing to make it appear, to have it declared and admitted, that he had not put an unnecessary question.

(*b.*) The whole reasoning of the Epistles to the Romans and the Galatians proceeds on this understanding.

(*c.*) It is the concession of Biblical scholars, that—to use Wieseler's language[1]—"leaving out the contested passages (such as Rev. xxii. 11), there is not a passage in the New Testament, where δικαιοῦν means aught but declare."

Wieseler says: "δικαιοῦν in the Septuagint means 'make just' only in Dan. xii. 3, Isa. liii. 11, Ps. lxxiii. 13, (Sirach xviii. 22)." " In Rom. iii. 20, 'by the deeds of the law shall no flesh be justified before Him,' Gal. ii. 16 (same as Rom. iii. 20, omitting ἐνώπιον αὐτοῦ, and both from Ps. cxliii. 2,) and Gal. iii. 11, 'and that by the law no man is justified before God,' the meaning cannot *possibly* be, *make* just."

"So too δικαιοῦν is declared to be the same as λογισθῆναι εἰς δικαιοσύνην in Rom. iv. 3, 5, 9, 23, 24; Gal. iii. 6; *i. e.*, justitia imputata, non infusa."

"Even in James the two phrases are used as equivalent: viz., δικαιοῦσθαι in James ii. 21, 24, 25; and λογισθῆναι εἰς δικαιοσύνην in James ii. 23."

---

[1] Galaterbrief, 1859, pp. 176-204. He cites Clem. of Rome in 1 Cor. ch. 32; Chrysostom, as so interpreting Rom. viii. 33; Theodoret, Rom. iii. 24, and Augustine, De Spir. et Littera. c. 16, "justum habere," though afterwards "justum facere" (Cf. on this, Nitzsch, Theol. Stud. u. Kritik., 1834, p. 481ff).

"Again in 1 Cor. i. 30, vi. 11, ἁγιασμός and ἡγιάσθητε are named with and distinguished from δικαιοσύνη and ἐδικαιώθητε." Justification involves acquittal from all the penalty and inheritance of all the blessings which come under the law.

CHAPTER III.

Justification (δικαίωσις) involves a righteousness (δικαιοσύνη) as its ground.

This is the reasoning of Paul in Romans and Galatians.

That it does so is evident:

1. From the nature of the case. (*a.*) If justification be not mere pardon; (*b.*) if the believer is declared just and admitted to the favor of a holy God; (*c.*) if God is a moral Governor, having supreme regard to holiness as the end of the law; (*d.*) if no one can be saved unless as righteous in God's sight.

2. From Scripture. If it is not so, there is no significance in the term δικαιοῦν, the Scripture need only have said "pardon." Rom. x. 4; Phil. iii. 9; Rom. iv. 6; 2 Cor. v. 21; Rom. v. 18, 19; Rom. iii. 26.

"God will not justify without a righteousness, nor without a righteousness which does honor to his law and sets its authority high in the sight of the universe" (Dr. Richards, p. 390).

CHAPTER IV.

This righteousness which is the ground of justification is not that of the sinner, personally fulfilling the demands of the law. It is not a legal justification, by which each is treated according to his personal deserts—not a legal justification in the sense of distributive justice.

1. It cannot be so, on account of the sinner's moral state. (*a.*) As a matter of fact, he is in a sinful, guilty condition, liable

to the just condemnation of the law. All men know this. (*b.*) If he should repent, he could not wipe out the past, the condemnation remains. (*c.*) So great is the power of sin in him that he lies morally unable to turn,—his natural ability does not avail for this, on account of the strength and power of sin. (*d.*) God cannot consistently merely pardon. (*e.*) Men cannot justify themselves by any denial of guilt. God accuses them, and God's law demands perfect holiness of them. (*f.*) Nor can man's faith, as evangelical obedience, be taken, on lower terms than those which demanded obedience in full. For if so, the obedience would still be our righteousness.

Man is in such a state, then, that he cannot merit heaven by the deeds of the law. (Even Pelagius could say, "lex ita mittit ad regnum cœlorum ut evangelium," only upon the understanding that the works of the law were external works.)

2. The Scripture declares that the personal righteousness of men cannot be the ground of their justification. The Law is always the same, always binding in its full extent. "All have sinned and come short of the glory of God." (*a.*) The Scripture declares that all are under condemnation. (*b.*) The "works of the law" of which the Apostle speaks are, the whole obedience which the law requires. They are contrasted with justification by faith alone, and not with mere legal performances. (*c.*) Express statements of Scripture: Rom. iii. 20, 28; Titus iii. 5, 7; Eph. ii. 8; Rom. iii. 24; Rom. iv. 5, 6, 7; Phil. iii. 9; Gal. iii. 10, 22; Rom. xi. 6.

CHAPTER V.

THE GROUND OF JUSTIFICATION.

Our justification can rest only upon one of two grounds. Ultimately, there are only two religions: that of works and that of faith in Christ.

The ground of justification must be a righteousness. It cannot be ours. Where and what is it?

Or: There must be a meritorious ground, under God's moral government, for our justification. It cannot be our merits. Whose merits, then?

Or: Justification is a procedure under God's moral government, not of his mere sovereignty. It is not a procedure resting on the personal merit of the justified person. It must be something taken instead of that, answering the same ends. That something is—the Atonement of Christ, his work for us.

§ 1. *Statements of Scripture as to the Ground of Justification.*
(*a.*) General Statements.—
Rom. v. 18. "Even so through the righteousness of one . . . . . upon all men unto justification of life."
Rom. v. 19. "So by the obedience of one shall many be made righteous."
Rom. x. 4. "Christ is *the end of the law for righteousness* to every one that believeth." (This is the most decisive statement of Scripture.)
2 Cor. v. 21. "For He hath made Him to be sin for us, who knew no sin; that we might be made the righteousness of God in Him."
Phil. iii. 9. "And be found in Him, not having mine own righteousness, which is of the law, but that which is through the faith of Christ, the righteousness which is of God by faith."

(*b.*) Justification is spoken of as an imputation.
Rom. iv. 6.—"the blessedness of the man, unto whom God imputeth righteousness without works."
Cf. Rom. v. 18, 19, above.
Rom. iv. 5. "To him that worketh not, but believeth on Him that justifieth the ungodly, his faith is counted for (λογίζεται) righteousness."

The meaning of impute is seen most distinctly in the usage of the compound ἐλλογέω. As in Philemon, verse 18, "if he hath wronged thee in anything . . . . τοῦτο ἐμοὶ ἐλλόγει,) put that on my account." So, Rom. v. 13, "but sin is not imputed (ἐλλογεῖται) when there is no law."

"To impute" does not involve the idea of a transfer of personal righteousness.

The imputation concerns the laying of our sins to the account of Christ as well as of his righteousness to our account.

(c.) Justification is spoken of as the result of Christ's obedience. (The distinction sometimes made between his active and passive obedience is not to be commended. It is said, that by his active obedience Christ satisfied the demands of the law for holiness; and by his passive, its demands for suffering. This distinction has not a Scriptural basis. The obedience of Christ's whole life, all that belongs to his work, is *imputed*, reckoned to our account for righteousness. It is thus that we "become the righteousness of God *in Him*.")

§ 2. *How Christ can be the Ground of our Justification.*

1. We are justified by what He did in, and in view of, a constituted relationship to us.[1]

2. The doctrine of union with Christ is fundamental as to the mode in which He can be the ground of our justification.

The Doctrine of the Vital or Mystical Union.—Larg. Cat., Q. 66: "The union which the elect have with Christ is the work of God's grace, whereby they are spiritually and mystically, yet really and inseparably, joined to Christ as their head and husband; which is done in their effectual calling."

Short. Cat., Q. 30. "The Spirit applieth to us the redemption purchased by Christ, by working faith in us, and thereby uniting us to Christ in our effectual calling."

This is the mystical union in the Calvinistic sense; it is found similarly expressed in other Confessions of the Reformation. It is something real, and not a mere figure; as real as the union between the branch and the vine. Though the branch and the vine be only a figure, yet the fact illustrated by the figure is not figurative.

The discussion proposed will state, I. The Scriptural Proof, II. The Proof derivable from other Doctrines and Analogies,

---

[1] This relationship is involved in a divine plan and is sometimes called "the covenant of redemption."

III. The Nature of this Union, IV. The Difference between the Calvinistic and other Modes of Viewing this Union.

I.—The Scriptural Proof.

The term "mystical," by which this union is denoted, is from Eph. v. 32. "This is a great mystery: but I speak concerning Christ and the church." Verse 31 closes with "and they two [husband and wife] shall be one flesh," and then follows the above, declaring that the union between Christ and his church is as close, as intimate as that between husband and wife; that the union between husband and wife is but the image, the lower realization, of the union between Christ and his people.

John vi. 56. "He that eateth my flesh, and drinketh my blood, dwelleth in me, and I in him." The reference is not to the sacrament to be instituted. The meaning is more than sacramental, viz., real.

John xiv. 23. "If a man love me, he will keep my words; and my Father will love him, and we will come unto him, and make our abode with him."

John xvii. 22, 23. "And the glory which thou gavest me I have given them; that they may be one, even as we are one: I in them, and thou in me, that they may be made perfect in one." —The union between Christ and his people is like that between Christ and the Father. If the real union between Christ and his followers is denied, then that between Christ and the Father must be denied also.

1 John ii. 5. "But whoso keepeth his word, in him verily is the love of God perfected: hereby know we that we are *in Him*." Verse 6: "He that saith he *abideth in Him* ought himself also so to walk, even as He walked."

1 John iv. 12. "If we love one another, God dwelleth in us, and his love is perfected in us."

The assumption of our nature is also part of the proof. John i. 14: "The word was made flesh."

Paul, as well as John, sets forth the mystical union.

Eph. v. 23–32, referred to above.

Rom. viii. 10. "And if *Christ be in you*, the body is dead because of sin; but the Spirit is life because of righteousness." (It is also shown, from the context here, that the union with Christ is mediated by the Spirit: verse 9, "if any man have not the Spirit of Christ"—verse 11: "But if the Spirit of Him that raised up Jesus from the dead dwell in you.")

Col. i. 27—"what is the riches of the glory of this mystery among the Gentiles; which *is Christ in you, the hope of glory*."

Eph. iii. 17. "That Christ may dwell in your hearts by faith."

Gal. iii. 27. "For as many of you as have been baptized into Christ have put on Christ."

1 Cor. vi. 14, 15. "And God hath both raised up the Lord, and will also raise up us by his own power. Know ye not that your bodies are the members of Christ?" Also, v. 17: "But he that is joined unto the Lord is one spirit."

There may also be cited:

2 Peter i. 4: "that by these ye might be ($\gamma\acute{\epsilon}\nu\eta\sigma\vartheta\epsilon$) partakers of the divine nature."

The figure of the branch and the vine, John xv.

Results from the Scriptural Evidence.

(*a.*) As a matter of fact and reality, there is as truly a union between Christ and his followers, as between Christ and the Father, the husband and the wife, the trunk and the branches.

(*b.*) This union is not sacramental but spiritual: not immediate, but through and by the Holy Spirit uniting us to Christ our head. This makes the distinction between the Calvinistic view and that of the mystics and of the Sacramentarians.

(*c.*) The union extends to the body, so far as this—that through the life-giving Spirit, we, like Christ, are to be raised from the dead: because He lives we shall live also.

(*d.*) This union is on the basis of the covenant of grace, and through it the blessings of that covenant are imparted to us.

(*e.*) The life given by this union is none other than the life which the Holy Ghost imparts—yet it is a life, not of mere general divine influence, but in union with Christ.

(*f.*) This life is given through faith as the instrument of our justification; it is a life not excluding, but including, justification.

II.—Proof from other sources of doctrine and analogy.

(*a.*) From the doctrine of Justification by faith alone. In our effectual calling, by the Spirit through faith, we are justified; *i. e.*, on the ground of what Christ has done, we are accepted in Him, "elect in *Christ.*" There must then be some peculiar bond or tie, on the ground of which we can be thus received and accepted in another.

(*b.*) From the parallel between our death in Adam and our life in Christ: Rom. v. 12 seq. The race is one in Adam, and hence could sin in him and fall with him; human nature became corrupt in him. We are condemned thereby: the natural union with Adam is the ground of this procedure. In like manner, the spiritual union with Christ is the basis of our being accepted, and justified in him.

(*c.*) From the truth of the intimate, secret, unseen, yet real influence of the Holy Spirit in regeneration—in our effectual calling, uniting us to Christ by these sacred influences, reinstating us in the moral image of God. These influences are confessedly mysterious; they are the bond of our union with Christ. This union is at the ground of regeneration and justification.

(*d.*) From the nature of love to Christ, faith in Christ, implying the closest personal relationship between Christ and ourselves—a union.

(*e.*) From the analogy of other works of God, and facts in our other relations.

Through all nature, if we are theists, we believe in a perpetual presence of God, everywhere, not merely in power, but in reality. Through all second causes the great First Cause is ever at work. Acts xvii. 28.

In each of the several tribes of creation there is a special, common character, whereby the tribe is made one, though also each individual is distinct from every other. There is a mystery and a fact here. The common nature and descent from one pair have a background of mysterious union, which is a background of fact also.

It is natural then to conclude from analogy, that in the new and higher kingdom of God's grace, for which all other things were made, there would be a *real union* in one head. This is given us in our union with Christ, through the influence of the gracious Spirit.

Thus, through the influences of the Holy Spirit, we are led to faith in Christ: to trust in Him; and in consequence of that we become partakers of all that Christ has done for us—are justified, *i. e.*, are both pardoned and adopted.

Now, as in the family there is a union of members, parents and children, so that all have the same liabilities, on the ground of the union; as in the race having its headship in Adam there is a union, with the same liabilities; so in our union to Christ through love and faith, a like union is implied.

III.—The nature of this union: (rather negatively than positively).

A general union with God is at the basis: Acts xvii. 28.

It involves also a union with the whole Trinity: John xiv. 23; xvii. 23; xvii. 21.

(*a*.) The union is not physical but spiritual.

(*b*.) It is not through the sacraments, but by the Spirit, through faith.

(*c*.) Not that the substance of Christ passes over into us, so that our natures are made divine with his divinity (Cf. Calvin's Instit. III. xi. 10).

(*d*.) Not that his theanthropic life, considered as his specific substance, or nature, is infused into us.

(*e*.) But, it is a vital, personal union:—mystical, because it cannot be further defined than as a fact, and by the consequent benefits. But though mystical, yet *real*.

(*f*.) Hence it is more than

(a^1.) Union of affection and aim. This is included, but this is the consequence of the union and not the union itself.

(b^1.) Than a merely external, constituted, arbitrary relation —than a mere union of compact; though this is also included. Just as with Adam the moral headship is based on the physical, the covenant is carried out through the natural relationship, so is the covenant of grace through this spiritual union.

(*g*.) The effect of faith in uniting to Christ is thus stated by

Augustine (Serm. 144): "Qui ergo in Christum credit, credendo in Christum, *venit in eum* Christus, et *quodammodo* unitur in eum, et membrum in corpore ejus efficitur." (The *credere in Christum* he shows to be very different from, *credere ipsum esse Christum*, and, *credere de Christo*,—devils may do this). Further: "Ille enim credit in Christum, qui et sperat in Christum et diligit Christum. Nam si fidem habet sine spe ac sine dilectione, Christum esse credit, non *in* Christum credit."

IV.—Classification and criticism of opinions as to the nature of our relation to Christ.

The great difference of theological systems comes out here. Since Christianity is redemption through Christ, our mode of conceiving that will determine the character of our whole theological system.

1. The humanitarian (Socinian) view. Christ is an example and a teacher. There is no other relationship than there is between us and other examples and teachers, excepting that He is the highest and best. There is between Him and us no living bond or tie. (Socinus admits that Christ confers immortality.) This is a bare, ethical, natural system, with no supernatural elements.

2. The other extreme is, Transubstantiation: through the sacraments, by transubstantiation of the elements of bread and wine, the very body and blood of Christ are received. (This view has a greatly modified form in the Lutheran doctrine of Consubstantiation.)

3. The Sacramental Theory (particularly of the Oxford School). The Sacraments are an extension of the Incarnation, and vehicles of grace. Through the Sacraments we receive, not the very body and blood, but the theanthropic life of Christ. The Holy Spirit works in the bestowal of this life, but—works through the Sacraments. There is a real, spiritual reception of the very substance of the Logos. (See Mercersb. Rev., Oct. 1854).

4. The Spiritual Life Theory. This drops the Sacraments. We receive from Christ a new, spiritual life; the communica-

tion of such a life is the great end of the Incarnation. The Atonement is merged in the Incarnation; the object of the Incarnation is the giving of life, rather than making atonement (Schleiermacher, Coleridge).

5. The general Calvinistic view. The union with Christ is mediated *by his Spirit* (it is not direct, not through sacraments), whence we are both renewed and justified. The great fact of objective Christianity is, Incarnation in order to Atonement: the great fact of subjective Christianity is, Union with Christ, whereby we receive the Atonement. The Sacraments are expressions, not vehicles of grace.

Our new life is hid with Christ in God. The Incarnation has the same relation to the new life that Creation has to the old. Yet this new life is by the distinct operation of the Holy Spirit. We stand in as close a relation to the second as to the first Adam—though it be spiritual and not natural.

Calvin (Works, Brunswick ed., 1870, vol. ix. p. 30, on the Defence of the Doctrine of the Sacraments) says: "The flesh of Christ is life-bringing. . . . We coalesce with Christ in a sacred unity, and that same flesh (caro) breathes life into us. . . . by a secret virtue of the Holy Spirit, we have, implanted into the body of Christ, a common life with Him. For from the hidden fountain of Deity, life is wonderfully infused into the flesh of Christ, that thence it might flow to us. . . . ."

6. The Governmental Theory. This denies the reality of such union with Christ, takes the expressions of Scripture relating to it as metaphors, and denies also the reality of justification on this basis. We become like Christ by choosing the same end that He did. His atonement removed the obstacles, so that we can now go directly to God. Justification is pardon only, for Christ's sake: or, if more, we are justified on the ground of our inherent state of love, or, because it is foreseen by God that we shall become wholly just by and by. Christ presents to us an exhibition of God's hatred of sin and love of holiness; and this moves us to be and do right more than anything else.

---

[1] If any one hesitates over this expression, there may perhaps be substituted for the term "flesh" the term "humanity," with no detriment to the force of the argument.

All this is true enough as far as it goes. But it condemns as a figment, as visionary and unreal, the grand fact of personal, vital union with Christ, through faith, as the basis of our justification, and the beginning of our new life.

In fine and sum—the question being, How can the lost favor of God be restored?—

The first theory says: It is enough for God to come and help us somewhat.

The second says: We are restored by partaking of Christ's very flesh and blood.

The third says: We are restored by partaking of the divine humanity—though not of the literal flesh and blood—through the Sacraments.

The fourth: by partaking of the life of Christ, not necessarily through the Sacraments.

The fifth: only through justification and regeneration, effected by the Holy Spirit, uniting us to Christ.

The sixth: through justification, *i. e.*, pardon, not including a real union with Christ, to produce effects, influences on us.

§ 3. *In what Way does what Christ has done avail to the Believer through this Union, for his Justification . . . . . as a Righteousness?*

How does it avail?

1. Not legal justification in the sense of distributive justice as defined. . . . . Not under the law in the restricted usage that it demands works as the condition of life. "The ungodly" are justified ("Legal justification occurs when one accused is vindicated by showing either that he did not do the act or had a right to do it." Barnes, p. 74).

Justification is contrasted with this expressly. The law requires uniform obedience: Rom. iii. 21. The law, of itself, has no provision for justification. Not as excluding all righteousness or merits, as the ground of justification. Proved in Chap. III.

2. Not a transfer of personal righteousness—Christ's righteousness to the believer: the believer and Christ being considered as separate.

3. But that Christ having satisfied the end of the law for righteousness, in man's behalf (made an atonement as already explained) *i. e.*, secured holiness, we, through union with Him, become partakers of all the benefits of his work. Here is the mystery of the work.

4. Though the demands of distributive justice are not directly met (*i. e.*, as the ultimate point of view in our justification[1]), yet the end to be gained by distributive justice, *i. e.*, the maintenance of holiness, is secured.

Considered in themselves, out of Christ, men are guilty, deserving condemnation.

5. For Christ's sake—because we are one with Him—we are treated "as if" righteous: but we could not be so treated unless there were in Christ a sufficient ground for this "*as if*": his merits.

CHAPTER VI.

THE INSTRUMENTAL CAUSE OF JUSTIFICATION.

§ 1. *Faith, and Faith alone.*

The Roman Catholic view is that justification is through the sacraments as well, *i. e.*, by baptism and by penance as restoring the forfeited grace of baptism. The Arminian view: the means of justification is faith as including love and future holiness. God perceives, in the act of faith, love and holiness following, and declares the person just, not on the ground of Christ's merit, but of the foreseen merits of the believer.

The Scriptures declare faith to be the only act of the soul on which justification is conditioned. Rom. i. 16; v. 1; Gal. ii. 16;

---

[1] If tenpence is due a man and he is paid a dollar, the tenpence is more than satisfied. Christ's work more than satisfies distributive justice, while directly and in the strictest sense, it does not and cannot "satisfy" it. Its *end* is more fully reached—holiness is made supreme and triumphant.

Phil. iii. 9; John iii. 18 asserts that faith is necessary to the obtaining eternal life.

§ 2. *The Idea of Faith.*

(*a.*) In a loose popular sense, Faith is belief in any truth on any ground.

(*b.*) In a general and somewhat abstract sense, it is belief in what is beyond the sphere of the senses.

(*c.*) It is belief, on the ground of testimony, in what we have not ourselves seen or known—belief on the ground of authority. The same truth may be known in different ways—by reason and by testimony too, *e. g.*, immortality.

(*d.*) More particularly, in a general Scriptural usage, Faith is trusting in God's testimony—receiving all that God has revealed to us. Roman Catholics say: It is belief in God's testimony, as witnessed by the church; it merits grace, of congruity, through the sacraments; being "formed" by love, it is directly meritorious and accumulates merits.

(*e.*) The special sense of Faith, the sense in which it is used in the doctrine of justification is, the receiving, resting in, and trusting upon Christ. Not mere abstract truth, but *Christ* is its object. It is not merely relying upon what God has testified in regard to all truth, but trusting in and receiving Christ as our Saviour—relying upon Him.

As such—

1. It is an act of the whole soul—not of the intellect, nor will, nor sensibilities, alone, but of all combined. The whole soul goes out in the act of faith in Christ. Faith is one of the most concrete of acts, yet in direct consciousness is an act perfectly simple.

2. It also includes in germ all other graces. It does this *because* it is an energy of the whole mind. "Worketh by love," Gal. v. 6. It involves repentance. "Show faith by works,' James ii. 18.

3. It is itself a holy act, involving trust and love, yet it is not as holy that it is the means of justification, but as being the act in which we receive Christ.

4. Thus it is properly called the instrumental cause of justification. The meritorious ground is Christ. Faith is not the highest of the virtues, but love is. Justification is not without works, yet not by works,—not without love, yet not by love, —not without assent, yet not as though the assent were meritorious.

§ 3. *Some Questions in regard to Faith.*

I.—Does faith always involve explicit; in distinction from implicit, knowledge? Must there always be a full and defined knowledge of what Christ is?

Some degree of knowledge is involved in every conscious act of faith. This is essential to it. Roman Catholics contend that faith may be implicit to a large extent, *i. e.*, a man may have saving faith without knowing specially anything about the work of Christ. Faith may be simply general trust in God and belief in the Bible—and especially in the church. Thus a man may say he believes what the church says, even if he does not know what that is, and he is to be considered as having faith in what the church holds.

But (1) We really assent only so far as we know the meaning of the statement which we accept. We may be ready to receive whatever else can be shown to rest upon the same authority. (2) The Scriptures interchange faith and knowledge.

II.—Whether the act of faith be a moral or intellectual act? The question here is between those who affirm that it is solely intellectual, and those who affirm that it involves the affections and the will (in part) as well as the intellect.

(1) It is an act of the soul in respect to moral and religious truth, accepting it, trusting it, and resting in it. If so, it must have a moral character. It is not mere perception, but involves assent. (2) Hence, it cannot be exercised without the affections. There is no possible element of trust entering into an act where the affections are not involved. It involves something of love. It is giving the soul to that which is presented. (3) A mere traditional or historical faith cannot be enough. As an intellectual act, it would be historical faith or receiving what came

down in the way of tradition. But we have to do here with something more than historical evidence. There is the influence of the Holy Spirit, the assent of the soul to divine truth. The Scriptures speak of those who believe, as taught of the Spirit. All the effects of faith are such as to show it to have a moral character as well as historical. They impose an obligation in respect to it, and this implies a moral, spiritual character belonging to it. Unbelief would not be a sin unless it involved that which is immoral.

III.—(Involved in the preceding.) Does trust belong to faith? This is denied by Romanists.

(1) Not, as applied to abstract doctrines, *e. g.*, the divinity of Christ. (2) But saving faith rests ultimately in persons, in God, in Christ. Most specifically, it is a direct reliance on Christ for salvation.

IV.—Does faith involve the assurance of personal salvation? Does such assurance belong to the essence of faith,—to the essence in distinction from the products of faith?

Sir Wm. Hamilton (Discussions, p. 493), arguing against Archdeacon Hare on Luther's doctrines, has affirmed very boldly that the doctrine of assurance—the feeling certain that God is propitious to me—that my sins are forgiven, was long held by the Protestant communities to be the criterion of a saving faith. Luther says, "He who hath not assurance spews faith out," and Melancthon makes it a distinction between Christianity and heathenism. Hamilton further says that this position was maintained by Calvin, by Arminius, and by all the Protestant Confessions down to the Westminster, when assurance was for the first time declared to be not of the essence of faith. He adds that then one of the great distinctions between Protestants and Roman Catholics was obliterated. These statements show that a great philosopher may be mistaken in departments where he is not well acquainted. By some of the earlier Reformers, as by Luther, it was undoubtedly asserted that faith involves assurance, and this was urged in part against the Roman Catholic view, which leads to the conclusion that no one can be assured of his salvation in this life, because salvation is dependent upon sanctification; in opposition to which Protestants argued that in faith itself was the ground and assurance of our salvation, and that we might have from the simple act of faith assurance of personal salvation. Calvin speaks guardedly. He says that there are doubts and difficulties, and that it is not necessary to have assurance in order to be a believer. Even the Synod of Dort did not include this among its decrees. It is not explicitly asserted in any of the Reformed Confessions, except in the Heidelberg Catechism,—not in the French, nor in that of Basel, nor in the Helvetic. The Westminster Confession, c. xviii. § 3, says, "This infallible assurance doth not so belong to the essence of faith, but that a true believer may wait long, and conflict with many difficulties before he be partaker of it." Turretine draws the distinction clearly. It is said to be not the essence of faith but its ripest product. This doctrine of assurance has been revived in Switzerland through Dr. Malan, whose tract has been published by the Reformed Dutch Board. He makes assurance to be not merely necessary to gospel peace, but to belong to faith, so that one cannot have faith without having assurance of faith. President Edwards met this point in a letter to Ebenezer Erskine of Scotland, where the controversy had been started in connection with the publication of the "Marrow of Divinity." He puts it substantially in this form: "Faith is belief, in its general sense, of what God has revealed to us in the gospel. He has revealed to us that all who believe will be saved, and we must believe that on the ground of the gospel assertion: but He has not revealed to us in the gospel that I, Jonathan Edwards, of Northampton, shall be saved, and therefore that does not belong to the essence of faith. The essence of faith consists in receiving what God has revealed."

§ 4. *Is Man responsible for his Belief*—i. e., *for his Unbelief?*

Those who assert that man is not responsible, do it because they hold that faith is a merely intellectual act, and depends on the amount of evidence which is brought before the mind, so that if a man has sufficient evidence, he cannot help believing; and if he has not, he cannot attain to belief. They argue the question on the ground of a general definition of faith—assent to testimony: and say, where the testimony is present, assent is compelled, and where it is not, assent is impossible.

The general position to be taken in respect to the matter is, that man is responsible for his unbelief so far as sin in any form or way keeps him from believing. If there is a want of opportunity or of natural capacity, he is not to be held responsible. But so far as any selfishness, any worldliness, any pride, any evil desire, any wrong affection, keeps him from submitting to the righteousness of God, just so far he is responsible. This is applied as follows: (1) To the evidence for the being of God. Faith, reliance, trust in the divine existence, is not a merely intellectual act; it is an act of the whole soul turning to God. Wherever there is atheism, the fact shows that the moral nature is benumbed. (2) To the evidences of Christianity. These are addressed partly to the intellect, but chiefly to man's moral wants, because Christianity presents itself as a remedy for man's moral disorders, and all that prevents any from receiving it is the absence of the sense of need of salvation. It is a moral hindrance. (3) To faith in Christ. This is essentially a moral act, an act of the whole soul. It is not merely an act of the intellect, but it is from a conscious need of redemption; and that which keeps any one from trusting in Christ is his lack of a proper sense of his sinfulness and need of a Saviour. (4) To the final condemnation of the sinner. In perhaps almost all minds, that which keeps from the acknowledgment of this, is the want of a proper sense of sin and of its just desert.[1]

§ 5. *Why is the high Office assigned to Faith of being the instrumental Cause of Justification?*

1. It is not because faith is the highest of the virtues: 1 Cor. xiii. 13.

2. It is because faith is the only way in which man can receive Christ. The act of the soul trusting Christ is the only mode in which the soul can be saved. Faith is the only con-

---

[1] Wardlaw, in reply to Brougham, has written on the question, Is man responsible for his belief? See Princ. Rev., vol. xviii. p. 53.

ceivable act by which the sinner can be united to Christ. It brings us to rest in God, to renounce self, to turn from self to Christ, and it is the only act of the mind by which this can be achieved. Both the simplicity and the power of faith are to be taken into consideration.[1]

CHAPTER VII.

THE DIFFERENCE BETWEEN THE ROMAN CATHOLIC AND PROTESTANT VIEWS OF JUSTIFICATION.

They agree in holding that justification is the consequence or result of the sinner's return to God under the influence of the Holy Spirit. They differ in their notion of justification, in their view of the point at which justification takes place, in their view of the nature of faith, of good works, and of works of supererogation.

1. The difference in the notion of justification. The Roman Catholic says, that this includes not only forgiveness and adoption, but also sanctification, that it involves the internal change of the sinner into a just person—an infusion of divine justice as the property of the soul. Sometimes they call it a physical act. This is connected with their view of the primitive endowments of man. They hold that man was endowed with all the capacities of human nature, and that in addition grace was imparted or infused—superadded to the primitive endowments; that by the fall, superadded, infused grace was lost; that the object of the gospel is to restore that lost grace, and that this is effected through the sacraments—baptism, penance and the Lord's Supper. It is restored substantially—physically—to man, and it is on account of this restored grace that man is justified, and this grace includes faith and sanctification. . The Protestant view

---

[1] Faith in relation to Justification, Edwards, ii. 628. Faith in relation to Perseverance, Ibid. iii. 510. Sermons on Justification, Ibid. iv. 64, cf. 36. (N. Y. Edition, 1868).

is, that justification in its essential notion is not the making just, but the declaring just, on the ground of faith alone. It is a forensic act, *i. e.*, an act in the form of a declaration before a judicial tribunal, and not in its first aspect declarative of character.

2. The difference as to the point at which justification occurs. They agree that justification is grace "per Christum," but the Roman Catholic says that God is moved by the faith, repentance, good purposes, and good works of man to make him just; that God makes him capable of doing good works, and in proportion to the amount of good works he does, justification advances, so that the justification is gradual, is constantly increasing, is never completed until sanctification is complete. The cause of justification is admitted to be Christ's merits, but the necessary condition is man's acts, man's works, man's sanctification. The Protestant view is that justification is in and by a simple act of faith. Man trusts in the pardoning grace of God through Christ, and good works are the fruit of that.

3. The question whether justification is by faith *alone*. Roman Catholics deny this. In doing this they give a different idea of faith. Faith, they say, is the assent by which we receive those things which are divinely revealed and promised, especially that the wicked are justified by the grace of God and the redemption of Christ. This is necessary to justification, but is not all that is necessary,—it must not be found alone. The Roman Catholic ground is: (1) God is the efficient cause of justification. (2) Christ is the meritorious ground. (3) Inherent righteousness, or our sanctified state, is the formal cause—the necessary condition of it. (4) Merit of condignity, in repentance, penance, good works, is necessary to justification. (5) The means by which all this is applied are the sacraments of the church, especially baptism. The Protestant view is, that the faith by which we receive Christ involves no mixture of our own works, that the simple faith and trust is the sole instrument of justification. In the Protestant view, justification is a single act of trust; in the Catholic, it is a process, and a long one.

4. The difference as to the relation of good works to justi-

fication. They agree that good works are not to be separated *in re* from justification, but differ as to their relation to it. The Protestant view is, that good works bring no merit or desert in respect to salvation or the title to eternal life. In every other point of view they insist upon good works, which are the fruit and consequence of justifying grace. Roman Catholics hold that good works bring an increase of grace, an increase of title to eternal life and heavenly felicity, and that in proportion to the amount of good works is the strength of the title to eternal life.

5. The difference as to the so-called works of supererogation. Roman Catholics hold that the regenerated may not only keep the commands of God entirely, but that they may keep more, —not only what is enjoined in the law but also the "evangelical counsels," things recommended but not binding—poverty, vows of chastity, etc. They may attain to a higher moral perfection and merit before God by these works. This is carried out in the whole system of monasticism, which has here its theoretic root—that in it a higher degree of religion[1] can be practiced. These monastic saints in this way go through life, obeying their voluntary vows and laying up a treasury of merit, which is committed by Christ to the keeping of the church. These are the works of supererogation, the merit of which is dispensed by the church in dispensations, etc., from the treasury of grace laid up from its departed supererogatory heroes. The general Protestant view is, that so far from there being any works of supererogation, not even the renewed can perfectly keep the commands of God, and the whole monastic life is rejected so far as it claims a higher perfection and special degree of merit.

[1] This goes so far that in the Roman Catholic system the word religion is restricted to the monastic life.

CHAPTER VIII.

HISTORICAL STATEMENTS RESPECTING THE DIFFERENT THEORIES OF JUSTIFICATION.

Each theological system and party must have its view of justification, and that view is modified by the fundamental peculiarity of each system. In the early Christian church, to the time of the Augustinian and Pelagian controversy, there was for the most part a simple Scriptural statement of the doctrine. It had not yet been brought out through controversy. The elements of it were not analyzed. In the anthropological controversy, between Pelagius and Augustine, the doctrine was brought to a statement, in connection with the doctrines of grace. The Pelagian view was, that our moral state is the only ground of justification,—corresponding to the general ethical tendency of Pelagius. In the Mediæval theology, among the Scholastics, originated the theory that justification, means to make just—in distinction from its being a declarative act—based in part on the etymology of the word justification, as used in the Latin language. This continued to be the prevalent doctrine until the Reformation controversies. It was then that the doctrine first came to a full discussion and articulate statement. Some of the Reformers speak of justification as equivalent to pardon, and use the terms pardon and justification as synonymous. But that was not in view of controversies like ours; it was with reference to the Roman Catholic position. This was, that justification consisted in pardon *and* sanctification. Luther, Melancthon and Calvin said, justification consists in pardon, but without ever denying that it likewise includes the title to eternal life. This is involved in the doctrine of assurance which they held, though statements which seem to make it merely pardon may be extracted from the writings of Calvin, etc. In the course of the Arminian controversy in Holland, at the beginning of the seventeenth century, coming to its consummation at the

Synod of Dort, 1618-19, the doctrine of justification was thoroughly debated, and the position of the Arminians was substantially as follows: Justification is declarative, the sinner is not made just inherently or relatively in the eye of the law, but is restored to his standing through God's favor; that, however, the ground of justification is not Christ's righteousness imputed, but is personal faith, including what was called evangelical obedience—a lower obedience than that required by the law, which is accepted instead of legal obedience. While asserting that faith, as including this evangelical obedience, is the proper ground of justification, they had no scruple in saying that the justification was gratuitous, on the ground that God for Christ's sake was willing to accept this imperfect, instead of perfect, obedience. This included the position that faith holds in its grasp all the future good works of the justified person. According to this system, it is quite apparent that the law of God in its strictness is virtually set aside. Christ does not act under that law, but outside of it, and the sinner does not obey that law, but renders an evangelical obedience; so that the law is simply set aside as far as Christ is concerned in his obedience, and the sinner in his obedience. Under this system sinners were told to do as well as they could, and trust God's mercy.

There have been some modifications of the doctrine in the discussions in our own country. The elder Edwards held to the doctrine of justification in the sense of the Protestant symbols. The only modification which he made—which is not a departure from the symbols but simply from one form of Calvinistic theology—was in emphasizing the statement that our real union with Christ is the basis of the justifying process, that our union with Christ is the ground of the legal procedure. The younger Edwards, in a sermon before the Conn. Association, 1786, on the subject, "Christ our righteousness," enters into an explanation of the nature of the union with Christ as vital in affection, making us one with Him or causing us to be treated as if one, on the ground of that union, and then he proceeds to consider the notion of justification itself. Of this he makes pardon to be an essential part, not limiting justification, however, to that, and then he goes on to say that it is the act of the sovereign, beside and above the law, and not the act of the judge, which latter position, he says, subverts the grace of the gospel. He is explicit in the statement that the satisfaction and obedience of Christ is the meritorious cause of justification. When he denies that it is the act of a judge, he must be understood to mean that it is not under the law in the strictest sense of distributive justice. He should not be taken as meaning that justification has not respect to the great ends of the law. By the act of a judge, he means simply a legal declaration as to the personal desert of each individual, and then of course justification cannot be the act of God as a judge. This subject has entered into later discussions, and by some writers of the so-called New School bodies, justification was made to be simply equivalent to pardon. Dr. Richards, however, (p. 389 seq.) takes a different ground and the ground on which the New School in general may be said to stand. He also says that the law is not made the rule of judgment, and the declaration of justification is not according to law, that God acts above the law: but he evidently takes law and judicial proceeding in the same sense with the younger Edwards: law means simply what is incumbent *on each* and what may be demanded of each. There is another modification in respect to the ground and the conditions of justification, in Mr. Finney's lectures on theology. (1) From the ground of justification he excludes Christ's obedience in our stead and our own obedience—whether under the law or the gospel, and anything and everything in the Mediatorial work, including the Atonement. The Atonement itself is not the fundamental reason of justification. The simple ground is the disinterested and infinite love of God. All Calvinists say that the source of justification is to be found in God's infinite love. By the ground of justification is usually meant, the specific reason of pardon and acquittal. (Mr. Finney uses the word *ground* in the sense of *source.*) (2) As to the conditions of justification, he holds that the Atonement is one condition, *i. e.*, is a *sine qua non*, and that faith, repentance, and sanctification are all conditions equally.— In making these to be just as important as the work of Christ, he destroys justification as a specific doctrine. His position resolves justification into sanctification or regeneration, and leaves it no validity of its own. He is consistent in requiring entire sanctification.

CHAPTER IX.

OBJECTIONS TO THE DOCTRINE OF JUSTIFICATION.

Obj. I.—It makes good works unnecessary.—But good works are excluded only in one aspect, *i. e.*, in relation to justification. They are as much as ever necessary in our holiness and Christian life. We are created in Christ Jesus unto good works.

Obj. II.—Justification makes salvation to be a matter of right and debt, on the ground of Christ's obedience in our stead; and this excludes it from being an act of grace.—But this can be maintained only on the ground of the mercantile theory of the Atonement—that Christ, in dying for the elect only, paid for them an exact *quid pro quo*. The fact is that salvation comes entirely from grace. It is God's grace which is made glorious by the Atonement.

Obj. III.—Justification is a merely external transaction.—But we are justified by faith, and faith is not external but internal.

Obj. IV.—There is a conflict in this matter between Paul and James.—But James commends faith as holy. What he is speaking against is a dead faith—merely intellectual—and he enjoins upon the disciples to show their faith by their works, so that faith is the primitive thing even with him. He starts (ii. 24) from morality to find its roots: if there is no morality there is no root. Paul goes from the faith to the works. With him the sap is first, with James, the fruit. James reprobates a dead faith, Paul urges a living faith.[1]

Obj. V.—Righteousness is not transferable.—We assent, and

---

[1] See Dr. Woods, and his citation from Wardlaw, that Paul is speaking of the justification of the sinner, and James of the justification of the believer.

say that Christ's personal righteousness is not transferred. On account of his righteousness we are treated as if righteous.

Obj. VI.—Christ's obedience can be no part of our justification, because He owed his obedience for himself.—But Christ did not owe an obedience for himself unto death, and He did not owe for himself to take the place which He took in the moral administration of the world, but He took it in our stead.

Obj. VII.—Believers although justified are still punished.—They are not punished in the strict sense, but in the sense in which punishment is necessary for reformation. Their punishments become chastisements.

Obj. VIII.—The Scriptures declare that in the Last Judgment, works will be made the basis of adjudication.—But there must be a proper conception of the Last Judgment. It is not the declaring of the sentence of the law, but is the final sentence itself. It is for the manifestation of character and state. It has not to do with our condemnation under the law immediately, because we are condemned under the law all along. That view which makes the Judgment parallel with a human tribunal, where the guilt or innocence is first pronounced, is not the view of Scripture. It cannot be reconciled with the view that all the world is already under condemnation. The Last Judgment is the winding up of the present sphere of things. It is the assignment of all who have lived to their final condition, and what that is to be is manifested in their works.

Obj. IX.—The Scriptures speak of other grounds of acceptance, besides the merits of Christ—such conditions as our forgiveness of others, our repentance, etc. But they do not speak of these in the same relation that they do of Christ's work.

BOOK III.

REGENERATION AND REPENTANCE.

We combine these, because they give us respectively the divine and the human side of the new life. The original usage of the term regeneration is of the new life as ascribed to Christ. Repentance refers to the new life as it comes into human consciousness. The new life is a life in Christ, and regeneration involves union with Christ and not a change of heart without relation to Him. In this doctrine we come into the sphere of the direct influences of the Holy Spirit. Regeneration is the Spirit's work in man, turning him from sin to holiness, from self to Christ.

CHAPTER I.

INTRODUCTORY STATEMENTS.

§.1. *The Doctrine as held in some of the different Systems.*

Each ecclesiastical and theological system has its doctrine of regeneration, the statement of which is determined by the fundamental principles of each system. The central point of each system will define the doctrine of regeneration. Each system must have it in some form, because it is contained in the Scriptures so plainly.

1. The Roman Catholic system makes regeneration to be through the church and sacraments. It is effected by sacramental grace, which can be conveyed only through the channels of the church. Baptism has an inherent efficacy in removing moral pollution. It infuses what is called in the technical language of theology a new habit,[1] what we now call a new state.

2. In the Church of England, in conformity with the liturgy, the doctrine of baptismal regeneration is maintained. In the order for baptism, the minister, after the service is performed, is to say: "this child is regenerate—." This, however, is

---

[1] *Habitus*, something which one has.

inconsistent with the XXXIX. Articles. Accordingly the evangelical portion of the church define regeneration in an external sense. They distinguish it from conversion, and define it as a change of external state, as an introduction into the church as an external body, as we put a cadet into West Point. This takes from it its spiritual import, and substitutes the outward for the inward.

3. The Pelagian view puts regeneration solely in an executive act of the human will. It makes regeneration to be the result of an act of choice. Holiness is conferred by the choice or preference of the individual. This runs into

4. The rationalistic theory, which reduces regeneration to a conformity to moral requirements, and chiefly to those which concern our relation with our fellow beings. The change is a natural one, is explained by the laws of the human mind. Moral improvement is regeneration.

5. Some theories of parties in this country.

(*a.*) The strict exercise scheme, as held by Dr. Emmons. Regeneration is an act or choice or volition, one of a series; of such series a moral being is made up, there being nothing behind these. Moreover this volition is in every case, whether it be sinful or holy, by direct divine efficiency: God creates it. It is an exercise, but the product of an immediate divine change. The later exercise scheme is different. It makes the exercises to be not the result of the divine efficiency, but of the man's agency. It puts in a soul behind the volitions, which is their source, and a will which brings the exercises into being.

(*b.*) The taste theory. Hopkins, Bellamy, Dwight and Burton make regeneration to consist not in an exercise, but in a new relish implanted. The heart, the affections are essentially involved in it.

These two opinions divided the older Hopkinsianism.

(*c.*) The theory that regeneration consists in a change in the governing purpose. This asserts that all that is moral is found in the governing purpose. The change in this is what makes the renewal of the soul. It is a choice. There may be motives and feelings and the action of the heart, but the renewal is in the governing purpose. This theory takes two forms: (1) That this governing purpose involves essentially an affection, and is not an act of bare will,—not a mere purpose, but a purpose which includes an affection, so that it is a combination of the sensibilities and the will. The purpose is a preference or love. (2) Others hold that the governing purpose may be without the affections,—that the affections lead to it, but are not comprised in the purpose. Psychologically, the difference would be this: Man is made up of intellect, feeling, and will. All agree that there must be presentation of truth to the intellect, that there must also be an awakening of the susceptibilities, and that this must lead to a new governing purpose. They differ as to whether this purpose takes the affections with it, or whether it may have the affections outside of it. Those who hold this latter position have always said that that purpose may be formed without any affection appearing in it,—that all the affections may be towards the world, while the purpose is towards God. And this is the logical result of the system.

(*d.*) The "self-love" theory, presented in an article in The Christian Spectator, 1829. It advocated the self-love theory of morals in connection with the subject of regeneration. The object of the article was to show how the sinner is regenerated, as far as this is psychologically possible. It says that in self-love is the prompting to all action, meaning by this our natural desire for happiness. There cannot be any moral action which is not from and for self-love, because such self-love is instinctive, and enters into all our moral acts. We are happy in loving God, and that is the ultimate subjective motive for loving Him. We love the world because we are happy in the world. On this basis, the article proceeds to the theory of regeneration. The first thing is to arouse in the mind this desire for happiness, and to fix it on some future good, on heaven,—to represent the Christian scheme as the only one which can confer happiness, and to make that the radical motive. Then all the doctrines and motives of the gospel are brought up—the feelings are aroused—the aroused feeling produces a sharper view of truth— that again stirs the feelings more and more, and thus the play is between the intellect and the feelings, until the sinner is brought to the point where he suspends the rushing tide of evil desire, and then the Holy Spirit comes in and renews the soul.

Remarks on this Theory. (1) Why would it not be as well to introduce the operation of the Spirit just before—and indeed all along before—as well as at the nodus? Why is it not more Scriptural to say that at all the points the Spirit operates? (2) Self-love, presented here as the ultimate motive and that which is to do the work of renewal, can never account for regeneration. If the ultimate decision be made in view of self-love—exalt that to what height we may—if that be the ultimate motive, then the soul is still in sin, because the ultimate motive has been the desire after its own happiness, and that is of the essence of sin. (3) It is equally difficult to see how this suspension of sinful activity is brought about or can be. How can the sinner, with his heart still unrenewed, be induced to suspend the tide of evil desires? He must do this, in order to get a chance for the putting forth of a holy volition. Suppose it suspended: it was from a motive good, bad, or indifferent. If the motive was good, the thing had been done already; if bad, it involves sin; if indifferent, there could be no suspension. (4) There is another supposable case: the person decides without a motive. Then the decision could not have any moral character. To suppose that a man can for a moment suspend his sinful nature, and remain for an instant without any character, is an inconceivability. (5) It might be added that even in unrenewed human nature there are better elements than self-love or desire for happiness: conscience, spiritual and moral susceptibilities, which are appealed to.

6. The general evangelical doctrine of regeneration. We give here the several heads which are to be debated in what follows.

(*a.*) Regeneration is a supernatural change of which God is the author, which is wrought by the Holy Spirit.

(*b.*) In its idea it is instantaneous, although not always so in conscious experience.

(*c.*) In adults it is wrought most frequently by the word of

God as the instrument. Believing that infants may be regenerated, we cannot assert that it is tied to the word of God absolutely.

(*d.*) It involves the renewal of the whole man—not merely of one of his faculties. It gives a new direction to all his faculties.

(*e.*) There is no antecedent co-operation on man's part in the change itself. The efficiency in the change is not human, it is in the Holy Spirit. The act of the will on man's part does not produce, but indicates the change.

(*f.*) Regeneration, in the New Testament sense, is on the basis of Christ's work, and consists essentially in the application of what Christ has done, to the human soul, through the Holy Spirit.

(*g.*) This new state shows itself in faith, repentance, and good works.

Negatively—

(*h.*) Regeneration is not a physical change but a change in the moral state. It does not impart new faculties, it gives direction to our faculties.

(*i.*) It does not consist in the executive acts of the will as distinguished from the immanent preference, but it is essentially found in the latter. Nor is it in the conscious, as distinguished from the unconscious, moral states of man. We know it in its results, not in its essence.

§ 2. *Of the Terms employed.*

1. Repentance is used often as synonymous with conversion. It implies a change of mind as conversion also denotes an act of turning. Regeneration is usually employed most strictly to denote that divine agency, in and upon the human soul, which insures a certain mode of action in man's powers in the direction of holiness. Regeneration is thus the divine side of the whole event, and if the divine agency alone is regarded, man may be said to be passive; but when it is viewed as upon the soul, it involves an activity of the soul. It cannot be said that man is passive *in the change*, because if there is a change it implies an

activity; but in the origination of the change, in the efficient cause, man is not the agent. The Holy Spirit is the agent, but as soon as the Holy Spirit acts, there must be activity in the soul. If regeneration is confined to the divine agency simply, without including its effect in the soul, man is said to be passive, because he is not the author of the act; but so soon as that agency is exerted there is activity in the soul, which is usually called conversion or repentance. The controversy in respect to activity and passivity is really one without much significance when explanations are made, if the parties are agreed on this point—that the Holy Spirit is the dominant cause and factor. The controversy is of importance if the agency of the Holy Spirit is denied.

2. The term Regeneration, in its strictest sense, may be said to signify or have reference to an instantaneous act, an act of the Holy Spirit in a moment of time, whereby the soul is renewed, changed from the love of sin to the love of holiness; and as such an instantaneous work of the Holy Spirit, it is distinct from conversion and repentance, and also from sanctification, which is the continued development of what is begun in regeneration.

3. Regeneration is often used in a much wider sense. In the writings of the Fathers it is equivalent to baptism—the sign being taken as equivalent to the thing signified. This was easier to be done at a time when the profession of Christ required of a person to forsake everything in the world, and when willingness to be baptized constituted a good evidence of true regeneration. The term is also used, as we have seen, by evangelical Anglicans, but by a forced interpretation, made to enable them to accept their liturgy. It is also used as designating the whole Christian life in its beginning and effects, including sanctification and the final glorified condition.

4. Some Scriptural representations of this renewed life: It is described as a renewal after the image of God; a being in Christ; a new creature or creation; a resurrection from the dead; light in contrast with darkness; life in contrast with death; a translation into a new kingdom, into the kingdom of God's dear Son; a

being born again of the Spirit; a new heart. Ezek. xxxvi. 26; John iii. 3; Deut. xxx. 6 in connection with Rom. ii. 29; Eph. ii. 1-10; i. 18; 2 Cor. v. 17; Gal. vi. 15; Eph. iv. 23, 24.

§ 3. *Connection of the Doctrine of Regeneration with other Truths.*
1. The term regeneration is often used in an abstract way, as designating the general element of the renewed life. Sometimes it is reduced to a single affection or purpose or feeling. There is undoubtedly such a general element, which can be stated in an abstract form. We can single out the term holiness as expressing the nature of the new state—as contrasted with the term sin as expressing moral evil—and can then say that regeneration is a change from the love of sin to the love of holiness. But in doing this, we ought to be careful not to sever regeneration from the other truths, so as to leave the way open for the inference that there can be a real regeneration which does not involve faith in Christ, a belief in his atoning work, and the renewing agency of the Holy Spirit.[1]

2. Regeneration includes, and in a Christian sense cannot be used without reference to, the relation to Christ, to the union of the soul by faith to Christ. The union with Christ is vital, and is what constitutes the new life. The Spirit which effects the change is the Spirit of Christ. There need not always be a conscious apprehension of Christ at the time. Calvin defines regeneration as coming to us by participation in Christ. The Scriptural statements are such as the following: 1 Cor. i. 30; Col. iii. 9, 10; Eph. ii. 10; Rom. viii. 2; 2 Cor. v. 17.

---

[1] Dr. Samuel Hopkins, who was one of the most orthodox of men, defined the new state resulting from regeneration as disinterested benevolence. He held strongly to the Trinity, the Atonement, and indeed to the highest and most pungent Calvinism. Dr. Channing, who was brought up under him, took his definition of the new life. Channing's mind worked upon it thus: That which is essential to a Christian is to have such benevolence. If I have that, of course I am a Christian. What essential need is there then for my believing also in the Trinity, Atonement, and Justification?—With any other abstract definition of regeneration such a result might be reached. It has been defined as the choice of the highest good. But the pantheist makes choice of the highest good from his point of view. Such statements may be taken as good abstract statements, but not as including the whole truth.

CHAPTER II.

THE NECESSITY OF REGENERATION.

1. The doctrine of depravity proves the necessity of regeneration. If the depravity of man be such as we have seen it, then, in order that he may attain to a holy state, he must be born again. There is no way of his coming into this new condition except by regeneration of the soul.

2. Regeneration is necessary if men are to enjoy what is perfectly holy here and hereafter. To be in the presence of the glories of heaven with a depraved heart, would be no joy to the sinner.

3. It is necessary in order that the atoning work of Christ be applied and received. This takes effect upon us only through regeneration. The receiving of his atoning work is the renewal of the soul.

4. It is necessary for the exercise of the specific graces of the Christian character. All the graces of the Christian life flow from this birth,—all true happiness, peace, and humility.

5. The Scriptures assert emphatically the necessity of regeneration: Matt. xviii. 3; John iii. 3.

CHAPTER III.

THE SUBJECTIVE CHARACTERISTICS OF REGENERATION.

1. Regeneration is not a physical change. The term physical, as used in respect to regeneration, is differently defined. It may mean what belongs to the external material world, or what belongs to the essence and faculties of man. Regeneration is not physical as implying a change in the essence or faculties of man. There is no dispute about this. Besides the essence and faculties, what else is there in man? Where does regeneration come? Those who hold strictly to the exercise scheme reason thus: There are in man, (1) the essence, (2) the faculties, (3) the acts or exercises of the faculties. Regenera-

tion is not in the 1st or 2d, therefore it must be in the 3d.—A better analysis gives this statement: There are in man, 1st, the essence, 2dly, the faculties, 3dly, the generic tendencies, 4thly, the actions. The regeneration then will take effect in the 3d and 4th,—not merely in the specific acts, but in the ground or source of those acts. Take, e. g., the case of Adam before he acted. He had the substance or essence of humanity in all the faculties of human nature. He acted. We will suppose that his first act was an act of trust in God. Now was there in him anything between the faculties and the choice of the acts? Advocates of the exercise scheme would say, No; but it is more Scriptural and philosophical to say, that before any act there was a bias or principle on the ground or basis of which his choice was made; and that this principle or tendency is not a faculty, but a state or direction of the faculties; and that was expressed in the first holy act or choice. In the child now there is not merely the essence with its faculties, but also a bias or tendency.

2. Regeneration does not have to do with the executive acts of the will, merely. The executive acts of the will are the determination to do something. They have respect to something to be achieved. They carry out the underlying preference. The freedom in these acts is the freedom from constraint, but they all presuppose a motive or bias or tendency. They are not the true seat of character, but express character.

3. Nor does regeneration consist in an immanent preference as the product of an executive act. This seems to be impossible, although many of the exhortations to repentance appear to imply the possibility of forming an immanent preference by an executive act. A man is told that he can repent as easily as he can walk. A man walks because he has made a determination to walk and the walking follows the choice, but the act of repentance cannot follow a choice. It is in the ‘choice itself. There is as much difference as between love and the motion of the hand. The change is the choice and the choice the change.

4. Regeneration does not have to do with the heart, to the exclusion of the will and the other powers of man. It is not merely in the sensibilities.

5. Regeneration has to do with the immanent preference. We have seen that the will has two main and very different functions: (*a.*) The immanent preferences, (*b.*) the executive volitions. In the immanent preference is the seat of true morality, spirituality, and it is this which when brought into a right state discloses the great end of man. In order to its renewal, there are necessary the vision of divine things, and then the love for divine things as the ruling principle. Love, which is the immanent preference, itself includes both the affections and the will. In love to God, for instance, there is the strongest current of affection and the most undoubted preference or choice. This of course has for its result the living for the end chosen, and the highest delight in it. In short, regeneration in its full measure and extent involves a new direction of all the human powers from the world and towards God,—an illumination of the understanding, a current of the affections, and a choice of the will. This position is fully sustained by the Scriptures: Jer. xxiv. 7; xxxi. 33; Ezek. xi. 19; Eph. iv. 24; John iii. 6; Eph. iv. 22, 23; 1 Cor. ii. 14; 2 Cor. iv. 6; 1 John ii. 10; John xiv. 15. The Scriptures also represent this renewal as shown in all the life as well as in all the faculties: John xiv. 23.

6. According to the Scriptural statements and what we derive from experience, it is evident that the deepest ground in us, on which the influence of the Holy Spirit is exerted, does not come into immediate consciousness. The work can be known by its fruits and results; and not by immediate consciousness: John iii. 8.

7. It is still further apparent that this work must be instantaneous,—not in conscious experience, but as the work of the Spirit. In conscious experience it may be far from instantaneous. The reason for insisting upon its being instantaneous, is the utter difference between sin and holiness. We cannot make the transition from the one to the other, because they are opposed to each other. There must be some point in the movement of the soul where it turns from darkness to light. We may not be able to discern it, but from the nature of the case there must be such a time. This alone is conformable with the Scriptural

statements: the account of the conversion of Paul, the expressions, "new life," "new creation," "being born again," and the like. The reasons why other views have been held are: (*a.*) The word regeneration is used by some in a broad and loose sense, as including all that God does in bringing man to himself—prevenient grace, providence,—but this is not the Scriptural sense of regeneration. (*b.*) What precedes is sometimes taken as a part of the renewal, *e. g.*, the conviction of sin, which may be very deep where there is no renewal of the soul, which may be conviction from a sense of fear rather than from a sense of holiness. (*c.*) There is sometimes an unwillingness to ascribe the work in its utmost essence to God. There is a tendency to the viewing it exclusively in its human relations, and as it comes out in man's experience. (*d.*) Regeneration is made to be entirely analogous to changes in moral character, which are often gradual. But in the renewal of the soul, there is more than a moral work, there is a spiritual process. There is more than the operation of man's faculties, there is a divine agency. From the sphere of morals we can derive only a partial analogy, incomplete as to the central point. Mere prudential motives are enough to produce a moral change, but they cannot produce a spiritual change. They do not reach the heart, the root of the matter.

CHAPTER IV.

THE AUTHOR OF REGENERATION.

The Scriptural representation is that regeneration is the work of the Holy Spirit, a proper efficient cause, setting in motion all other occasional influences and causes.

1. The positive Scriptural statements: Ps. li. 10; Jer. xxiv. 7; Eph. ii. 10; John i. 13; James i. 18.

2. Scripture represents that in this God acts not arbitrarily but as a sovereign: Rom. ix. 16; 1 Cor. i. 30, 31; iv. 7.

3. Scripture represents that a special power of God is exercised in the renewal of the soul, a power which is supernatural

rather than miraculous. A direct agency of God is implied in the whole phraseology of a new heart, new birth, and the ascription of the holiness in man to God: 1 Cor. ii. 14.

4. To confirm this the doctrine of divine providence leads to the inference that all the circumstances and influences, in respect to regeneration, are under the divine agency and control. The whole of providence, so far as that has to do with the work, is the work of God.

5. It is rational that God should be the author of regeneration. This highest work in man is most naturally ascribed to Him. The analogy of all the other works and ways of God leads to the inference. His power works in all nature, much more in the spiritual realm. Here is the highest good, the chief blessing.

CHAPTER V.

HOW DOES THE SPIRIT REGENERATE THE SOUL?

All God's modes of action are mysterious in the kingdom of nature and providence, and it is especially probable that there will be mystery in his highest and deepest work, in the realm of grace. Any theory of regeneration which explains it all must be false, because it assumes that the finite can compass the ways of Omnipotence. As far as any statements can be made with proper reserve, the following are probably most in accord with Scripture:

1. In all regeneration, whether of infants or adults, there must be essentially the same operation of the Spirit. There cannot be two kinds of regeneration, although there may be a diversity of modes.

2. The work of the Spirit is properly called supernatural rather than miraculous. Miraculous implies a divine intervention against the ordinary methods of God's working, both in the kingdom of nature and of grace. A supernatural work implies that the cause is above nature, but that it may and does work through natural channels in the order of providence, according to appointed methods in the kingdom of grace. In a super-

natural work there is a use of means through which the supernatural element courses. Although the influence itself is beyond means, yet it is through and by means. In the kingdom of God's grace there are ordinary methods or channels through which that grace courses.

3. These means may be various as far as consciousness extends: the course of providence, crises of life, sorrow, even joy. Often some of the means least valued are those which God uses. In many cases, perhaps in almost every case, of the revival of God's work, the means used for bringing it about are what were not anticipated. This has been exemplified in the history of revivals in our own country.

4. The ultimate act in regeneration is without instrumentality. That is, it is a direct influence of the Holy Spirit. If there be renewal of infants, this must be the case. Infants are saved; therefore they must be regenerated by an act which is without any apparent instrumentality. And if regeneration be always the same, there must be the same essential element in all other cases. It is sometimes made a test question whether a person can be regenerated in his sleep. If it is made a question whether God can renew a soul when that soul is unconscious, we should say, Yes, and any other view than that would imply that the human element is the prime factor. But we also say, that while the divine influence may work upon a mind which is unconscious, it will express itself when the mind becomes conscious in a change of preference, and that that will be the first conscious act of the individual.

5. The ultimate regenerating act is not properly to be called resistible, because it secures the will. The will is with it. The very word resistible implies that the will is undecided. All that precedes the renewing act can be called resistible, and so can what most persons call regeneration. But if we come to the central point—the influence of the Spirit securing the will—we cannot speak of its being resistible any more than we can speak of the possibility of a person making a different choice from one which he is making. He might do it the instant before, but now the will is secure.

6. The nature of activity and passivity. Both active and passive elements are involved in regeneration. The active elements, however, are to be viewed as the result of the Spirit's influences. The great law of action and reaction applies here. The activity of the sinner is the result or manifestation or the index of the influence of the Holy Spirit.

CHAPTER VI.

THE MEANS OF REGENERATION.

§ 1. *External providential Means.*

There is, in God's providence, a large mass of external means, including the church and the ministry—their instructions and all their influence.

§ 2. *Acts of the Sinner as among the Means.*

There are also certain acts of the sinner himself, to which he is to be exhorted, as coming among the means.

I.—He is to be exhorted to fix his attention upon the truth as it is presented to him in the Scriptures, religious books, or preaching. In the essay in the Christian Spectator to which we have referred, this and similar exhortations are drawn out so as to give the whole conscious process of the soul in renewal, and the matter is there stated thus: There are certain acts in themselves neither right nor wrong. The sinner is to be exhorted to make use of certain parts of complex acts, particularly to fix the mind upon those motives which come from self-love or the instinctive desire of happiness, and that is to be the main working element. The attention is not to be mainly on the truth, but on the truth as related to the sinner's happiness; and the love of happiness being instinctive, the sinner can feel the force of that motive and make use of it. That motive is neither holy nor sinful; it is indifferent, because from it either a holy or a sinful being may act. Out of all his other acts, the sinner is to single this one—desire of happiness, self-love, and the mind is to be fixed upon it until the future life with all its weal and woe is brought into vision. In order that this may be done, one other point is necessary, viz., that the tide of evil desires be suspended, and the sinner is to do this in order that he may fix his attention on his future happiness so that it may act properly.

On this representation we make the following remarks: (1) The proposal that one part shall be separated from the mind's complex acts would cause the acts to cease to be complex, and would present a single motive before the mind. That would be all that the mind had in view. The desire of happiness will be a single motive, not a part of the complex acts of the soul. (2) When thus singled out and separated as the supposed effectual motive, it must have either a holy or sinful character. It is inconceivable that it should remain indifferent. As it is in his mind, it must be either holy or sinful, because his own mind is in a certain moral state all the time, and we cannot single out a motive from the mind's activities, and say that that motive in the mind shall remain indifferent, any more than one can cast a stick into a current, and say that it shall remain suspended. The accompanying project, therefore, of suspending this sinful current, so that we may get an indifferent motive, is impossible to be achieved. No one ever did or can do it. (3) The proper exhortation in the case is, that the mind fix its attention not upon its own act at all, but upon God, and so turn to Him. Attention is to be fixed not on what the soul is doing, but upon God; not upon one's own interest, but upon the divine command; not on one's own will, but upon that to which the Holy Spirit influences; and so alone can the effectual and sufficient motive be found. The thoughts must be upon the object.

II.—Another mode of exhortation used is, that the sinner shall perform certain acts, which are in themselves indifferent, with his present motives: shall read the Bible, attend church and religious meetings, etc., with the motives which at present influence him.—This is an exhortation which cannot be consistently allowed. These acts are right, but with sinful motives and desires one cannot perform them aright. All that can be said is, that in doing this he is more likely to be brought under the in fluences of the Holy Spirit. These acts may be urged, not as if they themselves would lead to regeneration, but simply in the view that possibly by these acts the soul may come under renewing influences.[1]

III.—The exhortation to the sinner then should be this: to perform any and all acts with a right spirit. He should never be led to feel that he can be content or at peace, or that he is not in great and increasing guilt, until his acts are performed in a right spirit. Thus almost any of the acts, to which it is natural to exhort him, may be the turning-point. Any act performed in the right spirit is the turning-point. It may be the reading of the Scriptures, but it is more generally prayer, and this is the safest exhortation, because there the soul is brought face to face with God. The two elements—the divine and the human—coalesce: the human element turns to God.

§ 3. *Of the Truth as a means of Regeneration.*

The representations respecting the truth as a means of regeneration apply in their strictness to adult regeneration, or to the regeneration of those who have come to an age to understand the truth.

1. The truth is almost always the means, the occasional cause, of regeneration, in what precedes and leads to the regenerative act. The Spirit employs the truth in the previous processes.

2. It is also the fact that the truth is before the mind as motive in choosing, in the act of choice in which the conversion is consummated—yet it is not there as merely abstract, intellectual truth, but as truth in the Scriptural sense, in its fulness and power. It is not truth as belonging to my intellect alone, but as revealed by God and accompanied by the divine illumination.

---

[1] There was a long controversy between the old Calvinists and the Hopkinsians on this point. The former were in the habit of exhorting the sinner to read the Bible, go to church, etc.—and there the exhortations stopped, with the implication that God might come to his aid. The Hopkinsians made the staple of their exhortation to be, the call to immediate repentance on the ground of imperative obligation. They did not say that a person should not employ these means, but that he should not rely upon them, and that the exhortation should be as to the right spirit in which they should be performed. This, more than anything else, was the source of the success of the Hopkinsians at the beginning of the present century. It had also formed a part of the discussion which led to the first schism of the Presbyterian church in 1740.

3. The truth then may be called the chief occasional cause of regeneration in the ordinary course of divine providence.

4. The Scriptures thus represent it: James i. 18; 1 Pet. i. 23; 1 Cor. i. 18; Eph. vi. 17; Heb. iv. 12.

5. Regeneration by the truth does not make truth the efficient agency. God is the ultimate efficient agent in the case. It is the truth as wielded by the Spirit leading to the choice.

6. Truth in itself, bare and abstract, except as the instrument of the Spirit, cannot have moral efficacy sufficient to regenerate the soul. In the unrenewed heart there is no love for the specific truth of the gospel, but rather opposition to it. Truth as moral suasion is inadequate, as we have seen. As a general fact men resist the truth and life.

7. In speaking of the truth as a means of regeneration, we should be careful to use it in its specific Scriptural sense. The Scriptures never disjoin it from Christ and God and the Holy Spirit. Christ is the Truth. It is truth in the sense that truth and reality are one—the truth proclaimed and enforced by the Spirit as a living power unto salvation. To talk of man's being renewed by the truth without the Spirit, is the same as to talk of a man's being killed by a sword when the sword is in nobody's hands. There is this connection between the divine and human agency, and we cannot separate the two.

CHAPTER VII.

THE EXHORTATION: MAKE TO YOURSELF A NEW HEART.[1]

1. It is obligatory. It is an enforcement of the command or injunction of the divine law, that each one should love God with all his heart.

2. It is within the possible extent of man's natural capacities. It is no more than what his capacities may reach unto. It is within the compass of natural ability, using natural ability in the

[1] Ezek. xviii. 31.

sense of the possible extent of man's natural capacities,—not as what the will of man itself may do without the other faculties, not as power to the contrary, but what is in the possibility, as to extent, of man's constitution and faculties.

3. The only obstacle in the way of obeying the invitation and command is in the sinner's depraved heart.

4. The exhortation does not assert or imply that the sinner can comply without divine grace. It no more implies that a sinner can do this without divine grace, than that a Christian can.

5. The exhortation must be interpreted in harmony with the petition, "Create in me a clean heart, O God; and renew a right spirit within me." These two are counterparts.

6. The injunction must be preached so as to make men feel the obligation, the necessity, and the reasonableness of it.

7. It must be so preached that men shall feel that their reliance is not to be upon their own act, but upon divine grace, for the doing of what is enjoined,—so that they shall yield to divine grace, and not attempt the work without it.

CHAPTER VIII.

THE CONSCIOUS PROCESSES OF THE SOUL IN REGENERATION.

These vary somewhat according to the particular state of mind and the previous education, and some changes will be more marked and violent, and others more gradual. There will be, usually, serious meditation on the truth of God; the thoughts will be called in from the world and fixed upon divine truth; then there will be a feeling of want, of need, a feeling that the soul lacks that which is most important to it,—the sense of the need of coming into a different moral state, of turning from the world and unto God. Accompanying these there will be a conviction of sin, coming from the view of the sinner's own nature and character as opposed to the divine holiness, a wrestling of the soul under that conviction, and that conviction rising to a sense of moral pollution. Then, in almost all experience, there will be found the endeavor to renew one's self, to transform one's self into a righteous and holy condition by one's own strength and power. The result will be a feeling of helplessness, running back into the main points on which it is grounded, viz., (*a.*) The impossibility of atoning for the past by one's own works, which will continue to be a ground of condemnation. The helplessness there is entire and absolute. (*b.*) The conviction of moral helplessness. What he would that he does not, and what he would not that he does. This is what is known as the work of the law, the law as a schoolmaster leading to this condition, and in this condition Christ is offered as all that the soul wants, the call to turn and yield is made, and the turning-point will be the yielding to Christ, receiving Him as the personal Saviour, so that the object before the mind is Christ.

Practical Remarks:

1. The preacher should always be careful not to intimate that anything which precedes giving the whole soul to God is right, or can be rested in, or affords any ground of hope. *I. e.,* in the language of the old controversy between the Presbyterians and Congregationalists, "unregenerate doings are not to be allowed."

2. The preacher should likewise never say that any or all the acts the sinner can perform can be rightly performed without the aid of the Holy Spirit. It must always be claimed that all that is good is from the moving of God. We must ascribe all that tends to renewal to the working of the Divine Spirit in the soul. This is the great point of relief in the preaching of regeneration. It is the hope we have, that if there are any good influences within the soul, this is the work of the Holy Spirit, and that if the sinner will yield to them he may be saved. There is a co-operation of the human and divine elements, and religious safety lies in exalting the divine influences, and saying that what the sinner has to do is to yield to those influences. This gives a stronger basis to press an exhortation than the exaltation of human ability or of the power to the contrary.

3. The guilt of remaining in a convicted state should also be enforced. The helplessness which the sinner feels is the proof

of his guilt. The greatness of this helplessness shows the greatness of his guilt. This was the chief service of the Hopkinsian preaching—to insist that the helplessness was guilt.

4. The ability of the sinner should be preached and proclaimed so far as to show his guilt and the greatness of it, but not as the ground of his reliance internally. That reliance must be on God and on divine grace.

5. In preaching there should be a constant observance of, and reference to, the great psychological law, that the mind is not to be fixed upon its own acts, but on the object in view of which it acts.

6. No precise order of experience should be insisted upon as absolutely necessary—no one emotion or experience as the turning-point. This may be different in different minds. The receiving of Christ and resting in Him will be, after all, the grand test.

7. The exhortation to the sinner should be, to yield, to submit to the divine influences, to come to Christ, to yield to the grace that comes from Christ. How he can do this is the last question, and the answer is, he can do it by yielding. As to the how, it is in the act itself.

CHAPTER IX.

REPENTANCE.

This is the human side. The principal word translated repentance in our version ($\mu\varepsilon\tau\acute{a}\nu o\iota a$) signifies change of mind, the process of renewal viewed from the human side, and culminating in the human act. Accompanying it there is a feeling of the evil of sin and godly sorrow, but these do not make it. It is the act of renouncing the old and putting on the new.

One of the great differences between the Roman Catholics and Protestants is on this article of repentance. The whole of Protestant theology makes it an inward work. In the Roman Catholic system it is combined with external works, and repentance comes to have the significance of doing penance. The sacrament of penance is instituted to restore the grace of baptism lost by subsequent sin. In baptism the guilt of original sin is taken away. If a person sins after that, falls, *i. e.*, into "mortal sin," the sinful state must be amended by the sacrament of penance. In this, different parts are distinguished: Contrition, which with most is the imperfect antecedent purpose; Confession, which must be to the priest and must be a particular confession of mortal sins;[1] Satisfaction,[2] which is to be by meritorious works, giving money to the church, saying prayers, etc. The works of supererogation of deceased saints can be made over to help in this satisfaction; then, finally, Absolution,[3] as the act of the church, the judicial declaration that the soul is free from the guilt of these sins. So that the simple Scriptural doctrine of repentance runs through all these processes, binding each sinner to the church and to its sacraments.

§ 1. *Some general Statements of the Protestant View.*
1. Repentance is an internal change.
2. As the human side of regeneration, it implies regeneration, whenever it is real and true. It implies that there is in it the regeneration of the soul. To say that a person can repent without grace who cannot be regenerated without grace, is to state an anomaly; for if there be real repentance there is regeneration, and if a person may repent of himself he may regenerate himself.
3. Some of the elements which are reckoned to repentance—as conviction, sorrow for sin—may exist before there is actual, conscious renewal of the soul: though if the conviction be real and godly, the soul in that conviction is renewed although not conscious of it, and there is doubtless often a renewal before there is peace in the soul.

[1] The confession of venial sins is "useful."
[2] Christ does not free from temporal punishment. Meritorious acts are counseled, not absolutely required.
[3] Absolution is (*a.*) not merely declaratory, but judicial and effective, (*b.*) not a prayer, (*c.*) not conditional as to the future, (*d.*) in it the priest represents God.—In what goes before, however, if there is not contrition, at least in the form of attrition, natural sorrow, "the matter of the sacrament of penance is wanting,' and the form—absolution—does not avail.

4. Repentance, in the common usage of the term, is the exercise of the soul in view of all sin,—turning from it and unto God; and hence, Christians should daily repent. Here, of course, it is not used in its highest, strictest, central sense.

§ 2. *Repentance should be immediate.*

1. This is implied in the Scriptural exhortations.

2. It is an immediate inference from the impossibility of a neutral state.

3. It is involved in the obligatory character of repentance. Duty obliges at every point always.

4. The contrary supposition would allow a man to continue in sin, more or less.

5. As the turning from self to God, it must be immediate.

Insisting upon repentance being immediate does not imply that it can be without grace. On the contrary, the most effectual preaching should ever imply the present grace of God's Spirit. Even if there were no grace, repentance would still be a duty, because it does not surpass the extent of man's natural capacities, because the only hindrance to it is man's sinful heart.

§ 3. *Some special Works and Signs of Repentance.*

1. It is in view of the divine law,—acknowledging its justice and holiness and the justice of the sinner's condemnation under it.

2. It is not only in view of the law, but of God: Ps. li. 4.

3. There is a sense of the futility of all the sinner's pleas in extenuation of his guilt.

4. It includes the sense of moral pollution which comes from the conviction that the sinner as a sinner loves the worst thing in the universe.

5. It includes the sense of one's helpless condition, of which we have spoken.

6. It includes confession of sin, with petition, under the sense that our only help is in God and in his sovereign grace.

7. It issues in, and is, the turning to God, in view of his sovereignty and grace.

BOOK IV.

SANCTIFICATION AND PERFECTION.

CHAPTER I.

SANCTIFICATION.

Sanctification is the carrying to completion the work begun in regeneration. It is the completed union of the soul with Christ, so that as face answereth to face, the renewed soul answers to Christ. Christ is said especially to be made unto us sanctification: 1 Cor. i. 30. In short, sanctification is the work of overcoming the old man by the new.[1] It is the victory of the spirit over the flesh, of grace over sin. It is putting on Christ, becoming wholly like Him.

§ 1. *The Nature of Sanctification according to the Scriptures.*

There are two general descriptions in Scripture: the reinstating of the divine moral image, and the becoming like to Christ; and these two are one, the perfection of our moral being. The divine image in man was lost by the fall, so far as the divine image involves holiness, righteousness. The whole of the divine image is lost, because that image comprehends our spiritual capacities as our spiritual perfections. The capacity, the possibility of perfection remains, notwithstanding the fall. But in the strict and complete sense of the divine image, it was lost when original righteousness was lost, and it is the reinstating of this which is the work of sanctification.

But apart from these general statements the Scriptures have more explicit positions.

1. They represent sanctification as a work upon and in the human heart: Ps. li. 10. There is a continued dependence on God.

2. As far as the Persons of the Trinity are concerned, sanctification is the special work of the Holy Spirit, as regeneration is, although the whole Trinity is concerned in it.

---

[1] It is "the expulsive power of a new affection" (Chalmers).

3. It is of God's free grace, still and ever, not by our merits or deserts.

4. Yet it is through our agency: Phil. ii. 12.

5. Sanctification differs from merely moral reformation (a.) in that it is from God, and in a peculiar sense, of grace, (b.) in that the whole course of sanctification implies our constant dependence on Christ.

6. Sanctification is of the whole person,—intellect, heart, will; the body also becomes the temple of the Holy Ghost, and, through union with Christ, is raised again glorious and incorruptible.

7. All the means of grace are means of sanctification: Faith, the Word, Prayer, the Sacraments.

§ 2. *The Difference between Justification, Regeneration, and Sanctification.*

I.—Justification	precedes:		Sanctification	results;	
	"	is judicial:		"	is moral;
	"	is an act:		"	is a work;
	"	is once for all:		"	is gradual;
	"	causes change of state:		"	causes change of character;
In	"	sins are pardoned:	In	"	sins are subdued;
	"	is equal in all:		"	is unequal;
	"	is from guilt:		"	is from defilement;
In	"	Christ's righteousness is imputed:	In	"	inherent righteousness is given;
	"	gives title to heaven:		"	gives fitness for heaven.
II.—Regeneration gives			Sanctification gives		
		spiritual life:			spiritual growth;
		the seed:			the development;
		the babe in Christ:			the perfect man in Christ.

§ 3. *Of good Works and Sanctification.*

(a.) Good works are involved in sanctification: Eph. ii. 10. (b.) They are both internal and external. (c.) Good works are relatively such; they are not perfectly good, unmixed with sin. (d.) They are necessary: (1) As the proof of faith. They are not necessary to justification, but necessary to the working out of the faith which justifies. (2) They are necessary to the accomplishment of redemption in us. If there are no good works, there is no evidence of our being Christians. (3) They are expressly commanded to believers, in the Bible. (4) But eternal life is not merited by them. Eternal life is given for Christ's sake. Good works fit us for eternal life. This again is in contrast with the Roman Catholic view, which makes the merit of good works to be a part of the title to everlasting life.

§ 4. *The Means of Sanctification.*

All the means of grace are likewise means of sanctification. (1) The Word of God. Truth controls and guides the sanctification. This position is in contrast with the pretentions of fanatics and mystics who make their inward light to be above the Word. (2) Prayer. In its most general aspect, prayer includes praise to God, confession of sin, petition for grace, and supplication for benefits, with submission to the divine will. "Not my will, but thine be done" is the essence of every petition. In a more restricted sense, it is the utterance of holy desires before God. No prayer is possible except to a personal God. Those who pray otherwise are in a state of reverie and not of prayer. Some say that all prayer is in works. While it is true that there is no right prayer which does not lead to works, and that in works there may be petition, yet the two things are entirely distinct, and those who find prayer in works are without prayer. (3) The exercise of the virtues of the Christian character. (4) Works of beneficence and charity. (5) The observance of the ordinances of the church, especially the sacrament of the Lord's Supper.

As to the *Objections to Prayer.* These are two. (1) It is said that as we cannot stay the course of nature, which is uniform, prayer is needless in respect to all external objects. There is a settled order in regard to all physical cause and effect, with which prayer cannot interfere.—In regard to this: (*a.*) What is meant by the course of nature? It is a certain order of natural phenomena, antecedent and consequent, in the natural world. The formula for the natural world is: The same causes, in the same circumstances, will produce the same effects. But when prayer comes in, then, besides the causes in external nature, there may be another cause introduced. The course of nature has reference simply to facts. If new influences come in, the course of nature is no objection, as far as these influences may go, because a new influence may produce a new consequence, even in the arrangement of the physical order, as the mere external consequences of phenomena may be interrupted by our actions.[1] (*b.*) This position is still further strengthened by considering that nature is under and for divine providence. Nature is not ultimate. It is guided by divine providence for the ends of that providence, and the natural world is made subservient to the moral world. Divine Providence may use the same laws and give them different combinations and directions, in order to secure moral ends. This must be admitted if God and his providence are admitted. (*c.*) Any given prayer in the course of that providence may be a part of that series of causes which will issue in certain effects. It may have been appointed by God in his plan. If man can interrupt the course of nature, *i. e.*, can make new combinations, so that what nature would have done is not done, much more God may. And if God may in his plan embrace the prayer of any individual as one of the causes leading to certain effects, then there is no objection at all, from the course of nature, to the possibility of prayer and the answer to prayer. (2) The second objection is made on the ground of the unlimited promises of Scripture. This objection is sometimes in the form of an assertion as to the prayer of faith. Many interpret the prayer of faith as unlimited, on the ground of the promises, and then the objection comes, that such prayer secure of the answers would interfere with the divine order. A strong poetic way of stating it is, that prayer moves the hand that moves the world; but the theological order would be, the hand that moves the world moves prayer. The promises in question are such as that in Luke xvii. 6, which probably refers to miraculous works, and John xiv. 13, 14. In respect to such assurances, we need to make a distinction between a merely personal private desire and prayer as it is the matter of the promises. The prom

---

[1] If there were not a roof to a house, the rain would come in, and in this sense the course of nature is interrupted.

ises of Scripture are to be understood in harmony with all the rest of Scripture. Promises are not to give what each individual may ask for himself, but what is asked in faith and in the name of Christ. The question then is, What is real prayer? And here it must be said: (*a.*) The soul of prayer is the desire for the union of man's will with God's. (*b.*) It is based on God's word and promise. (*c.*) It is of the whole soul, expressing its inmost desire. (*d.*) It is and must be in trust and submission.—The prayer to which the promise is given is not the mere individual wish, desire, and petition, but that wish, desire, and petition as a part of the plan of God, with ultimate respect to God's will and kingdom. "In the name of Christ" includes the meaning, In the spirit of Christ. "In faith" includes, In submission to God.[1]

Practical Suggestions. (1) The habit of prayer should be that which leads us to engage in it daily and hourly. *I. e.*, the state of mind, in which we are as Christians, should be one of constant supplication, looking to God for his guidance and blessing. While there should be stated seasons for prayer, prayer should go with us all the day. (2) It is well to cultivate a habit of ejaculatory petition; *i. e.*, in any pauses of intercourse or of study, to look up to God with petition for guidance and blessing.

CHAPTER II.

PERFECTIONISM.

The question here is not whether it is conceivable that a man might become perfect. It is not what is the possible extent of our natural capacities, aided by grace—whether they might not attain unto perfection; for that theoretically must be conceded. Nor is it on the point of our obligation to be perfect.

[1] In the well-known case of Monica, the mother of Augustine, whose prayer that her son might not go to Rome on account of the dissipation there, was answered by his going to Rome and being converted, we have a striking instance of the answer to the soul and purport of prayer. Spiritual blessing is the soul and ultimate aim of every particular prayer.

The question is simply this: Are we authorized by experience and the word of God to expect perfection in this life? Perfection is nothing less than the complete sanctification of the whole man—in the intellect, heart, and will, so that he is in all his powers perfectly conformed to the will of God, so that even the spontaneous desire for what is sinful is excluded. It may be defined positively and negatively, *i. e.*, as entire conformity to the will of God, and as entire freedom from sin.

§ 1. *The older Theories.*

1. The Pelagian. This asserts that man's native capacities and powers are not injured by the fall. They may be weakened, but are not morally injured. There is no sin but actual transgression, and man is fully able to keep the divine law. The existence of divine grace is granted as a matter of fact, but it is made to be external rather than internal. Though it is not the general fact that men do it, yet it is true that they may live free from sin. In respect to the prayer, "Forgive us our debts," Pelagius said it did not apply to saints.

2. The Arminian. This makes perfection or complete sanctification to be loving God as much as He requires us to do in the gospel. It is a perfection which is simply proportionate to our present powers, and to the present demands of the law upon us under the gospel. Under the gospel dispensation, the demands of the law are relaxed. It does not demand perfect holiness, but as much as man can attain to, with his present powers in their present state. The older Arminians do not claim absolute sinlessness, but a state in which there should be no voluntary transgression. Imperfections may remain, but these they call infirmities.[1]

3. The Roman Catholic. This is connected with their general view of the sacraments and of sacramental grace. That original sin, which is the heritage of the human race, is taken away in baptism. The demand made upon those baptized and

---

[1] Fletcher disclaims perfection as demanded by the Paradisiacal law, and views it as only love to Christ constantly in the soul; whatever else comes up in the soul being regarded as imperfection simply, because it is not of the nature of the ruling principle in the heart.

thus received into the church is, obedience to all external morality. There is also a higher grade of virtue which may become the possession of some elect ones. That higher grade is found in yielding obedience to the "evangelical counsels" in the New Testament. Voluntary poverty, separation from the world, etc., are declared to be a higher degree of virtue and to be, in the eminent sense, religion. And by such obedience not only may perfection be reached, but also works of supererogation may be performed.

§ 2. *The modern View of Perfectionism.*

Some forty years ago this was the subject of earnest discussion among our Western churches. This view differs from the Pelagian, in allowing for a depravity of nature, though it is not decided whether that shall be called a moral state or a physical condition. It differs from the Arminian view, in denying gracious ability. The ability relied upon is not gracious, but man's natural capacity. The perfection to which man can attain consists in this: the choice of the highest good, and, as the result of that choice, the full and perfect discharge of all our duty. The perfection, however, is ultimately to be resolved into the choice. It is a choice which is according to our ability, in the present circumstances, as we now are. The perfection is not an absolute, but a relative perfection, a perfection which is just on a line with our present ability, so that the ability becomes the measure of our obligation, instead of the obligation being the measure of the ability. The main point in the theory, however, is this, that there is no moral character in anything in man, but the choice of an ultimate end,—that all except that does not come under the sphere of what is moral. The whole of character is in the governing purpose. In the discussions in respect to obligation and ability, matters have taken a singular turn at different periods of the controversy. The old New England position said that man had both natural ability and moral inability, that the obligation is the prime thing in the case, and that the obligation is to the full possible extent of our natural capacity. In the later speculations, natural ability is taken to amount to this: what a man can do in his depraved, diseased, and corrupt condition, just as it is; and the view carried out comes to the position that there is no moral inability at all, that that is a vicious phrase, and the perfection is that which man can attain by his natural powers.

I.—The Arguments for this View.

1. On the ground of ability. The command to be perfect implies the ability, and not only the possibility but the actuality of perfection. We are as much bound, on the ground of the command, to preach perfection as we are to preach repentance to the sinner. Perfection is as much attainable by the Christian as repentance by the sinner.—If the doctrine of natural ability be held without the check of moral inability, we do not see but that this argument is valid. Those who hold that the sinner can repent without divine grace must, on the same ground, preach absolute perfection, and that it is attainable in the case of every Christian. The only escape from this conclusion is by modifying the statement of natural ability in regard to repentance.

2. From the promises of God. It is said that God promises the perfection of his children.—But it is to be considered that the promises of God are conditional, and run through all time. They are not fixed to any particular time, or to this life distinctively. They relate to complete and final sanctification.

3. From the provision of the gospel. It is said that this is such for sanctification or entire holiness, that we may expect it in this life.—The argument proves too much. The fulness of the provision would not be our warrant for expecting entire sanctification, any more than the general atonement is a warrant for expecting a universal redemption. The provision in the divine order is always beyond what it is applied unto.

4. From prayer. We are to pray for entire sanctification.—Our prayer, however, is to be with trust. We are warranted, on the ground of the promise, in expecting entire sanctification, but that does not involve that it will come to us in this life.

5. An appeal to facts—as certified by Scripture.—This is to be viewed as part of the statement under the next head.

6. From Scripture. 1 John ii. 5; iv. 17; iii. 5 and seq.; Col. ii. 10.—These passages however set forth what is the true nature or character of Christians, what it is they are regenerated for, *i. e.*, for entire perfection, and do not declare or announce the fact that Christians themselves are at the present time perfect, although they ought to be so. The declaration is in respect to the idea of the Christian, rather than of the actual Christian life or experience. The Apostle John says, "If we say that we have no sin, we deceive ourselves" (1 John i. 8), and the other passages are to be interpreted in harmony with this. He proceeds to give the true idea of a Christian, but he does not say that Christians are actually conformed to this. The case in which perfection would be most likely to be found, if anywhere, is that of the Apostle Paul, and it is said that he claims perfection for himself in such passages as Acts xx. 26; Gal. ii. 20; 1 Cor. ii. 16; 2 Cor. i. 12; 1 Thess. ii. 10; 2 Tim. i. 3.—But these are to be taken as statements of Paul's general position and character. The "holily and justly and unblameably" of 1 Thess. ii. 10, is in reference to his conduct in the world, and not to his inward sanctification. The same Apostle says, Phil. iii. 12: "Not as though I had already attained, either were already perfect." Advocates of perfectionism interpret him as speaking here of the resurrection, and understand him to say that he had not yet attained unto the resurrection of the body. But that was a very needless thing for him to say. Other passages cited are: Phil. iii. 15—but here "perfect" means, thoroughly instructed in divine things; 1 Cor. ii. 6—but here again "perfect" means, having knowledge of divine things. Luke i. 6 would be a much stronger passage. If any one was perfect, Zacharias was; but even perfectionists interpret this of outward conformity, because it was a perfection under the old economy.

II.—Objections to Perfectionism.

1. On the ground of the radical theory of this modern perfectionism, if any Christians are perfect, all are perfect. Perfection, they say, consists in the choice of the highest good, and whatever else there may be in man is not of a moral sort. Then, as all Christians have chosen the highest good, and as all else

that is in them is not moral and has nothing to do with the question, it follows that all are perfect.

2. Even if anybody was perfect, he could not prove the fact. Who knows his own sinfulness? Who can know his secret sins? The one fact of secret sins alone should prevent any one from asserting that he is perfect. There may be sins which are sinful in the eye of God, which are not disclosed to us in their vileness.[1]

3. The effect of the doctrine, as held and preached, is to lower the standard of the divine law. In order to make the doctrine consistent, it is necessary to bring down that law to our present actual capacities, and in doing this it is lowered and made to be different in its demands upon each one.

4. The doctrine has, in the same way, a tendency to lower our view of the nature of sin. Its constant tendency is, to lead us to look for sin only in deliberate acts, in volitions.

5. The Scriptural argument against it is very strong: Job ix. 20; Ps. xix. 12; James iii. 2; John iii. 7, where a process is indicated; Phil. iii. 12; 1 John i. 8; Gal. v. 17–23; Heb. xii. 7; Ps. xvii. 15, showing *where* perfection is to be looked for; and especially, Rom. vii., throughout which chapter Paul speaks in the present tense, and has for the object of his argument to show that under and by the law no human being can be justified or obtain peace or salvation. Even to such a Christian as Paul, the law is such a condemning power as is set forth in verses 13, 14. We judge that in this chapter neither the regenerate nor the unregenerate is distinctively and exclusively in view, but that the chapter contains this general position, that no member of the human family, even one who is saved by Christ, can, when judged by the divine law, obtain peace by conformity to its requirements.

6. The manifest faults of Christians in this life are arguments against this doctrine. The tendency of those who hold it is to palliate these faults, and to say that they do not come under

---

[1] It may be supposed that if ever any one approached perfection, it was the wife of Jonathan Edwards, yet her holy exercises were mingled with the strongest wrestlings with sin.

the term sin—they are excusable imperfections. Some who have been wild and fanatical have said that for them, as Christians, there is no sin. Some perfectionist communities have run riot in the indulgence of fleshly lusts, on this ground.

7. The tendency of the doctrine is still further to lead to reliance upon conformity to law, and not upon the pure grace of God as the ground of peace and hope. The very claim of perfection implies that we measure ourselves by the law as a standard, and that withdraws us relatively from simple trust in Christ.

8. The doctrine rests in theory upon a delusive psychology, viz., that in one act or one governing moral state is the whole of character, and that everything else which is in us does not belong to character, and does not come under the categories either of sin or holiness. This is against Christian consciousness, and is practically delusive and false.

9. Christian experience, as a whole, is opposed to it. We have the confessions of the best men in the church, that they have had to struggle with sin.

10. Opposed to it likewise are the prayers for perfection which are enjoined upon us in Scripture as our duty: 1 Thess. iii. 10–13; v. 23; Heb. xiii. 21; Matt. vi. 12, in respect to which it may be asked, Into what state in this life can a Christian come in which the prayer "Forgive us our debts" may not be repeated?

11. The Scripture represents Christ as the only perfect man.

CHAPTER III.

PERSEVERANCE OF THE SAINTS.

The doctrine of the saints' perseverance is this: that those who have been really and truly renewed will persevere unto the end through a progressive sanctification. This sanctification is the work of God. The perseverance is through divine grace. The doctrine expresses a fact and not a mere theory. Perseverance is presented in Scripture as a duty incumbent on the saints. There is also contained a promise, on condition of the performance of the duty, and the promise culminates in the assurance of the fact that all true saints will perform the duty, and so persevere to the end.

§ 1. *Arguments in favor of the Doctrine.*

1. The promises of God to Christ as our Head: John vi. 37, 39; xvii. 2, 12.

2. God's promises to his people: Ps. xxxvii. 28; Jer. xxxi. 31; xxxii. 40; 1 Pet. i. 5.

3. From the nature of grace. It is implied in grace that there is an everlasting covenant, and it so described: Isa. lv. 3; Jer. xxxii. 40. It is exhibited as showing God's great love to the human race, and a gift which, from its nature, He would not be likely to withdraw. There is a union with Christ on the ground of the covenant, and from his love who shall separate us?

4. From the nature of the eternal life which is promised. Christ is to give eternal life to as many as the Father gives Him. Now what is eternal life? It is the continuance to eternity of what is given here in the seed and the germ. The life already begun is an eternal life: 1 John v. 11–13; John iii. 16.

5. From Christ's intercession: 1 John ii. 1; John xvii. 24, where the "I will" is emphatic, implying Christ's purpose.

6. It is implied in the doctrine of decrees as including election. Heb. vi. 17–19. "The immutability of his counsel."

§ 2. *Explanations of the Doctrine.*

It involves two elements: on the one hand, God's agency in preserving; on the other hand, the saints' agency in persevering. Neither of these by itself is the doctrine, but both together constitute it. It does not imply that salvation is given without conditions, but that the conditions of salvation are to be fulfilled. It is not meant that true believers shall be saved at any rate, without their own continued activity. The doctrine is that of the perseverance of the saints, that their activity shall be continued. It does not imply that true believers may not fall into sin.—It asserts that though they may fall into sin, they will not abide therein and be lost: Matt. xxiv. 24,—if possible, the elect,—but it is not possible. Phil. i. 6.— Believers are not to be saved because they deserve salvation: it is of grace.—Nor yet is the doctrine that those about whom it is doubtful whether they are Christians will be saved, but that those whom God has truly renewed will be.—In order then to disprove the doctrine, it must be shown that some real saints have apostatized,—not that some church members have, or some apparent saints, but some whom God has called.

§ 3. *Objections to the Doctrine.*

Obj. I.—From passages of Scripture representing apostasy as possible. The argument here is unsound, in that it infers a reality from a possibility. Ezek. xviii. 24 is a statement of possibility and consequence. John xv. 2 is to be understood of such as are united to Christ simply externally, and do not receive of the sap of the vine. Their not bearing fruit is a proof that they are not really united to Christ. The sense of Gal. v. 4 is, that any who depend on the law for justification cannot rely upon grace. Their depending on the law shows that they have not a part in the grace which alone can save them. In the parable of The Virgins, the five who were foolish probably represent those who make false professions, rather than apostates. The strongest passage is Heb. vi. 4 seq. This is a statement of an impossibility. In case those once enlightened should fall away, there is no possibility of their being brought again to repentance. This is to be taken as literally true. If any one does that, he cannot be saved. The door of salvation will be shut to him entirely. But the passage does not declare what is needed in order to prove the objection, and so disprove the doctrine,—that any who have been thus enlightened have actually fallen away.[1] Heb. x. 29; 2 Pet. ii. 20, 21, are general warnings, and do not include the point necessary to refute the doctrine. In Rev. xxii. 19 "taking away his part

---

[1] In the sense in which the Methodists hold to falling away and subsequent restoration, this passage is directly against them, for it says that if any do thus fall away, they cannot be renewed.

out of the book of life" is to be understood of the part which he would otherwise have had—not of what he actually had.

Obj. II.—On the ground of free agency. Man, being free, may fall away. But here, again, all that can be deduced from free agency is possibility, while what must be proved in order to refute the objection is actuality. It is admitted that falling away is possible so far as man is concerned: the doctrine is that, through God's faithfulness, it is certain that the falling away will not occur.

Obj. III.—On the ground of the effects of the doctrine. It is said that it tends to make Christians careless. But the doctrine is that of the *perseverance* of the saints in a holy life, and if Christians are over confident and careless, it is in spite of the doctrine and against its precise terms. It is a perversion of the doctrine to put it in the form which Cromwell is said to have done—that he knew he would be saved because he was once a Christian; because if a man lose present evidence, it casts a doubt on his previous experience.

Obj. IV.—That Adam and the angels fell, although holy. This is no objection to the doctrine, for we do not know that any promise was made to them that they should be kept. The promise is to those who are redeemed and regenerated out of a sinful state.

Obj. V.—On the ground of certain instances mentioned in Scripture, as Hymeneus and Philetus, Alexander, etc. The probability is that these were not real Christians.

Obj. VI.—The instances of David and Peter are cited. But these prove the doctrine: in spite of their sins they persevered, so far as we know.

Practical Remarks. (1) No past experience of the Christian can be taken as absolute, as giving him the unqualified certainty that he will be saved. (2) The evidence of any one being in a gracious condition must be found chiefly in his continuous sanctification, in his growing in grace and in the knowledge of Christ. (3) The doctrine calls upon us in preaching to emphasize the danger of deception in relation to one's being in a gracious state. (4) The doctrine is a source of great comfort

THE KINGDOM OF REDEMPTION. 589

to those who are in spiritual despondency. It may be the means of raising up those who are bowed down. (5) The ground of the doctrine is in God's promise and grace, and not in what man of himself can be or do: and therefore the application of the doctrine, or our right to apply it, will be in proportion to our reliance upon the divine promise and grace. (6) Warnings to Christians are useful and necessary. The doctrine does not prevent our uttering the most solemn warnings on the danger of falling away. (7) The assurance of perseverance can be had only by those who persevere. The perseverance itself is the only ground for putting ourselves individually under this doctrine. Rom. ii. 7; 2 Pet. i. 10; 1 Cor. ix. 27; Heb. iv. 1.

PART II.

THE UNION BETWEEN CHRIST AND HIS CHURCH.

[The author gave no lectures upon this part of the theological system. His general view, however, can be seen in the following statements, which are drawn from other parts of his manuscripts.]

§ 1. *Of the fundamental and germinant Idea of the Church of the Lord Jesus Christ.*

We derive this most fully from Eph. i. 22, 23. The church is the body of which Christ is the soul, the organism of which He is the life, the outward form of which He is the inward and formative principle. It is said to be the fulness of Him who filleth all with all things. That is, the church is filled up by and with Christ, with all his blessings, all his grace, and all his glory. And Christ being the one who in the universe filleth all things with all things, being the Word, the Creator, the Head and the End of all, His church filled with Him is filled with all. The plenitude of spiritual being and beatitude is poured forth from the eternal throne where He ever reigneth in regal dominion, and vitalizes, shapes, and guides that church, wherever found, in heaven or on earth. The church is the veritable mystical *body* of Christ. The union of soul and body is at once the most mysterious and the most patent fact about man's own nature. The sacred image of God is not only appareled in, but united with, the fragile vestments of mortality, and the immortal soul doubtless shapes, fills, and governs the transient tabernacle. And even thus it is with Christ in relation to his church. He who filleth all things—who made, preserves, and governs the universe, also, and in an eminent sense, fills his church, replenishing it with the abounding riches of his grace, and imparting to it that spiritual life which is the source and pledge of a bliss ful immortality. This is indeed the divine side of the church, but then the divine side is the real side.

This intimate alliance of the church with its Head is set forth and reiterated in varied modes throughout the Scriptures, and always in images that express the closest espousal, the most tender and yearning love: Isa. xliii. 1–7; xlix. 15; John xv. 5; Eph. v. 25, 29. Expositors in all ages have taken the Song of Songs, which depicts as does no other lyric the intense longing of the most chaste earthly affection, and applied all its oriental luxuriance in a supereminent and spiritual sense to celebrate the hymeneal union of the celestial Bridegroom and the terrestrial bride, whom the Bridegroom himself ransomed and clothed in white raiment, that she might share in his ineffable and divine love. And of earthly wedlock itself, the most logical of the apostles tells us that it is only a fugitive image of the eternal union between the Redeemer and the redeemed. And this is the real basis, and so gives us the true formative, organic idea of the Christian church: it is the body of Christ, the fulness of Him that filleth all with all.

§ 2. *Of the Nature of the Church as seen in the Light of this radical and central Idea.*

I.—The distinction between the invisible and the visible church. This distinction is not Protestant alone, but essentially Christian. The vital union of the soul with Christ is the formative element of the church. Wherever that is found, there the church is; where that is not, the true church is not. And this union is essentially spiritual, and so invisible. The invisible church is the true church—the only church to which belong prophecy, promise, victory, and full and final redemption. This and this alone has the three grand marks or notes of the church of Christ—catholicity, infallibility, and sanctity.

II.—The unreal and nugatory character of all prelatical claims. The church is made up of believers; the visible church is made up of all who are baptized; the invisible church of all who believe, whether baptized or not. The indwelling Spirit of Christ alone makes, alone can make, a Christian. A bishop cannot do it; a minister cannot do it; baptism cannot do it. They may help in it; but the work itself is God's work, his divine prerogative. If man could do it, there would be no need of God; and if God does it, man is only an instrument and not the real agent. The pretence that anything external, outward, and visible can make the internal and spiritual, that any outward form and means can directly impart inward and spiritual grace, is, in the last result and analysis, a materialistic hypothesis. It amounts to saying that mind can be the product of matter. The believer must always be left in the position of coming directly to Christ for salvation. What is external may be a means, a help, a stimulus, but can never be that mystic bond which unites the soul with its Lord and Master. This principle cuts deep and sharp, but it is the irresistible logic of the Divine Logos—that Christ may be all in all.

III.—This principle must shape our theory as to the nature and functions of the visible church organization. Any attempt to locate the essence of the church in bishops or even in the ministry, or in presbyteries or associations and the like, is utterly inconsistent with the radical idea and fact of the Christian system. The Spirit of God does not dwell peculiarly or exclusively in bishops, ministers, or presbyteries; and where the Spirit acts, there is the true church-building power. Any particular visible church is a company of believers (and their baptized children) united by covenant, where the Word is truly preached, and the Sacraments, as occasion serves, are duly administered. As to its particular constitution, much is left by the Word of God to the fitness of times and places—the general principles being duly cared for. These points are not finally settled by any *jure divino* warrant. The local church is doubtless the unit of the system; and the principle of unity, among those who have the same faith and order, must also in some way be secured. But when any such organization calls itself, by way of emphasis, *the* church, it emphasizes the wrong word, and so changes the vital sense of the other word. It is an arrogant claim, without Scriptural warrant, especially when it puts the essence of the church in some figment of an apostolical succession, which no texts can prove or history verify. The church is made by Christ and not by man. Where Christ dwells, there and there only is the church—for it is his body.

IV.—From the same principle—that the church is the body of Christ—it follows, that the church has and guards his truth, that it jealously preserves and defends whatever is essential and fundamental in Christian doctrine, as well as what is needful for the Christian life. For in Him are hid all the treasures of wisdom and knowledge. He is the King of Truth. The doctrines that center in Him are not mere theories, abstract opinions, but they express the essential facts about his person and work. The church can no more thrive without them, than morality can prosper without precepts and prohibitions. The attempt to separate Christian doctrine from the Christian life is vain. The two are as vitally connected as are the principle of life and the formative principle in the case of every seed or embryo. In the last analysis, perhaps, the truth is a reflex of the life, because the life is a manifestation of the truth. The relation is akin to that of the Scriptures and the Spirit; the Spirit works through and by the word; we are begotten of the truth.

Hence all churches have felt the need of public, authorized, and authentic confessions of faith, as a declaration of truth, a protest against error, a bond of union, and a means of instruction and growth. And in the midst of the incessant conflicts of modern denominations, especially in our own land, and of the insurgent pressure of all forms of error and infidelity—to call upon us to strike down our symbols is like calling on an army to strike down its flag in the face of the foe. No one can overestimate the influence of such a document, for example, as the Westminster Assembly's Shorter Catechism. It has made our church members strong in definite thought upon the weightiest themes. It has given them a consistent body of divinity in the midst of the fluctuations of opinion. It has been a spiritual and catholic bond of union, especially in connection with the theological treatises of the elder Edwards, between two of the most intelligent and powerful bodies of Christians in our country, the Congregational and Presbyterian, differing indeed on sundry unessential points of church order, but radically one in the common professed faith. It has done more to shape and train this land for its high evangelical mission than anything else except the inspired Word of God, which is the only divine rule of faith and practice.

The church, as the body of Christ, has the deposit of divine truth as its most sacred charge to keep, defend, and propagate. Its very life depends upon its faithfulness. To yield it is apostasy.

V.—The principle that the church is the body of Christ involves also this: that the church contains within itself the law and the means of its own growth. As a body, an organized society, in the midst of the human race, if it is to live, it must also grow. And unless it is to remain virtually stationary, its growth must be always gaining upon its loss. And there are two modes in which, in the divine order, this growth is to advance; it grows from within, by birth and infant baptism, and from without, by conversion of the unbaptized (or by reclaiming those who have forfeited the grace which baptism was designed to signify and seal). Apart from the Scriptural and historical argument for infant baptism, its fitness and necessity result from the very idea and nature of the church, as a form of human life, of human history, of human society. In a sinful race, the church is an exotic. That it may take root and thrive, it needs to make use of the strongest ligaments that bind man to man. The closest earthly bond, uniting the physical and moral, is found in the parental and filial relation. The family is the native root of the state; no less should the church be rooted in it. It is fitting that the mightiest human ties should be enlisted in the service of the church,—that the church should begin in the household. And this is one reason for infant baptism.—We must consider also the fact, that by their natural descent from the first parents of the human race, all mankind are involved in the penal evils of the first apostasy. The law of sin and death, which rules in the race, is mighty and universal because it takes in the law of birth. If now an economy of redemption is to be provided, it is eminently fitting that, so far as is possible, the same law should be turned into the service of redemption. Why should sin have all the advantage in appropriating the deepest instincts of the human soul? Why may not redemption, as well as sin, be connected in some way with the family constitution? Why may not the church receive the full benefit of those native and hallowed ties by which the successive generations of men live one life? Your children were unclean, argues Paul, if you were un believing, but because you believe now are they holy. And here is the profound meaning of the Abrahamic covenant.

The children of a believing parent or parents are to be baptized. Baptism is the sacrament whereby the subject of it is received into and made a member of the visible church. Baptized children are members of the church even as all children belong to the country in which they are born; they are under its watch and care, to be trained for its service. The name of God has been named upon them. They are included in the covenant. The covenant antedates and is the ground of the baptism; and this baptism makes them members of the visible, not necessarily of the invisible, church. Baptism incorporates into the external form and order of the body of Christ. Regeneration is not external but internal, so that there is no proper baptismal regeneration, any more than there is a material soul. Regeneration may or may not accompany the rite which is its sign and seal; it is not tied to it.

There are three theories on this point. One, the Baptist, view is, that baptism is to be applied only to the regenerate; a person must be regenerated before he is baptized. Another, the sacramental theory, says, that baptism is, or involves, regeneration; baptism regenerates and so admits into the visible church. The third view, that of the Reformed churches, neither confounds baptism and regeneration, as does the latter, nor sunders them, as does the former; it recognizes the fact, that baptism, on the ground of the parental relation, admits the child into the external order of the church, and that it is also a sign and seal of the ingrafting into Christ, who said, Suffer little children to come unto Me. And many of the Reformed Confessions expressly admit, that the grace of baptism is not tied to the moment of time when it is administered; but that whenever conversion takes place, it is connected with the grace signed and sealed in the baptismal covenant.

The church is to grow from without as well as from within. By the faithful preaching of the Word and all other duly appointed and wise methods, it is to strive to win those that have wandered from it, or those that never knew it.

VI.—The church, being the body of Christ, is rightfully independent of the civil power or the state, in respect to its proper spiritual functions, whether these concern doctrine, order, or discipline. The true relation of the church to the state is the unsolved problem of human history. The Hebrew nation identified the two; for it was a theocracy. The early Christian church had no recognized relation to the state; for it was a church in the catacombs, though in the catacombs it undermined the throne of the Cæsars. The mediæval Roman church tried to solve the problem by so enlarging the spiritual power as to bring princes and nations under its domination; but in doing this, it became corrupt, despotic, and anti-Christian. Modern Protestant Europe has tried to solve the problem by establishing national churches; but this brings the church into pecuniary and political dependence upon the powers that be. The heart of the present conflicts of Europe is in this struggle; England is now passing through it: Scotland's Free Church Presbyterians have done manful battle against this Erastianism. In this country our Puritan fathers attempted in some sort a revival of the old Jewish theocracy; but the course of events and our Revolution dissolved this unchristian marriage, by which the church lost its inherent rights, while the state had too much to do. And the influence of this separation is seen and felt in the beneficent and increased activity and power of both church and state, each having its specified and proper functions.

VII.—The principle that the church is the body of Christ leads to the position that his kingdom must have ultimate universality and supremacy. He who filleth all with all must needs fill his own body with all the riches of wisdom, grace, and glory. The vision of the redeemed church as the body of Christ and of the resplendent glories of its final consummation is at once the most ideal and the most real of all the hopes and prophecies of the future. That to which the church is destined is a fulness of wisdom, of faith, and of love. Of wisdom: for when we know the truth as it is in Jesus, we know all other truth aright. Reason and faith are at one. Of faith: that faith which allies the soul to God, that justifies the soul, that gives the victory over the world. Of love: such as binds together all holy beings and makes a universal brotherhood, an eternal kingdom, the love which is the sum and last name of all the virtues, and abideth forever.

And because this fulness of the church is a fulness of wisdom, faith, and love, it also must be a fulness in power and dominion. The most inspiring hope for the human race is in the sublime victories of Christ's kingdom. All power, said our Lord, has been given unto me, in heaven and on earth, and this imperial claim to universal dominion has been going into fulfilment ever since. In comparing the church with other forms of organized social life, we see that every human empire, state, republic, shall and must at last pass away, and that the church of Christ is the only institution which is to pass undissolved through the gates of death. This church is the only form of human society that has existed in the world from the beginning: it has seen the downfall of the hoary despotisms of the East; it witnessed the youthful glories of Greece and also its decline; it was in being when Romulus built the walls of Rome, and was mightier still when the last Roman Emperor was driven from the eternal city; it assisted in the formation and also in the destruction of the Germanic Empire; it laid the foundations of the civilization of France, England, Russia, and America; it has given all the strength they have to all these nations: they have prospered in proportion as they have served Christ's kingdom, and if they will not obey the law of Christ, they are like to be dashed in pieces or crumble in decay.—All this is not theory but historic fact. The prophecy is on the basis not only of God's word, but also of all the past facts of the annals of our race: it is of the consummation of what has been going on from the beginning, the complete outworking of the one principle, that the church is the body of Christ, the fulness of Him that filleth all with all.

PART III.

THE CONSUMMATION OF THE KINGDOM OF REDEMPTION IN TIME AND IN ETERNITY. THE ESCHATOLOGY.

CHAPTER I.

OF DEATH AND IMMORTALITY.

§ 1. *Death.*

As waking and sleeping mark our temporal life, so death and the resurrection are spoken of in regard to the eternal life: John xi. 13; Ps. xiii. 13. The departed are called souls in Scripture: Rev. vi. 9; xx. 4; Ps. xlix. 19. Hence, death is, separation of soul and body. The violence of the rupture is the fruit of sin.[1] Yet it is introductory to another state.[2] Its chief terror for man lies in its being the symbol of future penalty.[3]

§ 2. *Of Immortality.*

I.—Scriptural Arguments.

1. The Old Testament view. Some Socinians interpret the Old Testament as denying immortality, or as not containing the doctrine. Warburton, in his Divine Legation of Moses, endeavored to construct the system on that basis. His argument is that Moses had and must have had a *divine* mission, because he did not enforce his religion by the rewards and sanctions of a future life. The intimations of immortality are undoubtedly less full and definite in the Old Testament than in the New; but they increase in definiteness in the progress of the Old Testament dispensation. Christ against the Sadducees, Matt. xxii. 23–33, uses an argument which implies, if it implies anything, the

---

[1] "Der Tod ist nicht der rein negative abstracte Gegensatz des Lebens, er ist der *positive, concrete* Gegensatz desselben:.... er ist Auflösung des gottgesetzten Sein." (Delitzsch, Apologetik, s. 133.)

[2] "Appropinquante morte anima multo est divinior." (Cicero.)

[3] The fear of death, *when dying*, is rare. (Sir Benj. Brodie, Psychol. Inq's., i. 132.)

revelation of a future life in the Old Testament. "God is not the God of the dead, but of the living." That alone would be sufficient. The translation of Enoch, Gen. v. 24, supposes a continued existence.[1]

There are the taking away of Elijah, 2 Kings ii., and the miracles of Elijah and Elisha, restoring the dead, 1 Kings xvii.; 2 Kings iv. Whence could the soul return? The vivification of the dead, Ezek. xxxvii., "implies knowledge of the resurrection." Isa. xiv. 9; Ps. xvii. 15; xlix. 15; lxxiii. 24, recognize immortality. There are also passages which imply and involve the notion of a resurrection, which of course implies immortality. Isa. xxvi. 19; Dan. xii. 2; Job xix. 25 (this is a contested passage; some refer it to the resurrection; the least that can be made of it is confidence in God's vindication, not merely in the present, but in a future life); Eccl. xii. 7.

2. The New Testament view. Here there is no doubt about immortality. Matt. x. 28; John xi. 25; 2 Cor. v. 8, are specimens of the testimony.

II.—Philosophical Argument.

[Only the heads of argument are given.]

(1) The consensus gentium. It is the presumption among all nations. (2) The simplicity of the soul takes away any counter presumption. (3) The moral argument: (*a.*) Retribution, which is not completed in this life. (*b.*) The educability of man: his powers are not completely unfolded. His highest powers as a moral being are not reached in this life. His is an incomplete destiny, if there is not an immortality. He has been made in vain as to the ultimatum of his existence. (*c.*) In the distinct conscious personality of man, there is the strongest metaphysical ground for the position of his immortality. Brutes have not that personal moral being. They have individualized existence, but not moral personality. And so far as analysis can reach, this is absolutely simple. To this may be added the natural longing of mankind for the continuance of existence, which is inexplicable if man is not to live forever. (4) There is a moral

---

[1] Warburton finds difficulty in disposing of this case. He suggests that Moses knew about Enoch and kept it veiled from the people.

system; there is a God; He will bring the system to its completeness: hence, immortality.

§ 3. *Annihilation.*

The theory of annihilation has been brought forward in modern times, especially in connection with the theory of future punishment. It has been supposed to do away with some of the difficulties of that doctrine. The position has been taken that the impenitent dead are annihilated, and that death spoken of in relation to them means a literal cessation of being. As far as the Scriptures are concerned, the whole plausibility of the position arises from the use of the word, death. It sometimes means a cessation of conscious being in a certain condition. This is applied analogically to future existence. There is no instance, however, in which any other word can be found which implies this absolute cessation of being. And against this representation, and in favor of the ordinary view of death, in the future life,—that it implies suffering, all the passages that prove distinct future punishment stand. Matt. xxv. 31-46. The parallel in verse 46 implies the continued existence of both righteous and wicked, and what is asserted is, bliss for the one and punishment for the other. The parallel would not hold at all, if, with the wicked, it were to be a cessation of all being. Moreover, the very notion of punishment and suffering which is involved in the use of the word fire, verse 41, implies continued consciousness. So the description of the judgment, 2 Cor. v. 10, implies perpetuity of being. In Rom. ii. 6-11, the expressions, tribulation and anguish, cannot be taken at all for annihilation. In Rev. xxii. 11, the continuance of moral pollution implies the continuance of conscious being.

Other arguments adduced for annihilation are simply theoretical and metaphysical possibilities: *e. g.*, that the soul is not naturally indestructible, that God could annihilate it. That may be granted, but the question is not one of possibility, but of fact; and there is nothing better settled in Scripture than that death means penal suffering.[1]

[1] See Pres. Bartlett, Theory of the Extinction of the Wicked, New Englander, Oct. 1871. Also, Life and Death Eternal.

§ 4. *Objections to Immortality.*

Obj. I.—From the analogy of the vegetable and animal world. Vegetables die; they lose not only their present form, but the distinctive principle of life is apparently evaporated, when they cease to be. So of the animal creation. There is no evidence of the continued existence of the animal soul. On this basis an analogy is framed; if other living beings thus die, man may.—The analogy, granting it the fullest application, would hold only in respect to the material portion of man—what might be called the animal soul in man. The power of the analogy as to any further application is broken by the fact that man is also a moral, personal, spiritual agent, which the brutes are not, and it is entirely unwarrantable to apply from a lower to a higher sphere an analogy which has place only in the lower.

Obj. II.—From the decay of the faculties in old age.

As we come to the term of being here, the faculties apparently decline in vigor.—On this point what is said in Butler's Analogy is fair and conclusive. The faculties of the bodily constitution decay, *i. e.*, the body decays. The means of exercising the soul in this world die out. That is all that can be proved. As far as the higher faculties of the soul are concerned—its spiritual discernment, its reasoning powers—all that most concerns man as a spiritual being, the facts are not according to the statement. That decays which is to be laid aside. Still further, most of the human race die before any such change is at all apparent. The large majority die in infancy; very few live to the decline of their faculties; and any such argument would at the best have a very limited application.

Obj. III.—Immortality is a fact, and cannot be proved by mere reason.—All that we attempt to do by the use of reason is to attain a probability and moral certainty. Everything looks that way as far as reason is concerned. We do not establish it as a fact by reasoning, but as a moral certainty, in view of which we are to act. As far as it is a question of fact, we appeal to that which establishes the fact, the testimony of Christ and his apostles—the revelation of God.

Obj. IV.—It is said that as far as the moral argument goes, its demands are met by the continued existence of the race,—that it would only prove the continued existence of a race of moral beings here, and does not reach to the conclusion of a personal immortality, and that any judgment upon individuals is not fair. Judgment upon men is simply their character handed down. This is the general pantheistic position of Fichte, Strauss, etc. A moral argument for immortality is granted, but is resolved into the immortality of the race. The judgment is made to be the moral judgment of posterity upon those who have gone before.—But this is doing away with the proper sense of moral retribution, which, in its specific form, is the rendering to each according to his deserts. To resolve it into the retributions of human opinion is to do violence to the utterances of conscience. The righteous deserve more than a good name, and the wicked more than a bad name.

Obj. V.—It is said that the longing for immortality is satisfied by such continued fame among men.—But that is to disconnect the longing for immortality from personal being and personality, and when this is done, the essence of the longing is destroyed. What men desire and long for is, continued existence, not that they may be spoken of after death. This suggestion is from the pantheistic policy of resolving specific doctrines into general ideas.[1]

CHAPTER II.

OF THE INTERMEDIATE STATE.

By the intermediate state is meant the state of departed souls between death and the resurrection. That there is such a state, all believe who believe in the resurrection and final judgment. The differences of opinion are as to the character of the

[1] This is the whole of the skill of the pantheistic reconstruction of Christian truth. As it deals with the Christian doctrine of immortality, so it does with the doctrine of redemption. That is, the doctrine of the redemption of the individual soul. The pantheist says, it is the redemption of the soul from its lower and sensual form of existence, bringing it into its higher spiritual relations, etc.

state itself: chiefly, in controversy with the Romanists, whether it is of a purgatorial character; also in part in controversy with those who maintain the sleep of souls; and also in part there is involved the question of the possibility of repentance for those who die impenitent.

§ 1. *Historic Facts as to the Doctrine.*

In the Old Testament the general name for the place of departed souls is Sheol; in the New, Hades. It is represented in other forms of expression as the place to which the fathers are gathered, and[1] as the under-world. It is sometimes used in contrast with heaven. The departed are in a state where the dead are not yet in a blissful condition, but one of comparative darkness and silence. In the later Jewish speculations, after the Maccabees, we find a division of this under-world into the two abodes of Gehenna, a place of torment, and Paradise—or being in Abraham's bosom—a place of happiness.[2] In the time of the early Christians, next after the Apostolic age, we find in Marcion the first definite statements, with the avowal of the position that Christ went to the under-world and preached. Subsequently, Irenæus and Tertullian began to say that the object of Christ's going to the grave was to preach to the just patriarchs, etc., who had not known fully of salvation, but had died with only a dim knowledge of Christ. These views are soon connected with the phraseology, *limbus patrum, limbus infantum, i. e.*, a restricted abode of the fathers who died not having known Christ fully, and of infants who died, not being yet redeemed, but in a condition in which they would receive Christ when offered to them. The object of Christ's going was to reveal himself to them. That going was not yet connected with the notion that those who died in iniquity could be redeemed by Christ's labors among them. The simple view was, that there were those who did not know Christ, but awaited the proclamation of Him. Clement of Alexandria and Origen extended the doctrine so as to include the Gentiles and Christ's announcement of himself to them in

---

[1] As in the Egyptian mythology.
[2] See Dr. Geo. Campbell, "The Four Gospels," Prelim. Diss. VI., Part II.

Hades.[1] In the process of development in the third century, the doctrine becomes somewhat enlarged; it is extended so as to represent Christ descending into the grave in order to have a personal contest with Satan, and to rescue souls that were held captive. Some thought that Satan did not yet know about Christ's having made satisfaction for sin, and that Christ announced it in the contest. Augustine, in the fifth century, though receiving the opinion that Christ goes to the underworld, makes no reference to the possibility of any repentance there. Punishment and reward in his view begin at death. Some of the arguments for the doctrine are framed to account for what Christ did between his death and resurrection: to show that He was not in an unconscious state. Another reason was, that they might hold to the view that those who depart without conscious faith are saved, and yet connect their salvation with Christ. The clause in the Apostles' Creed, He descended into hell—or the world of departed spirits—came into the creed in the fourth century. It has received a variety of interpretations. Some, as the Westminster Confession, understand by it, simply, death: others connect with it the whole doctrine of the intermediate state. In the development of the Roman Catholic system, the doctrine assumed the further form of the complete purgatorial system. Luther in several passages seems to imply a literal conquest over the realm of the dead by Christ in his entering Hades. The view of Calvin is peculiar. He says, Inst. II. xvi. 10, that the descent into hell means that Christ suffered the torments of hell really and truly,—that his object was not to deliver others but himself,—to suffer the full extent of the divine wrath.

§ 2. PROPOSITION. *There is no sufficient Scriptural Warrant for such an Intermediate State as described, i. e.*, a state in which destiny is not yet decided, and is to be decided.

The only Scriptural passages are:

Eph. iv. 9, 10; but the object here is simply to show that

[1] They cited Ps. lxviii. 18. Origen is the first Christian writer who quotes 1 Pet. iii. 18–21 as setting forth Christ's work in the under-world. The appearing of the saints at the time of Christ's crucifixion, Matt. xxvii. 52, is also applied to this view.

Christ is Lord of all—of the realm below as well as the realm above,—that He conquered death in death. Nothing more can be fairly deduced from the passage.

Eph. iv. 8 (Ps. lxviii. 18); but this means nothing more than taking his enemies captive, not, delivering others from penal suffering.

Matt. xii. 40. This merely expresses the fact of death.

Acts ii. 27 (Ps. xvi. 10). This simply declares that death should not prevail over Christ, but that He should prevail over it.

1 Pet. iii. 18-21. "Being put to death in the flesh;" there is no doubt about that. "Quickened in the spirit;" this, with the foregoing clause, asserts in respect to Christ a fleshly state and the beginning of a spiritual state: "in the spirit" sets forth the complete domination of the spiritual and cessation of the fleshly as far as connected with this life. "In which" spirit, *i. e.*, "He went and preached unto the spirits in prison." When? The passage does not imply that He did it while in the state of death. "When they were sometime disobedient." Not that He preached to them in the interval of his death, which is not asserted. It is only said that it was "in the days of Noah." If the preaching referred to was the preaching at this time in Hades, why are Noah's times mentioned?—The object of the passage is, to connect the two facts that Christ, the Being who is now put to death in the flesh and quickened in the spirit, by that same spirit has been always preaching. He preached even in the days of Noah. "Those who were disobedient:" the mass rejected his preaching, but he preached so as to save eight souls. "And by the like figure, baptism, we are saved now." The object is, to connect the work of Christ with the whole mediatorial scheme. The other view compels us to say that the reason why Christ preached in Hades to these persons was because they refused to obey in Noah's time; which is a very singular reason for Christ's going to preach to them. Even if this other interpretation were allowed, all that could be got from it would be merely a proclamation of truth to them, without any mention of its effect.[1]

[1] [This interpretation of 1 Pet. iii. 18-21 is found only in a note-book. There are no hints in the manuscripts to aid in making a fuller statement of the author's view.]

§ 3. *Of Purgatory.*

The Roman Catholic Church has built up a doctrine of purgatory on a few passages of Scripture. As fully developed in the later dogmatic statements, the doctrine is as follows: That before Christ no one was in heaven. All were in an intermediate state. This had two regions: Paradise or Abraham's bosom for the perfect, Purgatory for the imperfect, including the different divisions of the *limbus patrum* and the *limbus infantum*. The doctrinal position connected with this is, that though Christ made full redemption for man so as to deliver from eternal woe, yet there is a class of sins from which persons are to obtain deliverance and pardon by means of ecclesiastical satisfactions; that the church has laid up a treasury of grace from the merits of Christ and the saints, which she may dispense; and that she dispenses these in order to relieve men from the temporal penalties of sin, the eternal penalties, as they grant, being taken away by Christ. During his life a man may accumulate hundreds of thousands of years of suffering, by his sins. The church may deliver him, by passing over to his credit merits from the store which she has in charge.

The only Scriptural basis which is suggested for this doctrine is Matt. iii. 11; 1 Cor. iii. 15; Jude 23. None of these has any bearing upon the doctrine. Newman presents this doctrine as one of the clearest instances of "development" from a slight Scriptural germ, but it is really an instance of the development from a germ of what was never in it, as if from a mustard seed one could develop an apple.

§ 4. *The Sleep of Souls.*

In the early church there were some who held the doctrine of the sleep of souls. Origen is said to have refuted certain advocates of this opinion at a council in Africa. Tertullian argued against them. One of the earlier works of Calvin, 1534, was against this doctrine. Many of the earlier Anabaptists and Socinians maintained the view. Luther shows a proclivity to it in some of his writings, but is undecided upon the whole. In later English literature, a somewhat similar doctrine has been taught by Isaac Taylor and by Archbishop Whately,—that between death and the resurrection there is a semi-conscious or semi-unconscious state of the soul, and that only at the resurrection are the full powers of the soul called out. Time, they say, is all annulled between death and the resurrection. The philosophical attempt to defend this has been on the ground that the soul cannot act without the body, and that therefore it must wait for the body.

Against the doctrine lie such considerations as the following: (1) The nature of the soul, implying constant activity. Sleep is in connection with the exigencies of the bodily constitution: when the soul is delivered from these, we should expect a more intense activity. (2) The doctrine has a cheerless aspect. It makes the future to be a blank and would cause a total loss in the instances where persons are taken from the earth in the height of their career,—from a condition where they are performing good service, and carried to a state where there is no activity. (3) Christian experience in the article of death is opposed to it: the bright visions of the future, apparent converse with the forms of the blessed, ardent expectations of immediate bliss. All Christian experience, as far as it reaches, is of an immediate entrance into a state of higher activity than mere slumber. (4) The Scriptures are against it. The representations of the life of the Christian here,—John v. 24, everlasting life is already begun; Phil. iii. 20, we are partakers already of the heavenly citizenship. The passages which speak of an immediate blessing,—Acts vii. 59, *i. e.*, Receive it now; Phil. i. 23, If he was to depart and be in unconsciousness, he would not be willing to give up his glorious labors for Christ; 2 Cor. v. 8, "Absent from the body" and "present with the Lord" are equivalent, and "present with the Lord" is not unconsciousness. To these may be added Heb. xii. 23, Luke xxiii. 43.

CHAPTER III.

THE SECOND ADVENT.

1.—The Millenarian Hypothesis.

Some advocates of this include more particulars, some less; the Millenarians best known as such, maintain substantially the following:[1] (1) Christ's personal advent precedes the millennium, (2) the resurrection of saints occurs at this advent, (3) the saints are to reign with Him, while mankind is still in the body, subject to disease and death, (4) this dispensation is to continue one thousand years, in which Jews and Gentiles are to be converted. —The doctrine involves these positions: (*a.*) The millennium is not an expansion of the present, but a new dispensation; (*b.*) It is not to be introduced by present agencies; all will wax worse and worse: the gospel will not convert the world; (*c.*) The Son of God will have a visible reign and majesty in the world. Christ and his saints will dwell in a new Jerusalem, of which Rev. xxi. gives the description, over and on the earthly Jerusalem; the temple will be rebuilt, the Jews restored, the center of worship will be at Jerusalem; (*d.*) There are two resurrections, one, of the holy dead, at the beginning,—another, of the wicked dead, at the close of the millennium; (*e.*) There will be no general Judgment; the Judgment is in two parts, one before, and one after, the millennium; (*f.*) Then the world is to be refitted and forever inhabited.

The Scriptural basis is Rev. xx. 4.—A period between the Ascension of Christ and the Second Advent is intercalated and said to be overlooked in Old Testament prophecy.

II.—Objections to this hypothesis.

1. The end of the world is not viewed as near in the New Testament.

2. Christ remains in heaven till the *end of all.* Acts iii. 21; Heb. x. 12, 13; Luke xix. 13.

---

[1] Lord, Lit. and Theol. Journal, July, 1850; see also Princ. Rev., Jan. 1853.

THE KINGDOM OF REDEMPTION. 609

3. The Bible brings into view only one final Judgment. Matt. xiii. 39; xxiv. 36; xxv. 31-46; 2 Thess. i. 6-10 (—the judgment of the righteous and of the wicked simultaneous).

4. The connection of the coming of Christ, the resurrection, and the judgment, is too explicit to admit their separation by the millennium. (*a.*) The connection of the second coming with the end of the world: Matt. xxiv. 3; 2 Pet. iii. 3-7. (*b.*) The connection of the second coming with the resurrection: 1 Thess. iv. 16, 17; John v. 28; Phil. iii. 20, 21; 1 Cor. xv. 22. (*c.*) The connection of the second advent with the judgment: Matt. xvi. 27; xxv. 31; 2 Tim. iv. 1; iv. 8; 2 Thess. i. 6-10; 1 Cor. iv. 5; Rev. i. 7; xxii. 12; Jude 6. (*d.*) The connection of the second advent with the resurrection. John vi. 39; xi. 24. (*e.*) The connection of the end of the world and the judgment. Matt. xiii. 36-43; xiii. 49; John xii. 48. (*f.*) The connection of the resurrection and the judgment. Dan. xii. 2; John v. 28, 29; Rev. xx. 13.

5. The resurrection is to be of a spiritual body, 1 Cor. xv. 44; but the pre-millennial resurrection is to a reign in the world as now constituted.

6. The kingdom of Christ has already come. Acts ii. 30, 31; iii. 15; iv. 26; v. 30, 31; Heb. x. 12; Rev. iii. 7; Matt. xiii. 31. ("Comings"[1] are (*a.*) General exertions of God's power: Isa. xix. 1; Dan. vii. 13; (*b.*) End of age or æon:[2] Matt. xxv. 28; 2 Thess. ii. 8; (*c.*) Death: Phil. i. 6; 1 Thess. v. 23; (*d.*) The final coming to judge the world and end the present state.)

---

[1] [This remark on "Comings" is found only in the author's papers; it was not given in the lectures in class. There is some doubt whether it contains his view or a view which he reserved for consideration.]

[2] Three æons reckoned by the Jews: before the law—under—and the time of Messiah.

CHAPTER IV.

RESURRECTION OF THE BODY.

The words translated resurrection—to awake from the dead, to raise up—are sometimes used to denote coming to life after death, but they are used distinctly with reference to the resurrection of the body. The doctrine was a common one among the Jews at the time of Christ. The Pharisees believed, and the Sadducees denied it. The doctrine is of prime importance in connection with the system of redemption in its wide application. Redemption is completed with the resurrection. Redemption is of the whole man, body as well as soul, and is not merely pardon or deliverance from spiritual suffering.

I.—In the Old Testament, the doctrine is anticipated rather than clearly defined. There is an intimation of it in Isa. xxvi. 19, where the restoration of the Jewish people is compared to a resurrection from the dead. Ezek. xxxvii. 1-14, implies a conviction of a resurrection. Dan. xii. 2 asserts the doctrine. From Job xix. 25, the Vulgate, Luther, and the English version teach the doctrine. The difficulty about it is in connection with the history of its interpretation. The Jewish teachers and Christ did not refer to this passage.[1] Perhaps the rendering in our version makes the reference more distinct than the Hebrew will warrant, but in our judgment the passage at least looks forward to a resurrection. Otherwise it would refer only to Job's recovery from sickness, which makes it rather tame in its connection.

II.—The New Testament. There is here a general and a specific recognition of the doctrine.

1. The general recognition. Matt. xxii. 23; Luke xx. 27; Acts xxiii. 6, speak of the opposing beliefs of the Pharisees and Sadducees; John xi. 24; v. 21, 25; 1 Cor. xv. 22; Acts xxiv. 15.

2. The specific statements. These lead to the definition of the *modus*, as far as that is possible. 2 Cor. v. 1-4; 1 Cor. xv.,—

---

[1] Some of the later Jewish interpreters explain it of the resurrection. See Notes and Queries, 1854, p. 428.

here the resurrection of the body is compared with Christ's resurrection; this is the most important point in the whole doctrine; the doctrine is to be constructed in view of that comparison; 1 Thess. iv. 14; Acts iv. 2; Acts xxvi. 23; 1 Cor. xv. 20; vi. 14.

III.—As to the *modus* of the resurrection.

The Scriptures treat this in the way of comparison and analogy, which is perhaps the only way in which it can be treated. There are only two passages—and a third one illustrative—from which anything in regard to the mode can be derived. Phil. iii. 20, 21,—here the comparison is with the resurrection of Christ. If He arose with the same body, we shall arise with the same body, but changed by the working of a mighty power; John xii. 24,—this suggests the analogy which is further carried out in 1 Cor. xv. 35-49,—here the question, How? is directly put and met. The response is, Death is necessary in order to this resurrection, and as the seed though the same is raised in a new form, so is it with the resurrection of the dead. From this passage all that can be stated is this: That it is the same body which is put in the grave which shall be raised, but it shall be raised in a different form,—not necessarily with identity of particles any more than there is identity of particles in the plant which grows from the seed. The difference is described by the difference between corruptible and incorruptible, between that which is a natural body and that which is a spiritual.—The objection which may be raised is on the question of identity. *What is the identity?* What is identity in any living and organized being? It implies a comparison of the being in one state with the being in another state. The identity consists in the following particulars: (1) The same central, identical principle of life remains. (2) There is, connected with this, the same formative principle. In connection with the principle of life, there must always be supposed the *nisus formativus*, that which makes the particular individuality of any particular plant or animal. These two gather about themselves whatever may tend to develop or nourish the body. The identity of a plant or human body is thus entirely different from that of a stone, which is the identity of the same particles.

Therefore the principle of life and the formative principle may remain the same, and yet gather around them other particles which may serve to form the new spiritual body. This view avoids the grossness of the merely sensuous view of the resurrection, and also avoids evaporating the doctrine into the simple statement that the same person continues to live after death.

IV.—Remarks.

1. The whole doctrine of the resurrection is resolved into the doctrine of immortality by the Swedenborgians.[1] This is refuted by two points: (*a.*) The Scriptural assertions that the resurrection is future, is to be at the Last Day, in connection with the Judgment. Immortality is immediate, but the resurrection is future. (*b.*) All the illustrations given in Scripture imply that it is the same body that is raised, and that Christ, to whose resurrection ours is compared, was raised with the same body.

2. The doctrine of the resurrection meets a deep-seated longing in human nature,—the identity as to form as well as in respect to soul.

3. It is on the basis of this doctrine that we may look for a renewal of our knowledge of the persons we have known, in the personal aspects.

4. The doctrine gives us a more living view of our eternal state than we should otherwise have.

CHAPTER V.

THE LAST JUDGMENT.

The Scriptures teach that there is a resurrection to judgment. Socinians and Swedenborgians view the last judgment as figurative, as equivalent merely to the final awards to each, with no scene, no congregation. Millenarians generally teach a judgment of nations, before the particular judgment of individuals.

---

[1] See also the later writings of Bush.

According to the Scriptures, the judgment follows the resurrection and is contemporaneous with the end of the world.

Scriptural passages on which the doctrine rests: Rev. xx. 12; Acts xvii. 31; 2 Thess. i. 7-10; Matt. xi. 24; xxv. 31-46. In 2 Pet. iii. 7-13 the judgment is connected with the end of the world.

The circumstances of the Judgment: (1) Christ is to be the Judge: John v. 22-25; Acts xvii. 31; Matt. xvi. 27. (2) The time is not known: 2 Pet. iii. 10; 1 Thess. v. 2; Matt. xxv. 13. (3) The sentence is to be passed on all: Matt. xxv. 32; Rom. ii. 6; 2 Cor. v. 10.—And even the angels are reserved for their doom. (4) The judgment is final: Rev. xxii. 11.

This Judgment is not the first passing of judgment, but the final manifestation of it. It is the end of a mediatorial kingdom, the consummation of an economy. The position that at The Judgment the first passing of judgment will occur, uproots the Scriptural doctrine of sin and of the penalty of death which has already begun to be inflicted upon men.

CHAPTER VI.

THE AWARDS OF THE LAST DAY.

Eternal blessedness is to be assigned by Christ to the righteous, and endless punishment to the wicked.

The first marked controversy on the doctrine of endless punishment was between Doctor Chauncey and the younger Edwards. The reply of Edwards is one of the ablest metaphysical discussions we have on the subject. Joseph Huntingdon, settled for a time in Rhode Island, left a work which was published after his death, entitled Calvinism Improved. The improvement consisted in denying the endlessness of future punishment. Almost all the earlier Universalists were of Calvinistic stock. Such were Murray and Winchester, under whom began the Universalist movement in this country. In later times Universalists have tended to become Unitarians, and to say that the Scriptures do not reveal anything at all about the future state, that all the expressions about it refer to the æon or age which is now existing. This, by the way, is the only defensible position on the Universalist side.[1] Maurice—to Jelf—argues that eternal implies a moral condition, and not a future state. Theodore Parker acknowledges that Christ taught the doctrine of endless punishment, and makes this one of the arguments in proof of the position that Christ was not perfect, but still had the Jewish prejudices lingering about him.

The question here is primarily one of fact and not one of theory. It is a fact about which our only means of knowing is the declaration of One who knows the future and what will be man's condition hereafter. It is a solemn, alarming, fearful truth: but to hold it is essential to the integrity of the whole system of faith, and also to the taking Scripture as the rule of faith. The denial of it leads to the undermining of the whole doctrine of sin and redemption. Universalism, in its theoretical grounds, all runs back into the ethical position that happiness is the great good and suffering the great evil in the universe. This is its proper philosophical basis. As soon as holiness is made to be the great good and sin the great evil, the basis of Universalism is undermined; because where there is sin there must be punishment, for the maintenance of the divine holiness. In fact, the chief objections to the doctrine of endless punishment are made on theoretical and not on exegetical grounds. The chief effort has been to show that Scripture may possibly be so interpreted.[2]

§ 1. *The Scriptural Testimony as to Endless Punishment.*

We do not now argue of future, but of everlasting punishment.

I.—The doctrine of endless punishment is a natural inference

---

[1] Prof. Stuart's Essays, 1830, republished in 1867, give the best philological reply to the Universalist positions. Article also by Prof. Barrows, Bib. Sac., July, 1858. Andrew Fuller's tract on Endless Punishment is a good discussion.

[2] *E. g.*, John Foster's famous letter: it contains no Scriptural argument, but is a general statement on the ground of the divine benevolence. See Woods, in his Lectures; Cheever, in Bib. Sac., viii. 471, x. 544.

from the fact that in the Scriptures there is not a hint of the possible future salvation of those who die impenitent.

II.—It is involved in the awards of the Last Day, as final: Matt. xxv. 41-44.

III.—It is an inference from the position that Christ's mediatorial kingdom is described as coming to an end, when of course all hope and possibility of recovery must cease.[1]

IV.—There are also special declarations.

1. The class of positive declarations as to the duration of destruction and torment: 2 Thess. i. 8, 9, where we have ὄλεθρον, destruction, αἰώνιον, eternal, and ἀπὸ προσώπου τοῦ κυρίου, *from the presence* of the Lord; Rev. xiv. 11.

2. Descriptions of suffering. Mark ix. 43; Luke xvi. 19-26;

3. The case of the devil and his angels. If a condition of endless punishment by suffering is established in their case, the theoretical argument against its possibility is overthrown. Rev. xx. 10; Matt. xxv. 41.

4. The description in Rev. xxii. 11, where the history of the world is carried to its consummation, and the last scenes are introduced. This involves the position that in the consummation of the whole order of things there is a final separation between the just and the unjust.

5. The second death is spoken of—an intensive way of describing the penalty.[2]

6. To these positions and statements must be added what is said of the sin against the Holy Ghost, Mark iii. 29[3] (Matt. xii. 31, 32; Luke xii. 10). The argument from what is said of the sin against the Holy Ghost is perhaps one of the most conclusive.[4] Forgiveness is excluded in the world to come from those who sin against the Holy Ghost (οὔτε ἐν τῷ μέλλοντι, Matt. xii. 32). The force of this statement *does not depend* upon what we may

---

[1] Prof. Stuart regarded this as one of the very strongest Scriptural arguments.

[2] [Rev. Vers.: "This is the second death, *even* the lake of fire." Rev. xx. 14.]

[3] [ἁμαρτήματος accepted as the reading. Rev. Vers.—"hath never forgiveness, but is guilty of an eternal sin."]

[4] Tholuck, who once was inclined to accept the doctrine of restitution, came back to the Scriptural faith in wrestling with the passages in regard to the sin against the Holy Ghost.

say the sin against the Holy Ghost is. (There are four leading views. (1) It is a single sin, an impious word which blasphemes the Holy Ghost, implying that the sinner has come to a state in which he resists God's last influences. Döderlein, Cramer, Reinhard, Michælis, Bretschneider, Harless, etc. (2) Any actual sin against a conscience which is illumined by God's Spirit. Weiss.—This is making it too general. (3) Some one, in the general class of "mortal sins." Lücke, Böhmer. (4) The most common and perhaps the best view: it is an internal state of the highest sinfulness which cannot be changed and which shows itself in speech or action, resisting or deliberately setting the soul against the influences of the Holy Ghost. Stier, Tholuck, Olshausen, Hahn, J. Müller,[1] Hofmann.[2])

Also there must be added what is said in 1 John v. 16, ἔστιν ἁμαρτία πρὸς θάνατον. There is sin for which prayer cannot avail.

7. It is to be noted, that these strong passages as to eternal perdition are in the New Testament and not in the Old.[3]

V.—The doctrine of final condemnation and eternal punishment is implied in other Scriptural doctrines. The theoretical possibilities here:

1. The doctrine of the nature and desert of sin includes the position that the punishment is to be everlasting. Sin as the worst thing is to be accompanied by that which will show it to be the worst. If there is any case of continued sin, it is a just inference that there will be continued punishment. Hence, in order to disprove the doctrine of eternal punishment, it must be shown that sin will be extirpated absolutely. Unless this is done, it cannot be shown that punishment will cease. The final Judgment shows the continuance of sin.

2. The doctrine of repentance as necessary to salvation involves theoretically the possibility of final and everlasting condemnation. If there is no repentance, there cannot be salva-

---

[1] Sünde, ii. 598, ed. 5.
[2] Schriftb., ii., 2, 315.—Augustine: "Duritia cordis usque ad finem hujus vitæ, vel impœnitentia finalis, quæ ipsa cum irremissibilitate necessarie conjuncta est." So, Luther.
[3] Urged by Dr. John Owen.—See Maurice, Essays, p. 336.

tion. If any remain impenitent, they cannot be finally saved, and must be punished forever. Those who preach the necessity of repentance also preach that if men do not repent, their final and everlasting condemnation will be just.

3. The same is the case with respect to the kindred point—salvation through Christ alone. If any do not believe, they must be lost. The necessity of believing in Christ in order to salvation implies the position that if any continue unbelieving their everlasting punishment is just and right. In order to escape from the theoretical possibility, we must escape from the absolute necessity of repentance and of faith in Christ. Admitting these to be absolutely essential, the inference is clear that in case there is not repentance and faith, there must be punishment as long as the absence of them continues.—Consequently, the Universalists come off these Scriptural grounds.

There is, in fact, no sense in salvation, as the bestowal of eternal life, unless it be a fact that without the salvation there would be eternal death. If the eternity of future punishment is not rational, eternal life as a gift of grace is irrational. If it be not just to condemn men to everlasting death for sin, it is not an act of grace to confer upon them endless blessedness. No one can believe in redemption unto endless beatitude, unless he believes in a state of condemnation which must be eternal, were it not for that redemption.

§ 2. *Objections to the Doctrine of Endless Punishment.*

The objections, being mostly on theoretical grounds, are not adequate to overthrow the testimony as to fact.

Obj. I.—That the word αἰώνιος does not signify time, but intensity. It designates a state rather than continued being.[1]— The position cannot be sustained from the usage.[2] A state is included, but duration is implied. If we do not infer from the word the endless punishment of the wicked, we cannot infer the endless blessedness of the righteous.

---

[1] Maurice's position.
[2] Stuart, p. 46, enumerates the cases in which αἰώνιος occurs. The proper translation is everlasting, not "œonian."

Obj. II.—To the *eternity* of punishment, as if that were a particular kind of punishment.—It is simply the continued existence of what is already begun. If penal suffering for transgression now is justifiable, it is justifiable as long as sin exists. If it is not justifiable hereafter, it is not justifiable here.

Obj. III.—From the power of God: his power is adequate to take away evil and suffering, and therefore He will ultimately exclude them from the universe.—But the power of God is not mere omnipotence, but power in connection with a moral government. It is in the service of his wisdom and holiness: to promote the holiness of his subjects is his great aim. Besides the argument would prove too much: it would prove that He should exclude sin and suffering now as well as in the future.

Obj. IV.—From the divine benevolence.—As we have already shown, God's Benevolence has ultimate respect to holiness, and not to the production of happiness. It is shown in providing a way of salvation. If this be rejected, no impeachment of the divine benevolence can remain.

Obj. V.—That sin is a negation, an imperfection, which will be thrown off in the progressive development of mankind. This is the Pantheistic view, and is the heart of all objections to the doctrine, *i. e.*, that sin is not the violation of a known law of holiness, but that it is a part of education. We have already considered this. If carried out, it overthrows the whole doctrine of sin and redemption and the entire Christian scheme. All becomes a mere process of development.

§ 3. *Of the Restitution of all Things.*

Some who deny everlasting punishment, rest their denial on the assertion that the Scriptures teach the restitution of all things, and the final reconciliation of all moral beings to God.— The previous argument refutes this. It only remains to consider some of the passages quoted in favor of this particular view. The position to be taken here is, that all these passages can be interpreted in harmony with the doctrine that there are some who will be forever punished, while, on the other hand, the passages which teach final condemnation cannot be interpreted in harmony with the position that there is to be such a restitution of all things. Some of the passages taken alone and without their connections might teach restitution; but we have to interpret the Scripture harmoniously.

Rom. v. 18. This is to be interpreted as a comparison of the two systems—as systems. As by the one system judgment comes upon all, so by the righteousness of One (or by one righteous deed) the free gift comes upon all. It satisfies the connection to interpret this of a superabounding provision in Christ for all, a provision generally for the whole human race.

Rom. viii. 19–24. Here all that is created is represented as looking forward to a time of redemption. The economy of redemption is contrasted with the economy of sin. "Creation" is most naturally interpreted, not of Christians, nor of moral beings, but of the whole creation, in consequence of sin, appointed in regard to a redemption, which is the grand issue. It is not inconsistent with the fact that some will not come under these provisions.

Col. i. 19, 20.—This also is general; it brings into view the grand effects and results; it does not deny that there may be exceptions. Christ's triumph is also said to consist in "putting under foot," destroying, punishing.

1 Tim. ii. 4. Here we must understand, not the "will" of efficient purpose, but—of benevolent desire, as shown in provision, plan, and arrangements.

Heb. ii. 9. Universality of provision[1] is asserted.

Phil. ii. 9. This is one of the strongest passages, because it is distributive: "Every knee," etc. We think it is a fair interpretation that the passage describes the issue of Christ's kingdom generally, and has respect to the honor to be paid to Him, the glory to accrue to Him rather than to the universality of hearty and loving allegiance. The burden of the passage is that He shall be glorified. It is fairly interpreted of—those who are under his dominion. Especially is this true when we take with it 1 Cor. xv. 24, which, describing the end of his mediatorial king-

[1] If all for whom Christ died are to be saved, then this passage would teach universal salvation. It does teach—a general atonement.

dom, speaks of the enemies under his feet, implying that there are those who are in a state of punishment.

It follows that the interpretation of Acts iii. 21, ἀποκαταστάσεως πάντων, as teaching universal salvation is not sustained by the Scriptures.

§ 4. *Position and Relations of the Doctrine of Future Punishment.*

1. The principles in the case are not made or altered by the fact of the eternity of the punishment. If proper strict punishment be admitted—punishment not as reformatory or disciplinary but penal—the principle is admitted. And then

2. The question is one of fact, of Scriptural interpretation: Whether the Bible really teaches that all will be saved.

3. The denial of the doctrine leads to other denials, and ultimately, if those who deny are logical, to doing away with the redemptive system; because the redemption is from *eternal* death; and if so, eternal death was right and righteous, as redemption is of grace. Hence

4. Denial of the doctrine leads to the denial of strict *moral* government as well. Sin is taken as negative, punishment as corrective. Naturalism is the consequence. These practical effects are seen as a matter of fact.

5. As to the numbers of the saved and lost we have no revelation.

6. The orthodox evangelical system exhibits much more of God's benevolence and mercy than does this universalism. It sets forth *a system of grace*, to all that hear the gospel offer. If any *such* are lost, it is because they refused the proffered grace.

7. The doctrine is to be preached always with solemnity and awe; and so as to give the strongest motives and power to the offer of salvation, which it is the *office* of the preacher to make to all.

§ 5. *The Award of Eternal Blessedness to the Righteous.*

The King shall say unto them on his right hand, Come ye blessed of my Father. The gates of the Paradise of God are opened wide to the redeemed and reëmbodied soul. Christ sees then of the travail of his soul, and is satisfied. Those who suffered with Him shall also reign with Him. They are heirs of God and joint-heirs with Christ.

This blessedness is in the vision of God; 1 Cor. xiii. 12; 2 Cor. v. 7; Matt. v. 8; 1 John iii. 2. God will then be revealed to the soul, as now the world is to the senses.

It is in the fellowship with Christ. Phil. i. 23.

It is in the complete indwelling of the Holy Spirit.

The creation will be transformed into its final condition of glory: Rom. viii. 19–32; 2 Pet. iii. 13; Rev xxi. 1.

The glory of human nature will be fully attained: the image of God will be perfectly realized, as it cannot be here on earth: 1 Cor. xiii. 12; 1 John iii. 2.

All created spirits will be united in one vast spiritual empire— a harmonized universe. As Jew and Gentile were brought into the unity of the Christian church, so human and angelic beings, all ages and all histories, are brought to a headship and eternal unity in Christ.

Of this the new song is the testimony and expression. Rev. v. 13: And every created thing which is in the heaven, and on the earth, and under the earth and on the sea, and all things that are in them, heard I saying, unto Him that sitteth on the throne, and unto the Lamb, be the blessing, and the honor, and the glory, and the dominion, for ever and ever.

In the eternal melody of that song, resounding for evermore, making heaven vocal with praise deeper and tenderer than any other,—in and with that melody, Christian Theology forever closes.

INDEX.

A.

Abbott, Ezra, 393.
Abelard, 21, 467.
Ability, natural, 326–336; moral, 328.
Adam, his headship, 344-347.
Advent, Second, 608, 609.
Alexander, Dr., 214.
Ambrose, 167.
Angels, 98, 99; evil, 99-101.
Annihilation, 600.
Anselm, 307, 363, 467.
Antecedents of Redemption, 3 et seq.
Anthropology, Christian, 160 et seq.
Anthropomorphism, 9.
Anthropopathism, 9.
Apollinaris, 396.
Apologetics (vol.) 3, 4, 8.
Aquinas, 82, 83, 104, 143, 174, 180, 307, 363.
Arian objections to Divinity of Christ, 63-65.
Arianism, 73, 74, 77, 397.
Arians, 5, 392.
Aristotle, 162, 196, 205, 226, 240, 277, 298, 307, 363, 494.
Arminian controversy in Holland, 548; position on justification, 539, 549.
Arminianism, 239, 242, 243.
Arminians, 198; question between them and Calvinists, 119.
Arnold, Dr., 360.
Assurance of salvation, 542, 543, Sir Wm. Hamilton, Luther, Melancthon, Calvin, Arminius, on, 542.
Athanasius, 74, 390.
Atonement, the, 437-477 et seq.; usage of the word, and terms clustering round it, 437, 438; its necessity, 438-442; represented as sacrificial; 442-461; theories of, as a moral influence, 464-466; a satisfaction to distributive justice, 466-469; to general justice, 469, 470; to public or essential justice, 470; remarks on these theories, 471-476; views of Kant, Robertson, Bushnell, Coleridge, Campbell, and Rothe, 465; of Anselm, Abelard, 467; of A. A. Hodge, 468; extent of, 478–481.
Attributes, divine, 12–47.

Augustine, 6, 167, 255, 256, 259, 298, 322, 350, 362, 363, 390, 536, 604, 616.
Austin, Samuel, 127.
Awards of the last day, 613–621.

B.

Baptism, 593; of infants, 594, 595.
Bartlett, Pres., 600.
Beecher, Edward, 7, 303, 310, 313.
Beecher, Lyman, 322.
Beings, created, different orders of, 98-101.
Bellamy, Dr., 215, 257, 305, 516, 554.
Benevolence, divine, 38–43; definition of, 38–40; sources of proof of, 40; objections to and theories, from existence of evil, 40–43.
Bengel, 388.
Bentham, 205.
Berkeley, 5, 103.
Bernard, 390.
Birks, 158.
Bledsoe, 124, 240, 509.
Blessedness, Eternal, of the Righteous, 620, 621.
Boethius, 18, 82.
Bonaventura, 143.
Brandis, 298.
Breckinridge, Dr., 16.
Bretschneider, 127, 144, 252.
Brodie, Sir Benj., 598.
Brown, 179.
Brown, Bishop, 5.
Brown's Theol. Tracts, 126, 191.
Brownson, O. A., 322.
Bull, Bishop, 252, 522.
Burke, Edm., 178.
Burton, Dr., 127, 554.
Bush, Dr., 612.
Bushnell, Horace, 48, 194, 247, 465.
Butler, Bish., 179, 180, 512.

C.

Cabbalists, 431.
Call, the gospel, 515-521; the external, 515, 516; the internal, 516.
Calvin, 11, 23, 29, 102, 124, 143, 307, 350, 363, 367, 431, 543, 548, 606.
Calvinistic bodies, 397; theologians, 143; theology, 31; its two princi-

ples, 377, 378; view of our union with Christ, 537.
Calvinists, their questions with Arminians, 119, 239, 243; with Hopkinsians, 568.
Campbell, Dr. George, 98, 603.
Campbell, McLeod, on Atonement, 465.
Candlish, R. S., 89, 364.
Carlyle, 277.
Cartesian philosophy, 104, 164.
Catechisms, Westminster, *see Westminster*.
Cave, Alfred, 438, 442.
Chalmers, Dr., 360, 496, 512, 575.
Channing, Dr., 559.
Chase, Prof., 113.
Chauncey, Dr., 613.
Chemnitz, 396.
Christ, his divinity, 53 et seq.; his divine attributes, 53-56; designated as divine, 56-60; the object of religious worship, 60-62; Arian objections, 63-65; his person and work, 341 et seq.; the perfect man, 354-358, teachings of Scripture concerning, 386-396; his divinity, 387-389; miraculous conception, 389-392; complete humanity, 392, 393; both divine and human, 393, 394, 421; one person and his personality from the divine nature, 394, 395, 421, 422; early heretical views concerning, 396; later objections and differences 397-421; general object of his coming, 430 et seq.; Prophet, Priest and King, 431-436; his sufferings and death, sacrificial, 447-461, vicarious, 450-453; Scriptural statements of, analyzed, 461-464; his Intercession, 481-487; union between, and the believer, 529-538; union between, and the church, 590-597.
Christian Cosmology, 91-159.
Christianity, superiority of, to Pantheism, 375.
Chrysostom, 431.
Church, the, fundamental and germinant idea of, 590; visible and invisible, 591; prelatical claims unreal, 591, 592; nature and functions of its organization, 592, 593; preserves and defends the truth, 593, 594; law and means of its growth contained within itself, 594-596; independent of the state, 596; its ultimate universality and supremacy, 596, 597.
Cicero, 26, 298, 598.
Clark, Adam, 26.
Clarke, Samuel, 16.
Clarke, 199.
Clement of Alexandria, 603.
Coleridge, 179, 182, 298, 465, 537.

Conception, miraculous, its proof from Scripture, 389-392; in it the Logos assumed a true and complete humanity, 392, 393.
Confessions of Faith, importance of, 593.
Conscience, 178-190; definitions of, 178, 179; elements of, 179, 180; Scripture testimony concerning it, 180, 181; proof of a moral law, 181; implies an immutable morality, 181, 182; feeling of obligation, 183; involves moral approval or disapproval, 183; personal accountability, 184; its domain, 184-186; is it right in its decisions, 186-190; its possession does not confer personal righteousness, 190.
Consciousness, 171.
Consequents of Redemption, 491 et seq.
Continued Creation, theories of, 103-105.
Continuity of the mental states, 172.
Cosmology, Christian, 91-159.
Cosmos, the divine, 54, 91, 92.
Covenant of Life, 258, 259; of works, 378; of redemption, 378; of grace, 378.
Covenants, the, 377, 378, 388.
Crawford, 318.
Created beings, different orders of, 98-101.
Creation, theories in regard to, 93-95; relation of God to, 95; a plan not a development, 95, 96; preservation of, 102-105; continued, 103, 104.
Creationism, 167, 169.
Creator and Creation, 91-96.
Cudworth, 5, 164, 199.
Cyril, 167.

D.
Day, Pres., 124, 126, 133, 138, 178, 238, 246, 252, 331.
Dalgairns' Theory of the Soul, 165.
Death, 598; temporal, 266, 267; spiritual, 267-271; eternal, 271-273.
De Bow, 261.
Decrees of God, 114-126; characteristics of, 117-119, proof of doctrine of, 120-122; objections to considered, 122-126.
Delitzsch, 598.
Depravity, universal, 275, 276; total, 276, 277; native, 277-282; objections to, 278-280; physical, 309-312.
Descartes, 246.
Designations, Scriptural, of divine nature, 10, 11; Theological, 11, 12.
De Wette, 281.
Dichotomy, 163.
Distinctions in the Godhead, 50-73; these essential, 73-90; personal, 79, 80.

Divine, Benevolence, 38-43; Efficiency, 103; Holiness, 34-36; Image, 255-258; Justice, 44-47; Knowledge, objects of, 24, 25; Love, 37-43; Nature and Attributes, 3-47; Prescience, 26-28; Providence, 106-114; Reason, 28, 29; Unity, 50-53; Veracity, 43, 44.
Divinity and Distinct Personality of the Father, 51-53; of the Son, 53-65; of the Spirit, 65-72.
Divinity of Christ, cumulative proof of, 53-63; Arian objections to, 63-65.
Docetæ, 392.
Docetism, 396.
Dorner, 59, 287, 294, 299, 363, 524.
Dort, Synod of, 117, 543, 549.
Douglass, James, 107.
Duns, John, 261,
Dwight, Pres., 127, 134, 208, 210, 218, 252, 257, 554.

E.

Ebionitism, 396, 397.
Ebrard, 66, 127, 144, 252, 287, 387, 431.
Edwards, Jonathan, 6, 350, 364; on Adam's primitive state, 257; divine benevolence, 38, 39; divine decrees, 120, 123; end of God in creation, 126, 128, 131, 132, 133, 138, 140, 141, 145; imputation, 308, 317; justification, 524, 543, 545; natural ability, 327, 329; nature of virtue, 127, 141, 198, 206, 213-218, 230; necessity, 250, 252; original sin, 259, 260, 277, 280, 287, 317; redemption, 384; the will, 120, 124, 174, 233, 236, 238-240, 243, 246-248, 250, 252.
Edwards, Jonathan, Jr., 39, 123, 124, 145, 251, 304, 545, 549, 550, 613.
Efficiency, divine, theory of, 308, 309.
Elect infants, 318, 322.
Election, doctrine of, 501, 505-514; theories of, 506-508.
Ellicott, 281.
Ellis, George E., 312.
Emmons, Dr., 103, 234, 257, 263, 308, 309, 312, 319, 523, 554.
End of God in creation, 126-146.
Epicurus, 146.
Episcopius, 85.
Eschatology, 598 et seq.
Essential Trinity, 73-90.
Eutyches, 396.
Eusebius, 431.
Evil angels, 99-101.
Exercise scheme, 554.

F.

Faith, the idea of, 540; questions concerning, 541-544; the only way of receiving Christ, 544, 545; Is man responsible for want of? 543, 544.

Faith and Philosophy, (vol.), 239, 243, 310, 330, 510.
Fall, the, historically viewed, 260-264.
Father, the, divinity and distinct personality of, 51-53.
Finney, Dr., 206, 550.
Fisher, George P., 311.
Fletcher, 589.
Flint's Philosophy of History, 109.
Flörke, W., 362.
Fonseca, note, 25.
Foster, John, 614.
Franciscans, the, 363.
Free-agency, does it account for sin? 149-153.
Fuller, Andrew, 516, 614.

G.

Gennadius, 167.
Gerhard, 29.
Gess, 398.
God, knowledge of, 3-6; definition of, 7; mode of our conception of, 7-9; Scriptural designations of, 10, 11; theological definitions of, 11, 12; attributes of, 12-16; as Pure Essence or Being, 16-23; as the Supreme Reason or Understanding, 23-29; his Will, 29-32; his Omnipotence, 32-34; his Holiness, 34-37; his Love, 37-43; his Veracity, 43, 44; his Justice, 44-48; Trinity of, 48-90; as Creator, 91-96; his Providence, 106-114; his Decrees, 114-126; his end in Creation, 126-146; his Law, and its requirements, characteristics and ends, 191-195.
God-man, the, Person of, 385 et seq.
Gonzales, 390.
Good, the highest, 195-198.
Governmental theory of our union with Christ, 537, 538; of Atonement, 469.
Grace, effectual, 520, 521.
Greek Fathers, 255.
Gregory Nazianzen, 143.
Gregory of Nyssa, 167.
Grinfield, E. W., note, 54, 92, 252.
Grote, John, 209.
Grotius, 469.
Güder, 180.

H.

Hahn, 12, 16.
Hall, Robert, 216.
Hamartology, 260 et seq.; the fall, 260-264; its penalty, 264-273; its consequences, 273-283; original sin, 283-302, 323-325; counter representations in Scripture and experience, 302-304; theories for solving the problem of sin, 304-325; power of sin over the human will, 326-336.
Hamilton, Sir Wm., 237, 246, 252, 542.

Hampden, Dr., 522.
Happiness theories, 205–214.
Harless, 281.
Harris, John, 127.
Hase, 16, 431.
Havernick, 10.
Headships, the two, 344–352.
Hegel, 4, 15, 136, 162, 251, 298.
Hegelians, 398.
Hengstenberg, 10, 259.
Heraclius, 397.
Hickok, Dr., 203, 326, 395.
Highest good, 195–198.
Hilary, 167.
Hodge, A. A., 468.
Hodge, Charles, 284, 320, 325, 398, 442.
Hofmann, 252.
Holiness, 234, 236; divine, 34–36; definitions of, 34; questions raised, 35–36.
Holy Ghost, sin against, views concerning, of Döderlein, Cramer, Reinhard, Michælis, Bretschneider, Harless, Weiss, Lücke, Böhmer, Stier, Tholuck, Olshausen, J. Müller, Hofmann, 616.
Holy Love, theories of, 214–218.
Holy Spirit, the, divine and a distinct Person from the Father and the Son, 65–72; objections, 69–71.
Hopkins, Dr. Samuel, 308, 309, 312–319, 554, 559.
Hopkinsian School, 31, 103.
Hopkinsianism, 234, 308, 309, 346, 554.
Hortensius, 298.
Howe, John, 293.
Huntingdon, Joseph, 613.
Hutterus Redivivus, 252.
Hypostases, 79.

I.
Idealism, 164.
Ignatius, 384.
Immaculate Conception, 390–392.
Immediate Imputation, theory of, 304–308.
Immortality, 598–600; Scriptural arguments for, 598, 599; philosophical, 599; objections to, 601, 602.
Imputation, 283–316; immediate, 284–286, 304–308; mediate, 284, 285, 314–323.
Inability, moral, 326–336; natural, 327, 328.
Incarnation, the, 341 et seq.; in its relation to sin, 343–352; possible, from the constitution of the divine nature, 352; fact and not doctrine, 353; its relation to man's needs, 354–362; gives us the model of a perfect man, 354–358; gives us access to God, 358–360; in order to redemption, 360–362; on the part of God, 362–368; different views of, 369–372; Socinian or Humanitarian, 369; Roman Catholic, 370; Oxford, 370; Arminian, 370; general Protestant, 371; outside of Christianity, 371; historical, 369–372; philosophical, 373–377; related to divine sovereignty and the covenants, 377, 378; as unfolding the possibilities of human nature, 379–384.
Infants, elect, 318, 322; salvation of, 322.
Intercession of Christ, 481–487; both kingly and priestly, 481, 482; his qualifications for it, 482, 483; in what it consists, 483–486; its fruits, 486, 487.
Intermediate State, 602–607; historic facts as to doctrine of, 603, 604; no scriptural warrant for, 604, 605; purgatory 606; sleep of souls, 606, 607; views of Marcion, Irenæus, Tertullian, Clement of Alexandria, Origen, Augustine, Roman Catholic Church, Luther, Calvin, 603, 604.
Interpreting Scripture, right mode of, 402, 406.
Introduction to Christian Theology, (vol.), 341, 353, 374.
Irenæus, 362, 363, 603.

J.
John of Damascus, 79, 390.
Jerome, 167.
Judgment, the last, 612.
Justice, divine, 44–47; general idea of, 44, 45; proofs of, 45; distinctions in respect to, 45; punitive, why exercised, four theories, 46, 47.
Justification, 522–552; preliminary explanations, 522–525; general and scriptural sense of the term and idea, 526–528; involves a righteousness, not personal, as its ground; 528, 529; Christ its ground, 529–531; how, 531–538; through faith, 539–545; difference between Roman Catholic and Protestant views of, 545–547; historical statements of 548–551; objections to doctrine of, 551, 552.
Justin Martyr, 143.
Justinian, 167.

K.
Kant, 127, 128, 137. 144, 179, 187, 203, 298, 465.
Kenosis, 398, 418, 425.
Keil, 388.
King, Arch., 150.
Kingdom of Redemption, 491–621; its consummation in time and in eternity, 598–621.
Knapp, 26.

Knowledge, divine, objects of, 24, 25.
Krabbe, 268.
Krummacher, 431.
Kurtz, 363.

L.

Lactantius, 146, 220.
Lasaulx, 168.
Last Judgment, 612.
Launoy, 391.
Law, moral, its two main ends, 472; in relation to divine holiness, 472, 473; to Christ's atonement, 473-476; of God, its requirements, characteristics and ends, 191-195.
Liebner, 363, 398.
Leibnitz, 150, 154, 164, 248, 298.
Leighton, Dr., 360.
Leo the Great, 167.
Lewis, Tayler, 231.
Liberty and Necessity, 250-252.
Limborch, 102.
Locke, 246
Logos, the, 28, 73, 74, 75, 87, 88, 392, 393.
Love, divine, 37-43; definitions of, 37; proofs of, 37: divisions of, as to its objects, 38; modifications of, 38; as benevolence, 38-43.
Love, Holy, Theories of, 214-218.
Luther, 11, 124, 167, 307, 542, 548, 606, 616.

M.

Mackintosh, 179.
Maclaurin, John, 206.
Magee, 452.
Malan, Dr. Cæsar, 543.
Man, as a moral being, 161-191; his relation to the Creator, 161; to the rest of the material creation, 161; to the spiritual realm, 161, 162; to his race, 162; his individuality, 163; union of his body and soul, 163, 164; his soul's origin, 166; his personality, 170; powers and faculties of his soul, 173-176; its original tendencies, 176-178; his conscience, 178-190; his highest spiritual capacities, 190, 191; as a moral agent, his personal relations to the law of God, 232-236; his primeval moral state, 252-258; his destination if he had continued obedient, 258, 259; as fallen, 273 et seq.; his redemption, 341 et seq.
Manning, Archb., 238, 240.
Marcion, 603.
Marsh, Pres., 300.
Martensen, 169, 252, 363, 431, 481.
Martin, (R. C.,) his Via Futura, 322.
Martin, John, 127.
Martyr, Justin, 167.

Materialism, 164, 346.
Maurice, F. D., 171, 614, 617.
McCosh, Dr., 220.
Mediate Imputation, 284, 285, 314-323.
Mediator, the, person of, 385 et seq.; work of, 430 et seq.; three-fold office of, 431 et seq.
Melancthon, 167, 307, 543, 548.
Messiah, the, 379, 381, 382, 383, 431-434.
Methodists, 26.
Mill, John Stuart, 209.
Millenarian hypothesis, 608; objections to, 608, 609.
Modalism, 73.
Molinos, 25.
Monophysites, 396.
Monothelites, 396, 397.
Moral, ability, 328; character, seat of, 236-250; inability, 326-336; law, 472-476; Science, Wayland's, 179, 193.
Morell, 164.
Mozley, 509, 510.
Müller, Julius, 124, 192, 194, 221, 229, 240, 241, 243, 252, 260, 268, 281, 282, 287, 310, 313, 333, 365, 390, 431, 616.

N.

Natural ability, 326-336.
Nature and attributes, divine, 3-47.
Neander, 287.
Necessity, Natural, 250; Moral, 250; Metaphysical or Philosophical, 250.
Nestorianism, 396.
New Platonists, 93.
Newton, note, 19.
Nicene Creed, 362.
Nitzsch, 431.
Norton, Andrews, 322.

O.

Omnipotence of God, 32-34; idea of, 32; definition of, 32; proof of, 32, 33; limits of, 33; Schleiermacher's definition of, 33, 34; objects of, 34.
Orders of created beings, 98-101.
Origen, 143, 167, 395, 603, 606.
Original sin, 283-323; objections, 323-325; Tendencies of man's soul, 176-178.
Owen, John, 317, 364, 522, 616.

P.

Paley, 40, 206.
Pantheism, 136, 346.
Parker, Theodore, 614.
Pascal, 89, 352, 382, 383.
Payne, Dr., 317.
Pelagian, views, 279, 312, 517.
Pelagianism, 255, 267.
Pelagius, 167, 322, 529; his controversy with Augustine, 548.

Penalty of sin, 264-273.
Perfectionism, 579-585; Pelagian theory of, 580; Arminian, 580; Roman Catholic, 580; modern, 581-583; objections to, 583-585.
Perrone, 322, 390, 391.
Perseverance of the saints, 585; arguments for the doctrine, 586; explanations of, 586-587; objections to, 587.
Person of Christ, 341 et seq.; (See Christ); Savoy and Westminster Confessions concerning, 385; heresies, objections, and difficulties concerning, 396-421; entire result as to, 421-429.
Personal distinctions in the Trinity, 79-90; identity, 171, 172; relations, man's, to the Law of God, 232-236.
Personality, 170.
Philo, 4, 167, 344, 369.
Philosophy of Christianity, 73, 373-377.
Plato, 4, 11, 93, 167, 168, 297, 494.
Power to the contrary, 329, 330.
Powers and faculties of the soul, 173-176.
Prayer, 577-579.
Predestination, 501-504, objections to, 509-514.
Pre-established harmony, theory of, 164.
Pre-existence, 167; hypothesis of, 313, 314.
Prentiss, George L., 322.
Preservation of Creation, 102-105; sources of proof of the doctrine, 102; its purport, 102, 103.
Primeval state of man, 252-258; of innocence, 253; of the divine image, 253, 254; not of confirmed holiness, 552.
Principia, Newton's, 19.
Prophet, Priest, and King, 431-436.
Providence, divine, General statements in regard to the doctrine, 106, 107; proof of, 108-110; distinction as to general and particular, 110, 111; modes of, 111-114.
Prudentius, 167.
Punishment, endless, 614-618; relations of doctrine of, 620.

Q.
Quenstedt, 127.
Quintilian, 277.

R.
Realism and Nominalism, 288, 319.
Realists and Nominalists, 13.
Reason, divine, 28, 29.
Redemption, antecedents of, 3-337; itself, 341 et seq.; Kingdom of, 491-501; Christianity looks forward to its realization, 492-495; contrast between this and human inventions, 495-498; some of its characteristics, 498-500; its glory and beauty, 500.
Reformation, the, 256.
Reformed Confessions, on assurance of faith, 543.
Regeneration, 553-574; Roman Catholic view of, 553; Church of England, 553; Pelagian, 554; Rationalistic, 554; exercise scheme, 554; taste theory, 554; change in governing purpose, 554; self-love, theory of, 555, 556; evangelical view of, 556, 557; Scriptural representations of, 558, 559; its connection with other truths, 559; its necessity, 560; its characteristics, 560-563; its author, 563, 564; its method, 564-566; its means, 566-569; obligatory, 569, 570; conscious processes of the soul in, 570-572.
Relations, personal, of man to the law of God, 232, 236.
Renan, 383.
Repentance, difference between Roman Catholic and Protestant views of, 572, 573; Protestant view stated, 573, 574.
Reprobation, 508, 509.
Resurrection of the body, 610-612.
Reubelt, 398.
Richards, Dr., 240, 252, 528, 550.
Ridgeley, 435.
Robertson, 465.
Roman Catholic view of faith, 541, 542, 548; of grace, 256; of justification, 539; of regeneration, 553.
Rothe, 26, 221, 366, 431, 465.

S.
Sabellianism, 73, 74; remarks on, 77-79.
Sacramental view of our union with Christ, 536.
Sacrifices, pagan, 443-445; vicarious, 446 et seq.; Old Testament, 445-447; Old Testament prophecies of sacrificial sufferings of Christ, 447, 448; New Testament witness to, 448-453; objections stated and answered, 453-461; Scriptural statements of, analyzed, 461-464.
Sanctification, 575-585; its nature, 575, 576; its means, 577-579.
Sartorius, 258.
Satan, 99-101.
Saumur, 308.
Saybrook, Wm. Hart, 218.
Scientia Media, 25, 26.
Schelling, 251, 398.
Scheme, selfish, 206, 207; of tendency to greatest happiness, 207-210; self-love, 210-213.
Schleiermacher, 13, 14, 15, 33, 100, 251, 390, 398, 431, 537.

Schœttgen, 431.
Scholastics, 104, 167.
Schneckenburger, 484.
Schweizer, 127, 144.
Scotus, 363.
Scripture, right mode of interpreting, 402-406.
Second Advent, 608, 609.
Self-existence of God, 16, 17.
Selfish scheme, 206.
Seneca, 297.
Sensibilities, the, 176.
Servetus, 363.
Sin, permission of, 146-159; is it the necessary means of the greatest good, 147-149; does free agency account for it, 149-153; reasons for its permission are beyond our knowledge, 153-156; definitions of, 234-236; doctrine concerning, see *Hamartology*, 260 et seq.; original, 283-325.
Smalley, 191, 257, 326.
Smith, Henry Boynton, reference to, his Christian Apologetics, 3, 4, 8; Faith and Philosophy, 239, 243, 310, 330; Introduction to Christian Theology, 109, 341, 353, 374; Realism and Nominalism, (art.), 319; Rev. of Whedon on the Will, 239.
Smith, John Pye, 24, 438.
Socinian view of our relation to Christ, 536.
Socinians, 397, 598.
Socinus, 363.
Socrates, 297, 379.
Son, the, Divinity and distinct personality of, 53-65.
Sophocles, 297.
South, Dr., 258, 453.
Sovereignty, divine, 377.
Spinoza, 4, 14, 375.
Spiritual Life theory of our union with Christ, 536, 537.
Spring, Dr., 126, 133.
Stapfer, 144, 308, 317.
Stearns, J. F., 523.
Stewart, Dugald, 180.
Stier, 268.
Strauss, 127.
Stuart, Moses, 308, 320, 614, 615, 617.
Sublapsarian view, 263.
Supererogation, 547.
Supralapsarianism, 117, 263.
Swedenborg, 9.
Swedenborgians, 612.
Synesius, 167.
Synod of Dort, 543, 549.

T.

Taste theory, 554.
Taylor, Isaac, 607.
Taylor, N. W., 149, 150, 210, 281, 296, 310, 312, 336, 470.
Temptation, the, 260, 264.
Tendencies, original, of man's soul, 176-178.
Tennyson quoted, 213.
Tertullian, 9, 167, 390, 603, 606.
Theodicy, the, 146-159.
Theodoretus, 167, 431.
Theology, Christian, Introduction to, (vol.), 341, 353, 374.
Theories, Holy Love, 214-218.
Tholuck, A., 281, 284, 287, 615.
Thomasius, 170, 252, 287, 362, 398.
Townley, H. C., 322.
Traducianism, 168, 169.
Transubstantiation, 536.
Trichotomy, 166.
Trinity, 48-90; preliminary remarks on, 48-50; outline of course on, 50; manifested, 50-73; permanent, 72; essential, 73-90.
Turretine, 543.
Twesten, 22, 101, 127, 131, 287.
Tyler, B., 252.
Tyler, William S., 297.

U.

Union between Christ and the believer, 502 et seq., 531; its proof from Scripture, 532, 533; from other doctrines and analogies, 534, 535; its nature, 535, 536; opinions concerning classified and criticised, 536-539.
Unitarian view of depravity, 312.
Unitarians, 56.
Unity of God, 48-51.
Universalism, 613, 614.
Universe, the, created, as set forth in Scripture, 96-98.
Upham, Prof. T., 248.
Utilitarianism, 209, 210.

V.

Veracity, divine, 43-44.
Vestiges of Creation, 95.
Vicarious sufferings and death of Christ, 450-453; objections to considered, 453-461.
Virtue, nature of, formal theories concerning, 198-218; acting according to fitness of things, 198, 199; promoting the end of our being, 199; conformity to relations of things, 199, 200; conformity to the Will of God, 200, 203; Kant's theory, 203; Hickok's, 203, 204; happiness, 205-214; holy love theories, 214-218; hints as to a theory of, 218-231.
Von Lasaulx, 441.
Von Orelli, 388.

W.

Warburton, 598, 599.
Wardlaw, 544.
Waterland, 438.
Wayland, 179, 193, 199, 208, 209.
Wendelin, 144.
Wessel, 363.
Western Church, 255.
Westminster standards, on assurance, 542, 543; divine providence, 106; elect infants, 318; election, 505; the fall, 260, 263, 273; foreordination, 250, 252; Hades, 604; justification, 525; liberty of choice, 243; mystical union, 531; new birth, 517; person of Christ, 385.
Whately, Arch., 150, 359, 607.
Whedon on the Will, Review of, 239.
Wiescler, 527.

Will, the, 176, 236-250; idea of, 237, 238; power of, 238, 239; its self-determination, 239; its modes of action, 240, 241; its liberty or freedom, 242-245; motives, 245-250; Divine, attributes of, 29, 32; idea of, 29; definitions of, 29, 30; distinctions of, as to its objects, 30; other distinctions, 31, 32.
Wisdom, divine, 28; proof of, 28; definition of, 28, 29.
Wisner, W. C., 126, 127, 130.
Wolff, 11.
Woods, Leonard, 104, 240, 551.

X.

Xenophon, 297.

Z.

Zwingle, 143.

HENRY BOYNTON SMITH:
His Life and Work.

EDITED BY HIS WIFE.

With a fine Portrait on Steel, by Ritchie. One Vol., 8vo, 500 pages. Cloth, $2.50. (*Copies sent by mail, post-paid, on receipt of price.*)

This Memoir of the lamented Prof. Smith, gives a faithful picture of his character and public career. The story is deeply interesting, and while it fully justifies his reputation as one of the most accomplished scholars and theologians, it also shows him to have been a man of very rare personal attractions. The volume is enriched with recollections of him by Prof. Park, President Seelye, of Amherst; Prof. A. S. Packard, of Bowdoin; Rev. Dr. Withington, Dr. Cyrus Hamlin, Prof. Park, of Andover; Prof. F. A. March, of Lafayette, and the Rev. Drs. T. H. Hastings and M. R. Vincent, of New York. Rev. Dr. Goodwin, of Philadelphia, and Rev. Dr. Prentiss have assisted in the preparation of the work.

EXTRACTS FROM NOTICES OF THE MEMOIR.

Philadelphia Presbyterian says: "Dr. Smith's life is here narrated largely in his own language. His letters are frank, bright, full, and frequent. These give to the book much of the interest of an autobiography—all the more interesting because he did not consciously compose it."

N. Y. Tribune: "This book is a picture of a character, and not of an intellect merely—others besides scholars may profitably read it—the beauty of Prof. Smith's character fully answered to the strength of his intellect and the richness of his culture—as the record of a scholarly career he had few equals on this side of the Atlantic."

N. Y. Evangelist: "The book is indeed one of the most attractive pieces of religious biography that we have ever read. The character of the departed scholar is outlined with great delicacy by the loving hand of her who knew him best."

N. Y. Christian Union: "This account of the man himself has a permanent value. The life was worthy of noble monuments and lasting fame, and no one can read this book without an impulse to higher effort and purer living; and this will be more pleasing to the ransomed spirit—more in harmony with the wishes of his life here than sculptured marbles."

N. Y. Observer: "Dr. Smith's life was full of incident and adventure. His education was splendid. Foreign travel in youth broadened his view, enlarged his acquaintance with universities, with men, books, and life. The brightest intellects discerned his greatness. As a pastor, preacher, teacher, lecturer and professor, as a reviewer and editor, he always made the mark of a first rate workman, doing everything well. The loving hand of the wife has fitly held out to the eyes of the world, and bound up in this bundle such evidence of his greatness and worth, that the present generation and posterity will know something of what the Church lost when this light went out before eventide."

A. C. ARMSTRONG & SON, 714 Broadway, New York.

APOLOGETICS.

A COURSE OF LECTURES

By Henry B. Smith, D.D., LL.D.

Edited by William S. Karr, D.D.

In one volume, 12mo. Price, $1.00. *Sent by mail, post-paid, on receipt of price.*

"No treatise on Apologetics contains within the same narrow limits so much material for the defence of Christianity. Students and teachers of Apologetics will join on upon the systematizing here done for them by this able apologete, and follow out the lines of defence which he indicates. *In this way it must prove to be a stimulating and reproductive work.*"—*Presbyterian Quarterly Review.*

"We cannot commend this book too highly. It is the matured thought of one of our maturest thinkers, on some of the most vital issues of our day. Believers and unbelievers who can appreciate clear definition, ponderous thought and cogent logic, ought alike to read this work. It is tonic to both intellect and faith."—*N. Y. Examiner.*

"No teacher in this country, and few anywhere, had a more thorough acquaintance with this large and abstruse subject, and with its enormous literature. His severe and carefully trained logical faculty, his cool and dispassionate judgment, his extensive learning, and his nervous and transparent style, lend to this, as to all his other productions, a profound interest and a peculiar charm. *It will be an invaluable manual, not only to the professional student, but to every thoughtful reader who seeks to justify the ways of God to man.*"—*New York Tribune.*

"Compact and vigorous, characteristic of the mind and method of the lamented scholar and theologian. The Lectures relate to the following fundamental points: the supernatural in general, the knowableness of the supernatural, the supernatural in miracles. It seems to us that many intelligent persons, who have never been able to interest themselves in theological or metaphysical discussions, would nevertheless find much pleasure and profit in reading these chapters— so concise, distinct, natural and informing."—*N. Y. Observer.*

"They show a thorough mastery of the subject and of the literature bearing upon it, especially that of more recent date. Prof. Smith was one of this country's strongest theological thinkers."—*N. Y. Churchman.*

"Taken as a whole, this is the best book of its kind which has yet come from any American divine. It demands and is worth study."—*Standard of the Cross.*

A. C. ARMSTRONG & SON, 714 BROADWAY, NEW YORK.

CHOICE STANDARD WORKS.

A NEW AND HANDSOME LIBRARY EDITION
OF

MILMAN'S COMPLETE WORKS,

With Table of Contents and Full Indexes.

IN 8 VOLS., CROWN 8VO, CLOTH.

PRICE, $12.00 PER SET. (Reduced from $24.50.

(Bound in Half Calf extra, $25.00 per set.)

THIS EDITION OF MILMAN'S WORKS, THOROUGHLY REVISED AND CORRECTED, COMPRISES

The History of the Jews, 2 Vols.
The History of Christianity, 2 Vols.
History of Latin Christianity, 4 Vols.

DR. MILMAN has won lasting popularity as a historian by his three great works, HISTORY OF THE JEWS, HISTORY OF CHRISTIANITY, and HISTORY OF LATIN CHRISTIANITY. These works link on to each other, and bring the narrative down from the beginning of all history to the middle period of the modern era. They are the work of the scholar, a conscientious student, and a Christian philosopher. DR. MILMAN prepared this new edition so as to give it the benefit of the results of more recent research. In the notes, and in detached appendices to the chapters, a variety of very important questions are critically discussed.

The author is noted for his calm and rigid impartiality, his fearless exposure of the bad and appreciation of the good, both in institutions and men, and his aim throughout, to utter the truth always in charity. The best authorities on all events narrated have been studiously sifted and their results given in a style remarkable for its clearness, force and animation.

MILMAN'S WORKS HAVE TAKEN THEIR PLACE AMONG THE APPROVED CLASSICS OF THE ENGLISH LANGUAGE. The general accuracy of his statements, the candor of his criticisms and the breadth of his charity are everywhere apparent in his writings. His search at all times seems to have been for truth, and that which he finds he states with simple clearness and with fearless honesty. HIS WORKS ARE IN THEIR DEPARTMENT OF HISTORY AS VALUABLE AS THE VOLUMES OF GIBBON ARE IN SECULAR HISTORY. THEY DESERVE A PLACE IN EVERY LIBRARY IN THE LAND. THIS NEW EDITION, in 8 vols., contains AN AVERAGE OF OVER 900 PAGES per volume. PRICE, $12.00 PER SET. (Formerly published in 14 vols. at $24.50.)

Sent on receipt of price, charges prepaid, by

A. C. ARMSTRONG & SON, 714 BROADWAY, NEW YORK.

NEW AND IMPORTANT BOOKS.

I.
Chas. Loring Brace's New Work,
GESTA CHRISTI;
Or, A History of Humane Progress Under Christianity.

1 vol., octavo, 500 pages, $2.50.

This work is designed to show the practical effect of Christianity on the laws, customs, and morals—1st, of the Roman period; 2d, of the Middle Ages; 3d, of the Modern Period. The position of Woman, Slavery, Serfdom, Parental Rights, and similar subjects in each period are treated of: in the Middle Ages, such as Feud, the Peace of God, Judicial, Duel, Ordeal, Torture, Private War, and Arbitration are discussed. In the Modern Period, the Influence of Christianity on International Law, Arbitration, the Limitation of War, and Modern Reforms are examined, as well as on Education and Liberal Government, the Distribution of Property, Temperance and Chastity. A brief comparison is made with the influence of the Hindoo, Buddhist, Chinese, Mohammedan religions on the position of women and humane progress. The closing chapter considers objections and examines the relation of Christianity to Evolution and future progress of mankind. The book is an effort to make plain the great Christian ideas of the age, and to show both what the Christian religion has done for progress in humane practices, and what it is adapted to do.

"THIS WORK CONTAINS A VAST AMOUNT OF USEFUL AND HELPFUL KNOWLEDGE OF THESE GREAT SUBJECTS. IT IS LIKELY TO BE ONE OF THE MOST EFFECTIVE CHRISTIAN APOLOGETICS OF THE AGE."—N. Y. Christian Union.

II.
REVIVALS: HOW AND WHEN?

By Rev. W. W. NEWELL, D. D. With steel portrait. 1 vol., 12mo. $1.25.

This is no ordinary book on the subject of Revivals of Religion. It does not commend great excitement followed by depressing apathy. It favors a religious quickening and an ingathering of souls every passing year. It does not commend a theory. It is eminently practical. It gives the exact experience of persons who, in the greatest variety of seemingly hopeless conditions, have been taught of the Lord just how to secure a spiritual blessing. It shows how the Revival has been secured and conducted in the Church, the Household, the Bible-class, the Sabbath-school, the Missionary and the Temperance circle.

Copies sent by mail, post-paid, on receipt of price, by
A. C. ARMSTRONG & SON, 714 BROADWAY, NEW YORK.

NEW AND IMPORTANT WORKS.

The Parabolic Teaching of Christ.

A Systematic and Critical Study of the Parables of our Lord.

By Rev. Prof. A. B. BRUCE, D.D.

1 vol., Octavo, 527 pages, Cloth, $2.50.

"A work which will at once take its place as a classic on the Parables of our Saviour. No minister should think of doing without it."—*Presbyterian Review*.

"A book which all students of theology should welcome. Prof. Bruce brings to his task the learning, and the liberal and finely sympathetic spirit, which are the best gifts of an expositor of Scripture. His treatment of his subject is vigorous and original, and, though he is evidently well read in the literature which belongs to it, he avoids the capital mistake of overlaying his exegesis with a mass of other men's views."
—*London Spectator*.

The New York *Christian Advocate* says: "Not since Trench's well-known work on the Parables has a volume of equal merit on the same subject been given to the Christian public until now. It is scholarly in every line, and its value for homiletic purpose is greater than that of any other book."

A New and Revised Edition, with New Maps and Illustrations, of

STANLEY'S SINAI AND PALESTINE,

IN CONNECTION WITH THEIR HISTORY.

By DEAN A. P. STANLEY.

With 7 NEW and Beautifully Colored Maps, and other Illustrations. One Large Crown 8vo Vol., 640 Pages. Price, $2.50.

The late Dean Stanley published a new and revised edition of his "SINAI AND PALESTINE." In it he made considerable additions and corrections, giving the work the final impress of his scholarship, taste and ability. This edition has been carefully conformed to the last English edition—including the new colored maps and illustrations, and is herewith commended anew AS THE MOST READABLE AS WELL AS THE MOST ACCURATE WORK ON THE SUBJECT IN THE ENGLISH LANGUAGE.

By HENRY B. SMITH, D.D., LL.D.

INTRODUCTION TO CHRISTIAN THEOLOGY.

Comprising: I. A General Introduction. II. The Special Introduction; or, The Prolegomena of Systematic Theology. Edited by Prof. Wm. S. Karr, D.D. 1 vol., 12mo, $1.00.

(Uniform with "Lectures on Apologetics," by same author.)

"The work is edited by Prof. W. S. Karr, D.D., of the Hartford Seminary. Prof. Smith's reputation as, perhaps, the foremost exponent of philosophic theology which our country has produced, will, doubtless, secure for this volume a wide circle of readers outside of those especially interested in theological studies. He boldly claimed for theology the position of the queen of sciences, and no one understood better than he what was meant by that claim."

Sent on receipt of price, charges prepaid, by

A. C. ARMSTRONG & SON, 714 BROADWAY, NEW YORK.

REV. DR. WM. M. TAYLOR'S WORKS.

Contrary Winds and Other Sermons.

Crown 8vo Volume, Cloth. $1.75. 3d Edition.

"This work touches on numerous phases of life and thought and experience, showing that the author has lived through a vast deal and has been made the richer and stronger by it. It leaves the impression of wisdom that comes from actual experience, dealing with life rather than speculations, and so comes home to the heart and conscience. IT SHOWS A WIDE RANGE OF READING AND CLOSE GRAPPLE WITH THE DIFFICULT PROBLEMS OF OUR TIME. Such preaching is tonic and invigorating. It strengthens the heart and fortifies the will to overcome trials and conquer temptations and achieve victory."—*N. Y. Christian at Work.*

The Congregationalist says: "Its variety of theme and the never-failing intellectual power which it illustrates, the author's reverent positiveness of faith, his broad and intimate knowledge of human nature, and the richness of his personal spiritual experiences—never obtruded but always underlying his words—render it a volume of rare and precious value to the Christian believer, and A CAPITAL SPECIMEN OF MANLY, BUSINESS-LIKE DISCUSSION TO ALL OTHERS WHO CARE TO READ WHAT A CHRISTIAN HAS TO SAY FOR HIS RELIGION."

N. Y. Churchman: "Sermons practical in their nature, full of deep thought and wise counsel. They will have as they deserve a wide circulation."

Now Ready—4th Edition of

THE LIMITATIONS OF LIFE

AND OTHER SERMONS.

By WM. M. TAYLOR, D.D.

WITH A FINE PORTRAIT ON STEEL BY RITCHIE. CROWN 8VO VOL., EXTRA CLOTH, $1.75.

"In variety of theme, in clearness and penetration of vision, in distinctness of aim, in intensity of purpose, in energy and well-directed effort, etc., this volume is perhaps without its equal in the language."
—*The Scotsman.*

Providence Journal: "The directness, earnestness, descriptive and illustrative power of the preacher, and his rare gift for touching the conscience and the heart, are fully exemplified in these eloquent discourses."

N. Y. Evangelist: "They have the noble simplicity and clearness of the truth itself, and which, fixing the attention of the reader from the beginning, holds it to the end. It is impossible to read them without the constant sense of the personality of the author."

Copies sent on receipt of price, post-paid, by
A. C. ARMSTRONG & SON, 714 BROADWAY, NEW YORK.

www.ingramcontent.com/pod-product-compliance
Lightning Source LLC
Chambersburg PA
CBHW021221300426
44111CB00007B/391